A
Bibliography
of
Macmillan
of Canada
Imprints
1906 - 1980

by
Bruce Whiteman
Charlotte Stewart
Catherine Funnell

Dundurn Press
Toronto and London
1985

Dundurn Canadian Historical Document Series: No. 4

Acknowledgements

The preparation of this manuscript and the publication of this book were made possible because of assistance from several sources. The author and publisher are particularly grateful to the Social Sciences and Humanities Research Council of Canada. The publisher acknowledges the ongoing generous financial support of the Canada Council and the Ontario Arts Council.

J. Kirk Howard, Publisher

Design and Production: Ron and Ron Design Photography
Printing and Binding: Les Ateliers Graphiques Marc Vielleux, Canada

Dundurn Press
Canada:
P.O. Box 245, Station F
Toronto, Ontario
M4Y 2L5

United Kingdom:
71 Great Russell Street
London WC1B 3BN
England

Canadian Cataloguing in Publication Data.
Whiteman, Bruce, 1952–

   A bibliography of Macmillan of Canada imprints 1906–1980

(Dundurn Canadian historical document series;
publication no. 4)
ISBN 0-919670-89-X

1. Macmillan Company of Canada – Bibliography.
2. Canada – Imprints.   I. Stewart, Charlotte, 1947–   II. Funnell, Catherine, 1954–
III. Title.   IV. Series.

Z483.M32W48 1985   015.71'03
C85-099005-X

British Library Cataloguing in Publication Data.
A Bibliography of Macmillan of Canada Imprints, 1906 –1980
   (Dundurn Canadian historical document series; no. 4)
   1. Canada—Imprints
   I. Macmillan of Canada   II. McMaster
University
   015.71 Z1365

ISBN 0-919670-89-X

A
Bibliography
of
Macmillan
of Canada
Imprints
1906 - 1980

by
Bruce Whiteman
Charlotte Stewart
Catherine Funnell

Preface

In the Fall of 1979, McMaster University acquired the archives of the Macmillan Company of Canada Ltd., which included the company's archival library of printed books. Dating back to the time when Sir Wilfrid Laurier was Prime Minister, the collection as a whole is an impressive one, and an important resource for the study of Canadian literary and publishing history.

This bibliography forms a descriptive record of the publishing activity of Macmillan of Canada, one of the most important Canadian publishers of the twentieth century. Many of the books that are identified and described here are present in the collection now housed in our Library. However, the passage of seventy-five years in a busy publishing house has left its mark on the collection, for it became clear when the library was first inventoried on arrival that its completeness was somewhat notional. The compilers have made every reasonable effort to remedy this shortcoming in the course of their work, so that the present volume might be of significant service to those who will use it.

Bibliographic work can seldom be done in isolation, especially in a research library environment, where the advice and assistance of many able people is readily available. Assistance was willingly given by both individuals and organizations to the compilers, Charlotte Stewart and Bruce Whiteman, who strove with singular dedication to advance this project while carrying demanding workloads in the library. Word processing and typesetting technology was capably and creatively used by Marju Kraav, Rose Marie Muli, Sue Fletcher and the staff of the University's Printing Department to produce the typeset copy. Members of our staff, too numerous to mention individually, responded willingly to requests for help both large and small. The Interlibrary Loan Department provided extensive assistance in obtaining many publications from other libraries.

Generous financial assistance was obtained through a grant from the Social Sciences and Humanities Research Council of Canada, and Catherine Funnell gave invaluable assistance to the compilers at the painstaking stage of identifying, locating and describing items for inclusion.

The publication of this bibliography documents an important part of our national literary heritage, and we hope that it will stimulate further research in the field of Canadian writing and publishing.

Graham R. Hill,
University Librarian,
McMaster University,
Hamilton, Ontario,
Canada.

Photograph of St. Martin's House (Headquarters of Macmillan of Canada 1910 to 1980).
Credit: Metropolitan Toronto Library Board

Introduction

The Macmillan Company of Canada, like a number of Canadian publishing houses founded in the twenty year period preceding the First World War, was started initially as what is known today as a "branch plant". Until 1905, the London head office had employed the Copp, Clark Company as its Canadian representative, and it was Copp's responsibility to sell English Macmillan books in the Dominion in much the same way that the Canadian house would later represent other British and American publishers. (The American branch of the company retained the Morang Educational Company in Canada in the same capacity.) It was not to be expected, however, that an agent, whatever he may have had to gain, would have been as able or willing to develop as extensive a market for his client's books as a subsidiary company would be. Copp, Clark, as a publisher, would naturally have been at greatest pains to sell its own books; its agency work, however useful it may have been as a relatively risk-free addition to incoming capital, must in the nature of things have always taken second place to the publishing and marketing of Copp's own list.

In part for this reason, and in part because of changes in copyright legislation, the Macmillan Company in London decided in 1905 to establish a small subsidiary in Toronto whose main responsibility it would be to market the publications of the English and American houses. There was no thought at this time that the Toronto branch would publish its own books, though it was foreseen that the provincial governments might demand Canadian textbooks and that this would to some degree necessitate original publishing by Macmillan of Canada. It was not until the 1920s, however, that the Canadian company began in any large way to publish indigenous Canadian books; that they did then do so was in part a result of the coming of age of Canadian letters, and in part a reflection of the tastes and interests of Hugh Eayrs, who became president of Macmillan in 1921.

The company's Ontario charter was issued on December 15, 1905, but the office at 27 Richmond Street West officially opened on the first of January 1906. (In 1910 larger quarters were built at 70 Bond Street.) The first president of the company was Frank Wise, an Englishman who had ten years' experience working at the American branch of Macmillan in New York. Under Wise's direction the company expanded quickly, establishing itself as an educational publisher to be reckoned with and as an important marketer of fiction, medical and miscellaneous books. With the acquisition in June, 1912, of the stock and contracts of the Morang Educational Company Limited, Macmillan of Canada became one of the three major textbook publishers in Canada. Textbooks would always remain the financial mainstay of the company's business.

The years of the First World War brought hardships of various kinds to all publishers. Manpower and materials were scarce, and markets diminished somewhat, particularly for educational books. Macmillan of Canada survived the war years, but not without some serious losses, and by the end of 1920 the English directors felt that a change of command was necessary if the company was going to prosper.

Hugh S. Eayrs, who succeeded Wise on February 2, 1921, was largely responsible for the development of Macmillan's reputation as a publisher of important Canadian books. Beginning with the W.H. Blake translation of Louis Hémon's *Maria Chapdelaine*, Eayrs attracted to the house the books of a number of the best Canadian novelists and poets, including writers like Louise Morey Bowman, Marius Barbeau, Mazo de la Roche, E.J. Pratt, Frederick Philip Grove, Dorothy Livesay, Raymond Knister, Stephen Leacock, Morley Callaghan, Grey Owl and others. The Eayrs years were notable also for an expansion of Macmillan's agency business, both Alfred A. Knopf and Archibald Constable being added to an already substantial list of foreign publishers whom the Canadian company represented.

Eayrs' early death at 46 on April 29, 1940 deprived the company of its head at a critical time. The house had weathered the depression largely on the basis of its strong educational list; but Eayrs' death, the loss of two senior employees (John Gray and Frank Upjohn) into the armed forces, and the privations of various kinds consequent on the war, all combined to make the Macmillan list during the war years a somewhat undistinguished one. Robert Huckvale (as president) and Ellen Elliot (the company secretary) oversaw the administration and editorial business during those five years, but it would not be inaccurate to describe the company as being "on hold" at the time. In John Gray's words, Macmillan was "travelling in a ship without an effective captain and with a first mate who didn't know anything, or care much, about navigation; and the weather forecast was stormy."[1]

On Huckvale's retirement as president in June, 1946, John Gray was made General Manager. Gray oversaw the most prosperous and successful

---

[1] John Morgan Gray, *Fun Tomorrow: Learning to be a Publisher and Much Else* (Toronto: Macmillan of Canada, 1978), p. 344.

period in the company's history, and among the important authors whom Macmillan published in the post-war years were James Reaney, Donald Creighton, Adele Wiseman, Hugh MacLennan, W.O. Mitchell, and Robertson Davies. Gray himself was an accomplished writer, and in an article published in 1967 in *Canadian Literature* he summed up many of the changes and problems in Canadian publishing in the twenty years following World War II.[2] In general, the agreeable changes outweighed the continuing problems, and the expansion of the Macmillan list bears witness to the improving climate for Canadian publishing in those years. Among the contributing factors to this positive growth must be counted the creation of The Canada Council in 1957 and a burgeoning nationalism — both political and literary — in Canada.

The publication of John Gray's article coincided with a remarkably buoyant year in the Canadian publishing industry, it being of course the year in which Canada celebrated the centenary of Confederation. But following on this high point there began a gradual deterioration in Macmillan's financial health, and by 1973 the company was in sufficient difficulty that its English directors decided to sell control to Maclean-Hunter Ltd. The takeover was finalized at almost the precise moment that the Report of the Ontario Royal Commission on Book Publishing (*Canadian Publishers & Canadian Publishing*) was released, and the commissioners could hardly have asked for ampler proof of their contention that the industry was in very poor shape indeed.

The character of the Macmillan list changed radically after the sale to Maclean-Hunter. Not unexpectedly there was a marked increase in the number of titles dealing with business and finance, a decrease in literary titles, and — rather surprisingly — a greater preponderance of academic books, largely Canadian editions of English scholarly works. Yet in spite of these changes, Maclean-Hunter was unable to improve the company's financial picture, and in the spring of 1980 it was announced that Macmillan of Canada would be sold to Gage Publishing. The sale was finalized in July, and from that point forward Macmillan was no longer an independent Canadian publisher. Although the imprint was retained, it now represented merely the trade division of a large diversified publishing house.

During all but eight of the seventy-five years of publishing which this bibliography encompasses, Macmillan of Canada was controlled by the head office in London (although the American branch, until its severance from the English house in 1952, also played an important role in the Canadian branch's affairs). Nevertheless the Toronto office was relatively free to direct its own operations,[3] and given this comparative degree of

---

[2] John Morgan Gray, "Canadian Books: A Publisher's View," *Canadian Literature* #33 (Summer 1967), pp. 25-36.

[3] John Gray once described the company as being "close to and largely owned by Macmillan (Holdings) of London. They leave us free to develop as a Canadian publishing house; they don't control us — but they could." (Gray to DuBarry Campeau, letter of December 15, 1965, Macmillan Archive, McMaster University Library).

self-regulation the company developed into one of the major Canadian publishers of this century. Only the Ryerson Press and McClelland and Stewart have contributed as much to the development of Canadian publishing, and of these three publishers Macmillan was, in theory at any rate, the least independent to pursue the encouragement of native writing. In practice, however, the company made an enormous contribution to the literary culture of Canada through its determination to bring important books into print, even when the financial returns were small or non-existent.

This bibliography attempts to list all books published by the Macmillan Company of Canada Limited, *i.e.* books which have some form of the Macmillan of Canada imprint on the title-page (or elsewhere in the case of non-book material).[4] The books so issued may have been published by Macmillan in the fullest sense of the word (that is to say the Canadian branch would have overseen the complete editorial and production process). Just as often, however, the books were manufactured elsewhere for a different publisher, and Macmillan of Canada would import sheets or bound stock and would issue the work with their own title-page (sometimes integral and sometimes in the form of a cancel). Books which Macmillan merely distributed as the agency representative of another house, *e.g.* Charles and Adam Black, Cambridge University Press, Constable etc., have been excluded, even when, as frequently happens, the Canadian branch is listed as distributor on the verso of the title-page or half-title.[5] Various in-house ephemera such as newsletters and sales catalogues have also been excluded, although a few items printed for private circulation are listed.

The bibliography is arranged chronologically, beginning in 1906 and concluding with those books published up to July 1980, when the house was sold to Gage. Within each year the entries are sub-arranged alphabetically by author (or title when appropriate). The body of an individual entry consists of the following elements: (1) a transcription of the title-page (lightly punctuated to facilitate legibility); (2) a collation note indicating pagination and size in millimetres (blank pages are counted, but blank leaves are ignored); (3) a general note section, in which re-impressions are indicated (where known), as well as previous publication by Morang and any other pertinent information on the book's publication history with Macmillan of Canada, including cross-references to earlier and/or later editions; and (4) a series note when appropriate. Books can be assumed to have been issued only in cloth unless otherwise indicated.

All editions of a title are given individual entries, reprints being noted

[4]Some books published during the seven years in which Macmillan was owned by Maclean-Hunter were issued under the imprint of the "Maclean-Hunter Learning Materials Company" (e.g. 2327). As this imprint was closely associated with Macmillan's Educational Division, these books have been included here.

[5]In the very early years, imported books were sometimes rubber-stamped with Macmillan of Canada's name and address on the title-page above the imprint. Although this is arguably a form of cancellation, such books have not been included in the bibliography.

only in the notes section. When a book was reprinted more than five times, the phrase "reprinted frequently" has been used; otherwise subsequent impressions are recorded by date. Sometimes it was not possible physically to locate a copy of the first impression of a book. In these cases the book will be found under the date of the earliest impression seen, with a note indicating the year of its first publication. (In all instances the phrase "First published in..." indicates first publication *by Macmillan of Canada*.) A few fugitive items turned up at the eleventh hour, necessitating the use of subnumerals in some instances (108A etc.) and the cancellation of numbers in others. The index provides access by author, title, contributor, illustrator and series.

No book is included which has not been physically examined. A number of sources, including Tod and Cordingley's *Check List of Canadian Imprints* and Watters' *Checklist of Canadian Literature 1628-1960*, list items purportedly bearing the Macmillan of Canada imprint but which, on examination, were found to be English or American Macmillan books. In addition, early reviewing journals, such as *The Canadian Bookman*, frequently attributed to Macmillan the publication of books which they merely distributed. Although such leads have been followed up as assiduously as possible, a great many of them turned out in fact to be ghosts, or at any rate to be unlocatable.

The compilers would be the first to acknowledge that a bibliography on this scale will contain errors both of omission and commission. Compiling a bibliography of a publisher's imprints presents its own particular difficulties, especially as most existing catalogues and reference works are not arranged in a fashion to facilitate searching by imprint. Although the compilers have had the comparative luxury of access to the company's archive and house library, neither is in any sense complete (approximately 70% of the books listed are present in the library). Two classes of books have been particularly elusive. The first comprises Canadian issues of novels manufactured elsewhere (mostly, but not exclusively, in the United States) to which Macmillan of Canada added their title-page. Many of these books are not listed in the *National Union Catalog* nor are copies recorded in the Union Catalogue of the National Library of Canada. Few are mentioned even in individual author bibliographies, and undoubtedly therefore some are missing from this bibliography. The second group is the earlier editions and reprints of textbooks, which libraries tend not to keep, and which booksellers normally ignore, making them very difficult to locate. Corrections and additions to this bibliography are welcome, and should be addressed to the Director, William Ready Division of Archives and Research Collections, Mills Memorial Library, McMaster University, Hamilton, Ontario, Canada, L8S 4L6.

1906

1. KIPLING, Rudyard

Puck of Pook's Hill. By Rudyard Kipling. Toronto: The Macmillan Company of Canada, Limited, 1906.

x, 306 pp.; 198 × 135 mm.

2. LE QUEUX, William

The Invasion of 1910, With A Full Account Of The Siege Of London. By William Le Queux. Naval Chapters By H.W. Wilson. Introductory Letter By Field-Marshall Earl Roberts, K.G., K.P., Etc. Toronto: The Macmillan Company Of Canada, Limited 1906. All rights reserved.

xiv, 550 pp.; 194 × 128 mm.

2A LOTI, Pierre

Disenchanted (Désenchantées). By Pierre Loti. Translated By Clara Bell. Toronto: The Macmillan Company Of Canada, Limited 1906. All rights reserved.

[6], 380, [2] pp.; 194 × 135 mm.

3. SMITH, Goldwin

In Quest Of Light. By Goldwin Smith. Toronto: Macmillan Company of Canada, Ltd. New York: The Macmillan Company 1906.

x, 177, [1] pp.; 190 × 125 mm.

4. TENNYSON, Alfred

Poetical Works of Alfred Lord Tennyson, Poet Laureate. Toronto: The Macmillan Company of Canada, Limited, 1906. All rights reserved.

viii, 646, [2] pp.; 188 × 126 mm.

1907

5. DAVIS, William Stearns

A Victor Of Salamis: A Tale Of The Days Of Xerxes, Leonidas And Themistocles. By William Stearns Davis, Author Of "A Friend Of Caesar," "God Wills It," "Belshazzar," Etc. [Quotation]. Toronto: The Macmillan Company of Canada, Ltd. New York: The Macmillan Company 1907.

viii, 450, [4] pp.; 195 × 130 mm.

6. LONDON, Jack

Before Adam. By Jack London, Author Of "The Call Of The Wild," "The Sea Wolf," "People Of The Abyss," "White Fang," Etc., Etc. With Numerous Illustrations By Charles Livingston Bull. Toronto: The Macmillan Company of Canada, Ltd. 1907.

viii, 242, [4] pp.; 195 × 132 mm.

7. MITCHELL, George W.

An Introduction to Latin Prose. By George W. Mitchell, M.A. Assistant
Professor of Latin and Greek, Queen's University, Kingston, Ontario. To-
ronto: The Macmillan Company of Canada, Limited. London: Macmillan
& Co., Limited. New York: The Macmillan Company, 1907.

294 pp.; 183 × 120 mm.
New edition with revisions and additions published in 1920 (see 157).

8. PATTERSON, J.H.

The Man-Eaters Of Tsavo And Other East African Adventures. By Lieut,-Col.
J.H. Patterson, D.S.O. With A Foreword By Frederick Courteney Selous.
With Illustrations. Toronto: The Macmillan Co. of Canada.

xx, 351, [1] pp.; 180 × 120 mm.

9. *The University Magazine*. Volume VI. 1907. The Macmillan Company Of
Canada.

Paginated as a serial; 245 × 167 mm.
First published (from 1901) by A.T. Chapman as *The McGill University Magazine*.
Issued by Macmillan as *The University Magazine* from Vol. 6, No. 1 (February 1907)
to Vol. 8, No. 4 (December 1909). Ceased publication with Vol. 19 (1920).

10. WADDELL, John

A School Chemistry. Intended For Use In High Schools And In Elementary
Classes In Colleges. By John Waddell B.A.(Dal. Coll.), B.Sc.(Lond.),
PH.D.(Heidelberg), D.Sc.(Edin.). Member of The American Chemical
Society, Formerly Assistant To The Professor Of Chemistry In Edinburgh
University; Assistant Professor In Chemistry In The School Of Mining,
Kingston. Second Edition, Revised And Enlarged. Toronto: The Macmil-
lan Company of Canada, Ltd. 1907.

xvi, 288, [2] pp.; 190 × 130 mm.

1908

11. CHURCHILL, Winston

Mr. Crewe's Career. By Winston Churchill. Author Of "Richard Carvell,"
"The Crisis," "The Crossing," "Coniston," Etc. Illustrated. Toronto: The
Macmillan Company Of Canada, Ltd.; Western Depository, Clark Brothers
& Co., Ltd., Winnipeg.

x, 498 pp. + ads.; 196 × 132 mm.

12. DUNCAN, Sara Jeannette

Cousin Cinderella: A Canadian Girl in London. By Mrs. Everard Cotes (Sara
Jeannette Duncan). Toronto: The Macmillan Company of Canada, Ltd.,
1908.

vi, 365, [1] pp. + ads.; 195 × 131 mm.

13. HALL, H.S.

Junior Algebra For Schools. Containing A Full Treatment of Graphs. With
Answers. By H.S. Hall, M.A. And S.R. Knight, B.A., M.B., Ch.B. Special
Canadian Edition Authorized By The Minister of Education For Ontario.
Price 50 CENTS. The Macmillan Company of Canada, Ltd. Toronto 1908.

viii, 415, [1] pp.; 170 × 115 mm.
Reprinted frequently.

14. KIPLING, Rudyard

Letters to the Family (Notes on a recent trip to Canada). By Rudyard Kipling.
Toronto: The Macmillan Company of Canada, Limited 1908.

72 pp.; 170 × 120 mm.
Second edition published in 1910 (see 35).

15. TRACY, Frank Basil

*The Tercentenary History Of Canada: From Champlain To Laurier
MDCVIII-MCMVIII*. By Frank Basil Tracy. With Many Full-Page Illust-
rations, Portraits and Maps Especially Made For This Work. Volume I.
Toronto: The Macmillan Co. of Canada, Ltd. 1908.

[2], 382 pp.; 205 × 138 mm.

16. TRACY, Frank Basil

*The Tercentenary History Of Canada: From Champlain To Laurier
MDCVIII-MCMVIII*. By Frank Basil Tracy. With Many Full-Page Illust-
rations, Portraits and Maps Especially Made For This Work. Volume II.
Toronto: The Macmillan Co. of Canada, Ltd. 1908.

[2], 383-772 pp.; 205 × 138 mm.

17. TRACY, Frank Basil

*The Tercentenary History Of Canada: From Champlain To Laurier
MDCVIII-MCMVIII*. By Frank Basil Tracy. With Many Full-Page Illust-
rations, Portraits and Maps Especially Made For This Work. Volume III.
Toronto: The Macmillan Co. of Canada, Ltd. 1908.

[2], 773-1172 pp.; 205 × 138 mm.

18. WELLS, H.G.

Tono-Bungay. A Novel. By H.G. Wells. Toronto: The Macmillan Company
of Canada, Ltd. 1908.

[6], 460 pp.; 192 × 125 mm.
Duffield imprint on spine.

19. WRONG, George M.

*A Canadian Manor and Its Seigneurs: The Story of a Hundred Years 1761-
1861*. By George M. Wrong M.A., Professor of History in the University of
Toronto. With Illustrations. Toronto: The Macmillan Company of Canada,
Limited 1908.

xvi, 295, [1] pp.; 237 × 160 mm.
Second edition published in 1926 (see 301).

20.   YOXALL, J.H.

Château Royal. By J.H. Yoxall. [Quotation]. Toronto: The Macmillan Co.
Of Canada, Ltd., 1908.

   [4], 335, [1] pp.; 190 × 130 mm.

1909

21.   BEALBY, J.T.

Canada. By J.T. Bealby, B.A. With twelve Full-Page Illustrations in Colour
By T. Mower Martin, R.C.A., C.M. Manly, Hy. Sandham, Allan Stewart,
W. Cotman Eade & Mortimer Menpes. The Macmillan Company of Canada,
Limited Toronto, Canada 1909.

   vii, 87, [1] pp.; 195 × 135 mm.

22.   DENISON, George T.

The Struggle for Imperial Unity: Recollections and Experiences. By Colonel
George T. Denison, President of the British Empire League in Canada.
Author of "Modern Cavalry," "A History of Cavalry," "Soldiering in
Canada," &c. Macmillan and Co., Limited, St. Martin's Street, London.
The Macmillan Co. of Canada, Ltd., Toronto. The Macmillan Company,
New York.

   xii, 422 pp.; 210 × 135 mm.

23.   KIPLING, Rudyard

Actions and Reactions. By Rudyard Kipling. Toronto: The Macmillan Company of Canada, Ltd., 1909.

   [6], 301, [1] pp.; 222 × 130 mm.

24.   MACHRAY, Robert

*Life of Robert Machray D.D., LL.D., D.C.L. Archbishop of Rupert's Land,
Primate of all Canada, Prelate of the Order of St. Michael and St. George*. By his
nephew Robert Machray, Sometime Canon of St. John's, Winnipeg. Toronto: The Macmillan Company of Canada Ltd., 1909.

   xx, 468 pp.; 228 × 145 mm.

25.   OLDMEADOW, Ernest

Antonio. By Ernest Oldmeadow. Toronto: The Macmillan Company Of
Canada, Ltd., 1909.

   508, [2] pp.; 197 × 137 mm.

26.   *Ontario High School Chemistry*. Pupils' Text-Book. Authorized by The
Minister of Education for Ontario. Price 40 Cents. Toronto: The Macmillan
Company of Canada, Ltd. 1909.

   viii, 191, [1] pp.; 188 × 127 mm.

27. *Ontario High School Laboratory Manual In Chemistry*. Authorized by The Minister of Education for Ontario. Price 20 cents. Toronto: The Macmillan Company of Canada, Ltd. 1909.

> [2], 60 pp.; 188 × 120 mm.
> Reprinted in 1910, 1913 and 1915.

28. SINCLAIR, Samuel Bower

Introductory Educational Psychology: A Book For Teachers in Training. By Samuel Bower Sinclair, M.A., Ph.D., Head of the School for Teachers, Macdonald College, P.Q. Author of "First Year at School," "The Possibility of a Science of Education," etc. And Frederick Tracy, B.A., Ph.D., Associate Professor of Philosophy in the University of Toronto. Author of "The Psychology of Childhood," "Geschichte der Kinderpsychologie in England und Nord Amerika," etc. Toronto: The Macmillan Company of Canada, Ltd. 1909.

> xii, 180 pp.; 188 × 125 mm.
> Reprinted in 1912.

29. THOMPSON, Gordon Boyce

The Kulturkampf: An Essay. By Gordon Boyce Thompson, M.A. With a Prefatory Note by George M. Wrong, M.A., Professor of History in the University of Toronto. Toronto: The Macmillan Co. of Canada, Limited 1909.

> viii, 141, [1] pp.; 208 × 140 mm.

1910

30. ATHERTON, Gertrude

Patience Sparhawk And Her Times: A Novel. By Gertrude Atherton. The Macmillan Co. Of Canada, Ltd.

> [4], 488 pp. + ads.; 192 × 136 mm.

30A BUTLER, William Francis

The Great Lone Land: A Tale of Travel and Adventure in the North-West of America. By Lieut.-General Sir William Francis Butler, G.C.B., Author Of "The Wild North Land" And "Red Cloud; A Tale Of The Great Prairie," Etc. [Quotation]. With Illustrations And Route Map. Seventeenth Edition. Toronto: The Macmillan Company Of Canada, Ltd., 1910.

> [2], xii, 386 pp.; 198 × 133 mm.
> Earlier editions not located.

31. CHURCHILL, Winston

The Crossing. By Winston Churchill, Author of "Richard Carvell," "The Crisis," "The Celebrity," Etc. Etc. With Illustrations By Sydney Adamson and Lilian Bayliss. Toronto: The Macmillan Co. of Canada, Ltd., 1910.

> viii, 598 pp. + ads.; 190 × 130 mm.

32.   CHURCHILL, Winston

A Modern Chronicle. By Winston Churchill, Author of "Richard Carvell," "The Crisis," "Mr. Crewe's Career," Etc. Illustrated by J.H. Gardner Soper. Toronto: The Macmillan Co. of Canada, Ltd., 1910.

[2], viii, 524 pp. + ads.; 190 × 130 mm.

32A CRAWFORD, F. Marion

Fair Margaret: A Portrait. By F. Marion Crawford, Author of "Saracinesca," "Sant' Ilario," "Whosoever Shall Offend," Etc., Etc. With Illustrations By Horace T. Carpenter. Toronto: The Macmillan Co. Of Canada, Ltd. 1910.

[6], 383, [1] pp. + ads.; 194 × 132 mm.

33.   [DE MILLE, James]

A Strange Manuscript found in a Copper Cylinder. Toronto: The Macmillan Co. of Canada Ltd. 1910.

vi, 291, [1] pp.; 188 × 125 mm.

34.   HAMILTON, D. Wiley

Common Weeds of Canada: A Pocket Guide. By D. Wiley Hamilton, M.A., Ph.D., Provincial Normal School, Fredericton, N.B. Toronto: The Macmillan Company of Canada Limited, 1910.

[4], 139, [1] pp. + ads.; 188 × 124 mm.

35.   KIPLING, Rudyard

Letters to the Family: Notes on a Recent Trip to Canada. By Rudyard Kipling. Toronto: The Macmillan Company of Canada Ltd. 1910.

94 pp.; 195 × 130 mm.
First published in 1908 (see 14).

36.   KIPLING, Rudyard

Rewards and Fairies. By Rudyard Kipling. With Illustrations By Frank Craig. Toronto: The Macmillan Company of Canada, Ltd. 1910.

xii, 338 pp.; 196 × 130 mm.

37.   LONDON, Jack

Illustrated by Philip R. Goodwin and Charles Livingston Bull. *The Call Of The Wild*. By Jack London. Toronto: The Macmillan Co. Of Canada Ltd, 1910. Decorated by Chas. Edw. Hooper.

[4], 9-231, [1] pp. + ad.; 198 × 132 mm.
A later edition was published in 1933 (see 532) and a school edition in 1964 (see 1682).

38.   LONDON, Jack

The Iron Heel. By Jack London. Author Of "The Call of the Wild," "White Fang," Etc. Toronto: The Macmillan Co. Of Canada, Ltd. 1910.

xvi, 354 pp. + ads.; 192 × 130 mm.

39. LONDON, Jack

The Sea-Wolf. By Jack London. Author Of "The Call Of The Wild," "People Of The Abyss," "Children Of The Frost," Etc. With Illustrations By W.J. Aylward. Toronto: The Macmillan Co. Of Canada, Ltd., 1910.

viii, 366 pp. + ads.; 197 × 132 mm.

40. WISE, Frank

The Empire Day by Day: A Calendar Record of British Valour and Achievement on Five Continents and on the Seven Seas. Compiled and Arranged by Frank Wise. Toronto: The Macmillan Company of Canada, Ltd., 1910.

31, [1] pp.; 184 × 142 mm.

1911

41. ARNOLD, Matthew

Morang's Ten Cent Series, *Arnold's Sohrab and Rustum*. Edited with Notes by John Jeffries, B.A., English Specialist, Jarvis Collegiate Institute, Toronto. Toronto: Morang Educational Company Limited 1911.

41, [1] pp.; 170 × 115 mm.

The original Morang wrapper has been replaced with a Macmillan Company of Canada wrapper. Issued in paper.

42. BAILEY, L.H.

Beginners' Botany. By L.H. Bailey. Toronto: The Macmillan Co. of Canada, Ltd. 1911.

x, 208, x pp. + ads.; 192 × 131 mm.
Reprinted frequently. Some later printings bear the cover-title *Ontario High School Beginners' Botany*.
Macmillan's Canadian School Series.

43. EDEN, Thomas Watts

A Manual of Midwifery. By Thomas Watts Eden, M.D., C.M. Edin., F.R.C.P. Lond., F.R.C.S. Edin., Obstetric Physician With Charge of Out-Patients and Lecturer On Practical Midwifery and Gynaecology, Charing Cross Hospital, Physician to Out-Patients, Queen Charlotte's Lying-In Hospital, Surgeon to In-Patients, Chelsea Hospital for Women, Examiner in Midwifery and Diseases of Women to the University of Oxford and to the Royal Army Medical College. With 339 Illustrations in the Text. Third Edition. Toronto: The Macmillan Company of Canada Ltd. 1911.

x, 709, [1] pp.; 226 × 148 mm.
Earlier editions not located. Fourth edition published in 1915 (see 82).

44. HARPELL, James J.

Canadian National Economy: The Cause of High Prices and Their Effect Upon the Country. By James Harpell. Toronto: The Macmillan Co. of Canada Ltd., 1911.

182 pp.; 213 × 143 mm.
Issued in paper.

45.   KOCHER, Theodor

Text-book of Operative Surgery. By Dr. Theodor Kocher, Professor of Surgery and Director of the Surgical Clinic in the University of Bern. Third English Edition. Authorized Translation From The Fifth German Edition By Harold J. Stiles, M.B., F.R.C.S. Edin., Surgeon to the Chalmers Hospital, Edinburgh, Surgeon to the Royal Edinburgh Hospital For Sick Children, Lecturer On Applied Anatomy, University of Edinburgh, And C. Balfour Paul, M.B., F.R.C.S. Edin., Assistant Surgeon, Royal Edinburgh Hospital For Sick Children. With 415 Illustrations. In Two Vols. Vol. I. Toronto: The Macmillan Company of Canada, Ltd. [and] London: Adam and Charles Black, 1911.

xxiv, 382 pp.; 248 × 172 mm.
Earlier editions not located.

46.   KOCHER, Theodor

Text-book of Operative Surgery. By Dr. Theodor Kocher, Professor of Surgery and Director of the Surgical Clinic in the University of Bern. Third English Edition. Authorized Translation From The Fifth German Edition By Harold J. Stiles, M.B., F.R.C.S. Edin., Surgeon to the Chalmers Hospital, Edinburgh, Surgeon to the Royal Edinburgh Hospital For Sick Children, Lecturer On Applied Anatomy, University of Edinburgh, And C. Balfour Paul, M.B., F.R.C.S. Edin, Assistant Surgeon, Royal Edinburgh Hospital For Sick Children. With 415 Illustrations. In Two Vols. Vol. II. Toronto: The Macmillan Company of Canada, Ltd. [and] London: Adam and Charles Black, 1911.

xiv, 383-723, [1] pp.; 248 × 172 mm.
Earlier editions not located.

1912

47.   BATTLE, William Henry

Clinical Lectures On The Acute Abdomen. By William Henry Battle, F.R.C.S. Surgeon To St. Thomas's Hospital, And Joint Lecturer On Systematic Surgery In The Medical School; Formerly Surgeon To The Royal Free Hospital; Assistant Surgeon To The East London Hospital For Children; Hunterian Professor Of Surgery At The Royal College Of Surgeons Of England; "Orator" of The Medical Society Of London, 1910; Author (With Mr. E.M. Corner) Of "The Surgery Of The Diseases Of The Appendix Vermiformis And Their Complications," Etc. Toronto: The Macmillan Company of Canada Ltd. 1912.

xii, 107, [1] pp.; 220 × 140 mm.

47A GALLON, Tom

Levity Hicks. By Tom Gallon. Toronto: The Macmillan Co. of Canada, Ltd.
320 pp.; 195 × 133 mm.

48. GILBERT, Grove Karl

High School Physical Geography. By Grove Karl Gilbert, Geologist, United States Geological Survey, And Albert Perry Brigham, Professor Of Geology In Colgate University. Authorized By The Minister Of Education For Ontario. Authorized For Use In Saskatchewan And Alberta. Revised Edition. Toronto: The Macmillan Company of Canada, Limited 1912.

> 351, [1] pp.; 195 × 130 mm.
> First published by Morang in 1909. Macmillan edition reprinted frequently.

49. KIPLING, Rudyard

Songs from Books. By Rudyard Kipling. Toronto: The Macmillan Company of Canada, Ltd. 1912.

> xii, 242, [2] pp.; 194 × 122 mm.

50. MINCHIN, Laurence H.J.

The King Edward Music Readers: First Reader. By Laurence H.J. Minchin, Formerly Supervisor of Music, Public Schools, Winnipeg. Authorized for use in the Public Schools of Manitoba, Saskatchewan and British Columbia. Fourth Edition Revised. Toronto: The Macmillan Co. of Canada, Ltd. 1912.

> 147, [1] pp.; 190 × 150 mm.
> First published by Morang in 1904. Macmillan edition reprinted in 1913.

51. MINCHIN, Laurence H.J.

The King Edward Music Readers: Second Reader. By Laurence H.J. Minchin, Formerly Supervisor of Music, Public Schools, Winnipeg. Authorized for use in the Public Schools of Manitoba, Saskatchewan and British Columbia. Toronto: The Macmillan Co. of Canada, Ltd. 1912.

> 192 pp.; 190 × 150 mm.
> First published by Morang in 1905.

52. MOREY, William C.

High School Ancient History. By William C. Morey, PH.D., D.C.L. Professor Of History And Political Science, University Of Rochester. Authorized By The Minister Of Education For Ontario. Toronto: The Macmillan Company of Canada, Ltd. 1912.

> 396 pp.; 190 × 130 mm.
> First published by Morang in 1909. Reprinted by Macmillan in 1913.

53. *Nova Scotia Readers: Third Reader*. Authorized for Use in Nova Scotia. Seventh Edition. Toronto: The Macmillan Co. of Canada Ltd., 1912.

> 190 pp.; 190 × 143 mm.
> First published by Morang in 1905.
> Nova Scotia Readers Series.

54. *Ontario Public School History Of Canada*. Authorized By The Minister Of Education For Ontario. Toronto: The Macmillan Company of Canada, Limited 1912.

306 pp.; 195 × 130 mm.
First published by Morang in 1910.

55.   TARR, Ralph

Tarr and McMurry Geographies. *Our Home and Its Surroundings: A First Book of Modern Geography*. Toronto: The Macmillan Company of Canada, Limited 1912. This book must not be imported into nor circulated in the United States of America or Great Britain.

viii, 152 pp.; 190 × 130 mm.

56.   WRONG, George M.

Ontario High School History Of England. By George M. Wrong, M.A. Professor Of History In The University Of Toronto. Authorized By The Minister Of Education For Ontario. Toronto: The Macmillan Company of Canada, Limited 1912.

viii, 536 pp.; 195 × 125 mm.
First published by Morang in 1911. Revised and enlarged in 1922 and reprinted in 1924, 1926, 1927 and 1928. See 357 for 1928 reprint of this edition.

1913

57.   *The British Journal of Surgery*. Under The Direction Of The Following Editorial Committee: Sir Berkeley G.A. Moynihan (Leeds), Chairman [etc.]. Volume I. July 1913 to April 1914. Numbers 1 to 4. Bristol: John Wright And Sons Ltd. London: Simpkin, Marshall, Hamilton, Kent And Co. Limited. Toronto: The Macmillan Co. Of Canada Ltd. [etc.].

Paginated as a serial; 255 × 180 mm.
Issued quarterly at first, subsequently six and then twelve times per year. The Macmillan of Canada imprint is on the title-page from Vol. 1 (1913) to Vol. 60 (1973).

58.   HAGARTY, E.W.

Macmillan's Canadian School Series, *Introductory Latin Grammar and First Latin Reader*. By E.W. Hagarty, M.A., Principal, Harbord Collegiate Institute,Toronto. Authorized for use in Manitoba. Toronto: The Macmillan Company of Canada Limited 1913.

xiv, 430 pp.; 193 × 127 mm.
First published by Morang in 1903.
Macmillan's Canadian School Series.

59.   HAWTHORNE, Nathaniel

Macmillan's Literature Series, *Tanglewood Tales*. (Complete). Edited with Notes by John C. Saul, M.A. Toronto: The Macmillan Company of Canada Limited 1913.

[4], 202, [2] pp.; 175 × 120 mm.
First published by Morang in 1906. Macmillan edition reprinted frequently. Issued in limp cloth.
Macmillan's Literature Series.

60.   HEATHERINGTON, Lynn A.
The Princess Elizabeth and Other Stories. By L.H.
71, [1] pp.; 200 × 145 mm.

61.   HERRINGTON, Walter S.
History of the County of Lennox and Addington. By Walter S. Herrington, K.C., Author of "Heroines of Canadian History," "Martyrs of New France," "The Evolution of the Prairie Provinces." Illustrated with eighty-three half-tones, taken from daguerreotypes and photographs. Toronto: The Macmillan Company of Canada, Limited 1913.
xii, 427, [1] pp.; 245 × 160 mm.

62.   JARVIS, W.H.P.
The Great Gold Rush: A Tale of the Klondike. By W.H.P. Jarvis, Author of "Letters of a Remittance Man". Toronto: The Macmillan Co. of Canada Limited 1913.
xii, 335, [1] pp.; 190 × 125 mm.
Reprinted in 1913.

63.   *Ontario Public School History Of England*. Authorized By The Minister Of Education For Ontario For Use In Forms IV And V Of The Public Schools. Fourth Edition. Toronto: The Macmillan Company of Canada, Ltd. 1913.
320 pp.; 195 × 125 mm.
First published by Morang in 1910. Macmillan edition reprinted frequently.

64.   WATSON, Albert D.
Love and the Universe: The Immortals and Other Poems. By Albert D. Watson. With introduction by Katherine Hale [pseud.]. Toronto: The Macmillan Company of Canada, Ltd., at St. Martin's House MCMXIII.
xviii, 191, [1] pp.; 212 × 140 mm.

1914

65.   BAILEY, L.H.
First Course in Biology. By L.H. Bailey. Part I. Plant Biology. And Walter M. Coleman. Part II. Animal Biology. Part III. Human Biology. Toronto: The Macmillan Co. Of Canada, Ltd. 1914.
xxvi, 204, 224, 164, x pp. + ads.; 191 × 135 mm.
Macmillan's Canadian School Series.

66.   BAKER, Arthur E.
A Concordance to the Poetical and Dramatic Works of Alfred, Lord Tennyson: Including the Poems Contained in the "Life of Alfred, Lord Tennyson" and the "Suppressed Poems" 1830-1868. By Arthur E. Baker, F.R.Hist.S., F.L.A., Secretary and Librarian, Taunton. Author of "A Brief Account of the Public

Library Movement in Taunton," Etc. Toronto: The Macmillan Company of
Canada Ltd. at St. Martin's House MCMXIV.

xvi, 1212 pp.; 233 × 215 mm.

67.   BATTLE, William Henry

The Acute Abdomen. By William Henry Battle, Senior Surgeon to St.
Thomas's Hospital. Formerly Joint Lecturer on Systematic Surgery, and on
Practical Surgery to St. Thomas's Hospital Medical School; Surgeon to the
Royal Free Hospital; Assistant Surgeon to the East London Hospital for
Children; Hunterian Professor, Royal College of Surgeons; Orator to the
Medical Society of London, etc.; Joint Author (with Mr. Corner) of the
Surgical Diseases of the Vermiform Appendix and their Complications (2nd
ed.), etc. Second Edition. Enlarged And Illustrated. The Macmillan Com-
pany of Canada, Ltd., Toronto 1914.

xii, 295, [1] pp.; 225 × 140 mm.
First edition not located.

68.   BOYD, John

*Sir George Etienne Cartier Bart: His Life and Times: A Political History of
Canada From 1814 Until 1873*. By John Boyd. In Commemoration of the One
Hundredth Anniversary of Sir George Etienne Cartier's Birth. Illustrated.
The Macmillan Company of Canada, Ltd. at St. Martin's House Toronto
MCMXIV.

xxii, 439, [1] pp.; 245 × 160 mm.
Reprinted in 1917 (Bonne Entente Edition).

69.   COOK, Edward

[Cover-title:] *Why the Empire is at War: The Causes And The Issues*. Set out, in
brief form, from the Diplomatic Correspondence and Speeches of Ministers.
By Sir Edward Cook. Toronto: The Macmillan Company of Canada, Ltd.,
at St. Martin's House. Price, Five Cents Post paid.

16 pp.; 235 × 150 mm.
Subsequently published in French (see 80). Issued in paper.

70.   KERR, W.A.R.

Macmillan's Canadian School Series, *A French Grammar*. By W.A.R. Kerr,
M.A., PH.D. Dean of the Faculty of Arts and Science and Professor of
Modern Language in the University of Alberta. And Edward Sonet, B.Ès.L.
Lecturer in French in the University of Alberta. Toronto: The Macmillan
Co. of Canada, Limited, 1914.

x, 267, [1] pp.; 185 × 123 mm.
Macmillan's Canadian School Series.

71.   KING, John

McCaul: Croft: Forneri: Personalities of Early University Days. By John
King, M.A., K.C. [Quotation]. Toronto: The Macmillan Company of
Canada Limited, at St. Martin's House, MCMXIV.

256 pp.; 207 × 140 mm..

72. McCULLY, Laura E.
     Mary Magdalene and Other Poems. By Laura E. McCully. Toronto: The
     Macmillan Company of Canada, Ltd. at St. Martin's House, MCMXIV.
       [6], 99, [1] pp.; 188 × 163 mm.

73. MITCHELL, George W.
     Macmillan's Canadian School Series, *Latin Composition Based on Caesar*. By
     George W. Mitchell, M.A. Professor of Classics, Queen's University,
     Kingston. Toronto: The Macmillan Company of Canada, Limited 1914.
       [4], 190 pp.; 183 × 118 mm.
       First published in 1908. Earlier printings not located.
       Macmillan's Canadian School Series.

74. *Nova Scotia Readers: First Reader*. Authorized for Use in the Province of
     Nova Scotia. Eighth Edition. Toronto: The Macmillan Co. of Canada, Ltd.
     1914.
       96 pp.; 187 × 141 mm.
       First published by Morang in 1905.
       Nova Scotia Readers Series.

75. *Nova Scotia Readers: Second Reader*. Authorized for Use in Nova Scotia.
     Eighth Edition. Toronto: The Macmillan Company of Canada, Ltd. 1914.
       127, [1] pp.; 190 × 143 mm.
       First published by Morang in 1905.
       Nova Scotia Readers Series.

1915

76. *The Alexandra Readers: Phonic Primer*. Authorized by the Departments of
     Education for Use in the Schools of Alberta and Saskatchewan. PRICE 10
     CENTS. Toronto: The Macmillan Company of Canada, Limited 1915.
       64 pp.; 183 × 128 mm.
       First published by Morang in 1900. Macmillan edition reprinted in 1918. Issued in
       limp cloth.

77. BLAKE, W.H.
     Brown Waters and Other Sketches. By W.H. Blake. [Quotation]. Toronto:
     The Macmillan Company of Canada Limited, at St. Martin's House,
     MCMXV.
       264 pp.; 195 × 130 mm.
       Other editions published in 1925 (see 237) and 1940 (see 861).

78. BURLEND, T.H.
     Macmillan's Canadian School Series, *A First Book of Zoology*. By T.H.
     Burlend, M.A., B.Sc. Lecturer in Histology and Embryology in the Univer-
     sity College of South Wales and Monmouthshire. Adapted for Canadian
     Schools by George A. Cornish, B.A. Lecturer in Science, University of

Toronto. Toronto: The Macmillan Company of Canada, Ltd. 1915.

vi, 180 pp.; 185 × 120 mm.
Macmillan's Canadian School Series.

79. CHURCHILL, Winston

A Far Country. By Winston Churchill. Author of "The Inside of the Cup" Etc. Illustrated by Herman Pfeifer. Toronto: The Macmillan Co. of Canada, Ltd., 1915.

[4], 509, [1] pp.; 127 × 183 mm.

80. COOK, Edward

[Cover-title:] *Pourquoi L'Empire est en Guerre: Naissance et Développement du Conflit*. Exposé rapide d'après la correspondance diplomatique et les discours des ministres. Traduction du livre écrit par Sir Edward Cook. The Macmillan Company of Canada, Limited, Éditeurs. Maison St. Martin, 70 Bond Street, Toronto. Prix, 10 Cents, franco.

16 pp.; 235 × 154 mm.
Originally published in English (see 69). Issued in paper.

81. CRAWFORD, J.T.

High School Algebra. By J.T. Crawford, B.A. Chief Instructor in Mathematics, University Schools, Lecturer in Mathematics, Faculty of Education, University of Toronto. Authorized by The Minister of Education for Ontario. Toronto: The Macmillan Company of Canada Limited, 1915.

xvi, 398 pp.; 192 × 130 mm.
Revised in 1916 (see 102A). Issued in the Western Canada Series in 1921. Revised in 1939 (see 832) and 1954 (see 1310).

82. EDEN, Thomas Watts

A Manual of Midwifery. By Thomas Watts Eden M.D., C.M. Edin., F.R.C.P. Lond., F.R.C.S. Edin., Obstetric Physician and Lecturer on Midwifery and Gynaecology, Charing Cross Hospital, Consulting Physician to Queen Charlotte's Lying-in Hospital, Surgeon to In-Patients, Chelsea Hospital for Women. Fourth Edition. With 5 Plates and 354 Illustrations in the Text. Toronto: The Macmillan Company of Canada Ltd., 1915.

x, 777, [1] pp.; 227 × 145 mm.
Third edition published in 1911 (see 43).

83. *The Fourth Golden Rule Book*. Recommended by the Minister of Education for use in the Public & Separate School Libraries of Ontario. Toronto: The Macmillan Company of Canada Ltd., at St. Martin's House, MCMXV.

x, 415, [1] pp.; 185 × 123 mm.

84. "GOOSEQUILL"

As Others See Us: Being the Diary of a Canadian Debutante. By "Goosequill". Toronto: The Macmillan Company of Canada, Ltd. at St. Martin's House, MCMXV.

299, [1] pp.; 187 × 127 mm.

85. HALES, B.J.

Macmillan's Canadian School Series, *Selected Western Flora: Manitoba,
Saskatchewan, Alberta*. By B.J. Hales B.A., Principal, Normal School, Bran-
don. Authorized by the Advisory Board of the Department of Education for
Use in High Schools and Collegiate Institutes in Manitoba. Toronto: The
Macmillan Company of Canada, 1915.

xvi, 181, [1] pp.; 190 × 127 mm.
This title is also found bound with L.H. Bailey's *Beginners' Botany*.
Macmillan's Canadian School Series.

86. Macmillan's Canadian School Series, *A Handbook to the Manitoba Readers*.
Specially Prepared for the Use of Teachers in Manitoba. The Macmillan
Company of Canada Ltd. at St. Martin's House, Toronto, MCMXV.

viii, 345, [13] pp.; 248 × 164 mm.
Macmillan's Canadian School Series.

87. HERRINGTON, Walter S.

Pioneer Life Among the Loyalists in Upper Canada. By W.S. Herrington K.C.,
Author of "History of the County of Lennox and Addington", "Heroines of
Canadian History," Etc. Illustrated. Toronto: The Macmillan Company of
Canada, Ltd. at St. Martin's House, MCMXV.

107, [1] pp.; 187 × 120 mm.
Reprinted in 1916, 1924 and 1938.

88. HUNTINGTON, Tuley Francis

Macmillan's Canadian School Series, *Elementary English Composition*. By
Tuley Francis Huntington M.A., Litt.D. Authorized by the Advisory Board
of the Department of Education for Use in the Collegiate Institutes and High
Schools of the Province of Manitoba. Toronto: The Macmillan Company of
Canada Limited 1915.

xiv, 345, [1] pp.; 188 × 125 mm.
First published in 1907. Reprinted in 1915. Earlier printings not located.
Macmillan's Canadian School Series.

89. HUNTINGTON, Tuley Francis

Macmillan's Canadian School Series, *Elements of English Composition*. By
Tuley Francis Huntington M.A., Litt.D. Authorized by the Advisory Board
of the Department of Education for use in the High Schools and Collegiate
Institutes of the Province of Manitoba. Toronto: The Macmillan Co. of
Canada, Limited, 1915.

xii, 355, [1] pp.; 188 × 127 mm.
First published in 1911. Reprinted in 1912, 1913 and 1915. Earlier printings not
located.
Macmillan's Canadian School Series.

90. KIPLING, Rudyard

[Cover-title:] *The Fringes Of The Fleet*. By Rudyard Kipling. Toronto: The
Macmillan Company Of Canada, Ltd., At St. Martin's House, 1915. Price 25
Cents.

[4], 70, [2] pp. + ad.; 160 × 114 mm.
Macmillan of Canada imprint on cover; London imprint on title-page. Issued in
paper.

91. ROBERTS, Charles G.D.

Macmillan's Canadian School Series, *A History of Canada*. For High Schools
And Academies. By Charles G.D. Roberts. Toronto: The Macmillan Co. of
Canada, Limited 1915.

xxiv, 492 pp.; 193 × 132 mm.
Reprinted in 1922 and 1927.
Macmillan's Canadian School Series.

92. ROHOLD, S.B.

*The War and the Jew: A Bird's Eye View of the World's Situation and the Jew's
Place in It*. By the Rev. S.B. Rohold, F.R.G.S. Pastor, Christian Synagogue,
Toronto. President Hebrew Christian Alliance of America. Ass't. Editor
"Missionary Review of the World", Missionary Editor "Jewish Era". Intro-
duction by the Rev. T.B. Kilpatrick, D.D. Professor of Systematic Theol-
ogy, Knox College, Toronto. Toronto: The Macmillan Company of Canada,
Limited, 1915.

xiv, 98 pp.; 175 × 117 mm.

93. RUSSELL, H.J.

Macmillan's Canadian Text-Books, *Canadian Commercial Correspondence and
Business Training*. By H.J. Russell, Commercial Master, St. John's Technical
High School, Winnipeg. Toronto: The Macmillan Company of Canada,
Ltd. 1915.

295, [1] pp.; 185 × 130 mm.
Reprinted in 1917. Revised in 1923 (see 210A). New edition published in 1944 under
title *The Competent Secretary* (see 1021).
Macmillan's Canadian Text-Books Series.

94. Macmillan's Canadian School Series, *Selected Narrative Poems*. Coleridge,
Wordsworth, Byron, Tennyson, Browning. Toronto: The Macmillan Company of Canada, Ltd. 1915.

238 pp.; 183 × 128 mm.
Reprinted in 1923 in paper.
Macmillan's Canadian School Series.

95. Macmillan's Canadian Text-Books, *Steps to Literature: A Fifth Reader*.
[Quotation]. Toronto: The Macmillan Company of Canada, Ltd. 1915.

439, [1] pp.; 185 × 120 mm.
Macmillan's Canadian Text-Books Series.

96. WELLS, H.G.

The Research Magnificent. By H.G. Wells, Author of "The Wife Of Sir Isaac
Harman," Etc. Toronto: The Macmillan Company of Canada, Limited
1915.

vi, 460 pp. + ads.; 190 × 125 mm.

97. WETHERELL, J.E.

Macmillan's Canadian School Series, *Fields Of Fame In England and Scotland*. By J.E. Wetherell, B.A. Inspector of High Schools for Ontario. Toronto: The Macmillan Company of Canada, Ltd., at St. Martin's House MCMXV.

xii, 171, [1] pp.; 192 × 128 mm.
Reprinted in 1923.
Macmillan's Canadian School Series.

98. WETHERELL, J.E.

Macmillan's Literature Series, *Poems Of The Love Of Country*. Selected And Edited By J.E. Wetherell, B.A. Inspector Of High Schools For The Province of Ontario. Toronto: The Macmillan Company of Canada, Limited 1915.

144 pp.; 168 × 108 mm.
First published by Morang in 1905. Issued in limp cloth.
Macmillan's Literature Series.

1916

99. AGER, Clarus

The Farmer and the Interests: A Study in Economic Parasitism. By Clarus Ager. [Quotation]. Toronto: The Macmillan Company of Canada Limited, at St. Martin's House, MCMXVI.

162 pp.; 195 × 135 mm.
Issued in paper.

100. BAUMBACH, Rudolph

Macmillan's German Classics, *Waldnovellen: Six Tales*. By Rudolph Baumbach. With Notes, Exercises, and Vocabulary by A.E. Lang, M.A. Professor of German Language and Literature, Toronto. Toronto: The Macmillan Company of Canada, Limited, 1916.

[6], 129, [1] pp.; 175 × 118 mm.
First published by Morang in 1908. Issued in paper.
Macmillan's German Classics Series.

101. BROWNING, Robert

Macmillan's Literature Series, *Selections From Browning, Tennyson and Arnold*. With introductions and Notes. Toronto: The Macmillan Company of Canada, Limited, 1916.

[8], 116, [2] pp.; 172 × 118 mm.
Reprinted in 1922.
Macmillan's Literature Series.

102. CHURCHILL, Winston

The Inside Of The Cup. By Winston Churchill, Author Of "Richard Carvell," "The Crisis," "A Modern Chronicle," Etc., Etc. Toronto: The Macmillan Co. of Canada, Ltd. 1916.

vi, 513, [1] pp.; 190 × 125 mm.
First published in 1913. Earlier printings not located. Reprinted frequently.

102A CRAWFORD, J.T.

High School Algebra. By J.T. Crawford, B.A., Chief Instructor In Mathematics, University Schools, Professor Of Mathematics, Ontario College Of Education, University Of Toronto. Revised Edition. Toronto: The Macmillan Company Of Canada, Limited.

xvi, 398, [2] pp.; 195 × 125 mm.
First published in 1915 (see 81). This revised edition issued in the Western Canada Series in 1921. Also issued, with additional chapters, as *The New Brunswick School Algebra* and *The Nova Scotia High School Algebra* and reprinted frequently. Revised in 1939 (see 832) and 1954 (see 1310).

103. CURTIS, Lionel

The Problem of the Commonwealth. By Lionel Curtis. Toronto: The Macmillan Company of Canada, Ltd., at St. Martin's House. Macmillan and Co., Limited. London, Bombay, Calcutta, Madras [and] Melbourne 1916.

xii, 247, [1] pp.; 214 × 140 mm.
Issued in cloth and paper.

104. LABICHE, Eugène

Macmillan's French Classics, *Le Voyage de Monsieur Perrichon*. Comédie en quatre actes. Par Labiche et Martin. Edited with Introduction, Notes, Exercises and Vocabulary by Pelham Edgar Ph.D., Professor of French, Victoria College, University of Toronto. Toronto: The Macmillan Company of Canada, Limited, 1916.

[4], 119, [1] pp.; 178 × 118 mm.
First published by Morang in 1908. Macmillan edition reprinted frequently. Reprinted in the French Matriculation Readers Series under the General Editorship of F.C.A. Jeanneret in 1934.
Macmillan's French Classics Series.

105. WOOD, S.T.

Macmillan's Lakeside Series, *How We Pay Each Other: An Elementary Reader in the Simple Economics of Daily Life*. By S.T. Wood. Toronto: The Macmillan Company of Canada, Limited, 1916.

xviii, 149, [3] pp.; 173 × 115 mm.
Macmillan's Lakeside Series.

1917

106. BEMISTER, Margaret

Macmillan's Lakeside Series, *Thirty Indian Legends*. By Margaret Bemister. Toronto: The Macmillan Company of Canada, Ltd., 1917.

182 pp.; 190 × 130 mm.
First published in 1912. Earlier printings not located.
Macmillan's Lakeside Series.

107. BIGGAR, E.B.

The Canadian Railway Problem. By E.B. Biggar, Former Editor "Canadian Engineer". Author Of "Canada: A Memorial Volume": "Reciprocity": "The Wool Problem Of Canada": "Canada's Forestry Problem": "History Of Canadian Journalism". The Macmillan Company of Canada, Limited at St. Martin's House, Toronto MCMXVII.

viii, 258 pp.; 200 × 130 mm.

108. BROWNE, T.A.

The Belgian Mother And Ballads of Battle Time. By T.A. Browne. Toronto: The Macmillan Company of Canada Limited, at St. Martin's House, MCMXVII.

viii, 106, [2] pp.; 200 × 135 mm.
Reprinted in 1917.

109. CORNISH, George A.

Macmillan's Canadian School Series, *A Laboratory Manual To Accompany Chemistry: A Text-Book For High Schools*. By George A. Cornish, B.A. Lecturer In Science, Faculty Of Education, University Of Toronto, And Chief Instructor In Science, University Schools Toronto. Assisted by Arthur Smith, B.A. Instructor In Chemistry, Central Technical School, Toronto. Authorized In Saskatchewan And Ontario. Toronto: The Macmillan Company of Canada, Limited 1917.

viii, 135, [5] pp.; 192 × 130 mm.
Another edition published in 1921 (see 163).
Macmillan's Canadian School Series.

110. DE LA RAMÉE, Marie Louise

Macmillan's Eclectic Series, *A Dog of Flanders*. By Marie Louise De la Ramée (Ouida). With Introduction and Notes. Toronto: The Macmillan Company of Canada, Limited, 1917.

58 pp.; 172 × 115 mm.
Issued in paper.
Macmillan's Eclectic Series.

111. EMERY, J.W.

The Library the School and the Child. By J.W. Emery, B.A., D.Paed. Normal School, Stratford, Ont. [Quotation]. The Macmillan Company of Canada, Limited at St. Martin's House, Toronto MCMXVII.

x, 216 pp.; 203 × 137 mm.

112. GOLDSMITH, Oliver

Macmillan's Eclectic Series, *The Deserted Village and The Traveller*. By Oliver Goldsmith. With Introduction and Notes. Toronto: The Macmillan Company of Canada, Limited, 1917.

52 pp.; 172 × 118 mm.
Issued in paper.
Macmillan's Eclectic Series.

113.   HALL, H.S.

Macmillan's Canadian School Series, *Lessons in Experimental and Practical Geometry*. By H.S. Hall, M.A. and F.H. Stevens, M.A. Authorized for use in The Public Schools of Saskatchewan. Toronto: The Macmillan Company of Canada, Limited, 1917.

[4], 128 pp.; 195 × 128 mm.
There are two other printings of this title containing minor variations on their title pages. In 1922, with the appearance of the first reprint, the series title was changed to The Western Canada Series. This applies to the 1937 reprint as well.
Macmillan's Canadian School Series.

114.   KENRICK, Frank B.

An Elementary Laboratory Course in Chemistry. By Frank B. Kenrick, M.A. PH.D., Associate Professor of Chemistry, University of Toronto, And Ralph E. De Lury, M.A. PH.D., Fellow in Chemistry, University of Toronto. Second Edition Revised. Toronto: The Macmillan Company of Canada, Limited, 1917.

[6], 89, [1] pp.; 246 × 166 mm.
First published by Morang in 1907. Reprinted in 1932.

115.   LASH, Z.A.

Defence and Foreign Affairs: A Suggestion for the Empire. By Z.A. Lash, K.C., LL.D. With a Prefatory Note by Sir Edmund Walker, C.V.O., LL.D., D.C.L. Toronto: The Macmillan Company of Canada, Ltd. 1917.

86 pp.; 215 × 143 mm.

116.   McINTYRE, W.A.

Macmillan's Canadian School Series, *Spelling and Dictation*. By W.A. McIntyre and A.W. Hooper, Provincial Normal School, Winnipeg. The Macmillan Company of Canada Ltd. Toronto, MCMXVII.

304 pp.; 188 × 144 mm.
New edition published in 1919 (see 146, 147, 148, 149).
Macmillan's Canadian School Series.

117.   MERRITT, William Hamilton

Canada and National Service. By Colonel William Hamilton Merritt, President, The Canadian Defence League. Toronto: The Macmillan Company of Canada, Limited, at St. Martin's House, MCMXVII.

xvi, 247, [1] pp.; 205 × 135 mm.

118.   *Selected Narrative Poems*. Arnold, Burns, Rosetti, Browning [and] Ballads. Toronto: The Macmillan Company of Canada, Ltd. 1917.

128 pp.; 154 × 120 mm.
Issued in paper.
Macmillan's Canadian School Series.

119.   SINCLAIR, Samuel Bower

Learning to Read: Phonics Made Easy For Primary Teachers and Mothers. By

Samuel Bower Sinclair, M.A., PH.D. Author of "First Year at School", "The Possibility of a Science of Education", "Introductory Educational Psychology." Stories by Anna E. Sinclair, B.A. Toronto: The Macmillan Co. of Canada, Limited, 1917.

> x, 118 pp.; 188 × 135 mm.

120. SISLER, W.J.

Macmillan's Canadian School Series, *Spelling and Language Lessons For Beginners in English*. By W.J. Sisler, Principal, Strathcona School, Winnipeg. Toronto: The Macmillan Company of Canada, Limited, 1917.

> 176 pp.; 193 × 140 mm.
> First published in 1915. Earlier printings not located. Revised edition published in 1927 (see 328).
> Macmillan's Canadian School Series.

121. *The Third Golden Rule Book*. Recommended by the Minister of Education for use in the Public and Separate School Libraries of Ontario. Toronto: The Macmillan Company of Canada, Ltd., at St. Martin's House, MCMXVII.

> x, 352 pp.; 185 × 123 mm.

122. WELLS, H.G.

The Soul of a Bishop. By H.G. Wells, Author of "Mr. Britling Sees it Through" etc. Frontispiece by C. Allan Gilbert. The Macmillan Company of Canada, Limited, at St. Martin's House, Toronto MCMXVII.

> [6], 341, [1] pp.; 195 × 133 mm.

123. WOOD, R.C.

The Soldier's First Aid: A Simple Treatise on How to Treat a Sick or Wounded Comrade. By R.C. Wood, Q.-M.S., Army Medical-Corps. Chief Instructor of "First Aid" to Overseas Battalions and Stretcher Bearers of Military District No. 2, Toronto, Canada. Toronto: The Macmillan Company of Canada, Limited, [And] London: Macmillan & Co., Ltd., 1917.

> 93, [1] pp. + ads.; 168 × 108 mm.
> Issued in limp cloth.

124. WORDSWORTH, William

Macmillan's Literature Series, *Selections From Wordsworth and Tennyson*. Edited with Introduction and Notes by Pelham Edgar, PH.D. Professor of English, Victoria Coll., Univ. of Toronto. Toronto: The Macmillan Company of Canada, Limited, 1917.

> 159, [1] pp.; 177 × 117 mm.
> Issued in limp cloth.
> Macmillan's Literature Series.

1918

125. ADAMI, J.G.

Medical Contributions To The Study Of Evolution. By J.G. Adami M.D.,
F.R.S., F.R.C.P. The Macmillan Co. of Canada, Ltd. Toronto 1918.

xviii, 372 pp.; 215 × 135 mm.

126. BOTSFORD, George Willis

Macmillan's Canadian School Series, *A History of the World: For High
Schools*. By George Willis Botsford and Joy Barrett Botsford. Authorized by
the Advisory Board of the Department of Education for Use in Manitoba.
The Macmillan Company of Canada Limited, at St. Martin's House, Toronto
MCMXVIII.

iv, 518 pp.; 195 × 130 mm.
Macmillan's Canadian School Series.

127. CHISHOLM, Murdoch

Glimpses of Destiny: From "The Book". By Murdoch Chisholm, M.D.,
L.R.C.P. Lond. Toronto: The Macmillan Company of Canada, Limited, at
St. Martin's House, MCMXVIII.

x, 157, [1] pp.; 190 × 130 mm.
First published in 1917. Earlier printings not located.

128. COLERIDGE, S.T.

Macmillan's Canadian School Series, *Selected Poems of Coleridge and Tennyson*. Edited with introduction and notes by Pelham Edgar, PH.D., Professor
of English, Victoria College, University of Toronto. Toronto: The Macmillan Company of Canada, Limited, 1918.

208 pp.; 173 × 118 mm.
Issued in limp cloth.
Macmillan's Canadian School Series.

129. DUNCAN, David M.

Macmillan's Canadian School Series, *A History of Canada for Public Schools*.
By David M. Duncan, M.A., Major, 43rd Battalion, C.E.F., Assistant-
Superintendent of Schools, Winnipeg. Toronto: The Macmillan Company
of Canada, Limited, 1918.

viii, 344 pp.; 190 × 130 mm.
Macmillan's Canadian School Series.

130. EAYRS, Hugh Sterling

Sir Isaac Brock. By Hugh S. Eayrs. The Macmillan Company of Canada Ltd.
Toronto MCMXVIII.

xii, 108 pp.; 178 × 118 mm.
Revised in 1924 (see 219A).
Canadian Men of Action Series.

131.   HALL, H.S.

Macmillan's Canadian School Series, *A School Geometry*. By H.S. Hall, M.A.
And F.H. Stevens, M.A. Revised Canadian Edition. Authorized by the
Department of Education for use in Saskatchewan. Toronto: The Macmillan Company of Canada, Limited, 1918.

viii, 100 pp.; 186 × 123 mm.
This edition is Part 1. Part I and II issued in a separate edition (see 132). Reprinted
frequently. In 1931 the series title changed to the Western Canada Series.
Macmillan's Canadian School Series.

132.   HALL, H.S.

Macmillan's Canadian School Series, *A School Geometry*. By H.S. Hall, M.A.
And F.H. Stevens, M.A. Revised Canadian edition. Authorized by the
Department of Education for use in Saskatchewan. Toronto: The Macmillan Company of Canada, Limited, 1918.

xiv, 267, [1] pp.; 188 × 125 mm.
Reprinted frequently. Part I and II found bound in this edition. Part I issued
separately (see 131). In 1931 the series title changed to the Western Canada Series.
Macmillan's Canadian School Series.

133.   HUNT, John D.

The Dawn of a New Patriotism: A Training Course in Citizenship. By John
Hunt, Clerk of the Executive Council, Alberta. Second Edition. Revised and
Enlarged. [Quotation]. Toronto: The Macmillan Company of Canada, Limited, at St. Martin's House, MCMXVIII.

xx, 410 pp.; 207 × 135 mm.
First published in 1917. First edition not located.

134.   HUNT, John D.

Democracy in Canada. By John D. Hunt, Clerk of the Executive Council,
Alberta. Toronto: The Macmillan Company of Canada, Limited, at St.
Martin's House: MCMXVIII.

56 pp.; 200 × 130 mm.

135.   KIPLING, Rudyard

Twenty Poems From Rudyard Kipling. [Quotation]. The Macmillan Company
of Canada, Ltd. Toronto MCMXVIII.

[6], 38 pp.; 170 × 110 mm.
Issued in paper.

136.   LEAKE, Albert H.

The Vocational Education Of Girls And Women. By Albert H. Leake, Inspec-
tor Of Manual Training And Household Arts, Ontario, Canada. Author Of
Industrial Education — Its Problems, Methods, And Dangers, And The
Means And Methods Of Agricultual Education. Toronto: The Macmillan
Co. of Canada, Ltd. 1918.

xx, 430, [6] pp.; 190 × 125 mm.

137. PARSONS, Lydia Mary

Mrs. Parson's Manual For Women's Meetings. By Lydia Mary Parsons, Official Lecturer to Women's Institutes. Toronto: The Macmillan Company of Canada Ltd. at St. Martin's House, 1918.

vi, 90 pp.; 140 × 130 mm.

138. PATERSON, Maude Elizabeth

A Child's Garden of Stories. By Maude Elizabeth Paterson. Illustrated by Estelle M. Ker. Toronto: The Macmillan Company of Canada Limited, 1918.

x, 160 pp.; 192 × 125 mm.
First published by Morang in 1911. Macmillan edition reprinted in 1926 and 1931.

139. SMITH, Francis Drake Lewellyn

[Cover-title:] *The Achievements of A Modest Old Gentleman*. Smith. Macmillan. Toronto.

13, [1] pp.; 163 × 115 mm.
Issued in paper.

140. WELLS, H.G.

Joan and Peter: The Story of an Education. By H.G. Wells, Author of "Mr. Britling Sees It Through," etc. Toronto: The Macmillan Co. Of Canada, Ltd., 1918.

[6], 594 pp. + ads.; 192 × 130 mm.

141. WELLS, H.G.

Mr. Britling Sees It Through. By H.G. Wells, Author of "The Wife of Sir Isaac Harmon," "The Research Magnificent," "What Is Coming," Etc. With Frontispiece. Toronto: The Macmillan Company of Canada, Ltd., At St. Martin's House, 1918.

[4], 443, [1] pp.; 196 × 130 mm.
First published in 1916. Earlier printings not located. Reprinted frequently.

1919

142. BELL, W. Blair

The Pituitary: A Study Of The Morphology, Physiology, Pathology, And Surgical Treatment Of The Pituitary, Together With An Account Of The Therapeutical Uses Of The Extracts Made From This Organ. By W. Blair Bell B.S., M.D. Lond., Gynaecological Surgeon, Royal Infirmary, Liverpool; Lecturer In Clinical Gynaecology In The University Of Liverpool; Sometime Examiner In Gynaecology And Obstetrics To The Royal Colleges Of Physicians And Surgeons, England, And To The Universities Of Durham And Belfast; Arris And Gale Lecturer, And Hunterian Professor, Royal College Of Surgeons, England. Toronto: The Macmillan Company of Canada Ltd 1919. All rights reserved.

xx, 348 pp.; 230 × 160 mm.

142A BURROUGHS, John

Macmillan's Literature Series, *Sharp Eyes And Other Essays*. By John Burroughs. Toronto: The Macmillan Company Of Canada, Limited, 1919.

106 pp.; 172 × 121 mm.
First published by Morang in 1910. Wrapper reads "Macmillan's Prairie Classics".
Issued in paper.
Macmillan's Literature Series.

143. *Canada's Song Book for the Middle School and Singing Clubs*. Arranged for Two-Part Singing. Toronto: The Macmillan Company of Canada, Ltd., at St. Martin's House, 1919.

63, [1] pp.; 195 × 154 mm.
Reissued in 1920 with one additional song on page [64].

144. CRAWFORD, J.T.

Macmillan's Canadian School Series, *Solutions of the Examples in the Crawford Algebras*. By J.T. Crawford, B.A., Chief Instructor in Mathematics, University Schools. Assistant Professor of Mathematics, Faculty of Education, University of Toronto. Toronto: The Macmillan Company of Canada, Limited, 1919.

145, [1] pp.; 188 × 123 mm.
Macmillan's Canadian School Series.

145. DUNCAN, David M.

Macmillan's Canadian School Series, *The Story of the Canadian People*. By David M. Duncan, M.A. Assistant-Superintendent of Schools, Winnipeg. Authorized for use in the provinces of Manitoba, Saskatchewan, Alberta and British Columbia. Toronto: The Macmillan Company of Canada, Limited, 1919.

xxviii, 428 pp.; 190 × 125 mm.
First published by Morang in 1904. A new edition published in 1920 (see 164A).
Macmillan's Canadian School Series.

146. McINTYRE, W.A.

Macmillan's Canadian School Series, *Spelling and Dictation*. By W.A. McIntyre and A.W. Hooper, Provincial Normal School, Winnipeg. Grade 2. The Macmillan Company of Canada, Ltd. Toronto MCMXIX.

42 pp.; 188 × 140 mm.
First published in 1917 (see 116). New edition in 1919. Reprinted in 1920. The 1919 edition issued in limp cloth.
Macmillan's Canadian School Series.

147. McINTYRE, W.A.

Macmillan's Canadian School Series, *Spelling and Dictation*. By W.A. McIntyre and A.W. Hooper, Provincial Normal School, Winnipeg. Grade Two and Three. The Macmillan Company of Canada, Ltd. Toronto MCMXIX.

88 pp.; 188 × 140 mm.
First published in 1917 (see 116). New edition in 1919. Issued in limp cloth.
Macmillan's Canadian School Series.

148.   McINTYRE, W.A.

Macmillan's Canadian School Series, *Spelling and Dictation*. By W.A. McIntyre and A.W. Hooper, Provincial Normal School, Winnipeg. Grade 2, 3, 4,
5. The Macmillan Company of Canada Ltd. Toronto MCMXIX.

172 pp.; 188 × 140 mm.
First published in 1917 (see 116). New edition in 1919. Issued in limp cloth.
Macmillan's Canadian School Series.

149.   McINTYRE, W.A.

Macmillan's Canadian School Series, *Spelling and Dictation*. By W.A. McIntyre and A.W. Hooper, Provincial Normal School, Winnipeg. Grade 3, 4,
and 5. The Macmillan Company of Canada Ltd. Toronto MCMXIX.

140 pp.; 188 × 140 mm.
First published in 1917 (see 116). New edition in 1919. Issued in limp cloth.
Macmillan's Canadian School Series.

150.   "M.P."

The Young Men's Parliamentary Guide. By "M.P." Toronto: The Macmillan
Company of Canada Ltd. at St. Martin's House 1919.

vi, 90 pp.; 142 × 105 mm.
The same text also published in 1919 under the title *The Canadian Parliamentary
Guide*, by M.P.

151.   PETERSON, C.W.

Wake Up, Canada! Reflections on Vital National Issues. By C.W. Peterson.
Toronto: The Macmillan Company of Canada Ltd., at St. Martin's House
MCMXIX.

365, [1] pp.; 205 × 136 mm.

152.   WOOD, William

Flag and Fleet: How the British Navy Won the Freedom of the Seas. By
William Wood. Lieutenant-Colonel, Canadian Militia; Member of the Cana-
dian Special Mission Overseas; Editor of "The Logs of the Conquest of
Canada"; Author of "All Afloat: A Chronicle of Craft and Waterways";
"Elizabethan Sea Dogs: A Chronicle of Drake and his Companions"; and
"The Fight for Canada: A Naval and Military Sketch". With a Preface by
Admiral-of-the Fleet The Earl Beatty, G.C.B., O.M., G.C.V.O., Etc., Etc.
Toronto: The Macmillan Company of Canada, Ltd., at St. Martin's House
1919.

xiv, 301, [3] pp.; 187 × 127 mm.
Issued in cloth and limp cloth.

1920

153.   BROWN, John

Rab and His Friends and Our Dogs. By Dr. John Brown. Toronto: The
Macmillan Company of Canada, Limited, 1920.

53, [3] pp.; 177 × 115 mm.
First published by Morang in 1909. Macmillan edition issued in paper.

154. **HARDY, E.A.**

Selections From the Canadian Poets. Chosen and edited by E.A. Hardy, B.A. [Quotation]. Toronto: The Macmillan Company of Canada Limited, at St. Martin's House MCMXX.

128 pp.; 195 × 133 mm.
First published by Morang in 1909. Macmillan edition reprinted frequently.

155. **McINTYRE, Alexander**

A Modern Arithmetic: Book I. By Alexander McIntyre B.A., Vice-Principal, Normal School, Winnipeg. Authorized by the Advisory Board for Use in Manitoba. Revised Edition. Toronto: The Macmillan Co. of Canada Ltd., 1920.

viii, 244 pp.; 188 × 128 mm.
First published by Morang in 1904. Macmillan edition issued in limp cloth.

156. **McINTYRE, Alexander**

A Modern Arithmetic: Book II. By Alexander McIntyre B.A., Vice-Principal, Normal School, Winnipeg. Authorized by the Advisory Board for Use in Manitoba. Revised Edition. Toronto: The Macmillan Co. of Canada Ltd., 1920.

viii, 331, [1] pp.; 183 × 125 mm.
First published by Morang in 1904. Macmillan edition issued in limp cloth.

157. **MITCHELL, George W.**

Macmillan's Canadian School Series, *An Introduction to Latin Prose*. Revised Edition. By George W. Mitchell M.A., Professor of Classics, Queen's University, Kingston, Ontario. Toronto: The Macmillan Company of Canada, Limited 1920.

366 pp.; 192 × 125 mm.
First published in 1907 (see 7).

158. **RAWLING, Louis Bathe**

Landmarks And Surface Markings Of The Human Body. By L. Bathe Rawling, M.B., B.C. (Cant.), F.R.C.S., Surgeon, Senior Demonstrator Of Operative Surgery, Late Senior Demonstrator Of Anatomy, St. Bartholomew's Hospital; Examiner In Surgery At Cambridge University. With Thirty-One Illustrations. Fifth Edition (Sixth Reprint). Toronto: The Macmillan Company Of Canada, Ltd., 1920.

viii, 96 pp.; 218 × 138 mm.
Earlier editions not located. Reprinted in 1922.

159. **RUSKIN, John**

The King of the Golden River or The Black Brothers: A Legend of Stiria. By John Ruskin, M.A. Illustrated by Richard Doyle. Toronto: The Macmillan Co. of Canada, Limited, 1920. (Canadian Copyright Edition).

64 pp.; 175 × 118 mm.
First published by Morang in 1905. Macmillan edition issued in paper.
Macmillan's Eclectic Series.

1921

160.   [BRIDLE, Augustus]
The Masques of Ottawa. By "Domino". [Quotation]. Toronto: The Macmillan Company of Canada, Ltd., at St. Martin's House. MCMXXI.

283, [1] pp.; 220 × 142 mm.

161.   BRYCE, James
Canada: An Actual Democracy. By James Bryce (Viscount Bryce), Author of "Modern Democracies," "The Holy Roman Empire," Etc. Toronto: The Macmillan Company of Canada, Ltd., at St. Martin's House 1921.

[2], 54 pp. + ads.; 225 × 143 mm.

162.   COLEMAN, Walter M.
Beginners' Zoology. By Walter M. Coleman. Authorized by the Minister of Education for Ontario. Toronto: The Macmillan Co. of Canada, Limited 1921.

[4], 229, [1] pp.; 190 × 130 mm.
Reprinted in 1922, 1923 and 1924.

163.   CORNISH, George A.
Macmillan's Western School Series, *A Laboratory Manual To Accompany Chemistry: A Text-Book For High-Schools*. By George A. Cornish B.A., Assistant Professor in Science, College of Education, University of Toronto and Chief Instructor in Science, University Schools, Toronto. Assisted by Arthur Smith, B.A., Chief Instructor in Physics, Central Technical School, Toronto. Authorized in Alberta, British Columbia, Manitoba and Saskatchewan. Toronto: The Macmillan Company of Canada, Limited 1921.

vi, 95, [3] pp.; 195 × 130 mm.
Another edition published in 1917 (see 109). Reprinted frequently. Series title varies.
Macmillan's Western School Series.

164.   DALY, George Thomas
Catholic Problems in Western Canada. By George Thomas Daly, C.SS.R. With Preface by the Most Reverend O.E. Mathieu, Archibishop of Regina. Toronto: The Macmillan Company of Canada, Ltd., at St. Martin's House, 1921.

352 pp.; 208 × 138 mm.

164A DUNCAN, David M.
Macmillan's Western Canada Series, *The Story of the Canadian People*. New Edition. By David M. Duncan, M.A., Assistant-Superintendent of Schools, Winnipeg. Note: This edition is for use during the School Year of 1920-21 in the Province of Manitoba only. Toronto: The Macmillan Company of Canada, Limited, 1920.

viii, 291, [1] pp.; 193 × 128 mm.
First published by Macmillan in 1919 (see 145). Reprinted in 1921, 1922 and 1923 with index. Issued in limp cloth.
Western Canada Series.

165. FERGUSON, W.C.

The Ontario High School French Reader. Edited by W.C. Ferguson, B.A. Ontario College of Education. And H.S. McKellar, B.A. University College, Toronto. Authorized by The Minister of Education for Ontario. Toronto: The Macmillan Company of Canada, Limited, 1921.

151, [1] pp.; 193 × 123 mm.
Reprinted frequently.

166. HALDANE, Richard Burdon

The Reign of Relativity. By Viscount Haldane. Toronto: The Macmillan Company Of Canada, Limited, 1921.

xxiv, 430 pp.; 227 × 146 mm.

167. HÉMON, Louis

Maria Chapdelaine. By Louis Hémon. A Translation By W.H. Blake, Author of "Brown Waters," etc. Toronto: The Macmillan Company of Canada Limited, 1921. All rights of this translation reserved.

263, [1] pp.; 189 × 124 mm.
Reprinted frequently. Issued in French in 1931 (see 460). Issued in the St. Martin's Classics series in 1932 and reprinted often. Reset and reissued with an introduction by Hugh Eayrs in 1938 (see 800). Reissued again in 1965 (see 1729).

168. HUGHES, Edward A.

Britain and Greater Britain in the Nineteenth Century. By Edward A. Hughes, M.A., Assistant Master at the Royal Naval College, Dartmouth, Sometime Major Scholar of Trinity College, Cambridge. The Macmillan Co. of Canada, Limited St. Martin's House, Toronto MCMXXI.

[8], 295, [1] pp.; 190 × 120 mm.
First published in 1919. Earlier printings not located.

169. LAUT, Agnes C.

Canada at the Cross Roads. By Agnes C. Laut, Author of "The Fur Trade in North America", Etc. Etc. Toronto: The Macmillan Company of Canada, Ltd., at St. Martin's House, MCMXXI.

[6], 279, [1] pp. + ads.; 203 × 138 mm.

170. McINTYRE, W.A.

The Alexandra Readers: Primer. By W.A. McIntyre, B.A., LL.D. Principal, Normal School, Winnipeg. And John C. Saul, M.A. Authorized by the Departments of Education for Use in the Schools of Alberta and Saskatchewan. Toronto: The Macmillan Company of Canada, Limited, 1921.

100 pp.; 188 × 132 mm.
First published by Morang in 1908. Earlier printings not located.

171. McINTYRE, W.A.

The Alexandra Readers: First Reader. By W.A. McIntyre, B.A., LL.D. Principal, Normal School, Winnipeg. And John C. Saul, M.A. Authorized by the Departments of Education for Use in the Schools of Alberta and

Saskatchewan. Toronto: The Macmillan Company of Canada, Limited, 1921.

144 pp.; 188 × 132 mm.
First published by Morang in 1908. Earlier printings not located.

172. McINTYRE, W.A.

The Alexandra Readers: Second Reader. By W.A. McIntyre, B.A., LL.D. Principal, Normal School, Winnipeg. John Dearness, M.A. Vice-Principal, Normal School, London. And John C. Saul M.A. Authorized by the Departments of Education for Use in the Schools of Alberta and Saskatchewan. Toronto: The Macmillan Company of Canada, Limited, 1921.

224 pp.; 188 × 132 mm.
First published by Morang in 1908. Earlier printings not located.

173. McINTYRE, W.A.

The Alexandra Readers: Third Reader. By W.A. McIntyre, B.A., LL.D. Principal, Normal School, Winnipeg. John Dearness, M.A. Vice-Principal, Normal School, London. And John C. Saul, M.A. Authorized by the Departments of Education for Use in the Schools of Alberta and Saskatchewan. Toronto: The Macmillan Company of Canada, Limited, 1921.

388 pp.; 188 × 132 mm.
First published by Morang in 1908. Earlier printings not located.

174. McINTYRE, W.A.

The Alexandra Readers: Fourth Reader. By W.A. McIntyre, B.A., LL.D. Principal, Normal School, Winnipeg. John Dearness, M.A. Vice-Principal, Normal School, London. And John C. Saul, M.A. Authorized by the Departments of Education for Use in the Schools of Alberta and Saskatchewan. Toronto: The Macmillan Company of Canada, Limited, 1921.

416 pp.; 188 × 132 mm.
First published by Morang in 1908. Earlier printings not located.

1922

175. BEER, Thomas

The Fair Rewards. Thomas Beer. [Quotations]. Toronto: The Macmillan Company of Canada, Ltd., at St. Martin's House, MCMXXII.

292 pp.; 198 × 136 mm.

176. BLAKE, W.H.

In a Fishing Country. By W.H. Blake, Author of "Brown-Waters" &c. Toronto: The Macmillan Company of Canada Ltd., at St. Martin's House, MCMXXII.

263, [1] pp.; 195 × 130 mm.

177. BOTSFORD, George Willis

High School Ancient History. By George Willis Botsford, PH.D. Professor of History, Columbia University. Authorized by the Minister of Education for Ontario. The Macmillan Company of Canada, Limited at St. Martin's House, Toronto, MCMXXII.

xvi, 467, [1] pp.; 193 × 127 mm.
Wrapper title is *The Ontario High School Ancient History.* First published in 1917. Reprinted in 1918,1919,1920,1921, and 1922. Earlier printings not located. This is a revised edition of the author's *History of the Ancient World.*

178. BOWMAN, Louise Morey

Moonlight and Common Day. By Louise Morey Bowman. Toronto: The Macmillan Company of Canada Limited, at St. Martin's House, MCMXXII.

63, [1] pp.; 220 × 175 mm.

179. *The Canadian Readers: Book One: A Primer and First Reader.* The Macmillan Company of Canada Limited, Toronto, 1922.

160 pp.; 195 × 135 mm.
Reprinted frequently.

180. CATHER, Willa

One of Ours. Willa Cather. [Quotation]. Toronto: The Macmillan Company of Canada, Ltd., At St. Martin's House, 1922.

[10], 459, [1] pp.; 195 × 132 mm.

181. COWPER, E.E.

Two On The Trail: A Story Of Canada Snows. By E.E. Cowper. Author of "The Moonrakers," "Kittiwake's Castle," "Crew of The Silver Fish," Etc. With A Frontispiece By W. Paget. London: The Sheldon Press, Northumberland Avenue, W.C. 2. New York And Toronto: The Macmillan Company.

160 pp.; 195 × 125 mm.

181A CRAWFORD, J.T.

Macmillan's Canadian School Series, *Senior High School Algebra.* By J.T. Crawford, B.A., Chief Instructor in Mathematics, University Schools, Assistant Professor of Mathematics, College of Education, University of Toronto, Author of "The High School Algebra", Joint Author of "The High School Arithmetic". Toronto: The Macmillan Company of Canada, Limited 1922.

x, 262 pp.; 195 × 128 mm.
Reprinted frequently.
Macmillan's Canadian School Series.

182. *General Science: A Handbook to Accompany the Prescribed Syllabus.* Authorized by the Advisory Board of the Department of Education for use in High Schools and Collegiate Institutes in Manitoba. Toronto: The Macmillan Company of Canada Limited, 1922.

[6], 202 pp.; 188 × 123 mm.
Issued in paper. Reprinted in 1923, 1924 and 1925.

183. HAYWARD, Victoria

Romantic Canada. By Victoria Hayward. Illustrated with Photographs by Edith S. Watson. With an Introduction by Edward J. O'Brien. Toronto: The Macmillan Company of Canada, Ltd. at St. Martin's House, 1922.

xvi, 254 pp.; 273 × 195 mm.

184. LOFTHOUSE, J.

A Thousand Miles From A Post Office Or, Twenty Years' Life And Travel In The Hudson's Bay Regions. By The Right Rev. J. Lofthouse, D.D. (Late) Bishop Of Keewatin. With A Preface By The Archbishop Of Canterbury. With Illustrations. London: Society For Promoting Christian Knowledge. New York And Toronto: The Macmillan Co. 1922.

viii, 183, [1] pp.; 195 × 123 mm.

185. PERTWEE, Roland

Men of Affairs. Roland Pertwee. Toronto: The Macmillan Company of Canada, Ltd., At St. Martin's House, 1922.

viii, 285, [1] pp.; 193 × 130 mm.

186. REAMAN, George Elmore

Teacher's Manual To Accompany Wall Charts of English For New Canadians. By George Elmore Reaman, M.A., B.Paed., PH.D., Director of Education, Y.M.C.A., Toronto. Toronto: The Macmillan Company of Canada Ltd., at St. Martin's House 1922.

[4], 28 pp.; 190 × 128 mm.
Issued in limp cloth.

187. RITCHIE, Mary Christine

Major General Sir Geoffrey Twining, K.C.M.G., C.B., M.V.O.: A Biographical Sketch and the Story of His East African Diaries. By Mary Christine Ritchie. [Quotation]. Montreal: A.T. Chapman [and] Toronto: The Macmillan Company of Canada Limited 1922.

102 pp.; 188 × 121 mm.
Issued in paper.

188. ROTHNEY, William Oliver

Character Education in the Elementary School. By William Oliver Rothney. Inspector of Protestant Schools, Quebec, and Professor of Education, University of Bishop's College, Lennoxville, Quebec, Canada. 1922, Toronto: The Macmillan Company of Canada Ltd., at St. Martin's House.

x, 157, [1] pp.; 193 × 130 mm.

189. SCOTT, Walter

Ivanhoe. By Sir Walter Scott, Bart. Abridged and Edited with Introduction, Notes, Glossary, &c by Fanny Johnson, Formerly Head Mistress of Bolton High School. Toronto: The Macmillan Company of Canada Limited, 1922.

xx, 290 pp.; 179 × 120 mm.
Reprinted frequently. Reprinted in the St. Martin's Classics Series in 1932.

190. WARD, James Edward

The Wayfarer: Leaves from a Wanderer's Log. By James Edward Ward.
Toronto: The Macmillan Company of Canada Limited, 1922.

[14], 231, [1] pp.; 188 × 133 mm.

191. WELLS, H.G.

The Secret Places of the Heart. By H.G. Wells. Toronto: The Macmillan
Company of Canada Limited, at St. Martin's House, 1922. All rights reserved.

[6], 287, [1] pp.; 192 × 130 mm.

1923

192. BARBEAU, Marius

Indian Days in the Canadian Rockies. By Marius Barbeau. Illustrations by W.
Langdon Kihn. Toronto: The Macmillan Company of Canada Limited, at
St. Martin's House, MCMXXIII.

[8], 208 pp.; 220 × 160 mm.

193. BLAKE, W.H.

A Fisherman's Creed. By W.H. Blake, Author of "In a Fishing Country" etc.
Toronto: The Macmillan Company of Canada Limited 1923.

[6], 40 pp.; 165 × 124 mm.

194. BROADUS, Edmund Kemper

A Book of Canadian Prose and Verse. Compiled and Edited by Edmund
Kemper Broadus (Professor of English in the University of Alberta) And
Eleanor Hammond Broadus. Toronto: The Macmillan Company of Canada
Limited, 1923.

xvi, 390 pp.; 195 × 130 mm.
Reprinted in 1924 and 1925. Revised edition published in 1934 (see 565). Also issued
in Macmillan's Western Canada Series.

195. *A Canadian Publishing House.* [Quotation]. The Macmillan Company of
Canada Limited, St. Martin's House — Toronto, 1923.

39, [1] pp.; 202 × 140 mm.

196. CATHER, Willa

A Lost Lady. By Willa Cather. [Quotation]. Toronto: The Macmillan Company Of Canada, Ltd., At St. Martin's House, 1923.

173, [1] pp.; 195 × 135 mm.

197. DE LA MARE, Walter

The Riddle and Other Tales. By Walter de la Mare. Toronto: The Macmillan
Company of Canada, Ltd., At St. Martin's House, 1923.

[6], 290 pp.; 194 × 130 mm.

198.   DE LA ROCHE, Mazo

Possession. By Mazo De La Roche. Toronto: The Macmillan Company of Canada, Ltd., St. Martin's House, MCMXXIII.

[8], 289, [1] pp.; 195 × 133 mm.

199.   DELL, Floyd

Janet March. A Novel by Floyd Dell, Author of *Moon-Calf* and *The Briary-Bush*. Toronto: The Macmillan Company Of Canada, Ltd., At St. Martin's House, 1923.

[6], 457, [1] pp.; 197 × 135 mm.

200.   *Essays Selected for Class Use*. By the English Staff of the University of Toronto. Toronto: The Macmillan Company of Canada Limited, at St. Martin's House, 1923.

[4], 203, [1] pp.; 193 × 125 mm.

200A FREDERICK, John T.

Druida. John T. Frederick. With seven woodcuts by Wilfred Jones. Toronto: The Macmillan Company Of Canada, Ltd., At St. Martin's House, 1923.

[4], 286 pp.; 196 × 135 mm.

201.   GOGGIN, D.J.

The Canadian Citizen. Edited by D.J. Goggin. Toronto: The Macmillan Company of Canada Limited, at St. Martin's House, 1923.

viii, 179, [1] pp.; 190 × 125 mm.
Reprinted in Macmillan's Canadian School Series in 1925.

202.   HARDY, E.A.

Talks on Education. By E.A. Hardy, B.A., D.Paed. Head of the Department of History, Jarvis Street Collegiate Institute, Toronto; Editor, "Selections from Canadian Poets," "Selected Poems of Wordsworth and Tennyson"; Author, "The Public Library: Its Place in Our Educational System." Toronto: The Macmillan Company of Canada Limited, at St. Martin's House, 1923.

[10], 101, [1] pp.; 189 × 126 mm.

203.   KIRK, R.G.

Six Breeds. By R.G. Kirk. With illustrations by Charles Livingston Bull. Toronto: The Macmillan Company Of Canada, Ltd., At St. Martin's House, 1923.

266 pp.; 197 × 137 mm.

204.   LIVESAY, Florence Randal

Shepherd's Purse. By Florence Randal Livesay, Author of "Songs from Ukraina". Toronto: The Macmillan Company of Canada Limited, at St. Martin's House MCMXXIII.

66, [2] pp.; 190 × 130 mm.

205. LOUDON, W.J.

Studies of Student Life. By W.J. Loudon. The Macmillan Company of Canada Limited, 1923.

[8], 110 pp.; 175 × 115 mm.

206. MacTAVISH, Newton

Thrown In. By Newton MacTavish. With an Introduction by J.D. Logan, Ph.D., Hon. Litt.D. Toronto: The Macmillan Company of Canada Limited, at St. Martin's House, 1923.

xii, 196 pp.; 195 × 125 mm.

207. MANSFIELD, Katherine

Bliss and Other Stories. By Katherine Mansfield. The Macmillan Company of Canada, Toronto.

[8], 279, [1] pp.; 189 × 115 mm.

208. MANSFIELD, Katherine

The Doves' Nest And Other Stories. By Katherine Mansfield. The Macmillan Company Of Canada, Toronto.

xxiv, 196, [2] pp.; 190 × 115 mm.
Reprinted in 1923. First printing not located.

209. MARSH, E.L.

Where the Buffalo Roamed: The Story of the Canadian West. By E.L. Marsh, Author of *The Story of Canada* and *Birds of Peasemarsh*. With illustrations from Paintings by Paul Kane and from photographs and drawings. Toronto: The Macmillan Company of Canada Limited, 1923.

[6], 257, [1] pp.; 189 × 125 mm.

210. OSBORNE, Marian

The Song of Israfel and Other Poems. By Marian Osborne. Erskine Macdonald Ltd. London W.C.1., Toronto: The Macmillan Co. of Canada, 1923.

67, [1] pp.; 195 × 125 mm.

210A RUSSELL, H.J.

Canadian Commercial Correspondence and Business Training, With Which is Incorporated *A Manual of Shorthand Dictation*. By H.J. Russell, Commercial Master, St. John's Technical High School, Winnipeg, Lecturer In Business English, Evening Courses, University of Manitoba. New And Completely Revised Edition. Toronto: The Macmillan Company Of Canada Limited 1923.

xx, 323, [1] pp.; 190 × 130 mm.
First published in 1915 (see 93). Reprinted in 1930. New edition published in 1944 under title *The Competent Secretary* (see 1021).

211.   SADLEIR, Michael
Desolate Splendour. By Michael Sadleir. Toronto: The Macmillan Company
of Canada Limited, at St. Martin's House, 1923.
[8], 320 pp.; 190 × 125 mm.

211A   SIWERTZ, Sigfrid
Downstream. By Sigfrid Siwertz. Toronto: The Macmillan Company Of
Canada, Ltd., At St. Martin's House, 1923.
[6], 405, [1] pp.; 196 × 138 mm.

212.   SMYTHE, Albert Ernest Stafford
The Garden of the Sun. By Albert Ernest Stafford Smythe. Toronto: The
Macmillan Company of Canada Limited, at St. Martin's House,
MCMXXIII.
81, [1] pp.; 192 × 135 mm.

213.   WELLS, H.G.
Men Like Gods. A Novel By H.G. Wells. The Macmillan Company of
Canada, Ltd. St. Martin's House, Bond Street, Toronto, 1923. All rights
reserved.
viii, 327, [1] pp.; 190 × 125 mm.

1924

213A   ASHWORTH, Edward Montague
La Roux. By Johnston Abbott [pseud.]. Toronto: The Macmillan Company
Of Canada, Limited, At St. Martin's House, 1924.
[6], 348 pp.; 195 × 134 mm.

214.   [BAGNOLD, Enid]
Serena Blandish, or The Difficulty of Getting Married. By A Lady of Quality.
The Macmillan Company of Canada, Limited, Toronto.
[4], 222, [2] pp.; 204 × 142 mm.

215.   BOWMAN, Louise Morey
Dream Tapestries. By Louise Morey Bowman, Author of "Moonlight and
Common Day". [Quotation]. Toronto: The Macmillan Company of Canada
Limited, at St. Martin's House, MCMXXIV.
91, [1] pp.; 195 × 130 mm.

216.   BRIDLE, Augustus
Hansen: A Novel of Canadianization. By Augustus Bridle. Author of "Masques of Ottawa", and "Sons of Canada". Toronto: The Macmillan Company
of Canada Limited, at St. Martin's House, 1924.
viii, 368 pp.; 195 × 130 mm.

217. CRAWFORD, J.T.

Solutions Of The Examples In Senior High School Algebra. By J.T. Crawford, B.A., Chief Instructor In Mathematics, University Schools, Associate Professor Of Mathematics, College Of Education, University Of Toronto. Author Of "The High School Algebra". Author Of "Senior High School Algebra". Joint Author Of "The High School Arithmetic". Toronto: The Macmillan Company of Canada Limited 1924.

iv, 152 pp.; 195 × 125 mm.

218. DALTON, A.C.

Flame and Adventure. By A.C. Dalton, Author of "The Marriage of Music and Other Poems". With illustrations by C.A. Ferguson. Toronto: The Macmillan Company of Canada Limited, at St. Martin's House, 1924.

[10], 73, [1] pp.; 182 × 115 mm.

219. DUNHAM, B. Mabel

The Trail of the Conestoga. By B. Mabel Dunham. With Foreword by The Rt. Hon. W.L. Mackenzie King. Toronto: The Macmillan Company of Canada Limited, at St. Martin's House, MCMXXIV.

[10], 342 pp.; 195 × 125 mm.
Reprinted in 1933.

219A EAYRS, Hugh Sterling

Sir Isaac Brock. By Hugh S. Eayrs. Revised Edition. Toronto: The Macmillan Company of Canada Limited, 1924.

xii, 108 pp.; 185 × 125 mm.
First published in 1918 (see 130). Reprinted in 1926.
Canadian Men of Action Series.

220. GARNETT, David

A Man in the Zoo. By David Garnett. Illustrated with wood engravings by R.A. Garnett. Toronto: The Macmillan Company of Canada Limited, 1924.

[6], 93, [3] pp.; 193 × 130 mm.

221. HANNA, D.B.

Trains of Recollection: Drawn from Fifty Years of Railway Service in Scotland and Canada and told to Arthur Hawkes. By D.B. Hanna, First President of the Canadian National Railways. Toronto: The Macmillan Company of Canada Ltd., at St. Martin's House, MCMXXIV.

xii, 340 pp.; 228 × 142 mm.

222. HERGESHEIMER, Joseph

Joseph Hergesheimer. *Balisand*. [Quotation]. Toronto: The Macmillan Company Of Canada, Ltd., At St. Martin's House, MCMXXIV.

371, [1] pp. + ads.; 192 × 131 mm.

223. JEFFRIES, John

Macmillan's Literature Series, *Longer Narrative Poems*. Edited with Notes by

John Jeffries, B.A. English Specialist, Jarvis Collegiate Institute, Toronto. Toronto: The Macmillan Company of Canada, Limited, 1924.

136 pp.; 175 × 120 mm.
First published by Morang in 1909. Macmillan edition issued in paper.
Macmillan's Literature Series.

223A MacGIBBON, Duncan Alexander

An Introduction to Economics for Canadian Readers. By Duncan Alexander MacGibbon, Professor of Political Economy in the University of Alberta. Toronto: The Macmillan Company of Canada Limited 1924.

xii, 203, [1] pp.; 188 × 125 mm.
Revised in 1929 and in 1935 (see 646A). Reprinted frequently. Revised in 1946 and reprinted in 1947 and 1948 (see 1189).

224. MACHEN, Arthur

Dog and Duck. Arthur Machen. Toronto: The Macmillan Company of Canada, Ltd., at St. Martin's House, 1924.

226 pp.; 196 × 135 mm.

225. MACKENZIE, Compton

Santa Claus in Summer. By Compton Mackenzie. With drawings by A.H. Watson. The Macmillan Company Of Canada, Toronto.

viii, 298 pp.; 201 × 135 mm.

226. MANN, Thomas

Buddenbrooks. Translated from the German of Thomas Mann by H.T. Lowe-Porter. Volume I. Toronto: The Macmillan Company Of Canada, Ltd., At St. Martin's House, 1924.

[6], 389, [1] pp.; 195 × 135 mm.

227. MANN, Thomas

Buddenbrooks. Translated from the German of Thomas Mann by H.T. Lowe-Porter. Volume II. Toronto: The Macmillan Company Of Canada, Ltd., At St. Martin's House, 1924.

[2], 359, [1] pp.; 195 × 135 mm.

228. MANSFIELD, Katherine

Something Childish and Other Stories. By Katherine Mansfield. [Quotation]. The Macmillan Company of Canada, Toronto.

x, 258, [2] pp.; 190 × 124 mm.

229. Macmillan's Canadian Text Books, *A Modern Phonic Primer: Part I: The Green Primer*. Authorized by the Advisory Board of the Department of Education for Use in the Public Schools of Manitoba. Toronto: The Macmillan Company of Canada, Limited, 1924.

64 pp.; 180 × 125 mm.
First published by Morang in 1900. Macmillan edition issued in limp cloth.
Macmillan's Canadian Text-Books Series.

230.   MOFFAT, Gertrude MacGregor

A Book of Verses. By Gertrude MacGregor Moffat. Toronto: The Macmillan Company of Canada Limited, at St. Martin's House, 1924.

xvi, 139, [1] pp.; 180 × 113 mm.

231.   ROBERTS, Charles G.D.

The Western Canada Series, *Neighbours Unknown*. By Charles G.D. Roberts. Author of "Kings in Exile", "The Backwoodsmen", "The House in the Water", Etc. Illustrated By Paul Bransom. Authorized for Use in the Province of Manitoba. Toronto: The Macmillan Company of Canada Limited, 1924.

x, 266 pp.; 189 × 120 mm.
Reprinted frequently. Also issued in the St. Martin's Classics Series in 1924 and 1933.
Western Canada Series.

232.   ROBERTSON, John K.

X-Rays and X-Ray Apparatus: An Elementary Course. By John K. Robertson, Associate Professor of Physics, Queen's University, Kingston, Canada. Toronto: The Macmillan Company of Canada, Limited, At St. Martin's House, 1924.

xii, 228 pp.; 233 × 157 mm.

233.   Macmillan's Literature Series, *Selected Poems From Wordsworth, Coleridge, Tennyson, and Browning*. With Brief Biographical Sketches and Notes. Authorized for Use in Saskatchewan. Toronto: The Macmillan Company of Canada Limited, 1924.

142 pp.; 175 × 120 mm.
Issued in limp cloth.
Macmillan's Literature Series.

234.   SUCKOW, Ruth

Country People. Ruth Suckow. Toronto: The Macmillan Company of Canada, Ltd., at St. Martin's House, 1924.

213, [1] pp.; 192 × 135 mm.

235.   WALLACE, W. Stewart

Sir John Macdonald. By W. Stewart Wallace, Librarian of the University of Toronto. Toronto: The Macmillan Company of Canada Limited, 1924.

[10], 132 pp.; 180 × 125 mm.
Macmillan's Canadian Statesmen Series.

1925

236.   BLACK, Newton Henry

Practical Chemistry: Fundamental Facts and Applications to Modern Life. By N. Henry Black, A.M. and James Bryant Conant, PH.D. Adapted for use in

the Schools of British Columbia by R.R. Clark. Toronto: The Macmillan
Company of Canada Limited, at St. Martin's House, 1925.

xii, 392 pp.; 190 × 130 mm.
Reprinted in 1932 and revised in 1937 (see 726).

237. BLAKE, W.H.

Brown Waters and Other Sketches. Together with a Fragment and Yarns. By
W.H. Blake. With an introduction by Vincent Massey. [Quotation]. Toronto: The Macmillan Company of Canada Limited, at St. Martin's House,
1925.

xiv, 249, [1] pp.; 185 × 125 mm.
First published in 1915 (see 77). Third edition published in 1940 (see 861).

238. BLUMENSTEIN, J.H.

McGill University Economic Studies: No. 3: National Problems of
Canada: *The Taxation of Corporations in Canada*. J.H. Blumenstein, M.A.
Published at St. Martin's House, Toronto, by The Macmillan Company of
Canada, Limited, for the Department of Economics and Political Science,
McGill University, Montreal. Price 40¢.

58 pp.; 216 × 140 mm.
Issued in paper.
McGill University Economic Studies Series.

239. BRADY, Alexander

Thomas D'arcy McGee. By Alexander Brady. Lecturer in Political Science,
University of Toronto. Toronto: The Macmillan Company of Canada Limited, 1925.

[8], 182 pp.; 180 × 125 mm.

240. BURNETT, Eliza Moore

Macmillan's Canadian School Series, *Manual of Method To Accompany The
Canadian Reader—Book 1*. By Eliza Moore Burnett. For the use of Primary
Teachers in British Columbia, Alberta, Saskatchewan and Manitoba. The
Macmillan Company of Canada Limited, St. Martin's House Toronto, 1925.

[6], 83, [7] pp.; 187 × 135 mm.
Macmillan's Canadian School Series.

241. CATHER, Willa

The Professor's House. By Willa Cather. [Quotation]. Toronto: The Macmillan Company of Canada, Ltd., at St. Martin's House MCMXXV.

283, [1] pp.; 192 × 130 mm.

242. CHARLESWORTH, Hector

Candid Chronicles: Leaves from the Note Book of a Canadian Journalist. By
Hector Charlesworth. Toronto: The Macmillan Company of Canada Limited, at St. Martin's House, 1925.

xvi, 404 pp.; 223 × 155 mm.

243. DE LA ROCHE, Mazo

Low Life: A Comedy in One Act. By Mazo de la Roche. Author of "Explorers of the Dawn", and "Passion". Toronto: The Macmillan Company of Canada Limited, at St. Martin's House, MCMXXV.

[10], 37, [1] pp.; 185 × 120 mm.
Also found bound with other plays (see 369). Issued in paper.

244. DELL, Floyd

This Mad Ideal. A Novel by Floyd Dell. Toronto: The Macmillan Company Of Canada, Ltd., At St. Martin's House, 1925.

246 pp. + ads.; 197 × 135 mm.

245. FAIR, L.M.

McGill University Economic Studies: No. 1: National Problems of Canada: *The Transportation of Canadian Wheat to the Sea*. L.M. Fair, M.A. Published at St. Martin's House, Toronto, by The Macmillan Company of Canada, Limited, for the Department of Economics and Political Science, McGill University, Montreal. Price 40¢.

76 pp.; 216 × 140 mm.
Issued in paper.
McGill University Economic Studies Series.

246. GARNETT, David

The Sailor's Return. By David Garnett. With a frontispiece by Ray Garnett. Toronto: The Macmillan Company Of Canada Limited, 1925.

[8], 162, [2] pp. + ads.; 195 × 133 mm.

247. GLASSEY, D.A.

Ontario High School Latin Reader. By D.A. Glassey, B.A. Harbord Collegiate Institute, Toronto, J.C. Robertson, M.A. Victoria College, University of Toronto, [and] J.S. Bennett, B.A. Humberside Collegiate Institute, Toronto. Authorized by the Minister of Education. Toronto: The Macmillan Company of Canada Limited, 1925.

vi, 200 pp.; 193 × 123 mm.

248. HAGARTY, E.W.

Macmillan's Canadian Classics, *Caesar for Junior Matriculation: Caesar: De Bello Gallico, IV, 20-38* [and] V, 1-23. Edited with Introduction, Notes, Exercises and Vocabularies by E.W. Hagarty M.A., Principal, Harbord Collegiate Institute, Toronto. Toronto: The Macmillan Company of Canada, Limited, 1925.

vi, 122 pp.; 175 × 120 mm.
First published by Morang in 1906. Macmillan edition reprinted in 1929.
Macmillan's Canadian Classics Series.

249. HALES, B.J.

Forests and Trees. By B.J. Hales, B.A. LL.B., Principal, Normal School,

Brandon, Man. Toronto: The Macmillan Company of Canada Ltd., at St. Martin's House, 1925.

x, 239, [1] pp.; 188 × 125 mm.
First published in 1919. First edition not located. This edition revised.

250.   HALES, B.J.

Macmillan's Canadian School Series, *Selected Western Flora: Manitoba, Saskatchewan, Alberta*. By B.J. Hales, B.A. Principal, Normal School, Brandon. Authorized by the Advisory Board of the Department of Education for Use in High Schools and Collegiate Institutes in Manitoba. Toronto: The Macmillan Company of Canada, Limited, 1925.

xvi, 196 pp.; 190 × 127 mm.
First published in 1915. Reprinted in 1916, 1919, 1922 and 1925. Earlier printings not located. The 1925 edition contains additional material.
Macmillan's Canadian School Series.

250A HAMSUN, Knut

Segelfoss Town. Translated from the Norwegian of Knut Hamsun by J.S. Scott. Toronto: The Macmillan Company of Canada, Ltd., at St. Martin's House, 1925.

368 pp.; 194 × 133 mm.

251.   HUXLEY, Aldous

Along The Road: Notes & Essays of a Tourist. By Aldous Huxley. Toronto: The Macmillan Company Of Canada Limited, 1925.

viii, 259, [1] pp. + ads.; 193 × 121 mm.

252.   HUXLEY, Aldous

Those Barren Leaves. By Aldous Huxley. Toronto: The Macmillan Company Of Canada Limited, 1925.

[6], 379, [1] pp.; 194 × 127 mm.

253.   JACOB, Fred

Day Before Yesterday. A Novel. By Fred Jacob, Author of "One Third of a Bill". The Macmillan Company of Canada Limited, at St. Martin's House, Toronto, 1925.

319, [1] pp.; 195 × 125 mm.

254.   JACOB, Fred

One Third of a Bill: Five Short Canadian Plays. By Fred Jacob. The Macmillan Company of Canada Limited, at St. Martin's House, Toronto, 1925.

x, 140 pp.; 190 × 125 mm.

255.   LOUDON, W.J.

Studies of Student Life. By W.J. Loudon. [Volume II: An Examination in Logic]. The Macmillan Company of Canada Limited, 1925.

[6], 169, [1] pp.; 175 × 115 mm.

256.   MacTAVISH, Newton
The Fine Arts in Canada. By Newton MacTavish, M.A., A Trustee of The
National Gallery of Canada. Toronto: The Macmillan Company of Canada
Limited, at St. Martin's House, 1925.
  xvi, 181, [1] pp.; 260 × 180 mm.

257.   McGill University Economic Studies: No. 2: National Problems of
Canada: *Ocean and Inland Water Transport*. The 1925 Graduating Class in
Commerce. Published at St. Martin's House, Toronto, by The Macmillan
Company of Canada, Limited, for the Department of Economics and Politi-
cal Science, McGill University, Montreal. Price 40¢.
  52 pp.; 216 × 140 mm.
  Issued in paper.
  McGill University Economic Studies Series.

258.   *Ontario Teachers' Manuals: Manual Training*. Authorized by the Minister
of Education. Toronto: The Macmillan Company of Canada Limited, 1925.
  211, [1] pp.; 245 × 165 mm.
  Reprinted frequently.

259.   OSBORNE, Marian
Flight Commander Stork and Other Verses. By Marian Osborne. With illustrations by F.A. Kerr. Toronto: The Macmillan Company of Canada Limited,
1925.
  [8], 48 pp.; 217 × 175 mm.

260.   McGill University Economic Studies: No. 4: National Problems of
Canada: *Reciprocal and Preferential Tariffs*. The 1925 Graduating Class in
Commerce. Published at St. Martin's House, Toronto, by The Macmillan
Company of Canada, Limited for the Department of Economics and Political
Science, McGill University, Montreal. Price 40¢.
  40 pp.; 216 × 140 mm.
  Issued in paper.
  McGill University Economic Studies Series.

261.   SCOTT, Stanley
Making God Vital or Jesus' Idea of God For Religious Education. By Stanley
Scott, D.B., Ph.D. Toronto: The Macmillan Company of Canada Limited,
at St. Martin's House, 1925.
  xii, 135, [1] pp.; 195 × 130 mm.

262.   SCOTT, Walter
The Lay of the Last Minstrel. By Sir Walter Scott. Edited with Notes by John
C. Saul, M.A. Toronto: The Macmillan Company of Canada Limited, 1925.
  viii, 123, [1] pp.; 173 × 120 mm.
  First published by Morang in 1906. Macmillan edition issued in limp cloth.
  Macmillan's Literature Series.

263. SHARMAN, Lyon
The Sea-Wall and Other Verse. By Lyon Sharman. Toronto: The Macmillan Company of Canada Limited, at St. Martin's House, MCMXXV.
79, [1] pp.; 175 × 135 mm.

264. SULLIVAN, Archibald
The Laughing Birds and Other Stories. By Archibald Sullivan. Toronto: The Macmillan Company of Canada Limited, at St. Martin's House, MCMXXV.
x, 283, [1] pp.; 193 × 130 mm.

265. TROTTER, Beecham
A Horseman and the West. By Beecham Trotter With Arthur Hawkes Assisting. Toronto: The Macmillan Company of Canada, Ltd., at St. Martin's House. MCMXXV.
304 pp.; 185 × 125 mm.

266. WALLACE, W. Stewart
The Western Canada Series, *A New History of Great Britain and Canada*. Two Volumes in One. By W. Stewart Wallace, M.A., Librarian, University of Toronto. Authorized by the Department of Education for Alberta. Toronto: The Macmillan Company of Canada Limited, at St. Martin's House, MCMXXV.
xii, 171, [1] pp.; 190 × 125 mm.
A supplement was published in 1926 (see 299).
Western Canada Series.

267. WARD, James Edward
The Window of Life. By James Edward Ward, Author of "The Wayfarer". Toronto: The Macmillan Company of Canada Limited at St. Martin's House, 1925.
xii, 113, [1] pp.; 187 × 123 mm.
Issued in paper.

268. WEAVER, Emily P.
The Only Girl: A Tale of 1837. By Emily P. Weaver. Toronto: The Macmillan Company of Canada Limited, at St. Martin's House, 1925.
[6], 298 pp.; 190 × 125 mm.
Reprinted frequently.

1926

269. AIKMAN, C. Howard
McGill University Economic Studies: No. 8: National Problems of Canada: *The Automobile Industry of Canada*. By C. Howard Aikman M.A., Published at St. Martin's House, Toronto, by The Macmillan Company of Canada, Limited for the Department of Economics and Political Science,

McGill University, Montreal. Price 75¢.

48 pp.; 218 × 145 mm.
Issued in paper.
McGill University Economic Studies Series.

270. CATHER, Willa

My Mortal Enemy. Willa Cather. The Macmillan Co. Of Canada, Ltd. At St.
Martin's House. Toronto 1926.

122, [2] pp.; 211 × 130 mm.

271. DE LA ROCHE, Mazo

Delight. By Mazo De La Roche. Author of "Possession," etc. Toronto: The
Macmillan Company of Canada, Limited, at St. Martin's House, 1926.

viii, 232 pp.; 195 × 130 mm.

272. FISHER, Olive M.

Seatwork for Primary Grades. By Olive M. Fisher, Instructor in Primary
Methods, Calgary Normal School, And Gertrude J. Wright, Junior Inspector
of Schools, Calgary. Toronto: The Macmillan Company of Canada Limited,
at St. Martin's House, 1926.

[4], 68 pp.; 188 × 134 mm.
Issued in limp cloth.

273. FORSEY, Eugene

McGill University Economic Studies: No. 5: National Problems of
Canada: *Economic and Social Aspects of the Nova Scotia Coal Industry*. By
Eugene Forsey, M.A. Published at St. Martin's House, Toronto, by The
Macmillan Company of Canada, Limited, for the Department of Economics
and Political Science, McGill University, Montreal. Price 75¢.

126 pp.; 215 × 145 mm.
McGill University Economic Studies Series.

274. FORTIER, Cora B.

Unknown Fairies of Canada. By "Maxine" [pseud.]. Toronto: The Macmillan Company of Canada Limited at St. Martin's House, 1926.

[8], 98 pp.; 250 × 174 mm.
First published by Macmillan in 1918. Earlier printings not located.

275. GARVIN, Amelia Beers

Canadian Houses of Romance. By Katherine Hale [pseud.]. With drawings by
Dorothy Stevens. Toronto: The Macmillan Company of Canada Limited, at
St. Martin's House, MCMXXVI.

xvi, 213, [1] pp.; 218 × 147 mm.

276. GIBBON, John Murray

Eyes of a Gypsy. By John Murray Gibbon. [Quotation]. Toronto: The
Macmillan Company of Canada Limited, at St. Martin's House, 1926.

255, [1] pp.; 194 × 130 mm.

277. HAMMOND, M.O.

Canadian Footprints: A Study in Foreground and Backgrounds. By M.O.
Hammond, Author of *Confederation and its Leaders*. Illustrated from photographs. Toronto: The Macmillan Company of Canada Limited, at St. Martin's House, MCMXXVI.

xvi, 305, [1] pp.; 225 × 150 mm.

278. HERGESHEIMER, Joseph

Joseph Hergesheimer. *Tampico: a Novel*. Toronto: The Macmillan Company Of Canada, Ltd., At St. Martin's House, MCMXXVI.

vi, 328, [2] pp.; 191 × 133 mm.

279. HOUSSER, Frederick B.

A Canadian Art Movement: The Story of the Group of Seven. By F.B. Housser.
Toronto: The Macmillan Company of Canada Limited, at St. Martin's
House, MCMXXVI.

221, [1] pp.; 214 × 137 mm.
Reprinted in 1927 and 1974.

280. HOWARD, Hilda

The Glamour Of British Columbia. By H. Glynn-Ward [pseud.]. Illustrated
With Photographs By the Author. Toronto: The Macmillan Company of
Canada Limited, at St. Martin's House, 1926.

xiv, 238 pp.; 190 × 130 mm.

281. HUXLEY, Aldous

Two Or Three Graces And Other Stories. By Aldous Huxley. The Macmillan
Co. Of Canada Ltd., At St. Martin's House, Toronto, 1926.

[6], 271, [1] pp.; 194 × 130 mm.

282. LANGTON, John

*Early Days in Upper Canada: Letters of John Langton from the Backwoods of
Upper Canada and the Audit Office of the Province of Canada*. Edited by W.A.
Langton. Toronto: The Macmillan Company of Canada Limited at St.
Martin's House, 1926.

x, 310 pp.; 222 × 150 mm.

283. LEACOCK, Stephen

Winnowed Wisdom. By Stephen Leacock. The Macmillan Company of
Canada Ltd., at St. Martin's House Toronto, 1926.

xvi, 264 pp.; 180 × 123 mm.

284. LLWYD, J.P.D.

Mysticism and Other Essays. By The Very Reverend J.P.D. Llwyd, D.C.L.,
Dean of Nova Scotia. Toronto: The Macmillan Company of Canada Limited, at St. Martin's House, 1926.

viii, 108 pp.; 187 × 118 mm.

285. LOUDON, W.J.

Studies of Student Life. By W.J. Loudon. [Volume III: Silas Smith of Coboconk]. The Macmillan Company of Canada Limited, 1926.

[6], 272 pp.; 175 × 115 mm.

286. MACDONALD, W.L.

English Prose Selections. Edited by W.L. Macdonald, M.A., PH.D. Associate Professor of English, University of British Columbia. Toronto: The Macmillan Company of Canada Limited, at St. Martin's House, MCMXXVI.

xii, 456 pp.; 167 × 108 mm.

287. MASSEY, Vincent

Canadian Plays From Hart House Theatre. Edited by Vincent Massey. Volume 1. Toronto: The Macmillan Company of Canada Limited, at St. Martin's House, 1926.

x, 216 pp.; 195 × 125 mm.

288. *Ontario Teachers' Manuals: Writing*. Authorized by the Minister of Education. Toronto: The Macmillan Company of Canada Limited, 1926.

vi, 98 pp.; 190 × 125 mm.
Reprinted in 1928.

289. OSBORNE, Marian

Sappho and Phaon. By Marian Osborne. Author of "Poems", "The Song of Israfel", "Flight Commander Stork", Etc. Toronto: The Macmillan Company of Canada Limited, at St. Martin's House, 1926.

68 pp.; 188 × 127 mm.

290. PATERSON, Isabel

The Fourth Queen. By Isabel Paterson. [Quotation]. The Macmillan Company of Canada Ltd. at St. Martin's House: Toronto MCMXXVI.

315, [1] pp.; 190 × 130 mm.

291. PRATT, E.J.

The Witches' Brew. By E.J. Pratt. With Decorations by John Austen. Toronto: The Macmillan Company of Canada Ltd., at St. Martin's House, MCMXXVI.

31, [1] pp.; 185 × 125 mm.

292. REICH, Nathan

McGill University Economic Studies: No. 7: National Problems of Canada: *The Pulp and Paper Industry in Canada*. (With special reference to the export of pulpwood.) Nathan Reich, M.A. Published at St. Martin's House, Toronto, by The Macmillan Company of Canada, Limited, for the Department of Economics and Political Science, McGill University, Montreal. Price 75¢.

78 pp.; 219 × 145 mm.
Issued in paper.
McGill University Economic Studies Series.

293. SCHREINER, Olive

From Man To Man, or Perhaps Only... By Olive Schreiner. (With An Introduction By S.C. Cronwright-Schreiner). [Quotation]. Toronto: The Macmillan Company, 1926.
    483, [1] pp.; 190 × 128 mm.

294. SHARMAN, Lyon

A Somersault to Love: A Comedy of Changing Manners in China, In One Act.
By Lyon Sharman, Author of "The Sea-Wall and Other Verse." Toronto:
The Macmillan Company of Canada Limited, at St. Martin's House,
MCMXXVI.
    [6], 48 pp.; 185 × 125 mm.

295. STEVENSON, Lionel

Appraisals of Canadian Literature. By Lionel Stevenson. Toronto: The
Macmillan Company of Canada Limited, at St. Martin's House,
MCMXXVI.
    xviii, 272 pp.; 192 × 130 mm.

296. TOMBS, Laurence Chalmers

McGill University Economic Studies: No. 6: National Problems of
Canada: *The Port of Montreal*. Laurence Chalmers Tombs, M.A. Published
at St. Martin's House, Toronto, by The Macmillan Company of Canada,
Limited, for the Department of Economics and Political Science, McGill
University, Montreal. Price 75¢.
    178 pp.; 219 × 145 mm.
    Issued in paper.
    McGill University Economic Studies Series.

297. TROTTER, Reginald George

Canadian History: A Syllabus and Guide to Reading. By Reginald George
Trotter, PH.D. Associate Professor of History, Queen's University. Sometime Parker Travelling Fellow in Canadian History, Harvard University, and
Assistant Professor of History, Stanford University. Toronto: The Macmillan Company of Canada Limited, at St. Martin's House, 1926.
    xiv, 162 pp.; 228 × 150 mm.

298. WALLACE, W. Stewart

The Dictionary of Canadian Biography. Compiled by W. Stewart Wallace,
M.A., Librarian of the University of Toronto. Toronto: The Macmillan
Company of Canada Limited, at St. Martin's House, 1926.
    vi, 433, [1] pp.; 237 × 160 mm.
    Revised and enlarged in 1945 in two volumes (see 1094 and 1095). Third edition
    published in 1963 (see 1657). Fourth edition published in 1978 (see 2606).

299. WALLACE, W. Stewart

Supplement Containing Additions to the 1925 Edition of A New History of Great Britain and Canada. Two Volumes in One. By W. Stewart Wallace, M.A., Author of "Sir John Macdonald", "The United Empire Loyalists", "The Family Compact", Etc. Authorized by the Department of Education for Alberta. Toronto: The Macmillan Company of Canada Limited, at St. Martin's House, MCMXXVI.

32 pp.; 185 × 125 mm.
For the book to which this is a supplement, see 266.

300. WETHERELL, J.E.

Aesop In Verse. By J. E. Wetherell, B.A., Author of "Fields of Fame" etc. Drawings by E. L. Thomson. [Quotation]. Toronto: The Macmillan Company of Canada Limited, at St. Martin's House, 1926.

xvi, 199, [1] pp.; 192 × 137 mm.

301. WRONG, George M.

A Canadian Manor and Its Seigneurs: The Story of a Hundred Years. By George M. Wrong, Professor of History in the University of Toronto. With illustrations. Toronto: The Macmillan Company of Canada Limited, at St. Martin's House, MCMXXVI.

xx, 295, [1] pp.; 243 × 163 mm.
First published in 1908 (see 19). Of this second edition there is a trade issue and an author's issue, the latter numbered and signed by the author.

1927

302. BEVAN, Molly

Gifts of the Year And Other Poems. By Molly Bevan. Toronto: The Macmillan Company of Canada Limited, at St. Martin's House 1927.

viii, 67, [1] pp.; 195 × 130 mm.

303. CHARLESWORTH, Hector

The Canadian Scene: Sketches: Political and Historical. By Hector Charlesworth. Author of "Candid Chronicles". Toronto: The Macmillan Company of Canada Limited, at St. Martin's House 1927.

[14], 235, [1] pp.; 193 × 130 mm.

304. COHEN, J.L.

Mothers' Allowance Legislation in Canada: A Legislative Review And Analysis With a Proposed "Standard" Act. By J.L. Cohen, Barrister-at-Law. Toronto: The Macmillan Company of Canada Limited, at St. Martin's House 1927.

134 pp.; 190 × 130 mm.
Issued in cloth and paper.

305.   CORNISH, George A.

Chemistry Manual. By George A. Cornish, B.A. Associate Professor in Science, Faculty of Education, University of Toronto, and Chief Instructor in Science, University Schools, Toronto. Assisted By Arthur Smith, B.A. Director of Physics, Central Technical Schools, Toronto. Authorized by The Minister of Education for Ontario. Price 25 cents. Toronto: The Macmillan Company of Canada, Limited 1927.

iv, 99, [3] pp.; 190 × 125 mm.
Reprinted frequently.

306.   DALY, George Thomas

Catholic Action. By George Thomas Daly, C.SS.R. Toronto: The Macmillan Company of Canada Limited, at St. Martin's House 1927.

166 pp. + ads.; 205 × 140 mm.
Issued in cloth and paper.

307.   DE LA ROCHE, Mazo

Come True. By Mazo De La Roche. Toronto: The Macmillan Company of Canada Limited, at St. Martin's House MCMXXVII.

[8], 47, [1] pp.; 185 × 120 mm.
Also issued with two other plays (see 369). Issued in paper.

308.   DE LA ROCHE, Mazo

Jalna. By Mazo De La Roche. Toronto: The Macmillan Company of Canada Limited, at St. Martin's House, MCMXXVII.

[8], 347, [1] pp.; 195 × 130 mm.
New edition published in 1947 (see 1128).

309.   DEWITT, Norman W.

Ancient History for High Schools. By Norman DeWitt, Ph.D. Professor of Latin, Victoria College, University of Toronto. Authorized by the Minister of Education for Ontario. Price 50 cents. Toronto: The Macmillan Company of Canada Limited 1927.

vi, 234 pp.; 192 × 125 mm.
Reprinted in 1928.

310.   DORLAND, Arthur Garratt

A History of the Society of Friends (Quakers) in Canada. By Arthur Garratt Dorland, Ph.D., Professor of History in the University of Western Ontario. Toronto: The Macmillan Company of Canada Limited, at St. Martin's House 1927.

xiv, 343, [1] pp.; 220 × 152 mm.

311.   DUNHAM, B. Mabel

Toward Sodom. By B. Mabel Dunham, Author of "The Trail of the Conestoga". Toronto: The Macmillan Company of Canada Limited, at St. Martin's House MCMXXVII.

viii, 336 pp.; 195 × 130 mm.

312. EDGAR, Pelham

Henry James: Man and Author. Toronto: The Macmillan Company of Canada Limited, at St. Martin's House 1927.

351, [1] pp.; 225 × 147 mm.

313. EVANS, Hubert

The New Front Line. By Hubert Evans. Toronto: The Macmillan Company of Canada Limited, at St. Martin's House 1927.

[8], 291, [1] pp.; 190 × 125 mm.

314. FALLON, Michael Francis

Little Manuals of Holy Scripture. *The Parables of Our Lord*. With an Introduction and Comments by Michael Francis Fallon, Bishop of London. Toronto: The Macmillan Company of Canada Limited, at St. Martin's House 1927.

[8], 56 pp.; 143 × 85 mm.
Little Manuals of Holy Scripture Series.

314A FLETCHER, J.S.

The Green Rope. By J.S. Fletcher. Toronto: The Macmillan Company Of Canada, Ltd., At St. Martin's House, MCMXXVII.

285, [1] pp.; 192 × 134 mm.

315. GROVE, Frederick Philip

Our Daily Bread. A Novel. By Frederick Philip Grove. [Quotation]. Toronto: The Macmillan Company of Canada Limited, at St. Martin's House MCMXXVII.

, vi, 390 pp.; 195 × 130 mm.

316. HALES, B.J.

Prairie Birds. By B.J. Hales, B.A., LL.B. Principal, Normal School, Brandon, Manitoba. Toronto: The Macmillan Company of Canada Limited, at St. Martin's House 1927.

xviii, 334 pp.; 190 × 123 mm.

317. The Western Canada Series, *History of England for Public Schools*. Authorized by the Departments of Education for Manitoba, Saskatchewan, Alberta and British Columbia. Toronto: The Macmillan Company of Canada, Limited 1927.

336 pp.; 190 × 125 mm.
First published by Morang in 1910. Reprinted by Macmillan in 1912 and frequently thereafter. Earlier printings not located.
Western Canada Series.

318. KING, W.L. Mackenzie

The Message of the Carillon And Other Addresses. By The Right Honourable W.L. Mackenzie King, C.M.G., LL.D., D.C.L., M.P. Prime Minister of Canada, Author of "Industry and Humanity", "The Secret of Heroism",

Etc. Toronto: The Macmillan Company of Canada Limited, at St. Martin's House 1927.

x, 274 pp.; 220 × 145 mm.

319. KIRBY, William

Annals of Niagara. By William Kirby, F.R.S.C. Edited with Introduction and Notes by Lorne Pierce. [Quotation]. Toronto: The Macmillan Company of Canada Limited, at St. Martin's House MCMXXVII.

xviii, 329, [1] pp.; 233 × 155 mm.

320. MANN, Thomas

Thomas Mann. *The Magic Mountain [Der Zauberberg].* Volume One. Translated from the German by H.T. Lowe-Porter. The Macmillan Company Of Canada, Ltd., Toronto, At St. Martin's House, 1927.

xii, 434, [2] pp.; 195 × 136 mm.

321. MANN, Thomas

Thomas Mann. *The Magic Mountain [Der Zauberberg].* Volume Two. Translated from the German by H.T. Lowe-Porter. The Macmillan Company Of Canada, Ltd., Toronto, At St. Martin's House, 1927.

[8], 437-900, [2] pp.; 195 × 136 mm.

322. MASSEY, Vincent

Canadian Plays From Hart House Theatre. Edited by Vincent Massey. Volume II. Toronto: The Macmillan Company of Canada Limited, at St. Martin's House 1927.

[8], 193, [1] pp.; 193 × 127 mm.

323. NIVEN, Frederick

Wild Honey. By Frederick Niven. The Macmillan Company of Canada Limited, at St. Martin's House — Toronto MCMXXVII.

[4], 251, [1] pp.; 190 × 130 mm.

324. PRATT, E.J.

The Iron Door: An Ode. By E.J. Pratt. Toronto: The Macmillan Company of Canada Limited, at St. Martin's House MCMXXVII.

30 pp.; 200 × 135 mm.

In addition to the trade issue of 900 copies, there is a limited issue of 100 copies, numbered and signed by Pratt.

325. SEQUEIRA, James H.

Diseases Of The Skin. By James H. Sequeira, M.D. Lond., F.R.C.S.Eng., Physician to the Skin Department and Lecturer on Dermatology and Syphilology at the London Hospital [etc.]. Fourth Edition. With 56 Plates in Colour and 309 Text-Figures. Toronto: The Macmillan Company Of Canada Ltd., 1927.

xii, 644 pp.; 242 × 160 mm.

Earlier editions not located.

326. **SHAKESPEARE, William**

Macmillan's Literature Series, Shakespeare's *Julius Caesar*. Edited with Notes by F.C. Colbeck, B.A. Principal, Humberside Collegiate Institute, Toronto. Toronto: The Macmillan Company of Canada, Limited 1927.

x, 78 pp.; 170 × 115 mm.
First published by Morang in 1906. Macmillan edition issued in limp cloth.
Macmillan's Literature Series.

327. **SHAKESPEARE, William**

Macmillan's Literature Series, Shakespeare's *The Merchant of Venice*. Edited with Notes by Gertrude Lawler, M.A. English Specialist, Harbord Collegiate Institute, Toronto. Toronto: The Macmillan Company of Canada, Limited 1927.

xvi, 81, [1] pp.; 170 × 115 mm.
First published by Morang in 1906. Macmillan edition issued in limp cloth.
Macmillan's Literature Series.

328. **SISLER, W.J.**

Macmillan's Canadian School Series, *Spelling and Language Lessons For Beginners in English*. By W.J. Sisler, B.Sc. (Ed.) Principal, Isaac Newton Junior High School, Winnipeg. Toronto: The Macmillan Company of Canada Limited 1927.

[6], 170 pp.; 193 × 140 mm.
First published in 1915. Reprinted in 1917 (see 120).
Macmillan's Canadian School Series.

329. **STERN, Gladys B.**

The Dark Gentleman. By G.B. Stern. Toronto: The Macmillan Company of Canada, Ltd., At St. Martin's House, 1927.

[4], 179, [1] pp.; 195 × 130 mm.

330. **WALLACE, W. Stewart**

The Growth of Canadian National Feeling. By W. Stewart Wallace, Librarian of the University of Toronto. Toronto: The Macmillan Company of Canada Limited 1927.

[8], 85, [1] pp.; 180 × 123 mm.

331. **WRONG, Hume**

Sir Alexander Mackenzie: Explorer and Fur-Trader. By Hume Wrong, Assistant Professor of History, University of Toronto. Toronto: The Macmillan Company of Canada Limited 1927.

[6], 171, [1] pp.; 180 × 125 mm.
Canadian Men of Action Series.

1928

332. ASHWORTH, Edward Montague

The Seigneurs of La Saulaye: Gentlemen Adventurers of New France Two Centuries Ago. By Johnston Abbott [pseud.]. Toronto: The Macmillan Company of Canada Limited, at St. Martin's House 1928.

   [6], 379, [1] pp.; 193 × 133 mm.

333. BARBEAU, Marius

The Downfall of Temlaham. By Marius Barbeau, Author of "Indian Days in the Canadian Rockies", etc. Illustrations by A.Y. Jackson, Edwin H. Holgate, W. Langdon Kihn, Emily Carr and Annie D. Savage. Toronto: The Macmillan Company of Canada Limited, at St. Martin's House 1928.

   xii, 253, [1] pp.; 220 × 165 mm.

334. BURRELL, Martin

Betwixt Heaven and Charing Cross. By Martin Burrell. Toronto: The Macmillan Company of Canada Limited, at St. Martin's House MCMXXVIII.

   x, 328 pp.; 215 × 140 mm.

335. BUTCHART, Reuben

The Lyric Flute And Other Poems. By Reuben Butchart. Toronto: The Macmillan Company of Canada Limited, at St. Martin's House 1928.

   viii, 78 pp.; 190 × 134 mm.

336. *Canadian Agriculture For High Schools*. Authorized by the Department of Education for Alberta. Toronto: The Macmillan Company of Canada Limited, at St. Martin's House 1928.

   x, 479, [1] pp.; 190 × 130 mm.

337. CARSON, George S.

Stories From The Life of Jesus. Illustrated From The Great Painters. Told in the Words of the Bible, with Connecting Notes. By George S. Carson, B.A., D.D. With an Introduction by Sir Robert Falconer, K.C.M.G., President of the University of Toronto. Toronto: The Macmillan Company of Canada Limited, at St. Martin's House 1928.

   xvi, 173, [1] pp.; 205 × 138 mm.

338. CHARLESWORTH, Hector

More Candid Chronicles: Further leaves from the Note Book of a Canadian Journalist. By Hector Charlesworth. Toronto: The Macmillan Company of Canada Limited, at St. Martin's House 1928.

   xvi, 429, [1] pp.; 220 × 153 mm.

339. CORBETT, Percy Ellwood

Canada and World Politics: Study of the Constitutional and International Relations of the British Empire. By Percy Ellwood Corbett, M.C., M.A. Dean of the Faculty of Law and Gale Professor of Roman Law in McGill University, Montreal; formerly Fellow of All Souls College, Oxford; Assistant Legal Adviser to the International Labour Office, League of Nations, And Herbert Arthur Smith, M.A. Barrister-at-Law; Professor of International Law in the University of London; late Professor of Constitutional Law in McGill University, Montreal; formerly Fellow of Magdalen College, Oxford. Toronto: The Macmillan Company of Canada Limited, at St. Martin's House MCMXXVIII.

xvi, 244 pp.; 220 × 140 mm.

340. CULLITON, John Thomas

McGill University Economic Studies: No. 9: National Problems of Canada: *Assisted Emigration and Land Settlement; With Special Reference to Western Canada*. John Thomas Culliton, M.A. Published by the Federated Press Limited, Montreal, for the Department of Economics and Political Science, McGill University, Montreal, 1928.

79, [1] pp.; 216 × 145 mm.
Correspondence in the Macmillan Archive verifies the publication of this book by the House, though the imprint does not indicate it.
McGill University Economic Studies Series.

341. DICKENS, Charles

Macmillan's Literature Series, *The Cricket on the Hearth: A Fairy Tale of Home*. By Charles Dickens. Edited with notes by J.F. Van Every, B.A. Toronto: The Macmillan Company of Canada, Limited 1928.

124, [4] pp.; 175 × 120 mm.
First published by Morang in 1909.
Macmillan's Literature Series.

342. EAYRS, Hugh Sterling

Lines For Macmillans' First Christmas Party. By H.S.E. Toronto, December 14, 1928.

8 pp.; 238 × 155 mm.
Issued in paper.

343. FORSTER, J.W.L.

Under the Studio Light: Leaves from a Portrait Painter's Sketch Book. By J.W.L. Forster. Toronto: The Macmillan Company of Canada Limited, at St. Martin's House, 1928.

xiv, 244 pp.; 220 × 150 mm.

344. FOURNIER, Henri-Alban

Alain-Fournier [pseud.]. *The Wanderer*. (Le Grand Meaulnes). Translated from the French by Francoise Delisle. Toronto: The Macmillan Company of Canada Limited, at St. Martin's House, MCMXXVIII.

xxxii, 306 pp.; 195 × 127 mm.

345. HAMILTON, Patrick

Twopence Coloured. By Patrick Hamilton, author of *Craven House* etc. The Macmillan Company Of Canada Ltd., Toronto 1928.

viii, 373, [1] pp.; 194 × 130 mm.

346. HEAGERTY, John J.

Four Centuries Of Medical History In Canada: And A Sketch Of The Medical History Of Newfoundland. By John J. Heagerty, M.D., D.P.H. Department of Health, Canada. With A Preface By A.G. Doughty, C.M.G., F.R.S.C. Dominion Archivist. Volume I. Toronto: The Macmillan Company of Canada Limited, at St. Martin's House 1928.

xviii, 395, [1] pp.; 230 × 145 mm.

347. HEAGERTY, John J.

Four Centuries Of Medical History In Canada: And A Sketch Of The Medical History Of Newfoundland. By John J. Heagerty, M.D.,D.P.H. Department of Health, Canada. With A Preface By A.G. Doughty, C.M.G., F.R.S.C. Dominion Archivist. Volume II. Toronto: The Macmillan Company of Canada Limited, at St. Martin's House 1928.

viii, 374 pp.; 230 × 145 mm.

348. IRVING, Washington

Macmillan's Literature Series, *Rip Van Winkle and Other Essays from the Sketch Book*. By Washington Irving. Toronto: The Macmillan Company of Canada Limited 1928.

115, [1] pp.; 175 × 118 mm.
First published by Morang in 1909. Macmillan edition issued in paper.
Macmillan's Literature Series.

349. JACOB, Fred

Peevee. A Novel. By Fred Jacob. Author of *Day Before Yesterday*. The Macmillan Company of Canada Limited, at St. Martin's House Toronto 1928.

x, 400 pp.; 195 × 129 mm.

349A KNISTER, Raymond

Canadian Short Stories. Edited by Raymond Knister. Toronto: The Macmillan Company Of Canada Limited, At St. Martin's House, 1928.

xx, 340 pp.; 196 × 135 mm.
Reprinted in 1929.

350. LEACOCK, Stephen

Short Circuits. By Stephen Leacock. The Macmillan Company of Canada Ltd., at St. Martin's House Toronto 1928.

xii, 336 pp.; 190 × 125 mm.

351. LIVESAY, Dorothy

[Cover-title:] *Green Pitcher*. By Dorothy Livesay. (Copyright 1928).
[Quotation]. Toronto: The Macmillan Company of Canada Limited, at St.
Martin's House 1928.

l6 pp.; 190 × 128 mm.
Issued in paper.

352. LLWYD, J.P.D.

Poems of Nature, Childhood, and Religion. By J.P.D. Llwyd. Toronto: The
Macmillan Company of Canada Limited, at St. Martin's House 1928.

[10], 64 pp.; 192 × 130 mm.

353. MACMILLAN, Cyrus

Canadian Wonder Tales. By Cyrus Macmillan. With a Foreword by Sir
William Peterson, K.C.M.G. The Macmillan Company of Canada Ltd., at
St. Martin's House Toronto 1928.

xvi, 240 pp.; 170 × 112 mm.
Week-End Library.

353A MANSFIELD, Katherine

The Letters of Katherine Mansfield. Edited by J. Middleton Murry. Volume I.
The Macmillan Company Of Canada Ltd., Toronto 1928.

viii, 319, [1] pp.; 191 × 127 mm.
Volume II not located.

354. WALLACE, W. Stewart

A First Book of Canadian History. By W. Stewart Wallace, M.A. (Oxon.).
[Quotation]. Authorized by the Minister of Education for the Public Schools
of Ontario. Toronto: The Macmillan Company of Canada Limited, at St.
Martin's House 1928.

[8], 246 pp.; 188 × 123 mm.
Reprinted in 1929, 1931, 1932, 1933 and 1934. Used as basis for *Canada our
Country: Part 2* (see 1532).

355. WALLACE, W. Stewart

A New History Of Great Britain And Canada. Two Volumes In One. By W.
Stewart Wallace, M.A. Author Of "Sir John Macdonald", "The United
Empire Loyalists", "The Family Compact", Etc. Prepared For Use In The
Schools of British Columbia. Toronto: The Macmillan Company of Canada
Limited, at St. Martin's House 1928.

xii, 200 pp.; 190 × 125 mm.

356. WAUGH, W.T.

James Wolfe: Man and Soldier. By W.T. Waugh, M.A. Kingsford Professor
of History/McGill University. Toronto: The Macmillan Company of Canada
Limited, at St. Martin's House 1928.

333, [1] pp.; 240 × 160 mm.

357. WRONG, George M.

Ontario High School History of England. By George M. Wrong, Professor of
History in the University of Toronto. Authorized by the Minister of Educa-
tion for Ontario. Revised and Enlarged Edition. Toronto: The Macmillan
Company of Canada Limited 1928.

> xvi, 624 pp.; 195 × 125 mm.
> First published in 1912 (see 56). Revised and enlarged in 1922 and reprinted in 1924,
> 1926, 1927, 1928 and 1929. Earlier printings not located.

358. WRONG, George M.

The Rise and Fall of New France. By George M. Wrong. Volume One.
Toronto: The Macmillan Co. of Canada, Ltd. at St. Martin's House, 1928.

> xviii, 491, [1] pp.; 220 × 148mm.

359. WRONG, George M.

The Rise and Fall of New France. By George M. Wrong. Volume Two.
Toronto: The Macmillan Co. of Canada, Ltd., at St. Martin's House, 1928.

> xii, 493-925, [1] pp.; 220 × 148 mm.

1929

360. ARMITAGE, John

Wing Po: A Romance of Modern China. By Hin Me Geong (John Armitage).
Toronto: The Macmillan Company of Canada Limited, at St. Martin's
House, 1929.

> [10], 323, [1] pp.; 195 × 130 mm.

361. BEATTIE, Kim

"And You!". By Kim Beattie. Toronto: The Macmillan Company of Canada
Limited, at St. Martin's House, 1929.

> [10], 91, [1] pp.; 190 × 130 mm.

362. BOMPAS, Charlotte Selina

*A Heroine of the North: Memoirs of Charlotte Selina Bompas (1830-1917) Wife
of the First Bishop of Selkirk (Yukon). With Extracts From Her Journal and
Letters*. Compiled by S. A. Archer. Toronto: The Macmillan Company of
Canada Limited, at St. Martin's House, 1929.

> xvi, 187, [1] pp.; 188 × 120 mm.

363. BRETT, G.S.

Introduction To Psychology. G.S. Brett, Professor of Philosophy, University of
Toronto, Ontario. Authorized by The Minister of Education. Price 35 cents.
Toronto: The Macmillan Company of Canada Limited, at St. Martin's
House, 1929.

> viii, 193, [1] pp.; 190 × 130 mm.

364.   BROOKER, Bertram
Yearbook of the Arts in Canada 1928/1929. Edited by Bertram Brooker. The Macmillan Company of Canada Limited, at St. Martin's House: 1929.
[12], 306, [2] pp.; 255 × 175 mm.

365.   CAREY, Basil
Mountain Gold. By Basil Carey. The Macmillan Company Of Canada Ltd., Toronto 1929.
[6], 309, [1] pp.; 194 × 135 mm.

366.   COLEMAN, H.T.J.
A Rhyme For A Penny. By H.T.J. Coleman. With Drawings by Elisabeth Kerr. Toronto: The Macmillan Company of Canada Limited, at St. Martin's House, MCMXXIX.
x, 49, [1] pp.; 235 × 152 mm.

367.   CONSTANTIN-WEYER, M.
By M. Constantin-Weyer. Translated by Slater Brown. *A Man Scans His Past*. [Un Homme Se Penche Sur Son Passé]. Toronto: The Macmillan Company of Canada Limited, at St. Martin's House, MCMXXIX.
viii, 250 pp.; 194 × 133 mm.

368.   CRAWFORD, A.W.
Greater English Poets. Selected and Edited by A.W. Crawford, M.A., PH.D. (Cornell), Aaron J. Perry, M.A. (Yale), of the Department of English, University of Manitoba, [and] A.S.P. Woodhouse, M.A. (Havard) [sic], of the Department of English, University of Toronto. Toronto: The Macmillan Company of Canada Limited at St. Martin's House, 1929.
xvi, 826 pp.; 192 × 130 mm.

369.   DE LA ROCHE, Mazo
Low Life and Other Plays. By Mazo De La Roche. Toronto: The Macmillan Company of Canada Limited, at St. Martin's House, MCMXXIX.
[8], 109, [1] pp.; 190 × 130 mm.
Two of the three plays collected in this volume were separately issued (see 243 and 307).

370.   DE LA ROCHE, Mazo
Whiteoaks of Jalna. By Mazo De La Roche. Toronto: The Macmillan Company of Canada Limited, at St. Martin's House, 1929.
viii, 384 pp.; 197 × 130 mm.
Reprinted in 1929. New edition published as *Whiteoaks* in 1948 (see 1173).

371. DICKENS, Charles

A Christmas Carol in Prose: Being a Ghost Story of Christmas. By Charles
Dickens. Edited with Notes by J.F. Van Every, B.A. Toronto: The Macmillan Company of Canada Limited, at St. Martin's House, 1929.

> 119, [1] pp.; 175 × 115 mm.
> Issued in paper.
> St. Martin's Literature Series.

372. EAYRS, Hugh Sterling

Lines For Macmillans' Second Christmas Party. By H.S.E. Toronto, December 20, 1929.

> 8 pp.; 238 × 155 mm.
> Issued in paper.

373. ENGLAND, Robert

The Central European Immigrant in Canada. By Robert England, M.C. Toronto: The Macmillan Company of Canada Limited, at St. Martin's House,
MCMXXIX.

> xviii, 238 pp.; 188 × 126 mm.

374. EUSTACE, C.J.

The Scarlet Gentleman. By C.J. Eustace. Toronto: The Macmillan Company
of Canada Limited, at St. Martin's House, MCMXXIX.

> 286 pp.; 188 × 123 mm.

375. *Everyday Canadian Primer*. Illustrated by Maud and Miska Petersham.
Toronto: The Macmillan Company of Canada Limited, at St. Martin's
House, 1929.

> iv, 116 pp.; 183 × 140 mm.
> Everyday Canadian Readers Series.

376. FRASER, A.J.

Trauma, Disease, Compensation: A Handbook of their Medico-Legal Relations.
By A.J. Fraser, M.D. Chief Medical Officer, Workmen's Compensation
Board, Winnipeg. Toronto: The Macmillan Company of Canada Limited, at
St. Martin's House, 1929.

> xiv, 516 pp.; 234 × 154 mm.

377. GOMERY, Percy

End of the Circle. By Percy Gomery. Toronto: The Macmillan Company of
Canada Limited, at St. Martin's House, 1929.

> viii, 266 pp.; 194 × 127 mm.

378. GRIFFIN, Selwyn P.

Open Secrets: Off the Beaten Track in Canada's Story. By Selwyn P. Griffin.
With Illustrations by T.G. Greene. Toronto: The Macmillan Company of
Canada Limited, at St. Martin's House, 1929.

> viii, 328 pp.; 207 × 134 mm.

379. GROVE, Frederick Philip

It Needs to be Said.... By Frederick Philip Grove, Author of "Our Daily Bread". Toronto: The Macmillan Company of Canada Limited, at St. Martin's House, 1929.

[6], 163, [1] pp.; 190 × 128 mm.

380. HALL, H.S.

Elementary Trigonometry. By H.S. Hall M.A., Formerly Scholar of Christ's College Cambridge. And S.R. Knight B.A., M.B., CH.B., Formerly Scholar of Trinity College Cambridge. Adapted for use in Canadian Schools by G.W. Keith, B.A., J. McKellar, B.A., W.A. Skirrow, M.A., R.A. Gray, B.A., A.I.A., [and] C.W. Robb, B.A. Toronto: The Macmillan Company of Canada Limited, at St. Martin's House, 1929.

xviii, 382 pp.; 190 × 130 mm.
First published in 1928 and reprinted in 1928. First edition not located. Revised in 1929.

381. HAUFF, Wilhelm

Das Kalte Herz: Märchen. Von Wilhelm Hauff. With Notes and Vocabulary by A.E. Lang, University of Toronto. Toronto: The Macmillan Company of Canada Limited, at St. Martin's House 1929.

[8], 111, [1] pp.; 180 × 120 mm.

382. KNISTER, Raymond

White Narcissus. A Novel by Raymond Knister. [Quotation]. Toronto: The Macmillan Company of Canada Limited, at St. Martin's House MCMXXIX.

254 pp.; 195 × 127 mm.

383. LAUREYS, Henry

The Foreign Trade of Canada. By Henry Laureys, Doctor of Economic and Commercial Science of the University of Louvain, Doctor of Economic, Social and Political Science of the University of Montreal, Dean of the School of Higher Commercial Studies of Montreal. Translated from the French Edition by H.A. Innis, PH.D. Assistant Professor at the Department of Political Science of the University of Toronto, And Alexander H. Smith, M.A., Head of the English Department at the School of Higher Commercial Studies of Montreal. With a Preface by Stephen Leacock, Ph.D., Litt.D., LL.D., Professor of Political Economy at McGill University. Toronto: The Macmillan Company of Canada Limited, at St. Martin's House, MCMXXIX.

xvi, 325, [1] pp.; 217 × 140 mm.

384. LEACOCK, Stephen

The Iron Man & the Tin Woman: with other such futurities: A Book of Little Sketches of To-day and Tomorrow. By Stephen Leacock. Toronto: The Macmillan Company of Canada Limited, at St. Martin's House, 1929.

viii, 309, [1] pp.; 184 × 123 mm.

385.   LINNELL, John

Youth and Other Poems. By John Linnell. Toronto: The Macmillan Company of Canada Limited, at St. Martin's House, 1929.

[10], 76 pp.; 193 × 130 mm.

386.   McDOUGALL, John Easton

If you know what I mean. By John Easton McDougall. Toronto: The Macmillan Company of Canada Limited, at St. Martin's House, 1929.

[10], 91, [1] pp.; 193 × 130 mm.

387.   MELVILLE, Herman

St. Martin's Classics, *Moby Dick*. By Herman Melville. With introduction and notes by E.J. Pratt M.A., PH.D., Associate Professor of English, University of Toronto. Toronto: The Macmillan Company of Canada Limited, at St. Martin's House, 1929.

xxxii, 215, [1] pp.; 170 × 115 mm.
St. Martin's Classics Series.

388.   M'GILLIVRAY, Duncan

The Journal of Duncan M'Gillivray of the North West Company at Fort George on the Saskatchewan 1794-5. With Introduction, Notes and Appendix by Arthur S. Morton, Professor of History, University of Saskatchewan. Toronto: The Macmillan Company of Canada Limited, at St. Martin's House MCMXXIX.

lxxviii, 109, [1] pp.; 238 × 160 mm.

389.   MORGAN-POWELL, S.

Memories That Live. By S. Morgan-Powell. Toronto: The Macmillan Company of Canada Limited, at St. Martin's House, MCMXXIX.

x, 282 pp.; 220 × 140 mm.

390.   MUNRO, William Bennett

American Influences on Canadian Government. The Marfleet Lectures Delivered at the University of Toronto 1929 by William Bennett Munro. Toronto: The Macmillan Company of Canada Limited, at St. Martin's House, 1929.

xii, 153, [1] pp.; 188 × 125 mm.

391.   PIERCE, Lorne

Alfred, Lord Tennyson and William Kirby: Unpublished Correspondence to which are added some letters from Hallam, Lord Tennyson. By Lorne Pierce. Toronto: The Macmillan Company of Canada Limited at St. Martin's House, MCMXXIX.

71, [1] pp.; 235 × 160 mm.
Issued in a limited edition of 250 signed and numbered copies.

392. PIERCE, Lorne

William Kirby: The Portrait of a Tory Loyalist. By Lorne Pierce. [Quotation].
Toronto: The Macmillan Company of Canada Limited, at St. Martin's
House MCMXXIX.

    xiv, 477, [1] pp.; 235 × 155 mm.

393. PROCTOR, Frank

Fox Hunting in Canada and Some Men Who Made It. With 106 full page
Illustrations. Toronto: The Macmillan Company of Canada Limited, at St.
Martin's House, MCMXXIX.

    373, [1] pp.; 230 × 150 mm.

394. RANKIN, Duncan Joseph

A History of the County of Antigonish, Nova Scotia. By The Rev. D.J. Rankin.
Member of the Historical Society of Nova Scotia, And Vice-President of the
Historical Society of Cape Breton. Toronto: The Macmillan Company of
Canada Limited, at St. Martin's House. MCMXXIX.

    xii, 390 pp.; 257 × 195 mm.

395. SHACKLETON, Helen

Saucy and All. Verses by Helen Shackleton. [Quotation]. Illustrations by
Kathleen Shackleton. Toronto: The Macmillan Company of Canada Limited, 1929.

    [6], 48 pp.; 220 × 175 mm.

396. SHAKESPEARE, William

St. Martin's Shakespeare, *As You Like It.* Toronto: The Macmillan Company of Canada Limited, at St. Martin's House, 1929.

    xlviii, 171, [1] pp.; 170 × 110 mm.
    St. Martin's Shakespeare Series.

397. SHAKESPEARE, William

St. Martin's Shakespeare, *Julius Caesar.* Toronto: The Macmillan Company
of Canada Limited at St. Martin's House, 1929.

    lv, 145, [1] pp.; 170 × 110 mm.
    St. Martin's Shakespeare Series.

398. SHAKESPEARE, William

St. Martin's Shakespeare, *Macbeth.* Toronto: The Macmillan Company of
Canada Limited, at St. Martin's House, 1929.

    lx, 153, [1] pp.; 170 × 110 mm.
    St. Martin's Shakespeare Series.

399. SULLIVAN, Alan

Double Lives. By Sinclair Murray [pseud.]. The Macmillan Company of
Canada Toronto.

    318 pp.; 190 × 120 mm.

400.   SWEATMAN, Constance Travers

To Love and to Cherish. A novel by Constance Travers Sweatman. Toronto:
The Macmillan Company of Canada Limited, at St. Martin's House 1929.
vi, 342 pp.; 195 × 125 mm.

401.   WILLISON, Marjory

*Golden Treasury of Famous Books: A Guide to Good Reading for Boys and Girls
and for the Enjoyment of Those Who Love Books.* By Marjory Willison. Toronto: The Macmillan Company of Canada Limited, at St. Martin's House,
1929.
xvi, 264 pp.; 190 × 128 mm.

1930

402.   AIKIN, J. Alex

Economic Power For Canada. By J. Alex Aikin, M.A. Toronto: The Macmillan Company of Canada Limited, at St. Martin's House, 1930.
[2], 265, [1] pp.; 185 × 128 mm.

403.   ARMSTRONG, G.H.

The Origin and Meaning of Place Names in Canada. By G.H. Armstrong,
M.A. Toronto: The Macmillan Company of Canada Limited, at St. Martin's
House, 1930.
viii, 312 pp.; 218 × 148 mm.
Reprinted in 1972.

404.   AYLEN, Elise

Roses of Shadow. By Elise Aylen. With a Foreword by Duncan Campbell
Scott. [Quotation]. Toronto: The Macmillan Company of Canada Limited,
at St. Martin's House, 1930.
viii, 56 pp.; 200 × 133 mm.

405.   *Bible Readings For Schools.* Arranged by an Interdenominational Committee. Group I. Issued for the approval of School Boards by consent of the
Department of Education for Ontario. The Macmillan Company of Canada
Limited, at St. Martin's House, Toronto 1930.
xxviii, 235, [1] pp.; 190 × 125 mm.

406.   *Bible Readings For Schools.* Arranged by an Interdenominational Committee. Group II. Issued for the approval of School Boards by consent of the
Department of Education for Ontario. The Macmillan Company of Canada
Limited, at St. Martin's House, Toronto 1930.
xviii, 284 pp.; 190 × 125 mm.

407. *Bible Readings For Schools*. Arranged by an Interdenominational Commit-
      tee. Group III. Issued for the approval of School Boards by consent of the
      Department of Education for Ontario. The Macmillan Company of Canada
      Limited, at St. Martin's House, Toronto 1930.

      xviii, 304 pp.; 190 × 125 mm.

408. **BONAR, J.**

      The Heritage of The Spiritual "Keep". By J. Bonar. Toronto: The Macmillan
      Company of Canada Limited, at St. Martin's House 1930.

      [8], 251, [1] pp.; 190 × 125 mm.

409. **BOOS, A.W.**

      McGill University Economic Studies - No.12: *The Financial Arrangements
      Between the Provinces and the Dominion*. By A.W. Boos, M.A. One of the
      National Problems of Canada Series. Toronto: The Macmillan Company of
      Canada Limited, at St. Martin's House. Publishers for the Department of
      Economics and Political Science, McGill University. 1930 (copyright).

      [2], 99, [1] pp. + ads.; 218 × 150 mm.
      McGill University Economic Studies Series.

410. **BOUCHARD, Georges**

      Other Days Other Ways: Silhouettes of the Past in French Canada. Translated
      from Vieilles Choses Vieilles Gens of Georges Bouchard, M.P. Woodcut
      Decorations by Edwin H. Holgate. Toronto: The Macmillan Company of
      Canada Limited, at St. Martin's House 1930.

      189, [1] pp.; 205 × 155 mm.
      Carrier imprint on spine.

411. **CALLAGHAN, Morley**

      It's Never Over. By Morley Callaghan. Toronto: The Macmillan Company of
      Canada Limited, at St. Martin's House 1930.

      [8], 225, [1] pp.; 205 × 130 mm.
      Reprinted in the Laurentian Library (No. 13) in 1972.

412. **CICERO, Marcus Tullius**

      *Selections From Cicero: Pro Lege Manilia. (De Imperio Gnaei Pompei Oratio
      ad Quirites)*. With Introduction and Notes By R.O. Joliffe, B.A., Ph.D. and
      H.L. Tracy, B.A., Ph.D. This edition is prescribed by the Department of
      Education for the Province of Ontario for use for Upper School Examination.
      Toronto: The Macmillan Company of Canada Limited, at St. Martin's
      House 1930.

      xxviii, 88 pp.; 168 × 114 mm.

413. **CONSTANTIN-WEYER, M.**

      A Martyr's Folly. By Maurice Constantin-Weyer. With a critical introduction
      by Pelham Edgar, M.A., Ph.D. Toronto: The Macmillan Company of
      Canada Limited, at St. Martin's House 1930.

      x, 309, [1] pp.; 195 × 128 mm.

414. DE LA ROCHE, Mazo
Portrait of a Dog. By Mazo De La Roche. Illustrated by Morgan Dennis.
Toronto: The Macmillan Company of Canada Limited, At St. Martin's
House, 1930.
viii, 167, [1] pp.; 200 × 146 mm.

415. DENT, W. Redvers
Show Me Death. By W. Redvers Dent. Toronto: The Macmillan Company
of Canada, Limited, at St. Martin's House 1930.
[8], 375, [1] pp.; 193 × 130 mm.

416. DONOVAN, Peter
Late Spring. By Peter Donovan. The Macmillan Company of Canada Limited
at St. Martin's House Toronto 1930.
352 pp.; 187 × 122 mm.

417. EAYRS, Hugh Sterling
Lines For Macmillans' Third Christmas Party. By H.S.E. Toronto, December
19, 1930.
8 pp.; 238 × 165 mm.
Issued in paper.

418. GORDON, T.M.
McGill University Economic Studies - No. 11: *The Canadian Sales Tax*. By
T.M. Gordon, M.A. One of the National Problems of Canada Series. To-
ronto: The Macmillan Company of Canada Limited, at St. Martin's House.
Publishers for the Department of Economics and Political Science, McGill
University. 1930 (Copyright).
vi, 62 pp.; 215 × 150 mm.
McGill University Economic Studies Series.

419. GROVE, Frederick Philip
The Yoke of Life. By Frederick Philip Grove. Toronto: The Macmillan
Company of Canada Limited, at St. Martin's House 1930.
vi, 355, [1] pp.; 190 × 130 mm.

420. GUNN, J.J.
Echoes of the Red. By J.J. Gunn. A Reprint of Some of the Early Writings of
the Author Depicting Pioneer Days in the Red River Settlements. Illustrated
By Herbert Joseph. Toronto: The Macmillan Company of Canada Limited,
at St. Martin's House 1930.
x, 246 pp.; 182 × 127 mm.

421. HAHN, J.E.
The Intelligence Service Within the Canadian Corps 1914-1918. By Major J.E.
Hahn, D.S.O., M.C. Late General Staff, 4th Canadian Division, C.E.F.
Historical Resumé by General Sir Arthur Currie G.C.M.G., K.C.B.
Foreword by Major-General J.H. MacBrien, C.B., C.M.C., D.S.O. Chief of

the General Staff, Canadian Militia. Toronto: The Macmillan Company of Canada Limited, at St. Martin's House 1930.

xxiv, 263, [1] pp.; 225 × 150 mm.

422.   HARRIS, Theodore Herbert

McGill University Economic Studies - No. 13: *The Economic Aspects of the Crowsnest Pass Rates Agreement*. By Theodore Herbert Harris, M.A. One of the National Problems of Canada Series. Toronto: The Macmillan Company of Canada Limited, at St. Martin's House. Publishers for the Department of Economics and Political Science, McGill University. 1930 (Copyright).

viii, 86 pp.; 215 × 150 mm.
McGill University Economic Studies Series.

423.   HASELL, F.H. Eva

Canyons, Cans and Caravans. By F.H. Eva Hasell. Author of "Across the Prairie in a Motor Caravan" and "Through Western Canada in a Caravan". Illustrated from Photographs by the Author. London: Society for Promoting Christian Knowledge. New York and Toronto: The Macmillan Co., 1930.

x, 320 pp.; 188 × 122 mm.

424.   HAWTHORNE, Nathaniel

The Wonder Book. By Nathaniel Hawthorne. Edited with Notes by John C. Saul, M.A. Toronto: The Macmillan Company of Canada Limited, at St. Martin's House 1930.

vi, 138, [2] pp.; 170 × 110 mm.
St. Martin's Literature Series.

425.   HENDERSON, John

Howard Ferguson: The Romance of a Personality. By John Henderson. With illustrations by Jack McLaren. Toronto: The Macmillan Company of Canada Limited, at St. Martin's House 1930.

viii, 145, [1] pp.; 195 × 128 mm.

426.   LA RUE, Mabel Gwinnip

The F-U-N Book For Canadian Boys and Girls. By Mabel Gwinnip La Rue. Illustrated by Maud and Miska Petersham. Toronto: The Macmillan Company of Canada Limited, at St. Martin's House 1930.

iv, 110 pp.; 185 × 135 mm.

427.   LA RUE, Mabel Gwinnip

Under the Story Tree With Young Canada. By Mabel Gwinnip La Rue. Illustrated by Maud and Miska Petersham. Toronto: The Macmillan Company of Canada Limited, at St. Martin's House 1930.

iv, 139, [1] pp.; 185 × 135 mm.

428.   LATHAM, Allan Brockway

McGill University Economic Studies: No. 10: *The Catholic and National*

Labour Unions of Canada. By Allan Brockway Latham, M.A. One of the National Problems of Canada Series. Toronto: The Macmillan Company of Canada Limited, at St. Martin's House. Publishers for the Department of Economics and Political Science, McGill University. 1930 (Copyright).

vi, 104 pp. + ads.; 215 × 150 mm.
McGill University Economic Studies Series.

429. LEACOCK, Stephen

Economic Prosperity in the British Empire. By Stephen Leacock B.A, PH.D., LL.D., Litt.D., F.R.S.C. Head of the Department of Economics and Political Science, McGill University, Montreal. The Macmillan Company of Canada Ltd. Toronto 1930.

viii, 245, [1] pp.; 187 × 125 mm.

430. LIGHTHALL, W.D.

The Person of Evolution: The Outer Consciousness, The Outer Knowledge, The Directive Power. Studies of Instinct as Contributions to a Philosophy of Evolution. By W.D. Lighthall, LL.D. (McGill). Author of "The Outer Consciousness", "A New Utilitarianism", etc. Macmillan: Toronto-London-New York 1930.

216 pp.; 197 × 130 mm.
First published in 1930 by both Macmillan of Canada and Kennedy in Montreal. Reissued with a second appendix in 1931. A third edition published in 1933 (see 531).

431. LOUDON, W.J.

A Canadian Geologist. By W.J. Loudon, B.A. Toronto: The Macmillan Company of Canada Limited, at St. Martin's House 1930.

x, 257, [1] pp.; 220 × 142 mm.

432. LOUDON, W.J.

Studies of Student Life. By W.J. Loudon. [Volume VI: The Yellow Tortoise And Other Tales].

[8], 184 pp.; 175 × 115 mm.

433. MASSEY, Vincent

Good Neighbourhood and Other Addresses in the United States. By The Hon. Vincent Massey, P.C. (Can.), LL.D. His Majesty's Minister for Canada to the United States, 1927-1930. [Quotation]. Toronto: The Macmillan Company of Canada Limited, at St. Martin's House 1930.

xiv, 362 pp.; 198 × 137 mm.

434. MOORE, W.F.

Indian Place Names in Ontario. By Captain W.F. Moore, Formerly teacher in several schools in Ontario. Toronto: The Macmillan Company of Canada Limited, at St. Martin's House 1930.

48 pp.; 185 × 124 mm.

435. NORDEGG, Martin
The Fuel Problem of Canada. By Martin Nordegg. [Quotation]. The Macmillan Company of Canada Limited, at St. Martin's House, Toronto 1930.
x, 155, [1] pp.; 190 × 128 mm.

436. PEABODY, James Edward
Biology and Human Welfare. By James Edward Peabody, M.A. and Arthur Ellsworth Hunt, Ph.B. Canadian Edition. Adapted and Authorized by the Department of Education for Manitoba. Toronto: The Macmillan Company of Canada Limited, at St. Martin's House 1930.
viii, 379, [1] pp.; 200 × 135 mm.

437. PRATT, E.J.
St. Martin's Classics, *Verses of the Sea*. By E.J. Pratt. With an Introduction by Charles G.D. Roberts and Notes by the Author. Toronto: The Macmillan Company of Canada Limited, at St. Martin's House 1930.
xvi, 97, [1] pp.; 170 × 115 mm.
St. Martin's Classics Series.

438. RANKIN, Duncan Joseph
Our Ain Folk and Others. By The Rev. D.J. Rankin, Editor of "A History of the County of Antigonish", "Stray Leaves from Highland History" etc. Toronto: The Macmillan Company of Canada Limited, at St. Martin's House 1930.
viii, 208 pp.; 192 × 130 mm.

439. *Selected Stories From Canadian Prose*. Toronto: The Macmillan Company of Canada Limited, at St. Martin's House 1930.
xx, 274 pp.; 190 × 130 mm.
First published in 1929. First edition not located. Reprinted with corrections in 1929, 1930, 1931 and 1932. Reissued in St. Martin's Classics Series in 1932 and reprinted in 1933 (see 546).

440. SHEFFIELD, Philip H.
The Gateway Primer: For New Canadian Children Learning English. By Philip Sheffield, Inspector of Schools, Nelson, B.C. Illustrated by Eleanor Osborn Eadie and Elsie Deane. The Macmillan Company of Canada Limited, at St. Martin's House, Toronto 1930.
[4], 98 pp.; 190 × 140 mm.

441. STEVENSON, O.J.
Country Life Reader. O.J. Stevenson M.A., D. Paed. Professor of English, Agricultural College, Guelph. Recommended by the Minister of Education for use as a Supplementary Reader in the Elementary Schools of Ontario. Authorized by the Department of Education for use in the Schools of New Brunswick. Toronto: The Macmillan Company of Canada Limited 1930.
xii, 418 pp.; 186 × 125 mm.

442. SULLIVAN, Alan

Queer Partners. By Sinclair Murray [pseud.]. The Macmillan Company of Canada Toronto.

313, [1] pp.; 183 × 120 mm.

443. TENNYSON, Alfred

Gareth and Lynette (Idylls of the King). By Alfred, Lord Tennyson. With an Introduction and Notes. Toronto: The Macmillan Company of Canada Limited, at St. Martin's House 1930.

xx, 87, [1] pp.; 170 × 110 mm.
St. Martin's Literature Series.

444. WALKER, C.C.

The Biology of Civilization. By C.C. Walker. Toronto: The Macmillan Company of Canada Limited, at St. Martin's House 1930.

viii, 323, [1] pp.; 215 × 140 mm.

445. WILSON, Dorothy M.

Vocational Arithmetic For Girls. By Dorothy M. Wilson B.A., Instructor in Mathematics and Science at the Central Technical School, Toronto, and Lillian M. Black, B.A., Instructor in Mathematics and General Subjects at the Central Technical School, Toronto. Toronto: The Macmillan Company of Canada Limited, at St. Martin's House 1930.

viii, 233, [1] pp.; 195 × 124 mm.
Reprinted with corrections in 1933.

446. WILSON, George Ewart

Fractures And Their Complications. By George Ewart Wilson M.B. (Tor.)., F.R.C.S.(Eng.), F.A.C.S. Surgeon-in-Chief, St. Michael's Hospital, Toronto; Assistant Professor of Surgery, University of Toronto; Formerly Surgeon in charge of Emergency and Outpatient Department, Toronto General Hospital. [Quotation]. Toronto: The Macmillan Company of Canada Limited, at St. Martin's House 1930.

viii, 415, [1] pp.; 230 × 145 mm.

1931

447. ABBOTT, Maude E.

History of Medicine in the Province of Quebec. By Maude E. Abbott, B.A., M.D., McGill University, Montreal, Canada. Author of "An Historical Sketch of the Medical Faculty of McGill University"; "McGill's Heroic Past"; etc. Toronto: The Macmillan Company of Canada Limited, at St. Martin's House 1931.

97, [1] pp.; 265 × 180 mm.

448. ASHLEY, C.A.

An Introduction to Auditing for Canadians. By C.A. Ashley, B.Com., Associate of the Institute of Chartered Accountants of England and Wales and of Ontario. Assistant Professor of Accounting in the University of Toronto. Toronto: The Macmillan Company of Canada Limited, at St. Martin's House 1931.

x, 160 pp.; 190 × 125 mm.

449. BAKER, Franklin T.

Everyday Canadian Second Reader. By Franklin T. Baker, Ashley H. Thorndike and Mildred Batchelder. Illustrated by Maud and Miska Petersham. Adapted for use in Canadian Schools by H.H. Mackenzie, B.A. Toronto: The Macmillan Company of Canada Limited, at St. Martin's House 1931.

xx, 230 pp.; 185 × 135 mm.
Everyday Canadian Readers Series.

450. BELL, Jack Mackintosh

Far Places. By Jack Mackintosh Bell M.A., Ph.D., LL.D., Fellow of the Geological Society of America, Fellow of the Royal Geographical Society, Fellow of the Royal Society of Canada. Author of *The Wilds of Maoriland*, *Tales of the Red Children*, *Sidelights on the Siberian Campaign*. Toronto: The Macmillan Company of Canada Limited, at St. Martin's House 1931.

xvi, 174 pp.; 215 × 140 mm.

451. BROWN, Audrey Alexandra

A Dryad In Nanaimo. By Audrey Alexandra Brown. Toronto: The Macmillan Company of Canada Ltd. At St. Martin's House 1931.

vi, 70 pp.; 230 × 145 mm.
An enlarged edition was published in 1934 (see 566).

452. BURKE, Thomas

The Pleasantries of Old Quong. By Thomas Burke. The Macmillan Company Of Canada Ltd., Toronto, 1931.

viii, 279, [1] pp.; 195 × 130 mm.

453. CRAMP, Mary

Eternal Youth: Addresses to Girls 1913-1930. By Mary Cramp and Maud C. Edgar B.A., Headmistresses of Miss Edgar's and Miss Cramp's School Inc., Montreal, Canada. Toronto: The Macmillan Company of Canada Limited, at St. Martin's House 1931.

viii, 262 pp.; 220 × 143 mm.

454. CUTHBERTSON, George A.

Freshwater: A History and a Narrative of the Great Lakes. Written and Illustrated by George A. Cuthbertson. Toronto: The Macmillan Company of Canada Limited, at St. Martin's House 1931.

[12], 315, [1] pp.; 237 × 155 mm.

455.   DAFOE, John W.

Clifford Sifton in Relation to his Times. By John W. Dafoe. Toronto: The
Macmillan Company of Canada Limited, at St. Martin's House 1931.

xxx, 552 pp.; 225 × 155 mm.

456.   DANIELS, E.G.

Dominion Language Series: Book One. By E.G. Daniels, B.A., Municipal
Inspector of Schools, Burnaby, B.C. T.R. Hall, B.A., Inspector of Schools,
Kelowna, B.C. A.F. Matthews, M.A., Inspector of Schools, Kamloops,
B.C. and H.H. Mackenzie, B.A., Inspector of Schools, Vancouver, B.C.
Authorized by the Minister of Education for British Columbia for use in
Grades Three and Four. Toronto: The Macmillan Company of Canada
Limited, at St. Martin's House 1931.

xviii, 306 pp.; 195 × 135 mm.
Dominion Language Series.

457.   DE LA ROCHE, Mazo

Explorers of the Dawn. By Mazo De La Roche. With a Foreword by Christopher Morley. Toronto: The Macmillan Company of Canada, Ltd., at St.
Martin's House MCMXXXI.

292 pp.; 190 × 125 mm.

457A   DE LA ROCHE, Mazo

Finch's Fortune. By Mazo De La Roche. Toronto: The Macmillan Company
of Canada Limited, at St. Martin's House 1931.

viii, 399, [1] pp.; 190 × 125 mm.
Revised in 1948 (see 1169).

458.   DUNN, Fannie Wyche

Everyday Canadian First Reader. By Fannie Wyche Dunn, Franklin T. Baker
and Ashley H. Thorndike. Illustrated by Maud and Miska Petersham.
Adapted for use in Canadian Schools by H.H. Mackenzie, B.A. Toronto:
The Macmillan Company of Canada Limited, at St. Martin's House 1931.

x, 181, [1] pp.; 183 × 138 mm.
Everyday Canadian Readers Series.

459.   GREY OWL

The Men of the Last Frontier. By Grey Owl. Toronto: The Macmillan
Company of Canada Limited, at St. Martin's House 1931.

xiv, 253, [1] pp.; 220 × 145 mm.
Reprinted frequently. Reprinted in the Laurentian Library (No. 37) in 1976.

460.   HÉMON, Louis

Maria Chapdelaine: Récit du Canada Français. Par Louis Hémon. With
Introduction, Notes, Questionnaire, Exercises, and Vocabulary. Toronto:
The Macmillan Company of Canada Limited, At St. Martin's House, 1931.

viii, 262 pp.; 185 × 122 mm.
Reissued with new apparatus by Albert A. Thibault and Morgan S. Kenney in 1958.
Macmillan French Series.

461. HENDERSON, John

Trails to Success. A collection of articles specially prepared by distinguished
Canadian authorities with the object of acquainting University and High
School Students as to the conditions existing, the prospects offered, and the
methods of entering various professions and callings suitable for educated,
ambitious young men and women. Collected and edited by John Henderson
and Alfred H. Allen. Toronto: The Macmillan Company of Canada Limited, at St. Martin's House 1931.

266 pp.; 215 × 140 mm.

462. HILTON, M.J.

A Book of General Science. By M.J. Hilton, Head of Science Department,
Edmonton Technical School. Authorized by the Ministers of Education for
Alberta and British Columbia. Toronto: The Macmillan Company of
Canada Limited, at St. Martin's House 1931.

xvi, 399, [1] pp.; 198 × 133 mm.
Revised edition published in 1939 (see 841).

463. JEANS, James

The Stars in Their Courses. By Sir James Jeans, M.A., D.Sc., LL.D., F.R.S.
Toronto: The Macmillan Company of Canada Limited, at St. Martin's
House 1931.

xii, 188 pp.; 192 × 130 mm.

464. MACBETH, R.G.

Sir Augustus Nanton: A Biography. By R.G. Macbeth, M.A., D.D., LL.D.
Author of "The Romance of Western Canada" and "The Romance of the
Canadian Pacific Railway" Etc. Toronto: The Macmillan Company of
Canada Limited, at St. Martin's House 1931.

x, 130 pp.; 220 × 140 mm.

465. MacIVER, R.M.

Society: Its Structure and Changes. By R.M. MacIver, Lieber Professor of
Political Philosophy and Sociology, Columbia University. Toronto: The
Macmillan Company of Canada Limited, at St. Martin's House 1931.

xvi, 569, [1] pp.; 218 × 140 mm.

466. POWER, Rhoda

Stories From Everywhere. By Rhoda Power. Illustrated by Nina K. Brisley.
Toronto: The Macmillan Company of Canada Limited, at St. Martin's
House 1931.

viii, 168 pp.; 230 × 163 mm.

467. SHAKESPEARE, William

St. Martin's Shakespeare, *The First Part of King Henry the Fourth*. Toronto:
The Macmillan Company of Canada Limited, at St. Martin's House 1931.

lviii, 186 pp.; 170 × 110 mm.
St. Martin's Shakespeare Series.

468.   SHAKESPEARE, William

St. Martin's Shakespeare, *A Midsummer Night's Dream*. Toronto: The Macmillan Company of Canada Limited, at St. Martin's House 1931.

lviii, 145, [1] pp.; 170 × 110 mm.
St. Martin's Shakespeare Series.

469.   STEVENSON, Andrew

Macmillan's Literature Series, *Selections From The Nature Poets*. Edited with Notes By Andrew Stevenson, B.A., Assistant Master, Normal School, London. Toronto: The Macmillan Company of Canada, Limited 1931.

128 pp.; 175 × 120 mm.
First published by Morang in 1906. Macmillan edition issued in paper.
Macmillan's Literature Series.

470.   SULLIVAN, Alan

The Golden Foundling. By Sinclair Murray [pseud.]. The Macmillan Company of Canada Toronto, 1931.

338 pp.; 193 × 127 mm.

471.   TAYLOR, R.W.

Statistical Contributions to Canadian Economic History. Volume II. Statistics of Foreign Trade. By R.W. Taylor, M.A. Assistant Professor of Political Economy, McMaster University. *Statistics of Prices*. By H. Michell, M.A. Professor of Political Economy, McMaster University. Toronto: The Macmillan Company of Canada, Limited 1931.

vi, 93, [1] pp.; 310 × 235 mm.

472.   WALLACE, W. Stewart

Murders and Mysteries: A Canadian Series. By W. Stewart Wallace. Toronto: The Macmillan Company of Canada Limited, at St. Martin's House 1931.

[8], 333, [1] pp.; 220 × 140 mm.

473.   WINTER, Charles F.

Lieutenant-General The Hon. Sir Sam Hughes K.C.B., M.D. Canada's War Minister 1911-1916. Recollections of Service as Military Secretary at Headquarters, Canadian Militia, prior to and during the early stages of the Great War. By Brigadier-General Charles F. Winter, R.O., (Canada). Toronto: The Macmillan Company of Canada Limited, at St. Martin's House 1931.

xviii, 182 pp.; 217 × 137 mm.

1932

474.   BARTLETT, Gertrude

"The White Bird" And Other Poems. By Gertrude Bartlett. With an Introduction by Robert Norwood. Toronto: The Macmillan Company of Canada Limited, at St. Martin's House 1932.

[14], 57, [1] pp.; 192 × 132 mm.

475. BOLLERT, Grace

Canadian Treasury Manuals: Book One: Grade 1. By Grace Bollert. The Ryerson Press [and] The Macmillans in Canada 1932.

iv, 314 pp.; 195 × 135 mm.
Revised in 1934 (see 564).
Treasury Readers Series.

476. BRADY, Alexander

Canada. By Alexander Brady. Associate Professor of Political Science in the University of Toronto. The Macmillan Company of Canada Limited, at St. Martin's House, Toronto 1932.

viii, 374 pp.; 220 × 140 mm.

477. BRUCE, Charles

Tomorrow's Tide. By Charles Bruce. Toronto: The Macmillan Company of Canada Ltd., at St. Martin's House 1932.

[6], 28 pp.; 194 × 130 mm.

478. CALLAGHAN, Morley

A Broken Journey. By Morley Callaghan. Toronto: The Macmillan Company of Canada Limited, at St. Martin's House 1932.

[8], 270 pp.; 190 × 130 mm.
Reprinted in the Laurentian Library (No. 36) in 1976.

479. DANIELS, E.G.

Dominion Language Series: Book Three. By E.G. Daniels, B.A., Municipal Inspector of Schools, Burnaby, B.C. T.R. Hall, B.A., Inspector of Schools, Kelowna, B.C. A.F. Matthews, M.A., Inspector of Schools, Kamloops, B.C. and H.H. Mackenzie, B.A., Inspector of Schools, Vancouver, B.C. Toronto: The Macmillan Company of Canada Limited, at St. Martin's House 1932.

xviii, 374 pp.; 195 × 135 mm.
Dominion Language Series.

480. DE LA ROCHE, Mazo

Lark Ascending. By Mazo De La Roche. Toronto: The Macmillan Company of Canada Limited, at St. Martin's House 1932.

[6], 303, [1] pp.; 195 × 130 mm.

481. DUNCAN, Eric

The Rich Fisherman And Other Sketches. By Eric Duncan. Toronto: The Macmillan Company of Canada Limited, at St. Martin's House 1932.

113, [1] pp.; 187 × 123 mm.

482. ÉNAULT, Louis

Louis Énault, *Le Chien du Capitaine*. Edited by Margaret de G. Verrall. Authorized in the Province of Ontario. Toronto: The Macmillan Company of Canada Limited, at St. Martin's House 1932.

viii, 172 pp.; 172 × 115 mm.
Reissued in 1935 with exercises (see 638).

482A FARNOL, Jeffery

Voices From The Dust: Being Romances of Old London and of That which Never Dies. [Quotation]. By Jeffery Farnol. With Illustrations By H.R. Millar. Toronto: The Macmillan Company Of Canada Limited, At St. Martin's House, 1932.

xii, 369, [1] pp. + ad.; 193 × 134 mm.

483. FINNEMORE, John

Social Life in England: From Saxon Times to the Present Day. By John Finnemore, Author of "Boys and Girls of Other Days," "Famous Englishmen," Etc. With Seventy-Five Illustrations and a Sketch-Map. The Macmillan Company of Canada, Ltd. St. Martin's House - 70 Bond Street Toronto.

288 pp.; 190 × 125 mm.

484. GRIFFIN, Frederick

Soviet Scene: A Newspaperman's Close-ups of New Russia. By Frederick Griffin. Toronto: The Macmillan Company of Canada Limited, at St. Martin's House 1932.

xii, 279, [1] pp.; 215 × 140 mm.
Reprinted in 1933.

485. IGNATIEFF, Nicholas

The Russian Emerges: A Native Assessment of the Soviet Experiment. By Nicholas Ignatieff. Toronto: The Macmillan Company of Canada Limited, at St. Martin's House 1932.

xvi, 112 pp.; 194 × 122 mm.

486. JONES, Harry A.

Metal-Work For Grades VII, VIII, and IX. By Harry A. Jones, Machine Shop Instructor, Technical School, Vancouver. Authorized for use in the Schools of British Columbia. Toronto: The Macmillan Company of Canada Limited, at St. Martin's House 1932.

[6], 112 pp.; 221 × 145 mm.
Issued in limp cloth.

487. KIRBY, William

St. Martin's Classics, *The Golden Dog (Le Chien D'or): A Romance of Old Quebec.* By William Kirby F.R.S.C. Shortened, With Introduction and Glossary by E.C. Woodley, M.A. Authorized by the Ministers of Education for British Columbia and Quebec. Toronto: The Macmillan Company of Canada Limited, at St. Martin's House 1932.

xii, 227, [1] pp.; 170 × 110 mm.
First published in the St. Martin's Classics Series in 1931. First printing not located.
Reprinted in 1932.
St. Martin's Classics Series.

488. LAMB, Charles
Tales From Shakespeare. By Charles and Mary Lamb. Edited with an Introduction, by the Rev. Alfred Ainger M.A. Toronto: The Macmillan Company of Canada Limited, at St. Martin's House 1932.
xx, 368 pp.; 155 × 104 mm.

489. LEACOCK, Stephen
Afternoons in Utopia: Tales of the New Time. By Stephen Leacock. The Macmillan Company of Canada Ltd., at St. Martin's House, Toronto 1932.
viii, 240 pp.; 188 × 125 mm.

490. LEACOCK, Stephen
Back to Prosperity: The Great Opportunity of the Empire Conference. By Stephen Leacock B.A., Ph.D., LL.D., Litt.D., F.R.S.C. Head of the Department of Economics and Political Science, McGill University, Montreal. Toronto: The Macmillan Company of Canada Limited, at St. Martin's House 1932.
[8], 108 pp.; 193 × 125 mm.

491. LIVESAY, Dorothy
Sign Post. By Dorothy Livesay. Toronto: The Macmillan Company of Canada Ltd. at St. Martin's House 1932.
x, 61, [1] pp.; 198 × 120 mm.

492. LOUDON, W.J.
Sir William Mulock: A Short Biography. By William James Loudon, Professor Emeritus in the University of Toronto. Toronto: The Macmillan Company of Canada Limited, at St. Martin's House 1932.
xii, 384 pp.; 225 × 150 mm.

493. MACDONALD, Adrian
Narrative Poems for Honour Matriculation. Edited with Notes and Questions by Adrian Macdonald, M.A., English Master, The Normal School, Peterborough, Ontario. These poems are authorized by the Department of Education of Ontario for use in Upper School Examinations. Toronto: The Macmillan Company of Canada Limited, at St. Martin's House 1932.
[8], 110 pp.; 174 × 120 mm.
Reprinted in 1935 in limp cloth.
Macmillan's Matriculation English Texts Series.

494. MacGIBBON, Duncan Alexander
The Canadian Grain Trade. By Duncan Alexander MacGibbon, M.A., Ph.D. Member of the Royal Grain Inquiry Commission, 1923-4; Member of the Board of Grain Commissioners for Canada; Sometime Professor of Political Economy at the University of Alberta. Toronto: The Macmillan Company of Canada Limited, at St. Martin's House 1932.
xvi, 503, [1] pp.; 213 × 138 mm.

495. MACKAY, Muriel A.

Dominion French Readers: Book One. By Muriel A. Mackay, B.A. And
Alfreda E. Thompson, B.A. Instructors in French, Kitsilano Junior and
Senior High Schools, Vancouver, B.C. Authorized by the Minister of Edu-
cation for British Columbia. Toronto: The Macmillan Company of Canada
Limited, at St. Martin's House 1932.

xxiv, 145, [1] pp.; 189 × 124 mm.

496. MARIE, Grand Duchess of Russia

A Princess in Exile. By Marie, Grand Duchess of Russia. Toronto: The
Macmillan Company of Canada Limited, at St. Martin's House 1932.

xii, 306 pp.; 243 × 160 mm.

497. MARJORIBANKS, Edward

Volume One. *The Life of Lord Carson*. By Edward Marjoribanks, author of
The Life of Sir Edward Marshall Hall. With a Preface by the Rt. Hon.
Viscount Hailsham, D.C.L., LL.D. 1932 Toronto: The Macmillan Com-
pany of Canada Limited, at St. Martin's House.

viii, 455, [1] pp.; 220 × 143 mm.

498. MOINAUX, Jules

Jules Moinaux, *Les Deux Sourds*. Edited with Notes, Exercises and Vocabulary by F.C.A. Jeanneret, Professor of French, University of Toronto. This
play is authorized by the Department of Education of Ontario for use in
Middle School Examinations. Toronto: The Macmillan Company of Canada
Limited, at St. Martin's House 1932.

viii, 65, [1] pp.; 182 × 120 mm.
Issued in limp cloth.
Macmillan's Matriculation French Series.

499. ORMOND, Frances L.

Canadian Treasury Manuals: Book Two: Grades II and III. By Frances L.
Ormond, Charlotte M. Ormond, and M.A. Beresford, B.A. The Ryerson
Press [and] The Macmillans in Canada.

[4], 154 pp.; 195 × 135 mm.
Revised in 1934 (see 600).
Treasury Readers Series.

500. PARGMENT, M.S.

La France et Les Français. Par M.S. Pargment. Authorized by The Minister
of Education for the Province of Ontario. Toronto: The Macmillan Company of Canada Limited, at St. Martin's House 1932.

[12], 372 pp.; 163 × 115 mm.
Macmillan's Matriculation French Series.

501. PIERCE, Lorne

The Canada Book of Prose and Verse: Book Two. By Lorne Pierce and Dora
Whitefield. The Ryerson Press [and] The Macmillans in Canada.

x, 423, [1] pp.; 200 × 140 mm.
Revised in 1935 (see 653). Further revised and reissued as *Life and Adventure* in 1948
(see 1205). Revised again in 1962 (see 1595). Reprinted frequently.
Canada Books of Prose and Verse Series.

502. PIERCE, Lorne

The Canada Book of Prose and Verse: Book Three. By Lorne Pierce and Dora
Whitefield. The Ryerson Press [and] The Macmillans in Canada.

xiv, 475, [1] pp.; 200 × 135 mm.
Revised in 1936 (see 714). Further revised and reissued as *Our Heritage* in 1948 (see
1203). Revised again in 1963 (see 1631). Reprinted frequently.
Canada Books of Prose and Verse Series.

503. PRATT, E.J.

Many Moods. By E.J. Pratt. Toronto: The Macmillan Company of Canada
Ltd., at St. Martin's House 1932.

viii, 53, [1] pp.; 225 × 148 mm.

504. PRIESTLEY, J.B.

J.B. Priestley, *Faraway*. Toronto: The Macmillan Company of Canada
Limited, at St. Martin's House 1932.

[6], 568 pp.; 220 × 146 mm.

505. *Songs For Canadian Boys: A Collection of Songs Especially Suitable for
Chorus Singing by Canadian Boys*. Compiled by a Committee Representing
the Quebec Provincial Council of the Boy Scouts Association. Published on
Behalf of the Montreal District Council Boy Scouts Association by The
Macmillan Company of Canada Limited, at St. Martin's House Toronto
1932.

vi, 124 pp.; 175 × 120 mm.
There is also a large edition containing substantially more material (see 506).

506. *Songs For Canadian Boys: A Collection of Songs Especially Suitable For
Chorus Singing by Canadian Boys*. Explanatory and Historical Notes on Each
of the More Important Songs are Also Included. Compiled by a Committee
Representing the Quebec Provincial Council of the Boy Scouts Association.
Published on Behalf of the Montreal District Council Boy Scouts Association
by The Macmillan Company of Canada Limited, at St. Martin's House,
Toronto 1932.

xvi, 297, [1] pp.; 250 × 165 mm.
For the edition containing words only, see 505.

507. STEVENSON, Robert Louis

St. Martin's Classics, *The Black Arrow: A Tale of the Two Roses*. By Robert
Louis Stevenson. With Illustrations by H.M. Brock, R.I. Authorized by the
Minister of Education for the Province of Quebec. Toronto: The Macmillan
Company of Canada Limited, at St. Martin's House 1932.

x, 286 pp.; 170 × 115 mm.
St. Martin's Classics Series.

508.   TROTTER, Reginald George

The British Empire-Commonwealth: A Study in Political Evolution. By Reginald George Trotter, Queen's University. [Quotation]. Toronto: The Macmillan Company of Canada Limited, at St. Martin's House 1932.

   x, 131, [1] pp.; 190 × 125 mm.

509.   URQUHART, H.M.

The History of the 16th Battalion (The Canadian Scottish) Canadian Expeditionary Force in the Great War 1914-1919. H.M. Urquhart, D.S.O., M.C., A.D.C. Lieutenant-Colonel, Reserve of Officers, Canadian Non-Permanent Active Militia. Published for The Trustees and Regimental Committee of the 16th Battalion (The Canadian Scottish), C.E.F. Toronto: The Macmillan Company of Canada Limited, at St. Martin's House 1932.

   xxii, 853, [1] pp.; 240 × 155 mm.

510.   WALLACE, Robert C.

A Liberal Education in A Modern World: The Burwash Lectures Delivered at Victoria University Toronto, 1932. By R.C. Wallace, President of the University of Alberta. Toronto: The Macmillan Company of Canada Limited, at St. Martin's House 1932.

   xiv, 114 pp.; 186 × 125 mm.

511.   WALLACE, W. Stewart

The Story of Laura Secord: A Study in Historical Evidence. By W.S. Wallace. Toronto: The Macmillan Company of Canada Limited, at St. Martin's House 1932.

   26 pp.; 235 × 150 mm.
   Issued in paper.

512.   WOLFENDEN, Hugh H.

The Real Meaning of Social Insurance: Its Present Status and Tendencies. By Hugh H. Wolfenden, Fellow of the Institute of Actuaries, Great Britain; Fellow of the Actuarial Society of America; Fellow of the Royal Statistical Society. Toronto: The Macmillan Company of Canada Limited, at St. Martin's House 1932.

   xvi, 227, [1] pp.; 193 × 125 mm.

513.   WOOTTON, Christina Dyde

Canadian Treasury Manuals: Book Three: Grades IV, V and VI. By Christina Dyde Wootton, M.A., B.C. Diltz, M.A. and Charles C. Bremner, M.A. The Ryerson Press [and] The Macmillans in Canada.

   vi, 253, [1] pp.; 195 × 135 mm.
   Revised edition issued in 1934 (see 616).
   Treasury Readers Series.

1933

514. ALEXANDER, W.H.

These Twenty-Five Years: A Symposium. By W.H. Alexander, E.K. Broadus, F.J. Lewis and J.M. Maceachran of the University of Alberta. Toronto: The Macmillan Company of Canada Limited 1933.

  viii, 113, [1] pp.; 218 × 138 mm.

515. BLACK, Newton Henry

New Practical Physics: Fundamental Principles And Applications To Daily Life. By Newton Henry Black and Harvey Nathaniel Davis. Revised and Adapted for Canadian Schools by James Grant Davidson, Physics Department, University of British Columbia. Authorized by the Departments of Education for British Columbia and Manitoba. Toronto: The Macmillan Company of Canada Limited, at St. Martin's House 1933. All rights reserved.

  viii, 648 pp.; 190 × 125 mm.
  First published in 1930. First edition not located.

516. BRUCE, E.L.

Mineral Deposits of the Canadian Shield. By E.L. Bruce, B.Sc., Ph.D., Miller Memorial Research Professor of Geology, Queen's University, Kingston. Toronto: The Macmillan Company of Canada Limited: at St. Martin's House 1933.

  xxiv, 428 pp.; 230 × 152 mm.

517. CARROLL, Gladys Hasty

As the Earth Turns. Gladys Hasty Carroll. Toronto: The Macmillan Company of Canada Limited, At St. Martin's House, 1933.

  [8], 339, [1] pp.; 200 × 137 mm.

518. COOPER, Irvin

Circle of Fifths: A Text Book on the Rudiments of Music. By Irvin Cooper, Mus. Bac. Associate of the Royal Manchester College of Music. Director of Music, West Hill High School, Montreal. Lecturer in Theory of Music, McGill University. Toronto: The Macmillan Company of Canada Limited, at St. Martin's House 1933.

  xii, 130 pp.; 190 × 128 mm.

519. DAY, John Percival

Considerations on the Demand for A Central Bank in Canada. By John Percival Day, B.A., B.Sc. (London), D. Phil. (St. Andrews). Professor of Economics in McGill University, Montreal. Published for McGill University by the Macmillan Company of Canada Limited, Toronto 1933.

  56 pp.; 223 × 155 mm.
  Issued in paper.

520.   DE LA ROCHE, Mazo

The Master of Jalna. By Mazo De La Roche. Toronto: The Macmillan Company of Canada Limited, at St. Martin's House 1933.

viii, 331, [1] pp.; 190 × 125 mm.
New edition published in 1948 (see 1170).

521.   DE SCHWEINITZ, Karl

Growing Up: The Story of How We Become Alive, Are Born, and Grow Up. By Karl de Schweinitz. Toronto: The Macmillan Company of Canada Limited, at St. Martin's House 1933.

111, [1] pp.; 207 × 138 mm.
First published in 1928 and reprinted frequently. Earlier printings not located.

522.   DUMAS, Alexandre

St. Martin's Classics, *The Three Musketeers*. By Alexandre Dumas. Abridged and Edited by C.J. Brown, M.A., Professor of English Literature, Lucknow University and H.S. Walker, M.A., Headmaster, St. Mary's School, Melrose. Toronto: The Macmillan Company of Canada Limited, at St. Martin's House 1933.

x, 154 pp.; 170 × 115 mm.
St. Martin's Classics Series.

523.   GATES, Arthur I.

Canadian Work-Play Books, *Round the Year*. By Arthur I. Gates and Miriam Blanton Huber. Illustrated by A. Gladys Peck. Authorized for use in the Province of British Columbia. Toronto: The Macmillan Company of Canada Limited, at St. Martin's House 1933.

viii, 167, [1] pp.; 185 × 140 mm.
Work-Play Books Series.

524.   JACKES, Lyman Bruce

The Romance of Canada's Money. By Paul Montgomery [pseud.]. Toronto: The Macmillan Company of Canada Limited, at St. Martin's House 1933.

[10], 29, [1] pp.; 220 × 150 mm.
Issued in limp cloth.

525.   KENNEDY, Leo

The Shrouding. Poems by Leo Kennedy. Toronto: The Macmillan Company of Canada Limited. . . at St. Martin's House 1933.

xiv, 59, [1] pp.; 224 × 145 mm.

526.   KEYNES, John Maynard

Essays in Biography. By John Maynard Keynes, Fellow of King's College, Cambridge. Toronto: The Macmillan Company of Canada Limited, at St. Martin's House 1933.

x, 318 pp.; 200 × 128 mm.

527.   KIRKWOOD, M.M.
Duty and Happiness in a Changed World. By M.M. Kirkwood, M.A., Ph.D.
Assistant Professor of English, University College, University of Toronto.
Toronto: The Macmillan Company of Canada Limited: at St. Martin's
House 1933.

[8], 207, [1] pp.; 194 × 129 mm.

528.   KNIGHT, G. Wilson
*The Christian Renaissance, With Interpretations of Dante, Shakespeare and
Goethe, And a Note on T.S. Eliot*, by G. Wilson Knight, Chancellors Professor of English, Trinity College, Toronto. Toronto: The Macmillan Company of Canada Limited, at St. Martin's House 1933.

x, 374 pp.; 224 × 143 mm.

529.   LABICHE, Eugène
Labiche et Jolly, *Le Baron de Fourchevif: Comédie en Un Acte*. Edited with
Notes, Exercises and Vocabulary by F.C.A. Jeanneret, Professor of French,
University College, University of Toronto. This play is prescribed by the
Department of Education for use in Middle School Examinations. Toronto:
The Macmillan Company of Canada Limited, at St. Martin's House 1933.

viii, 76 pp.; 182 × 120 mm.
Issued in limp cloth.
Macmillan's Matriculation French Series.

530.   LEACOCK, Stephen
*Stephen Leacock's Plan To Relieve the Depression in 6 Days, To Remove it in 6
Months, To Eradicate it in 6 Years*. Toronto: The Macmillan Company of
Canada Limited, at St. Martin's House 1933.

[2], 18 pp.; 225 × 150 mm.
Issued in paper.

531.   LIGHTHALL, W.D.
*The Person of Evolution: The Outer Consciousness, The Outer Knowledge, The
Directive Power*. By W.D. Lighthall, LL.D., (McGill). Definitive Edition
with Three Appendices: including A Theory of Atomic Life, Undying and
Evolutionary. Macmillan Toronto-London-New York, 1933.

246 pp.; 195 × 130 mm.
First published in 1930 (see 430).

532.   LONDON, Jack
St. Martin's Classics, *The Call of the Wild*. By Jack London. With an
Introduction, Notes, and Bibliography. Authorized for use in the Province of
Manitoba. Toronto: The Macmillan Company of Canada Limited at St.
Martin's House 1933.

xii, 197, [1] pp.; 170 × 110 mm.
First published in 1910 (see 37). A school edition, with study material prepared by
Linton D. Read, was published in 1964 (see 1682).
St. Martin's Classics Series.

533.   LONGSTRETH, T. Morris

In Scarlet and Plain Clothes: The History of the Mounted Police. By T. Morris
Longstreth, author of *The Silent Force*. Toronto: The Macmillan Company
of Canada Limited, at St. Martin's House 1933.

x, 365, [1] pp.; 200 × 135 mm.

534.   MACAULEY, Thomas Babington

Macmillan's Literature Series, Macaulay's *Lays of Ancient Rome*. Edited with
Notes By John C. Saul, M.A. Authorized by the Department of Education
for use in the Province of Manitoba. Toronto: The Macmillan Company of
Canada, Limited 1933.

135, [1] pp.; 175 × 117 mm.
First published by Morang in 1910. Macmillan edition issued in paper.
Macmillan's Literature Series.

535.   MACDONALD, Adrian

Longer Poems for Honour Matriculation 1933-34. Edited with Notes and
Questions by Adrian Macdonald, M.A. English Master, The Normal School,
Peterborough, Ontario. These poems are prescribed by the Department of
Education of Ontario for use in Upper School Examinations. Toronto: The
Macmillan Company of Canada Limited, at St. Martin's House 1933.

[8], 86 pp.; 175 × 119 mm.
Macmillan's Matriculation English Texts Series.

536.   MACDONALD, Adrian

St. Martin's Classics, *A Pedlar's Pack: Narrative Poetry For Secondary
Schools*. Edited, With Preface And Notes By Adrian Macdonald, M.A.
English Master, The Normal School, Peterborough, Ontario. Toronto: The
Macmillan Company of Canada Limited, at St. Martin's House 1933.

xiv, 240 pp.; 170 × 110 mm.
First published in 1932. Earlier printings not located. Reprinted frequently.
St. Martin's Classics Series.

537.   MacKENZIE, J.J.

*Number 4 Canadian Hospital: The Letters of Professor J.J. MacKenzie From
the Salonika Front: With a Memoir by his Wife Kathleen Cuffe MacKenzie*.
Toronto: The Macmillan Company of Canada Limited, at St. Martin's
House 1933.

[8], 247, [1] pp.; 218 × 142 mm.

538.   MOORE, William Henry

The Definite National Purpose. By William Henry Moore. Toronto: The
Macmillan Company of Canada Limited, at St. Martin's House 1933.

xvi, 161, [1] pp.; 188 × 128 mm.

539.   PEACOCK, Thomas Love

St. Martin's Classics, *Maid Marian*. By Thomas Love Peacock. With Introduction, Notes, Etc. by F.A. Cavenagh, M.A. Fellow of University College,

London, Assistant Master at King Edward VII School, Lytham. Toronto: The Macmillan Company of Canada Limited, at St. Martin's House 1933.

x, 139, [1] pp.; 170 × 110 mm.
St. Martin's Classics Series.

540.   Macmillan's Canadian School Series, *A Phonic Manual For the Use of Teachers*. To Be Used in Connection With Any Series of Authorized Readers Published in Canada. Toronto: The Macmillan Company of Canada Limited 1933.

[4], 92 pp.; 185 × 118 mm.
First published by Morang in 1902.
Macmillan's Canadian School Series.

541.   POWLEY, Edward B.

St. Martin's Classics, *A Hundred Years of English Poetry*. Selected by Edward B. Powley. Authorized for use by the Province of Quebec. Toronto: The Macmillan Company of Canada Limited, at St. Martin's House 1933.

xiv, 175, [1] pp.; 170 × 110 mm.
St. Martin's Classics Series.

542.   PRIESTLEY, J.B.

J.B. Priestley, *Wonder Hero*. 1933, Toronto: The Macmillan Company of Canada Limited, at St. Martin's House.

[8], 321, [1] pp.; 190 × 123 mm.

543.   RABINOWITCH, I.M.

Diabetes Mellitus: A Handbook of Simplified Methods of Diagnosis and Treatment. By I.M. Rabinowitch D.Sc., M.D., C.M., F.R.C.P.(C), Assistant Professor of Medicine and Lecturer in Biochemistry, McGill University. Director, The Department of Metabolism, The Montreal General Hospital. Consultant in Biochemistry to the Children's Memorial Hospital, Montreal, and to the Shriner's Hospital for Crippled Children, Montreal. With an Introduction by A.B. Macallum, M.A., M.B., Ph.D., Sc.D., LL.D., F.R.S. Toronto: The Macmillan Company of Canada Limited, at St. Martin's House 1933.

xviii, 246 pp.; 205 × 142 mm.

544.   ROBERTS, Charles G.D.

Eyes of the Wilderness. Charles G.D. Roberts. Toronto: The Macmillan Company of Canada Limited, at St. Martin's House 1933.

viii, 269, [1] pp.; 192 × 130 mm.

545.   ROBERTS, Leslie

So This is Ottawa. By Leslie Roberts. Author of "These Be Your Gods", and "When the Gods Laughed". Toronto: The Macmillan Company of Canada Limited, at St. Martin's House 1933.

xiv, 222 pp.; 215 × 145 mm.

546.   St. Martin's Classics, *Selected Stories From Canadian Prose*. Authorized by the Province of Alberta. Toronto: The Macmillan Company of Canada Limited, at St. Martin's House 1933.

>   xx, 274 pp.; 170 × 115 mm.
>   First published in 1929 and reprinted in 1929, 1930 (see 439), 1931 and 1932. First published in the St. Martin's Classics Series in 1932 and reprinted in 1933. Earlier printing not located.
>   St. Martin's Classics Series.

547.   SHAKESPEARE, William

Macbeth. Edited with Introduction, Notes and Questions by Adrian Macdonald, M.A. English Master, The Normal School, Peterborough, Ontario. Toronto: The Macmillan Company of Canada Limited, at St. Martin's House 1933.

>   xxviii, 144 pp.; 180 × 122 mm.
>   Issued in limp cloth and cloth.
>   Macmillan's Matriculation English Texts Series.

548.   SHAKESPEARE, William

The Merchant of Venice. Edited with Introduction, Notes and Questions by Adrian Macdonald, M.A. English Master, The Normal School, Peterborough, Ontario. Toronto: The Macmillan Company of Canada Limited, at St. Martin's House 1933.

>   xxx, 135, [1] pp.; 175 × 118 mm.
>   Macmillan's Matriculation English Texts Series.

549.   SUTTON, F.A.

One-Arm Sutton. Major-General F.A. Sutton. Toronto: The Macmillan Company of Canada Limited, at St. Martin's House 1933.

>   viii, 277, [1] pp.; 215 × 140 mm.

550.   THOMPSON, Norman

Canadian Railway Development From the Earliest Times. By Norman Thompson, Canadian Representative of the Railway and Locomotive Historical Society, And Major J.H. Edgar B.Sc., A.M.E.I.C., V.D. Toronto: The Macmillan Company of Canada Limited, at St. Martin's House 1933.

>   xvi, 402 pp.; 200 × 140 mm.

551.   VERNE, Jules

Voyage au Centre de la Terre. Par Jules Verne. Adapted and Edited by Eugene Pellissier, Formerly Assistant Master at Clifton College and Lecturer at University College, Bristol. Prescribed for use in the Province of Ontario. Toronto: The Macmillan Company of Canada Limited, at St. Martin's House 1933.

>   xii, 216 pp.; 175 × 115 mm.
>   Macmillan's Matriculation French Series.

552. WALLACE, W. Stewart

The Memoirs of the Rt. Hon. Sir George Foster P.C., G.C.M.G. By W. Stewart
Wallace, M.A. (Oxon). Toronto: The Macmillan Company of Canada Limited, at St. Martin's House 1933.

x, 291, [1] pp.; 218 × 140 mm.

553. WARD, James Edward

Indian Summer and Other Poems. James Edward Ward. Author of *The Wayfarer.* Toronto: The Macmillan Company of Canada Limited, at St. Martin's
House 1933.

79, [1] pp.; 225 × 145 mm.

554. WELLS, H.G.

H.G. Wells. *The Bulpington of Blup: Adventures, Poses, Stresses, Conflicts,
And Disaster in a Contemporary Brain.* Toronto: The Macmillan Company of
Canada Limited, At St. Martin's House, 1933.

x, 414 pp.; 203 × 136 mm.

555. WELLS, H.G.

The Shape of Things to Come. By H.G. Wells. Toronto: The Macmillan
Company of Canada Limited, at St. Martin's House 1933.

x, 431, [1] pp.; 220 × 140 mm.

556. WILSON, Clifford

Adventurers All: Tales of Forgotten Heroes in New France. By Clifford Wilson.
With Nine Illustrations by A. Sherriff Scott. Toronto: The Macmillan
Company of Canada Limited, at St. Martin's House 1933.

xviii, 244 pp.; 203 × 135 mm.

1934

557. ARMSTRONG, P.C.

City and Country: A Study in Fundamental Economics. By P.C. Armstrong
and F.E.M. Robinson. Toronto: The Macmillan Company of Canada Limited, at St. Martin's House 1934.

xii, 145, [1] pp.; 215 × 140 mm.

558. ASSELSTINE, R.W.

Canadian Treasury Readers: Book Four. By R.W. Asselstine. Authorized for
use in the Public Schools of Nova Scotia. The Macmillans in Canada [and]
The Ryerson Press.

vi, 346 pp.; 190 × 135 mm.

First published in 1932. Earlier printings not located. Reprinted in 1934, 1935,
1936, 1937, and 1938.

Treasury Readers Series.

559.   BARBEAU, Marius

Cornelius Krieghoff: Pioneer Painter of North America. By Marius Barbeau, Author of "Indian Days in the Canadian Rockies," "The Downfall of Temlaham"...etc. 1934, Toronto: The Macmillan Company of Canada Limited, at St. Martin's House.

[14], 152 pp.; 245 × 185 mm.

560.   BATES, E.S.

A Planned Nationalism: Canada's Effort. By E.S. Bates. Toronto: The Macmillan Company of Canada Limited, at St. Martin's House 1934.

xiv, 171, [1] pp.; 220 × 140 mm.

561.   BENNET, C.L.

The Canada Book of Prose and Verse: Book Four. By C.L. Bennet and Lorne Pierce. The Macmillans in Canada [and] The Ryerson Press.

xii, 573 pp.; 200 × 135 mm.
Revised and reissued as *The Golden Caravan* in 1948 (see 1163). Second revision published in 1962 (see 1558). Reprinted frequently.
Canada Books of Prose and Verse Series.

562.   BERESFORD, M.A.

Highroads to Reading: Book Three. By M.A. Beresford. Authorized for use in the Public Schools of Alberta, British Columbia, Manitoba and Saskatchewan. The Ryerson Press [and] The Macmillans in Canada.

viii, 280 pp.; 190 × 135 mm.
First published in 1932. Earlier printings not located. Reprinted in 1934, 1935 and 1937. A Quebec edition was published in 1937. Also published in The Treasury Readers Series under the title *Canadian Treasury Readers: Book Three*.
Treasury Readers Series.

563.   BERESFORD, M.A.

Highroads to Reading: Work and Play To Accompany Book Three. By M.A. Beresford, M.A. The Macmillans in Canada [and] The Ryerson Press.

48 pp.; 273 × 208 mm.
First published in 1932. Earlier printings not located. Reprinted in 1934 and 1937. Issued in paper.
Treasury Readers Series.

564.   BOLLERT, Grace

The Treasury Manual: Grade One. By Grace Bollert, Provincial Normal School, Vancouver. The Macmillans in Canada [and] The Ryerson Press.

vi, 287, [1] pp.; 185 × 130 mm.
First published in 1932 (see 475). Revised edition issued in paper.
Treasury Readers Series.

565.   BROADUS, Edmund Kemper

A Book of Canadian Prose and Verse. Compiled, and with Biographical Notes By Edmund Kemper Broadus, Professor of English in the University of Alberta, And Eleanor Hammond Broadus, Author of "Dante Vivo", etc.

New and Completely Revised With Additional Material. Toronto: The
Macmillan Company of Canada Limited, at St. Martin's House 1934.

xviii, 415, [1] pp.; 220 × 150 mm.
First published in 1923 (see 194).

566. BROWN, Audrey Alexandra

A Dryad in Nanaimo. (As originally published in 1931). Together With
Eleven New Poems. By Audrey Alexandra Brown. Toronto: The Macmillan
Company of Canada Limited, at St. Martin's House 1934.

viii, 120 pp.; 230 × 145 mm.
First published in 1931 (see 451).

567. BRUCE, Herbert A.

Our Heritage And Other Addresses. By Colonel The Hon. Herbert A. Bruce,
R.A.M.C., M.D., L.R.C.P., F.R.C.S. (Eng.), LL.D. Toronto: The Macmillan Company of Canada Limited, at St. Martin's House 1934.

xviii, 392 pp.; 225 × 150 mm.

568. BURRELL, Martin

Crumbs Are Also Bread. By Martin Burrell. Author of *Betwixt Heaven and
Charing Cross*, etc. Toronto: The Macmillan Company of Canada Limited,
at St. Martin's House 1934.

[12], 340 pp.; 230 × 138 mm.

569. CALLAGHAN, Morley

Such Is My Beloved. By Morley Callaghan. [Quotation]. Toronto: The
Macmillan Company of Canada Limited, At St. Martin's House, 1934.

[8], 288 pp.; 192 × 130 mm.

570. CHANT, Sperrin N.F.

Mental Training: A Practical Psychology. By Sperrin N.F. Chant, M.A.
Associate Professor of Psychology, University of Toronto; Member: Re-
search Staff, Canadian National Committee for Mental Hygiene. Toronto:
The Macmillan Company of Canada Limited, at St. Martin's House 1934.

xii, 195, [1] pp.; 200 × 138 mm.

571. CLARKE, George Herbert

Halt And Parley And Other Poems. By George Herbert Clarke. Author of
"The Hasting Day", etc. Toronto: The Macmillan Company of Canada
Limited, at St. Martin's House 1934.

[14], 30 pp.; 197 × 140 mm.

572. CORBETT, E.A.

Blackfoot Trails. By E.A. Corbett, M.A. Director of Department of Extension, University of Alberta. Toronto: The Macmillan Company of Canada
Limited, at St. Martin's House 1934.

[8], 139, [1] pp.; 215 × 142 mm.

573. DAWSON, C.A.

Canadian Frontiers of Settlement, Edited by W.A. Mackintosh and W.L.G.
Joerg In Nine Volumes. Volume VI: *The Settlement Of The Peace River
Country*. By C.A. Dawson, Professor of Sociology at McGill University.
Assisted by R.W. Murchie, Professor of Sociology at the University of
Minnesota. Toronto: The Macmillan Company of Canada Limited, at St.
Martin's House 1934.

xii, 284 pp.; 255 × 170 mm.
Canadian Frontiers of Settlement Series.

574. DE LA ROCHE, Mazo

Beside a Norman Tower. By Mazo De La Roche. Illustrations by A.H.
Watson. Toronto: The Macmillan Company of Canada Limited, at St.
Martin's House 1934.

x, 229, [1] pp.; 195 × 128 mm.

575. DICKENS, Charles

St. Martin's Classics, *David Copperfield*. By Charles Dickens. With an Intro-
duction by Evelyn McDonald, M.A., Bloor Collegiate Institute, Toronto.
Illustrations by "Phiz." Toronto: The Macmillan Company of Canada
Limited, at St. Martin's House 1934.

xiv, 923, [1] pp.; 170 × 110 mm.
St. Martin's Classics Series.

576. DICKENS, Charles

St. Martin's Classics, *A Tale of Two Cities*. By Charles Dickens. With an
Introduction by G.K. Chesterton And Notes and Questions by Guy Boas,
M.A. Authorized by the Minister of Education for the Province of Quebec.
Toronto: The Macmillan Company of Canada Limited, at St. Martin's
House 1934.

xxiv, 338 pp.; 175 × 115 mm.
St. Martin's Classics Series.

576A ELIOT, George

St. Martin's Classics, *Silas Marner*. By George Eliot. With introduction and
notes by G. Fred McNally, M.A., Supervisor of Schools, Edmonton. Authorized by the Minister of Education for the Province of Alberta. Toronto:
The Macmillan Company of Canada Limited, at St. Martin's House 1934.

xvi, 225, [1] pp.; 170 × 110 mm.
First published in 1930. Earlier printings not located. Reprinted in 1937.
St. Martin's Classics Series.

577. ELSON, John

Riders of the Dawn. By John Elson. Toronto: The Macmillan Company of
Canada Limited, at St. Martin's House 1934.

[6], 33, [1] pp.; 193 × 128 mm.

578. ERCKMANN, Émile

Erckmann-Chatrian, *Madame Thérèse*. Edited with Introduction, Notes and Vocabulary by Arthur Reed Ropes, M.A., Late Fellow of King's College, Cambridge. With Exercises by Jessie Muir, M.A., Lisgar Collegiate, Ottawa. This novel is prescribed by the Department of Education for use in Upper School Examinations. Toronto: The Macmillan Company of Canada Limited, at St. Martin's House 1934.

xvi, 301, [1] pp.; 170 × 115 mm.
Revised edition published in 1951 (see 1240).
Macmillan's Matriculation French Series.

579. GREY OWL

Pilgrims of the Wild. By Wa-Sha-Quon-Asin (Grey Owl). With a Foreword by Hugh Eayrs. Toronto: The Macmillan Company of Canada Limited, At St. Martin's House, 1934.

xxii, 281, [1] pp.; 221 × 143 mm.
Reprinted frequently. Reprinted in the Laurentian Library (No. 60) in 1978.

580. GROVES, Abraham

All in the Day's Work: Leaves from a Doctor's Case-book. By Abraham Groves, M.D. Formerly Medical Superintendent of the Royal Alexandra Hospital (now the Groves Memorial Hospital), Fergus, Ont. Life Member of the Ontario Medical Association. With a Foreword by Ambrose Lorne Lockwood, D.S.O., M.C., M.D., C.M., F.A.C.S., F.R.C.S.(C.). Toronto: The Macmillan Company of Canada Limited, at St. Martin's House 1934.

xviii, 181, [1] pp.; 220 × 142 mm.

581. HALL, H.S.

Plane Geometry. By H.S. Hall, M.A. And F.H. Stevens, M.A. Adapted and Authorized for use in the Schools of Saskatchewan. Toronto: The Macmillan Company of Canada Limited, at St. Martin's House 1934.

viii, 288 pp.; 188 × 129 mm.

582. HARDY, E.A.

The Canada Books Manual Accompanying The Canada Books of Prose and Verse: Book One Grades VII-IX. By E.A. Hardy, B.A., D.Paed., J.F. Van Every, B.A., B.Paed., [and] R.H. Wallace, M.A. The Ryerson Press [and] The Macmillans in Canada.

vi, 155, [1] pp.; 200 × 138 mm.
Canada Books of Prose and Verse Series.

583. HATHAWAY, E.J.

The Story of the Old Fort at Toronto. By E.J. Hathaway. Toronto: The Macmillan Company of Canada Limited, at St. Martin's House 1934.

[4], 35, [1] pp.; 225 × 150 mm.
Issued in limp cloth.

584. HEIGHINGTON, Wilfrid

Whereas and Whatnot. By Wilfrid Heighington, One of His Majesty's Coun-
sel, Member for St. David in the Legislative Assembly of Ontario, Captain,
2nd (Reserve) Battalion, Royal Grenadiers. Toronto: The Macmillan Company of Canada Limited, at St. Martin's House 1934.

viii, 152 pp.; 195 × 127 mm.

585. IRWIN, Alan Maurice

*'-and ships-and sealing-wax': A Chronicle of the Cruise of the Empress of
Britain, 1933-4.* By Alan Maurice Irwin. With photographs by the Author.
Toronto: The Macmillan Company of Canada Limited, at St. Martin's
House 1934.

[8], 285, [1] pp.; 223 × 145 mm.

586. LABICHE, Eugène

Labiche et Martin, *La Poudre aux Yeux.* Edited with Notes, Exercises and
Vocabulary by W.H. Williams, University of Toronto Schools, In consulta-
tion with F.C.A. Jeanneret, Professor of French, University of Toronto,
General Editor of the series, who also furnishes the Introduction. Toronto:
The Macmillan Company of Canada Limited, at St. Martin's House 1934.

[8], 129, [1] pp.; 184 × 124 mm.
Issued in limp cloth.
Macmillan's Matriculation French Series.

587. LANG, S.E.

The Story of Philosophy in Verse: A Handbook for Amateurs. By S.E. Lang.
Toronto: The Macmillan Company of Canada Limited, at St. Martin's
House 1934.

x, 101, [1] pp.; 215 × 140 mm.

588. LAWRENCE, Frieda

"Not I, But The Wind. . ." By Frieda Lawrence, geb. Freiin von Richthofen.
1934, Toronto: The Macmillan Company of Canada Limited, at St. Martin's
House.

xii, 297, [1] pp.; 205 × 130 mm.

589. LESLIE, Doris

Full Flavour. By Doris Leslie. The Macmillan Company of Canada Ltd. At
St. Martin's House Toronto.

506 pp.; 210 × 140 mm.

590. MACDONALD, Adrian

Poems for Honour Matriculation 1934-35. Edited with Notes and Questions by
Adrian Macdonald, M.A. English Master, The Normal School, Peterborough, Ontario. These poems are prescribed by the Department of Education of Ontario for use in Upper School Examinations. Toronto: The Macmillan Company of Canada Limited, at St. Martin's House 1934.

[10], 107, [1] pp.; 175 × 119 mm.
Issued in limp cloth.
Macmillan's Matriculation English Texts Series.

591. MACKENZIE, H.H.

Canadian Treasury Readers: Book Five. By H.H. Mackenzie and Lorne
Pierce. Authorized for use in the Public Schools of Nova Scotia. The Macmillans in Canada [and] The Ryerson Press.

viii, 354 pp.; 190 × 135 mm.
First published in 1932. Earlier printings not located. Reprinted in 1934, 1935, 1936
and 1938.
Treasury Readers Series.

592. MACKINTOSH, W.A.

Canadian Frontiers of Settlement, Edited by W.A. Mackintosh and W.L.G.
Joerg In Nine Volumes. Volume I: *Prairie Settlement: The Geographical
Setting*. By W.A. Mackintosh, Professor of Political and Economic Science,
Queen's University. Toronto: The Macmillan Company of Canada Limited,
at St. Martin's House 1934.

xvi, 242 pp.; 255 × 170 mm.
Canadian Frontiers of Settlement Series.

593. MacMURCHY, Helen

Sterilization? Birth Control?: A Book for Family Welfare and Safety. By Helen
MacMurchy, C.B.E., M.D., Author of *The Almosts, The Little Blue Books,
The Canadian Mother's Book*, &c. Toronto: The Macmillan Company of
Canada Limited, at St. Martin's House 1934.

[8], 156 pp.; 193 × 130 mm.

594. McAREE, J.V.

J.V. McAree, *The Fourth Column*. The Macmillan Company of Canada
Limited Toronto — 1934.

xviii, 332 pp.; 234 × 150 mm.

595. McNALLY, G. Fred

St. Martin's Classics, *A Book of Good Stories*. With Preface, Introduction and
Notes by G. Fred McNally, M.A., Supervisor of Schools, Edmonton. Toronto: The Macmillan Company of Canada Limited, at St. Martin's House
1934.

xvi, 318 pp.; 173 × 113 mm.
Reprinted in 1934, 1935, 1936 (twice) and 1937 (three times).
St. Martin's Classics Series.

596. MOODY, Irene H.

Wraiths. By Irene H. Moody, Author of *Delphine of the 'Eighties*. Toronto:
The Macmillan Company of Canada, Limited, at St. Martin's House.
xii, 66 pp.; 230 × 142 mm.

597. NEIL, Stephen

All the King's Men. By Stephen Neil. Toronto: The Macmillan Company of Canada Limited, at St. Martin's House 1934.

[4], 322 pp.; 193 × 127 mm.

598. ORMOND, Frances L.

Highroads to Reading: Book Two. By Frances L. Ormond. Authorized for use in the Public Schools of Alberta, British Columbia, Manitoba and Saskatchewan. The Ryerson Press [and] The Macmillans in Canada.

viii, 243, [1] pp.; 190 × 135 mm.
First published in 1932. Earlier printings not located. Also published in The Treasury Readers Series under the title *Canadian Treasury Readers: Book Two*. Treasury Readers Series.

599. ORMOND, Frances L.

Highroads to Reading: Work and Play To Accompany Book Two. By Frances L. Ormond and Charlotte M. Ormond. Illustrated by Belle Cameron Brown. The Macmillans in Canada [and] The Ryerson Press.

48 pp.; 273 × 208 mm.
Issued in paper.
Treasury Readers Series.

600. ORMOND, Frances L.

The Treasury Manual: Grades II and III. By Frances L. Ormond, Charlotte M. Ormond, and M.A. Beresford, M.A. The Macmillans in Canada [and] The Ryerson Press.

[4], 156 pp.; 185 × 130 mm.
First published in 1932 (see 499). This revised edition issued in paper.

601. PIERCE, Lorne

Canadian Treasury Readers: Book Six. By Lorne Pierce. Authorized for use in the Public Schools of Nova Scotia. The Macmillans in Canada [and] The Ryerson Press.

vi, 381, [1] pp.; 190 × 135 mm.
First published in 1932. Earlier printings not located. Reprinted in 1934 and 1936. Treasury Readers Series.

602. PRIESTLEY, J.B.

J.B. Priestley, *English Journey: Being a Rambling But Truthful Account of What One Man Saw and Heard and Felt and Thought During a Journey Through England During The Autumn of the Year 1933*. Toronto: The Macmillan Company of Canada, Limited, at St. Martin's House 1934.

[12], 336 pp.; 204 × 137 mm.

603. ROBERTSON, Douglas S.

To the Arctic With the Mounties. By Douglas S. Robertson. Toronto: The Macmillan Company of Canada Limited, at St. Martin's House 1934.

[12], 309, [1] pp.; 220 × 140 mm.

604. ROY, Elsie

Highroads to Reading: The Primer: Work and Play to Accompany "Jerry and Jane". By Elsie Roy [and] Henrietta Roy. Illustrated by Cynthia Clayton. The Macmillans in Canada [and] The Ryerson Press.

94 pp.; 277 × 205 mm.
Issued in paper.
Treasury Readers Series.

605. ROY, Elsie

Highroads to Reading: Work and Play To Accompany Book One. By Elsie Roy [and] Henrietta Roy. Illustrated by Cynthia Clayton. The Macmillans in Canada [and] The Ryerson Press.

80 pp.; 277 × 205 mm.
First published in 1932. Earlier printings not located. Also published in this series under the title *Work and Play: To Accompany Book One*. Issued in paper.
Treasury Readers Series.

606. ROY, Henrietta

Highroads to Learning: Jerry and Jane. By Henrietta Roy, Elsie Roy, P.H. Sheffield [and] Grace Bollert. Authorized for use in the Public Schools of Alberta, British Columbia, Manitoba and Saskatchewan. The Macmillans in Canada [and] The Ryerson Press.

vi, 122 pp.; 190 × 135 mm.
First published in 1932. First printing not located. Also published in The Treasury Readers Series under the title *Canadian Treasury Readers: Jerry and Jane*.
Treasury Readers Series.

607. SHAKESPEARE, William

As You Like It. Edited with Introduction, Notes and Questions by Adrian Macdonald, M.A. English Master, The Normal School, Peterborough, Ontario. Toronto: The Macmillan Company of Canada Limited, at St. Martin's House 1934.

xxviii, 151, [1] pp.; 177 × 119 mm.
Issued in limp cloth.
Macmillan's Matriculation English Texts Series.

608. SHAKESPEARE, William

Henry the Fourth: Part 1. Edited with Introduction, Notes and Questions by Adrian Macdonald, M.A. English Master, The Normal School, Peterborough, Ontario. Toronto: The Macmillan Company of Canada Limited, at St. Martin's House 1934.

xxii, 153, [1] pp.; 177 × 119 mm.
Issued in limp cloth.
Macmillan's Matriculation English Texts Series.

609. SHEFFIELD, Philip H.

Highroads to Reading: Book One. By P.H. Sheffield, Henrietta Roy, Elsie Roy, [and] Grace Bollert. Authorized for use in the Public Schools of Alberta, British Columbia, Manitoba and Saskatchewan. The Ryerson Press [and] The Macmillans in Canada.

vi, 153, [1] pp.; 190 × 133 mm.
First published in 1932. First printing not located. Also published under the title
Canadian Treasury Readers: Book One in The Treasury Readers Series.
Treasury Readers Series.

610. STEVENSON, Robert Louis

St. Martin's Classics, *Kidnapped*. By R.L. Stevenson. Illustrated by C.E.
Brock, R.I. Toronto: The Macmillan Company of Canada Limited, at St.
Martin's House 1934.

xxx, 271, [1] pp.; 170 × 115 mm.
St. Martin's Classics Series.

611. STEVENSON, Robert Louis

St. Martin's Classics, *Treasure Island*. By R.L. Stevenson. Illustrated by
H.M. Brock. Toronto: The Macmillan Company of Canada Limited, at St.
Martin's House 1934.

xxviii, 231, [1] pp.; 170 × 115 mm.
St. Martin's Classics Series.

612. STREET, A.G.

Farmer's Glory. By A.G. Street. Toronto: The Macmillan Company of
Canada Limited, at St. Martin's House 1934.

xviii, 294 pp.; 190 × 125 mm.

613. TURTON, M. Conway

Cassiar. By M. Conway Turton. Toronto: The Macmillan Company of
Canada Limited, at St. Martin's House 1934.

x, 123, [1] pp.; 218 × 140 mm.

614. WELLS, H.G.

*Experiment in Autobiography: Discoveries and Conclusions of a Very Ordinary
Brain (Since 1866)*. By H.G. Wells. Toronto: The Macmillan Company of
Canada Limited, at St. Martin's House 1934.

xii, 718 pp.; 238 × 155 mm.

615. WOLFENDEN, Hugh H.

Unemployment Funds: A Survey and Proposal. A Study of Unemployment
Insurance and Other Types of Funds for the Financial Assistance of the
Unemployed. By Hugh H. Wolfenden. Fellow of the Institute of Actuaries,
Great Britain; Fellow of the Actuarial Society of America; Fellow of the Royal
Statistical Society. Toronto: The Macmillan Company of Canada Limited,
at St. Martin's House 1934.

xviii, 229, [1] pp.; 215 × 140 mm.

616. WOOTTON, Christina Dyde

The Treasury Manual: Grades IV-VI. By Christina Dyde Wootton, M.A.,
B.C. Diltz, M.A., And Charles C. Bremner, M.A. The Macmillans in
Canada [and] The Ryerson Press.

vi, 218 pp.; 185 × 130 mm.
First published in 1932 (see 513). This revised edition issued in paper. Reprinted in 1936.
Treasury Readers Series.

1935

617. BARNARD, Leslie Gordon

Jancis. By Leslie Gordon Barnard. Toronto: The Macmillan Company of Canada Limited, at St. Martin's House 1935.

245, [1] pp.; 220 × 164 mm.

618. BAUTZMANN, Hermann

Learn to Ski! By Herman Bautzmann. Toronto: The Macmillan Company of Canada Limited, at St. Martin's House 1935.

x, 81, [1] pp.; 185 × 120 mm.

619. BEATTIE, Jessie L.

Hill-Top. By Jessie L. Beattie. Toronto: The Macmillan Company of Canada Limited, at St. Martin's House 1935.

[10], 276 pp.; 218 × 145 mm.

620. BELL, Charles W.

Who Said Murder? By Charles W. Bell, K.C. Toronto: The Macmillan Company of Canada Limited, at St. Martin's House 1935.

xiv, 403, [1] pp.; 230 × 150 mm.

621. BENNET, C.L.

The Canada Book of Prose and Verse: Book Five. By C.L. Bennet and Lorne Pierce. The Macmillans in Canada [and] The Ryerson Press.

xii, 596 pp.; 200 × 135 mm.
Revised and reissued as *Argosy to Adventure* in 1950 (see 1212). Revised again in 1963 (see 1610). Reprinted frequently.
Canada Books of Prose and Verse Series.

622. BIGELOW, Harold E.

Dominion Chemistry Manual: To Accompany Dominion High School Chemistry. By Harold E. Bigelow, Ph.D., F.R.S.C., Professor of Chemistry, Mount Allison University, Sackville, N.B. And Fred G. Morehouse, M.Sc., LL.D., Supervisor of Schools, Halifax, N.S. Authorized by the Department of Public Instruction for use in the Schools of Nova Scotia. Toronto: The Macmillan Company of Canada Limited, at St. Martin's House 1935.

xvi, 137, [1] pp.; 200 × 135 mm.

623.   BIGELOW, Harold E.

Dominion High School Chemistry. By Harold E. Bigelow, Ph.D., F.R.S.C.,
Professor of Chemistry, Mount Allison University, Sackville, N.B. And Fred
G. Morehouse, M.Sc., LL.D., Supervisor of Schools, Halifax, N.S. Au-
thorized by the Department of Public Instruction for use in the schools of
Nova Scotia. Toronto: The Macmillan Company of Canada Limited, at St.
Martin's House 1935.

   xiv, 587, [1] pp.; 200 × 135 mm.

624.   BOURINOT, Arthur S.

Selected Poems (1915-1935). By Arthur S. Bourinot. With a Note by Sir
Andrew Macphail. Toronto: The Macmillan Company of Canada Limited,
at St. Martin's House 1935.

   [12], 90, [2] pp.; 200 × 130 mm.

625.   BROADUS, Edmund Kemper

Saturday And Sunday. By Edmund Kemper Broadus. Toronto: The Macmillan Company of Canada Limited, at St. Martin's House 1935.

   [12], 260 pp.; 220 × 145 mm.

626.   BURPEE, Lawrence J.

*The Search For The Western Sea: The Story of the Exploration of North-Western
America*. By Lawrence J. Burpee. New and Revised Edition. Volume I.
Toronto: The Macmillan Company of Canada Limited, at St. Martin's
House.

   lxii, 304 pp.; 220 × 140 mm.
   First volume of two-volume set in slip-case.

627.   BURPEE, Lawrence J.

*The Search For the Western Sea: The Story of the Exploration of North-Western
America*. By Lawrence J. Burpee. New and Revised Edition. Volume II.
Toronto: The Macmillan Company of Canada Limited, at St. Martin's
House.

   x, 305-609, [1] pp.; 220 × 140 mm.
   Second volume of two-volume set in slip-case.

628.   CALLAGHAN, Morley

Morley Callaghan, *They Shall Inherit the Earth*. 1935. Toronto: The Macmillan Company of Canada Limited, at St. Martin's House.

   [6], 336, [2] pp.; 218 × 140 mm.

629.   CANBY, Henry Seidel

Dominion High School English. Henry Seidel Canby, John Baker Opdycke
[and] Margaret Gillum. Adapted for use in Canada. Authorized by the
Council of Public Instruction for use in Schools of N.S. Toronto: The
Macmillan Company of Canada Limited, at St. Martin's House 1935.

   xvi, 494 pp.; 200 × 135 mm.

630. CARRINGTON, C.E.

A History of England. By C.E. Carrington, M.A. formerly Lecturer in History at Pembroke College, Oxford and J. Hampden Jackson, M.A. Christ Church, Oxford, Assistant Master at Haileybury College. [Quotation]. Authorized by the Department of Public Instruction for use in the schools of Nova Scotia. Toronto: The Macmillan Company of Canada Limited, at St. Martin's House 1935.

xlii, 486 pp.; 197 × 137 mm.

631. CARSLEY, Sara E.

Alchemy And Other Poems. By Sara E. Carsley. Toronto: The Macmillan Company of Canada Limited, at St. Martin's House 1935.

viii, 61, [1] pp.; 200 × 135 mm.

631A CHASE, Mary Ellen

Silas Crockett. By Mary Ellen Chase. Toronto: The Macmillan Company Of Canada Limited, At St. Martin's House 1935.

xii, 404 pp.; 215 × 135 mm.

632. COLQUHOUN, A.H.U.

Press, Politics, And People: The Life and Letters of Sir John Willison, Journalist and Correspondent of The Times. By A.H.U. Colquhoun. Toronto: The Macmillan Company of Canada Limited, at St. Martin's House 1935.

[10], 306 pp.; 235 × 150 mm.

633. COLVIN, Ian

Volume Two. *The Life of Lord Carson*. By Ian Colvin. 1935 Toronto: The Macmillan Company of Canada Limited, at St. Martin's House.

446 pp.; 220 × 143 mm.

634. COOPER, Duff

Haig. By Duff Cooper. Author of *Talleyrand*. Toronto: The Macmillan Company of Canada Limited, at St. Martin's House 1935.

402 pp.; 232 × 150 mm.

635. CRUIKSHANK, E.A.

The Life of Sir Henry Morgan: With an Account of the English Settlement of the Island of Jamaica (1655-1688). By Brig.-General E.A. Cruikshank, LL.D., F.R.S.C., F.R.Hist.S. Toronto: The Macmillan Company of Canada Limited, at St. Martin's House 1935.

[12], 448 pp.; 220 × 140 mm.

636. DAVIDSON, James Grant

Physics Laboratory Manual & Work Book To Accompany Black, Davis & Davidson New Practical Physics. By James G. Davidson, University of British Columbia, With A Committee of High School Teachers. Authorised by The

Department of Education for Use in British Columbia. Toronto: The Macmillan Company of Canada Limited, at St. Martin's House 1935.

vi, 114 pp.; 270 × 203 mm.
Reprinted in 1937. Issued in paper.

637. DE LA ROCHE, Mazo

Young Renny. By Mazo De La Roche. Toronto: The Macmillan Company of Canada Limited, at St. Martin's House 1935.

viii, 277, [1] pp.; 190 × 125 mm.
New edition published in 1947 (see 1129).

638. ÉNAULT, Louis

Louis Énault, *Le Chien du Capitaine*. Edited by Margaret de G. Verrall. With Exercises by Helen B. St. John, Head of the Department of French, Jarvis Collegiate, Toronto. This novel is prescribed by the Department of Education of Ontario for reading in Middle School Examinations. Toronto: The Macmillan Company of Canada Limited, at St. Martin's House 1935.

viii, 205, [1] pp.; 190 × 125 mm.
First published in 1932 (see 482).
Macmillan's Matriculation French Series.

639. FOURNIER, Leslie T.

Railway Nationalization in Canada: The Problem of the Canadian National Railways. By Leslie T. Fournier, M.A., Ph.D., Assistant Professor of Economics, Department of Economics and Social Institutions, Princeton University, N.J. Toronto: The Macmillan Company of Canada Limited, at St. Martin's House 1935.

xiv, 358 pp.; 230 × 150 mm.
Volume V in a series published by the International Finance Section of the Department of Economics and Social Institutions in Princeton University.

640. HARDY, W.G.

Father Abraham. By W.G. Hardy. Toronto: The Macmillan Company of Canada Limited 1935.

416 pp.; 192 × 124 mm.

641. JACKSON, Gilbert

An Economist's Confession of Faith. By Gilbert Jackson. Toronto: The Macmillan Company of Canada Limited, at St. Martin's House 1935.

[10], 182 pp.; 200 × 135 mm.

642. KING, W.L. Mackenzie

Industry and Humanity: A Study in the Principles Underlying Industrial Reconstruction. By the Right Honourable W.L. Mackenzie King, M.P. New and Shorter Edition. The Macmillan Company of Canada Limited, at St. Martin's House 1935.

xxii, 269, [1] pp.; 220 × 145 mm.
Revised edition published in 1947 (see 1143).

643.   LARSEN, Thorlief

A Century of Short Stories (1824-1927). Edited by Thorlief Larsen, M.A., F.R.S.C. [and] W.L. Macdonald, M.A., Ph.D. Department of English, University of British Columbia. Authorized by the Minister of Education for British Columbia. Toronto: The Macmillan Company of Canada Limited, at St. Martin's House 1935.

xxiv, 327, [1] pp.; 200 × 135 mm.

644.   LIMPUS, George H.

Elementary General Science. By George H. Limpus, B.A. Head of the Department of General Science, Kitsilano Junior High School, Vancouver, B.C. And John W.B. Shore, B.A. Vice-Principal, Kitsilano Junior High School, Vancouver, B.C. Authorized for use in the provinces of British Columbia and Alberta. Toronto: The Macmillan Company of Canada Limited at St. Martin's House 1935.

xviii, 362 pp.; 193 × 130 mm.
Reprinted in 1936 and 1937.

645.   LIMPUS, George H.

General Science for the Intermediate School. By George H. Limpus, B.A. Head of the Department of General Science, Kitsilano Junior High School, Vancouver, B.C. And John W.B. Shore, B.A. Vice-Principal, Kitsilano Junior High School, Vancouver, B.C. Toronto: The Macmillan Company of Canada Limited, at St. Martin's House 1935.

xviii, 362 pp.; 200 × 135 mm.

646.   LOUGHEED, W.J.

Geometry For High Schools. By W.J. Lougheed, Professor of Methods in Mathematics, Ontario College of Education, And J.G. Workman, Instructor in Mathematics, University of Toronto Schools. Authorized by the Minister of Education for Ontario. PRICE 50 CENTS. Toronto: The Macmillan Company of Canada Limited, at St. Martin's House 1935.

x, 338 pp.; 190 × 125 mm.
Reprinted in 1935. Revised in 1940 (see 876).

646A   MacGIBBON, Duncan Alexander

An Introduction to Economics for Canadian Readers. Revised and Much Enlarged Edition. By Duncan Alexander MacGibbon. Authorized for use in the provinces of Alberta, Manitoba and Nova Scotia. Toronto: The Macmillan Company of Canada Limited 1935.

viii, 240 pp.; 190 × 125 mm.
First published in 1924 (see 223A). Revised in 1929. This edition reprinted frequently. Revised in 1946 and reprinted in 1947 and 1948 (see 1189).

647.   MACKINTOSH, W.A.

Canadian Frontiers of Settlement, Edited by W.A. Mackintosh and W.L.G. Joerg In Nine Volumes. Volume IV: *Economic Problems Of The Prairie*

Provinces. By W.A. Mackintosh, Professor of Political and Economic Science, Queen's University. Assisted by A.B. Clark, Formerly Professor of Political Economy, University of Manitoba, G.A. Elliott, Professor of Political Economy, University of Alberta, and W.W. Swanson, Professor of Economics, University of Saskatchewan. Toronto: The Macmillan Company of Canada Limited, at St. Martin's House 1935.

x, 308 pp.; 255 × 170 mm.
Canadian Frontiers of Settlement Series.

648. No entry.

649. MARSH, D'arcy

The Tragedy of Henry Thornton. By D'arcy Marsh. Toronto: The Macmillan Company of Canada Limited, at St. Martin's House 1935.

xvi, 293, [1] pp.; 220 × 145 mm.

650. MORLEY, Christopher

Hasta La Vista Or, A Postcard From Peru. By Christopher Morley. Toronto: The Macmillan Company of Canada Limited, at St. Martin's House.

x, 268 pp.; 200 × 130 mm.

651. NEVILLE, K.P.R.

A Book of Latin Prose Selections. Edited, with Introduction, Notes and Vocabulary by K.P.R. Neville, M.A., Ph.D., University of Western Ontario. E.A. Dale, M.A., University of Toronto. D. Breslove, M.A., Malvern Collegiate Institute, Toronto, And H.L. Tracy, B.A., Ph.D., Queen's University. Prescribed by the Department of Education for the Province of Ontario for use for Upper School Examination. Toronto: The Macmillan Company of Canada, Limited, at St. Martin's House 1935.

lvi, 336 pp.; 173 × 114 mm.

652. PIERCE, Lorne

The Canada Book of Prose and Verse: Book One. By Lorne Pierce and Dora Whitefield. The Ryerson Press [and] The Macmillans in Canada.

x, 410 pp.; 200 × 135 mm.
First published in 1932. This edition revised. Further revised and reissued as *Beckoning Trails* in 1948 (see 1209). Revised again in 1962 (see 1565). First edition not located. Reprinted frequently.
Canada Books of Prose and Verse Series.

653. PIERCE, Lorne

The Canada Book of Prose and Verse: Book Two. By Lorne Pierce and Dora Whitefield. The Ryerson Press [and] The Macmillans in Canada.

x, 446 pp.; 200 × 140 mm.
First published in 1932 (see 501). This edition revised. Further revised and reissued as *Life and Adventure* in 1948 (see 1205). Revised again in 1962 (see 1595). Reprinted frequently.
Canada Books of Prose and Verse Series.

654. PRATT, E.J.

The Titanic. By E.J. Pratt. Toronto: The Macmillan Company of Canada Limited, at St. Martin's House 1935.

[6], 42 pp.; 238 × 158 mm.

655. PRIESTLEY, J.B.

The Works of J.B. Priestley. *Three Plays And A Preface*. Toronto: The Macmillan Company Of Canada Limited, At St. Martin's House, 1935.

xx, 305, [1] pp.; 202 × 136 mm.

656. ROY, James A.

Joseph Howe: A Study in Achievement and Frustration. By James A. Roy, M.A., (Edin.). [Quotation]. Toronto: The Macmillan Company of Canada Limited, at St. Martin's House 1935.

xvi, 347, [1] pp.; 232 × 155 mm.

657. SHAKESPEARE, William

Shakespeare's *Julius Caesar*. Edited with Introduction, Notes and Questions by Adrian Macdonald, M.A. English Master, the Normal School, Peterborough, Ontario. Toronto: The Macmillan Company of Canada Limited, at St. Martin's House 1935.

xxviii, 137, [1] pp.; 175 × 118 mm.
Issued in limp cloth.
Macmillan's Matriculation English Texts Series.

658. STERN, Gladys B.

Shining And Free: A Day In The Life Of The Matriarch. By G.B. Stern. Toronto: The Macmillan Company Of Canada Limited, At St. Martin's House, 1935.

[12], 291, [1] pp.; 190 × 127 mm.

659. STRANGE, William

Sunset in Ebony. A Novel by William Strange. Toronto: The Macmillan Company of Canada Limited, at St. Martin's House 1935.

[6], 305, [1] pp.; 200 × 128 mm.

660. SULLIVAN, Alan

The Great Divide. Alan Sullivan. A Romance Of The Canadian Pacific Railway. Toronto: The Macmillan Company of Canada Limited, at St. Martin's House 1935.

417, [3] pp.; 195 × 125 mm.

661. VINING, Charles

Bigwigs: Canadians Wise and Otherwise. By R.T.L. (Charles Vining). With 37 illustrations by Ivan Glassco. Toronto: The Macmillan Company of Canada Limited, at St. Martin's House 1935.

[10], 149, [1] pp.; 257 × 190 mm.

662.   VOADEN, Herman

St. Martin's Classics, *A Book of Plays For Schools And Community Drama Groups in Canada*. Edited by Herman Voaden, M.A., Director of English and of The Play Workshop, Central High School of Commerce, Toronto. Editor of "Six Canadian Plays". Toronto: The Macmillan Company of Canada Limited, at St. Martin's House 1935.

xx, 316 pp.; 170 × 110 mm.
St. Martin's Classics Series.

663.   WALLACE, W. Stewart

A Reader in Canadian Civics. By W. Stewart Wallace M.A. Authorized by the Minister of Education for Ontario. Toronto: The Macmillan Company of Canada Limited, at St. Martin's House 1935. Price 28 cents.

xvi, 186 pp.; 188 × 125 mm.
Reprinted in 1942.

664.   WATSON, William R.

My Desire. By William R. Watson. With a Foreword by Dr. Robt. C. Wallace, President of the University of Alberta. Toronto: The Macmillan Company of Canada Limited, at St. Martin's House 1935.

85, [1] pp.; 192 × 130 mm.

665.   *What You Should Know About Cancer*. No. 1 in the "What You Should Know About —" Series. Under the General Editorship of Grant Fleming, M.C, M.D., D.P.H., F.R.C.P.(C.). Toronto: The Macmillan Company of Canada Limited, at St. Martin's House 1935.

[12], 41, [1] pp.; 155 × 105 mm.
"What You Should Know About" Series.

666.   *What You Should Know About Economical Cooking*. No. 2 in the "What You Should Know About—" Series. Under the general Editorship of Grant Fleming, M.C., M.D., D.P.H., F.R.C.P.(C.). Toronto: The Macmillan Company of Canada Limited, at St. Martin's House 1935.

[14], 82 pp.; 155 × 105 mm.
"What You Should Know About" Series.

667.   *What You Should Know About Tuberculosis*. No. 4 in the "What You Should Know About—" Series. Under the general Editorship of Grant Fleming, M.C., M.D., D.P.H., F.R.C.P.(C.). Toronto: The Macmillan Company of Canada Limited, at St. Martin's House 1935.

[12], 50 pp.; 155 × 105 mm.
"What You Should Know About" Series.

668.   *What You Should Know About Your Heart*. No. 3 in the "What You Should Know About—" Series. Under the general Editorship of Grant Fleming, M.C., M.D., D.P.H., F.R.C.P.(C.). Toronto: The Macmillan Company of Canada Limited, at St. Martin's House 1935.

[12], 45, [1] pp.; 155 × 105 mm.
"What You Should Know About" Series.

669. WILLIAMS, W.H.

Continuous Prose Exercises for Translation into French: Based on Pargment's La France et Les Français. By W.H. Williams, M.A., B. Paed., University of Toronto Schools. Toronto: The Macmillan Company of Canada Limited, at St. Martin's House 1935.

[4], 27, [1] pp.; 162 × 111 mm.
First published in 1934. Reprinted in 1934 and 1935. Earlier printings not located.
Issued in limp cloth.
Macmillan's Matriculation French Series.

670. WOOLLCOTT, Alexander

The Woollcott Reader: Bypaths In The Realms Of Gold. Toronto: The Macmillan Company Of Canada Limited, At St. Martin's House, 1935.

xii, 1010, [2] pp.; 219 × 146 mm.

671. WRIGHT, C.P.

The St. Lawrence Deep Waterway: A Canadian Appraisal. By C.P. Wright. Toronto: The Macmillan Company of Canada Limited at St. Martin's House 1935.

xxii, 450 pp.; 220 × 140 mm.

672. WRONG, George M.

Canada and the American Revolution: The Disruption of the First British Empire. By George M. Wrong. Toronto: The Macmillan Company of Canada Limited, at St. Martin's House 1935.

xiv, 497, [1] pp.; 220 × 146 mm.

1936

673. ARNOLD, Matthew

Representative Essays of Matthew Arnold. Edited with an introduction by E.K. Brown, Professor of English Literature, University of Manitoba. Toronto: The Macmillan Company of Canada Limited, at St. Martin's House 1936.

xlii, 240 pp.; 195 × 125 mm.
Reprinted in 1940.

674. BARBEAU, Marius

The Kingdom of Saguenay. By Marius Barbeau. Illustrations by A.Y. Jackson, George Pepper, Kathleen Daly, Peter and B. Cogill Haworth, André Biéler, Arthur Lismer, Gordon Pfeiffer, Yvonne Mckague, Rody Kenny Courtice and Albert Cloutier. Chapter heads by Marjorie Borden. Toronto: The Macmillan Company of Canada Limited, at St. Martin's House 1936.

[14], 167, [1] pp.; 238 × 160 mm.

675.   BARBEAU, Marius

Quebec: Where Ancient France Lingers. By Marius Barbeau. Illustrations by Marjorie Borden. Toronto: The Macmillan Company of Canada Limited at St. Martin's House 1936.

[14], 137, [1] pp.; 215 × 165 mm.
Issued in cloth and paper.

676.   BENNET, C.L.

The Canada Book of Prose and Verse: Book Six. By C.L. Bennet and Lorne Pierce. The Macmillans in Canada [and] The Ryerson Press.

xiv, 624, [2] pp.; 200 × 135 mm.
Canada Books of Prose and Verse Series.

677.   BENNETT, Ethel Hume

A Treasure Ship of Old Quebec. By Ethel Hume Bennett, Author of "Judy on York Hill," "Camp Conqueror," Etc. Illustrated by Hazel Boswell. Toronto: The Macmillan Company of Canada Limited, at St. Martin's House 1936.

[8], 266 pp.; 215 × 145 mm.

678.   BENTLEY, Phyllis

Freedom, Farewell! By Phyllis Bentley. Toronto: The Macmillan Company Of Canada Limited, At St. Martin's House, 1936.

viii, 484 pp.; 202 × 140 mm.

679.   BIGGAR, P.E.

Diesel Engines. By P.E. Biggar, M.S.A.E., M.I.A.E. Consulting Engineer. Toronto: The Macmillan Company of Canada Limited, at St. Martin's House 1936.

xii, 165, [1] pp.; 230 × 155 mm.

680.   BOSWELL, James

Boswell's Journal of a Tour to the Hebrides with Samuel Johnson LL.D. Now First Published from the Original Manuscript. Prepared for the Press, with Preface and Notes by Frederick A. Pottle and Charles H. Bennett. Toronto: The Macmillan Company of Canada Limited, at St. Martin's House 1936.

xviii, 435, [1] pp.; 237 × 161 mm.

681.   BRITTAIN, Vera

Honourable Estate. A Novel of Transition. By Vera Brittain. Toronto: The Macmillan Company of Canada Limited, at St. Martin's House 1936.

xiv, 601, [1] pp.; 205 × 135 mm.

682.   BROADUS, Edmund Kemper

The Story of English Literature. Edmund Kemper Broadus, Professor of English Language and Literature in the University of Alberta. Authorized by the Council of Public Instruction for use in the Schools of Nova Scotia. Toronto: The Macmillan Company of Canada Limited, at St. Martin's House, 1936.

> xiv, 814 pp.; 200 × 133 mm.
> First published in 1930. First edition not located.

683. BROOKER, Bertram

Yearbook of the Arts in Canada 1936. Edited by Bertram Brooker. The Macmillan Company of Canada Limited 1936.

> xxviii, 256 pp.; 258 × 173 mm.

684. CALLAGHAN, Morley

Now That April's Here and other stories. By Morley Callaghan. 1936 Toronto: The Macmillan Company of Canada Limited, at St. Martin's House.

> 316 pp.; 210 × 140 mm.

685. CLARKE, George Herbert

Ode On The Burial Of King George The Fifth. By George Herbert Clarke. Macmillan 1936.

> 4 pp.; 230 × 154 mm.
> Issued in paper.

686. COLLIN, W.E.

The White Savannahs. By W.E. Collin. Toronto: The Macmillan Company of Canada Limited, at St. Martin's House 1936.

> [10], 288 pp.; 220 × 147 mm.

687. COOPER, Duff

Haig. The Second Volume by Duff Cooper. Author of *Talleyrand*. Toronto: The Macmillan Company of Canada Limited at St. Martin's House 1936.

> xii, 483, [1] pp.; 232 × 150 mm.

688. CREIGHTON, Alan

Earth Call: A Book of Poems. By Alan Creighton. Toronto: The Macmillan Company of Canada Limited, at St. Martin's House 1936.

> x, 67, [1] pp.; 225 × 162 mm.

689. CRUIKSHANK, E.A.

The Political Adventures of John Henry: The Record of an International Imbroglio. By Brig.-General E.A. Cruikshank, LL.D., F.R.S.C., F.R.Hist.S. Toronto: The Macmillan Company of Canada Limited, at St. Martin's House 1936.

> [12], 206 pp.; 230 × 147 mm.

690. DAWSON, C.A.

Canadian Frontiers of Settlement, Edited by W.A. Mackintosh and W.L.G. Joerg In Nine Volumes. Volume VII: *Group Settlement: Ethnic Communities in Western Canada*. By C.A. Dawson, Professor of Sociology at McGill University. Toronto: The Macmillan Company of Canada Limited, at St. Martin's House 1936.

xxii, 395, [1] pp.; 255 × 170 mm.
Canadian Frontiers of Settlement Series.

691. DE KIRILENE, Louise

The Quintuplets' First Year: The Survival of the Famous Five Dionne Babies and its Significance for all Mothers. By Louise De Kirilene. Toronto: The Macmillan Company of Canada Limited, at St. Martin's House 1936.

xvi, 221, [1] pp.; 205 × 150 mm.

692. DE LA ROCHE, Mazo

Whiteoak Harvest. By Mazo De La Roche. Toronto: The Macmillan Company of Canada Limited, at St. Martin's House 1936.

vi, 329, [1] pp.; 200 × 130 mm.
New edition published in 1948 (see 1172).

693. DEACON, William Arthur

A Literary Map of Canada. As Compiled by William Arthur Deacon. Drawn and Embellished by the hand of Stanley Turner. Published by The Macmillan Company of Canada Limited, St. Martin's House Toronto. Copyright Canada MCMXXXVI. Printed in Canada by Rous and Mann Limited.

Broadside; 865 × 523 mm.

694. DURRANT, J.E.

A New Geometry: Analytic-Synthetic. By J.E. Durrant, Head of the Department of Mathematics, Collegiate-Vocational Institute, Guelph, Ontario, And H.R. Kingston, Head of the Department of Mathematics and Astronomy, University of Western Ontario, London, Ontario. Toronto: The Macmillan Company of Canada Limited, at St. Martin's House 1936.

xii, 62 pp.; 195 × 130 mm.
Revised in 1940 as *A New Analytic Geometry* (see 872). Second revised edition published in 1960 (see 1524).

695. FEUILLET, Octave

Octave Feuillet, *Le Roman d'un Jeune Homme Pauvre*. Edited with Notes, Exercises and Vocabulary by Norma Rochat, M.A., Humberside Collegiate, Toronto. Toronto: The Macmillan Company of Canada Limited, at St. Martin's House 1936.

viii, 292 pp.; 188 × 125 mm.
Reprinted in 1936.
Macmillan's Matriculation French Series.

696.   GOLDSMITH, Oliver

St. Martin's Classics, *The Vicar of Wakefield*. By Oliver Goldsmith. With an Introduction and Notes by J.F. Macdonald, M.A., Professor of English, University College, University of Toronto. Illustrated by Hugh Thomson. Toronto: The Macmillan Company of Canada Limited, at St. Martin's House 1936.

xxxii, 315, [3] pp.; 170 × 110 mm.
St. Martin's Classics Series.

697.   GRAVES, Robert

"Antigua, Penny, Puce". By Robert Graves. The Macmillan Company of Canada Ltd. Toronto 1936.

viii, 311, [1] pp.; 188 × 120 mm.

698.   GRAY, Henry M.W.

The Colon as a Health Regulator—From a Surgeon's Point of View: The effects and treatment of its developmental abnormalities. By Sir Henry M.W. Gray, K.B.E., C.B., C.M.G., LL.D. (Aberdeen), M.B., C.M. (Aberdeen), F.R.C.S. (Edinburgh) etc., Colonel, A.M.S., (retd.) late Consultant Surgeon, B.E.F., France, and Consultant in Special Military Surgery (orthopaedic), Home Service; Civil Surgeon, S. African War, 1899-1900; formerly Surgeon and Lecturer on Clinical Surgery, Aberdeen Royal Infirmary and Royal Hospital for Sick Children, Aberdeen; Surgeon in Montreal. Author of *Early Treatment of War Wounds*. Toronto: The Macmillan Company of Canada Limited, at St. Martin's House 1936.

xx, 100 pp.; 200 × 130 mm.

699.   GREY OWL

Tales of an Empty Cabin. By Wa-Sha-Quon-Asin (Grey Owl). Toronto: The Macmillan Company of Canada Ltd. And At St. Martin's House.

xvi, 335, [1] pp.; 221 × 143 mm.
Reprinted frequently. Reprinted in the Laurentian Library (No. 26) in 1975.

700.   GRIFFIN, Frederick

Variety Show: Twenty Years of Watching the News Parade. By Frederick Griffin. Author of *Soviet Scene*. Toronto: The Macmillan Company of Canada Limited, at St. Martin's House 1936.

xiv, 359, [1] pp.; 233 × 148 mm.

701.   HUXLEY, Aldous

Eyeless In Gaza. Aldous Huxley. Toronto: The Macmillan Company of Canada Limited, at St. Martin's House 1936.

[6], 619, [1] pp.; 205 × 135 mm.

702.   JAYCOCKS, T.G.

Camera Conversations. By "Jay" [pseud.]. With a Foreword by B.K. Sandwell. Toronto: The Macmillan Company of Canada Limited, at St. Martin's House 1936.

xvi, 298, [2] pp.; 270 × 182 mm.

703. KIPLING, Rudyard

St. Martin's Classics, *Kim*. By Rudyard Kipling. Illustrated by J. Lockwood
Kipling. Special edition exclusively for use in Canadian Schools: prescribed
by the Minister of Education for use in Ontario. Toronto: The Macmillan
Company of Canada Limited, at St. Martin's House 1936.

[6], 422 pp.; 170 × 110 mm.
Reprinted in 1937 (three times), 1938 and 1939.
St. Martin's Classics Series.

704. LANE, Wilmot B.

Quebec. By Wilmot B. Lane. Toronto: The Macmillan Company of Canada
Limited, at St. Martin's House 1936.

[8], 40 pp.; 205 × 140 mm.

705. LEACOCK, Stephen

*The Gathering Financial Crisis in Canada: A Survey of the Present Critical
Situation*. By Stephen Leacock Ph.D., Litt.D., LL.D., D.C.L. Sometime
Head of the Department of Economics and Political Science and now Profes-
sor Emeritus, of McGill University, Montreal. Toronto: The Macmillan
Company of Canada Limited, at St. Martin's House 1936.

[8], 24 pp.; 225 × 150 mm.
Issued in paper.

706. LESLIE, Doris

Fair Company. Doris Leslie. The Macmillan Company of Canada Ltd. At St.
Martin's House Toronto.

x, 466, [4] pp.; 200 × 135 mm.

707. LOWER, A.R.M.

Canadian Frontiers of Settlement, Edited by W.A. Mackintosh and W.L.G.
Joerg In Nine Volumes. Volume IX: *Settlement And The Forest Frontier In
Eastern Canada*. By A.R.M. Lower, Professor of History, Wesley College,
Winnipeg, Manitoba. *Settlement And The Mining Frontier*. By Harold A.
Innis, Professor of Political Economy, University of Toronto. Toronto: The
Macmillan Company of Canada Limited, at St. Martin's House 1936.

xiv, 424 pp.; 255 × 170 mm.
Canadian Frontiers of Settlement Series.

708. MACDONALD, Adrian

Upper School Poems. Edited with Notes and Questions by Adrian Macdonald, M.A. The Normal School, Toronto. These poems are prescribed by
the Department of Education of Ontario for use in Upper School Examinations. Toronto: The Macmillan Company of Canada Limited, at St. Martin's
House 1936.

[8], 85, [1] pp.; 177 × 119 mm.
Reprinted in 1936 and 1939. Issued in limp cloth.
Macmillan's Matriculation English Texts Series.

709. McCOWAN, Daniel

Animals of the Canadian Rockies. By Dan McCowan. Illustrated from photographs by the author. Frontispiece by Carl Rungius. Toronto: The Macmillan Company of Canada Limited, At St. Martin's House, 1936.

x, 302 pp.; 221 × 149 mm.
Reprinted in 1941 and 1950.

710. MITCHELL, Margaret

Gone With The Wind. By Margaret Mitchell. Toronto: The Macmillan Company Of Canada Limited, At St. Martin's House, 1936.

[6], 1037, [1] pp.; 221 × 149 mm.
Reprinted frequently. A "Motion Picture Edition" was issued in 1939 (see 852).

711. MOODY, Irene H.

Attar of Song And Other Poems. By Irene H. Moody. Toronto: The Macmillan Company of Canada Limited, at St. Martin's House 1936.

viii, 70 pp.; 235 × 160 mm.

712. MURCHIE, R.W.

Canadian Frontiers of Settlement, Edited by W.A. Mackintosh and W.L.G. Joerg In Nine Volumes. Volume V: *Agricultural Progress on the Prairie Frontier*. By R.W. Murchie, Professor of Rural Sociology, University of Minnesota. Assisted by William Allen, Professor of Farm Management, University of Saskatchewan, [and] J.F. Booth, Commissioner of Agricultural Economics, Dominion Department of Agriculture. Toronto: The Macmillan Company of Canada Limited, at St. Martin's House 1936.

xii, 344 pp.; 255 × 170 mm.
Canadian Frontiers of Settlement Series.

713. PARKER, Dorothy

Dorothy Parker, *Collected Poems: Not So Deep As A Well*. Decorated by Valenti Angelo. 1936 The Macmillan Company of Canada Ltd.

xii, 210 pp.; 216 × 135 mm.

714. PIERCE, Lorne

The Canada Book of Prose and Verse: Book Three. By Lorne Pierce and Dick Whitefield. The Ryerson Press [and] The Macmillans in Canada.

xii, 489, [1] pp.; 200 × 135 mm.
First published in 1932 (see 502). This edition revised. Further revised and reissued as *Our Heritage* in 1948 (see 1203). Revised again in 1963 (see 1631). Reprinted frequently.
Canada Books of Prose and Verse Series.

715. St. Martin's Classics, *Poems of Yesterday and To-day*. Authorized by the Protestant Committee of the Council of Education for the Province of Quebec. Toronto: The Macmillan Company of Canada Limited, at St. Martin's House 1936.

xiv, 144, [2] pp.; 170 × 110 mm.
St. Martin's Classics Series.

716. PRIESTLEY, J.B.

They Walk in the City: The Lovers in the Stone Forest. By J.B. Priestley. [Quotation]. Toronto: The Macmillan Company of Canada Limited, at St. Martin's House 1936.

[6], 515, [1] pp.; 200 × 135 mm.

717. ROBERTON, Thomas B.

T.B.R. Newspaper Pieces. By Thomas B. Roberton. Reprinted from the *Winnipeg Free Press.* Toronto: The Macmillan Company of Canada Limited, at St. Martin's House 1936.

xvi, 142 pp.; 195 × 125 mm.

718. RUSSELL, G. Stanley

The Road Behind Me. By G. Stanley Russell, M.A., D.D., Author of *The Monastery by the River, The Church in the Modern World, The Face of God and Other Sermons.* Toronto: The Macmillan Company of Canada Limited, at St. Martin's House 1936.

xii, 287, [1] pp.; 215 × 140 mm.

719. SCOTT, F.R.

New Provinces: Poems of Several Authors. Toronto: The Macmillan Company of Canada Limited, at St. Martin's House 1936.

x, 77, [1] pp.; 208 × 125 mm.

720. STERN, Gladys B.

Monogram. By G.B. Stern. Toronto: The Macmillan Company of Canada Limited, at St. Martin's House.

[14], 293, [1] pp.; 225 × 145 mm.

721. THOMSON, J.J.

Recollections and Reflections. By Sir J.J. Thomson, O.M., D.Sc., F.R.S., etc. Master of Trinity College, Cambridge. Toronto: The Macmillan Company of Canada Limited, at St. Martin's House 1936.

viii, 451, [1] pp.; 235 × 150 mm.

722. TYRER, Alfred Henry

Sex Marriage and Birth-Control: A Guide-book to a Satisfactory Sex-Life in Marriage. By Alfred Henry Tyrer. Illustrated. A Practical Handbook for the guidance of members of the Medical, Nursing and Legal Professions, the Clergy and Social Workers. Toronto: The Macmillan Company of Canada Limited, at St. Martin's House 1936.

xvi, 128 pp.; 200 × 135 mm.

1937

723. BANNON, R.V.

Eastland Echoes. By R.V. Bannon. Toronto: The Macmillan Company of
Canada Limited, at St. Martin's House 1937.

[8], 44 pp.; 230 × 155 mm.

724. BARBEAU, Marius

Romancero Du Canada. By Marius Barbeau. Toronto: The Macmillan Company of Canada Limited at St. Martin's House 1937.

254 pp.; 238 × 175 mm.

725. BERESFORD, M.A.

The Treasury Readers, *Work and Play To Accompany Book Three*. By M.A.
Beresford, M.A. The Ryerson Press [and] The Macmillans in Canada.

48 pp.; 274 × 207 mm.
First published in 1932. Reprinted in 1934, 1935, 1936 and 1937. Earlier printings
not located. Issued in paper.
Treasury Readers Series.

726. BLACK, Newton Henry

New Practical Chemistry: Fundamental Principles Applied to Modern Life.
Newton Henry Black [and] James Bryant Conant. Authorized by the De-
partment of Education for use in the Schools of Alberta. Toronto: The
Macmillan Company of Canada Limited, at St. Martin's House 1937.

xii, 347, [1] pp.; 204 × 135 mm.
First published in 1925 (see 236).

727. BOLLERT, Grace

A Picture Book For Jerry and Jane. By Grace Bollert. Toronto: The Ryerson
Press and The Macmillan Company of Canada Limited 1937.

20 pp.; 180 × 140 mm.
First published in 1932. Reprinted in 1937. Earlier printings not located. Issued in
paper.

728. BRIFFAULT, Robert

Europa In Limbo. Robert Briffault. Toronto: The Macmillan Company of
Canada Limited, at St. Martin's House 1937.

[8], 476 pp.; 220 × 155 mm.

729. BROWN, Audrey Alexandra

The Tree of Resurrection and Other Poems. By Audrey Alexandra Brown,
Author of "A Dryad in Nanaimo". Toronto: The Macmillan Company of
Canada Limited, at St. Martin's House 1937.

viii, 151, [1] pp.; 220 × 130 mm.

730. BRUCE, Herbert A.

Friendship: The Key To Peace And Other Addresses. By Herbert A. Bruce,
R.A.M.C., M.D., L.R.C.P., F.R.C.S. (Eng.), LL.D. Toronto: The Macmillan Company of Canada Limited, at St. Martin's House 1937.

xiv, 364 pp.; 225 × 148 mm.

731. CAIRNCROSS, A.S.

St. Martin's Classics, *Fact and Fiction*. Selected and Edited by A.S.
Cairncross, M.A., D.Litt. Authorized for use by the Department of Educa-
tion of British Columbia. Toronto: The Macmillan Company of Canada
Limited, at St. Martin's House 1937.

xiv, 276, [4] pp.; 170 × 110 mm.
St. Martin's Classics Series.

732. CHARLESWORTH, Hector

I'm Telling You: Being the Further Candid Chronicles of Hector Charlesworth.
Author of *Candid Chronicles*, *The Canadian Scene*, etc., etc. Toronto: The
Macmillan Company of Canada Limited, at St. Martin's House 1937.

xvi, 344 pp.; 223 × 155 mm.

733. CLARKE, George Herbert

Hymn To The Spirit Eternal. (Seranus Memorial Prize, 1937). By George
Herbert Clarke. Macmillan.

4 pp.; 230 × 154 mm.
Issued in paper.

734. COULTER, John

The Family Portrait. By John Coulter. Toronto: The Macmillan Company of
Canada Limited, at St. Martin's House 1937.

[6], 124 pp.; 197 × 120 mm.
Issued in paper.

735. COULTER, John

The House in the Quiet Glen. By John Coulter. Toronto: The Macmillan
Company of Canada Limited, at St. Martin's House 1937.

[8], 36, [2] pp.; 198 × 122 mm.
The half-title reads *The House in the Quiet Glen and The Family Portrait*, although
only the former is present. Issued in paper.

736. COULTER, John

The House in the Quiet Glen and The Family Portrait. By John Coulter.
Toronto: The Macmillan Company of Canada Limited, at St. Martin's
House 1937.

[8], 36, [4], 124 pp.; 200 × 125 mm.

737. COULTER, John

Radio Drama is Not Theatre. By John Coulter and Ivor Lewis. Toronto: The
Macmillan Company of Canada Limited, at St. Martin's House 1937.

x, 10 pp.; 205 × 143 mm.
Issued in paper.
Canadian Broadcasting Series.

738.   DAILEY, Helen S.

The Treasury Readers, *Work and Play To Accompany Book Two*. By Helen S. Dailey. Illustrated by Cynthia Clayton. The Ryerson Press [and] The Macmillans in Canada.

96 pp.; 274 × 207 mm.
First published in 1932. Reprinted in 1934, 1935, 1936 and 1937. Earlier printings not located. Issued in paper.
Treasury Readers Series.

739.   No entry.

740.   DE LA ROCHE, Mazo

The Very House. By Mazo De La Roche. Toronto: The Macmillan Company of Canada Limited, at St. Martin's House 1937.

[4], 257, [1] pp. + ads.; 190 × 128 mm.

741.   DE WITT, Norman W.

A Brief World History. By Norman W. De Witt, Ph.D., F.R.S.C. Professor of Latin, Victoria College, University of Toronto. Authorized by the Department of Education for use in Alberta. Toronto: The Macmillan Company of Canada Limited, at St. Martin's House 1937.

xii, 832 pp.; 200 × 133 mm.
Reprinted with corrections in 1937.

742.   No entry.

743.   ENGLAND, Robert

The Threat to Disinterested Education: A Challenge. By Robert England, M.C., M.A. Director of University Extension and Associate Professor of Economics of the University of British Columbia. Toronto: The Macmillan Company of Canada Limited, at St. Martin's House 1937.

[4], 28 pp.; 173 × 124 mm.
Issued in paper.

744.   FIELDHOUSE, H.N.

The Spanish Civil War: A Long Term View. By H.N. Fieldhouse, M.A., Department of History, University of Manitoba. Toronto: The Macmillan Company of Canada Limited, at St. Martin's House 1937.

31, [1] pp.; 213 × 139 mm.
Issued in paper.

745.   FOLEY, Pearl

Pearl Foley, *The Yellow Circle*. Toronto: The Macmillan Company of Canada Limited, at St. Martin's House 1937.

315, [1] pp.; 195 × 130 mm.

746. GLOVER, T.R.

A Corner of Empire: The Old Ontario Strand. By T.R. Glover and D.D. Calvin. Toronto: The Macmillan Company of Canada. Cambridge, England: At the University Press 1937.

xii, 178 pp.; 220 × 140 mm.

747. GREY OWL

The Tree. By Wa-sha-quon-asin (Grey Owl). Toronto: The Macmillan Company of Canada Limited, at St. Martin's House 1937.

62 pp.; 197 × 125 mm.

748. HARDY, Thomas

St. Martin's Classics, *Under the Greenwood Tree or the Mellstock Quire: A Rural Painting of the Dutch School.* By Thomas Hardy. Edited by E.J. Pratt. Toronto: The Macmillan Company of Canada Limited, at St. Martin's House 1937.

xxviii, 279, [3] pp.; 170 × 110 mm.
St. Martin's Classics Series.

749. HIND, E. Cora

Seeing For Myself: Agricultural Conditions Around the World. By E. Cora Hind. Toronto: The Macmillan Company of Canada Limited, at St. Martin's House 1937.

xxii, 347, [1] pp.; 227 × 153 mm.

750. HOUSSER, Frederick B.

Views and Reviews of Finance and Economics. By Fred B. Housser. Reprinted from *The Toronto Star.* Edited by E. Burnham Wyllie, M.A., Ph.D., Sometime Fellow in Philosophy, Queen's University, Canada. Toronto: The Macmillan Company of Canada Limited, at St. Martin's House 1937.

xviii, 322, [4] pp.; 228 × 148 mm.

751. KING, H.B.

A History of Britain. By H.B. King. Authorized by the Minister of Education for use in British Columbia. Toronto: The Macmillan Company of Canada Limited, at St. Martin's House 1937.

xii, 567, [1] pp.; 213 × 138 mm.

752. LODGE, R.C.

Manitoba Essays. Written in Commemoration of the Sixtieth Anniversary of the University of Manitoba. By Members of the Teaching Staffs of the University and its Affiliated Colleges. R.C. Lodge, Editor. Toronto: The Macmillan Company of Canada Limited, at St. Martin's House 1937.

xvi, 432 pp.; 223 × 147 mm.

753. LUDWIG, Emil

The Nile: The Life-Story of a River. Emil Ludwig. Translated By Mary H. Lindsay. 1937 Toronto: The Macmillan Company of Canada Limited, at St. Martin's House.

xvi, 619, [1] pp.; 240 × 155 mm.

754. MacCORKINDALE, H.N.

Mathematics for the Junior High School. By H.N. MacCorkindale, Superintendent of Schools, Vancouver, B.C. Book II Grade Eight. Authorized by the Minister of Education for use in British Columbia. Toronto: The Macmillan Company of Canada Limited, at St. Martin's House 1937.

xviii, 274 pp.; 190 × 130 mm.
Reprinted in 1938, 1939, 1942, 1943 and 1944.

755. No entry.

756. MACKAY, Muriel A.

Dominion French Readers: Book Two. By Muriel A. Mackay, B.A. And Alfreda E. Thompson, B.A. Authorized by the Minister of Education for use in the Province of British Columbia. Toronto: The Macmillan Company of Canada Limited, at St. Martin's House 1937.

xx, 578 pp.; 190 × 125 mm.

757. MACMILLAN, Harold

[Cover-title:] *Europe Today: Prospect And Retrospect*. An Address Delivered to the Empire Club of Canada, in Toronto, March 11th, 1937 by Harold Macmillan, M.P. Privately printed for their friends by The Macmillans In Canada.

12 pp.; 215 × 138 mm.
Issued in paper.

758. MacMURCHY, Marjorie

The Longest Way Round. By Lady Willison (Marjorie MacMurchy), Author of *The Child's House*, *Golden Treasury of Famous Books*, etc. Toronto: The Macmillan Company of Canada Limited, at St. Martin's House 1937.

[10], 325, [1] pp.; 197 × 130 mm.

759. MASON, Guy

The Canada Books Manual: Book Four, Accompanying The Canada Books of Prose and Verse Books IV to VI, for Grades X-XII. By Guy Mason, B.A., Provincial Normal College, Truro. The Ryerson Press [and] The Macmillans in Canada.

vi, 144 pp.; 200 × 138 mm.
Canada Books of Prose and Verse Series.

760. MAURA, Sister

Breath of the Spirit. By Sister Maura. Toronto: The Macmillan Company of Canada Limited, at St. Martin's House 1937.

x, 35, [1] pp.; 192 × 130 mm.

761.   McLAREN, Floris Clark

Frozen Fire. By Floris Clark McLaren. Toronto: The Macmillan Company of Canada Limited, at St. Martin's House 1937.

[8], 39, [1] pp.; 188 × 128 mm.

762.   MORRISON, Edith Lennox

William Tyrell of Weston. By Edith Lennox Morrison and J.E. Middleton. Toronto: The Macmillan Company of Canada Limited, at St. Martin's House 1937.

xvi, 152 pp.; 220 × 143 mm.

763.   MURPHY, Charles

1825—D'arcy McGee—1925: A Collection of Speeches and Addresses. Together with a Complete Report of the Centennial Celebration of the Birth of The Honourable Thomas D'arcy McGee at Ottawa, April 13th, 1925. Selected and Arranged by The Honourable Charles Murphy, K.C., LL.D. Toronto: The Macmillan Company of Canada Limited, at St. Martin's House 1937.

xvi, 366, [18] pp.; 245 × 155 mm.

764.   NEVILLE, K.P.R.

A Book of Latin Poetry. Edited with Introduction, Notes and Vocabulary by K.P.R. Neville, M.A., Ph.D., University of Western Ontario, R.O. Jolliffe, M.A., Ph.D., Queen's University, Kingston, E.A. Dale, M.A., University of Toronto, And D. Breslove, M.A., Malvern Collegiate Institute, Toronto. Prescribed by the Department of Education for the Province of Ontario for use for Upper School Examination. Authorized for use in the Province of Nova Scotia. Toronto: The Macmillan Company of Canada Limited, at St. Martin's House 1937.

liv, 366 pp.; 173 × 114 mm.
First published in 1931. Reprinted frequently. Earlier printings not located.

765.   PRATT, E.J.

The Fable of the Goats and Other Poems. By E.J. Pratt. Toronto: The Macmillan Company of Canada Limited, at St. Martin's House 1937.

viii, 47, [1] pp.; 230 × 150 mm.

766.   PRENTICE, J.D.

Teddy's Story. By J.D. Prentice, Commander, R.N. Illustrated by Steven Spurrier. Toronto: The Macmillan Company of Canada Limited, at St. Martin's House 1937.

356 pp.; 204 × 135 mm.

767.   ROBERTON, Thomas B.

A Second Helping of Newspaper Pieces. By Thomas B. Roberton ("T.B.R.").Toronto: The Macmillan Company of Canada Limited, at St. Martin's House 1937.

x, 157, [1] pp.; 193 × 125 mm.

768. ROCKLEY, Lady

Some Canadian Wild Flowers: Being the First Part of Wild Flowers of the Great Dominions. By Lady Rockley, C.B.E., Citizen and Gardener of London. Author of "A History of Gardening in England" (Hon. Alicia Amherst), "Children's Gardens", "London Parks and Gardens" (Hon. Mrs. Evelyn Cecil). Toronto: The Macmillan Company of Canada Limited, at St. Martin's House 1937.

    xii, 107, [1] pp.; 213 × 165 mm.

769. ROSEBOROUGH, Margaret M.

An Outline of Middle English Grammar. By Margaret M. Roseborough. Toronto: The Macmillan Company of Canada Limited, at St. Martin's House 1937.

    x, 112 pp.; 193 × 130 mm.

770. ROUX, Louis A.

Premier Cours de Français. Louis A. Roux, Officier d'Académie, Head of Department of French, Newark Academy, Newark N.J. With Drawings by A. Gladys Peck. Toronto: The Macmillan Company of Canada Limited, at St. Martin's House 1937.

    xvi, 431, [1] pp.; 202 × 135 mm.

771. SCHULL, Joseph

The Legend of Ghost Lagoon. By Joseph Schull. Toronto: The Macmillan Company of Canada Limited, at St. Martin's House 1937.

    [8], 178 pp.; 220 × 145 mm.

772. SHACKLETON, Helen

Saucy Again. Verses by Helen Shackleton. Illustrations by Edith B. MacLaren. [Quotation]. The Macmillan Company of Canada Limited Toronto 1937.

    [8], 49, [1] pp.; 220 × 175 mm.

773. SHAKESPEARE, William

Twelfth Night or What You Will. Edited with Introduction, Notes and Questions by Adrian Macdonald, M.A., English Master, the Normal School, Peterborough, Ontario. Toronto: The Macmillan Company of Canada Limited, at St. Martin's House 1937.

    xxx, 120 pp.; 177 × 120 mm.
    Issued in limp cloth.
    Macmillan's Matriculation English Texts Series.

774. SIME, J.G.

In a Canadian Shack. By J.G. Sime. Toronto: The Macmillan Company of Canada Limited, at St. Martin's House 1937.

    [8], 241, [1] pp.; 195 × 125 mm.

775.   SMITH, Anna Beatrice
Water From the Rock. By Anna Beatrice Smith (Imogen Carroll). Edited by
Dr. Mabel Cartwright. [Quotation]. Toronto: The Macmillan Company of
Canada Limited, at St. Martin's House 1937.
xxxii, 60 pp.; 190 × 130 mm.

776.   SPRIGGE, Elizabeth
The Son of the House. By Elizabeth Sprigge. Toronto: The Macmillan
Company of Canada Limited, at St. Martin's House 1937.
315, [1] pp.; 195 × 130 mm.

777.   SWANSON, W.W.
Rail, Road and River. By W.W. Swanson, Ph.D., Professor of Economics,
University of Saskatchewan. Toronto: The Macmillan Company of Canada
Limited, at St. Martin's House 1937.
x, 121, [1] pp.; 217 × 140 mm.

778.   WELLS, H.G.
H.G. Wells. *The Croquet Player*. Toronto: The Macmillan Company of
Canada Limited, At St. Martin's House, 1937.
[2], 98 pp.; 210 × 131 mm.

779.   WOOLLCOTT, Alexander
Woollcott's Second Reader. Toronto: The Macmillan Company Of Canada
Limited, At St. Martin's House, 1937.
x, 1056 pp.; 219 × 146 mm.

1938

780.   BEATTIE, Jessie L.
Three Measures. By Jessie L. Beattie, Author of "Hill-Top". Toronto: The
Macmillan Company of Canada Limited, at St. Martin's House 1938.
x, 295, [1] pp.; 210 × 140 mm.

781.   BENNETT, Ethel Hume
New Harvesting: Contemporary Canadian Poetry, 1918-1938. Chosen by
Ethel Hume Bennett, Author of "A Treasure Ship of Old Quebec", "Judy of
York Hill", "Camp Ken-Jockety" etc. Decorations by J.M. Donald. To-
ronto: The Macmillan Company of Canada Limited, at St. Martin's House
1938.
xx, 198 pp.; 220 × 140 mm.
Issued in the St. Martin's Classics Series in 1939.

782.   BENTLEY, Phyllis
Sleep in Peace. By Phyllis Bentley. Toronto: The Macmillan Company of
Canada Limited, At St. Martin's House, 1938.
557, [1] pp.; 200 × 130 mm.

783.   BICKNELL, Minnie Evans

Relief: A Play in One Act. By Minnie Evans Bicknell. Toronto: The
Macmillan Company of Canada Limited, at St. Martin's House 1938.

28 pp.; 165 × 100 mm.
Issued in paper.

784.   BORDEN, Robert

Robert Laird Borden: His Memoirs. Edited and with a Preface by Henry
Borden. With an introduction by Arthur Meighen. Toronto: The Macmillan
Company of Canada Limited, at St. Martin's House 1938.

xviii, 542 pp.; 230 × 150 mm.

785.   BOWMAN, Louise Morey

Characters in Cadence. By Louise Morey Bowman, Author of *Moonlight and
Common Day* and *Dream Tapestries.* Toronto: The Macmillan Company of
Canada Limited, at St. Martin's House 1938.

xii, 91, [1] pp.; 225 × 145 mm.

786.   BRITTAIN, Vera

Thrice a Stranger. Vera Brittain. The Macmillans in Canada Toronto — 1938.

xvi, 435, [1] pp.; 220 × 145 mm.

787.   BROWN, Audrey Alexandra

The Log of A Lame Duck. By Audrey Alexandra Brown. With a Foreword by
Lady Tweedsmuir. Toronto: The Macmillan Company of Canada Limited,
at St. Martin's House 1938.

viii, 292 pp.; 220 × 140 mm.

788.   BROWN, Cynthia

Cooking — With a Grain of Salt. By Cynthia Brown. With an Introduction by
Bernard K. Sandwell. Decorations by Ann Monkman. Toronto: The Macmillan Company of Canada Limited, at St. Martin's House 1938.

xvi, 382 pp.; 210 × 140 mm.

789.   CAMPBELL, Marjorie Wilkins

The Soil Is Not Enough. By Marjorie Wilkins Campbell. Toronto: The
Macmillan Company of Canada Limited, at St. Martin's House 1938.

[10], 285, [1] pp.; 195 × 130 mm.

790.   CASH, Gwen

I Like British Columbia. By Gwen Cash. Illustrated by J.M. Donald. Toronto: The Macmillan Company of Canada Limited, at St. Martin's House
1938.

xvi, 192 pp.; 234 × 150 mm.

791. CLAY, Charles

Swampy Cree Legends: Being Twenty Folk Tales from the Annals of a Primitive, Mysterious Fast-Disappearing Canadian Race. As told to Charles Clay, B.A., F.A.G.S., F.C.G.S., by Kuskapatches the Smokey One. Toronto: The Macmillan Company of Canada Limited, at St. Martin's House 1938.

xx, 95, [1] pp.; 200 × 125 mm.

792. DE LA ROCHE, Mazo

Growth Of a Man. By Mazo De La Roche. Toronto: The Macmillan Company of Canada Limited, at St. Martin's House 1938.

viii, 377, [1] pp. + ads.; 200 × 130 mm.

793. EAYRS, Hugh Sterling

The Barometer Points to Change. An Address delivered to the Toronto Branch of the Canadian Authors' Association on Friday, March 11th, 1938 by Hugh Eayrs. Privately printed for their friends by The Macmillans in Canada.

[4], 27, [1] pp.; 217 × 140 mm.
Issued in paper.

794. EDGAR, Marriott

Albert and The Lion And Other Incomparable Ditties. By Marriott Edgar. Performed by Stanley Holloway, George Patton, Etc. With illustrations by Anne Monkman and a Short, sharp word by Hugh Eayrs. Toronto: The Macmillan Company of Canada Limited, at St. Martin's House 1938.

[2], 30 pp.; 252 × 188 mm.
Reprinted frequently.

795. EGGLESTON, Wilfrid

The High Plains. By Wilfrid Eggleston. Toronto: The Macmillan Company of Canada Limited, at St. Martin's House 1938.

[10], 267, [1] pp.; 207 × 143 mm.

796. FARQUHARSON, Rica Mclean

They Meet Again: A Comedy in One Act. Rica Mclean Farquharson. Toronto: The Macmillan Company of Canada Limited, at St. Martin's House 1938.

[6], 26 pp.; 180 × 125 mm.
Issued in paper.

797. GREY OWL

A Book Of Grey Owl: Pages from the Writings of Wa-sha-quon-asin. With an Introduction by Hugh Eayrs. Toronto: The Macmillan Company of Canada Limited at St. Martin's House.

xxii, 324 pp.; 200 × 130 mm.
Reset and reissued in 1941 (see 907).

798. HARDY, W.G.

Turn Back the River. By W.G. Hardy. Toronto: The Macmillan Company of Canada Limited, at St. Martin's House 1938.

xii, 385, [1] pp.; 202 × 138 mm.

799. HARVEY, Jean-Charles

Sackcloth For Banner (Les Demi-Civilisés). By Jean-Charles Harvey. Translated by Lukin Barett. Toronto: The Macmillan Company of Canada Limited, at St. Martin's House 1938.

x, 262 pp.; 207 × 140 mm.

800. HÉMON, Louis

Maria Chapdelaine. By Louis Hémon. Translated by W. H. Blake. Illustrated by Thoreau Macdonald. With a Historical Introduction by Hugh Eayrs. Toronto: The Macmillan Company of Canada Limited, 1938.

173, [1] pp.; 209 × 157 mm.
First published in 1921 (see 167). Reissued in 1965 (see 1729).

800A HOUGHTON, Claude

Strangers. Claude Houghton. Toronto: The Macmillan Company Of Canada Limited, At St. Martin's House, 1938.

559, [1] pp.; 211 × 140 mm.

801. JACKSON, W.A.

General Mathematics: Book 1. By W.A. Jackson, Head of the Department of Mathematics, Oakwood Collegiate, Toronto. J.E. Dean, Director of Mathematics, Central Technical School, Toronto. And J.T. Crawford, Late Professor of Mathematics, Ontario College of Education, Toronto. Authorized by the Minister of Education for Ontario. Price 45 cents. Toronto: The Macmillan Company of Canada Limited, at St. Martin's House 1938.

xii, 394 pp.; 193 × 125 mm.

802. LABICHE, Eugène

Labiche et Jolly, *La Grammaire: Comédie-Vaudeville en Un Acte*. Edited with Notes, Idioms, Exercises and Vocabulary By F.C.A. Jeanneret, Professor of French, University College, University of Toronto. Toronto: The Macmillan Company of Canada, Limited, at St. Martin's House 1938.

[12], 81, [1] pp.; 180 × 124 mm.
Macmillan's Matriculation French Series.

803. LESLIE, Doris

Concord in Jeopardy. By Doris Leslie. The Macmillan Company of Canada Limited, Toronto 1938.

518 pp.; 190 × 130 mm.

804. [Cover-title:] *Lines Read at Macmillan's Annual Christmas Party*. December 16th, 1938.

4 pp.; 188 × 125 mm.
Issued in paper.

805.   LINK, Henry C.

The Rediscovery of Man. By Henry C. Link, Ph.D. Toronto: The Macmillan
Company of Canada Limited, at St. Martin's House 1938.

  xii, 257, [1] pp.; 203 × 134 mm.

806.   MacDERMOT, H.E.

Sir Thomas Roddick: His Work in Medicine and Public Life. By H.E. Mac-
Dermot, M.D. Toronto: The Macmillan Company of Canada Limited, at
St. Martin's House 1938.

  xiv, 160 pp.; 220 × 140 mm.

807.   No entry.

808.   MARSH, D'arcy

Democracy at Work: The Machinery of Parliament Hill and the Civil Service.
By D'arcy Marsh, Author of *The Tragedy of Henry Thornton*. Toronto: The
Macmillan Company of Canada Limited, at St. Martin's House 1938.

  [8], 100 pp.; 205 × 143 mm.

809.   MILNE, W.S.

*The Canada Books Manual, Accompanying The Canada Books of Prose and
Verse, Book One, Grade VII*. By W.S. Milne, M.A. The Ryerson Press [and]
The Macmillans in Canada.

  viii, 77, [1] pp.; 193 × 130 mm.
  First published in 1932. Revised in 1934 and 1938. Earlier editions not located.

810.   MORGAN-POWELL, S.

Down the Years. By S. Morgan-Powell. With a Foreword by E.J. Pratt.
Toronto: The Macmillan Company of Canada Limited, at St. Martin's
House 1938.

  xii, 90 pp.; 218 × 138 mm.

811.   MORTON, Arthur S.

Canadian Frontiers of Settlement, Edited by W.A. Mackintosh and W.L.G.
Joerg In Nine Volumes. *History of Prairie Settlement*. By Arthur S. Mor-
ton, Professor of History, University of Saskatchewan. *"Dominion Lands"
Policy*. By Chester Martin, Professor of History, University of Toronto.
Toronto: The Macmillan Company of Canada Limited, at St. Martin's
House 1938.

  xviii, 571, [1] pp.; 255 × 170 mm.
  Canadian Frontiers of Settlement Series.

812.   NORWOOD, Gilbert

Spoken in Jest. By Gilbert Norwood. Toronto: The Macmillan Company of
Canada Limited, at St. Martin's House 1938.

  viii, 209, [1] pp.; 222 × 145 mm.

813. ODLE, E.V.

Quest and Conquest: An Anthology of Personal Adventures. Compiled by E.V.
Odle. Toronto: The Macmillan Company of Canada Limited, at St. Martin's
House 1938.

xvi, 230 pp.; 117 × 110 mm.
St. Martin's Classics Series.

814. PRIESTLEY, J.B.

The Doomsday Men: An Adventure. By J.B. Priestley. Toronto: The Macmillan Company Of Canada Limited At St. Martin's House, 1938.

[8], 312 pp.; 194 × 130 mm.

815. RAVEN, Charles E.

War and The Christian. By Charles E. Raven, D.D., Regius Professor of
Divinity in the University of Cambridge and Canon of Ely. Author of *Jesus
and the Gospel of Love, Is War Obsolete?* etc. etc. Toronto: The Macmillan
Company of Canada Limited, at St. Martin's House 1938.

185, [1] pp.; 190 × 130 mm.

816. SCOTT, Walter

St. Martin's Classics, *The Talisman*. By Sir Walter Scott. Abridged and
Edited with Notes, Glossary, etc., by Fanny Johnson, Formerly Head Mis-
tress of Bolton High School. With an Introduction by J.F. Macdonald,
M.A., Associate Professor of English, University of Toronto. Toronto: The
Macmillan Company of Canada Limited, at St. Martin's House 1938.

xviii, 248, [2] pp.; 170 × 110 mm.
First published in 1935. Reprinted in 1938. Earlier printings not located.
St. Martin's Classics Series.

817. STERN, Gladys B.

The Ugly Dachshund. By G.B. Stern. With illustrations by K.F. Barker.
Toronto: The Macmillan Company Of Canada Limited, At St. Martin's
House, 1938.

147, [1] pp.; 194 × 125 mm.

818. STEVENSON, O.J.

The Unconquerable North and Other Poems. By O.J. Stevenson. Toronto:
The Macmillan Company of Canada Limited, at St. Martin's House 1938.

viii, 79, [1] pp.; 193 × 128 mm.

819. STUART, Grace

The Achievement of Personality In the Light of Psychology and Religion. By
Grace Stuart, M.A., B.Litt. With an Introduction by Professor L.W. Gren-
sted, D.D. Nolloth Professor of the Philosophy of the Christian Religion in
the University of Oxford; University Lecturer in the Psychology of Religion.
Toronto: The Macmillan Company of Canada Limited, at St. Martin's
House 1938.

192 pp.; 193 × 128 mm.

820. THOMSON, Lesslie R.

The Canadian Railway Problem: Some Economic Aspects of Canadian Trans-
portation and A Suggested Solution for the Railway Problem. By Lesslie R.
Thomson, Consulting Engineer. Toronto: The Macmillan Company of
Canada Limited, at St. Martin's House 1938.

xiv, 1080 pp.; 257 × 170 mm.

821. TURNBULL, Jane M.

Essential Traits of French-Canadian Poetry. By Jane M. Turnbull, M.A.,
Ph.D. Toronto: The Macmillan Company of Canada Limited, at St. Martin's House 1938.

xii, 225, [1] pp.; 215 × 140 mm.

822. WATSON, William R.

I Give You Yesterday. By William R. Watson. With a Preface by Bernard K.
Sandwell. Toronto: The Macmillan Company of Canada Limited, at St.
Martin's House 1938.

x, 238 pp.; 207 × 140 mm.

823. WOOD, H.G.

Did Christ Really Live? By H.G. Wood, Author of *The Truth and Error*
of Communism, Henry T. Hodgkin, Christianity and the Nature of History, etc
Toronto: The Macmillan Company of Canada Limited, at St. Martin's
House 1938.

191, [1] pp.; 193 × 127 mm.

824. WRONG, George M.

The Canadians: The Story of a People. George M. Wrong. Toronto: The
Macmillan Company of Canada Limited, at St. Martin's House 1938.

455, [1] pp.; 240 × 157 mm.
Revised and reprinted in 1938.

1939

825. BAILEY, Josh

The Old Country Under Fire. By Josh Bailey. Toronto: The Macmillan
Company of Canada Limited, at St. Martin's House 1939.

xiv, 197, [1] pp.; 215 × 142 mm.

826. BAIRD, Irene

Waste Heritage. By Irene Baird. Toronto: The Macmillan Company of
Canada Limited, At St. Martin's House, 1939.

[8], 329, [1] pp.; 217 × 145 mm.
Reprinted in paper in 1973, and in the Laurentian Library (No. 18) in 1973.

827. **BEARD, Charles A.**

America In Midpassage. By Charles A. Beard & Mary R. Beard. Drawings by Wilfred Jones. Volume III [of] The Rise of American Civilization. Toronto: The Macmillan Company Of Canada Limited, At St. Martin's House, 1939.

[10], 977, [1] pp.; 222 × 150 mm.

828. **BOURINOT, Arthur S.**

Under the Sun: Poems. By Arthur S. Bourinot. Toronto: The Macmillan Company of Canada Limited, at St. Martin's House 1939.

[12], 69, [1] pp.; 190 × 130 mm.
Issued in paper.

829. **CHARTERS, W.W.**

Health Through Science. By W.W. Charters, Ph.D., Dean F. Smiley, M.D., [and] Ruth M. Strang, PH.D. Revised for use in Canadian Schools by Rae Chittick, B.Sc., R.N., Instructor in Health Education, Provincial Normal School, Calgary, Alberta. Authorized by the Department of Education for use in Alberta. Toronto: The Macmillan Company of Canada Limited, at St. Martin's House 1939.

x, 524 pp.; 188 × 135 mm.

830. **CLARKE, George Herbert**

Ode on The Royal Visit to Canada 1939. By George Herbert Clarke. Macmillan.

4 pp.; 220 × 145 mm.
Issued in paper.

831. **COCKBURN, Russell R.**

Mally: The Story Of A Dog. By Russell R. Cockburn. Toronto: The Macmillan Company of Canada Limited, at St. Martin's House 1939.

[8], 248 pp.; 210 × 154 mm.

832. **CRAWFORD, J.T.**

A New Algebra for High Schools. By J.T. Crawford, Late Professor of Mathematics, Ontario College of Education, Toronto. As Completely Revised by J.E. Dean, Director of Mathematics, Central Technical School, Toronto and W.A. Jackson, Head of the Department of Mathematics, Oakwood Collegiate, Toronto. Authorized by the Minister of Education for Ontario. Price 55 cents. Toronto: The Macmillan Company of Canada Limited, at St. Martin's House 1939.

xii, 382 pp.; 193 × 128 mm.
First published in 1915 (see 81). Revised in 1916 (see 102A). Third revision published in 1954 (see 1310).

833. **CREIGHTON, Alan**

Cross-Country. By Alan Creighton. Toronto: The Macmillan Company of Canada Limited, at St. Martin's House 1939.

viii, 68 pp.; 232 × 154 mm.

834. DE LA ROCHE, Mazo

The Sacred Bullock and Other Stories of Animals. By Mazo De La Roche.
Illustrated by Stuart Tresilian. Toronto: The Macmillan Company of
Canada Limited, at St. Martin's House 1939.

    x, 221, [3] pp.; 193 × 130 mm.

835. EAYRS, Hugh

It Isn't Good Enough. An Address delivered to the Annual Meeting of the
Canadian Authors' Association on July 3rd, 1939 by Hugh Eayrs. Privately
printed for their friends by The Macmillans in Canada.

    [2], 16 pp.; 217 × 140 mm.
    Issued in paper.

836. EISENDRATH, Maurice N.

The Never Failing Stream. Maurice N. Eisendrath. Toronto: The Macmillans in Canada 1939.

    xviii, 398 pp.; 220 × 140 mm.

837. FLENLEY, R.

Essays in Canadian History. Presented to George Mackinnon Wrong for his
eightieth birthday. Edited by R. Flenley. Toronto: The Macmillan Company of Canada Limited, at St. Martin's House 1939.

    xii, 372 pp.; 220 × 140 mm.

838. FLETCHER, B.A.

Studies of the Institute of Public Affairs at Dalhousie University, *The Next
Step in Canadian Education: An Account of the Larger Unit of School Administration*. By B.A. Fletcher, M.A., B.Sc., O.E. Smith Professor of Education, Dalhousie University, Nova Scotia, Canada. Toronto: The Macmillan Company of Canada Limited, at St. Martin's House 1939.

    xviii, 202 pp.; 220 × 140 mm.
    Dalhousie University Institute of Public Affairs Series.

839. GUILLET, Edwin

The Pathfinders of North America. By Edwin and Mary Guillet. With 73
illustrations. Toronto: The Macmillan Company of Canada Limited, at St.
Martin's House 1939.

    xiv, 304 pp.; 200 × 145 mm.
    Reprinted in 1942, 1945, 1946 and 1948. Revised in 1957 (see 1399).

840. HETT, Francis Paget

*Georgina: A Type Study of Early Settlement and Church Building in Upper
Canada*. By Francis Paget Hett. [Quotation]. Toronto: The Macmillan
Company of Canada Limited, at St. Martin's House MCMXXXIX.

    xvi, 128 pp.; 218 × 172 mm.

841. HILTON, M.J.

A Book of General Science. By M.J. Hilton, Head of Science Department,
Edmonton Technical School. Authorized by the Minister of Education for

Alberta. Toronto: The Macmillan Company of Canada Limited, at St. Martin's House 1939.

xvi, 399, [1] pp.; 200 × 130 mm.
First published in 1931 (see 462). This edition revised.

842. HIND, E. Cora

My Travels and Findings. By E. Cora Hind, Author of "Seeing For Myself". Toronto: The Macmillan Company of Canada Limited, at St. Martin's House 1939.

xviii, 185, [1] pp.; 208 × 130 mm.

843. HUXLEY, Aldous

After Many A Summer. A Novel by Aldous Huxley. 1939. Toronto: The Macmillan Company Of Canada Limited, At St. Martin's House.

[6], 314 pp.; 194 × 127 mm.

844. KIPLING, Rudyard

St. Martin's Classics, *'Captains Courageous': A Story of the Grand Banks*. By Rudyard Kipling. Special edition exclusively for use in Canadian Schools. Authorized by the Department of Public Instruction, Province of Quebec. Toronto: The Macmillan Company of Canada Limited, at St. Martin's House 1939.

vi, 282, [2] pp.; 117 × 110 mm.
Another school edition was published in 1964 (see 1649).
St. Martin's Classics Series.

845. LeROSSIGNOL, J.E.

The Habitant-Merchant. By J.E. LeRossignol, Author of *The Flying Canoe*, *The Beauport Road*, etc. With Motif Illustrations by B. Cogill Haworth and a wrapper design from a painting by Dorothy Stevens. Toronto: The Macmillan Company of Canada Limited, at St. Martin's House 1939.

258 pp.; 230 × 152 mm.

846. LOUGHEED, W.J.

General Mathematics: Book II. By W.J. Lougheed, Professor of Methods in Mathematics, Ontario College of Education, And J.G. Workman, Instructor in Mathematics, University of Toronto Schools. Authorized by the Minister of Education for Ontario. Price 50 cents. Toronto: The Macmillan Company of Canada Limited, at St. Martin's House 1939.

x, 284 pp.; 188 × 123 mm.

847. McDOWELL, Franklin Davey

The Champlain Road. By Franklin Davey McDowell. Toronto: The Macmillan Company of Canada Limited, at St. Martin's House 1939.

xiv, 421, [1] pp.; 205 × 140 mm.
Reprinted in 1939 and 1940 (twice). A French translation was published in 1942 (see 952). A Huronian edition was published in 1949 (see 1204).

848. McINNES, Graham

A Short History of Canadian Art. By Graham McInnes. Toronto: The Macmillan Company of Canada Limited, at St. Martin's House 1939.

> xiv, 125, [1] pp.; 220 × 140 mm.
> A revised and enlarged edition was published in 1950 under the title *Canadian Art* (see 1226).

849. MERCER, Samuel A.B.

The Tell El-Amarna Tablets. Edited by Samuel A.B. Mercer, Professor of Semitic Languages and Egyptology, Trinity College in the University of Toronto. With the Assistance of Professor Frank Hudson Hallock in the final Revision of the Manuscript. Vol. I. Toronto: The Macmillan Company of Canada Limited, at St. Martin's House 1939.

> xxiv, 441, [1] pp.; 238 × 162 mm.

850. MERCER, Samuel A.B.

The Tell El-Amarna Tablets. Edited by Samuel A.B. Mercer, Professor of Semitic Languages and Egyptology, Trinity College in the University of Toronto. With the Assistance of Professor Frank Hudson Hallock in the final Revision of the Manuscript. Vol. II. Toronto: The Macmillan Company of Canada Limited, at St. Martin's House 1939.

> [6], [443]-908, [2] pp.; 238 × 162 mm.

851. MILNE, W.S.

The Canada Books Manual, Accompanying The Canada Books of Prose and Verse: Book Two, Grade VIII. By W.S. Milne, M.A. The Ryerson Press [and] The Macmillans in Canada.

> vi, 76 pp.; 193 × 130 mm.
> First published in 1932. Revised in 1939. First edition not located.
> Canada Books of Prose and Verse Series.

852. MITCHELL, Margaret

Gone With The Wind. Motion Picture Edition. By Margaret Mitchell. Toronto: The Macmillan Company of Canada Limited, At St. Martin's House, 1939.

> [6], 391, [1] pp.; 240 × 179 mm.
> First published in 1936 (see 710). Issued in paper.

853. PARKER, Dorothy

Here Lies: The Collected Stories of Dorothy Parker. Toronto: The Macmillan Company of Canada Limited, at St. Martin's House 1939.

> viii, 362 pp.; 208 × 130 mm.

854. PRIESTLEY, J.B.

Rain Upon Godshill: A Further Chapter of Autobiography. By J.B. Priestley. Toronto: The Macmillan Company of Canada Limited, at St. Martin's House 1939.

> [4], 330, [2] pp.; 218 × 140 mm.

855. RICHTER, L.

Studies of the Institute of Public Affairs at Dalhousie University, *Canada's Unemployment Problem*. By H.M. Cassidy, W.L. Jacobsen, W.M. Jones, Dorothy King, A. McNamara, L. Richter, S.A. Saunders, H.A. Weir, [and] Charlotte Whitton. Edited by L. Richter, Dalhousie University. With a Foreword by Hon. Norman McL. Rogers, Minister of Labour. Toronto: The Macmillan Company of Canada Limited, at St. Martin's House 1939.

xvi, 414 pp.; 220 × 140 mm.
Dalhousie University Institute of Public Affairs Series.

856. ROBERTS, Leslie

We Must Be Free: Reflections of a Democrat. By Leslie Roberts. Toronto: The Macmillan Company of Canada Limited, at St. Martin's House 1939.

xx, 248 pp.; 220 × 144 mm.

857. SAUNDERS, S.A.

Studies of the Institute of Public Affairs at Dalhousie University, *Studies in the Economy of the Maritime Provinces*. By S.A. Saunders. With a Preface by H.A. Innis. Toronto: The Macmillan Company of Canada Limited, at St. Martin's House 1939.

xiv, 266 pp.; 220 × 140 mm.
Dalhousie University Institute of Public Affairs Series.

858. SMITH, Reed

Learning to Write. By Reed Smith. Canadian Edition Completely Revised and Reset. Authorized by the Minister of Education for use in the Schools of Ontario. Toronto: The Macmillan Company of Canada Limited, at St. Martin's House 1939.

xii, 484 pp.; 205 × 140 mm.
Reprinted frequently. Revised in 1947 (see 1155). Second revised edition published in 1961 (see 1556).

859. STEINBECK, John

The Grapes of Wrath. John Steinbeck. Toronto: The Macmillan Company of Canada Limited, At St. Martin's House.

[6], 619, [1] pp.; 207 × 138 mm.

860. STOKES, Milton L.

The Bank of Canada: The Development and Present Position of Central Banking in Canada. By Milton L. Stokes, M.A., LL.B., Ph.D., Professor of Economics, Lebanon Valley College. With Foreword by F. Cyril James, B. Com. (London); PH.D., Director of the School of Commerce, McGill University. Toronto: The Macmillan Company of Canada Limited, at St. Martin's House 1939.

xiv, 382 pp.; 220 × 150 mm.

1940

861.   BLAKE, W.H.

Brown Waters. By W.H. Blake. With a Preface by Lord Tweedsmuir. Illustrations by Clarence A. Gagnon. [Quotation]. Toronto: The Macmillan
Company of Canada Limited 1940.

[16], 168 pp.; 227 × 180 mm.
First published in 1915 (see 77). Second edition published in 1925 (see 237).

862.   BOAS, Guy

The School Book of English Verse. Chosen by Guy Boas, M.A., Headmaster,
Sloane School, Formerly Senior English Master, St. Paul's School. Au-
thorized by the Minister of Education for use in the schools of Ontario.
Toronto: The Macmillan Company of Canada Limited, at St. Martin's
House 1940.

xviii, 569, [1] pp.; 185 × 128 mm.
Reprinted in 1945. Revised in 1949 (see 1200).

863.   *The British Commonwealth at War*. The Macmillan Company of Canada
Limited, 70 Bond Street Toronto, 1940.

[2], 24 pp.; 230 × 150 mm.
Issued in paper.
Round Table War Pamphlets Series.

864.   BRITTAIN, Vera

Testament Of Friendship: The Story of Winifred Holtby. By Vera Brittain.
Toronto: The Macmillan Company Of Canada Limited, At St. Martin's
House, 1940.

xiv, 442 pp. + ad.; 202 × 136 mm.

865.   BUCK, Pearl S.

Other Gods: An American Legend. By Pearl S. Buck. Toronto: The Macmillan Company Of Canada Limited, At St. Martin's House, 1940.

[6], 430, [2] pp.; 195 × 135 mm.

866.   CLARKE, George Herbert

McMaster University 1890-1940: Commemoration Ode. By George Herbert
Clarke. 1940.

4 pp.; 230 × 155 mm.
This pamphlet is attributed to Macmillan by Watters (p. 42). Issued in paper.

867.   COOK, Alexander J.

Geometry For Today. Based on *A Junior Geometry* by A.W. Siddons and R.T.
Hughes. By Alexander J. Cook, Associate Professor of Mathematics, Univer-
sity of Alberta. Authorized by the Department of Education for Alberta.
Toronto: The Macmillan Company of Canada Limited, at St. Martin's
House 1940.

x, 260 pp.; 195 × 130 mm.

868. DAWSON, C.A.

Canadian Frontiers of Settlement, Edited by W.A. Mackintosh and W.L.G.
Joerg In Nine Volumes: Volume VIII. *Pioneering in the Prairie Provinces:
The Social Side of the Settlement Process*. By C.A. Dawson, Professor of
Sociology at McGill University, And Eva R. Younge, Social Research Assis-
tant at McGill University. Toronto: The Macmillan Company of Canada
Limited, at St. Martin's House 1940.

xiv, 338 pp.; 255 × 170 mm.
Canadian Frontiers of Settlement Series.

869. DE LA ROCHE, Mazo

Whiteoak Heritage. By Mazo De La Roche. Toronto: The Macmillan Company of Canada Limited, at St. Martin's House 1940.

viii, 283, [1] pp.; 195 × 132 mm.

870. DEACON, William Arthur

Sh-h-h...Here Comes the Censor! An address to the Ontario Library Association, March 26, 1940. By William Arthur Deacon. Macmillan.

16 pp.; 175 × 140 mm.
Issued in paper.

871. DONALD, J.M.

Quebec Patchwork. By J.M. Donald. Illustrated by the author. Toronto: The
Macmillan Company of Canada Limited, at St. Martin's House 1940.

[8], 368 pp.; 217 × 158 mm.

872. DURRANT, J.E.

A New Analytic Geometry. By J.E. Durrant, Head of the Department of
Mathematics, Vice-Principal, Collegiate-Vocational Institute, Guelph, Ontario, And H.R. Kingston, Head of the Department of Mathematics and
Astronomy, Director of Summer School and Extramural Studies, University
of Western Ontario, London, Ontario. Toronto: The Macmillan Company
of Canada Limited, at St. Martin's House 1940.

x, 348 pp.; 193 × 130 mm.
First published in 1936 as *A New Geometry: Analytic-Synthetic* (see 694). Second
revised edition published in 1960 (see 1524).

873. GRAY, John M.

Prose of Our Day. Selected and edited by John M. Gray and Frank A.
Upjohn. Toronto: The Macmillan Company of Canada Limited, at St.
Martin's House 1940.

xvi, 331, [1] pp.; 170 × 110 mm.
Revised in 1940 (see 874).

874. GRAY, John M.

St. Martin's Classics, *Prose of Our Day*. Selected and edited by J.M. Gray,
F.A. Upjohn and J.J. Knights. Revised edition. Toronto: The Macmillan
Company of Canada Limited, at St. Martin's House 1940.

xiv, 367, [1] pp.; 170 × 110 mm.
First published in 1940 (see 873). Revised edition reprinted frequently.
St. Martin's Classics Series.

875.   KEYNES, John Maynard

How To Pay For the War: A Radical Plan For the Chancellor of the Exchequer.
By John Maynard Keynes. Toronto: The Macmillan Company of Canada
Limited, At St. Martin's House, 1940.

viii, 88 pp.; 187 × 125 mm.
Issued in card covers.

876.   LESLIE, Doris

Royal William: The Story of a Democrat. By Doris Leslie. Toronto: The
Macmillan Company of Canada Limited, at St. Martin's House 1940.

372, [4] pp.; 200 × 130 mm.

877.   LOUGHEED, W.J.

A Modern Geometry For High Schools. By W.J. Lougheed, Professor of
Methods in Mathematics, Ontario College of Education, And J.G. Workman, Instructor in Mathematics, University of Toronto Schools. Authorized
by the Minister of Education for Ontario. PRICE 50 CENTS. Toronto: The
Macmillan Company of Canada Limited, at St. Martin's House 1940.

xviii, 269 pp.; 193 × 127 mm.
First published in 1935 as *Geometry For High Schools* (see 646). This edition revised.

878.   MILLER, Norman

An Advanced Course in Algebra. By Norman Miller, Ph.D., Professor of
Mathematics in Queen's University, Kingston, And Robert E.K. Rourke,
A.M., Assistant Headmaster and Instructor in Mathematics at Pickering
College, Newmarket. Toronto: The Macmillan Company of Canada Li-
mited, at St. Martin's House 1940.

xvi, 326 pp.; 207 × 140 mm.
Revised in 1947 (see 1144).

879.   MOODY, Irene H.

Lava. [Quotation]. By Irene H. Moody. Toronto: The Macmillan Company
of Canada Limited, at St. Martin's House 1940.

xii, 96 pp.; 240 × 160 mm.

880.   MORGAN, Charles

The Voyage. By Charles Morgan. [Quotation]. Toronto: The Macmillan
Company of Canada Limited, at St. Martin's House 1940.

[8], 508 pp.; 215 × 140 mm.

881. MORGAN-POWELL, S.

This Canadian Literature. Being an address delivered before the Toronto Branch of the Canadian Authors' Association at Toronto, on May 11th, 1940. By S. Morgan-Powell, Editor and Literary Editor of the Montreal Daily Star. Privately printed for their friends by The Macmillans in Canada.

[2], 14 pp.; 214 × 140 mm.
Issued in paper.

882. PANNETON, Philippe

Ringuet [pseud.], *Thirty Acres*. Translated by Felix and Dorothea Walter. Toronto: The Macmillan Company of Canada Limited, at St. Martin's House 1940.

[6], 324 pp.; 192 × 130 mm.
There are two distinct editions of this book, both published in 1940. The first uses the English sheets and has the Macmillan of Canada logo on the title-page. The second was printed in Canada from a new setting of type, and lacks the logo on the title-page. Its pagination also varies slightly, being [6], 329, [1] pp.

883. PRATT, E.J.

Brébeuf and His Brethren. By E.J. Pratt. Toronto: The Macmillan Company of Canada Limited, at St. Martin's House 1940.

[6], 65, [1] pp.; 220 × 140 mm.
Revised edition published in 1940 (see 884). New edition in paper published in 1966 (see 1804).

884. PRATT, E.J.

Brébeuf and His Brethren. By E.J. Pratt. Toronto: The Macmillan Company of Canada Limited, at St. Martin's House 1940.

[6], 66 pp.; 238 × 160 mm.
First published in 1940 (see 883). This edition slightly revised with new epilogue and limited to five hundred copies, numbered and signed and issued in a slip-case. Also issued in trade format in 1941. A new edition in paper published in 1966 (see 1804).

885. PRIESTLEY, J.B.

Let The People Sing. By J.B. Priestley. Toronto: The Macmillan Company of Canada Limited, at St. Martin's House 1940.

[10], 418 pp.; 200 × 130 mm.
First published in 1939. Reprinted in 1940. First printing not located.

886. SIME, J.G.

The Land of Dreams. By J.G. Sime. Toronto: The Macmillan Company of Canada Limited 1940.

xii, 273, [1] pp.; 205 × 140 mm.

887. SINCLAIR, Upton

World's End. Upton Sinclair. Toronto: The Macmillan Company Of Canada Limited, At St. Martin's House, 1940.

[10], 740, [2] pp.; 219 × 145 mm.

888.   STERN, Gladys B.
A Lion In The Garden. By G.B. Stern. Toronto: The Macmillan Company Of
Canada Limited, At St. Martin's House, 1940.
   287, [1] pp.; 192 × 132 mm.

889.   STEWART, Herbert Leslie
From a Library Window: Reflections of a Radio Commentator. By Herbert
Leslie Stewart M.A. (Oxon.), PH.D., Professor of Philosophy, Dalhousie
University. Toronto: The Macmillan Company of Canada Limited 1940.
   x, 323, [1] pp.; 220 × 145 mm.

890.   TRAQUAIR, Ramsay
The Old Silver of Quebec. By Ramsay Traquair, McGill University. With
sixteen pages of illustrations from photographs. Published under the Auspices of The Art Association of Montreal. Toronto: The Macmillan Company of Canada Limited 1940.
   xii, 169, [3] pp.; 250 × 165 mm.

891.   WOOLF, Virginia
Roger Fry: A Biography. Virginia Woolf. Toronto: The Macmillan Company of Canada Limited, at St. Martin's House 1940.
   307, [1] pp.; 220 × 140 mm.

1941

892.   BAIRD, Irene
He Rides the Sky. By Irene Baird. Toronto: The Macmillan Company of
Canada Limited 1941.
   [12], 241, [1] pp.; 205 × 135 mm.

893.   BAIRD, Irene
The North American Tradition. By Irene Baird. Toronto: The Macmillan
Company of Canada Limited 1941.
   32 pp.; 178 × 120 mm.
   Issued in paper.
   Macmillan War Pamphlets (Canadian Series).

894.   BLACK, Newton Henry
Elementary Practical Physics. Newton Henry Black [and] Harvey Nathaniel
Davis. Authorized by the Council of Public Instruction for use in the schools
of Nova Scotia. Toronto: The Macmillan Company of Canada Limited 1941.
   x, 710 pp.; 208 × 138 mm.

895.   BLOCHIN, Anne Elizabeth
That Dog of Yours. By Anne Elizabeth Blochin. Toronto: The Macmillan
Company of Canada Limited 1941.
   [14], 183, [1] pp.; 230 × 135 mm.

896. BOWMAN, F.B.

Everyday Proctology. By F.B. Bowman, M.B., F.R.C.P. (Canada). Proctologist, Hamilton General Hospital and Mountain Sanatorium; Member, American Proctologic Society. Illustrated by the Author. Toronto: The Macmillan Company of Canada Limited 1941.

xiv, 123, [1] pp.; 220 × 140 mm.

897. BRITTAIN, Vera

England's Hour. By Vera Brittain. [Quotation]. Toronto: The Macmillan Company Of Canada Limited, At St. Martin's House, 1941.

xviii, 301, [1] pp.; 197 × 132 mm.

898. BROWN, Audrey Alexandra

Poetry And Life. An Address given at the Canadian Authors' Association in Vancouver, on August 24th, 1941 by Audrey Alexandra Brown. Privately printed for their friends by The Macmillans In Canada.

[4], 10 pp.; 215 × 140 mm.
Issued in paper.

899. BUCKLEY, Beatrice Barron

Songs of Weeny Gopher. Music and Lyrics by Beatrice Barron Buckley. The Macmillan Company of Canada Limited 1941.

60 pp.; 300 × 234 mm.
Issued in paper.

900. COX, Leo

North Star. By Leo Cox. Toronto: The Macmillan Company of Canada Limited 1941.

viii, 56 pp.; 208 × 137 mm.

901. DULEY, Margaret

Highway to Valour. Margaret Duley, Author of *The Eyes of the Gull*, *Cold Pastoral*. [Quotation]. Toronto: The Macmillan Company of Canada Limited, at St. Martin's House 1941.

[8], 324 pp.; 215 × 140 mm.

902. EISENDRATH, Maurice N.

Reading in War-Time. By Maurice N. Eisendrath. Toronto: The Macmillan Company of Canada Limited 1941.

31, [1] pp.; 178 × 120 mm.
Issued in paper.
Macmillan War Pamphlets (Canadian Series).

903. ELLIOTT, Ellen

Publishing in Wartime. An Address delivered to the twentieth Anniversary Convention of the Canadian Authors' Association on Friday, August 22nd, 1941. By Ellen Elliott. Privately printed by The Macmillans in Canada for their friends.

[2], 27, [1] pp.; 217 × 145 mm.
Issued in paper.

904.   GIBBON, John Murray

The New Canadian Loyalists. By John Murray Gibbon. Toronto: The Macmillan Company of Canada Limited 1941.

   39, [1] pp.; 178 × 120 mm.
   Issued in paper.
   Macmillan War Pamphlets (Canadian Series).

905.   GOLDEN, Lou L.L.

Conscription. By "Politicus" (L.L.L. Golden). Toronto: The Macmillan
Company of Canada Limited 1941.

   32 pp.; 178 × 120 mm.
   Issued in paper.
   Macmillan War Pamphlets (Canadian Series).

906.   GRAY, John M.

The One-Eyed Trapper. By John Morgan Gray. Illustrated by D.L. Mayes.
The Macmillan Company of Canada Ltd. Toronto 1941.

   256 pp.; 194 × 137 mm.
   Reprinted in 1946 and 1955.

907.   GREY OWL

A Book of Grey Owl: Pages from the Writings of Wa-Sha-Quon-Asin. Edited
by E.E. Reynolds. With Preface by Lovat Dickson. The Macmillan Company of Canada Limited.

   xvi, 272 pp.; 188 × 125 mm.
   First published in 1938 (see 797). This edition reset. Reprinted frequently . Issued in
   paper in 1974 and in the Laurentian Library (No. 35) in 1975.

908.   HEATON, T.G.

Artificial Pneumothorax in Pulmonary Tuberculosis. By T.G. Heaton, M.B.,
Chest Clinician, Toronto Western Hospital; Visiting Physician, St. Michael's
Hospital, Toronto; Formerly Resident Physician, Mountain Sanatorium,
Hamilton; and since outbreak of war, Major in charge of Medical Service at
Toronto Military Hospital. With an Introduction by Dr. C.D. Parfitt. The
Macmillan Company of Canada Limited 1941.

   xiv, 217, [1] pp.; 220 × 140 mm.
   Revised in 1947 (see 1141).

909.   HUXLEY, Aldous

Grey Eminence: A Study in Religion and Politics. By Aldous Huxley. 1941.
Toronto: The Macmillan Company Of Canada Limited, At St. Martin's
House.

   viii, 278, [2] pp.; 205 × 133 mm.

910.   IRWIN, Margaret

The Gay Galliard: The Love Story of Mary, Queen of Scots. By Margaret
Irwin. Toronto: The Macmillan Company of Canada Limited, at St. Martin's House 1941.

   viii, 423, [1] pp.; 205 × 134 mm.

911. KING, W.L. Mackenzie

Canada at Britain's Side. By The Right Honourable W.L. Mackenzie King, M.P. Toronto: The Macmillan Company of Canada Limited 1941.

xii, 332 pp.; 218 × 139 mm.

912. MACBETH, John Douglas

Somewhere in England: War Letters of a Canadian Officer on Overseas Service. By John Douglas Macbeth. Toronto: The Macmillan Company of Canada Limited 1941.

32 pp.; 178 × 120 mm.
Issued in paper.
Macmillan War Pamphlets (Canadian Series).

913. MacDERMOT, H.E.

Maude Abbott: A Memoir. By H.E. MacDermot, M.D., F.R.C.P.(C). Toronto: The Macmillan Company of Canada Limited, at St. Martin's House 1941.

xiv, 264 pp.; 220 × 143 mm.

914. MACDONALD, J.F.

St. Martin's Classics, *Twenty-One Modern Essays*. Edited, With Preface and Notes by J.F. Macdonald, Department of English, University College, University of Toronto. Toronto: The Macmillan Company of Canada Limited, at St. Martin's House 1941.

xii, 132, [4] pp.; 170 × 110 mm.
St. Martin's Classics Series.

915. MacGOWAN, S.J.

Jouons! By S.J. MacGowan, Supervisor of French, Protestant Board of School Commissioners, Montreal and R.C. Amaron, Supervisor of French in the Protestant Schools of the Province of Quebec. Drawings by Anne Savage. Authorized for use in the Protestant Schools of the Province of Quebec. The Macmillan Company of Canada Limited 1941.

viii, 139, [1] pp.; 208 × 155 mm.
Revised in 1954 (see 1315 and 1316).

916. MARY ST. PAUL, Mother

From Desenzano to "The Pines": A Sketch of the history of the Ursulines of Ontario, With a brief history of the Order compiled from various sources. By Mother M. St. Paul, O.S.U. of the Ursuline Community of "The Pines", Chatham, Ontario, Canada. With Foreword by The Right Reverend A.P. Mahoney, D.P., Vicar General of the Diocese of London. Toronto: The Macmillan Company of Canada Limited 1941.

xviii, 387, [1] pp.; 225 × 140 mm.

917.   McCOWAN, Daniel

A Naturalist in Canada. By Dan McCowan, F.Z.S. Illustrated from Photographs by the Author. Frontispiece by Carl Rungius. Sketches by Bruce Horsfall. Toronto: The Macmillan Company of Canada Limited 1941.

xiv, 284 pp.; 220 × 140 mm.
Enlarged edition published in 1946. Reprinted in 1948 (see 1193).

918.   MITCHELL, G.D.

Soldier in Battle. By Capt. G.D. Mitchell, M.C., D.C.M., Author of *Backs to the Wall* and *The Awakening.* Canadian Edition. Toronto: The Macmillan Company of Canada Limited 1941.

174 pp.; 135 × 103 mm.

919.   MITCHELL, John

The Yellow Briar: A Story of the Irish on the Canadian Countryside. By Patrick Slater [pseud.]. Toronto: The Macmillan Company of Canada Limited 1941.

[10], 293, [1] pp.; 205 × 135 mm.
Reprinted in 1945 and 1951. First paperback edition published in 1963. A school edition was published in 1966 (see 1796). Another edition, with an account of the author by Dorothy Bishop, was published in 1970 (see 2071).

920.   PLUMPTRE, A.F.W.

Mobilizing Canada's Resources For War. By A.F.W. Plumptre. Toronto: The Macmillan Company of Canada Limited 1941.

xxiv, 306 pp.; 218 × 140 mm.

921.   PRATT, E.J.

Dunkirk. E.J. Pratt. Toronto: The Macmillan Company of Canada Limited 1941.

[2], 13, [1] pp.; 215 × 135 mm.
Issued in an envelope. A special edition of 300 numbered copies in cloth was issued at Christmas, 1941, "for Messrs. Johnston, Everson & Charlesworth."

922.   PRATT, E.J.

St. Martin's Classics, *Heroic Tales in Verse.* Edited, With Preface and Notes By E.J. Pratt, Department of English, Victoria College, University of Toronto. Toronto: The Macmillan Company of Canada Limited, at St. Martin's House 1941.

xvi, 217, [3] pp.; 170 × 110 mm.
St. Martin's Classics Series.

923.   PRIESTLEY, J.B.

Postscripts. By J.B. Priestley. Toronto: The Macmillan Company Of Canada Limited, At St. Martin's House, 1941.

viii, 100 pp.; 190 × 128 mm.

924.   SILCOX, Claris Edwin

The War and Religion. By Claris Edwin Silcox. Toronto: The Macmillan
Company of Canada Limited 1941.

>   30 pp.; 178 × 120 mm.
>   Issued in paper.
>   Macmillan War Pamphlets (Canadian Series).

925.   SINCLAIR, Upton

Between Two Worlds. Upton Sinclair. Toronto: The Macmillan Company Of
Canada Limited, At St. Martin's House, 1941.

>   x, 859, [3] pp.; 221 × 146 mm.

926.   SMITH, I. Norman

The British Commonwealth Air Training Plan. By I. Norman Smith. Toronto:
The Macmillan Company of Canada Limited 1941.

>   [4], 28 pp.; 210 × 135 mm.
>   Issued in paper.
>   Macmillan War Pamphlets Series.

927.   STRANGE, Harry

Never a Dull Moment. By Harry and Kathleen Strange. [Quotations]. Toronto: The Macmillan Company of Canada Limited 1941.

>   x, 373, [1] pp.; 220 × 140 mm.

928.   STRANGE, William

Into the Blitz: A British Journey. By William Strange. With a Foreword by
the Honourable Angus L. Macdonald, Minister of Defence for Naval Services. Toronto: The Macmillan Company of Canada Limited 1941.

>   xvi, 318 pp.; 210 × 135 mm.

929.   *Voices of Victory: Representative Peotry of Canada in War-time*. Toronto:
The Macmillan Company of Canada Limited 1941.

>   xiv, 97, [1] pp.; 220 × 140 mm.
>   Second edition published in 1942 (see 948).

930.   WALLING, S.A.

Aircraft Mathematics. By S.A. Walling, Senior Master, R.N. (Ret.) and J.C.
Hill, B.A.(Cantab.), Educational Department, Cambridge University Press.
Toronto: The Macmillan Company of Canada Limited 1941.

>   189, [1] pp.; 195 × 126 mm.

931.   WAVELL, Archibald

Generals and Generalship. The Lees Knowles Lectures delivered at Trinity
College, Cambridge in 1939 by General Sir Archibald Wavell. With a
foreword by General Sir John Dill, Chief of the Imperial General Staff.
Toronto: The Macmillan Company of Canada Limited 1941.

>   [4], 27, [1] pp.; 213 × 135 mm.
>   Issued in paper.
>   Macmillan War Pamphlets Series.

932.   WILLIS, John

Studies of the Institute of Public Affairs at Dalhousie University, *Canadian Boards at Work*. By D.W. Buchanan, J.A. Corry, T. Norman Dean, George Farquhar, Jacob Finkelman, S.J. Mclean, R.B. Whitehead, E.F. Whitmore, [and] R.L. Winton. Edited by John Willis, Dalhousie University. Toronto: The Macmillan Company of Canada Limited, at St. Martin's House 1941.

xl, 190 pp.; 220 × 140 mm.
Dalhousie University Institute of Public Affairs Series.

933.   WOODSWORTH, Charles J.

Canada and the Orient: A Study in International Relations. By Charles J. Woodsworth, B.A., Ph.D., (Econ. London). Issued under the auspices of The Canadian Institute of International Affairs. Toronto: The Macmillan Company of Canada Limited 1941.

xiv, 321, [1] pp.; 220 × 140 mm.

1942

934.   BARTLETT, E.H.

The Royal Canadian Navy. By E.H. Bartlett, Lieutenant, R.C.N.V.R. With an Introduction by The Honourable Angus L. Macdonald, Minister of National Defence for Naval Services. Toronto: The Macmillan Company of Canada Limited 1942.

30 pp.; 210 × 138 mm.
Issued in paper.
Macmillan War Pamphlets (Canadian Series).

935.   BUCK, Pearl S.

Dragon Seed. By Pearl S. Buck. Toronto: The Macmillan Company of Canada Limited 1942.

[6], 378 pp.; 210 × 140 mm.

936.   CANBY, Henry Seidel

Junior High School English: First And Second Years. Henry Seidel Canby, Olive I. Carter [and] Helen Louise Miller. Canadian Abridgement by Arthur S. Robinson [and] Harry M. Grant. Authorized by the Department of Education for New Brunswick. Toronto: The Macmillan Company of Canada Limited 1942.

xx, 481, [1] pp.; 204 × 135 mm.

937.   CASH, Gwen

A Million Miles From Ottawa. By Gwen Cash. Author of *I Like British Columbia*. Toronto: The Macmillan Company of Canada Limited 1942.

xii, 152 pp.; 200 × 130 mm.

938.   COULTER, John

[Cover-title:] *These Are The Words Of Transit Through Fire*. Written By John
Coulter For Music By Healey Willan [etc.]. Format and lay-out designed by
John Coulter and Published by The Macmillan Company of Canada Limited.

[8] pp.; 310 × 224 mm.
Issued in paper. Imprint on p. [2].

939.   [Cover-title:] *Doctor's Simplex System*. The Macmillan Company of
Canada, Limited Toronto.

[Unpaginated ledger]; 310 × 260 mm.
Issued in card-cover.

940.   FINNIE, Richard

Canada Moves North. By Richard Finnie, Author of *Lure of the North*.
Illustrated. 1942. Toronto: The Macmillan Company of Canada Limited, At
St. Martin's House.

xii, 227, [1] pp.; 220 × 148 mm.
Revised edition published in 1948 (see 1174).

941.   GRAYSON, Ethel Kirk

Fires in the Vine. By Ethel Kirk Grayson. Toronto: The Macmillan Company
of Canada Limited 1942.

[12], 497, [1] pp.; 208 × 139 mm.

942.   HALLACK, Cecily

La Confession et la Communion des Touts-Petits. Arrangement de Cecily Hallack. Illustrations de Dom Pedro Subercaseaux-Errazuriz, O.S.B. Toronto:
The Macmillan Company of Canada Limited at St. Martin's House | Quebec:
Louis-Alexandre Belisle, 4, Rue St. Jacques. 1942.

28 pp.; 178 × 130 mm.
Issued in paper.

943.   HAMILTON, T. Glen

*Intention and Survival: Psychical Research Studies and the Bearing of Inten-
tional Actions by Trance Personalities on the Problem of Human Survival*. By T.
Glen Hamilton, M.D., F.A.C.S. Edited by J.D. Hamilton, M.A. Toronto:
The Macmillan Company of Canada Limited 1942.

xx, 292 pp.; 210 × 140 mm.

944.   HARDY, W.G.

W.G. Hardy, *All the Trumpets Sounded: A novel based on the life of Moses*. The
Macmillan Company of Canada Limited Toronto 1942.

[8], 501, [1] pp.; 208 × 140 mm.

945.   HILTON, James

James Hilton, *Random Harvest*. Toronto: The Macmillan Company Of
Canada Limited, 1942.

[6], 326, [2] pp.; 209 × 140 mm.
Reprinted in 1942 and 1943.

946.   HOOD, Robert Allison

The Case of Kinnear. By Robert Allison Hood, Author of *The Chivalry of Keith Leicester*, *The Quest of Alistair*, etc. Toronto: The Macmillan Company of Canada Limited 1942.

x, 329, [1] pp.; 202 × 138 mm.

947.   HUMPHREY, John P.

The Inter-American System: A Canadian View. By John P. Humphrey, B.Com., B.A., B.C.L., Associate Professor of Law, McGill University, formerly Carnegie Fellow in International Law. Issued under the auspices of The Canadian Institute of International Affairs. Toronto: The Macmillan Company of Canada Limited 1942.

xiv, 329, [1] pp.; 220 × 140 mm.

948.   KING, Amabel

Voices of Victory: Representative Poetry of Canada in Wartime. Compiled by Amabel King. Donated to the Imperial Order Daughters of the Empire in aid of their work. Toronto: The Macmillan Company of Canada Limited 1942.

xiv, 94 pp.; 217 × 138 mm.
First published in 1941 (see 929).

949.   KIPLING, Rudyard

A Choice of Kipling's Verse. Made by T.S. Eliot. With an essay on Rudyard Kipling. Toronto: The Macmillan Company of Canada Limited, at St. Martin's House 1942.

306 pp.; 205 × 132 mm.

950.   KNIGHT, Vera

Air Raid Precautions for Canada. Vera Knight. Illustrations by Margot Bodwell and J.R. Sandham. Toronto: The Macmillan Company of Canada Limited 1942.

[6], 76 pp.; 160 × 105 mm.

951.   MacGOWAN, S.J.

Avançons. By S.J. MacGowan, Supervisor of French, Protestant Board of School Commissioners, Montreal, R.C. Amaron, Supervisor of French in the Protestant Schools of the Province of Quebec and Evelyn M. Eaton, Assistant Supervisor of French, Protestant Board of School Commissioners, Montreal. Drawings by Anne Savage. Authorized for use in the Protestant Schools of the Province of Quebec. Toronto: The Macmillan Company of Canada Limited 1942.

xii, 208 pp.; 208 × 154 mm.
Revised in 1950 (see 1224). Revised in two books in 1961 and 1962 (see 1525 and 1567).

952.   McDOWELL, Franklin Davey

La Route de Champlain. (Traduction de "The Champlain Road" publié originairement en anglais). Par Franklin Davey McDowell. Traduit de l'anglais par Georges Panneton, S.A.C.E. de Paris. Toronto: The Macmillan

Company of Canada Limited, at St. Martin's House | Quebec: Louis-Alexandre Belisle, Editeur, 4 Rue St.-Jacques.

xx, 492 pp.; 208 × 144 mm.
First published in English in 1939 (see 847). A Huronian edition was published in 1949 (see 1204). Issued in paper.

953.   SHARMAN, Lyon

Town and Forest. By Lyon Sharman, Author of *The Sea-Wall and Other Verse, A Somersault to Love: A Comedy in One Act, Sun Yat-Sen: His Life and Its Meaning*. Toronto: The Macmillan Company of Canada Limited 1942.

73, [1] pp.; 150 × 115 mm.
Issued in paper.

954.   SONET, Édouard

Veille D'Examen. Fantaisie en un acte, jouée pour la première fois par les étudiants de l'Université d'Alberta, à l'occasion d'une réunion des membres du Club France-Canada et du Cercle francais, le 21 Mars 1937 à Edmonton, Alberta, Canada. By E. Sonet. Cette fantaisie a été écrite en mémoire des heureux jours où l'humour de mes deux amis Douglas Killam et Robert Gordon faisait la joie de leurs collègues de l'Université d'Alberta. Toronto: The Macmillan Company Of Canada Limited 1942.

[4], 28 pp.; 188 × 125 mm.
Issued in cloth and paper.

955.   STRUTHER, Jan

Mrs. Miniver. By Jan Struther. Toronto: The Macmillan Company of Canada Limited 1942.

vi, 213, [1] pp.; 190 × 125 mm.

956.   WALES, Julia Grace

Democracy Needs Education. Julia Grace Wales, Ph.D. Macmillan.

[10], 107, [1] pp.; 175 × 110 mm.

957.   WHITTON, Charlotte

Canadian Women in the War Effort. By Charlotte Whitton. Toronto: The Macmillan Company of Canada Limited 1942.

[6], 57, [1] pp.; 212 × 137 mm.
Issued in paper.
Macmillan War Pamphlets (Canadian Series).

958.   WOLFENDEN, Hugh H.

The Fundamental Principles of Mathematical Statistics: With Special Reference to the Requirements of Actuaries and Vital Statisticians and An Outline of a Course in Graduation. By Hugh H. Wolfenden, Fellow of the Institute of Actuaries, Great Britain, Fellow of the Actuarial Society of America, Fellow of the American Institute of Actuaries, Fellow of the Royal Statistical Society. Published for the Actuarial Society of America, New York, By The Macmillan Company of Canada Limited Toronto 1942.

xviii, 379, [1] pp.; 220 × 144 mm.

1943

959. BARBEAU, Marius

The Indian Speaks. By Marius Barbeau and Grace Melvin. 1943. The Caxton
Printers, Ltd., Caldwell, Idaho, and The Macmillan Company of Canada,
Ltd., Toronto, Ontario.

   117, [1] pp.; 230 × 155 mm.

960. BARTLETT, Vernon

Tomorrow Always Comes. By Vernon Bartlett. Toronto: The Macmillan
Company of Canada Limited 1943.

   127, [1] pp.; 194 × 124 mm.

961. BRADY, Alexander

*Canada After The War: Studies in Political, Social and Economic Policies For
Post-War Canada*. Edited by Alexander Brady, Professor of Political
Economy, University of Toronto, and F.R. Scott, Professor of Civil Law,
McGill University. Issued under the auspices of The Canadian Institute of
International Affairs. Toronto: The Macmillan Company of Canada Li-
mited 1943.

   xii, 348 pp.; 220 × 140 mm.

962. BROWN, Audrey Alexandra

Challenge To Time And Death. By Audrey Alexandra Brown, Author of *A
Dryad in Nanaimo*, *The Tree of Resurrection*, and *The Log of a Lame Duck*.
Toronto: The Macmillan Company of Canada Limited 1943.

   viii, 55, [1] pp.; 235 × 155 mm.

963. BRYANT, Arthur

Dunkirk (A Memorial). By Arthur Bryant. All profits are to be devoted to the
Daily Sketch War Relief Fund. Toronto: The Macmillan Company of
Canada Limited 1943.

   16 pp.; 180 × 120 mm.
   Issued in paper.

964. BUCK, Pearl S.

The Promise. By Pearl S. Buck. Toronto: The Macmillan Company of
Canada Limited 1943.

   [6], 248 pp.; 220 × 142 mm.

965. CHALMERS, Harvey

West To The Setting Sun. By Harvey Chalmers. Toronto: The Macmillan
Company of Canada Limited 1943.

   xii, 362 pp.; 220 × 145 mm.
   Reprinted in 1944, and in 1946 with additions.

966. CROSS, Austin F.

The People's Mouths. By Austin F. Cross. [Quotation]. Toronto: The Macmillan Company of Canada Limited 1943.

[8], 171, [1] pp.; 206 × 138 mm.

967. ENGLAND, Robert

Discharged: A Commentary on Civil Re-establishment of Veterans in Canada. By Robert England, M.C., M.A. Toronto: The Macmillan Company of Canada Limited 1943.

xxii, 468 pp.; 232 × 150 mm.
A supplement was published in 1944 (see 1000).

968. GODSELL, Philip H.

Arctic Trader: The Account of Twenty Years With the Hudson's Bay Company. By Philip H. Godsell, F.R.G.S., Former Field Officer, Hudson's Bay Company. Author of "Famous Forts of Fur Land". Illustrated. Toronto: The Macmillan Company of Canada Limited 1943.

xii, 322 pp.; 220 × 140 mm.
Reprinted frequently.

969. GOULD, Mona

Tasting the Earth. Mona Gould. The Macmillan Company of Canada Limited Toronto 1943.

[12], 44 pp.; 214 × 134 mm.

970. GUERNSEY, Isabel Russell

Free Trip to Berlin. By Isabel Russell Guernsey. Toronto: The Macmillan Company of Canada Limited 1943.

xii, 230 pp.; 204 × 137 mm.

971. HENDERSON, Velyien E.

Materia Medica. Velyien E. Henderson, M.A., M.B., F.R.S.C., F.R.C.P. and Winnifred L. Chute, B.A., Reg.N. Toronto: The Macmillan Company of Canada Limited 1943.

xii, 160 pp.; 203 × 133 mm.

972. HILTON, James

Lost Horizon. By James Hilton. Toronto: The Macmillan Company of Canada Limited 1943.

[6], 237, [1] pp.; 170 × 106 mm.
School edition published in 1965 (see 1730).

973. HUXLEY, Aldous

The Art of Seeing. By Aldous Huxley. 1943. Toronto: The Macmillan Company Of Canada Limited, At St. Martin's House.

viii, 143, [1] pp.; 194 × 127 mm.

974.   KING, Amabel

The New Crusaders and Other Poems. By Amabel King. Original Drawings by
Wilson MacDonald. Toronto: The Macmillan Company of Canada Limited
1943.

xii, 66 pp.; 203 × 160 mm.

975.   KNOX, Olive E.

By Paddle and Saddle. By Olive Elsie Knox. Toronto: The Macmillan
Company of Canada Limited 1943.

xii, 270 pp.; 203 × 136 mm.
Reprinted in 1946.

976.   MacDONALD, Wilson

Greater Poems of the Bible. Metrical Versions, Biblical Forms and Original
Poems. By Wilson MacDonald. Toronto: The Macmillan Company of
Canada Limited 1943.

xxvi, 277, [1] pp.; 235 × 155 mm.

977.   MacINTYRE, Mary

Skippy and Others. By Mary MacIntyre. Illustrations by Georgette
Berckmans. Toronto: The Macmillan Company of Canada Limited 1943.

[8], 131, [1] pp.; 198 × 148 mm.
Reprinted in 1944.

978.   McDOWELL, Franklin Davey

Forges of Freedom. Franklin Davey McDowell. Illustrations by Franklin
Carmichael, R.C.A., O.S.A. Toronto: The Macmillan Company of Canada
Limited 1943.

xvi, 542 pp.; 233 × 154 mm.

979.   MILLER, Norman

Plane Trigonometry and Statics. By Norman Miller, Professor of Mathematics
in Queen's University, Kingston, And Robert E.K. Rourke, Associate
Headmaster and Instructor in Mathematics at Pickering College, Newmarket. Toronto: The Macmillan Company of Canada Limited 1943.

xiv, 427, [1] pp.; 205 × 140 mm.

980.   MURCH, N.L.

Continuous Prose Exercises Based on Louis Hémon's Maria Chapdelaine.
Prepared by N.L. Murch, University of Toronto Schools. Toronto: The
Macmillan Company of Canada Limited 1943.

[4], 27, [1] pp.; 162 × 114 mm.
Issued in paper.

981. NEWNHAM, J.A.
By Water and the Word: A Transcription of the Diary of the Right Reverend J.A. Newnham, M.A., D.D., LL.D. While Plying the Waters and Ice-Fields of Northern Canada in the Diocese of Moosonee. By Mrs. F.P. Shearwood. Toronto: The Macmillan Company of Canada Limited 1943.

xii, 215, [1] pp.; 195 × 138 mm.

982. PRATT, E.J.
Still Life and Other Verse. E.J. Pratt. Toronto: The Macmillan Company of Canada Limited 1943.

[8], 40 pp.; 217 × 137 mm.

983. PRIESTLEY, J.B.
Daylight on Saturday: A Novel About an Aircraft Factory. By J.B. Priestley. Toronto: The Macmillan Company of Canada Limited 1943.

vi, 306 pp.; 210 × 140 mm.
Reprinted in 1943 and 1944.

984. SANSOM, Clive
Speech Rhymes: Book 1. Edited by Clive Sansom. Toronto: The Macmillan Company of Canada Limited 1943.

48 pp.; 170 × 122 mm.
Issued in paper.

985. SAUNDERS, Hilary St. George
Combined Operations: The Official Story of the Commandos. With a Foreword by Vice-Admiral Lord Louis Mountbatten, Chief of Combined Operations. 1943. Toronto: The Macmillan Company of Canada Limited, at St. Martin's House.

xvi, 155, [1] pp.; 205 × 135 mm.

986. SYMONS, Harry
Friendship. By Harry Symons. [Quotation]. Toronto: The Macmillan Company of Canada Limited 1943.

xx, 265, [1] pp.; 225 × 165 mm.

987. WATT, Frederick B.
Who Dare To Live. By Frederick B. Watt, Lt.-Cmdr., R.C.N.V.R. Toronto: The Macmillan Company of Canada Limited 1943.

[8], 68 pp.; 220 × 140 mm.
Reprinted in 1943 (twice) and 1944.

988. WHITTON, Charlotte
The Dawn of Ampler Life. By Charlotte Whitton, C.B.E. Toronto: The Macmillan Company of Canada Limited 1943.

vi, 154 pp.; 225 × 148 mm.

1944

989. BARBEAU, Marius
Mountain Cloud. By Marius Barbeau. Illustrations by Thoreau MacDonald.
1944. The Caxton Printers, Ltd., Caldwell, Idaho, And The Macmillan
Company of Canada Ltd. Toronto.
   300 pp.; 235 × 155 mm.

990. BARTHOLOMEW, Wallace Edgar
The Business Man's English: Spoken and Written. By Wallace Edgar Bar-
tholomew, Formerly Specialist in Commercial Education, New York State
Education Department, And Floyd Hurlbut, Superintendent of Schools,
Bay Shore N.Y. Revised Edition. Toronto: The Macmillan Company of
Canada Limited 1944.
   x, 357, [1] pp.; 183 × 130 mm.
   Reprinted in 1949.

991. BASKINE, Gertrude
Hitch-hiking the Alaska Highway. By Gertrude Baskine, M.A., Fellow of
R.C.G.S., (First woman to receive a military permit to cover overland the
Alaska Military Highway while it was still under construction). Toronto:
The Macmillan Company of Canada Limited 1944.
   x, 317, [1] pp.; 215 × 145 mm.

992. BISHOP, William A.
Winged Peace. By Air Marshal William A. Bishop, Royal Canadian Air
Force, V.C., C.B., D.S.O. and Bar, M.C., D.F.C., Legion of Honour, Croix
de Guerre. Toronto: The Macmillan Company of Canada Limited 1944.
   xxii, 175, [1] pp.; 220 × 150 mm.

993. BURPEE, Lawrence J.
The Discovery of Canada. By Lawrence J. Burpee. Drawn end papers by
James Sim. Toronto: The Macmillan Company of Canada Limited 1944.
   x, 280 pp.; 210 × 135 mm.
   Reprinted in 1946 and 1948.

994. CARR, William Guy
Checkmate In The North: The Axis Planned to Invade America. By William
Guy Carr, LT.-CMDR., R.C.N.R. Toronto: The Macmillan Company of
Canada Limited 1944.
   [12], 304 pp.; 217 × 148 mm.

995. CEKOTA, A.
The Battle of Home: Some Problems of Industrial Community. By A. Cekota.
Illustrated by Joseph Lenhard. Toronto: The Macmillan Company of
Canada Limited 1944.
   xvi, 373, [1] pp.; 234 × 155 mm.

996. COULTER, John

Deirdre of the Sorrows. An ancient and noble tale retold by John Coulter for music by Healey Willan. Toronto: The Macmillan Company of Canada Limited 1944.

    xii, 72 pp.; 215 × 138 mm.
    Revised in 1965 under the title *Deirdre* (see 1710).

997. DANIELS, E.G.

Dominion Language Series: Book Two. By E.G. Daniels, B.A., Inspector of Schools, New Westminster, B.C., T.R. Hall, B.A., Inspector of Schools, Kelowna, B.C., A.F. Matthews, M.A., Inspector of Schools, Kamloops, B.C. and H.H. Mackenzie, B.A., Inspector of Schools, Vancouver, B.C. Authorized by the Minister of Education for British Columbia for Use in Grades five and six. Toronto: The Macmillan Company of Canada Limited, at St. Martin's House 1944.

    xviii, 310 pp.; 195 × 135 mm.
    First published in 1932. Reprinted frequently. Earlier printings not located.
    Dominion Language Series.

998. DE LA ROCHE, Mazo

The Building of Jalna. By Mazo De La Roche. Toronto: The Macmillan Company of Canada Limited 1944.

    [10], 381, [1] pp.; 205 × 138 mm.
    Reprinted in 1945. New edition published in 1948 (see 1168).

999. *Dixon's Victory Atlas: The World at War...1939-1945*. A Canadian Atlas from a Canadian point of view. 19 pages. An essential Guide to Current Events. 14 up-to-date War maps in 8 colours, covering all war areas in full detail. 5 year war record, September 1st 1939 to June 1st 1944 with introduction and conclusion. Useful information, well indexed, up-to-the minute. The Macmillan Company of Canada Limited, 70 Bond Street, Toronto 2, Ontario. For Home, Office and Classroom Reference.

    19, [1] pp.; 277 × 200 mm.

1000. ENGLAND, Robert

Canadian Re-establishment Benefits for Veterans. Supplement to Discharged: A Commentary on Civil Re-establishment of Veterans in Canada. By Robert England. Toronto: The Macmillan Company of Canada Limited 1944.

    [8], 17, [3] pp.; 225 × 138 mm.
    Issued in paper.

1001. GROSSMAN, Vladimir

The Pan-Germanic Web: Remaking Europe. By Vladimir Grossman. Toronto: The Macmillan Company of Canada Limited 1944.

    x, 179, [1] pp.; 197 × 130 mm.

1002.   GROVE, Frederick Philip
The Master of the Mill. By Frederick Philip Grove. Toronto: The Macmillan
Company of Canada Limited 1944.
   [8], 393, [1] pp.; 220 × 145 mm.
   Reprinted in 1945.

1003.   JORGENS, Norma
Jack and Jill. Designed by Norma Jorgens. [On back cover:] The Macmillan
Company of Canada Limited Copyright 1944.
   [10] pp.; 170 × 145 mm.

1004.   JORGENS, Norma
Little Bo-Peep. Designed by Norma Jorgens. [On back cover:] The Macmillan Company of Canada Limited Copyright 1944.
   [10] pp.; 170 × 145 mm.

1005.   JORGENS, Norma
Little Miss Muffet. Designed by Norma Jorgens. [On back cover:] The
Macmillan Company of Canada Limited Copyright 1944.
   [10] pp.; 170 × 145 mm.

1006.   JORGENS, Norma
Old Mother Hubbard. Designed by Norma Jorgens. [On back cover:] The
Macmillan Company of Canada Limited Copyright 1944.
   [10] pp.; 170 × 145 mm.

1007.   JORGENS, Norma
There Was a Crooked Man. Designed by Norma Jorgens. [On back cover:]
The Macmillan Company of Canada Limited Copyright 1944.
   [10] pp.; 170 × 145 mm.

1008.   JORGENS, Norma
Three Little Kittens. Designed by Norma Jorgens. [On back cover:] The
Macmillan Company of Canada Limited Copyright 1944.
   [10] pp.; 170 × 145 mm.

1009.   KING, W.L. Mackenzie
Canada and the Fight for Freedom. By The Right Honourable W.L. Mackenzie King, M.P. Toronto: The Macmillan Company of Canada Limited 1944.
   xxvi, 326 pp.; 215 × 140 mm.

1010.   LINKLATER, Eric
The Wind on The Moon: A Story for Children. By Eric Linklater. Nicholas
Bentley drew the pictures. Toronto: The Macmillan Company of Canada
Limited, at St. Martin's House 1944.
   [6], 363, [1] pp.; 190 × 122 mm.

1011. LIVINGSTONE, Richard

On Education. By Sir Richard Livingstone, President of Corpus Christi College, Oxford. Containing two books previously published separately, *The Future in Education* and *Education For a World Adrift*. With a Foreword by Virginia C. Gildersleeve, Dean of Barnard College. Toronto: The Macmillan Company of Canada Limited 1944.

x, 158 pp.; 150 × 110 mm.

1012. LUDWIG, Emil

Mackenzie King: A Portrait Sketch. By Emil Ludwig. Illustrated. Toronto: The Macmillan Company of Canada Limited 1944.

[4], 62 pp.; 212 × 133 mm.

1013. McLEOD, Carroll

Dat H'ampire H'air Train Plan. By Squadron Leader Carroll McLeod. Illustrations by Flying Officer H. Rickard. Toronto: The Macmillan Company of Canada Limited 1944.

85, [1] pp.; 283 × 216 mm.

1014. McRAE, D.G.W.

The Arts and Crafts of Canada. By D.G.W. McRae, B.Arch., M.F.A., A.R.I.B.A., M.R.A.I.C. Toronto: The Macmillan Company of Canada Limited 1944.

80 pp.; 275 × 215 mm.

1015. MYERSON, M.H.

Germany's War Crimes and Punishment: The Problem of Individual and Collective Criminality. By M.H. Myerson, "Flying Officer, R.C.A.F." (A.C.C.). Toronto: The Macmillan Company of Canada Limited 1944.

xiv, 272 pp.; 200 × 135 mm.

1016. PAGE, Patricia Kathleen

The Sun and The Moon. By Judith Cape [pseud.]. Toronto: The Macmillan Company of Canada Limited 1944.

[10], 200 pp.; 205 × 135 mm.

1017. PARTRIDGE, J.A.

Natural Science Through the Seasons: 100 Teaching Units. By J.A. Partridge, Formerly Principal, Provincial Normal School, North Bay, Ontario. Toronto: The Macmillan Company of Canada Limited 1944.

xxii, 522 pp.; 230 × 155 mm.
Reprinted in 1955.

1018. PRATT, E.J.

Collected Poems. By E.J. Pratt. Toronto: The Macmillan Company of Canada Limited 1944.

xii, 314 pp.; 220 × 145 mm.
Reprinted in 1946. Revised and enlarged edition published in 1958 (see 1443).

1019. RICKARD, T.A.

The Romance of Mining. By T.A. Rickard, A.R.S.M., D.Sc. Toronto: The
Macmillan Company of Canada Limited 1944.

[12], 450 pp.; 218 × 140 mm.
Reprinted in 1945 and 1947.

1020. ROBERTSON, E. Arnot

The Sign Post. By E. Arnot Robertson. Toronto: The Macmillan Company
of Canada Limited 1944.

313, [1] pp.; 205 × 135 mm.

1021. RUSSELL, H.J.

The Competent Secretary: Canadian Commercial Correspondence. By H.J.
Russell, F.C.I., A.C.I.S., Member of the Royal Society of Teachers. For
Stenographers, Correspondents, Civil Service Candidates and Executives.
Toronto: The Macmillan Company of Canada Limited 1944.

xii, 257, [1] pp.; 188 × 125 mm.
First published in 1915 under the title *Canadian Commercial Correspondence and
Business Training* (see 93). Revised in 1923 (see 210A).

1022. SCHULL, Joseph

I, Jones, Soldier. By Joseph Schull. Toronto: The Macmillan Company of
Canada Limited 1944.

[8], 62 pp.; 192 × 130 mm.

1023. SCOTT, F.R.

The Constitution and the Post-War World. By F.R. Scott, Professor of Civil
Law, McGill University. Issued under the auspices of The Canadian Institute
of International Affairs. Toronto: The Macmillan Company of Canada
Limited 1944.

[2], 28 pp.; 197 × 135 mm.
Issued in paper.

1024. WEATHERBY, Hugh

Tales the Totems Tell. By Hugh Weatherby. Illustrations by the Author.
Toronto: The Macmillan Company of Canada Limited 1944.

xii, 96 pp.; 210 × 155 mm.
Reprinted frequently.

1025. WERFEL, Franz

Franz Werfel, *The Song of Bernadette*. Translated by Ludwig Lewisohn.
Toronto: The Macmillan Company of Canada Limited 1944.

575, [1] pp.; 197 × 143 mm.

1026. WINSOR, Kathleen

Forever Amber. By Kathleen Winsor. Toronto: The Macmillan Company Of
Canada Limited, 1944.

[4], 972 pp.; 219 × 146 mm.

1027. WOOD, Alan

The Falaise Road. By Alan Wood. A Hurricane Book. The Macmillan Company of Canada Limited, Toronto 1944.

64 pp.; 185 × 125 mm.
Hurricane Books Series.

1028. WOOLLCOTT, Alexander

The Letters of Alexander Woollcott. Edited by Beatrice Kaufman and Joseph Hennessey. Toronto: The Macmillan Company of Canada Limited 1944.

xxvi, 410 pp.; 215 × 140 mm.

1945

1029. ALLEN, Erastus S.

Craftsmen's Library 24, *Wood Forms*. Erastus S. Allen. Written in Basic English. Edited by Ivan H. Crowell, Director of Handicrafts, McGill University, Macdonald College, P.Q. Macmillan.

16 pp.; 170 × 120 mm.
Issued in paper.
Craftsmen's Library.

1030. ASHLEY, C.A.

Corporation Finance. By C.A. Ashley, Professor of Accounting in the University of Toronto. Toronto: The Macmillan Company of Canada Limited 1945.

[10], 62, [2] pp.; 214 × 138 mm.
Revised in 1947 (see 1124). Second revision published in 1956 (see 1360). Issued in paper.

1031. *L'assurance sur la vie: Un manuel Canadien*. Toronto: The Macmillan Company of Canada Limited, 1945.

62 pp.; 208 × 135 mm.
Also published in English (see 1075). Issued in paper.

1032. AUSTIN, Peggy Johannsen

Craftsmen's Library 2, *Linoleum Block Printing*. Peggy Johannsen Austin. Edited by Ivan H. Crowell, Director of Handicrafts, McGill University, Macdonald College, P.Q. Macmillan.

16 pp.; 170 × 120 mm.
Issued in paper.
Craftsmen's Library.

1033. BARNARD, Leslie Gordon

So Near is Grandeur. By Leslie Gordon Barnard. Toronto: The Macmillan Company of Canada Limited 1945.

207, [1] pp.; 230 × 165 mm.

1034. BEAUDIN, Irene

Craftsmen's Library 15, *Cord Weaving*. Irene Beaudin. Edited by Ivan H. Crowell, Director of Handicrafts, McGill University, Macdonald College, P.Q. Macmillan.

> 16 pp.; 170 × 120 mm.
> Issued in paper.
> Craftsmen's Library.

1035. BLACKSTONE, A.M.

Craftsmen's Library 30, *Carving and Painting Birds*. A.M. Blackstone. Edited by Ivan H. Crowell, Director of Handicrafts, Department of Industry and Reconstruction, Fredericton, N.B. Macmillan.

> 16 pp.; 170 × 120 mm.
> Issued in paper.
> Craftsmen's Library.

1036. BORDEN, Alice

Craftsmen's Library 29, *Hand Carding and Spinning of Wool*. Alice Borden. Edited by Ivan H. Crowell, Director of Handicrafts, Department of Industry and Reconstruction, Fredericton, N.B. Macmillan.

> 16 pp.; 170 × 120 mm.
> Issued in paper.
> Craftsmen's Library.

1037. BRADFORD, John L.

Craftsmen's Library 1, *Small Animal Sculpturing*. John L. Bradford. Edited by Ivan H. Crowell, Director of Handicrafts, McGill University, Macdonald College, P.Q. Macmillan.

> 16 pp.; 170 × 120 mm.
> This series originated as the Macdonald College Handicraft Series. Fifty-six pamphlets were proposed though fifteen never went to press. The pamphlets were not published consecutively and this accounts for the missing numbers in the series. Numbers 31-40, 42, 43, 46, 53, 54, and 56 were never published.
> Craftsmen's Library.

1038. BURTON, J.W.

Craftsmen's Library 17, *Juniper Root Carving*. J.W. Burton. Edited by Ivan H. Crowell, Director of Handicrafts, McGill University, Macdonald College, P.Q. Macmillan.

> 16 pp.; 170 × 120 mm.
> Issued in paper.
> Craftsmen's Library.

1039. BYNG, Evelyn (Moreton)

Up The Stream of Time. By Viscountess Byng of Vimy. [Quotation]. Toronto: The Macmillan Company of Canada Limited 1945.

> [10], 274 pp.; 210 × 135 mm.

1040.   CAPLING, Gordon W.

Craftsmen's Library 13, *Care and Sharpening of Handicraft Tools*. Gordon W. Capling. Edited by Ivan H. Crowell, Director of Handicrafts, McGill University, Macdonald College, P.Q. Macmillan.

  20 pp.; 170 × 120 mm.
  Issued in paper.
  Craftsmen's Library.

1041.   CHRISTIE, R.C.

Craftsmen's Library 45, *Building Duck-Hunting Blinds*. R.C. Christie. Edited by Ivan H. Crowell, Director of Industry and Reconstruction, Fredericton, N.B. Macmillan.

  14 pp.; 170 × 120 mm.
  Issued in paper.
  Craftsmen's Library.

1042.   CHRISTIE, R.C.

Craftsmen's Library 20, *Making Duck Decoys*. R.C. Christie. Edited by Ivan H. Crowell, Director of Handicrafts, McGill University, Macdonald College, P.Q. Macmillan.

  16 pp.; 170 × 120 mm.
  Issued in paper.
  Craftsmen's Library.

1043.   COX, Merle Evans

Craftsmen's Library 47, *Cork Work*. Mrs. Merle Evans Cox. Edited by Ivan H. Crowell, Director of Handicrafts, Department of Industry and Reconstruction, Fredericton, N.B. Macmillan.

  15, [1] pp.; 170 × 120 mm.
  Issued in paper.
  Craftsmen's Library.

1044.   CROWELL, Ivan H.

Craftsmen's Library 5, *Chip Carving*. Ivan H. Crowell. Edited by Ivan H. Crowell, Director of Handicrafts, McGill University, Macdonald College, P.Q. Macmillan.

  16 pp.; 170 × 120 mm.
  Issued in paper.
  Craftsmen's Library.

1045.   CROWELL, Ivan H.

Craftsmen's Library 11, *Design and Hook Your Own Rugs*. Ivan H. Crowell. Edited by Ivan H. Crowell, Director of Handicrafts, McGill University, Macdonald College, P.Q. Macmillan.

  16 pp.; 170 × 120 mm.
  Issued in paper.
  Craftsmen's Library.

1046.   CROWELL, Ivan H.

Craftsmen's Library 7, *Finger Weaving Part 1*. Ivan H. Crowell. Edited by Ivan H. Crowell, Director of Handicrafts, McGill University, Macdonald College, P.Q. Macmillan.

    16 pp.; 170 × 120 mm.
    Issued in paper.
    Craftsmen's Library.

1047.   CROWELL, Ivan H.

Craftsmen's Library 18, *Horn Craft*. Ivan H. Crowell. Edited by Ivan H. Crowell, Director of Handicrafts, McGill University, Macdonald College, P.Q. Macmillan.

    16 pp.; 170 × 120 mm.
    Issued in paper.
    Craftsmen's Library.

1048.   CROWELL, Ivan H.

Craftsmen's Library 14, *Leather Belts*. Ivan H. Crowell. Edited by Ivan H. Crowell, Director of Handicrafts, McGill University, Macdonald College, P.Q. Macmillan.

    16 pp.; 170 × 120 mm.
    Issued in paper.
    Craftsmen's Library.

1049.   CROWELL, Ivan H.

Craftsmen's Library 48, *Smart Buttons, Buckles and Novelty Fastenings in Leather*. Ivan H. Crowell. Edited by Ivan H. Crowell, Director of Handicrafts, Department of Industry and Reconstruction, Fredericton, N.B. Macmillan.

    20 pp.; 170 × 120 mm.
    Issued in paper.
    Craftsmen's Library.

1050.   CURRIE, A.W.

Economic Geography of Canada. By A.W. Currie, Dr. Com. Sc.(Harvard), Associate Professor of Commerce, University of British Columbia. Toronto: The Macmillan Company of Canada Limited 1945.

    xvi, 455, [1] pp.; 215 × 140 mm.
    Reprinted in 1947.

1051.   DAFOE, John W.

The Voice of Dafoe: A Selection of Editorials on Collective Security, 1931-1944. By John W. Dafoe, Editor-in-chief, "Winnipeg Free Press", 1903-1944. [Quotation]. Edited by W.L. Morton. Toronto: The Macmillan Company of Canada Limited 1945.

    xxviii, 293, [1] pp.; 220 × 150 mm.

1052.   DAVIDSON, Enid

Craftsmen's Library 4, *Inkle Loom Weaving*. Enid Davidson. Edited by Ivan H. Crowell, Director of Handicrafts, McGill University, Macdonald College, P.Q. Macmillan.

16 pp.; 170 × 120 mm.
Issued in paper.
Craftsmen's Library.

1053.   EDGAR, Mary S.

Wood-Fire and Candle-Light. Mary S. Edgar. Toronto: The Macmillan Company of Canada Limited 1945.

xii, 121, [1] pp.; 187 × 125 mm.

1054.   EMORY, Florence H.M.

Public Health Nursing in Canada: Principles and Practice. By Florence H.M. Emory, Associate Director, School of Nursing, University of Toronto. Toronto: The Macmillan Company of Canada Limited 1945.

xx, 554 pp.; 214 × 144 mm.
Revised in 1953 (see 1292).

1055.   GARRARD, E.H.

Craftsmen's Library 9, *Portraits and Landscapes in Fine Veneer Woods*. E.H. Garrard. Edited by Ivan H. Crowell, Director of Handicrafts, McGill University, Macdonald College, P.Q. Macmillan.

16 pp.; 170 × 120 mm.
Issued in paper.
Craftsmen's Library.

1056.   GATES, Arthur I.

Good Times on Our Street. Today's Work-Play Books. Gates, Huber, Peardon, [and] Salisbury. The Macmillan Company of Canada Ltd. 1945.

[8], 201, [1] pp.; 200 × 153 mm.
Work-Play Books Series.

1057.   GATES, Arthur I.

Tags and Twinkle. Today's Work-Play Books. Gates, Huber, Peardon, [and] Salisbury. The Macmillan Company of Canada Ltd. 1945.

[8], 154 pp.; 200 × 150 mm.
Work-Play Books Series.

1058.   GREENLEES, Stephen

Craftsmen's Library 19, *How to Tie Trout Flies*. Stephen Greenlees. Edited by Ivan H. Crowell, Director of Handicrafts, McGill University, Macdonald College, P.Q. Macmillan.

16 pp.; 170 × 120 mm.
Issued in paper.
Craftsmen's Library.

1059.   HARMER, Bertha

Textbook of the Principles and Practice of Nursing. By Bertha Harmer, R.N.,
A.M., Late Director of the School for Graduate Nurses, McGill University,
Montreal, Canada; Formerly Instructor in the Toronto General Hospital
School of Nursing, Toronto, Canada, the Vassar Training Camp, Vassar
College, New York, St. Luke's Hospital School of Nursing, New York City,
and Assistant Professor, Yale University School of Nursing; and Virginia
Henderson, R.N., A.M., Instructor in Nursing Education, Teachers Col-
lege, Columbia University, New York City, Formerly Instructor in the
Norfolk Protestant Hospital, Norfolk, Virginia, and the Strong Memorial
Hospital, Rochester, New York. Fourth Edition, Revised. Toronto: The
Macmillan Company of Canada Limited, 1945.

xii, 1047, [1] pp.; 215 × 138 mm.
Earlier editions not located.

1060.   HEAPS, Leo

Escape from Arnheim: A Canadian Among the Lost Paratroops. By Leo Heaps.
Toronto: The Macmillan Company of Canada Limited 1945.

[8], 159, [1] pp.; 215 × 140 mm.

1061.   HECHT, Ethel

Craftsmen's Library 28, *The Marionette Stage*. Ethel Hecht. Edited by Ivan
H. Crowell, Director of Industry and Reconstruction, Fredericton, N.B.
Macmillan.

15, [1] pp.; 170 × 120 mm.
Issued in paper.
Craftsmen's Library.

1062.   HECHT, Ethel

Craftsmen's Library 44, *Marionettes*. Ethel Hecht. Edited by Ivan H.
Crowell, Director of Handicrafts, Department of Industry and Reconstruction, Fredericton, N.B. Macmillan.

16 pp.; 170 × 120 mm.
Issued in paper.
Craftsmen's Library.

1063.   HILL, Marjorie

Craftsmen's Library 12, *Glove Making*. Marjorie Hill, B.A., B.A.Sc. Edited
by Ivan H. Crowell, Director of Handicrafts, McGill University, Macdonald
College, P.Q. Macmillan.

16 pp.; 170 × 120 mm.
Issued in paper.
Craftsmen's Library.

1064.   HILTON, James

James Hilton, *So Well Remembered*. Toronto: The Macmillan Company of
Canada Limited 1945.

[4], 309, [1] pp.; 198 × 140 mm.
Reprinted in 1945 (twice).

1065. HILTON, James

The Story of Dr. Wassell. By James Hilton. Toronto: The Macmillan Company of Canada Limited 1945.

    xiv, 153, [1] pp.; 200 × 140 mm.

1066. HURST, George L.

Craftsmen's Library 22, *Classical Wood Carving.* Rev. George L. Hurst. Edited by Ivan H. Crowell, Director of Handicrafts, McGill University, Macdonald College, P.Q. Macmillan.

    16 pp.; 170 × 120 mm.
    Issued in paper.
    Craftsmen's Library.

1067. KIRNER, Ann A.

Craftsmen's Library 21, *Braided and Interbraided Rugs.* Ann A. Kirner. Edited by Ivan H. Crowell, Director of Handicrafts, McGill University, Macdonald College, P.Q. Macmillan.

    16 pp.; 170 × 120 mm.
    Issued in paper.
    Craftsmen's Library.

1068. KNOX, Olive E.

How We Hear [and] *Sewing Seams With Steel.* By Olive E. Knox, B.A. Toronto: The Macmillan Company of Canada Limited 1945.

    [6], 63, [1] pp.; 175 × 110 mm.
    Issued in paper.
    Radio Plays Series.

1069. KNOX, Olive E.

Penicillin [and] *Fresh Water From the Sea.* By Olive E. Knox, B.A. Toronto: The Macmillan Company of Canada Limited 1945.

    [6], 61, [1] pp.; 175 × 110 mm.
    Issued in paper.
    Radio Plays Series.

1070. KNOX, Olive E.

Wheels and Friction [and]*Sulfa Drugs.* By Olive E. Knox, B.A. Toronto: The Macmillan Company of Canada Limited 1945.

    [6], 54 pp.; 175 × 110 mm.
    Issued in paper.
    Radio Plays Series.

1071. LAPIERRE, Charles J.

Craftsmen's Library 49,*Care and Repair of Fishing Reels and Rods.* Charles J. Lapierre. Edited by Ivan H. Crowell, Director of Handicrafts, Department of Industry and Reconstruction, Fredericton, N.B. Macmillan.

    16 pp.; 170 × 120 mm.
    Issued in paper.
    Craftsmen's Library.

1072. LAURIE, Margaret

Craftsmen's Library 23, *The Cradle or Box Loom*. Margaret Laurie. Edited by Ivan H. Crowell, Director of Handicrafts, McGill University, Macdonald College, P.Q. Macmillan.

16 pp.; 170 × 120 mm.
Issued in paper.
Craftsmen's Library.

1073. LEECHMAN, Douglas

Craftsmen's Library 25, *Cutting and Polishing Small Stones*. Douglas Leechman. Edited by Ivan H. Crowell, Director of Handicrafts, McGill University, Macdonald College, P.Q. Macmillan.

16 pp.; 170 × 120 mm.
Issued in paper.
Craftsmen's Library.

1074. LENT, D. Geneva

Craftsmen's Library 10, *It's Fun to do Cross-Stitch and Needlepoint*. D. Geneva Lent. Edited by Ivan H. Crowell, Director of Handicrafts, McGill University, Macdonald College, P.Q. Macmillan.

16 pp.; 170 × 120 mm.
Issued in paper.
Craftsmen's Library.

1075. *Life Insurance: A Canadian Handbook*. Toronto: The Macmillan Company of Canada Limited 1945.

56 pp.; 210 × 137 mm.
Also published in French (see 1031). Issued in paper.

1076. MACDONALD, Grant

Sailors. By Grant Macdonald (Lieutenant R.C.N.V.R.). Published under the Auspices of The Navy League of Canada. Toronto: The Macmillan Company of Canada Limited 1945.

vi, 153, [1] pp.; 284 × 219 mm.

1077. McCOWAN, Daniel

Outdoors With A Camera In Canada. By Dan McCowan, F.Z.S. Toronto: The Macmillan Company of Canada Limited 1945.

102 pp.; 233 × 153 mm.
Reprinted in 1947.

1078. MUNRO, Ross

Gauntlet to Overlord: The Story of the Canadian Army. By Ross Munro. Toronto: The Macmillan Company of Canada Limited 1945.

xiv, 477, [1] pp.; 217 × 145 mm.

1079. NELSON, Eddie R.

Craftsmen's Library 27, *Jewellery-Making for Beginners*. Eddie R. Nelson. Edited by Ivan H. Crowell, Director of Handicrafts, Department of Industry and Reconstruction, Fredericton, N.B. Macmillan.

> 16 pp.; 170 × 120 mm.
> Issued in paper.
> Craftsmen's Library.

1080. POWELL, A.E.

Craftsmen's Library 6, *Whittling Novelties from Wood*. A.E. Powell. Edited by Ivan H. Crowell, Director of Handicrafts, McGill University, Macdonald College, P.Q. Macmillan.

> 16 pp.; 170 × 120 mm.
> Issued in paper.
> Craftsmen's Library.

1081. PRATT, E.J.

They Are Returning. E.J. Pratt. Toronto: The Macmillan Company of Canada Limited 1945.

> 15, [1] pp.; 225 × 150 mm.
> Issued in paper.

1082. PRIESTLEY, J.B.

Three Men in New Suits. By J.B. Priestley. Toronto: The Macmillan Company of Canada Limited 1945.

> [4], 170 pp.; 200 × 140 mm.

1083. RENZIUS, Rudy

Craftsmen's Library 55, *Built-Up Wood Carvings*. Rudy Renzius. Edited by Ivan H. Crowell, Director of Handicrafts, Department of Industry and Reconstruction, Fredericton, N.B. Macmillan.

> 16 pp.; 170 × 120 mm.
> Issued in paper.
> Craftsmen's Library.

1084. RENZIUS, Rudy

Craftsmen's Library 26, *Hammered Silver Flatware*. Rudy Renzius. Edited by Ivan H. Crowell, Director of Handicrafts, Department of Industry and Reconstruction, Fredericton, N.B. Macmillan.

> 16 pp.; 170 × 120 mm.
> Issued in paper.
> Craftsmen's Library.

1085. RENZIUS, Rudy

Craftsmen's Library 50, *Wrought-Iron Work Without a Forge*. Rudy Renzius. Edited by Ivan H. Crowell, Director of Handicrafts, Department of Industry and Reconstruction, Fredericton, N.B. Macmillan.

> 19, [1] pp.; 170 × 120 mm.
> Issued in paper.
> Craftsmen's Library.

1086.   ROWAND, Jessie

Craftsmen's Library 16, *Tooling Leather*. Jessie Rowand. Edited by Ivan H. Crowell, Director of Handicrafts, McGill University, Macdonald College, P.Q. Macmillan.

> 16 pp.; 170 × 120 mm.
> Issued in paper.
> Craftsmen's Library.

1087.   SANDERS, Byrne Hope

Emily Murphy: Crusader ("Janey Canuck"). By Byrne Hope Sanders. Toronto: The Macmillan Company of Canada Limited 1945.

> xx, 355, [1] pp.; 220 × 140 mm.

1088.   SANDYS-WUNSCH, T.V.

Craftsmen's Library 41, *Vegetable Dyeing for Beginners*. Byrtha L. Stavert. Edited by Ivan H. Crowell, Director of Handicrafts, Department of Industry and Reconstruction, Fredericton, N.B. Macmillan.

> 16 pp.; 170 × 120 mm.
> Issued in paper.
> Craftsmen's Library.

1089.   SEGALL, Jean Brown

Wings of the Morning. By Jean Brown Segall. [Quotation]. Toronto: The Macmillan Company of Canada Limited 1945.

> xviii, 151, [1] pp.; 210 × 140 mm.

1090.   SMITH, Gordon A.

Craftsmen's Library 32, *Silk Screen Printing*. Gordon A. Smith. Edited by Ivan H. Crowell, Director of Handicrafts, Department of Industry and Reconstruction, Fredericton, N.B. Macmillan.

> 16 pp.; 170 × 120 mm.
> Issued in paper.
> Craftsmen's Library.

1091.   STAVERT, Byrtha L.

Craftsmen's Library 41, *Vegetable Dyeing for Beginners*. Byrtha L. Stavert. Edited by Ivan H. Crowell, Director of Handicrafts, Department of Industry and Reconstruction, Fredericton, N.B. Macmillan.

> 16 pp.; 170 × 120 mm.
> Issued in paper.
> Craftsmen's Library.

1092.   STRANGE, Kathleen

With the West in Her Eyes: The Story of a Modern Pioneer. Kathleen Strange. [Quotation]. Toronto: The Macmillan Company of Canada Limited 1945.

> viii, 293, [1] pp.; 210 × 138 mm.
> Issued in cloth and paper.

1093. VOADEN, Herman

On Stage: Plays For School and Community. Edited by Herman Voaden, M.A., Director of English, Central High School of Commerce, Toronto. Editor of "Six Canadian Plays", "A Book of Plays", and "Four Good Plays to Read and Act". Toronto: The Macmillan Company of Canada Limited 1945.

xxviii, 445, [1] pp.; 190 × 120 mm.
Reprinted in 1946.

1094. WALLACE, W. Stewart

The Dictionary of Canadian Biography. By W. Stewart Wallace, M.A., Librarian of the University of Toronto. Second Edition, Revised and Enlarged. Volume I, A-K. Toronto: The Macmillan Company of Canada Limited, at St. Martin's House 1945.

x, 328 pp.; 237 × 155 mm.
First published in 1926 (see 298). Third edition published in 1963 (see 1657). Fourth edition published in 1978 (see 2606).

1095. WALLACE, W. Stewart

The Dictionary of Canadian Biography. By W. Stewart Wallace, M.A., Librarian of the University of Toronto. Second Edition, Revised and Enlarged. Volume II, L-Z. Toronto: The Macmillan Company of Canada Limited, at St. Martin's House 1945.

[4], 329-729, [1] pp.; 237 × 155 mm.
For publication history, see note to previous entry.

1096. WELSH, Nobert

The Last Buffalo Hunter. By Mary Weekes. As told to her by Norbert Welsh. Toronto: The Macmillan Company of Canada Limited 1945.

304 pp.; 193 × 135 mm.

1097. WINSLOW-SPRAGGE, Alice

Craftsmen's Library 52, *Canadian Handicraft Guild Loom*. Alice Winslow-Spragge. Edited by Ivan H. Crowell, Director of Handicrafts, McGill University, Macdonald College, P.Q. Macmillan.

20 pp.; 170 × 120 mm.
Issued in paper.
Craftsmen's Library.

1098. WREN, Frances

Craftsmen's Library 8, *Bill-folds, Purses and Under-arm Bags*. Frances Wren. Edited by Ivan H. Crowell, Director of Handicrafts, McGill University, Macdonald College, P.Q. Macmillan.

16 pp.; 170 × 120 mm.
Issued in paper.
Craftsmen's Library.

1099.   WREN, Frances

Craftsmen's Library 3, *Indian Slippers*. Frances Wren. Edited by Ivan H. Crowell, Director of Handicrafts, McGill University, Macdonald College, P.Q. Macmillan.

16 pp.; 170 × 120 mm.
Issued in paper.
Craftsmen's Library.

1946

1100.   AMARON, R. C.

Le Français Pratique: Book I. By R. Campbell Amaron, French Specialist, Quebec High School, Robert A. Peck, Supervisor of French in the Protestant Schools of the Province of Quebec, And Margaret E. Buchanan, Formerly Assistant Supervisor of French in the Protestant Schools of the Province of Quebec. Authorized for use in the Protestant Schools of Quebec. Toronto: The Macmillan Company of Canada Limited 1946.

x, 231, [1] pp.; 218 × 150 mm.
Revised in 1956 (see 1363).

1100A   AMARON, R.C.

Le Français Pratique: Book II. By R. Campbell Amaron, French Specialist, Quebec High School, Donald W. Buchanan, French Specialist, Town of Mount Royal High School, Robert A. Peck, Supervisor of French in the Protestant Schools of the Province of Quebec, And Margaret E. Buchanan, Formerly Assistant Supervisor of French in the Protestant Schools of the Province of Quebec. Authorized for use in the Protestant Schools of Quebec. Toronto: The Macmillan Company Of Canada Limited 1946.

xii, 230, [2] pp.; 218 × 150 mm.
Revised in 1956 (see 1363).

1101.   COLLARD, Edgar Andrew

Oldest McGill. Edgar Andrew Collard. Toronto: The Macmillan Company of Canada Limited 1946.

xvi, 135, [1] pp.; 230 × 155 mm.

1102.   DE LA ROCHE, Mazo

Return to Jalna. By Mazo De La Roche. Toronto: The Macmillan Company of Canada Limited 1946.

viii, 540 pp.; 200 × 140 mm.

1103.   EWING, John M.

Understanding Yourself and Your Society. By John M. Ewing, B.A.(Queens), D.Paed.(Toronto), Principal, and Head of the Department of Philosophy and Psychology, Victoria College, Victoria, B.C., Formerly Instructor in Educational Psychology, Provincial Normal School, Vancouver, B.C. Illustrations by Frances Neil. Toronto: The Macmillan Company of Canada Limited 1946.

xvi, 357, [3] pp.; 213 × 140 mm.
Revised in 1962 (see 1569).

1104. FERNE, Doris
Paschal Lamb and Other Poems. By Doris Ferne. Toronto: The Macmillan
Company of Canada Limited 1946.
[8], 39, [1] pp.; 187 × 128 mm.

1105. GATES, Arthur I.
Wide Wings. The New Work-Play Books. Arthur I. Gates, Miriam Blanton
Huber, Celeste Comegys Peardon. The Macmillan Company 1946.
vi, 344 pp.; 200 × 155 mm.
First published in 1939. Reprinted frequently. Earlier printings not located.
New Work-Play Books Series.

1106. GOULD, Mona
I Run with the Fox. By Mona Gould. Toronto: The Macmillan Company of
Canada Limited 1946.
x, 30 pp.; 186 × 130 mm.

1107. GROVE, Frederick Philip
In Search of Myself. By Frederick Philip Grove. [Quotation]. Toronto: The
Macmillan Company of Canada Limited 1946.
[10], 457, [1] pp.; 210 × 142 mm.

1108. HUDSON, Reba
Brief For Beauty. By Reba Hudson. Toronto: The Macmillan Company of
Canada Limited 1946.
[12], 28 pp.; 185 × 129 mm.

1109. LINEAWEAVER, Marion
Let's Ski!: A Book for Beginners. Marion Lineaweaver. Toronto: The Macmillan Company of Canada Limited 1946.
[6], 66 pp.; 210 × 135 mm.

1110. *Manuel de L'Infirmière Visiteuse*. Préparé par The National Organization
for Public Health Nursing. (Membre du National Health Council).
Troisième édition. Traduit de l'anglais par François Vézina. Toronto: The
Macmillan Company of Canada Limited 1946.
537, [1] pp.; 200 × 140 mm.
Earlier editions not located. Third edition (corrected) published in 1948 (see 1175).

1111. MATTHEW, Anne Irwin
Stories of Old London (57 B.C.-473 A.D.). By Anne Irwin Matthew. Illustra-
tions by R.M. Collins. Book I. Toronto: The Macmillan Company of
Canada Limited 1946.
[4], 46 pp.; 200 × 138 mm.
Issued in paper.

1112.   MATTHEW, Anne Irwin
Stories of Old London (516 A.D.-669 A.D.). By Anne Irwin Matthew. Illust-
rations by R.M. Collins. Book II. Toronto: The Macmillan Company of
Canada Limited 1946.

[4], 35, [1] pp.; 200 × 138 mm.
Issued in paper.

1113.   MATTHEW, Anne Irwin
Stories of Old London (734 A.D.-886 A.D.). By Anne Irwin Matthew. Illust-
rations by R.M. Collins. Book III. Toronto: The Macmillan Company of
Canada Limited 1946.

[4], 35, [1] pp.; 200 × 138 mm.
Issued in paper.

1114.   MATTHEW, Anne Irwin
Stories of Old London (897 A.D.-1016 A.D.). By Anne Irwin Matthew.
Illustrations by R.M. Collins. Book IV. Toronto: The Macmillan Company
of Canada Limited 1946.

[4], 36 pp.; 200 × 138 mm.
Issued in paper.

1115.   McLEISH, W.Y.
Education Through Mathematics: A Text-book for High Schools. By W.Y.
McLeish and J.E. Smith. Authorized by the Minister of Education in British
Columbia. Toronto: The Macmillan Company of Canada Limited 1946.

xii, 545, [1] pp.; 205 × 135 mm.

1116.   MILLER, Norman
Supplementary Exercises for An Advanced Course in Algebra. By Norman
Miller, Ph.D., Professor of Mathematics in Queen's University, Kingston
and Robert E.K. Rourke, A.M., Assistant Headmaster and Instructor in
Mathematics at Pickering College, Newmarket. The Macmillan Company of
Canada Limited 1946.

32 pp.; 205 × 137 mm.
Issued in paper.

1117.   PIERCE, Lorne
The New World Readers, *My World and I*. Editor-in-chief — Lorne Pierce.
General Editor — Frederick Minkler. **** *My World and I*, G.H. Dobrindt,
B.A., F.J. Gathercole, B.A., B.ED., Miriam Norton, M.A., Eleanor Boyce,
M.A. The Ryerson Press [and] The Macmillans in Canada. Copyright,
Canada, 1946 by The Ryerson Press and The Macmillan Company of
Canada, Limited.

x, 438 pp.; 200 × 148 mm.
Revised in 1958 (see 1430).
New World Readers Series.

1118.   PIERCE, Lorne

The New World Readers, *Over the Bridge*. Editor-in-chief — Lorne Pierce.
General Editor — Frederick Minkler. **** *Over the Bridge*, Margaret A.
Robinson, B.A., B.Paed. [and] Maud Blanchard Tomey. The Ryerson Press
[and] The Macmillans in Canada. Copyright, Canada, 1946 by The Ryerson
Press and The Macmillan Company of Canada, Limited.

> x, 406 pp.; 200 × 148 mm.
> Revised in 1958 (see 1446).
> New World Readers Series.

1119.   PIERCE, Lorne

The New World Readers, *Under the North Star*. Editor-in-chief — Lorne
Pierce. General Editor — Frederick Minkler. **** *Under the North Star*,
Clare B. Routley, M.A., Grace Morgan, B.A., B.Paed., Miriam Norton,
M.A. [and] Eleanor Boyce, M.A. The Ryerson Press [and] The Macmillans
in Canada. Copyright, Canada, 1946 by The Ryerson Press and The Mac-
millan Company of Canada, Limited.

> xii, 433, [1] pp.; 200 × 148 mm.
> Revised in 1958 (see 1449).
> New World Readers Series.

1120.   SHAW, Margaret Mason

He Conquered Death: The Story of Frederick Grant Banting. By Margaret
Mason Shaw. Toronto: The Macmillan Company of Canada Limited 1946.

> [14], 111, [1] pp.; 210 × 150 mm.

1121.   SWIFT, Jonathan

Gulliver's Travels. By Jonathan Swift. Introduction by G.L. Brodersen.
Toronto: The Macmillan Company of Canada Limited 1946.

> x, 351, [1] pp.; 185 × 125 mm.

1122.   WATT, Frederick B.

Landfall. By Lieut.-Commander Frederick B. Watt, M.B.E., R.C.N.(R.).
Toronto: The Macmillan Company of Canada Limited 1946.

> [12], 59, [1] pp.; 220 × 140 mm.

1947

1123.   ALFRED, Brother

Catholic Pioneers in Upper Canada. By Rev. Brother Alfred, F.S.C., LL.D.
President General of the Canadian Catholic Historical Association, Founder
of St. Joseph's College, University of Alberta, Edmonton; of De La Salle
Oaklands College, Avenue Road Hill, Toronto; and of "Benildus Hall", The
Christian Brothers' Study House, Toronto. Toronto: The Macmillan Com-
pany of Canada Limited 1947.

> xvi, 251, [1] pp.; 210 × 140 mm.

1124.   ASHLEY, C.A.

Corporation Finance. By C.A. Ashley, Professor of Commerce in the University of Toronto. Toronto: The Macmillan Company of Canada Limited 1947.

250 pp.; 218 × 138 mm.
The first five chapters of *Corporation Finance* were originally published as a pamphlet in 1945 (see 1030). Revised in 1956 (see 1360). Reprinted frequently.

1125.   BARBEAU, Marius

Alaska Beckons. By Marius Barbeau. Illustrated by Arthur Price. 1947. The Caxton Printers, Ltd. Caldwell, Idaho [and] The Macmillan Company of Canada.

343, [1] pp.; 234 × 157 mm.

1126.   BONE, P. Turner

When the Steel Went Through: Reminiscences of a Railroad Pioneer. By P. Turner Bone, C.E. Toronto: The Macmillan Company of Canada Limited 1947.

[12], 180 pp.; 210 × 145 mm.

1127.   BOWERS, Henry

Mathematics For Canadians Book 1. By Henry Bowers, Principal of the Normal School, Stratford, Norman Miller, Professor of Mathematics in Queen's University, Kingston, And Robert E.K. Rourke, Headmaster and Instructor in Mathematics at Pickering College, Newmarket. J.M. Dent And Sons (Canada) Ltd. And The Macmillan Company of Canada Limited 1947.

xvi, 448 pp.; 208 × 140 mm.
Mathematics For Canadians Series.

1128.   DE LA ROCHE, Mazo

Jalna. By Mazo De La Roche. Toronto: The Macmillan Company of Canada Limited 1947.

viii, 290 pp.; 190 × 120 mm.
First published in 1927 (see 308).

1129.   DE LA ROCHE, Mazo

Young Renny. By Mazo De La Roche. Toronto: The Macmillan Company of Canada Limited 1947.

viii, 247, [1] pp.; 187 × 120 mm.
First published in 1935 (see 637).

1130.   GATES, Arthur I.

The Pupils' Own Vocabulary Speller. Canadian Edition. Grade II. By Arthur I. Gates, Henry D. Rinsland, Ina C. Sartorius, [and] Celeste Comegys Peardon. Illustrated by Mary Highsmith. Authorized in Alberta and Saskatchewan. Toronto: The Macmillan Company of Canada Limited.

95, [1] pp.; 195 × 140 mm.
Also found bound with the Grade III volume. Authorization statement varies. Revised in 1951 (see 1242).
Pupils' Own Vocabulary Speller Series.

1131.   GATES, Arthur I.

The Pupils' Own Vocabulary Speller. Canadian Edition. Grade III. By Arthur
I. Gates, Henry D. Rinsland, Ina C. Sartorius, [and] Celeste Comegys
Peardon. Illustrated by Marjorie Thompson. Authorized in Alberta: permissively authorized in Saskatchewan. Toronto: The Macmillan Company
of Canada Limited.

95, [1] pp.; 195 × 140 mm.
Also found bound with the Grade II volume. Authorization statement varies.
Revised in 1951 (see 1243).
Pupils' Own Vocabulary Speller Series.

1132.   GATES, Arthur I.

The Pupils' Own Vocabulary Speller. Canadian Edition. Grade IV. By Arthur
I. Gates, Henry D. Rinsland, Ina C. Sartorius, [and] Celeste Comegys
Peardon. Illustrated by Mary Highsmith. Authorized in Alberta: permis-
sively authorized in Saskatchewan. Toronto: The Macmillan Company of
Canada Limited.

126 pp.; 195 × 140 mm.
Also found bound with the Grades V and VI volumes. Revised in 1951 (see 1244).
Pupils' Own Vocabulary Speller Series.

1133.   GATES, Arthur I.

The Pupils' Own Vocabulary Speller. Canadian Edition. Grade V. By Arthur
I. Gates, Henry D. Rinsland, Ina C. Sartorius, [and] Celeste Comegys
Peardon. Illustrated by Marjorie Thompson. Authorized in Alberta: permissively authorized in Saskatchewan. Toronto: The Macmillan Company
of Canada Limited.

128 pp.; 195 × 140 mm.
Also found bound with the Grades IV and VI volumes. Revised in 1951 (see 1245).
Pupils' Own Vocabulary Speller Series.

1134.   GATES, Arthur I.

The Pupils' Own Vocabulary Speller. Canadian Edition. Grade VI. By Arthur
I. Gates, Henry D. Rinsland, Ina C. Sartorius, [and] Celeste Comegys
Peardon. Illustrated by Mary Highsmith. Authorized in Alberta: permis-
sively authorized in Saskatchewan. Toronto: The Macmillan Company of
Canada Limited.

132 pp.; 195 × 140 mm.
Also found bound with the Grades IV and V volumes. Revised in 1951 (see 1246).
Pupils' Own Vocabulary Speller Series.

1135.   GATES, Arthur I.

The Pupils' Own Vocabulary Speller. Canadian Edition. Grade VII. By Arthur
I. Gates, Henry D. Rinsland, Ina C. Sartorius, [and] Celeste Comegys
Peardon. Illustrated by Marjorie Thompson. Authorized in Alberta: permissively authorized in Saskatchewan. Toronto: The Macmillan Company
of Canada Limited.

128 pp.; 195 × 140 mm.
Also found bound with the Grade VIII volume. Revised in 1951 (see 1247).
Pupils' Own Vocabulary Speller Series.

1136.   GATES, Arthur I.
The Pupils' Own Vocabulary Speller. Canadian Edition. Grade VIII. By
Arthur I. Gates, Henry D. Rinsland, Ina C. Sartorius, [and] Celeste Comegys
Peardon. Illustrated by Marjorie Thompson. Authorized in Alberta: per-
missively authorized in Saskatchewan. Toronto: The Macmillan Company
of Canada Limited.

> 139, [1] pp.; 195 × 140 mm.
> Also found bound with the Grade VII volume.
> Pupils' Own Vocabulary Speller Series.

1137.   GIBBON, John Murray
Three Centuries of Canadian Nursing. By John Murray Gibbon, Author of
Canadian Mosaic. In collaboration with Mary S. Mathewson, R.N., B.S.,
Director of Nursing, the Montreal General Hospital, formerly Assistant
Director of the School for Graduate Nurses, McGill University. Illustrated.
Toronto: The Macmillan Company of Canada Limited 1947.

> xxii, 505, [1] pp.; 234 × 155 mm.

1138.   GOLDBERG, Nathan R.
Coffee and Bitters. By Nathan Ralph [pseud.]. Author of *Twelve Poems*.
Toronto: The Macmillan Company of Canada Limited 1947.

> x, 37, [1] pp.; 185 × 128 mm.

1139.   GROVE, Frederick Philip
Consider Her Ways. By Frederick Philip Grove. [Quotation]. Toronto: The
Macmillan Company of Canada Limited 1947.

> xxxiv, 298 pp.; 200 × 140 mm.

1140.   HARRISON, Elizabeth
A Whip for Time. By Elizabeth Harrison. Toronto: The Macmillan Company
of Canada Limited 1947.

> [12], 28 pp.; 185 × 128 mm.

1141.   HEATON, T.G.
Artificial Pneumothorax in Pulmonary Tuberculosis. (Second Edition). By T.G.
Heaton, M.B.(Tor.), Chest Clinician, Toronto Western Hospital and Chris-
tie Street Hospital, Toronto. With an Introduction by Dr. C.D. Parfitt.
Toronto: The Macmillan Company of Canada Limited 1947.

> xvi, 292 pp.; 207 × 138 mm.
> First published in 1941 (see 908).

1142.   HILTON, James
James Hilton, *Nothing So Strange*. Toronto: The Macmillan Company of
Canada Limited 1947.

> [6], 308 pp.; 200 × 137 mm.

1143.   KING, W.L. Mackenzie

*Industry and Humanity: A study in the principles underlying Industrial Recon-
struction*. By the Right Honourable W.L. Mackenzie King, M.P. Toronto:
The Macmillan Company of Canada Limited 1947.

xxx, 270 pp.; 225 × 145 mm.
Abridged edition published in 1935 (see 642).

1144.   MILLER, Norman

An Advanced Course in Algebra. By Norman Miller, Professor of Mathematics
in Queen's University, Kingston, And Robert E.K. Rourke, Associate
Headmaster and Instructor in Mathematics at Pickering College, Newmarket. Revised Edition. Toronto: The Macmillan Company of Canada Limited, at St. Martin's House 1947.

xviii, 394 pp.; 203 × 134 mm.
First published in 1940 (see 878).

1145.   MITCHELL, W.O.

Who Has Seen the Wind. By W.O. Mitchell. Toronto: The Macmillan
Company of Canada Limited 1947.

[8], 344 pp.; 200 × 140 mm.
A school edition was published in 1960 (see 1501). Reprinted in paper in 1971 in the
St. Martin's Classics Series. Published in the Laurentian Library (No. 14) in 1972.
An edition with illustrations by William Kurelek was published in 1976 (see 2418A).

1146.   MOODY, Irene H.

Always the Bubbles Break. By Irene H. Moody. Toronto: The Macmillan
Company of Canada Limited 1947.

[8], 39, [1] pp.; 185 × 128 mm.

1147.   NORTON, Miriam

The Work and Study Book for My World and I. Grade Six Level. The New
World Readers. [Table of Contents]. [Miriam Norton, M.A. and Eleanor
Boyce, M.A.]. The Ryerson Press [and] The Macmillans in Canada.

[2], 88, [2] pp.; 255 × 196 mm.
Revised in 1965 (see 1708). Issued in paper.
New World Readers Series.

1148.   NORTON, Miriam

The Work And Study Book For Over the Bridge. Grade Four Level. The New
World Readers. [Table of Contents]. [Miriam Norton, M.A. and Eleanor
Boyce, M.A.]. The Ryerson Press [and] The Macmillans in Canada.

[2], 94 pp.; 255 × 196 mm.
There are two versions of this title (see 1153 for the second version). Revised in 1960
(see 1503). Issued in paper.
New World Readers Series.

1149.   PRATT, E.J.

Behind the Log. By E.J. Pratt. Drawings By Grant Macdonald. Toronto: The
Macmillan Company of Canada Limited 1947.

xvi, 47, [1] pp.; 233 × 150 mm.

1150. PRATT, E.J.

Ten Selected Poems. With Notes By E.J. Pratt, Department of English, Victoria College, University of Toronto. Toronto: The Macmillan Company of Canada Limited, at St. Martin's House 1947.

xii, 149, [1] pp.; 195 × 120 mm.
Also issued in the St. Martin's Classics Series in 1947. A later reprint lacks the date on the title-page.

1151. PRIESTLEY, J.B.

Jenny Villiers: A Story of the Theatre. By J.B. Priestley. Toronto: The Macmillan Company of Canada Limited 1947.

[4], 189, [1] pp.; 217 × 138 mm.

1152. ROBINSON, Margaret A.

The New World Readers, *Teacher's Handbook for Over the Bridge*. Margaret A. Robinson, B.A., B.Paed. The Ryerson Press [and] The Macmillans in Canada.

iv, 158 pp.; 194 × 133 mm.
Revised in 1960 as *Teacher's Manual for Over the Bridge* (see 1504). Reprinted frequently.
New World Readers Series.

1153. ROBINSON, Margaret A.

The Work And Study Book For Over The Bridge. Grade Four Level. The New World Readers. [Table of Contents]. [Margaret A. Robinson, B.A., B.Paed. and Maud Blanchard Tomey]. The Ryerson Press [and] The Macmillans in Canada.

[2], 102 pp.; 255 × 196 mm.
This is the second version of this title (see 1148 for the first one). Revised in 1960 (see 1503). Issued in paper.
New World Readers Series.

1154. ROUTLEY, Clare B.

The Work and Study Book for Under the North Star. Grade Five Level. The New World Readers. [Table of Contents]. [Clare B. Routley, M.A., Grace Morgan, B.A., B.Paed., Miriam Norton, M.A. and Eleanor Boyce, M.A.]. The Ryerson Press [and] The Macmillans in Canada.

[2], 94 pp.; 255 × 196 mm.
Revised in 1960 (see 1502). Issued in paper.
New World Readers Series.

1155. SMITH, Reed

Learning to Write. By Reed Smith. Canadian Edition Completely Revised and Reset. Authorized by the Minister of Education for use in the Schools of Ontario. Toronto: The Macmillan Company of Canada Limited, at St. Martin's House 1947.

xii, 511, [1] pp.; 205 × 140 mm.
First published in 1939 (see 858). Second revised edition published in 1961 (see 1556).

1156. SONET, Édouard

Maison de Pension Pour Étudiants. Comédie par Édouard Sonet. Cette comédie en un acte a été représentée pour la première fois le 9 Mars, 1945. Toronto: The Macmillan Company of Canada Limited 1947.

xvi, 131, [1] pp.; 190 × 118 mm.

1157. ST. JOHN, Helen B.

Livre de Lecture: An Intermediate French Reader. By Helen B. St. John, Ontario College of Education. Toronto: The Macmillan Company of Canada Limited 1947.

viii, 256 pp.; 170 × 115 mm.
Revised in 1951 (see 1258).

1158. STAPLES, Rj

Exploring the World of Music: Guide Book One. By Rj Staples, Provincial Supervisor of Music, Saskatchewan. Authorized for use in Saskatchewan. Toronto: The Macmillan Company of Canada Limited 1947.

xvi, 340 pp.; 230 × 160 mm.

1159. TAYLOR, Daphne

The Pompous Parrot And Other West Indian Tales. By Daphne Taylor. Illustrated by Nan Richards. Toronto: The Macmillan Company of Canada Limited 1947.

xii, 114 pp.; 282 × 205 mm.

1160. TRAQUAIR, Ramsay

The Old Architecture of Quebec: A Study of the Buildings Erected In New France From The Earliest Explorers To The Middle Of The Nineteenth Century. By Ramsay Traquair, M.A. (hon.), F.R.I.B.A., F.R.A.I.C., Professor Emeritus of Architecture, McGill University. Toronto: The Macmillan Company of Canada Limited, 1947.

xx, 324 pp.; 285 × 210 mm.

1161. WILSON, Alice E.

The Earth Beneath Our Feet. By Alice E. Wilson. Illustrated by C.E. Johnson. Toronto: The Macmillan Company of Canada Limited 1947.

[8], 294, [2] pp.; 205 × 130 mm.

1162. WILSON, Ethel

Hetty Dorval. By Ethel Wilson. Toronto: The Macmillan Company of Canada Limited 1947.

[8], 116 pp.; 198 × 135 mm.
Reprinted in the Laurentian Library (No. 6) in 1967.

1948

1163. BENNET, C.L.

The Golden Caravan. By C.L. Bennet, J.F. Swazye and Lorne Pierce. The Macmillans in Canada [and] The Ryerson Press.

x, 546 pp.; 200 × 138 mm.
First published in 1934 as *The Canada Book of Prose and Verse, Book Four* (see 561). Revised in 1962 (see 1558). Reprinted frequently.

1164. BENTLEY, Phyllis

Life Story. By Phyllis Bentley. Toronto: Macmillan 1948.

297, [1] pp.; 185 × 125 mm.

1165. CALLAGHAN, Morley

Morley Callaghan, *Luke Baldwin's Vow*. Illustrations by Michael Poulton. Macmillan of Canada/Toronto 1948.

[2], 187, [1] pp.; 222 × 138 mm.
Reprinted in 1974.

1166. CALLAGHAN, Morley

The Varsity Story. By Morley Callaghan. Illustrated by Eric Aldwinckle, O.S.A. Toronto: The Macmillan Company of Canada Limited 1948.

[8], 172, [2] pp.; 213 × 138 mm.

1167. CANBY, Henry Seidel

Applying Good English. Henry Seidel Canby, John Baker Opdycke [and] Margaret Gillum. Toronto: The Macmillan Company of Canada Limited, at St. Martin's House 1948.

xviii, 430 pp.; 205 × 140 mm.

1168. DE LA ROCHE, Mazo

The Building of Jalna. By Mazo De La Roche. Toronto: The Macmillan Company of Canada Limited 1948.

viii, 327, [1] pp.; 187 × 125 mm.
First published in 1944 (see 998).

1169. DE LA ROCHE, Mazo

Finch's Fortune. By Mazo De La Roche. Toronto: The Macmillan Company of Canada Limited 1948.

viii, 385, [1] pp.; 187 × 125 mm.
First published in 1931 (see 475A).

1170. DE LA ROCHE, Mazo

The Master of Jalna. By Mazo De La Roche. Toronto: The Macmillan Company of Canada Limited 1948.

viii, 336 pp.; 187 × 125 mm.
First published in 1933 (see 520).

1171. DE LA ROCHE, Mazo

Wakefield's Course. By Mazo De La Roche. Toronto: The Macmillan Company of Canada Limited 1948.

x, 370 pp.; 187 × 125 mm.

1172. DE LA ROCHE, Mazo

Whiteoak Harvest. By Mazo De La Roche. Toronto: The Macmillan Company of Canada Limited 1948.

x, 334 pp.; 187 × 125 mm.
First published in 1936 (see 692).

1173. DE LA ROCHE, Mazo

Whiteoaks. By Mazo De La Roche. Toronto: The Macmillan Company of Canada Limited 1948.

viii, 385, [1] pp.; 187 × 125 mm.
First published in 1929 as *Whiteoaks of Jalna* (see 370).

1174. FINNIE, Richard

Canada Moves North. Revised edition. By Richard Finnie. Author of *Lure of the North*. Illustrated. 1948. Toronto: The Macmillan Company of Canada Limited.

[8], 239, [1] pp.; 220 × 145 mm.
First published in 1942 (see 940).

1175. GARDNER, Mary Sewall

L'Infirmière Visiteuse. Par Mary Sewall Gardner, R.N., A.M. Membre de l'American Public Health Association, Présidente honoraire de la National Organization for Public Health Nursing, experte auprès de la Providence District Nursing Association. Traduit de l'anglais par Francois Vézina. Troisième édition corrigée. [Quotation]. Toronto: The Macmillan Company of Canada Limited 1948.

xii, 491, [1] pp.; 227 × 140 mm.
Third edition published 1946 (see 1110).

1176. GATES, Arthur I.

The Canadian Pupils' Own Vocabulary Speller: Text-Workbook Edition. Grade 2. Arthur I. Gates, Henry D. Rinsland, Ina C. Sartorius, [and] Celeste Comegys Peardon. Authorized in Alberta; permissively authorized in Saskatchewan. The Macmillan Company of Canada Limited.

96 pp.; 275 × 205 mm.
Issued in paper.
Pupils' Own Vocabulary Speller Series.

1177. GATES, Arthur I.

The Canadian Pupils' Own Vocabulary Speller: Text-Workbook Edition. Grade 3. Arthur I. Gates, Henry D. Rinsland, Ina C. Sartorius, [and] Celeste Comegys Peardon. Authorized in Alberta; permissively authorized in Saskatchewan. The Macmillan Company of Canada Limited.

96 pp.; 275 × 205 mm.
Issued in paper.
Pupils' Own Vocabulary Speller Series.

1178. GATES, Arthur I.

The Canadian Pupils' Own Vocabulary Speller: Text-Workbook Edition.
Grade 4. Arthur I. Gates, Henry D. Rinsland, Ina C. Sartorius, [and] Celeste
Comegys Peardon. Authorized in Alberta; permissively authorized in Sas-
katchewan. The Macmillan Company of Canada Limited.

96 pp.; 275 × 205 mm.
Issued in paper.
Pupils' Own Vocabulary Speller Series.

1179. GATES, Arthur I.

The Canadian Pupils' Own Vocabulary Speller: Text-Workbook Edition.
Grade 5. Arthur I. Gates, Henry D. Rinsland, Ina C. Sartorius, [and] Celeste
Comegys Peardon. Authorized in Alberta; permissively authorized in Sas-
katchewan. The Macmillan Company of Canada Limited.

96 pp.; 275 × 205 mm.
Issued in paper.
Pupils' Own Vocabulary Speller Series.

1180. GATES, Arthur I.

The Canadian Pupils' Own Vocabulary Speller: Text-Workbook Edition.
Grade 6. Arthur I. Gates, Henry D. Rinsland, Ina C. Sartorius, [and] Celeste
Comegys Peardon. Authorized in Alberta; permissively authorized in Sas-
katchewan. The Macmillan Company of Canada Limited.

96 pp.; 275 × 205 mm.
Issued in paper.
Pupils' Own Vocabulary Speller Series.

1181. GATES, Arthur I.

The Canadian Pupils' Own Vocabulary Speller: Text-Workbook Edition.
Grade 7. Arthur I. Gates, Henry D. Rinsland, Ina C. Sartorius, [and] Celeste
Comegys Peardon. Authorized in Alberta; permissively authorized in Sas-
katchewan. The Macmillan Company of Canada Limited.

99, [1] pp.; 275 × 205 mm.
Issued in paper.
Pupils' Own Vocabulary Speller Series.

1182. GATES, Arthur I.

The Canadian Pupils' Own Vocabulary Speller: Text-Workbook Edition.
Grade 8. Arthur I. Gates, Henry D. Rinsland, Ina C. Sartorius, [and] Celeste
Comegys Peardon. Authorized in Alberta; permissively authorized in Sas-
katchewan. The Macmillan Company of Canada Limited.

102 pp.; 275 × 205 mm.
Issued in paper.
Pupils' Own Vocabulary Speller Series.

1183. GIBSON, J. Douglas

Canada's Economy in a Changing World. Edited by J. Douglas Gibson. Issued under the auspices of the Canadian Institute of International Affairs under whose direction this book was written. Toronto: The Macmillan Company of Canada Limited 1948.

xvi, 380 pp.; 217 × 138 mm.

1184. GOOD, Mabel Tinkiss

Men of Valour. By Mabel Tinkiss Good. Illustrated by George Pepper. Toronto: The Macmillan Company of Canada Limited 1948.

xiv, 137, [1] pp.; 212 × 137 mm.

1185. KEIRSTEAD, B.S.

The Theory of Economic Change. By B.S. Keirstead, William Dow Professor of Political Economy in McGill University. Toronto: The Macmillan Company of Canada Limited 1948.

xii, 386 pp.; 213 × 136 mm.

1186. KIPLING, Rudyard

The Jungle Book. By Rudyard Kipling. With Illustrations by J. Lockwood Kipling, C.I.E., And W.H. Drake. Toronto: The Macmillan Company of Canada Limited.

viii, 276, [4] pp.; 173 × 110 mm.
St. Martin's Classics Series.

1187. KNOX, Olive E.

Red River Shadows. By Olive Knox. Toronto: Macmillan: 1948.

xii, 303, [1] pp.; 212 × 137 mm.

1188. LOGAN, H.A.

Trade Unions in Canada: Their Development and Functioning. By H.A. Logan, Department of Economics, University of Toronto. Toronto: The Macmillan Company of Canada Limited 1948.

xxii, 639, [1] pp.; 238 × 155 mm.

1189. MacGIBBON, Duncan Alexander

An Introduction to Economics for Canadian Readers. Revised and Much Enlarged Edition. By Duncan Alexander MacGibbon. Authorized for use in the provinces of Alberta, Manitoba and Nova Scotia. Toronto: The Macmillan Company of Canada Limited 1948.

xii, 203, [1] pp.; 190 × 125 mm.
First published in 1924 (see 223A). Revised in 1929. Revised in 1935 (see 646A). Revised in 1946 and reprinted in 1947 and 1948. Earlier printings not located.

1190. MacKAY, L.A.

The Ill-Tempered Lover And Other Poems. L.A. MacKay. Toronto: The Macmillan Company of Canada Ltd. 1948.

viii, 72 pp.; 228 × 160 mm.

1191. MacLENNAN, Hugh

St. Martin's Classics, *Barometer Rising*. Hugh MacLennan. Arranged for School reading and with Introduction, Notes and Questions. Toronto: The Macmillan Company of Canada Limited, at St. Martin's House 1948.

xiv, 377, [1] pp.; 173 × 112 mm.
Another school edition was published in 1969 (see 2000).
St. Martin's Classics Series.

1192. McCOWAN, Daniel

Hill-Top Tales. By Dan McCowan, F.Z.S. Illustrated from Photographs by the author and others. Toronto: The Macmillan Company of Canada Limited 1948.

xiv, 266 pp.; 220 × 140 mm.

1193. McCOWAN, Daniel

A Naturalist in Canada. By Dan McCowan, F.Z.S. Illustrated from Photographs by the Author. Frontispiece by Carl Rungius. Sketches by Bruce Horsfall. Toronto: The Macmillan Company of Canada Limited 1948.

xiv, 294 pp.; 220 × 140 mm.
First published in 1941 (see 917). Enlarged edition published in 1946. Reprinted in 1948. Earlier printing not located.

1194. McPHEDRAN, Marie

Golden North. By Marie McPhedran. Toronto: The Macmillan Company of Canada Limited 1948.

xiv, 192 pp.; 205 × 135 mm.
Reprinted in 1966.

1195. MINKLER, Frederick

Voluntary Reading Interests in Canadian Schools. Frederick Minkler, B.A., D.Paed. The Macmillan Company of Canada [and] The Ryerson Press.

xvi, 106 pp.; 273 × 210 mm.
Issued in paper.

1196. SITWELL, Osbert

Laughter In The Next Room. Sir Osbert Sitwell. Toronto: The Macmillan Company of Canada Limited: 1948.

[10], 400 pp.; 220 × 145 mm.

1197. WATSON, William R.

William R. Watson, *And All Your Beauty*. [Quotation]. Toronto: The Macmillan Company of Canada, Limited 1948.

xii, 385, [1] pp.; 210 × 137 mm.

1949

1198. No entry

1199. BICE, Clare

Across Canada: Stories of Canadian School Children. By Clare Bice. The Macmillan Company of Canada Limited Toronto.

[6], 122 pp.; 220 × 170 mm.
Reprinted in 1954 and 1957.

1200. BOAS, Guy

The School Book of English Verse. Chosen by Guy Boas, M.A., Headmaster, Sloane School, Formerly Senior English Master, St. Paul's School. Revised Canadian Edition. Authorized for use in the schools of Saskatchewan. Toronto: The Macmillan Company of Canada Limited, at St. Martin's House 1949.

xx, 604 pp.; 185 × 125 mm.
First published in 1940 (see 862).

1201. BOWERS, Henry

Mathematics For Canadians. Manitoba Edition. By Henry Bowers, Principal of the Normal School, Stratford, Norman Miller, Professor of Mathematics in Queen's University, Kingston, And Robert E.K. Rourke, Headmaster and Instructor in Mathematics at Pickering College, Newmarket. J.M. Dent and Sons (Canada) Ltd., and The Macmillan Company of Canada Limited 1949.

xvi, 473, [1] pp.; 208 × 140 mm.
Mathematics For Canadians Series.

1202. DE LA ROCHE, Mazo

Mary Wakefield. By Mazo De La Roche. Toronto: The Macmillan Company of Canada Limited 1949.

vi, 298 pp.; 200 × 133 mm.

1203. FYFE, C.T.

Our Heritage. By C.T. Fyfe and Lorne Pierce. The Ryerson Press [and] The Macmillans in Canada.

x, 531, [1] pp.; 200 × 135 mm.
First published in 1932 as *The Canada Book of Prose and Verse, Book Three* (see 502). Revised in 1936 (see 714). Further revised and reissued as *Our Heritage* in 1948. First printing not located. Revised again in 1963 (see 1631).
Canada Books of Prose and Verse Series.

1204. McDOWELL, Franklin Davey

The Champlain Road. By Franklin Davey McDowell. Huronian Edition. Toronto: The Macmillan Company of Canada Limited 1949.

xvi, 338 pp.; 215 × 140 mm.
First published in 1939 (see 847). Issued in French in 1942 (see 952).

1205.   PIERCE, Lorne

Life and Adventure. By Lorne Pierce. The Ryerson Press [and] The Macmillans in Canada 1949.

x, 454 pp.; 200 × 137 mm.
First published in 1932 as *The Canada Book of Prose and Verse, Book Two* (see 501). Revised in 1935 (see 653). Further revised and reissued as *Life and Adventure* in 1948. First printing not located. Revised again in 1962 (see 1595).
Canada Books of Prose and Verse Series.

1206.   No entry

1207.   TURNER, Arthur C.

Mr. Buchan, Writer: A Life of the First Lord Tweedsmuir. Arthur C. Turner, M.A. (Glasgow), M.A., B.Litt. (Oxford), Lecturer in History, University of Glasgow, Commonwealth Fund Fellow, University of California. [Quotation]. Toronto Macmillan 1949.

114 pp.; 185 × 120 mm.

1208.   WILSON, Ethel

The Innocent Traveller. By Ethel Wilson. [Quotation]. Toronto: The Macmillan Company of Canada, Limited 1949.

x, 276, [2] pp.; 188 × 123 mm.
Reprinted in cloth and paper in 1960.

1209.   YOUNG, Madeline

Beckoning Trails. By Madeline Young [and] Lorne Pierce. The Macmillans in Canada [and] The Ryerson Press.

x, 437, [1] pp.; 200 × 135 mm.
First published in 1932 as *The Canada Book of Prose and Verse, Book One*. Revised in 1935 (see 652). Further revised and reissued as *Beckoning Trails* in 1948. First printing not located. Revised again in 1962 (see 1565).
Canada Books of Prose and Verse Series.

1950

1210.   BARTON, Lucy

The Practice Book For Our Heritage. Lucy Barton, M.A., B.Paed. [and] J.J. Knights, M.A. The Ryerson Press and The Macmillan Company of Canada, Limited.

132 pp.; 260 × 205 mm.
Issued in paper.

1211.   BATES, J.C.

The Practice Book For Life and Adventure. J.C. Bates. The Ryerson Press and The Macmillan Company of Canada, Limited.

120 pp.; 257 × 200 mm.
Issued in paper.

1212.   BENNET, C.L.

Argosy to Adventure. By C.L. Bennet and Lorne Pierce. The Macmillans in Canada [and] The Ryerson Press.

xii, 603, [1] pp.; 198 × 135 mm.
First published in 1935 as *The Canada Book of Prose and Verse, Book Five* (see 621).
Revised again in 1963 (see 1610).
Canada Books of Prose and Verse Series.

1213.   BENNETT, John

St. Martin's Classics, *Master Skylark: A Story of Shakespeare's Time*. By John Bennett. Introduction Notes and Questions by H.W. Chrysler, M.A., Head of the Department of English, Oakwood Collegiate Institute, Toronto. Illustrations by Reginald B. Birch. Toronto: The Macmillan Company of Canada Limited, at St. Martin's House 1950.

xiv, 320 pp.; 170 × 115 mm.
St. Martin's Classics Series.

1214.   BIRKETT, Geraldine

Number Experiences: Book One. By Geraldine W. Birkett And Marian James. J.M. Dent & Sons (Canada) Limited, Toronto [and] Vancouver, And the Macmillan Company of Canada Limited Toronto.

[2], 94 pp.; 270 × 200 mm.
Reprinted in 1952. Issued in paper.
Number Experiences Series.

1215.   BOWERS, Henry

[Cover-title:] Department of Education, Province of Alberta. *Locus and the Circle*. Section B: Mathematics 20. By Henry Bowers, Norman Miller [and] Robert E.K. Rourke. Dent: Macmillan.

[1], 376-455, [1] pp.; 205 × 138 mm.
An offprint from *Mathematics for Canadians: Manitoba Edition: Book II* (see 1217).
Issued in paper.

1216.   BOWERS, Henry

Mathematics For Canadians: II. By Henry Bowers, Principal of the Normal School, Stratford, Norman Miller, Professor of Mathematics in Queen's University, Kingston, And Robert E.K. Rourke, Headmaster and Instructor in Mathematics at Pickering College, Newmarket. Authorized in the Province of Alberta. Approved for use in the Province of Ontario. J.M. Dent and Sons (Canada) Ltd. And The Macmillan Company of Canada Limited.

xiv, 365, [1] pp.; 210 × 140 mm.
Mathematics For Canadians Series.

1217. BOWERS, Henry

Mathematics For Canadians: Manitoba Edition: Book II. By Henry Bowers,
Principal of the Normal School, Stratford, Norman Miller, Professor of
Mathematics in Queen's University, Kingston, And Robert E.K. Rourke,
Headmaster and Instructor in Mathematics at Pickering College, Newmar-
ket. J.M. Dent and Sons (Canada) Ltd. And The Macmillan Company of
Canada Limited.

xiv, 580 pp.; 208 × 138 mm.
Mathematics For Canadians Series.

1218. BURWELL, F.M.

To You The Torch: Democracy For Young Canadians. By F.M. Burwell, B.A.
and F.J. Clute, B.A. Advisory Editor C.R. Macleod, B.A., B.Paed. Illustrated by H.D. Ariss. The Macmillan Company of Canada Limited Toronto.

xiv, 299, [1] pp.; 215 × 155 mm.

1219. CLARK, Catherine Anthony

The Golden Pine Cone. By Catherine Anthony Clark. Illustrated by Clare
Bice. The Macmillan Company of Canada Limited Toronto 1950.

[10], 181, [1] pp.; 235 × 157 mm.

1220. COOK, Lyn

The Bells On Finland Street. By Lyn Cook. Illustrated by Stanley Wyatt.
Toronto: The Macmillan Company of Canada Limited 1950.

[8], 197, [1] pp.; 215 × 145 mm.
Reprinted in 1962.

1221. DOBRINDT, G.H.

The New World Readers, *Teacher's Handbook for My World and I*. G.H.
Dobrindt [and] Martha Brand. The Ryerson Press [and] The Macmillans in
Canada.

x, 156 pp.; 200 × 135 mm.
Revised in 1961 as *Teacher's Manual for My World and I* (see 1517).
New World Readers Series.

1222. KNIGHTS, J.J.

Notes and Questions to accompany Jane Austen's Pride and Prejudice. By J.J.
Knights, M.A., Formerly Head of the Department of English, Upper
Canada College. Toronto: The Macmillan Company of Canada Limited, at
St. Martin's House 1950.

[2], 20, [2] pp.; 163 × 115 mm.
Issued in paper.

1223. LONGSTRETH, T. Morris

Showdown. T. Morris Longstreth. Toronto: 1950, The Macmillan Company of Canada Limited.

[6], 196 pp.; 215 × 145 mm.

1224. MacGOWAN, S.J.

Avançons. By S.J. MacGowan, Formerly Supervisor of French, Protestant Board of School Commissioners, Montreal, R.C. Amaron, Instructor of French, Quebec High School, and Evelyn M. Eaton, Supervisor of French, Protestant Board of School Commissioners, Montreal. Drawings by Anne Savage. Authorized for use in the Protestant Schools of the Province of Quebec. Toronto: The Macmillan Company of Canada Limited.

xii, 205, [1] pp.; 208 × 153 mm.
First published in 1942 (see 951). This edition revised. Revised again in two books in 1961 and 1962 (see 1525 and 1567).

1225. McCOURT, Edward

Home is the Stranger. By Edward A. McCourt. Toronto: The Macmillan Company of Canada Limited 1950.

[10], 268 pp.; 208 × 148 mm.

1226. McINNES, Graham

Canadian Art. By Graham McInnes. Toronto: The Macmillan Company of Canada Limited 1950.

xii, 140 pp.; 258 × 180 mm.
First published in 1939 under the title *A Short History of Canadian Art* (see 848). This edition revised and enlarged.

1227. MUSTARD, C.A.

By Map and Compass: An Introduction to Orienteering. Edited for Canadian Schools by Major C.A. Mustard, M.B.E., B.A., B.Paed. Toronto: The Macmillan Company of Canada Limited 1950.

64 pp.; 203 × 190 mm.
Issued in paper.

1228. NORTON, Miriam

The New World Readers, *Teacher's Handbook for Under the North Star*. Miriam Norton, M.A. [and] Eleanor Boyce, M.A., PH.D. The Ryerson Press [and] The Macmillans in Canada.

x, 166 pp.; 200 × 135 mm.
Revised in 1961 as *Teacher's Manual for Under the North Star* (see 1546).
New World Readers Series.

1229. *Poems For Senior Students*. With Notes and Questions. Authorized by the Minister of Education for Ontario. Toronto: The Macmillan Company of Canada Limited, at St. Martin's House 1950.

[6], 98 pp.; 172 × 113 mm.
Issued in limp cloth.

1230. STEINHAUER, David

Lectures Choisies pour Les Commençants. By David Steinhauer, B.A., Head of Modern Languages Department, Oakwood Collegiate Institute, Toronto. Illustrated by H.J. Ariss. Toronto: The Macmillan Company of Canada Limited.

xiv, 111, [1] pp.; 190 × 120 mm.

1231.   YOUNG, Madeline
> *The Practice Book For Beckoning Trails*. Madeline Young, M.A., B.Paed.,
> [and] Lucy Barton, M.A., B.Paed. The Ryerson Press and The Macmillan
> Company of Canada Limited.
>> 112 pp.; 260 × 205 mm.
>> Issued in paper.
>> Canada Books of Prose and Verse Series.

1951

1232.   BRUCE, Charles
> *The Mulgrave Road*. By Charles Bruce. Toronto: Macmillan: 1951.
>> viii, 39, [1] pp.; 225 × 160 mm.

1233.   CALLAGHAN, Morley
> *The Loved And The Lost*. A novel by Morley Callaghan. Toronto 1951 The
> Macmillan Company of Canada Limited.
>> [6], 234 pp.; 215 × 145 mm.
>> Reprinted in the Laurentian Library (No. 9) in 1970.

1234.   CLARK, Catherine Anthony
> *The Sun Horse*. By Catherine Anthony Clark. Illustrated by Clare Bice. The
> Macmillan Company of Canada Limited Toronto 1951.
>> [12], 209, [1] pp.; 215 × 140 mm.

1235.   COOK, Lyn
> *The Little Magic Fiddler*. By Lyn Cook. Illustrated by Stanley Wyatt. To-
> ronto: The Macmillan Company of Canada Limited 1951.
>> [4], 252 pp.; 215 × 140 mm.
>> Reprinted in 1959 and 1965.

1236.   DAVIS, Adelle
> *Vitality Through Planned Nutrition*. By Adelle Davis, A.B., M.S., Consulting
> Nutritionist. Revised Canadian Edition. Authorized in British Columbia.
> The Macmillan Company of Canada Limited Toronto, 1951.
>> xii, 498 pp.; 211 × 139 mm.

1237.   DE LA ROCHE, Mazo
> *Renny's Daughter*. By Mazo De La Roche. Toronto: The Macmillan Com-
> pany of Canada Limited, at St. Martin's House 1951.
>> [8], 363, [1] pp.; 213 × 140 mm.

1238.   DUVALL, Evelyn Millis

Family Living. Evelyn Millis Duvall, PH.D. Edited by Dora S. Lewis. Illustrated by Mabel J. Woodbury. Canadian editor Harold P. Johns, PH.D., Director of Educational and Vocational Guidance, Department of Education, British Columbia. Authorized in British Columbia. The Macmillan Company of Canada Limited, Toronto — 1951.

xviii, 390 pp.; 210 × 140 mm.

1239.   EMERY, Donald W.

English Fundamentals: Form A. By Don W. Emery and John M. Kierzek. Canadian Edition. Authorized in British Columbia. Toronto: The Macmillan Company of Canada Limited 1951.

x, 240 pp.; 228 × 155 mm.
Revised in 1953 (see 1291).

1240.   ERCKMANN, Émile

Erckmann-Chatrian, *Madame Thérèse*. Edited with Introduction, Notes and Exercises by Helen B. St. John, Ontario College of Education. Toronto: The Macmillan Company of Canada Limited 1951.

viii, 347, [1] pp.; 170 × 110 mm.
First published in 1934 in Macmillan's French Matriculation Series (see 578).

1241.   FORAN, M. Roy

The Story of Matter. M. Roy Foran, M.Sc., Professor of Industrial Chemistry, Nova Scotia Technical College, Halifax [and] H. Ritchie Chipman, M.A., Ph.D., Queen Elizabeth High School, Halifax. The Macmillan Company of Canada Limited, Toronto 1951.

xii, 721, [1] pp.; 218 × 140 mm.

1242.   GATES, Arthur I.

The Pupils' Own Vocabulary Speller. By Arthur I. Gates, Henry D. Rinsland, Ina C. Sartorius, [and] Celeste Comegys Peardon. Grade 2. Revised Canadian edition. Authorized in Ontario and Quebec. Toronto: The Macmillan Company of Canada Limited.

95, [1] pp.; 207 × 137 mm.
First published in 1947 (see 1130). Authorization statement varies. Also found bound with the Grade 3 volume.
Pupils' Own Vocabulary Speller Series.

1243.   GATES, Arthur I.

The Pupils' Own Vocabulary Speller. By Arthur I. Gates, Henry D. Rinsland, Ina C. Sartorius, [and] Celeste Comegys Peardon. Grade 3. Revised Canadian edition. Authorized in Ontario and Quebec. Toronto: The Macmillan Company of Canada Limited.

112 pp.; 207 × 137 mm.
First published in 1947 (see 1131). Authorization statement varies. Also found bound with the Grade 2 volume.
Pupils' Own Vocabulary Speller Series.

1244.   GATES, Arthur I.

The Pupils' Own Vocabulary Speller. By Arthur I. Gates, Henry D. Rinsland, Ina C. Sartorius, [and] Celeste Comegys Peardon. Grade 4. Revised Canadian edition. Authorized in Ontario and Quebec. Toronto: The Macmillan Company of Canada Limited.

   128 pp.; 207 × 137 mm.
   First published in 1947 (see 1132). Authorization statement varies. Also found bound with the Grades 5 and 6 volumes.
   Pupils' Own Vocabulary Speller Series.

1245.   GATES, Arthur I.

The Pupils' Own Vocabulary Speller. By Arthur I. Gates, Henry D. Rinsland, Ina C. Sartorius, [and] Celeste Comegys Peardon. Grade 5. Revised Canadian edition. Authorized in Ontario and Quebec. Toronto: The Macmillan Company of Canada Limited.

   140 pp.; 207 × 137 mm.
   First published in 1947 (see 1133). Authorization statement varies. Also found bound with the Grades 4 and 6 volumes.
   Pupils' Own Vocabulary Speller Series.

1246.   GATES, Arthur I.

The Pupils' Own Vocabulary Speller. By Arthur I. Gates, Henry D. Rinsland, Ina C. Sartorius, [and] Celeste Comegys Peardon. Grade 6. Revised Canadian edition. Authorized in Ontario and Quebec. Toronto: The Macmillan Company of Canada Limited.

   144 pp.; 207 × 137 mm.
   First published in 1947 (see 1134). Authorization statement varies. Also found bound with the Grades 4 and 5 volumes.
   Pupils' Own Vocabulary Speller Series.

1247.   GATES, Arthur I.

The Pupils' Own Vocabulary Speller. By Arthur I. Gates, Henry D. Rinsland, Ina C. Sartorius, [and] Celeste Comegys Peardon. Grade 7. Revised Canadian edition. Approved for use in the Province of Ontario; authorized in Alberta, Nova Scotia, Prince Edward Island, Quebec and Saskatchewan. Toronto: The Macmillan Company of Canada Limited.

   144 pp.; 207 × 137 mm.
   First published in 1947 (see 1135).
   Pupils' Own Vocabulary Speller Series.

1248.   GILL, J.L.

Prose for Senior Students: An Anthology of Short Stories and Essays. Selected and edited by J.L. Gill and L.H. Newell, Instructors in English, The University of Toronto Schools. Toronto: The Macmillan Company of Canada Limited 1951.

   viii, 447, [1] pp.; 213 × 138 mm.
   Revised in 1960 (see 1491). Issued in paper in 1977.

1249. HALL, T. Roy
Book One: Grade Two: Language Journeys. By T. Roy Hall [and] E.B.
Broome. The Macmillan Company of Canada Limited Toronto.
   xii, 214 pp.; 205 × 145 mm.
   Language Journeys Series.

1250. HILTON, James
James Hilton, *Morning Journey*. Toronto: The Macmillan Company of
Canada Limited 1951.
   [6], 345, [1] pp.; 211 × 143 mm.

1251. LIMPUS, George H.
Explorations in Science. By George H. Limpus, William T. Reid, [and] John
W.B. Shore. Illustrated by Robert Banks. Authorized for use in the Province
of British Columbia. Toronto: The Macmillan Company of Canada Limited.
   xiv, 419, [1] pp.; 232 × 152 mm.
   First published in 1935 as part of *Elementary General Science* (see 644).

1252. LIMPUS, George H.
Uses of Science. By George H. Limpus, William T. Reid [and] John W.B.
Shore. Illustrated by Robert Banks. Authorized for use in the Province of
British Columbia. Toronto: The Macmillan Company of Canada Limited.
   xvi, 479, [1] pp.; 232 × 152 mm.
   First published in 1935 as part of *Elementary General Science* (see 644).

1253. MacLENNAN, Hugh
Hugh MacLennan, *Each Man's Son*. [Quotation]. Toronto: The Macmillan
Company of Canada Limited 1951.
   xii, 244 pp.; 213 × 140 mm.
   Reprinted in the Laurentian Library (No. 11) in 1971.

1254. MacLENNAN, Hugh
Hugh MacLennan, *Two Solitudes*. Arranged for School reading and with
Introduction, Notes and Questions by Claude T. Bissell, M.A., Ph.D. The
Macmillan Company of Canada Limited.
   xxvi, 382 pp.; 190 × 125 mm.
   Reprinted (with variant title-page) in 1959. Trade edition issued in 1957 (see 1403).

1255. McCOWAN, Daniel
Tidewater to Timberline. By Dan McCowan. Illustrated From Photographs by
the Author. Toronto: The Macmillan Company of Canada Limited, at St.
Martin's House 1951.
   xiv, 205, [1] pp.; 218 × 140 mm.

1256.   MEWHORT, D.S.

Mathematics for Canadians 7. By D.S. Mewhort, B.A., B.Paed., Principal, Earlscourt School, Toronto, And R.S. Godbold, B.A., B.Paed., Principal, Norway Public School, Toronto. Illustrations by Victor Child. J.M. Dent and Sons (Canada) Ltd., [and] The Macmillan Company of Canada Limited.

viii, 344 pp.; 207 × 138 mm.
Mathematics for Canadians Series.

1257.   PHELAN, Josephine

The Ardent Exile: The Life and Times of Thos. Darcy McGee. Toronto: The Macmillan Company of Canada Limited 1951.

x, 317, [1] pp.; 215 × 137 mm.

1258.   ST. JOHN, Helen B.

Livre de Lecture: A French Reader For High Schools. By Helen B. St. John. Revised Edition. Toronto: The Macmillan Company of Canada Limited 1951.

x, 304 pp.; 175 × 115 mm.
First published in 1947 (see 1157). Also found with authorization statement.

1952

1259.   BIRKETT, Geraldine

Number Experiences: Book Three. By Geraldine Birkett And Marian James. J.M. Dent & Sons (Canada) Limited, Toronto [and] Vancouver, And The Macmillan Company of Canada Limited Toronto.

[4], 94, [14] pp.; 270 × 200 mm.
Issued in paper.
Number Experiences Series.

1260.   BOWERS, Henry

Mathematics for Canadians 9. By Henry Bowers, Principal of the Normal School, Stratford, Norman Miller, Professor of Mathematics in Queen's University, Kingston, Robert E.K. Rourke, Headmaster and Instructor in Mathematics at Pickering College, Newmarket, and George E. Wallace, Instructor in Mathematics, Leaside High School. J.M. Dent and Sons (Canada) Ltd., and The Macmillan Company of Canada Limited.

xvi, 413, [1] pp.; 210 × 140 mm.
Authorization statement varies.
Mathematics for Canadians Series.

1261.   BOWERS, Henry

Research In The Training of Teachers. By Henry Bowers, M.A., D.Paed., Principal, Normal School, Stratford. J.M. Dent & Sons (Canada) Limited [and] The Macmillan Company of Canada Limited.

viii, 167, [1] pp.; 190 × 135 mm.

1262. BROOME, E.B.

Language Journeys: Grade VII. By E.B. Broome [and] J. McGechaen. Illustrations by Robert Banks. The Macmillan Company of Canada Limited Toronto.

xviii, 298 pp.; 205 × 145 mm.
Language Journeys Series.

1263. BROOME, E.B.

Language Journeys: Grade VIII. By E.B. Broome [and] J. McGechaen. Illustrated by Nancy Caudle. The Macmillan Company of Canada Limited Toronto.

xviii, 363, [1] pp.; 205 × 145 mm.
Language Journeys Series.

1263A BROWN, Arthur E.

Mathematics In Practice. By Arthur E. Brown, B.A., B.Paed., Instructor in Mathematics, Danforth Technical School, Toronto, David E. Bridge, B.A.Sc., B.Paed., Director of Mechanical and Industrial Technology, Ryerson Institute of Technology, Toronto [and] Wallace J. Morrison, B.A., B.Paed., Head of the Mathematics Department, Danforth Technical School, Toronto. Toronto: The Macmillan Company Of Canada Limited 1952.

x, 329, [5] pp.; 215 × 150 mm.
Revised in 1954 (see 1306A). Second revision published in 1960 (see 1481). Alberta revision published in 1964 (see 1662).

1264. CHARTERS, W.W.

Today's Health and Growth Series, *A Sound Body.* W.W. Charters, PH.D., Director, The Research Service, Stephens College, Columbia, Missouri, Dean F. Smiley, M.D., Consultant in Health and Physical Fitness, American Medical Association, [and] Ruth M. Strang, PH.D., Professor of Education, Teacher's College, Columbia University. Illustrations edited by Byron Musser, Inc., New York. Posed Photographs by James Snyder. Revised Canadian Edition. Authorized in Nova Scotia. The Macmillan Company of Canada Limited Toronto 1952.

x, 341, [1] pp.; 210 × 148 mm.
First published in 1941. Revised in 1947. Reprinted in 1952. Earlier printings not located.
Today's Health and Growth Series.

1265. CREIGHTON, Donald

John A. Macdonald: The Young Politician. By Donald Creighton. Toronto: The Macmillan Company of Canada Limited 1952.

xiv, 524, [2] pp.; 220 × 150 mm.
Reprinted in 1956 (paper), 1965 (cloth), 1968 and 1974 (paper).

1266.   GATES, Arthur I.

Teacher's Manual to Accompany The Pupils' Own Vocabulary Speller. Revised
Canadian Edition. By Arthur I. Gates, Henry D. Rinsland, Ina C. Sartorius,
[and] Celeste Comegys Peardon. Grades II-III. Toronto: The Macmillan
Company of Canada Limited.

> xx, 65, [1] pp.; 207 × 138 mm.
> Issued in paper.
> Pupils' Own Vocabulary Speller Series.

1267.   GATES, Arthur I.

Teacher's Manual to Accompany The Pupils' Own Vocabulary Speller. Revised
Canadian Edition. By Arthur I. Gates, Henry D. Rinsland, Ina C. Sartorius,
[and] Celeste Comegys Peardon. Grades IV-V-VI. Toronto: The Macmillan
Company of Canada Limited.

> xx, 88 pp.; 207 × 138 mm.
> Issued in paper.
> Pupils' Own Vocabulary Speller Series.

1268.   GATES, Arthur I.

Teacher's Manual to Accompany The Pupils' Own Vocabulary Speller. Revised
Canadian Edition. By Arthur I. Gates, Henry D. Rinsland, Ina C. Sartorius,
[and] Celeste Comegys Peardon. Grades VII-VIII. Toronto: The Macmillan
Company of Canada Limited.

> xx, 51, [1] pp.; 207 × 138 mm.
> Issued in paper.
> Pupils' Own Vocabulary Speller Series.

1269.   HALL, T. Roy

Book One: Grade 3: Language Journeys. T. Roy Hall [and] E.B. Broome.
Illustrations by R.W. Major and Ron Jackson. The Macmillan Company of
Canada Limited Toronto.

> xii, 228 pp.; 205 × 145 mm.
> Revised in 1960 (see 1494).
> Language Journeys Series.

1270.   HALL, T. Roy

Grade 4: Language Journeys. By T. Roy Hall [and] E.B. Broome. Illustrations by R.J. Banks. The Macmillan Company of Canada Limited Toronto.

> xii, 240 pp.; 205 × 145 mm.
> Revised in 1959 (see 1469).
> Language Journeys Series.

1271.   JAMES, Marian D.

Number Experiences: Book One: Teachers' Edition. Marian James, Director
of Primary and Kindergarten Education, Greater Victoria Schools, Victoria,
B.C. and Geraldine Birkett, Provincial Normal School, Vancouver, B.C.
J.M. Dent & Sons (Canada) Limited Toronto and Vancouver, and The
Macmillan Company of Canada Limited Toronto.

[2], 174 pp.; 270 × 200 mm.
Issued in limp cloth.
Number Experiences Series.

1272.   JAMES, Marian D.

Number Experiences: Book Two. By Marian James And Geraldine Birkett.
J.M. Dent & Sons (Canada) Limited Toronto [and] Vancouver, And The
Macmillan Company of Canada Limited Toronto.

[2], 102 pp.; 270 × 200 mm.
Issued in paper.
Number Experiences Series.

1273.   JAMES, Marian D.

Number Experiences: Book Two: Teachers' Edition. Marian James, Director
of Primary and Kindergarten Education, Greater Victoria Schools, Victoria,
B.C. and Geraldine Birkett, Provincial Normal School, Vancouver, B.C.
J.M. Dent & Sons (Canada) Limited, Toronto and Vancouver, and The
Macmillan Company of Canada Limited, Toronto.

[2], 191, [3] pp.; 270 × 200 mm.
Issued in limp cloth.
Number Experiences Series.

1274.   JAMES, Marian D.

Number Experiences: Book Three: Teachers' Edition. Marian James, Director
of Kindergarten-Primary Education, Greater Victoria Schools, Victoria, B.C.
and Geraldine Birkett, Provincial Normal School, Vancouver, B.C. J.M.
Dent & Sons (Canada) Limited, Toronto and Vancouver, and The Macmillan Company of Canada Limited Toronto.

[2], 194 pp.; 270 × 200 mm.
Issued in limp cloth.
Number Experiences Series.

1275.   MACDONALD, Marianne

Black Bass Rock. Marianne Macdonald. 1952 Macmillan: Toronto.

223, [1] pp.; 188 × 124 mm.

1276.   McPHEDRAN, Marie

Cargoes on the Great Lakes. By Marie McPhedran. Illustrations by Dorothy
Ivens. Toronto: The Macmillan Company of Canada Limited 1952.

226 pp.; 210 × 142 mm.

1277.   MEWHORT, D.S.

Mathematics for Canadians 8. By D.S. Mewhort, B.A., B.Paed., Principal,
Earlscourt School, Toronto, And R.S. Godbold, B.A., B.Paed., Principal,
Norway Public School, Toronto. Illustrations by Victor Child. Approved for
use in the Province of Ontario. J.M. Dent and Sons (Canada) Ltd. And The
Macmillan Company of Canada Limited.

xii, 386 pp.; 207 × 138 mm.
Mathematics For Canadians Series.

1278.   POMEROY, Elsie

Teacher's Guidebook for Life and Adventure. Elsie Pomeroy. The Ryerson Press [and] The Macmillans in Canada.

> x, 80 pp.; 195 × 134 mm.
> Revised in 1963 (see 1646). Issued in paper.
> Canada Books of Prose and Verse Series.

1279.   PRATT, E.J.

Towards the Last Spike. By E.J. Pratt. A Verse-Panorama Of The Struggle To Build The First Canadian Transcontinental From The Time Of The Proposed Terms Of Union With British Columbia (1870) To The Hammering Of The Last Spike In The Eagle Pass (1885). Macmillan — 1952 — Toronto.

> [8], 53, [1] pp.; 233 × 155 mm.

1280.   THOMSON, Arthur David

[Cover-title:] *It's Fun To Write*. By A.D. Thomson, Assistant Superintendent of Schools, Winnipeg, Manitoba. The Macmillan Company of Canada Limited Toronto.

> [100] pp.; 255 × 200 mm.
> Reissued the same year as *It's Fun To Write: Book One*. Both versions issued in paper.

1281.   WILSON, Ethel

The Equations of Love: Tuesday and Wednesday [and] *Lilly's Story*. By Ethel Wilson. Toronto: Macmillan 1952.

> [6], 280 pp.; 187 × 125 mm.
> Reprinted in the Laurentian Library (No.19) in 1974.

1282.   YOUNG, Madeline

Teacher's Guidebook for Beckoning Trails. Madeline Young. The Macmillans in Canada [and] The Ryerson Press.

> xiv, 102 pp.; 195 × 133 mm.
> Revised in 1962 (see 1566). Issued in paper.
> Canada Books of Prose and Verse Series.

1953

1283.   AMBROSE, Kay

Beginners, Please! A Concentrated Primer for Ballet Students of all ages. By Kay Ambrose in Collaboration with Celia Franca. Toronto: Macmillan, 1953.

> 64, [2] pp.; 189 × 126 mm.

1284.   BENTLEY, Phyllis

The House of Moreys: A Romance. By Phyllis Bentley. Toronto: The Macmillan Company of Canada Limited, 1953.

> 283, [1] pp.; 190 × 125 mm.

1285. BOWERS, Henry

Mathematics For Canadians 10. By Henry Bowers, Principal of the Normal School, Stratford, Norman Miller, Professor of Mathematics in Queen's University, Kingston, Robert E.K. Rourke, Headmaster and Instructor in Mathematics at Pickering College, Newmarket, and George E. Wallace, Instructor in Mathematics, Leaside High School. Approved for use in the Province of Ontario. J.M. Dent and Sons (Canada) Ltd., and The Macmillan Company of Canada Limited.

vi, 344 pp.; 210 × 140 mm.
Mathematics For Canadians Series.

1286. BOWERS, Henry

Chapter XII of Mathematics For Canadians, Book III, *Systems of Equations*. By Henry Bowers, Norman Miller [and] Robert E.K. Rourke. Dent: Macmillan.

260-291 pp.; 205 × 138 mm.
An offprint from *Mathematics For Canadians*, Book III. Issued in paper.
Mathematics For Canadians Series.

1287. BOYLE, Joyce

Muskoka Holiday. By Joyce Boyle. Illustrated by Geoffrey Whittam. Toronto: Macmillan 1953.

[8], 216 pp.; 200 × 135 mm.
Reissued in 1959 with new illustrations.

1288. CHARTERS, W.W.

Today's Health And Growth Series, *Growing Up Healthy*. W.W. Charters, PH.D., Dean F. Smiley, M.D., [and] Ruth M. Strang, PH.D. Revised Canadian Edition. Authorized in Nova Scotia. Illustrations edited by Byron Musser, Inc., New York. Posed Photographs by James Snyder. The Macmillan Company of Canada Limited, Toronto.

x, 302 pp.; 217 × 155 mm.
Today's Health and Growth Series.

1289. COOK, Lyn

Rebel on the Trail. By Lyn Cook. Illustrated by Ruth M. Collins. Macmillan—1953—Toronto.

vi, 247, [1] pp.; 215 × 140 mm.
Reprinted in 1965 and 1969.

1290. DE LA ROCHE, Mazo

The Whiteoak Brothers: Jalna—1923. By Mazo De La Roche. Toronto: The Macmillan Company of Canada Limited 1953.

[8], 307, [1] pp.; 200 × 135 mm.

1291. EMERY, Donald W.

English Fundamentals: Form A. By Don W. Emery and John M. Kierzek. Canadian edition. Authorized in British Columbia. Toronto: The Macmillan Company of Canada Limited 1953.

xii, 240 pp.; 228 × 162 mm.
First published in 1951 (see 1239). This edition revised.

1292.   EMORY, Florence H.M.

Public Health Nursing in Canada: Principles and Practice. By Florence H.M.
Emory, Associate Director and Associate Professor, School of Nursing,
University of Toronto. Revised Edition. Toronto: The Macmillan Company
of Canada Limited 1953.

xxii, 397, [1] pp.; 212 × 138 mm.
First published in 1945 (see 1054).

1293.   GILL, J.L.

The Macmillan Book of Poetry: An Anthology of Shorter Poems. Selected and
edited by J.L. Gill and L.H. Newell, Instructors in English, The University
of Toronto Schools. Toronto: The Macmillan Company of Canada Limited
1953.

xiv, 285, [1] pp.; 213 × 140 mm.
Also issued as *Poetry for Senior Students: An Anthology of Shorter Poems* (see 1294).

1294.   GILL, J.L.

Poetry for Senior Students: An Anthology of Shorter Poems. Selected and
Edited by J.L. Gill and L.H. Newell, Instructors in English, The University
of Toronto Schools. Toronto: The Macmillan Company of Canada Limited
1953.

xiv, 285, [1] pp.; 213 × 140 mm.
Also issued as *The Macmillan Book of Poetry: An Anthology of Shorter Poems* (see
1293). Revised in 1958 (see 1431).

1295.   HALL, T. Roy

Grade 5: Language Journeys. By T. Roy Hall [and] E.B. Broome. Illustrations by R.J. Banks. The Macmillan Company of Canada Limited Toronto.

xii, 271, [1] pp.; 205 × 145 mm.
Revised in 1959 (see 1470).
Language Journeys Series.

1296.   HILTON, James

Time and Time Again. By James Hilton. Toronto: The Macmillan Company
of Canada Limited, 1953.

[8], 306 pp.; 209 × 140 mm.

1297.   LONGSTRETH, T. Morris

Great Stories of Canada, *The Scarlet Force: The Making of the Mounted Police*.
By T. Morris Longstreth. Illustrated by Ruth M. Collins. Toronto: 1953:
Macmillan.

x, 182 pp.; 213 × 138 mm.
Reprinted in 1954, 1958, 1960 and 1963. Revised in 1964 (see 1683). Second revised
edition published in 1974 (see 2276).
Great Stories of Canada Series.

1298.   MacINNIS, Grace

J.S. Woodsworth: A Man to Remember. By Grace MacInnis. Toronto: The
Macmillan Company of Canada Limited 1953.

xvi, 336 pp.; 219 × 137 mm.
Reprinted in the Laurentian Library (No. 23) in 1974.

1299.   MUNSTERHJELM, Erik

Erik Munsterhjelm, *The Wind and the Caribou: Hunting and Trapping in
Northern Canada*. Toronto: The Macmillan Company of Canada Limited,
1953.

vi, 234 pp.; 215 × 140 mm.
Reprinted in the Laurentian Library (No. 24) in 1974.

1300.   PRATT, E.J.

Poems For Upper School. With Notes and Questions by E.J. Pratt, Professor
Emeritus, Department of English, Victoria College, Toronto. Authorized by
the Minister of Education for Ontario. Macmillan—1953.

[6], 81, [1] pp.; 172 × 115 mm.
Issued in limp cloth.

1301.   RADCLIFF, Thomas

Authentic Letters From Upper Canada. Including an account of Canadian
Field Sports by Thomas William Magrath: The whole edited by The Rev.
Thomas Radcliff: Illustrated by Samuel Lover and Introduced by James
John Talman. Toronto: The Macmillan Company of Canada Limited 1953.

xxiv, 207, [1] pp.; 220 × 140 mm.
Pioneer Books Series.

1302.   SWAYZE, Beulah Garland

Teacher's Guidebook for Our Heritage. Beulah Swayze [and] J. Fred Swayze.
Canada Books of Prose and Verse. The Ryerson Press [and] The Macmillans
in Canada.

xiv, 134 pp.; 195 × 130 mm.
Issued in paper.
Canada Books of Prose and Verse Series.

1954

1303.   ALLEN, Ralph

The Chartered Libertine. *By Ralph Allen*. [Quotation]. Toronto: Macmillan:
1954.

[6], 270 pp.; 217 × 140 mm.

1304.   BERTON, Pierre

Great Stories of Canada, *The Golden Trail: The Story of the Klondike Rush*. By
Pierre Berton. Illustrated by Duncan Macpherson. Toronto: 1954: Macmillan.

[10], 147, [1] pp.; 213 × 134 mm.
Reprinted in 1959, 1962, 1964 and 1967. Revised in 1973 (see 2185).
Great Stories of Canada Series.

1305.   BICE, Clare

The Great Island: A Story of Mystery in Newfoundland. Written And Illustrated by Claire Bice. The Macmillan Company of Canada Limited, Toronto, 1954.

[8], 103, [1] pp.; 218 × 165 mm.
Reprinted in 1962.

1306.   BROWN, Arthur E.

Mathematics in Practice. Revised Edition with added material for second year work. By Arthur E. Brown, B.A., B.Paed., Instructor in Mathematics, Danforth Technical School, Toronto, David E. Bridge, B.A.Sc., B.Paed., Director of Mechanical and Industrial Technology, Ryerson Institute of Technology, Toronto, [and] Wallace J. Morrison, B.A., B.Paed., Head of the Mathematics Department, Danforth Technical School, Toronto. Toronto: The Macmillan Company of Canada Limited.

x, 450 pp.; 217 × 140 mm.
First published in 1952 (see 1263A). Second revision published in 1960 (see 1481). Alberta revision published in 1964 (see 1662).
Mathematics in Practice Series.

1307.   BROWN, Arthur E.

Supplement To Mathematics in Practice. (Original Edition). By Arthur E. Brown, B.A., B.Paed., Instructor in Mathematics, Danforth Technical School, Toronto, David E. Bridge, B.A.Sc., B.Paed., Director of Mechanical and Industrial Technology, Ryerson Institute of Technology, Toronto, [and] Wallace J. Morrison, B.A., B.Paed., Head of the Mathematics Department, Danforth Technical School, Toronto. Toronto: The Macmillan Company of Canada Limited.

iv, 120 pp.; 205 × 150 mm.
Issued in paper.
Mathematics in Practice Series.

1308.   BRUCE, Charles

The Channel Shore. By Charles Bruce. Toronto: 1954: Macmillan.

[6], 398 pp.; 220 × 140 mm.
Reprinted in paper in 1957.

1309.   CAMPBELL, Marjorie Wilkins

Great Stories of Canada, *The Nor'Westers: The Fight for the Fur Trade.* By Marjorie Wilkins Campbell. Illustrated by Illingworth Kerr. Toronto: 1954: Macmillan.

x, 176 pp.; 213 × 138 mm.
Reprinted in 1956, 1958, 1961, 1966 and 1971. Revised in 1974 (see 2245).
Great Stories of Canada Series.

1310. CRAWFORD, J.T.

A New Algebra for High Schools. By J.T. Crawford, Late Professor of
Mathematics, Ontario College of Education, Toronto. As Completely Re-
vised by J.E. Dean, Director of Mathematics, Central Technical School,
Toronto, and W.A. Jackson, Head of the Department of Mathematics,
Oakwood Collegiate, Toronto. Toronto: The Macmillan Company of
Canada Limited, at St. Martin's House 1954.

xii, 441, [1] pp.; 190 × 128 mm.
First published in 1915 (see 81). Revised in 1916 (see 102A). Second revised edition
published in 1939 (see 832).

1311. CREIGHTON, Donald

[Cover-title:] *Canada in the World*. Donald Creighton. [Verso:] 1954 The
Macmillan Company of Canada Limited.

227-254 pp.; 227 × 150 mm.
This paper is an offprint from *Canada's Tomorrow* (see 1320). Issued in paper.

1312. DE LA ROCHE, Mazo

Variable Winds at Jalna. By Mazo De La Roche. Toronto: The Macmillan
Company of Canada Limited 1954.

[10], 359, [1] pp.; 196 × 130 mm.

1313. DEAN, J.E.

Logarithms the Slide Rule and Tables. By J.E. Dean, M.A., B.Paed., C.D.A.,
Central Technical School, Toronto, And C.M. Rutledge, B.A., B.Paed.,
Danforth Technical School, Toronto. The Macmillan Company of Canada
Limited 1954.

x, 102 pp.; 210 × 135 mm.
Reprinted in *Senior Technical Mathematics* (see 1496). Issued in paper.

1314. EATON, Evelyn M.

Commençons: Course in French for Grade III. By Evelyn M. Eaton, Super-
visor of French, Protestant School Board of Greater Montreal, and S.J.
MacGowan, Former Supervisor of French, Protestant Board of School
Commissioners, Montreal. The Macmillan Company of Canada Limited.

iv, 84 pp.; 215 × 132 mm.

1315. EATON, Evelyn M.

Jouons: Book I. Evelyn M. Eaton, Supervisor of French, Protestant School
Board of Greater Montreal [and] S.J. MacGowan, Former Supervisor of
French, Protestant Board of School Commissioners, Montreal. Illustrated by
Gundega Janfelde. Authorized for use in the Protestant Schools of the
Province of Quebec. The Macmillan Company of Canada Limited.

x, 105, [1] pp.; 217 × 135 mm.
First published in 1941 (see 915). This edition revised.

1316.   EATON, Evelyn M.

Jouons: Book Two. Evelyn M. Eaton, Supervisor of French, Protestant
School Board of Greater Montreal [and] S.J. MacGowan, Former Supervisor
of French, Protestant Board of School Commissioners, Montreal. Illustrated
by Gundega Janfelde. Authorized for use in the Protestant Schools of the
Province of Quebec. The Macmillan Company of Canada Limited.

viii, 144 pp.; 217 × 135 mm.
First published in 1941 (see 915). This edition revised.

1317.   EATON, Evelyn M.

Teacher's Manual for Jouons: Books I and II. By Evelyn M. Eaton, Super-
visor of French, Protestant School Board of Greater Montreal and S.J.
MacGowan, Former Supervisor of French, Protestant Board of School
Commissioners, Montreal. The Macmillan Company of Canada Limited.

[8], 120 pp.; 216 × 135 mm.

1318.   FUSEE, M.A.L.

Arithmetic for Canadians 6. General Editor F.J. Gathercole, B.A., M.ED.
M.A.L. Fusee, R.S. Godbold, [and] D.S. Mewhort. Illustrations By
Lindsay, Marjorie And Victor Child. J.M. Dent And Sons (Canada) Limited
[and] The Macmillan Company of Canada Limited.

xiv, 335, [1] pp.; 205 × 150 mm.
Arithmetic For Canadians Series.

1319.   GARLAND, Aileen

Canada: Then and Now. By Aileen Garland. Based on *A First Book of
Canadian History* by W. Stewart Wallace. Illustrated by Robert Banks. The
Macmillan Company of Canada Limited.

x, 461, [1] pp.; 230 × 150 mm.

1320.   GILMOUR, G.P.

*Canada's Tomorrow: Papers and Discussion, Canada's Tomorrow Confer-
ence, Quebec City, November 1953*. Edited by G.P. Gilmour. Illustrations by
Eric Aldwinckle. Toronto: Macmillan 1954.

xii, 324 pp; 233 × 155 mm.

1321.   HALL, T. Roy

Grade 6: Language Journeys. By T. Roy Hall [and] E.B. Broome. Illustrations by R.J. Banks. The Macmillan Company of Canada Limited.

xiv, 306 pp.; 205 × 145 mm.
Revised in 1960 (see 1495).
Language Journeys Series.

1322.   LONGSTRETH, T. Morris

Great Stories Of Canada, *The Force Carries On: The Sequel to the Scarlet
Force*. By T. Morris Longstreth. Illustrated by Clare Bice. Toronto: 1954:
Macmillan.

x, 182 pp.; 213 × 138 mm.
Reprinted in 1964.
Great Stories of Canada Series.

1323. MacLENNAN, Hugh

Thirty & Three. By Hugh MacLennan. Edited by Dorothy Duncan.
[Quotation]. Toronto: The Macmillan Company of Canada Limited 1954.
x, 261, [1] pp.; 218 × 140 mm.

1324. McINNES, Graham

Lost Island: An Adventure. By Graham McInnes. Toronto: Macmillan 1954.
x, 229, [1] pp.; 193 × 130 mm.

1325. MILLER, Orlo

Great Stories Of Canada, *Raiders of the Mohawk: The Story of Butler's
Rangers*. By Orlo Miller. Illustrated by John Maclellan. Toronto: 1954:
Macmillan.
x, 182 pp.; 213 × 138 mm.
Reprinted in 1955.
Great Stories of Canada Series.

1326. PHELAN, Josephine

The Boy Who Ran Away. By Josephine Phelan. Illustrated by Vernon Mould.
Macmillan—Toronto—1954.
viii, 152 pp.; 210 × 136 mm.
Great Stories of Canada Series.

1327. ROBERTSON, John Ross

Old Toronto: A Selection of Excerpts From Landmarks of Toronto. By John
Ross Robertson. Edited, Integrated, and sometimes Emended by E.C. Kyte.
With an Index and Twenty-seven of the Original Illustrations. Toronto: The
Macmillan Company of Canada Limited 1954.
xii, 346 pp.; 220 × 140 mm.
Pioneer Books Series.

1328. STANLEY, George F.G.

Canada's Soldiers 1604-1954: The Military History of an Unmilitary People.
By George F.G. Stanley, Royal Military College of Canada. In collaboration
with Harold M. Jackson, Department of Veteran Affairs. Maps by C.C.J.
Bond, Historical Section, General Staff Army Headquarters. Toronto: The
Macmillan Company of Canada Limited 1954.
[12], 401, [1] pp.; 240 × 160 mm.
Revised in 1960 (see 1506). Second revision published in 1974 (see 2294).

1329. STEINHAUER, David

Les Maîtres Conteurs: An Anthology of French Short Stories. Selected and
Edited With Notes, Exercises and Vocabulary by David Steinhauer, B.A.,
Oakwood Collegiate Institute, Toronto. Macmillan Toronto 1954.
x, 225, [1] pp.; 213 × 140 mm.

1330. THOMSON, Arthur David

[Cover-title:] *It's Fun To Write: Book Two*. By A.D. Thomson, Assistant Superintendent of Schools, Winnipeg, Manitoba. The Macmillan Company of Canada Limited Toronto.

[96] pp.; 245 × 200 mm.
Issued in paper.

1331. WILSON, Ethel

Swamp Angel. By Ethel Wilson. Toronto: Macmillan 1954.

vi, 215, [1] pp.; 189 × 125 mm.
Reprinted in 1955.

1955

1332. CLARK, Catherine Anthony

The One-Winged Dragon. By Catherine Anthony Clark. Illustrated by Clare Bice. Toronto: Macmillan: 1955.

271, [1] pp.; 220 × 145 mm.

1333. COOK, Lyn

Jady and the General. Lyn Cook. Illustrated by Murray Smith. Macmillan Toronto 1955.

vi, 242 pp.; 215 × 140 mm.

1334. CRAIG, Gerald M.

Early Travellers In The Canadas 1791-1867. Selected and Edited with an Introduction by Gerald M. Craig. Toronto: The Macmillan Company of Canada Limited 1955.

xxxvi, 300 pp.; 210 × 130 mm.
Issued in cloth and paper.
Pioneer Books Series.

1335. CRANE, Stephen

St. Martin's Classics, *The Red Badge of Courage*. By Stephen Crane. Biographical Introduction, Questions and Notes by Bert Case Diltz, Professor of Methods in English and History, Ontario College of Education, University of Toronto. Toronto: The Macmillan Company of Canada Limited at St. Martin's House 1955.

[4], 223, [1] pp.; 170 × 110 mm.
St. Martin's Classics Series.

1336. CREIGHTON, Donald

John A. Macdonald: The Old Chieftain. By Donald Creighton. Toronto: The Macmillan Company of Canada Limited 1955.

xii, 630 pp.; 220 × 152 mm.
Reprinted in 1965, 1966 (paper), 1968, 1973 and 1979 (paper).

1337.   DE LA ROCHE, Mazo

The Song of Lambert. By Mazo de la Roche. Illustrated by Eileen A. Soper. Toronto: Macmillan 1955.

[4], 51, [1] pp.; 220 × 143 mm.

1338.   FARRAR, F.S.

Great Stories Of Canada, *Arctic Assignment: The Story of the St. Roch*. By Sgt. F.S. Farrar, R.C.M.P. Edited by Barrett Bonnezen. Illustrated by Vernon Mould. Toronto: 1955: Macmillan.

x, 180 pp.; 213 × 138 mm.
Reprinted in 1959, 1963 and 1967. Revised in 1973 (see 2200).
Great Stories of Canada Series.

1339.   HALE, R.L.

St. Martin's Classics, *The Open Road: Stories Essays and Travel Tales*. Selected and edited by R.L. Hale, Head of English Department, Peterborough Collegiate and Vocational School. Toronto: The Macmillan Company of Canada Limited, at St. Martin's House 1955.

xii, 205, [1] pp.; 172 × 110 mm.

1340.   HAMIL, Fred Coyne

Lake Erie Baron: The Story of Colonel Thomas Talbot. By Fred Coyne Hamil. Toronto: The Macmillan Company of Canada Limited 1955.

x, 326 pp.; 215 × 137 mm.

1341.   HARVEY, D.C.

Journeys To The Island Of St. John or Prince Edward Island 1775-1832. Edited by D.C. Harvey. Toronto: The Macmillan Company of Canada Limited 1955.

viii, 213, [1] pp.; 217 × 140 mm.
Pioneer Books Series.

1342.   HILTZ, Mary C.

Nutrition: An Elementary Text. By Mary C. Hiltz, B.S.(Columbia), M.A.(Tor.), Associate Professor of Foods and Nutrition, School of Home Economics, University of Manitoba. Toronto: The Macmillan Company of Canada Limited.

xiv, 175, [1] pp.; 215 × 138 mm.
Revised in 1965 (see 1731).

1343.   JAMES, Marian D.

Arithmetic for Canadians 3. By Marian D. James. General Editor F. Gathercole, B.A., M.Ed. Illustrated By Priscilla Hutchings And Jacqueline Valentine. J.M. Dent And Sons (Canada) Limited [and] The Macmillan Company of Canada Limited.

352 pp.; 205 × 150 mm.
Arithmetic For Canadians Series.

1344.   LEFROY, John Henry

John Henry Lefroy, *In Search Of The Magnetic North: A Soldier-Surveyor's Letters from the North-West, 1843-1844*. Edited by George F.G. Stanley. Toronto: The Macmillan Company of Canada Limited 1955.

> xx, 171, [1] pp.; 220 × 140 mm.
> Pioneer Books Series.

1345.   MACDONALD, Marianne

Smugglers Cove. Marianne Macdonald. Illustrated by Selwyn Dewdney. The Macmillan Company of Canada Limited Toronto 1955.

> [8], 208 pp.; 211 × 134 mm.

1346.   McCOURT, Edward

Great Stories Of Canada, *Buckskin Brigadier: The Story of the Alberta Field Force*. By Edward McCourt. Illustrated by Vernon Mould. Toronto: 1955: Macmillan.

> x, 150 pp.; 213 × 138 mm.
> Reprinted in paper in 1962 and 1968.
> Great Stories of Canada Series.

1347.   McCOWAN, Daniel

Upland Trails. By Dan McCowan. Illustrated From Photographs by the Author. Toronto: The Macmillan Company of Canada Limited, at St. Martin's House 1955.

> xvi, 158 pp.; 215 × 140 mm.

1348.   McKEOWN, Elizabeth

At Home and Abroad. By Elizabeth McKeown. Illustrations by Robert Banks and Selwyn Dewdney. The Macmillan Company of Canada Limited 1955.

> x, 236 pp.; 205 × 144 mm.
> Reprinted, with minor revisions, in 1958 (see 1440). Published in French in 1957 (see 1405).

1349.   McNABB, V.

Arithmetic for Canadians 4. V. McNabb. General Editor F.J. Gathercole, B.A., M.ED. Illustrations Stanley Wyatt And Lindsay, Marjorie And Victor Child. J.M. Dent And Sons (Canada) Limited [and] The Macmillan Company of Canada Limited.

> xiv, 322 pp.; 205 × 150 mm.
> Arithmetic For Canadians Series.

1350.   MCNABB, V.

Arithmetic for Canadians 4. V. McNabb. *Answer Book*. J.M. Dent and Sons (Canada) Limited [and] The Macmillan Company of Canada Limited.

> [2], 26 pp.; 197 × 147 mm.
> Issued in paper.
> Arithmetic for Canadians Series.

1351. PRATT, E.J.

[Cover-title:] *Magic in Everything*. E.J. Pratt.

6, [2] pp.; 164 × 103 mm.
Imprint on last page of text. Issued in paper.

1352. RIÈSE, Laure

L'âme de la Poésie Canadienne Francaise. Selected, edited and with Biographical Notes by Laure Rièse, Dip.d'Et. Sup., M.A., Ph.D., O.A., Associate Professor of French, Victoria University, Toronto. Toronto: The Macmillan Company of Canada Limited 1955.

xxxii, 263, [1] pp.; 217 × 140 mm.
Issued in cloth and paper.

1353. ROWÀT, Donald C.

Your Local Government: A Sketch of the Municipal System in Canada. By Donald C. Rowat, Head of the Department of Political Science, Carleton University, Ottawa. Toronto: The Macmillan Company of Canada Limited 1955.

xii, 148 pp.; 195 × 120 mm.
Reprinted in 1962, 1965 and 1968. Revised in 1975 (see 2352). Issued in paper.

1354. SULLIVAN, J.A.

Red Sails on the Great Lakes. By J.A. (Pat) Sullivan. Macmillan Toronto 1955.

x, 189, [1] pp.; 218 × 135 mm.
Issued in cloth and paper.

1355. WADE, Mason

The French Canadians 1760-1945. By Mason Wade. Toronto: The Macmillan Company of Canada Limited 1955.

xvi, 1136 pp.; 220 × 150 mm.
Reprinted (with corrections) in 1956. Revised in two volumes in 1968 (see 1963 and 1964). Revised and issued in the Laurentian Library in two volumes (No. 33 and 44) in 1975 and 1976.

1356. WILKINSON, Anne

Anne Wilkinson, *The Hangman Ties the Holly*. Toronto: Macmillan 1955.

[6], 57, [1] pp.; 222 × 142 mm.

1357. WILLISON, Gladys

Land of the Chinook: Stories of Early Alberta. By Gladys Willison. Illustrated by Vernon Mould. Toronto: The Macmillan Company of Canada Limited 1955.

viii, 197, [1] pp.; 217 × 140 mm.

1358. WOOD, Edgar Allardyce

Great Stories Of Canada, *The Map-Maker: The Story of David Thompson*. By Kerry Wood [pseud.]. Illustrated by William Wheeler. Toronto: Macmillan: 1955.

[6], 185, [1] pp.; 213 × 138 mm.
Reprinted in 1957, 1959, 1962, 1966 and 1968.
Great Stories of Canada Series.

1359. YONG, Pak Jong

Korean Boy. By Pak Jong Yong. With Jock Carroll. Toronto: The Macmillan Company of Canada Limited 1955.

[8], 184 pp.; 213 × 140 mm.

1956

1360. ASHLEY, C.A.

Corporation Finance in Canada. By C.A. Ashley, B.Com., F.C.A., Professor of Commerce, Department of Political Economy, University of Toronto [and] J.E. Smyth, M. Com., C.A., Associate Professor of Commerce and Administration, Queen's University. Toronto: The Macmillan Company of Canada Limited 1956.

253, [1] pp.; 220 × 140 mm.
The first five chapters were originally published in 1945 (see 1030). First revised edition published in 1947 (see 1124). Reprinted frequently.

1361. BICE, Clare

A Dog for Davie's Hill. Written and illustrated by Clare Bice. The Macmillan Company of Canada Limited Toronto 1956.

viii, 120 pp.; 210 × 165 mm.
Reprinted in 1958 and 1970.

1362. BOYCE, Eleanor

Teacher's Manual for Canada: Then and Now. Eleanor Boyce, M.A., Ph.D., [and] Aileen Garland, B.A., M.Ed. The Macmillan Company of Canada Limited.

vi, 69, [1] pp.; 225 × 145 mm.
Issued in paper.

1363. BUCHANAN, Donald W.

Le Français Pratique. Revised Edition. Donald W. Buchanan, M.A., D.de l'Univ., French Specialist, Town of Mount Royal High School, Margaret E.B. Buchanan, M.A., Formerly Assistant Supervisor of French in the Protestant Schools of the Province of Quebec, [And] Robert A. Peck, M.A., Supervisor of French, Westmount. Illustrated by Pat and Bill Wheeler. Authorized for use in the Protestant Schools of Quebec. The Macmillan Company of Canada Limited Toronto.

xii, 411, [1] pp.; 238 × 155 mm.
First published in 1946 in two volumes (see 1100 and 1100A).

1364.   CHALMERS, J.W.

Great Stories Of Canada, *Red River Adventure: The Story of the Selkirk Settlers*. By J.W. Chalmers. Illustrated by Lewis Parker. Toronto: 1956: Macmillan.

   158 pp.; 216 × 140 mm.
   Reprinted in 1959, 1962 and 1966.
   Great Stories of Canada Series.

1365.   CHITTICK, Rae

Health for Canadians. Rae Chittick, Director, School for Graduate Nurses, McGill University, Formerly Associate Professor of Education, University of Alberta. Toronto: The Macmillan Company of Canada 1956.

   x, 373, [1] pp.; 228 × 163 mm.
   Revised edition published in 1962 (see 1562).

1366.   CREIGHTON, Donald

The Empire of the St. Lawrence. By Donald Creighton. Toronto: The Macmillan Company of Canada Limited 1956.

   x, 441, [1] pp.; 227 × 157 mm.
   Reprinted in 1970 in paper and in 1972 in cloth.

1367.   EASTERBROOK, W.T.

Canadian Economic History. By W.T. Easterbrook, M.A., PH.D., Professor of Economics, Department of Political Economy, University of Toronto, And Hugh G.J. Aitken, M.A., Ph.D., Assistant Professor of Economics, Division of Social Sciences, University of California, Riverside. Toronto: The Macmillan Company of Canada Limited 1956.

   xiv, 606 pp.; 238 × 158 mm.
   Reprinted frequently.

1368.   GILL, J.L.

Invitation to Poetry: An Anthology for Junior Students. Selected and edited by J.L. Gill and L.H. Newell, Instructors in English, the University of Toronto Schools. Toronto: The Macmillan Company of Canada Limited, 1956.

   xii, 267, [1] pp.; 188 × 126 mm.

1369.   GOOD, Mabel Tinkiss

At the Dark of the Moon. By Mabel Tinkiss Good. Illustrated by Clare Bice. 1956 The Macmillan Company of Canada Limited Toronto.

   [10], 69, [1] pp.; 225 × 170 mm.
   Reprinted in 1966.

1370.   GRAY, Elma E.

Wilderness Christians: The Moravian Mission to the Delaware Indians. By Elma E. Gray in collaboration with Leslie Robb Gray. Illustrations by Clare Bice. Toronto: The Macmillan Company of Canada Limited 1956.

   xiv, 354 pp.; 237 × 155 mm.

1371.   HAIG-BROWN, Roderick

Great Stories Of Canada, *Captain of the Discovery: The Story of Captain George Vancouver*. By Roderick Haig-Brown. Illustrated by Robert Banks. Toronto: Macmillan: 1956.

[10], 181, [1] pp.; 213 × 138 mm.
Reprinted in 1959, 1964, 1967 and 1972. Revised in 1974 (see 2263).
Great Stories of Canada Series.

1372.   ISRAEL, Charles E.

How Many Angels. A Novel by Charles E. Israel. Toronto: Macmillan 1956.

vi, 329, [1] pp.; 200 × 130 mm.

1373.   JAMES, Marian D.

Arithmetic for Canadians 3. Marian D. James. *Answer Book*. J.M Dent and Sons (Canada) Limited [and] The Macmillan Company of Canada Limited.

[4], 47, [1] pp.; 197 × 147 mm.
Issued in paper.
Arithmetic For Canadians Series.

1374.   LAMBERT, R.S.

Great Stories Of Canada, *Redcoat Sailor: The Adventures of Sir Howard Douglas*. By R.S. Lambert. Illustrated by Adrian Dingle. Toronto: 1956: Macmillan.

160 pp.; 213 × 138 mm.
Reprinted in 1963 and 1967.
Great Stories of Canada Series.

1375.   McNABB, V.

[Cover-title:]*Arithmetic Workbook For Grade 4*. McNabb. J.M. Dent & Sons (Canada) Limited [and] The Macmillan Company of Canada Limited.

96 pp.; 275 × 213 mm.
Issued in paper.
Arithmetic For Canadians Series.

1376.   ORR, Andrew A.

Invitation to Drama: One-Act Plays For Secondary Schools. Selected and Edited by Andrew A. Orr, Head of English Department, Tillsonburg District High School. Toronto: The Macmillan Company of Canada Limited 1956.

viii, 208 pp.; 185 × 125 mm.
Revised in 1967 (see 1867).

1377.   PHELAN, Josephine

Great Stories Of Canada, *The Bold Heart: The Story of Father Lacombe*. By Josephine Phelan. Illustrated by Jerry Lazare. Toronto: 1956: Macmillan.

[10], 182 pp.; 213 × 138 mm.
Great Stories of Canada Series.

1378. *Poems For Upper School 1956-57. The Prologue to The Canterbury Tales* by Geoffrey Chaucer. With Notes and Questions by Charles W. Dunn, Formerly Professor of English, University College, Toronto. *The Roosevelt and the Antinoe* by E.J. Pratt. With Notes and Questions by the Macmillan Editors. Authorized by the Minister of Education for Ontario. The Macmillan Company of Canada Limited Toronto.

> [8], 50, [2] pp.; 185 × 125 mm.
> Issued in paper.

1379. VAN VLIET, M.L.

Physical Education For Junior and Senior High Schools. By M.L. Van Vliet, Ed.D., Director of the School of Physical Education, University of Alberta. The Macmillan Company of Canada Limited Toronto 1956.

> vi, 321, [1] pp.; 235 × 155 mm.
> Revised edition published in 1967 (see 1892).

1380. WEST, Rebecca

The Fountain Overflows. A Novel by Rebecca West. 1956 The Macmillan Company of Canada Limited Toronto.

> [8], 435, [1] pp.; 215 × 140 mm.

1381. WHALLEY, George

Writing in Canada: Proceedings Of The Canadian Writers' Conference, Queen's University, 28-31 July, 1955. Edited by George Whalley. With an Introduction by F.R. Scott. Toronto: The Macmillan Company of Canada Limited 1956.

> xii, 147, [1] pp.; 203 × 130 mm.
> Issued in cloth and paper.

1382. WILKINSON, Anne

Lions in the Way: A Discursive History of the Oslers. By Anne Wilkinson. [Quotation]. 1956, The Macmillan Company of Canada Limited Toronto.

> xii, 274 pp.; 220 × 140 mm.
> Issued in cloth and paper.

1383. WILSON, Ethel

Love and Salt Water. By Ethel Wilson. 1956 The Macmillan Company of Canada Toronto.

> x, 202, [2] pp.; 200 × 130 mm.

1384. WISEMAN, Adele

The Sacrifice. A novel by Adele Wiseman. 1956, The Macmillan Company of Canada Limited Toronto.

> 346 pp.; 218 × 145 mm.
> Reprinted in the Laurentian Library (No. 8) in 1968.

1957

1385. ALBION-MEEK, Peggy

The Great Adventurer. Peggy Albion-Meek, B.A. Introduction, Notes and Exercises by William J. Ellison, M.A., Head of the English Department, Weston Collegiate and Vocational School. Authorized in the Province of Saskatchewan. Toronto: The Macmillan Company of Canada Limited 1957.

viii, 154 pp.; 185 × 125 mm.

1386. BARBEAU, Marius

I Have Seen Quebec. By Marius Barbeau. Designed by Arthur Price. The Macmillan Company of Canada Limited Toronto 1957.

163, [1] pp.; 210 × 158 mm.
Issued in paper.

1387. BEKE, Laszlo

A Student's Diary: Budapest, October 16-November 1, 1956. By Laszlo Beke. Edited And Translated By Leon Kossar And Ralph M. Zoltan. Toronto 1957 The Macmillan Company of Canada Limited.

125, [1] pp.; 210 × 140 mm.

1388. BIRKETT, Geraldine

[Cover-title:] *Arithmetic For Canadians Book One*. Gerladine Birkett, Associate Professor of Education, University of British Columbia [and] Marian James, Director of Kindergarten and Primary Studies, Victoria, British Columbia. Illustrated by R. Van den Hoogen and others. Copyright, (Canada) 1957, by J.M. Dent & Sons (Canada) Limited and The Macmillan Company of Canada Limited.

104 pp.; 270 × 210 mm.
Issued in paper.
Arithmetic For Canadians Series.

1389. BIRKETT, Geraldine

[Cover-title:] *Arithmetic For Canadians Book Two*. Gerladine Birkett, Associate Professor of Education, University of British Columbia [and] Marian James, Director of Kindergarten and Primary Studies, Victoria, British Columbia. Illustrated by R. Van den Hoogen and others. Copyright, (Canada) 1957, by J.M. Dent & Sons (Canada) Limited and The Macmillan Company of Canada Limited.

120 pp.; 270 × 210 mm.
Issued in paper.
Arithmetic For Canadians Series.

1390. CAMPBELL, Marjorie Wilkins

The North West Company. Marjorie Wilkins Campbell. Toronto: The Macmillan Company of Canada Limited 1957.

xvi, 295, [1] pp.; 220 × 140 mm.
Revised in 1973 (see 2188).

1391. COOK, Lyn

Pegeen and the Pilgrim. By Lyn Cook. Illustrated by Pat and Bill Wheeler. Toronto: The Macmillan Company of Canada Limited 1957.

vi, 248 pp.; 215 × 140 mm.
Issued in cloth and paper. Reprinted in 1961 and 1970.

1392. CREIGHTON, Donald

Dominion of the North: A History of Canada. New Edition. By Donald Creighton. 1957 The Macmillan Company of Canada Limited Toronto.

xii, 619, [1] pp.; 220 × 153 mm.
New edition reprinted in 1962, 1966, 1967 and 1972.

1393. DE LA ROCHE, Mazo

Ringing the Changes: An Autobiography. By Mazo De La Roche. [Quotation]. Toronto: 1957: Macmillan.

xvi, 304 pp.; 220 × 140 mm.

1394. EUBANK, Howard L.

Basic Physics for Secondary Schools. Howard L. Eubank, Vice-Principal, Etobicoke Collegiate Institute, Toronto, Ontario, John M. Ramsay, Principal, Smith Falls Collegiate Institute, Smith Falls, Ontario, [and] Leslie A. Rickard, Head of Science Department, Forest Hill Collegiate Institute, Toronto, Ontario. Illustrations by Kenneth Dallison and Robert Kunz. The Macmillan Company of Canada Limited Toronto 1957.

xvi, 416 pp.; 240 × 158 mm.
Reprinted with corrections in 1958. Revised in 1963 (see 1627).

1395. FAIRLEY, T.C.

Great Stories Of Canada, *The True North: The Story of Captain Joseph Bernier*. By T.C. Fairley & J. Charles E. Israel. Illustrated by James Hill. Toronto: 1957: Macmillan.

160 pp.; 213 × 140 mm.
Great Stories of Canada Series.

1396. FIDLER, Vera

Chuckwagon of the Circle B. By Vera Fidler. Illustrated by Douglas Stephens. 1957 The Macmillan Company of Canada Limited Toronto.

174 pp.; 215 × 140 mm.

1397. GATHERCOLE, F.J.

Arithmetic for Canadians 5. F.J. Gathercole, R.S. Godbold, D.S. Mewhort. Illustrated by Lindsay, Marjorie And Victor Child, Kenneth Dallison [and] Stanley Wyatt. J.M. Dent And Sons (Canada) Limited [and] The Macmillan Company of Canada Limited.

380 pp.; 205 × 150 mm.
Revised in 1960 (see 1500).
Arithmetic For Canadians Series.

1398.   GATHERCOLE, F.J.

Teacher's Manual For Arithmetic For Canadians. F.J. Gathercole, B.A.,
M.Ed., Superintendent of Public Schools, Saskatoon. J.M. Dent & Sons
(Canada) Limited [and] The Macmillan Company of Canada Limited.

   iv, 75, [1] pp.; 201 × 150 mm.
   Issued in paper.
   Arithmetic For Canadians Series.

1399.   GUILLET, Edwin

The Pathfinders of North America. Edwin and Mary Guillet. Revised by
Marian Prueter. Maps by Robert Kunz—Illustrations by Lewis Parker. The
Macmillan Company of Canada Limited.

   x, 364 pp.; 207 × 150 mm.
   First published in 1939 (see 839).

1400.   HARMON, Daniel William

*Sixteen Years In The Indian Country: The Journal of Daniel William Harmon
1800-1816.* Edited with an Introduction by W. Kaye Lamb, Dominion
Archivist. Maps by C.C.J. Bond, Historical Section, General Staff, Army
Headquarters. Toronto: The Macmillan Company of Canada Limited 1957.

   xxx, 277, [1] pp.; 213 × 135 mm.
   Issued in cloth and paper.
   Pioneer Books Series.

1401.   HUTCHISON, Margaret

Tamarac. By Margaret Hutchison. Macmillan 1957 Toronto.

   [6], 282 pp.; 213 × 140 mm.

1402.   JAMIESON, Stuart

Industrial Relations in Canada. By Stuart Jamieson, University of British
Columbia. Toronto: The Macmillan Company of Canada Limited 1957.

   xii, 144 pp.; 213 × 140 mm.
   Second edition published in 1973 (see 2207).

1403.   MacLENNAN, Hugh

Two Solitudes. By Hugh MacLennan. 1957 The Macmillan Company of
Canada Limited Toronto.

   [10], 370 pp.; 207 × 136 mm.
   First published in a school edition in 1951 (see 1254). Reprinted in the Laurentian
   Library (No. 1) in 1967.

1404.   MARSHALL, John Stewart

Physics. John Stewart Marshall, Professor of Physics, McGill University
[and] Elton Roy Pounder, Associate Professor of Physics, McGill University.
The Macmillan Company of Canada Limited: Toronto 1957.

   viii, 906 pp.; 237 × 155 mm.
   Second edition published in 1967 (see 1860).

1405. McKEOWN, Elizabeth

Au Canada et A L'étranger. Par Elizabeth McKeown. Production de Louis Charbonneau. Illustrations par Robert Banks et Selwyn Dewdney. The Macmillan Company of Canada Limited.

x, 237, [1] pp.; 205 × 144 mm.
First published in English in 1955 (see 1348). Reprinted with minor revisions in 1958 (see 1440).

1406. MUNSTERHJELM, Erik

Erik Munsterhjelm, *Fool's Gold: A Narrative of Prospecting and Trapping in Northern Canada*. Toronto: The Macmillan Company of Canada Limited 1957.

250 pp.; 220 × 140 mm.

1407. OSLER, William

The Student Life: The Philosophy of Sir William Osler. Edited by Richard E. Verney, M.B., F.R.C.P.E., D.R., Physician in Charge, Department of Student Health, University of Edinburgh, and Nurses' Health Service, The Royal Infirmary of Edinburgh. With Forewords By John Bruce C.B.E., T.D., M.B., Ch.B., F.R.C.S. Ed., Regius Professor of Clinical Surgery, University of Edinburgh, And Alec H. Macklin, O.B.E., M.C., T.D., M.D. Physician, Student Health Service, University of Aberdeen. The Macmillan Company of Canada Limited Toronto 1957.

xiv, 214 pp.; 188 × 125 mm.

1408. PATRICK, Lynn

Let's Play Hockey! By Lynn Patrick and D. Leo Monahan. Illustrated by Lewis Parker. Toronto—Macmillan—1957.

vi, 79, [3] pp.; 200 × 125 mm.

1409. SCHULL, Joseph

Great Stories Of Canada, *The Salt Water Men: Canada's Deep-Sea Sailors*. By Joseph Schull. Illustrations by Ed McNally. Toronto: 1957: Macmillan.

144 pp.; 210 × 140 mm.
Reprinted in paper in 1960 and 1966.
Great Stories of Canada Series.

1410. SCOTT, F.R.

The Blasted Pine: An Anthology of Satire, Invective and Disrespectful Verse, Chiefly by Canadian Writers. Selected and Arranged and with an Introduction by F.R. Scott and A.J.M. Smith. Preface by David L. Thomson. Toronto: The Macmillan Company of Canada Limited 1957.

xx, 138 pp.; 210 × 136 mm.
Reprinted in 1960, 1962 and 1965. Revised in 1967 (see 1881).

1411. THURBER, Walter A.

Exploring Science: One. By Walter A. Thurber. Edited by Paul E. Smith. The Macmillan Company of Canada Limited Toronto.

160 pp.; 220 × 155 mm.
Exploring Science Series.

1412.   THURBER, Walter A.

Exploring Science: Two. By Walter A. Thurber. Edited by Paul E. Smith.
The Macmillan Company of Canada Limited Toronto.

176 pp.; 220 × 155 mm.
Exploring Science Series.

1413.   THURBER, Walter A.

Exploring Science: Three. By Walter A. Thurber. Edited by Paul E. Smith.
The Macmillan Company of Canada Limited Toronto.

192 pp.; 220 × 155 mm.
Exploring Science Series.

1414.   THURBER, Walter A.

Exploring Science: Four. By Walter A. Thurber. Edited by Paul E. Smith.
The Macmillan Company of Canada Limited Toronto.

224 pp.; 220 × 155 mm.
Exploring Science Series.

1415.   THURBER, Walter A.

Exploring Science: Five. By Walter A. Thurber. Edited by Paul E. Smith.
The Macmillan Company of Canada Limited.

320 pp.; 220 × 155 mm.
Exploring Science Series.

1416.   THURBER, Walter A.

Exploring Science: Six. By Walter A. Thurber. Edited by Paul E. Smith. The
Macmillan Company of Canada Limited Toronto.

352 pp.; 220 × 155 mm.
Exploring Science Series.

1417.   THURBER, Walter A.

Teachers' Manual for Exploring Science: One. By Walter A. Thurber, Professor of Science, Cortland State Teachers College, Cortland, New York. Edited
by Paul E. Smith. The Macmillan Company of Canada Limited Toronto.

95, [1], 160 pp.; 220 × 155 mm.
Exploring Science Series.

1418.   THURBER, Walter A.

Teachers' Manual for Exploring Science: Two. By Walter A. Thurber, Professor of Science, Cortland State Teachers College, Cortland, New York. Edited
by Paul E. Smith. The Macmillan Company of Canada Limited Toronto.

176 pp.; 220 × 155 mm.
Exploring Science Series.

1419.   THURBER, Walter A.

Teachers' Manual for Exploring Science: Three. By Walter A. Thurber,
Professor of Science, Cortland State Teachers College, Cortland, New York.
Edited by Paul E. Smith. The Macmillan Company of Canada Limited
Toronto.

192 pp.; 220 × 155 mm.
Exploring Science Series.

1420.   THURBER, Walter A.

Teachers' Manual for Exploring Science: Four. By Walter A. Thurber, Professor of Science, Cortland State Teachers College, Cortland, New York. Edited by Paul E. Smith. The Macmillan Company of Canada Limited Toronto.
224 pp.; 220 × 155 mm.
Exploring Science Series.

1421.   THURBER, Walter A.

Teachers' Manual for Exploring Science: Five. By Walter A. Thurber, Professor of Science, Cortland State Teachers College, Cortland, New York. Edited by Paul E. Smith. The Macmillan Company of Canada Limited Toronto.
320 pp.; 220 × 155 mm.
Exploring Science Series.

1422.   THURBER, Walter A.

Teachers' Manual for Exploring Science: Six. By Walter A. Thurber, Professor of Science, Cortland State Teachers College, Cortland, New York. Edited by Paul E. Smith. The Macmillan Company of Canada Limited Toronto.
352 pp.; 220 × 155 mm.
Exploring Science Series.

1423.   WEST, Rebecca

Rebecca West, *The Court and the Castle: Some treatments of a recurrent theme*. Toronto: Macmillan 1957.
[8], 319, [1] pp.; 205 × 130 mm.

1424.   WOOD, Edgar Allardyce

Great Stories Of Canada, *The Great Chief: Maskepetoon Warrior of the Crees*. By Kerry Wood [pseud.]. Illustrated by John A. Hall. Toronto: Macmillan: 1957.
160 pp.; 213 × 138 mm.
Reprinted in 1960, 1964 and 1967.
Great Stories of Canada Series.

1958

1425.   BOYLE, Joyce

The Stone Cottage Mystery. By Joyce Boyle. Toronto: Macmillan 1958.
[6], 151, [1] pp.; 215 × 135 mm.
Reprinted in 1961, 1966 and 1969 (paper).

1426.   CLARK, Catherine Anthony

The Silver Man. By Catherine Anthony Clark. Illustrated by Clare Bice. Toronto: Macmillan: 1958.
231, [1] pp.; 220 × 140 mm.

1427. DAVIES, Robertson
A Mixture of Frailties. By Robertson Davies. [Quotation]. Macmillan: 1958: Toronto.

[2], 379, [1] pp.; 212 × 140 mm.
Reprinted in the Laurentian Library (No. 7) in 1968.

1428. DE LA ROCHE, Mazo
Bill and Coo. By Mazo de la Roche. Illustrated by Eileen A. Soper. The Macmillan Company of Canada Limited Toronto 1958.

[4], 40 pp.; 220 × 140 mm.

1429. DE LA ROCHE, Mazo
Centenary at Jalna. By Mazo De La Roche. Toronto: The Macmillan Company of Canada Limited 1958.

viii, 302 pp.; 187 × 125 mm.

1430. DOBRINDT, G.H.
The New World Readers: A Basic Reading Programme for the Junior Grades, *My World and I*. G.H. Dobrindt, F.J. Gathercole [and] Campbell Hughes. Illustrators Clare Bice [and] Jerry Lazare. The Ryerson Press [and] The Macmillan Company of Canada Limited.

x, 438 pp.; 214 × 155 mm.
First published in 1946 (see 1117). This edition revised. Reprinted frequently.
New World Readers Series.

1431. GILL, J.L.
Poetry for Senior Students: An Anthology of Shorter Poems. Revised edition. Selected and edited by J.L. Gill and L.H. Newell, The University of Toronto Schools. Toronto: The Macmillan Company of Canada Limited 1958.

xiv, 272 pp.; 214 × 140 mm.
First published in 1953 (see 1294). Revised edition reprinted in 1959, 1962 and 1964.

1432. GOUGEON, Helen
The Best Tasted Recipes From Weekend Magazine: *Helen Gougeon's Good Food*. Illustrated by Carlo Italiano. Color photographs by Charles King. [Quotation]. The Macmillan Company of Canada Limited 1958.

[12], 236 pp.; 215 × 133 mm.

1433. HEARNE, Samuel
A Journey From Prince of Wales' Fort In Hudson's Bay To The Northern Ocean: 1769, 1770, 1771, 1772. By Samuel Hearne. Edited with an Introduction by Richard Glover, Professor of History, University of Manitoba. Toronto: The Macmillan Company of Canada Limited 1958.

lxiv, 301, [1] pp.; 212 × 130 mm.
Pioneer Books Series.

1434. ISRAEL, Charles E.
The Mark. A Novel by Charles E. Israel. Macmillan 1958 Toronto.

[8], 306 pp.; 210 × 138 mm.

1435. MACDONALD, Marianne

The Treasure Of Ur. By Marianne Macdonald. 1958 The Macmillan Company of Canada Limited Toronto.

222 pp.; 213 × 135 mm.

1436. MacLENNAN, Hugh

The Watch That Ends the Night. A novel by Hugh MacLennan. Macmillan of Canada Toronto 1958.

[6], 373, [1] pp.; 195 × 135 mm.
Reprinted in 1959. Reprinted in the Laurentian Library (No. 32) in 1975.

1437. McCOURT, Edward

Great Stories Of Canada, *Revolt in the West: The Story Of the Riel Rebellion*. By Edward McCourt. Illustrated by Jack Ferguson. Toronto: 1958: Macmillan.

159, [1] pp.; 213 × 138 mm.
Great Stories of Canada Series.

1438. McDOUGALL, Colin

Execution. Colin McDougall. The Macmillan Company of Canada Limited Toronto 1958.

227, [1] pp.; 216 × 135 mm.
Reprinted in the Laurentian Library (No. 2) in 1967.

1439. McIVOR, R. Craig

Canadian Monetary, Banking and Fiscal Development. R. Craig McIvor, M.A., Ph.D., Professor of Economics, McMaster University, Hamilton, Ontario. Toronto: The Macmillan Company of Canada Limited 1958.

xx, 263, [1] pp.; 240 × 155 mm.

1440. McKEOWN, Elizabeth

At Home and Abroad. By Elizabeth McKeown. Illustrations by Robert Banks and Selwyn Dewdney. Approved for Use in the Province of Ontario. The Macmillan Company of Canada Limited, 1958.

x, 237, [1] pp.; 205 × 150 mm.
First published in 1955 (see 1348). Published in French in 1957 (see 1405).

1441. ORMSBY, Margaret A.

Margaret A. Ormsby, *British Columbia: A History*. The Macmillans in Canada 1958.

x, 558 pp.; 240 × 160 mm.
Reprinted in 1959 and 1964. Revised in 1971 (see 2119).

1442. *Poems For Upper School 1958-59*. *Paradise Lost* by John Milton. With Notes and Questions by Gordon H. Bailey, York Mills Collegiate Institute, North York. *The Titanic* by E.J. Pratt. With Notes and Questions by the Macmillan Editors. Authorized by the Minister of Education for Ontario. The Macmillan Company of Canada Limited Toronto.

[4], 76 pp.; 184 × 125 mm.
Issued in paper.

1443. PRATT, E.J.

The Collected Poems of E.J. Pratt. Second Edition. Edited with an introduction by Northrop Frye. Published by the Macmillan Company of Canada Limited, Toronto, 1958.

xxviii, 395, [1] pp.; 235 × 140 mm.
First published in 1944 (see 1018). Reprinted in 1962.

1444. RADDALL, Thomas H.

Great Stories Of Canada, *The Rover: The Story of a Canadian Privateer*. By Thomas H. Raddall. Illustrated by Vernon Mould. Toronto: 1958: Macmillan.

156 pp.; 213 × 138 mm.
Great Stories of Canada Series.

1445. REANEY, James

A Suit of Nettles. James Reaney. Toronto: The Macmillan Company of Canada Limited 1958.

x, 54 pp.; 252 × 160 mm.

1446. ROBINSON, Margaret A.

The New World Readers: A Basic Reading Programme for the Junior Grades, *Over the Bridge*. Margaret Robinson. Illustrators Adrian Dingle [and] Ken Zealley. The Ryerson Press [and] The Macmillan Company of Canada Limited.

x, 406 pp.; 214 × 155 mm.
First published in 1946 (see 1118).
New World Readers Series.

1447. ROSS, Malcolm

Edited by Malcolm Ross, *The Arts in Canada: A Stock-Taking at Mid-Century*. Painting, Sculpture, Music, Ballet, Opera, Theatre in English-Speaking Canada, Le Théâtre au Canada-Français, Poetry, The Novel, Creative Scholarship, Film, Radio and Television, Tradition et Évolution au Canada Français, Architecture and Town Planning, Industrial Design, Handicrafts. The Macmillan Company of Canada Limited 1958.

viii, 176 pp.; 282 × 203 mm.

1448. ROSS, Sinclair

The Well. By Sinclair Ross. Macmillan: 1958: Toronto.

[6], 256 pp.; 212 × 135 mm.

1449. ROUTLEY, Clare B.

The New World Readers: A Basic Reading Programme for the Junior Grades, *Under the North Star*. Clare Routley [and] Grace Morgan. Illustrators Hilton Hassell [and] Priscilla Hutchings. The Ryerson Press [and] The Macmillan Company of Canada Limited.

x, 438 pp.; 214 × 155 mm.
First published in 1946 (see 1119).
New World Readers Series.

1450. SEARY, E.R.

Reading English: A Handbook For Students. By E.R. Seary and G.M. Story. The Macmillan Company of Canada Limited Toronto 1958.

x, 116 pp.; 202 × 128 mm.
Issued in cloth and paper. Reprinted in 1962. Revised in 1966 (see 1809).

1451. STEINBECK, John

The Pearl. John Steinbeck. With Illustrations by José Clemente Orozco. Notes by R.L. Hale, Formerly Head of the English Department, Peterborough Collegiate and Vocational School, And P.A. de Souza, Principal, St. Peter's High School, Peterborough, Ontario. The Macmillan Company of Canada Limited 1958.

[4], 138 pp.; 190 × 125 mm.
Also issued in 1963 bound with *The Red Pony* (see 1652).

1452. WHEELER-BENNETT, John W.

King George VI: His Life and Reign. By John W. Wheeler-Bennett. Toronto: The Macmillan Company of Canada Limited 1958.

xvi, 891, [1] pp.; 223 × 150 mm.

1453. WILLIS, H.L.

Invitation to Short Stories. H.L. Willis, B.A., Vice-Principal, Ottawa Technical High School [And] W.R. McGillivray, B.A., Head of English, Fisher Park High School, Ottawa. Illustrations Kenneth Dallison. Toronto: The Macmillan Company of Canada Limited 1958.

x, 221, [1] pp.; 185 × 125 mm.

1959

1454. ASHCROFT, C.C.

General Shop Work. Prepared by C.C. Ashcroft, B.A.Sc., B.Paed., P.Eng., and J.A.G. Easton, F.R.A.I.C., P.Eng. Revised Edition. The Macmillan Company of Canada Limited.

viii, 280 pp.; 280 × 215 mm.
First published in 1940. Earlier edition not located.

1455. BATES, Ronald

In memory of my Father. *The Wandering World*. By Ronald Bates. [Quotation]. Toronto 1959 The Macmillan Company of Canada Limited.

[4], 60 pp.; 205 × 128 mm.

1456. BRUCE, Charles

A Chronicle by Charles Bruce, *The Township of Time*. Toronto, 1959 The Macmillan Company of Canada Limited.

[6], 234 pp.; 218 × 138 mm.

1457.   CALLAGHAN, Morley
Morley Callaghan's Stories. Toronto: The Macmillan Company of Canada Limited 1959.
[14], 364 pp.; 215 × 150 mm.
Reprinted in the Laurentian Library (No. 5) in 1967.

1458.   CARELESS, J.M.S.
Brown of The Globe. Vol. One: The Voice of Upper Canada 1818-1859. J.M.S. Careless. Toronto. The Macmillan Company of Canada Limited 1959.
x, 354 pp.; 250 × 150 mm.
Issued in cloth and paper. Reprinted in paper in 1972.

1459.   CATLIN, George
The Atlantic Community. By George Catlin. The Macmillan Company of Canada Limited Toronto 1959.
[vi], 146 pp.; 188 × 124 mm.

1460.   CHEVRIER, Lionel
The St. Lawrence Seaway. By The Hon. Lionel Chevrier, M.P. The Macmillan Company of Canada Limited Toronto 1959.
x, 174 pp.; 240 × 150 mm.

1461.   CORNISH, John
John Cornish, *Olga*. 1959 The Macmillan Company of Canada Limited Toronto.
174 pp.; 190 × 123 mm.

1462.   DICKSON, Lovat
The Ante-Room. By Lovat Dickson. Toronto: The Macmillan Company of Canada Limited 1959.
[6], 270 pp.; 220 × 140 mm.
Reprinted in the Laurentian Library (No. 25) in 1974.

1463.   DIMOCK, Hedley G.
The Child in Hospital: A Study Of His Emotional And Social Well-Being. By Hedley G. Dimock. 1959 The Macmillan Company of Canada Limited Toronto.
xvi, 236 pp.; 218 × 138 mm.

1464.   EUBANK, Howard L.
Physics for Secondary Schools. Howard L. Eubank, Vice-Principal, Etobicoke Collegiate Institute, Toronto, Ontario, John M. Ramsay, Inspector of Science for Secondary Schools, Ontario, [and] Leslie A. Rickard, Head of Science Department, Forest Hill Collegiate Institute, Toronto, Ontario. Illustrations by Kenneth Dallison and Robert Kunz. Authorized in Alberta. The Macmillan Company of Canada Limited, Toronto.
xii, 192 pp.; 240 × 158 mm.

1465. FERGUSON, Robert D.

Great Stories of Canada, *Man from St. Malo: The Story of Jacques Cartier*. By Robert D. Ferguson. Illustrated By Douglas Sneyd. Toronto: 1959: Macmillan.

160 pp.; 216 × 140 mm.
Reprinted in 1961 and 1966. Revised in 1974 (see 2259).
Great Stories of Canada Series.

1466. FRASER, Frances

The Bear Who Stole the Chinook and other Stories. By Frances Fraser. Illustrated by Lewis Parker. 1959 The Macmillan Company of Canada Limited.

[8], 72 pp.; 233 × 150 mm.
Reprinted in 1969.

1467. GODBOLD, R.S.

Work Book To Accompany Mathematics for Canadians Grade VII. By R.S. Godbold, B.A., B.Paed., Inspector of Elementary Schools, Toronto. J.M. Dent & Sons (Canada) Limited [and] The Macmillan Company of Canada Limited.

[2], 91, [1] pp.; 275 × 215 mm.
Issued in paper.
Mathematics For Canadians Series.

1468. GREENE, Marion

Canal Boy. By Barion Greene. Illustrations by Vernon Mould. Toronto: The Macmillan Company of Canada Limited 1959.

[6], 152 pp.; 217 × 137 mm.

1469. HALL, T. Roy

Grade 4: Language Journeys. Revised Edition. T. Roy Hall [and] E.B. Broome. Authorized in the Province of Alberta. Illustrations by R.J. Banks. The Macmillan Company of Canada Limited Toronto.

xvi, 248 pp.; 205 × 145 mm.
First published in 1952 (see 1270).
Language Journeys Series.

1470. HALL, T. Roy

Grade 5: Language Journeys. Revised Edition. T. Roy Hall [and] E.B. Broome. Authorized in the Province of Alberta. Illustrations by R.J. Banks. The Macmillan Company of Canada Limited Toronto.

xvi, 284 pp.; 205 × 145 mm.
First published in 1953 (see 1295).
Language Journeys Series.

1471. HUMBLE, A.H.

Lyric And Longer Poems: Book 1. A.H. Humble, Head of English Department, Trinity College School, Port Hope. Toronto: The Macmillan Company of Canada Limited.

x, 197, [1] pp.; 188 × 124 mm.

1472. KEIRSTEAD, B.S.

Capital, Interest and Profits. B.S. Keirstead, Professor of Political Economy
in the University of Toronto. Toronto: The Macmillan Company of Canada
Limited 1959.

x, 180 pp.; 226 × 143 mm.

1473. MOODIE, Susanna

Life In The Clearings. By Susanna Moodie. To which is added this author's
Introduction to *Mark Hurdlestone*. Edited and Introduced by Robert J.
McDougall. Toronto: The Macmillan Company of Canada Limited 1959.

xxxvi, 298 pp.; 217 × 140 mm.
Reprinted in the Laurentian Library (No. 39) in 1976. There are at least two
printings of this title. One of these was issued in the Pioneer Books Series.
Pioneer Books Series.

1474. SMYTHE, James M.

Elements of Geography. James M. Smythe, M.A., Head of Geography Department, Earl Haig Collegiate Institute, Township of North York, [and]
Charles G. Brown, B.A., Head of Geography Department, Downsview
Collegiate Institute, Township of North York. 1959 The Macmillan Company of Canada Limited Toronto.

[16], 285, [1] pp.; 230 × 155 mm.
Revised in 1964 (see 1698) and in 1970 (see 2079). A special revised edition was
published in 1976 (see 2435). English and French metric editions appeared in 1978
and 1979 (see 2602 and 2655).

1475. STACEY, C.P.

C.P. Stacey, *Quebec 1759: The Siege and the Battle*. [Quotation]. 1959 The
Macmillan Company of Canada Limited Toronto.

xiv, 210 pp.; 235 × 150 mm.
Reprinted in 1966.

1476. STEINHAUER, David

Conteurs Modernes: An Anthology Of French Short Stories For Grade 12.
Selected and Edited With Exercises and Vocabulary by D. Steinhauer, B.A.
and T.J. Casaubon, B.A. Macmillan Toronto.

x, 147, [1] pp.; 214 × 140 mm.

1477. SWAYZE, J. Fred

Great Stories Of Canada, *Frontenac and the Iroquois: The Fighting Governor of
New France*. By Fred Swayze. Illustrated by Huntley Brown. Toronto:
1959: Macmillan.

158 pp.; 216 × 140 mm.
Great Stories of Canada Series.

1960

1478. BLANCHET, Guy
Search in the North. Guy Blanchet. The Macmillan Company of Canada Limited Toronto 1960.

197, [1] pp.; 224 × 144 mm.

1479. BOWDEN, Nancy J.
Basic Spelling For High School Students. Nancy J. Bowden, Formerly of the Department of English, Nova Scotia Teachers College. The Macmillan Company of Canada Limited, Toronto 1960.

x, 102 pp.; 210 × 150 mm.

1480. BRONTË, Emily
Wuthering Heights. Emily Bronte. Study Material Prepared By Linton D. Read, Head of the English Department, Moira Secondary School, Belleville, Ontario. Toronto: The Macmillan Company of Canada Limited.

[6], 353, [1] pp.; 190 × 125 mm.
An edition edited by F.T. Flahiff was published in 1968 (see 1906).

1481. BROWN, Arthur E.
Mathematics In Practice. Revised Edition. Arthur E. Brown, B.A., B.Paed., Principal, Danforth Technical School, Toronto, David E. Bridge, B.A.Sc., B.Paed., Technical Training Specialist, Vocational Training Branch, Department of Labour, Federal Government, [and] Wallace J. Morrison, B.A., B.Paed., Head of the Mathematics Department, Danforth Technical School, Toronto. The Macmillan Company of Canada Limited, Toronto 1960.

xii, 418 pp.; 235 × 155 mm.
First published in 1952 (see 1263A). Revised in 1954 and a supplement published (see 1306 and 1307). Alberta revision published in 1964 (see 1662).

1482. BUCHANAN, Donald W.
Revue Pratique de Grammaire. Donald W. Buchanan, M.A., D. de l'Univ., French Specialist, Town of Mount Royal High School, [and] Margaret E.B. Buchanan, M.A., Formerly Assistant Supervisor of French in the Protestant Schools of the Province of Quebec. Illustrated by Gordon Collins. Authorized for use in the Protestant Schools of Quebec. The Macmillan Company of Canada Limited Toronto.

xii, 172 pp.; 235 × 155 mm.

1483. BUCKLEY, Helen
Economics For Canadians. Helen Buckley, Economic Consultant [and] Kenneth Buckley, Professor of Economics, University of Saskatchewan. Toronto: The Macmillan Company of Canada Limited.

x, 224 pp.; 240 × 155 mm.
Revised in 1968 (see 1909).

1484. CALLAGHAN, Morley

Morley Callaghan, *The Many Colored Coat*. Macmillan: 1960: Toronto.
318 pp.; 220 × 145 mm.
Reprinted in the Laurentian Library (No. 12) in 1972.

1485. CANADIAN ASSOCIATION OF PROFESSORS OF
        EDUCATION

Canadian Association of Professors of Education, *Papers read at the Fifth Annual Conference Of The Canadian Association Of Professors Of Education*. Saskatoon, June 8, 9, 10, 1959. The Macmillan Company of Canada Limited.
[8], 62 pp.; 233 × 155 mm.

1486. FLOWER, George E.

The Macmillan Spelling Series: 2. General Editor: George E. Flower, Ontario College of Education. Authors: Sybil F. Shack, Principal, Lord Roberts School, Winnipeg, Manitoba, Robert F. Bornhold, Inspector of Public Schools, Halton County, Ontario, K.H.D. Hall, Superintendent of Public Schools, East York, Ontario, [and] Gordon F. Mann, Inspector of Public Schools, Windsor, Ontario. Copyright, Canada, 1960, by The Macmillan Company of Canada, Limited.
107, [1] pp.; 213 × 145 mm.
Revised in 1978 (see 2550).
Macmillan Spelling Series.

1487. FLOWER, George E.

The Macmillan Spelling Series: 2. Teachers' Edition. General Editor: George E. Flower, Ontario College of Education. Authors: Sybil F. Shack, Principal, Lord Roberts High School, Winnipeg, Manitoba, Robert F. Bornhold, Inspector of Public Schools, Halton County, Ontario, K.H.D. Hall, Superintendent of Public Schools, East York, Ontario, [and] Gordon F. Mann, Inspector of Public Schools, Windsor, Ontario. Copyright, Canada, 1960, by The Macmillan Company of Canada, Limited.
xxii, 137, [1] pp.; 213 × 145 mm.
The Teachers' Editions were issued interleaved with the basic speller (unpaginated), and some were also issued separately in paper.
Macmillan Spelling Series.

1488. FLOWER, George E.

The Macmillan Spelling Series: 3. General Editor: George E. Flower, Ontario College of Education. Authors: Robert F. Bornhold, Inspector of Public Schools, Halton County, Ontario, K.H.D. Hall, Superintendent of Public Schools, East York, Ontario, Gordon F. Mann, Inspector of Public Schools, Windsor, Ontario, [and] Sybil F. Shack, Principal, Lord Roberts School, Winnipeg, Manitoba. Copyright, Canada, 1960, by The Macmillan Company of Canada, Limited.
112 pp.; 213 × 145 mm.
Revised in 1977 (see 2512).
Macmillan Spelling Series.

1489. FRASER, Simon

The Letters and Journals of Simon Fraser 1806-1808. Edited with an Introduction by W. Kaye Lamb, Dominion Archivist. 1960 The Macmillan Company of Canada Limited Toronto.

viii, 292 pp.; 220 × 140 mm.
Pioneer Books Series.

1490. GARLAND, Aileen

Canada our Country Part 1. By Aileen Garland. Illustrated by Robert Banks And Joe Rosenthal. Based on *A First Book of Canadian History* By W. Stewart Wallace. The Macmillan Company of Canada Limited.

x, 348 pp.; 233 × 150 mm.
Part 2 was published in 1961 (see 1532).

1491. GILL, J.L.

An Anthology Of Short Stories And Essays: Prose for Senior Students. Revised Edition. Selected and Edited by J.L. Gill and L.H. Newell, Instructors in English, the University of Toronto Schools. The Macmillan Company of Canada Limited Toronto.

[10], 426 pp.; 212 × 135 mm.
First published in 1951 (see 1248). Issued in paper in 1977.

1492. GREENE, E.J.H.

Reflex French: A Comprehensive Course in Modern French Usage. By E.J.H. Greene, Professor of French and Head of the Department of Modern Languages, University of Alberta, Manoël Faucher, Associate Professor of French, University of Alberta, [and] Dennis M. Healy, Dean of the College of Liberal Arts and Science and Chairman of the Department of Modern Languages, Long Island University. Illustrations by François Bret. Toronto: The Macmillan Company of Canada Limited 1960.

xvi, 256 pp.; 220 × 140 mm.
Reprinted in 1962, 1963 and 1965. Integrated edition published in 1966. Reprinted in 1970 (see 2061).

1493. GREGG, Robert J.

A Students' Manual of French Pronunciation. By Robert J. Gregg, Associate Professor in the Department of Romance Studies and Director of the Language Laboratory at the University of British Columbia. Toronto: The Macmillan Company of Canada Limited 1960.

x, 155, [1] pp.; 188 × 124 mm.
Reprinted in paper in 1966.

1494. HALL, T. Roy

Grade 3: Language Journeys. Authorized in the Province of Alberta. Revised Edition. T. Roy Hall [and] E.B. Broome. Illustrations by R.W. Major and William Wheeler. The Macmillan Company of Canada Limited Toronto.

xvi, 244 pp.; 205 × 145 mm.
First published in 1952 (see 1269).
Language Journeys Series.

1495. HALL, T. Roy

Grade 6: Language Journeys. Approved for use in the Province of Ontario. Revised Edition. T. Roy Hall [and] E.B. Broome. Authorized in the Province of Alberta. Illustrations by R.J. Banks and W. Wheeler. The Macmillan Company of Canada Limited Toronto.

> xvi, 320 pp.; 205 × 145 mm.
> First published in 1954 (see 1321).
> Language Journeys Series.

1496. HEYWOOD, A.H.

Senior Technical Mathematics. Edited By A.H. Heywood, M.A. Toronto: The Macmillan Company of Canada Limited.

> xiv, 558 pp.; 216 × 138 mm.
> Reprinted with corrections in 1961.

1497. HODGETTS, J.E.

Canadian Public Administration. J.E. Hodgetts, Professor of Political Science, Queen's University, Kingston, Ontario, [and] D.C. Corbett, Senior Lecturer in Political Science, Canberra University College; Formerly Associate Professor, University of British Columbia. Toronto 1960 The Macmillan Company of Canada Limited.

> xiv, 575, [1] pp.; 235 × 147 mm.

1498. HUMBLE, A.H.

Lyric And Longer Poems: Book II. A.H. Humble, Head of English Department, Trinity College School, Port Hope. Toronto: The Macmillan Company of Canada Limited.

> xii, 210 pp.; 188 × 124 mm.

1499. MacLENNAN, Hugh

Hugh MacLennan, *Scotchman's Return and other Essays*. 1960 The Macmillan Company of Canada Limited Toronto.

> xiv, 279, [1] pp.; 216 × 140 mm.
> Reprinted in 1960 in paper.

1500. McKENZIE, Paul B.

Arithmetic for Canadians 5. Paul B. McKenzie. J.M. Dent And Sons (Canada) Limited [and] The Macmillan Company of Canada Limited.

> xvi, 240 pp.; 205 × 150 mm.
> First published in 1957 (see 1397). This edition revised. Reprinted in 1961.
> Arithmetic For Canadians Series.

1501. MITCHELL, W.O.

Who Has Seen the Wind. By W.O. Mitchell. Study Material Prepared by Ruth Godwin, Ed.D., Faculty of Education, University of Alberta. [Quotation]. Macmillan of Canada Toronto.

> [10], 317, [1] pp.; 185 × 120 mm.
> For the publishing history of this title, see 1145.

1502. NOBLE, George

The New World Readers. Lorne Pierce, Editor-in-chief. Frederick Minkler, General Editor. *The Workbook for Under the North Star*. George Noble/Harry Fisher. Illustrated by Marion Paton. Copyright Canada, 1948 and 1960, by The Ryerson Press and The Macmillan Company of Canada Limited.

120 pp.; 273 × 210 mm.
First published in 1948 (see 1154). Revised edition issued in paper.
New World Readers Series.

1503. ROBINSON, Margaret A.

The New World Readers. Lorne Pierce, Editor-in-Chief. Frederick Minkler, General Editor. *The Workbook for Over the Bridge*. M.A. Robinson/V. McNabb. Illustrated by W. Taylor. Copyright Canada, 1946 and 1960, by The Ryerson Press and The Macmillan Company of Canada Limited, 1960.

120 pp.; 273 × 210 mm.
First published in 1947 (see 1148 and 1153). Revised edition issued in paper.
New World Readers Series.

1504. ROBINSON, Margaret A.

The New World Readers, *Teacher's Manual for Over the Bridge*. M.A. Robinson/B. Dick. The Ryerson Press/The Macmillan Company of Canada Limited.

viii, 263, [1] pp.; 206 × 150 mm.
First published in 1947 as *Teacher's Handbook for Over the Bridge* (see 1152). Issued in paper.
New World Readers Series.

1505. SCHULL, Joseph

Great Stories Of Canada, *Battle for the Rock: The Story of Wolfe and Montcalm*. By Joseph Schull. Illustrated by Lewis Parker. Toronto: 1960: Macmillan.

158 pp.; 213 × 138 mm.
Great Stories of Canada Series.

1506. STANLEY, George F.G.

Canada's Soldiers: The Military History of an Unmilitary People. Revised Edition. By George F.G. Stanley, Royal Military College of Canada. In Collaboration with Harold M. Jackson, Department of Veterans Affairs. Maps by C.C.J. Bond, Historical Section, General Staff, Army Headquarters. The Macmillan Company of Canada Limited Toronto 1960.

[12], 449, [1] pp.; 235 × 155 mm.
First published in 1954 (see 1328). Second revised edition published in 1974 (see 2294).

1507. THOMSON, Dale C.

Dale C. Thomson, *Alexander Mackenzie: Clear Grit*. 1960 The Macmillan Company of Canada Limited Toronto.

xii, 436 pp.; 240 × 147 mm.

1508.   UNDERHILL, Frank H.
In Search of Canadian Liberalism. Frank H. Underhill. The Macmillan Company of Canada Limited Toronto 1960.

xiv, 282 pp.; 225 × 140 mm.
Issued in cloth and paper. Reprinted in 1961 and 1975.

1509.   VOADEN, Herman
Four Plays of Our Time. Edited by Herman Voaden, M.A., C.D.A., Director of English, Central High School of Commerce, Toronto. Toronto: The Macmillan Company of Canada Limited.

xiv, 399, [1] pp.; 185 × 123 mm.

1510.   VOADEN, Herman
Supplementary Notes for Four Plays of Our Time: Flight into Danger, I Remember Mama, Teahouse of the August Moon, An Enemy of the People. Edited by Herman Voaden, M.A., C.D.A., Director of English, Central High School of Commerce, Toronto. Toronto: The Macmillan Company of Canada Limited.

[2], 16 pp.; 275 × 213 mm.
Issued in paper.

1511.   WILLINSKY, A.I.
A.I. Willinsky, *A Doctor's Memoirs*. 1960 The Macmillan Company of Canada Limited Toronto.

xii, 183, [1] pp.; 218 × 137 mm.

1512.   WOOD, Edgar Allardyce
Great Stories Of Canada, *The Queen's Cowboy: Colonel MacLeod of the Mounties*. By Kerry Wood [pseud.]. Illustrated by Joe Rosenthal. Toronto: Macmillan: 1960.

157, [1] pp.; 213 × 138 mm.
Reprinted in 1963 and 1967.
Great Stories of Canada Series.

1961

1513.   AYRE, Robert
Sketco The Raven. By Robert Ayre. Illustrated By Philip Surrey. 1961 Toronto: The Macmillan Company of Canada Limited.

[6], 183, [1] pp.; 230 × 155 mm.
Reprinted in 1963 and 1967.

1514.   BARGEN, Peter Frank
The Legal Status of the Canadian Public School Pupil. By Peter Frank Bargen, M.A., PH.D., Superintendent of Public Schools, Jasper Place, Alberta. The Macmillan Company of Canada Limited Toronto.

xiv, 172 pp.; 234 × 155 mm.

1515.   BERTON, Pierre

The New City: a prejudiced view of Toronto. Photographed by Henri Rossier.
Written and Edited by Pierre Berton. Published by the Macmillan Company
of Canada Limited at Toronto 1961.

>   137, [1] pp.; 320 × 230 mm.
>   Issued in cloth and paper.

1516.   BLISHEN, Bernard R.

Canadian Society: Sociological Perspectives. Edited by Bernard R. Blishen,
Frank E. Jones, Kaspar D. Naegele, [and] John Porter. Toronto, The
Macmillan Company of Canada Limited, 1961.

>   xvi, 622 pp.; 232 × 155 mm.
>   Second edition (revised) published in 1964 (see 1661). Third edition (further re-
>   vised) published in 1968 (see 1904).

1517.   BOYCE, Eleanor

The New World Readers, *Teacher's Manual for My World and I*. Eleanor
Boyce/Miriam Norton. The Ryerson Press/The Macmillan Company of
Canada Limited.

>   viii, 194 pp.; 207 × 150 mm.
>   First published in 1950 as *Teacher's Handbook for My World and I* (see 1221).
>   Reprinted in 1962. Issued in paper.

1518.   BREWIS, T.N.

Canadian Economic Policy. T.N. Brewis, M.Com., Ph.D., Associate Profes-
sor of Economics, Carleton University, H.E. English, B.A., Ph.D., As-
sociate Professor of Economics, Carleton University, Anthony Scott,
B.Com., A.M., Ph.D., Associate Professor of Economics, University of
British Columbia, [and] Pauline Jewett, M.A., Ph.D., Associate Professor of
Political Science, Carleton University. With a Statistical Appendix by J.E.
Gander, M.A., Dominion Bureau of Statistics. The Macmillan Company of
Canada Limited, Toronto 1961.

>   xvi, 365, [1] pp.; 235 × 150 mm.
>   Issued in cloth and paper. Revised in 1965 (see 1709).

1519.   CALLAGHAN, Morley

A Passion in Rome. A Novel By Morley Callaghan. Macmillan: 1961:
Toronto.

>   352 pp.; 218 × 148 mm.
>   Reprinted in the Laurentian Library (No. 62) in 1978.

1520.   CONRAD, Joseph

Three Stories. By Joseph Conrad. Edited by Carlyle King, M.A., Ph.D.,
Head, Department of English, University of Saskatchewan, Saskatoon, Saskatchewan. Toronto: The Macmillan Company of Canada Limited 1961.

>   viii, 247, [1] pp.; 190 × 125 mm.

1521. COOK, Lyn

The Road to Kip's Cove. Lyn Cook. Illustrated by William Wheeler. The Macmillan Company of Canada Limited—Toronto—1961.

viii, 220 pp.; 215 × 140 mm.
Reprinted in 1962.

1522. CURTEIS, Thomas N.

Our Number World: Number Meaning 3. By Thomas N. Curteis, Principal of Willows Elementary School, Victoria, Marian D. James, Formerly Primary Supervisor, Greater Victoria Schools [and] Hugh E. Farquhar, Executive Assistant to the Principal, Victoria College, B.C. Illustrated by E. Bakowsky and W. Wheeler. J.M. Dent and Sons (Canada) Limited, [and] The Macmillan Company of Canada Limited.

[6], 357, [1] pp.; 227 × 143 mm.

1523. DEUTSCH, John J.

The Canadian Economy: Selected Readings. John J. Deutsch, Vice-Principal (Administration), Queen's University, Burton S. Keirstead, Professor of Political Economy, University of Toronto, Kari Levitt, Lecturer in Economics, McGill University, [and] Robert M. Will, Assistant Professor of Economics, University of British Columbia. Toronto, 1961. The Macmillan Company of Canada Limited.

xvi, 549, [1] pp.; 227 × 142 mm.
Revised in 1965 (see 1713).

1524. DURRANT, J.E.

A New Analytic Geometry. Revised Edition. By J.E. Durrant, B.A., B.Paed., F.R.S.A., Principal, Etobicoke Collegiate Institute, Toronto, Ontario, H.R. Kingston, M.A., Ph.D., LL.D., F.R.A.S., Formerly Head of the Department of Mathematics and Astronomy, Dean of Arts and Science and Principal of University College, University of Western Ontario, London, Ontario, J. Norman C. Sharp, M.A., Head of the Department of Mathematics, North Albion Collegiate, Etobicoke Township, [and] James W. Kerr, B.A., M.B.E., Vice-Principal, Leaside High School, Ontario. Toronto: The Macmillan Company of Canada Limited.

x, 362 pp.; 195 × 135 mm.
First published in 1936 as *A New Geometry: Analytic Synthetic* (see 694). Revised in 1940 (see 872).

1525. EATON, Evelyn M.

Avançons: Book 1. Evelyn M. Eaton, Former Co-ordinator of French, Protestant School Board of Greater Montreal, [and] S.J. MacGowan, Former Supervisor of French, Protestant Board of School Commissioners, Montreal. Illustrations by Fleda N.G. Peck. Toronto: The Macmillan Company of Canada Limited 1961.

xii, 201, [1] pp.; 233 × 147 mm.
First published in 1942 (see 951). Revised in 1950 (see 1224). Book I reprinted in 1961. Book II revised in 1962 (see 1567).

1526. EAYRS, James

James Eayrs, *Northern Approaches: Canada and the Search for Peace*. Toronto: 1961 The Macmillan Company of Canada Limited.

[12], 195, [1] pp.; 220 × 136 mm.
Issued in cloth and paper.

1527. FERGUSON, Robert D.

Great Stories Of Canada, *Fur Trader: The Story of Alexander Henry*. By Robert D. Ferguson. Illustrated by Douglas Sneyd. Toronto: 1961: Macmillan.

159, [1] pp.; 213 × 138 mm.
Great Stories of Canada Series.

1528. FINCH, Robert

Dover Beach Revisited And Other Poems. Robert Finch. 1961 The Macmillan Company of Canada Limited Toronto.

[8], 111, [1] pp.; 220 × 144 mm.

1529. FLOWER, George E.

The Macmillan Spelling Series: 4. General Editor: George E. Flower, Ontario College of Education. Authors: Gordon F. Mann, Inspector of Public Schools, Windsor, Ontario, Robert F. Bornhold, Inspector of Public Schools, Halton County, Ontario, K.H.D. Hall, Superintendent of Public Schools, East York, Ontario, [and] Sybil F. Shack, Principal, Lord Roberts School, Winnipeg, Manitoba. Copyright, Canada, 1961, by The Macmillan Company of Canada Limited. Approved for use in the Province of Ontario.

107, [1] pp.; 213 × 145 mm.
Revised in 1977 (see 2488).
Macmillan Spelling Series.

1529A FLOWER, George E.

The Macmillan Spelling Series: 5. General Editor: George E. Flower, Ontario College of Education. Authors: Robert F. Bornhold, Inspector of Public Schools, Halton County, Ontario, K.H.D. Hall, Superintendent of Public Schools, East York, Ontario, Gordon F. Mann, Inspector of Public Schools, Windsor, Ontario [and] Sybil F. Shack, Principal, Lord Roberts School, Winnipeg, Manitoba. Copyright, Canada, 1961, by The Macmillan Company Of Canada Limited.

110, [2] pp.; 213 × 145 mm.
Revised in 1978 (see 2595).
Macmillan Spelling Series.

1530. FLOWER, George E.

The Macmillan Spelling Series: 4. Teachers' Edition. General Editor: George E. Flower, Ontario College of Education. Authors: Gordon F. Mann, Inspector of Public Schools, Windsor, Ontario, Robert F. Bornhold, K.H.D. Hall, Superintendent of Public Schools, East York, Ontario, [and] Sybil F. Shack, Principal, Lord Roberts School, Winnipeg, Manitoba. Copyright, Canada, 1961, by The Macmillan Company of Canada Limited.

xxvi, 137, [1] pp.; 213 × 145 mm.
See note to 1487.
Macmillan Spelling Series.

1531.   FLOWER, George E.

The Macmillan Spelling Series: 6. General Editor: George E. Flower, Ontario College of Education. Authors: Sybil F. Shack, Principal, Lord Roberts School, Winnipeg, Manitoba, Robert F. Bornhold, Inspector of Public Schools, Halton County, Ontario, K.H.D. Hall, Superintendent of Public Schools, East York, Ontario, [and] Gordon F. Mann, Inspector of Public Schools, Windsor, Ontario. Copyright, Canada, 1961, by The Macmillan Company of Canada Limited.

111, [1] pp.; 213 × 145 mm.
Revised in 1978 (see 2564).
Macmillan Spelling Series.

1532.   GARLAND, Aileen

Canada our country: Part 2. By Aileen Garland. Illustrated by Robert Banks and Joe Rosenthal. Based on *A First Book of Canadian History* By W. Stewart Wallace. The Macmillan Company of Canada Limited.

x, 375, [15] pp.; 232 × 148 mm.

1533.   GARLAND, Aileen

Teacher's Manual For Canada our Country: Part 1. By Aileen Garland. [Table of Contents]. The Macmillan Company of Canada Limited.

[2], 69, [1] pp.; 217 × 150 mm.
Issued in paper.

1534.   GREER, Carlotta C.

Your Home and You. Carlotta Greer [and] Ellen P. Gibbs. Grateful acknowledgement is made to the staff of the School of Home Economics, University of Manitoba for the work done on measurements, Government regulations and reference materials of the Canadian edition of *Your Home and You*, revised edition. The Macmillan Company of Canada Limited.

viii, 504 pp.; 237 × 164 mm.

1535.   HAIG-BROWN, Roderick

The living land: An Account Of The Natural Resources Of British Columbia. Roderick Haig-Brown. Produced By The British Columbia Natural Resources Conference. Published by The Macmillan Company of Canada Limited Toronto 1961.

269, [1] pp.; 278 × 217 mm.

1536.   HALLETT, Fred H.

Machine Shop Theory and Practice. Fred H. Hallett, Head of the Technical Department and Supervisor of Evening Classes, Central Secondary School, Hamilton, Ontario. Illustrated by G. Fantuz. Toronto: The Macmillan Company of Canada Limited 1961.

[10], 141, [1] pp.; 226 × 156 mm.
Revised in 1969 (see 1985).
Macmillan Basic Technical Series.

1537. HILTZ, Mary C.

Fundamental Nutrition in Health and Disease. By Mary C. Hiltz, B.S.(Columbia), M.A.(Toronto). The Macmillan Company of Canada Limited Toronto.

xx, 299, [1] pp.; 215 × 138 mm.

1538. HORNE, Alistair

Canada And The Canadians. By Alistair Horne. Toronto: The Macmillan Company of Canada Limited 1961.

xiv, 329, [1] pp.; 220 × 140 mm.

1539. HUMBLE, A.H.

Lyric And Longer Poems: Book III. A.H. Humble, Head of English Department, Trinity College School, Port Hope. Toronto: The Macmillan Company of Canada Limited.

viii, 200 pp.; 188 × 124 mm.

1540. HUMBLE, A.H.

Lyric And Longer Poems: Book IV. A.H. Humble, Head of English Department, Trinity College School, Port Hope. Toronto: The Macmillan Company of Canada Limited.

x, 232 pp.; 188 × 124 mm.

1541. ISRAEL, Charles E.

A novel. *Rizpah*. By Charles E. Israel. Toronto: 1961: Macmillan.

[8], 534, [2] pp.; 220 × 140 mm.

1542. MacLENNAN, Hugh

Hugh MacLennan, *Seven Rivers of Canada: The Mackenzie, The St. Lawrence, The Ottawa, The Red, The Saskatchewan, The Fraser, The St. John*. Macmillan of Canada Toronto.

x, 170 pp.; 232 × 155 mm.
Reprinted in 1963, 1969 and 1972. Revised and enlarged in 1974 (see 2278).
Reprinted in the Laurentian Library (No. 49) in 1977.

1543. MacMILLAN, R.L.

The Ontario Heart Foundation and the Faculty of Medicine, University of Toronto. International Symposium: *Anticoagulants and Fibrindysins*. Edited by R.L. MacMillan and J.F. Mustard. Toronto, 1961 The Macmillan Company of Canada Limited.

xx, 449, [1] pp.; 238 × 158 mm.

1544. McPHEDRAN, Margaret G.

The Maternity Cycle: A Physiological Approach To Nursing Care. Margaret G. McPhedran, R.N., M.A., Associate Professor, School of Nursing, University of New Brunswick, Formerly Assistant Professor, School of Nursing, University of Toronto. 1961 The Macmillan Company of Canada Limited, Toronto.

xvi, 158 pp.; 188 × 125 mm.

1545. MITCHELL, W.O.

W.O. Mitchell, *Jake and the kid*. Toronto: The Macmillan Company of
Canada Limited 1961.

[6], 184 pp.; 215 × 140 mm.
Reprinted in the Laurentian Library (No. 21) in 1972.

1546. NOBLE, George

The New World Readers, *Teacher's Manual for Under the North Star*. George
Noble/Harry Fisher. The Ryerson Press/The Macmillan Company of
Canada Limited.

viii, 224 pp.; 203 × 150 mm.
First published in 1950 as *Teacher's Handbook for Under the North Star* (see 1228).
This revised edition reprinted in 1962. Issued in paper.
New World Readers Series.

1547. PATTERSON, Raymond M.

The Buffalo Head. By R.M. Patterson, Author of *Dangerous River*. The
Macmillan Company of Canada Limited Toronto 1961.

xiv, 273, [1] pp.; 215 × 144 mm.
Reprinted in paper in 1972. Reprinted in the Laurentian Library (No. 61) in 1978.

1548. *Poems For Upper School 1961-62. The Prologue to The Canterbury Tales* by
Geoffrey Chaucer. With Notes and Questions by Charles W. Dunn, For-
merly Professor of English, University College, Toronto. *The Death of The
Hired Man* by Robert Frost. With Notes and Questions by A.H. Humble.
Authorized by the Minister of Education for Ontario. The Macmillan Com-
pany of Canada Limited Toronto.

[6], 30 pp. + ads.; 184 × 125 mm.
Issued in paper.

1549. RICHMOND, John

A Tearful Tour of Toronto's Riviera of Yesteryear. By John Richmond. Photographs from the James Collection. Paintings and drwgs by Loraine Surcouf.
Macmillan Toronto 1961.

[44] pp.; 335 × 245 mm.

1550. RITCHIE, C.T.

Great Stories of Canada, *The First Canadian: The Story of Champlain*. By
C.T. Ritchie. Illustrated by William Wheeler. Toronto: 1961: Macmillan.

155, [1] pp.; 213 × 138 mm.
Great Stories of Canada Series.

1551. ROBERTSON, Duncan

Errors In Composition. Duncan Robertson, Assistant Professor of English,
Queen's University. Toronto, 1961 The Macmillan Company of Canada
Limited.

[2], 64, [8] pp.; 182 × 115 mm.
Revised in 1963 (see 1649). Issued in paper.

1552. ROSS, Aileen D.

Becoming a Nurse. Aileen D. Ross, Department of Sociology and Anthropology, McGill University. The Macmillan Company of Canada Limited Toronto 1961.

xvi, 420 pp.; 220 × 135 mm.

1553. SPEED, F.M.

Basic General Science: Book 1. F.M. Speed, University of Toronto Schools, Toronto, [and] H.M. Lang, Vice-Principal, Kipling Collegiate Institute, Toronto. Illustrations by G. Fantuz, W.E. Youmans, A.V. Bradshaw. The Macmillan Company of Canada Limited Toronto 1961.

xvi, 488 pp.; 225 × 155 mm.

1554. WARHAFT, Sidney

English Poems, 1250-1660. Sidney Warhaft [and] John Woodbury, University of Manitoba. 1961 The Macmillan Company of Canada Limited Toronto.

xvi, 227, [1] pp.; 233 × 140 mm.

1555. WILSON, Ethel

Mrs. Golightly and other stories. Ethel Wilson. Toronto: 1961 The Macmillan Company of Canada Limited.

[6], 209, [1] pp.; 208 × 140 mm.

1556. WINTER, Ernest H.

Learning to Write. Second Revised Edition. By Ernest H. Winter, M.A., Head of English Department, Eastdale Collegiate and Vocational Institute, Oshawa, Ontario. Original Author Reed Smith. The Macmillan Company of Canada Limited Toronto 1961.

xii, 504 pp.; 205 × 140 mm.

First published in 1939 (see 858). Revised in 1947 (see 1155).

1557. WORTHINGTON, Larry

A Biography Of Major-General F.F. Worthington C.B., M.C., M.M., 'Worthy'. By Larry Worthington. The Macmillan Company of Canada Limited Toronto 1961.

[10], 236 pp.; 220 × 140 mm.

1962

1558. BENNET, C.L.

The Canada Books of Prose and Verse, *Golden Caravan.* C.L. Bennet and J.Fred Swayze. The Ryerson Press—Toronto [and] The Macmillan Company of Canada Limited.

[10], 518 pp.; 235 × 165 mm.
First published in 1934 as *The Canada Book of Prose and Verse, Book Four* (see 561).
Revised and reissued as *The Golden Caravan* in 1948 (see 1163). This edition revised.
Reprinted frequently.
Canada Books of Prose and Verse Series.

1559. BESSETTE, Gérard

Not For Every Eye. A Novel by Gérard Bessette. Translated from the French
by Glen Shortliffe. Toronto: The Macmillan Company of Canada Limited
1962.

[6], 98 pp.; 215 × 135 mm.
Reprinted in the Laurentian Library (No. 53) in 1977.

1560. No entry.

1561. CHEAL, John E.

Educational Administration: The Role of the Teacher. John E. Cheal, Head of
Department of Educational Administration, Faculty of Education, University of Calgary, Harold C. Melsness, Former Associate Professor, Department of Educational Administration, Faculty of Education, University of
Alberta, [and] Arthur W. Reeves, Formerly Head of Department of Educational Administation, Faculty of Education, University of Alberta. The
Macmillan Company of Canada Limited Toronto 1962.

xxiv, 277, [1] pp.; 234 × 155 mm.

1562. CHITTICK, Rae

Health for Canadians. Rae Chittick, Emeritus Professor of Nursing, McGill
University, Formerly Associate Professor of Education, University of Al-
berta. Illustrations by Robert Kunz. Toronto: The Macmillan Company of
Canada Limited.

x, 373, [1] pp.; 228 × 165 mm.
First published in 1956 (see 1365).

1563. CLARK, Catherine Anthony

The Diamond Feather, or The Door in the Mountain: A magic tale for children.
By Catherine Anthony Clark. Illustrated by Clare Bice. Toronto: The
Macmillan Company of Canada Ltd. 1962.

224 pp.; 220 × 140 mm.

1564. COOPER, Suzanne

Contes français et légendes canadiennes. Editors Suzanne Cooper, Raymond
Bolla, Thomas Christmas, Gilbert H. King, Armand Tobaly [and] William
Trenholm. The Macmillan Company of Canada Limited Toronto 1962.

[8], 207, [1] pp.; 190 × 125 mm.

1565. DIEBEL, P.W.

Beckoning Trails. By P.W. Diebel And Madeline Young. The Ryerson Press
— Toronto [and] The Macmillan Company of Canada Limited.

[12], 483, [1] pp.; 233 × 153 mm.
First published in 1932 as *The Canada Book of Prose and Verse, Book One* (see 652).
Revised and reissued as *Beckoning Trails* in 1948 (see 1209). This edition revised.
Reprinted frequently.
Canada Books of Prose and Verse Series.

1566.   DIEBEL, P.W.

The Canada Books of Prose and Verse: Book 1, *The Teacher's Guidebook for Beckoning Trails*. P.W. Diebel, Inspector, Hamilton Public Schools, [and] Reginald McBurney, Master, Lakeshore Teachers' College, Ontario. The Ryerson Press [and] The Macmillan Company of Canada Limited.

xxii, 142 pp.; 208 × 150 mm.
First published in 1952 (see 1282). Revised edition issued in paper.
Canada Books of Prose and Verse Series.

1567.   EATON, Evelyn M.

Avançons: Book 2. Evelyn M. Eaton, Former Co-ordinator of French, Protestant School Board of Greater Montreal, [and] S.J. MacGowan, Former Supervisor of French, Protestant Board of School Commissioners, Montreal. Illustrations by William Wheeler. Toronto: The Macmillan Company of Canada Limited.

xii, 238 pp.; 233 × 155 mm.
First published in 1942 (see 951). Revised in 1950 (see 1224). Book 1 revised in 1961 (see 1525).

1568.   ELLIOTT, George

George Elliott, *The kissing man*. [Quotation]. Toronto 1962 The Macmillan Company of Canada Limited.

[8], 136 pp.; 217 × 137 mm.
Issued in cloth and paper. Reprinted in the Laurentian Library (No. 28) in 1975.

1569.   EWING, John M.

John M. Ewing's *Understanding Yourself and Your Society*. Revised by John Macdonald, M.A.(Edinburgh), Ed.B., Ph.D.(Glasgow), Faculty of Education, University of Alberta. Illustrations by G. Fantuz. Toronto: The Macmillan Company of Canada Limited.

[8], 248 pp.; 218 × 135 mm.
First published in 1946 (see 1103).

1570.   FLOWER, George E.

The Macmillan Spelling Series: 6. Teachers' Edition. General Editor: George E. Flower, Ontario College of Education. Authors: Sybil F. Shack, Principal, Lord Roberts School, Winnipeg, Manitoba, Robert F. Bornhold, K.H.D. Hall, Superintendent of Public Schools, East York, Ontario [and] Gordon F. Mann, Inspector of Public Schools, Windsor, Ontario. © The Macmillan Company of Canada Limited.

xxvi, 141, [1] pp.; 213 × 145 mm.
See note to 1487.
Macmillan Spelling Series.

1571.   FLOWER, George E.

The Macmillan Spelling Series: 7. General Editor: George E. Flower, On-
tario College of Education. Authors: K.H.D. Hall, Superintendent of Pub-
lic Schools, East York, Ontario, Robert F. Bornhold, Inspector of Public
Schools, Halton County, Ontario, Gordon F. Mann, Inspector of Public
Schools, Windsor, Ontario [and] Sybil F. Shack, Principal, Lord Roberts
School, Winnipeg, Manitoba. Copyright, Canada, 1962, by The Macmillan
Company of Canada Limited.

> 112 pp.; 213 × 145 mm.
> Revised in 1978 (see 2596).
> Macmillan Spelling Series.

1572.   FLOWER, George E.

The Macmillan Spelling Series: 7. Teachers' Edition. General Editor: George
E. Flower, Ontario Institute for Studies in Education. Authors: K.H.D.
Hall, Superintendent of Elementary Schools, East York, Ontario, Robert F.
Bornhold, Gordon F. Mann, Superintendent of Public Schools, Windsor,
Ontario [and] Sybil F. Shack, Principal, Isaac Brock School, Winnipeg,
Manitoba. Copyright, Canada 1962, by The Macmillan Company of Canada
Limited.

> xxvi, 141, [1] pp.; 213 × 145 mm.
> See note to 1487.
> Macmillan Spelling Series.

1573.   GOODSPEED, D.J.

The Conspirators: A Study of the Coup d'État. By D.J. Goodspeed. Toronto:
The Macmillan Company of Canada Limited 1962.

> xii, 252 pp.; 220 × 137 mm.
> Reprinted in the Laurentian Library (No. 3) in 1967.

1574.   GREASON, George K.

Canadian Democracy at Work. George K. Greason, Head of History Depart-
ment, Downsview Collegiate Institute, North York [and] Roy C. King,
Principal, C.B. Parsons Junior High School, North York. Drawings by
Dorothy Mould and Vernon Mould. Toronto: The Macmillan Company of
Canada Limited.

> [8], 101, [1] pp.; 225 × 145 mm.
> Revised in 1966 (see 1781A), 1969 (see 1984), 1971 (see 2099) and 1977 (2476A).
> Issued in paper.

1575.   HARDY, Thomas

*The Life And Death Of the Mayor of Casterbridge: A Story Of A Man of
Character.* By Thomas Hardy. Edited by Andrew A. Orr, M.A. and Vivian de
Sola Pinto. Toronto: The Macmillan Company of Canada Limited.

> x, 417, [3] pp.; 188 × 125 mm.
> Reprinted in paper in 1971.

1576.   HARLOW, Robert

Robert Harlow, *Royal Murdoch*. Toronto/1962 Macmillan of Canada.

> [6], 243, [1] pp.; 220 × 143 mm.

1577. HOLLAND, Elizabeth

A Separate Person. By Elizabeth Holland. [Quotation]. 1962 The Macmillan Company of Canada Limited Toronto.

[6], 247, [3] pp.; 200 × 130 mm.

1578. KUTHAN, George

Vancouver: sights & insights. Drawings By George Kuthan & Words By Donald Stainsby. Macmillan of Canada Toronto 1962.

[8], 139, [1] pp.; 258 × 200 mm.
Issued in cloth and paper.

1579. LABARGE, Margaret Wade

Simon De Montfort. By Margaret Wade Labarge. Toronto: The Macmillan Company of Canada Limited 1962.

xii, 312 pp.; 227 × 145 mm.

1580. LANG, H. Murray

Basic General Science: Book 2. H.M. Lang, Vice-Principal, Kipling Collegiate Institute, Toronto, [and] F.M. Speed, University of Toronto Schools, Toronto, Illustrations by A. Diana, K. King. The Macmillan Company of Canada Limited, Toronto.

xiv, 396 pp.; 225 × 155 mm.
Revised in 1968 (see 1929).

1581. LEITCH, Adelaide

The Great Canoe. By Adelaide Leitch. Illustrated by Clare Bice. Buckskin Books. 1962 Macmillan of Canada Toronto.

[6], 115, [1] pp.; 190 × 125 mm.
Buckskin Books Series.

1582. LONGSTRETH, T. Morris

The Calgary Challengers. Illustrated by William Wheeler. By T. Morris Longstreth. Macmillan of Canada: Toronto: 1962.

[8], 165, [1] pp.; 218 × 140 mm.

1583. MACPHERSON, Jay

Four Ages of Man: The Classical Myths. By Jay Macpherson. [Quotation]. 1962 The Macmillan Company of Canada Limited Toronto.

[10], 205, [1] pp.; 215 × 140 mm.
Also issued in a school edition.

1584. MANNING, Helen Taft

The Revolt Of French Canada 1800-1835: A Chapter in the History of the British Commonwealth. By Helen Taft Manning, Emeritus Professor of History, Bryn Mawr College, Pennsylvania. Toronto: The Macmillan Company of Canada Limited 1962.

xx, 426 pp.; 222 × 150 mm.

1585. MAY, Charles Paul
> *A Book of Canadian Animals*. By Charles Paul May. Illustrations by John Crosby. 1962 Toronto The Macmillan Company of Canada Limited.
>> [10], 115, [1] pp.; 210 × 135 mm.
>> Reprinted in 1975.

1586. McGREGOR, F.A.
> *The Fall and Rise of Mackenzie King: 1911-1919*. By F.A. McGregor. Macmillan of Canada/Toronto/1962.
>> [10], 358 pp.; 234 × 153 mm.

1587. McGUFFIN, Mervin J.
> *Automotive Mechanics: Principles And Operation*. Mervin J. McGuffin, Shop Co-ordinator, H.B. Beal Technical and Commercial High School, London, Ontario. Illustrated by Keith King. Toronto: The Macmillan Company of Canada Limited.
>> [12], 144 pp.; 226 × 156 mm.
>> Macmillan Basic Technical Series.

1588. McLAUGHLIN, Lorrie
> *West to the Cariboo*. By Lorrie McLaughlin. Illustrated by Joe Rosenthal. Buckskin Books. 1962 Macmillan of Canada Toronto.
>> [6], 122 pp.; 190 × 125 mm.
>> Buckskin Books Series.

1589. McNAMEE, James
> *My Uncle Joe*. By James McNamee. Illustrated by Lewis Parker. Macmillan of Canada 1962 Toronto.
>> [10], 63, [1] pp.; 232 × 154 mm.

1590. MEASURES, Howard
> Howard Measures, *Styles of Address: A Manual of Usage in Writing and in Speech*. Revised Edition. [Quotation]. 1962 The Macmillan Company of Canada Limited Toronto.
>> x, 150 pp.; 215 × 135 mm.
>> Third edition published in 1969 (see 2008).

1591. MILLER, H.G.
> *Hand And Machine Woodwork*. H.G. Miller, New Toronto Secondary School, New Toronto, Ontario. Illustrated by G. Fantuz [and] Keith King. Toronto: The Macmillan Company of Canada Limited.
>> [10], 196 pp.; 226 × 156 mm.
>> Revised in 1972 (see 2161). A metric edition was published in 1978 (see 2581).
>> Macmillan Basic Technical Series.

1592. MILLER, Orlo
> *The Donnellys Must Die*. By Orlo Miller. 1962 Macmillan of Canada Toronto.
>> [10], 244 pp.; 233 × 150 mm.
>> Reprinted in the Laurentian Library (No. 4) in 1967.

1593. MITCHELL, W.O.

W.O. Mitchell, *the Kite*. Macmillan of Canada Toronto 1962.

[6], 210 pp.; 213 × 135 mm.
Reprinted in the Laurentian Library (No. 20) in 1974.

1594. No entry

1595. PENNER, Philip G.

Life and Adventure. By Philip Penner and Edna Baxter. The Ryerson Press
—Toronto [and] The Macmillan Company of Canada Limited.

[12], 516 pp.; 235 × 155 mm.
First published in 1932 as *The Canada Book of Prose and Verse, Book Two* (see 501).
Revised in 1935 (see 653). Further revised and reissued as *Life and Adventure* in 1948
(see 1205). This edition revised. Reprinted frequently.
Canada Books of Prose and Verse Series.

1596. PRATT, E.J.

Here the Tides Flow. E.J. Pratt. Edited with Introduction, Notes and Questions by D.G. Pitt, M.A., PH.D., Department of English, Memorial University of Newfoundland, St. John's, Newfoundland. Toronto: The Macmillan
Company of Canada Limited 1962.

xiv, 169, [1] pp.; 182 × 123 mm.
Issued in paper.

1597. REANEY, James

James Reaney, *The Killdeer And Other Plays: The Killdeer, The Sun and the
Moon, One Man Masque, Night-blooming Cereus*. Toronto 1962 The Macmillan Company of Canada Limited.

viii, 224 pp.; 220 × 140 mm.

1598. SCHULL, Joseph

Great Stories of Canada, *Ships of the Great Days: Canada's Navy in World
War II*. By Joseph Schull. Illustrated by Ed McNally. Toronto: 1962:
Macmillan.

156 pp.; 213 × 138 mm.
Great Stories of Canada Series.

1599. SWAYZE, Beulah Garland

Father Gabriel's Cloak. By Beulah Garland Swayze. Illustrated by Douglas
Sneyd. Buckskin Books. 1962 Macmillan of Canada Toronto.

[6], 122 pp.; 190 × 125 mm.
Buckskin Books Series.

1600. WHALLEY, George

The Legend of John Hornby. George Whalley. Macmillan of Canada Toronto.

xiv, 367, [1] pp.; 220 × 136 mm.
Reprinted in the Laurentian Library (No. 51) in 1977.

1601. WILSON, Clifford

Great Stories of Canada, *Adventurers from the Bay: Men of the Hudson's Bay Company*. By Clifford Wilson. Illustrated by Lloyd Scott. Toronto: 1962: Macmillan.

159, [1] pp.; 213 × 138 mm.
Great Stories of Canada Series.

1602. WILSON, John Francis

The Story of the Migration of Skivins and his first year in Western Canada. Written and Illustrated by John Francis Wilson. 1962 The Macmillan Company of Canada Limited Toronto.

43, [1] pp.; 233 × 310 mm.

1603. WOOD, Edgar Allardyce

Wild Winter. By Kerry Wood [pseud.]. Illustrated by Victor Mays. 1962 The Macmillan Company of Canada Limited Toronto.

[10], 175, [1] pp.; 210 × 137 mm.

1604. WOODS, H.D.

Labour Policy and Labour Economics in Canada. H.D. Woods, McGill University [and] Sylvia Ostry, University of Montreal. Macmillan of Canada Toronto 1962.

xviii, 534 pp.; 235 × 147 mm.
Reprinted in 1967. Revised in 1972 (see 2169) and 1973 (see 2232).

1963

1605. AFFLECK, Muriel A.

Language Journeys: Grades I and II: A Handbook for Teachers. Muriel A. Affleck, Associate Professor of Elementary Education, University of Alberta, Elsie Bradshaw, Reading Specialist, Public School Board of Edmonton, Annie C. Roberts, Division I Consultant, Public School Board, Edmonton [and] Katherine G. Thierrien, Director of Elementary Grade Instruction, Separate School Board, Edmonton. The Macmillan Company of Canada Limited Toronto.

x, 181, [1] pp.; 206 × 144 mm.
Language Journeys Series.

1606. ANBUREY, Thomas

Edited and With an Introduction by Sydney Jackman, F.R. HIST. S., *With Burgoyne from Quebec: An Account of the Life at Quebec and of the Famous Battle at Saratoga*. First published as Volume One of *Travels Through the Interior Parts of North America*. By Thomas Anburey. With illustrations from the first edition and a map specially drawn by C.C.J. Bond. Macmillan of Canada/Toronto/1963.

[12], 220 pp.; 220 × 136 mm.
Pioneer Books Series.

1607. ASHLEY, C.A.

C.A. Ashley, *The first twenty-five years: A Study of Trans-Canada Airlines*.
1963 The Macmillan Company of Canada Limited Toronto.

xii, 72, [4] pp.; 195 × 120 mm.
Issued in paper.

1608. BALLANTYNE, Lareine

The Scout Who Led an Army. By Lareine Ballantyne. Illustrated by Lee
Clifton. Buckskin Books. 1963 Macmillan of Canada Toronto.

[10], 106, [8] pp.; 190 × 125 mm.
Reprinted in 1966.
Buckskin Books Series.

1609. BENHAM, Leslie

The Heroine of Long Point. By Leslie and Lois Benham. Illustrated by Vernon
Mould. Buckskin Books. 1963 Macmillan of Canada Toronto.

[10], 113, [5] pp.; 190 × 125 mm.
Buckskin Books Series.

1610. BENNET, C.L.

The Canada Books of Prose and Verse, *Argosy to Adventure*. C.L. Bennet.
The Ryerson Press — Toronto, [and] The Macmillan Company of Canada
Limited.

[10], 558 pp.; 235 × 165 mm.
First published in 1935 as *The Canada Book of Prose and Verse, Book Five* (see 621).
Revised and reissued as *Argosy to Adventure* in 1950 (see 1212). This edition revised.
Reprinted frequently.
Canada Books of Prose and Verse Series.

1611. BRAMWELL, Barbara

Adventure at the Mill. By Barbara and Heather Bramwell. Illustrated by
William Lytle. Buckskin Books. 1963 Macmillan of Canada Toronto.

[10], 113, [5] pp.; 190 × 125 mm.
Buckskin Books Series.

1612. BROWN, Gwethalyn Graham

Dear Enemies: A Dialogue On French And English Canada. By Gwethalyn
Graham [pseud.] And Solange Chaput Rolland. Toronto 1963 The Macmillan Company of Canada Limited.

xiv, 112 pp.; 216 × 136 mm.
Issued in cloth and paper.

1613. CALLAGHAN, Morley

That Summer in Paris. Morley Callaghan. Memories of Tangled Friendships
With Hemingway, Fitzgerald, And Some Others. Toronto Macmillan of
Canada 1963.

255, [1] pp.; 218 × 148 mm.
Reprinted in paper in 1973 and in the Laurentian Library (No. 40) in 1976.

1614.   CARELESS, J.M.S.

Brown of The Globe. Vol. Two: Statesman of Confederation 1860-1880. J.M.S.
Careless. Toronto: The Macmillan Company of Canada Limited 1963.

x, 406 pp.; 250 × 150 mm.
Issued in cloth and paper. Reprinted in 1972 in paper.

1615.   CARELESS, J.M.S.

Canada: A Story of Challenge. By J.M.S. Careless, Chairman of the Department of History, University of Toronto. The Macmillan Company of Canada
Limited Toronto.

xiv, 444 pp.; 185 × 125 mm.
Reprinted in 1970 and in the Laurentian Library (no. 30) in 1974.

1616.   CHAMBERS, Robert

A Book of Essays. Edited By Robert Chambers And Carlyle King. Toronto
1963 The Macmillan Company of Canada Limited.

[8], 151, [1] pp.; 200 × 125 mm.

1617.   CHEAL, John E.

*Investment in Canadian Youth: An Analysis of Input-Output Differences Among
Canadian Provincial School Systems.* By John E. Cheal, Associate Professor,
Faculty of Education, Department of Educational Administration, Univer-
sity of Alberta. This study was conducted under the auspices of the Midwest
Administration Center, University of Chicago. The Macmillan Company of
Canada Limited Toronto.

xiv, 167, [1] pp.; 235 × 155 mm.

1618.   CLARK, Catherine Anthony

The Man With Yellow Eyes. By Catherine Anthony Clark. Illustrated by
Gordon Rayner. Buckskin Books. 1963 Macmillan of Canada Toronto.

[6], 122 pp.; 190 × 125 mm.
Buckskin Books Series.

1619.   COLLINS, Herbert F.

Les Beaux Jours: A French Reader for Junior Forms. By Herbert F. Collins,
M.A.(Lond.). Illustrated by Jennetta Vise. The Macmillan Company of
Canada Limited Toronto.

vi, 106 pp.; 183 × 130 mm.
First published in 1956. Reprinted in 1957, 1961, 1963 and 1966. Earlier printings
not located. Issued in limp cloth.

1620.   *Conference across a Continent: An Account Of H.R.H. The Duke Of Edin-
burgh's Second Commonwealth Study Conference On The Human Consequences
Of The Changing Industrial Environment In The Commonwealth And Empire.
Canada: May 13-June 6, 1962.* Macmillan of Canada 1963.

[12], 521, [1] pp.; 232 × 155 mm.

1621. COOK, Lyn

Samantha's Secret Room. Lyn Cook. Illustrated by Bill McKibbin. 1963 The Macmillan Company of Canada Limited Toronto.

x, 210 pp.; 218 × 140 mm.
Reprinted in 1966, 1968 and 1978 (paper).

1622. COVELL, Harold M.

[Cover-title:] Ryerson/Macmillan. The Canada Books of Prose and Verse, *Reading Study Book One*. Harold M. Covell [and] John McGechaen.

96 pp.; 275 × 210 mm.
At the foot of p. [1] it is noted that this Reading Study book is for *Beckoning Trails*.
Issued in paper.
Canada Books of Prose and Verse Series.

1623. DICKSON, Lovat

The House of Words. By Lovat Dickson. Toronto: The Macmillan Company of Canada Limited 1963.

[8], 304 pp.; 220 × 140 mm.

1624. DOWNEY, Lawrence W.

The Canadian Secondary School: An Appraisal and a Forecast. A Collection of the papers delivered at the Conference on the Canadian High School sponsored by the Department of Secondary Education, University of Alberta. Edited by Lawrence W. Downey and L. Ruth Godwin. The Macmillan Company of Canada Limited and W.J. Gage Limited Toronto.

xiv, 128 pp.; 225 × 145 mm.
Issued in paper.

1625. EATON, Evelyn M.

Teachers' Manual for Avançons: Books I and II. By Evelyn M. Eaton, Co-ordinator of French, Protestant School Board of Greater Montreal. The Macmillan Company of Canada Limited.

[10], 173, [1] pp.; 218 × 140 mm.

1626. ENNS, Frederick

The Legal Status of the Canadian School Board. By Frederick Enns, B.E.D., M.E.D., PH.D., Assistant Professor of Educational Administration, University of Alberta.

xviii, 213, [1] pp.; 235 × 152 mm.

1627. EUBANK, Howard L.

Basic Physics For Secondary School. Revised Edition. Howard L. Eubank, Principal, Woburn Collegiate Institute, Scarborough, Ontario, John M. Ramsay, Inspector of Secondary Schools, Ontario [and] Leslie A. Rickard, Head of Science Department, Forest Hill Collegiate Institute, Toronto, Ontario. Illustrations by Robert Kunz and Kenneth Dallison. The Macmillan Company of Canada Limited, Toronto.

xvi, 454 pp.; 238 × 158 mm.
First published in 1957 (see 1394).

1628.   FLOWER, George E.

The Macmillan Spelling Series: 3. Teachers' Edition. General Editor: George
E. Flower, Ontario College of Education. Authors: Robert F. Bornhold,
Inspector of Public Schools, Halton County, Ontario, K.H.D. Hall,
Superintendent of Public Schools, East York, Ontario, Gordon F. Mann,
Inspector of Public Schools, Windsor, Ontario [and] Sybil F. Shack, Princi-
pal, Lord Roberts School, Winnipeg, Manitoba. © The Macmillan Company
of Canada Limited, 1963.

> xxvi, 141, [1] pp.; 213 × 145 mm.
> See note to 1487.
> Macmillan Spelling Series.

1629.   FLOWER, George E.

The Macmillan Spelling Series: 8. General Editor: George E. Flower, On-
tario Institute for Studies in Education. Authors: Sybil F. Shack, Principal,
Isaac Brock School, Winnipeg, Manitoba, Robert F. Bornhold, K.H.D.
Hall, Superintendent of Elementary Schools, East York, Ontario, [and]
Gordon F. Mann, Superintendent of Public Schools, Windsor, Ontario.
© The Macmillan Company of Canada Limited, 1963.

> 116 pp.; 213 × 145 mm.
> Revised in 1978 (see 2565).
> Macmillan Spelling Series.

1630.   FUMERTON, H.S.

Petits Contes de l'Histoire canadienne. By H.S. Fumerton, Northmount Junior
High School, North York. Illustrated by William Lytle. Macmillan of
Canada Toronto.

> [8], 72 pp.; 183 × 122 mm.
> Issued in limp cloth.

1631.   FYFE, C.T.

Our Heritage. By C.T. Fyfe and F.F. Sutherland. The Ryerson Press —
Toronto [and] The Macmillan Company of Canada Limited.

> [10], 533, [1] pp.; 232 × 155 mm.
> First published in 1932 as *The Canada Book of Prose and Verse, Book Three* (see 502).
> Revised in 1936 (see 714). Further revised and reissued in 1948 as *Our Heritage* (see
> 1203). This edition revised. Reprinted frequently.
> Canada Books of Prose and Verse Series.

1632.   GARLAND, Aileen

Teacher's Manual For Canada our Country: Part 2. By Aileen Garland. [Table
of Contents]. The Macmillan Company of Canada Limited.

> [2], 62 pp.; 217 × 150 mm.
> Issued in paper.

1633.   GILBERT, Robin

Pierre Et Les Cambrioleurs: A Modern School Reader. By Robin Gilbert, B.A.
Illustrations by B. Biro. The Macmillan Company of Canada Limited Toronto.

> 61, [1] pp.; 180 × 130 mm.
> Issued in limp cloth.

1634. GRAY, John M.
Lord Selkirk of Red River. John Morgan Gray. 1963 The Macmillan Company of Canada Limited Toronto.
   xx, 388 pp.; 225 × 145 mm.

1635. HARRIS, John Norman
The Weird World of Wes Beattie. John Norman Harris. Macmillan of Canada Toronto.
   [8], 216 pp.; 208 × 143 mm.

1636. ISRAEL, Charles E.
Who Was Then the Gentleman? A Novel By Charles E. Israel. Toronto: 1963: Macmillan.
   [4], 297, [1] pp.; 220 × 138 mm.

1637. LAMBERT, R.S.
Great Stories Of Canada, *Mutiny in the Bay: Henry Hudson's Last Voyage*. By R.S. Lambert. Illustrated by Joe Rosenthal. Toronto 1963 Macmillan.
   160 pp.; 213 × 138 mm.
   Reprinted in 1966.
   Great Stories of Canada Series.

1638. MacEWEN, Gwendolyn
Julian The Magician. A novel by Gwendolyn MacEven [sic]. Toronto: The Macmillan Company of Canada Limited 1963.
   [6], 151, [1] pp.; 200 × 138 mm.

1639. MacNUTT, W.S.
New Brunswick, A History: 1784-1867. W.S. MacNutt. Macmillan of Canada Toronto 1963.
   xvi, 496 pp.; 233 × 151 mm.
   Issued in cloth and paper.

1640. MASSEY, Vincent
What's Past Is Prologue: The Memoirs of the Right Honourable Vincent Massey, C.H. The Macmillan Company of Canada Limited Toronto 1963.
   [18], 540 pp.; 220 × 147 mm.

1641. McCLELLAND, Hugh
The Magic Lassoo. Written and Illustrated by Hugh McClelland. St. Martin's Press New York [and] The Macmillan Company of Canada Limited Toronto.
   39, [1] pp.; 230 × 175 mm.

1642. McKELLAR, Hugh D.
Beyond the Footlights: One-Act Plays For Secondary Schools. Selected and Edited by Hugh D. McKellar, B.A., B.L.S., Mus. Bac. Toronto: The Macmillan Company of Canada Limited.
   x, 239, [1] pp.; 190 × 125 mm.

1643. PALARDY, Jean

Jean Palardy, *The early furniture Of French Canada*. Translated From The French By Eric McLean. Macmillan of Canada Toronto 1963.

411, [1] pp.; 208 × 160 mm.
Reprinted in cloth in 1965 and in paper in 1971, 1974 and 1978.

1644. PENNER, Philip G.

Chapters VI and VII From Learning English. Philip G. Penner [and] Ruth E. McConnell, University of British Columbia. The Macmillan Company of Canada Limited Toronto 1963.

[4], 181-288 pp.; 207 × 130 mm.
An offprint from *Learning English* (see 1645). Issued in paper.

1645. PENNER, Philip G.

Learning English. Philip G. Penner [and] Ruth E. McConnell, University of British Columbia. The Macmillan Company of Canada Toronto.

xviii, 487, [1] pp.; 215 × 140 mm.
Revised in 1977 as *Learning Language* (see 2507).

1646. PENNER, Philip G.

The Canada Books of Prose and Verse, Book 2: *The Teacher's Guidebook for Life and Adventure*. P.G. Penner, Faculty and College of Education, University of British Columbia [and] E.L. Baxter, Faculty and College of Education, University of British Columbia. Editor-in-Chief: Reginald McBurney. 7: *Beckoning Trails*, 8: *Life and Adventure*, 9: *Our Heritage*. The Ryerson Press [and] The Macmillan Company of Canada Limited.

xxvi, 120 pp.; 205 × 150 mm.
First published in 1952 (see 1278).
Canada Books of Prose and Verse Series.

1647. *Poems For Upper School 1963-64*. *The Titanic* by E.J. Pratt. With Notes and Questions by the Macmillan Editors. *An Epistle* by Robert Browning. With Notes and Questions by Julia Gray, Richview Collegiate Institute, Islington, Ontario. The Macmillan Company of Canada Limited Toronto.

[4], 76 pp.; 184 × 125 mm.
Issued in paper.

1648. RITCHIE, C.T.

Great Stories of Canada, *Runner of the Woods: The Story Of Young Radisson*. By C.T. Ritchie. Illustrated By William Wheeler. Toronto: 1963: Macmillan.

160 pp.; 213 × 138 mm.
Great Stories of Canada Series.

1649. ROBERTSON, Duncan

Errors In Composition. Duncan Robertson, Department of English, Queen's University. Toronto, 1963 The Macmillan Company of Canada Limited.

xiv, 70, [4] pp.; 182 × 120 mm.
First published in 1961 (see 1551). This edition revised. Issued in paper.

1650. SAVAGE, James

James Savage, *Resources For Tomorrow*. Macmillan of Canada Toronto.
x, 246 pp.; 230 × 145 mm.

1651. SPRY, Irene M.

Irene M. Spry, *The Palliser Expedition: An Account Of John Palliser's British North American Expedition 1857-1860*. Toronto/1963 The Macmillan Company of Canada Limited.
x, 310 pp.; 225 × 155 mm.
Reprinted in paper in 1973.

1652. STEINBECK, John

The Red Pony. By John Steinbeck. With Illustrations by Wesley Dennis. Study Material Prepared By C.J. Porter, B.A., Head of the English Department, Cobourg District Collegiate Institutes. Macmillan of Canada: Toronto.
128 pp.; 190 × 125 mm.
Also found bound with *The Pearl* (see 1451).

1653. STIRLING, Norman

Introduction to Technical Drawing. Norman Stirling, Technical Director, Courtice High School, Courtice, Ontario. Toronto: The Macmillan Company of Canada Limited 1963.
[10], 256 pp.; 258 × 182 mm.
Revised in 1970 (see 2080). A metric edition was published in 1977 (see 2517).
Macmillan Basic Technical Series.

1654. THOMPSON, Frances C.

Danger in the Coves. By Frances C. Thompson. Illustrated by Lloyd Scott. Buckskin Books. 1963 Macmillan of Canada Toronto.
[6], 122 pp.; 190 × 125 mm.
Buckskin Books Series.

1655. TROOP, Robert

Robert Troop, *The Sound of Vinegar*. 1963 Macmillan of Canada Toronto.
243, [1] pp.; 190 × 125 mm.

1656. TWAIN, Mark

The Adventures of Huckleberry Finn. Mark Twain. Study Material Prepared By C.J. Porter, B.A., Head Of The English Department, Cobourg District Collegiate Institutes. The Macmillan Company of Canada Limited Toronto.
[6], 330 pp.; 188 × 125 mm.
Issued in cloth and paper.

1657. WALLACE, W. Stewart

The Macmillan Dictionary Of Canadian Biography. By W. Stewart Wallace, Librarian Emeritus of the University of Toronto. Third Edition — Revised and Enlarged. 1963 London Macmillan Toronto. St. Martin's New York.

[10], 822, [2] pp.; 240 × 163 mm.
First published in 1926 (see 298). Revised and enlarged in 1945 (see 1094 and 1095).
Fourth edition published in 1978 (see 2606).

1658. WOOD, Edgar Allardyce

The Boy and the Buffalo. By Kerry Wood [pseud.]. Illustrated by Audrey
Teather. Buckskin Books. 1963 Macmillan of Canada Toronto.

[10], 120 pp.; 190 × 125 mm.
Buckskin Books Series.

1659. WRIGHT, Richard

Andrew Tolliver. By Richard Wright. Illustrated by Lewis Parker. Macmillan
of Canada Toronto.

[8], 105, [1] pp.; 175 × 118 mm.
Buckskin Books Series.

1964

1660. BENNET, C.L.

A Treasury of Prose and Verse. By C.L. Bennet [and] Lorne Pierce. The
Macmillans in Canada [and] The Ryerson Press.

xiv, 625, [1] pp.; 200 × 140 mm.
First published in 1936. Earlier printings not located. Reprinted frequently.
Canada Books of Prose and Verse Series.

1661. BLISHEN, Bernard R.

Canadian Society: Sociological Perspectives. Revised Editon. Edited by Bernard R. Blishen, Frank E. Jones, Kaspar D. Naegele, [and] John Porter.
1964 Macmillan of Canada/Toronto, Macmillan & Co Ltd./London, St.
Martin's Press/New York.

xvi, 541, [1] pp.; 232 × 155 mm.
First published in 1961 (see 1516). Third edition (further revised) published in 1968
(see 1904).

1662. BROWN, Arthur E.

Mathematics in Practice. Revised Edition. Authorized in the Province of
Alberta. Arthur E. Brown, B.A., B.Paed., Principal, Danforth Technical
School,Toronto, David E. Bridge, B.A.Sc., B.Paed., Technical Training
Specialist, Vocational Training Branch, Department of Labour, Federal
Government, [and] Wallace J. Morrison, B.A., B.Paed., Head of the
Mathematics Department, DanforthTechnical School, Toronto. The Mac-
millan Company of Canada Limited, Toronto.

xii, 428 pp.; 235 × 155 mm.
First published in 1952 (see 1263A). Revised in 1954 and a supplement published
(see 1306 and 1307). Second revision published in 1960 (see 1481).

1663. BROWN, N.E.

Consumer Education. N.E. Brown, Co-ordinator of Social Studies, Wetaski-win High School. Toronto: The Macmillan Company of Canada Limited.

[8], 80 pp.; 225 × 140 mm.
Revised in 1967 (see 1828). Issued in paper.

1664. BROWNLEE, Raymond B.

Brownlee. Fuller. Hancock. Sohon. Whitsit. *Elements of Chemistry*. Revised by Paul J. Boylan, Associate Professor of Chemistry and Physics, State College, Boston, Mass., Physical Science Lecturer, Northeastern University. Macmillan of Canada Toronto.

viii, 696, [2] pp.; 238 × 160 mm.

1665. CAMU, Pierre

Economic Geography of Canada. With An Introduction To A 68-Region System. Pierre Camu, Vice-President, St. Lawrence Seaway Authority, E.P. Weeks, Executive Director, Atlantic Development Board, Canada [and] Z.W. Sametz, Director, Economic and Social Research Division, Department of Citizenship and Immigration, Canada. 1964 Macmillan of Canada Toronto, Macmillan & Co. Ltd. London, St. Martin's Press New York.

xviii, 393, [1] pp.; 245 × 180 mm.

1666. CARMICHAEL, William H.

[Cover-title:] *Topics For Grade Eleven Mathematics, Arts and Science Branch, Four Year Course. Applications of Percentage, Common Statistical Terms*. Wm. H. Carmichael, Wm. W. Fraser, Elizabeth D. McArthur, Board of Education for the Township of York. The Macmillan Company of Canada Limited.

[4], 80 pp.; 270 × 208 mm.
Issued in paper.

1667. CONRAD, Joseph

Youth. Joseph Conrad. Study Material Prepared by Ernest H. Winter, M.A., Head of the English Department, O'Neill Collegiate and Vocational Institute, Oshawa, Ontario. [Quotation]. Toronto: The Macmillan Company of Canada Limited.

viii, 54 pp.; 180 × 120 mm.
Issued in paper.

1668. COVELL, Harold M.

[At bottom of page:] The Canada Books of Prose and Verse, *Reading Study Book for Life and Adventure*. Harold M. Covell [and] John McGechaen. Illustrated by Gus Fantuz. © The Ryerson Press and the Macmillan Company of Canada Limited, 1964 [etc.].

103, [1] pp.; 275 × 210 mm.
Issued in paper.
Canada Books of Prose and Verse Series.

1669.   CREIGHTON, Donald

The Road to Confederation: The Emergence Of Canada, 1863-1867. Donald Creighton. 1964 Macmillan of Canada Toronto.

[12], 489, [1] pp.; 225 × 150 mm.

1670.   CURRAN, Verna I.

Passeport au français. Selected and edited by Verna I. Curran, M.A., PH.D., Head of Modern Language Department, William Lyon Mackenzie Collegiate Institute, North York. Illustrated by Leo Rampen. The Macmillan Company of Canada Limited Toronto.

[12], 203, [1] pp.; 190 × 125 mm.

1671.   DOW, Marguerite R.

Light From Other Windows. Study Material Prepared By Marguerite R. Dow, Head Of The English Department, Laurentian High School, Ottawa. Toronto: The Macmillan Company of Canada.

[12], 235, [1] pp.; 188 × 125 mm.
Reissued subsequently with author's credentials changed to Associate Professor of English, Althouse College of Education, University of Western Ontario.

1672.   FAIT, Hollis F.

Health And Fitness For Modern Living. Hollis F. Fait. The Macmillan Company of Canada Limited Toronto. Revised Canadian Edition 1964.

x, 417, [1] pp.; 238 × 159 mm.

1673.   FALLE, G.G.

Three Restoration Comedies. *The Country Wife* By William Wycherley. *The Way of the World* By William Congreve. *The Rehearsal* By George Villiers, Second Duke of Buckingham. Edited by G.G. Falle, Trinity College, University of Toronto. Macmillan of Canada - Toronto, Macmillan & Co. Ltd. - London, St. Martin's Press - New York.

[8], 342 pp.; 182 × 122 mm.
Issued in paper.
College Classics in English Series.

1674.   FLOWER, George E.

The Macmillan Spelling Series: 5. Teachers' Edition. General Editor: George E. Flower, Ontario College of Education. Authors: Robert F. Bornhold, K.H.D. Hall, Superintendent of Public Schools, East York, Ontario, Gordon F. Mann, Inspector of Public Schools, Windsor, Ontario [and] Sybil F. Shack, Principal, Lord Roberts School, Winnipeg, Manitoba. © The Macmillan Company of Canada Limited, 1964.

xxvi, [139], [1] pp.; 213 × 145 mm.
Macmillan Spelling Series.

1675.   GALBRAITH, John Kenneth

The Scotch. By John Kenneth Galbraith. With illustrations by Samuel H. Bryant. The Macmillan Company of Canada Ltd. Toronto 1964.

xiv, 145, [1] pp.; 215 × 145 mm.

1676. GOODSPEED, D.J.

Great Stories of Canada, *The Good Soldier: The Story of Isaac Brock*. By D.J. Goodspeed. Illustrated by Jack Ferguson. Toronto: 1964: Macmillan.

156 pp.; 213 × 138 mm.
Reprinted in 1967.
Great Stories of Canada Series.

1677. GOODSPEED, D.J.

Redcoat Spy. John Redmayne [pseud.]. Illustrated by John Lawrence. 1964 Macmillan of Canada Toronto.

163, [1] pp.; 200 × 130 mm.
John Redmayne is a pseudonym for D.J. Goodspeed and Herbert F. Wood.

1678. GREASON, George K.

The Citizen and Local Government. George K. Greason, Vice-Principal, Downsview Secondary School, North York [and] Roy C. King, Principal, C.B. Parsons Junior High School, North York. Drawings by William Lytle. Toronto: The Macmillan Company of Canada Limited.

[8], 88 pp.; 225 × 143 mm.
Issued in limp cloth.

1678A GREIG, James W.

Over the Horizon. Edited by James W. Greig, North York Board of Education. The Macmillan Company Of Canada Limited Toronto.

[12], 308 pp.; 233 × 155 mm.
Revised edition published in 1977 (see 2477).
Passport to Reading Series.

1679. KIPLING, Rudyard

Captains Courageous: A Story of the Grand Banks. Rudyard Kipling. Study material prepared by Hume Wilkins, Vice-Principal, Cornwall Collegiate Institute and Vocational School, Cornwall, Ontario. The Macmillan Company of Canada Limited.

191, [1] pp.; 188 × 126 mm.
First published in 1939 (see 844). This edition reissued in paper in 1972.

1680. LAFITTE, Lucette

Lucette Lafitte, *Antoine Chasseur*. Dessins de Walter Groetz. The Macmillan Company of Canada Limited Toronto.

61, [1] pp.; 185 × 124 mm.
Issued in limp cloth.

1681. LEITCH, Adelaide

Lukey Paul from Labrador. By Adelaide Leitch. Illustrated by Joe Rosenthal. Buckskin Books. 1964 Macmillan of Canada Toronto.

[8], 116 pp.; 190 × 125 mm.
Buckskin Books Series.

1682. LONDON, Jack

The Call Of The Wild. Jack London. Study Material Prepared By Linton D.
Read, Vice-Principal, Moira Secondary School, Belleville, Ontario. Toronto:
The Macmillan Company of Canada Limited.

vii, 126 pp.; 188 × 125 mm.
First published in 1910 (see 37). Reissued in Macmillans' St. Martin's Classics series
in 1933 (see 532). Issued in cloth and paper.

1683. LONGSTRETH, T. Morris

Great Stories Of Canada, *The Scarlet Force: The Making Of The Mounted
Police*. By T. Morris Longstreth. Illustrated By Lloyd Scott. Toronto:
1964: Macmillan.

x, 182 pp.; 213 × 138 mm.
First published in 1953 (see 1297). Second revised edition published in 1974 (see
2276).
Great Stories of Canada Series.

1684. MAY, Charles Paul

A Second Book of Canadian Animals. By Charles Paul May. Illustrations By
John Crosby. Toronto 1964 The Macmillan Company of Canada Limited.

[8], 109, [1] pp.; 207 × 130 mm.
Reprinted in 1967 and 1977.

1685. MILLER, S.H.

Michel et Le Loup. S.H. Miller, B.A., Lutterworth Grammar School,
Leicestershire, And C. Jacob, B.A., Bilborough Grammar School, Nottin-
gham. The Macmillan Company of Canada Limited Toronto.

32 pp.; 230 × 174 mm.
Issued in limp cloth.

1686. MONTROSE, Anne

The Winter Flower and Other Fairy Stories. By Anne Montrose. Illustrated by
Mircea Vasiliu. Macmillan of Canada Toronto.

143, [1] pp.; 235 × 158 mm.

1687. OHEARN, Peter J.T.

Peter J.T. Ohearn, Q.C., *Peace, Order and Good Government: A New
Constitution For Canada*. 1964 The Macmillan Company of Canada Limited
Toronto.

x, 325, [1] pp.; 215 × 135 mm.

1688. ORMSBY, William

Crisis in the Canadas, 1838-1839: The Grey Journals And Letters. Edited by
William Ormsby. 1964 Macmillan of Canada Toronto.

[12], 244 pp.; 218 × 137 mm.
Issued in cloth and paper.
Pioneer Books Series.

1689. PENNER, Philip G.

Canadian Reflections: An Anthology Of Canadian Prose. Philip Penner And John McGechaen. Toronto: The Macmillan Company of Canada Limited.

xii, 329, [1] pp.; 190 × 125 mm.

1690. ROBINS, Patricia

Any time at all. By Patricia Robins. Illustrated by Lauretta Rix. 1964 Macmillan of Canada Toronto.

63, [1] pp.; 207 × 143 mm.

1691. ROSENTHAL, Joe

Old Markets, New World. Drawn by Joe Rosenthal. Described by Adele Wiseman. © Joe Rosenthal and Adele Wiseman 1964. Printed in Canada by The Bryant Press Limited 1964. The Macmillan Company of Canada Limited/Toronto.

64, [8] pp.; 302 × 230 mm.

1692. RULE, Jane

The Desert of the Heart. By Jane Rule. 1964 The Macmillan Company of Canada Limited Toronto.

254 pp.; 200 × 131 mm.

1693. SCOTT, Frank

Quebec States Her Case: Speeches and articles from Quebec in the years of unrest. Edited by Frank Scott and Michael Oliver. 1964/Macmillan of Canada/ Toronto.

[10], 165, [1] pp.; 215 × 135 mm.
Reprinted in paper in 1964, 1966 and 1968.

1694. SHUTE, Nevil

Pied Piper. Nevil Shute. Study Material Prepared by C.M. Irwin, Vice-Principal, Centennial Secondary School, Belleville, Ontario. Toronto: The Macmillan Company of Canada Limited.

vi, 250 pp.; 190 × 125 mm.
Reprinted in 1977 in paper.

1695. SIMONSON, H.P.

Health and Fitness for Canadian Youth. H.P. Simonson, B.Sc., B.Ed., Principal, Ottewell Junior High School, Edmonton, E.A. Hastie, B.A., Formerly Associate Professor, Faculty of Education, University of Alberta, [and] H.A. Doherty, M.Ed., Executive Assistant, Alberta Teachers' Association. Illustrated by G. Fantuz. The Macmillan Company of Canada Limited/Toronto.

[10], 201, [1] pp.; 235 × 165 mm.

1696. SIMONSON, H.P.

Health For Young Canadians. H.P. Simonson, B.Sc., B.Ed., Principal, Ottewell Junior High School, Edmonton, E.A. Hastie, B.A., Formerly Associate Professor, Faculty of Education, University of Alberta, [and] H.A. Doherty, M.Ed., Executive Assistant, Alberta Teachers' Association. The Macmillan Company of Canada Limited/Toronto. Illustrated by G. Fantuz.

[10], 164 pp.; 235 × 165 mm.

1697. SMYTH, W.M.

Poems Of Spirit And Action: Voice of Poetry. Revised Canadian Edition. This book is substantially based on *Poems of Spirit and Action* and *Further Poems of Spirit and Action* by permission of the editor W.M. Smyth and Edward Arnold (publishers). Toronto: The Macmillan Company of Canada Limited.

[8], 208 pp.; 175 × 120 mm.

1698. SMYTHE, James M.

Revised Edition, *Elements of Geography*. James M. Smythe, M.A., Head of the Geography Department, Earl Haig Secondary School, North York, Charles G. Brown, B.A., Principal, Earl Haig Secondary School, North York, [and] Eric H. Fors, B.A., Head of the Geography Department, Downsview Secondary School, North York. Maps and Diagrams by A. Diana. Macmillan of Canada/Toronto.

xiv, 466 pp.; 235 × 165 mm.
First published in 1959 (see 1474). Second revision published in 1970 (see 2079). A special revised edition was published in 1976 (see 2435). English and French metric editions appeared in 1978 and 1979 (see 2602 and 2655).

1699. VARLEY, Peter

Canada. Photographed By Peter Varley. Introduction By Kildare Dobbs. 176 Photogravure Plates. 8 Plates in Colour. Toronto: Macmillan of Canada.

57, [3] pp. + plates; 310 × 215 mm.
Revised in 1965 (see 1757). Second revised edition published in 1969 (see 2034).

1700. WATERSTON, Elizabeth

Composition for Canadian Universities. Elizabeth Waterston, University of Western Ontario, [and] Munro Beattie, Carleton University. With an appendix by R.G. Baldwin on grading freshman essays. 1964 The Macmillan Company of Canada Limited Toronto.

xii, 332 pp.; 207 × 138 mm.
Issued in paper.

1701. WEVILL, David

Birth of a Shark. Poems By David Wevill. Toronto: Macmillan of Canada 1964.

viii, 56 pp.; 220 × 140 mm.

1702. **WILKINSON, H.**

Basic Sheet Metal Work. H. Wilkinson, Formerly Instructor of Sheet Metal Work, Central Technical School, Toronto, Ontario. Illustrated by Wray Youmans. Toronto: The Macmillan Company of Canada Limited.

[10], 155, [1] pp.; 226 × 156 mm.
Macmillan Basic Technical Series.

1703. **WOOD, Edgar Allardyce**

Mickey The Beaver and other stories. By Kerry Wood [pseud.]. Illustrated by Audrey Teather. 1964 Macmillan of Canada Toronto.

vi, 74 pp.; 195 × 158 mm.

1704. **ZASLOW, Morris**

The Defended Border: Upper Canada And the War of 1812. A collection of writings giving a comprehensive picture of the War of 1812 in Upper Canada: the military struggle, the effects of the war on the people, and the legacies of war. Edited for the Ontario Historical Society by Morris Zaslow, Department of History, University of Toronto. Assisted by Wesley B. Turner. 1964 Toronto, The Macmillan Company of Canada Limited.

xiv, 370 pp.; 233 × 150 mm.
Issued in cloth and paper.

1965

1705. **ASHLEY, C.A.**

C.A. Ashley/R.G.H. Smails, *Canadian Crown Corporations: Some Aspects Of Their Administration And Control*. Toronto/1965. The Macmillan Company of Canada Limited.

x, 360 pp.; 214 × 134 mm.

1706. **BACON, Francis**

Francis Bacon: A Selection Of His Works. Edited by Sidney Warhaft, University of Manitoba. *Essayes, 1597. Essaies, Vol 2. The Essayes or Counsels, Civill and Morall, 1625. The Proficience and Advancement of Learning. The Wisdom of the Ancients. The Great Instauration. The New Organon. Of the Dignity and Advancement of Learning. New Atlantis Letters*. Macmillan of Canada - Toronto [and] Macmillan & Co. Ltd - London.

[12], 497, [1] pp.; 180 × 120 mm.
Issued in paper.
College Classics in English Series.

1707. **BICE, Clare**

Hurricane Treasure. Written and Illustrated by Clare Bice. Macmillan of Canada Toronto.

190 pp.; 208 × 140 mm.
Reprinted in 1976.

1708.   BOYCE, Eleanor

The New World Readers. Lorne Pierce, Editor-in-Chief. Frederick Minkler, General Editor. *The Workbook for My World and I*. Miriam Norton/Eleanor Boyce. Illustrated by W. Taylor. Copyright Canada, 1946 and 1960, by The Ryerson Press and The Macmillan Company of Canada Limited 1965.

112 pp.; 273 × 210 mm.
First published in 1947 (see 1147). Revised edition published in 1960. Earlier printing not located. Issued in paper.
New World Readers Series.

1709.   BREWIS, T.N.

Revised Edition, *Canadian Economic Policy*. T. N. Brewis, M.Com., Ph.D., Department of Economics, Carleton University, H.E. English, B.A., Ph.D., Secretary, Private Planning Association of Canada (on leave from Department of Economics, Carleton University), Anthony Scott, B.Com., B.A., A.M., Ph.D., Department of Economics and Political Science, University of British Columbia, [and] Pauline Jewett, M.A., Ph.D., M.P., Department of Political Science, Carleton University. With a Statistical Appendix by J. E. Gander, M.A., Director of Research, Tariff Board. The Macmillan Company of Canada Limited Toronto.

xvi, 463, [1] pp.; 235 × 150 mm.
First published in 1961 (see 1518).

1710.   COULTER, John

Deirdre. An ancient and noble tale retold by John Coulter for music by Healey Willan, being the revised version of their *Deirdre of the Sorrows*. Revised for presentation by the Opera School, Royal Conservatory of Music, University of Toronto, April, 1965. © John Coulter 1965. The Macmillan Company of Canada Limited takes pleasure in contributing this souvenir printing of the libretto on the occasion of the stage production of this Canadian opera.

32 pp.; 214 × 140 mm.
First published in 1944 under the title *Deirdre of the Sorrows* (see 996). Revised edition reprinted in 1966. Issued in paper.

1710A CREIGHTON, Donald

The Story Of Canada. By Donald Creighton. 1965 The Macmillan Company of Canada Limited Toronto.

291, [1] pp.; 223 × 138 mm.
First published in 1959. Reprinted in 1965. Earlier printing not located. Revised edition published in 1971 (see 2090).

1711.   CREIGHTON, Luella Bruce

Great Stories Of Canada, *Tecumseh: The Story Of The Shawnee Chief*. By Luella Bruce Creighton. Illustrated by William Lytle. Toronto: 1965: Macmillan.

159, [1] pp.; 213 × 138 mm.
Great Stories of Canada Series.

1712. DALY, Ronald C.

The Macmillan School Atlas. Ronald C. Daly, B.A., M.Ed., Vice-Principal, Dundas Public School, Junior, Toronto, Formerly Social Studies Consultant, Toronto Board of Education. Maps and illustrations by John R. Waller. The Macmillan Company of Canada Limited Toronto.

114 pp.; 274 × 215 mm.
Metric edition published in 1976 (see 2379).

1713. DEUTSCH, John J.

Revised Edition, *The Canadian Economy: Selected Readings*. John J. Deutsch, Chairman, Economic Council of Canada, Burton S. Keirstead, Professor of Economics, University of Toronto, Kari Levitt, Assistant Professor of Economics, McGill University, [and] Robert M. Will, Associate Professor of Economics, The University of British Columbia. Toronto: The Macmillan Company of Canada Limited.

xiv, 518 pp.; 227 × 142 mm.
First published in 1961 (see 1523). Issued in cloth and paper.

1714. DICKENS, Charles

Great Expectations. By Charles Dickens. Edited by R. D. McMaster, University of Alberta. Macmillan of Canada Toronto.

xxviii, 484 pp.; 183 × 124 mm.
Reprinted in 1965, 1966, 1968 and 1975.
College Classics in English Series.

1715. DICKENS, Charles

Great Expectations. Charles Dickens. Study Material Prepared By Ernest H. Winter, M.A., Head of the English Department, Eastdale Collegiate and Vocational Institute, Oshawa, Ontario. Illustrated By B. Stanley-Jones. Toronto: The Macmillan Company of Canada Limited.

[8], 518 pp.; 188 × 125 mm.

1716. DIEBEL, P.W.

A Parade of Poems. Selected and annotated by P.W. Diebel [and] R. McBurney. Illustrated by Karl Rix. Toronto: Macmillan of Canada.

xii, 283, [1] pp.; 185 × 125 mm.

1717. DOCTER, Grace M.

Outward Bound. Edited by Grace M. Docter, B.A., Formerly Head of Guidance Department, Central High School of Commerce, Toronto. *Passport To Reading*: A multi-level reading series. General editor: Harold M. Covell, B.ED., M.A., ED.D., Professor of Reading Education, Faculty of Education, University of British Columbia. Associate editors: V. Laurence Davidson, B.A., B.ED., Caledonia Junior High School, Dartmouth, Nova Scotia, L. Ruth Godwin, M.ED., ED.D., Language Arts Consultant, North York Board of Education, James W. Greig, B.A., ED.D., The Faculty of Education, University of Toronto, Josephine V. Harris, B.A., B. ED., Supervisor of Curriculum, Schools Administration Office, Dartmouth,

Nova Scotia, Dorothy Rizer, B.A., M.ED., Faculty of Education, University of British Columbia, [and] Tory I. Westermark, B.ED., M.ED., D.ED., Faculty of Education, University of British Columbia. The Macmillan Company of Canada Limited Toronto.

[12], 304 pp.; 234 × 155 mm.
Passport To Reading Series.

1718. DODDS, Donald G.

Wild Captives. By Donald G. Dodds. Illustrated by Ronald Andrews. Macmillan of Canada Toronto.

[12], 110 pp.; 217 × 139 mm.
Reprinted in 1967.

1719. DUDEK, Louis

Poetry Of Our Time: An Introduction To Twentieth-Century Poetry Including Modern Canadian Poetry. Edited by Louis Dudek. Toronto: The Macmillan Company of Canada Limited.

xxiv, 376 pp.; 208 × 130 mm.
Reprinted in 1966, 1971, 1972, 1974 and 1977. Issued in cloth and paper.

1720. GODDEN, Rumer

Breakfast With the Nikolides. Rumer Godden. London Toronto Macmillan 1965.

[10], 291, [1] pp.; 202 × 134 mm.

1721. GODDEN, Rumer

Gypsy Gypsy. By Rumer Godden. Macmillan London Melbourne Toronto 1965.

[6], 289, [1] pp.; 202 × 134 mm.

1722. GODDEN, Rumer

Kingfishers Catch Fire. By Rumer Godden. Macmillan London Melbourne Toronto 1965.

[6], 293, [1] pp.; 190 × 125 mm.

1723. GODFREY, Denis

A Novel By Denis Godfrey, *No Englishman Need Apply*. Macmillan of Canada/Toronto.

[8], 272 pp.; 220 × 140 mm.

1724. GOODSPEED, D.J.

D.J. Goodspeed, *Bayonets at St. Cloud: The Story of The 18th Brumaire*. The Macmillan Company of Canada Limited Toronto 1965.

192 pp.; 220 × 140 mm.

1725. GOODSPEED, D.J.

Substitute General. A Peter Maclean Story. John Redmayne [pseud.]. Illustrated by John Lawrence. 1965 Macmillan of Canada Toronto.

[4], 158 pp.; 200 × 130 mm.
John Redmayne is a pseudonym for D.J. Goodspeed and Herbert F. Wood.

1726. GRAVEL, Jean-Paul
Jean-Paul Gravel, Head of the Science Department, Two Mountains Regional High School, Two Mountains, Quebec, *Objective Review Questions for Basic Physics for Secondary Schools*. The Macmillan Company of Canada Limited.
[4], 96 pp.; 275 × 215 mm.
Issued in paper.

1727. GRISWOLD, A. Whitney
The Fine Arts and the University. A. Whitney Griswold, John P. Coolidge, F. Curtis Canfield, Vincent J. Scully [and] Edward F. Sekler. The Macmillan Company of Canada Limited, Toronto [and] St. Martin's Press, New York, In Association with York University.
xii, 89, [1] pp.; 220 × 140 mm.

1728. HARLOW, Robert
Robert Harlow, *A Gift of Echoes*. Toronto: Macmillan of Canada.
[8], 248 pp.; 223 × 140 mm.

1729. HÉMON, Louis
Maria Chapdelaine. By Louis Hémon. Translated by W. H. Blake. Illustrated by Thoreau MacDonald. 1965 Macmillan of Canada Toronto.
xiv, 161, [1] pp.; 220 × 142 mm.
First published in 1921 (see 167). Reissued in 1938 (see 800). This edition issued simultaneously in a school edition with study material by N.F. McTeague. Reprinted in the Laurentian Library (No. 17) in 1973.

1730. HILTON, James
Lost Horizon. James Hilton. Study Material Prepared By Linton D. Read, Vice-Principal, Moira Secondary School, Belleville, Ontario. Toronto: The Macmillan Company of Canada Limited.
[6], 186 pp.; 188 × 125 mm.
First published in 1943 (see 972).

1731. HILTZ, Mary C.
Nutrition: An Introductory Text. By Mary Catherine Hiltz, B.S.(Columbia), M.A.(Toronto), Formerly Associate Professor of Foods and Nutrition, School of Home Economics, University of Manitoba. Toronto: The Macmillan Company of Canada Limited.
xiv, 169, [1] pp.; 217 × 136 mm.
First published in 1955 (see 1342). This edition revised.

1732. HOOLE, Arthur H.
The Fundamentals Of Clear Writing. Arthur H. Hoole, St. John's College, University of Manitoba. Toronto: The Macmillan Company of Canada Limited.

[8], 184 pp.; 200 × 130 mm.
Reprinted in 1965. Reissued with exercises in 1967 (see 1851). Issued in paper.

1733. HUMBLE, A.H.
Thought and Style: An Introduction to Literary Criticism for Senior Students. By
A. H. Humble, M.A.(Oxon.) And T.W. Lawson, M.A.(Cantab.), Trinity
College School, Port Hope. Macmillan of Canada Toronto.
[10], 92 pp.; 181 × 120 mm.
Issued in paper.

1734. ISRAEL, Charles E.
Shadows on a Wall. A novel by Charles E. Israel. Macmillan of Canada
Toronto.
350 pp.; 215 × 141 mm.

1735. JACKSON, Agatha
Steps to Better English. Agatha Jackson. The Macmillan Company of Canada
Limited Toronto.
[10], 182 pp.; 188 × 125 mm.

1736. KROETSCH, Robert
But We Are Exiles. [Quotation]. A Novel By Robert Kroetsch. Macmillan of
Canada Toronto.
[8], 145, [1] pp.; 210 × 138 mm.
Reprinted in the Laurentian Library (No. 45) in 1977.

1737. LABARGE, Margaret Wade
A Baronial Household of the Thirteenth Century. Margaret Wade Labarge.
1965 Toronto The Macmillan Company of Canada Limited.
235, [1] pp.; 202 × 128 mm.

1738. LALANDE, Lionel
Invitation à lire: An Anthology of French Prose and Verse. Selected and edited
with exercises, vocabularies, and biographical notes by Lionel Lalande & Eva
Lalande. Illustrated by Leo Rampen. The Macmillan Company of Canada
Limited Toronto.
[10], 245, [1] pp.; 188 × 123 mm.

1739. MASSEY, Norman Bland
Patterns For The Teaching Of Science. By Norman Bland Massey, Formerly
Science Master, London Teachers' College, London, Ontario. The Macmil-
lan Company of Canada Limited Toronto.
[8], 253, [1] pp.; 220 × 140 mm.
Revised in 1969 (see 2004).

1740. MASSEY, Vincent
*Confederation on the March: Views On Major Canadian Issues During The
Sixties*. The Right Honourable Vincent Massey, C.H. Macmillan of Canada
Toronto 1965.
[8], 101, [1] pp.; 245 × 164 mm.

1741. McCOURT, Edward

The Road Across Canada. Edward McCourt. Illustrated by John A. Hall.
1965 Macmillan of Canada Toronto.

[8], 199, [1] pp.; 218 × 140 mm.

1742. McGRATH, W.T.

Crime and Its Treatment in Canada. Edited by W.T. McGrath. 1965 Macmillan of Canada Toronto [and] St. Martin's Press New York.

[16], 510 pp.; 230 × 150 mm.
Reprinted in 1970 in paper. Second edition published in 1976 (see 2416).

1743. PARR, Michael

The Green Fig Tree. Michael Parr. 1965 Macmillan of Canada Toronto.

[12], 83, [1] pp.; 217 × 140 mm.

1744. PEARCE, Donald

Donald Pearce, *Journal Of A War: North-West Europe 1944-1945.* 1965 Macmillan of Canada Toronto.

[10], 188 pp.; 215 × 140 mm.

1745. REANEY, James

The Boy With An R In His Hand: A tale of the type riot at William Lyon Mackenzie's printing office in 1826. By James Reaney. Illustrated by Leo Rampen. 1965 Macmillan of Canada Toronto.

x, 101, [1] pp.; 214 × 135 mm.

1746. SCHULL, Joseph

Laurier: The First Canadian. By Joseph Schull. 1965 Macmillan of Canada Toronto.

[14], 658 pp.; 225 × 150 mm.

1747. SHERMAN, Paddy

Cloud Walkers: Six Climbs on Major Canadian Peaks. Paddy Sherman. Maps by John A. Hall. 1965 Macmillan of Canada Toronto.

[10], 161, [1] pp.; 225 × 155 mm.

1748. SHOULTZ, Kenneth G.

Basic Electricity: Theory and Practice. Kenneth G. Shoultz, Principal, Ontario Vocational Centre, Ottawa, Ontario, Former Technical Director and Supervisor of Evening Classes, Lakeport Secondary School, St. Catharines, Ontario. Illustrated by A. Diana. The Macmillan Company of Canada Limited, St. Martin's Press, New York.

[10], 214 pp.; 226 × 155 mm.
Macmillan Basic Technical Series.

1749.   SIMCOE, Elizabeth

Edited by Mary Quayle Innis, *Mrs. Simcoe's Diary*. With illustrations from the original manuscript. 1965 Macmillan of Canada Toronto [and] St. Martin's Press New York.

[8], 223, [1] pp.; 219 × 140 mm.
Reprinted in the Laurentian Library (No. 65) in 1971.

1750.   SMITH, J. Percy

The Unrepentant Pilgrim: A Study of the Development of Bernard Shaw. J. Percy Smith. Macmillan of Canada Toronto 1965.

xiv, 274 pp.; 210 × 140 mm.

1751.   STEVENSON, Robert Louis

The Black Arrow. Robert Louis Stevenson. Study Material Prepared By James Henderson, M.A., Head of the English Department, Oakville-Trafalgar High School, Oakville, Ontario. Toronto: The Macmillan Company of Canada Limited.

x, 308 pp.; 185 × 125 mm.

1752.   SWAYZE, J. Fred

The Rowboat War On The Great Lakes, 1812-1814. Fred Swayze. Illustrated by Paul Liberovsky. Macmillan of Canada Toronto.

[8], 120 pp.; 210 × 135 mm.
Issued in cloth and paper.
Great Stories of Canada Series.

1753.   SWIFT, Jonathan

Jonathan Swift: A Selection Of His Works. Edited by Philip Pinkus, University of British Columbia. *Gulliver's Travels*. *The Tale of a Tub*. *The Battle of the Books*. *A Modest Proposal*. Poems. Macmillan of Canada - Toronto, Macmillan & Co. Ltd. - London, St. Martin's Press - New York.

xxx, 517, [1] pp.; 187 × 123 mm.
Issued in paper. Reprinted in 1965, 1966, 1967, 1969 and 1972.
College Classics in English Series.

1754.   TAYLOR, Norman Burke

Basic Physiology and Anatomy. Norman Burke Taylor, M.D. in collaboration with Margaret McPhedran, R.N., M.A. The Macmillan Company of Canada Limited Toronto.

xviii, 648 pp.; 240 × 165 mm.

1755.   TREASE, Geoffrey

Word To Caesar. Geoffrey Trease. Study material prepared by R.L. Hale, Head of the English Department, Peterborough Collegiate and Vocational School. Macmillan of Canada Toronto.

[6], 270 pp.; 195 × 128 mm.
Reprinted in paper in 1972.

1756. URQUHART, M.C.

Historical Statistics Of Canada. M.C. Urquhart, Editor. K.A.H. Buckley, Assistant Editor. Sponsored by Canadian Political Science Association and Social Science Research Council of Canada. Cambridge: At the University Press [and] Toronto: Macmillan Company of Canada Ltd 1965.

xvi, 672 pp.; 293 × 230 mm.

1757. VARLEY, Peter

Canada. Photographed By Peter Varley. Introduction By Kildare Dobbs. 176 Photogravure Plates. 9 Plates in Colour. Toronto: Macmillan of Canada.

57, [3] pp. + plates; 310 × 215 mm.

First published in 1964 (see 1699). Second revised edition published in 1969 (see 2034).

1758. VOADEN, Herman

Drama IV. Edited by Herman Voaden, M.A., C.D.A., F.R.S.A., Formerly Director of English, Central High School of Commerce, Toronto. Toronto: The Macmillan Company of Canada Limited.

xiv, 401, [1] pp.; 190 × 125 mm.

1759. WAIN, John

The Contenders: A Novel. By John Wain. Macmillan London Melbourne Toronto [and] St. Martin's Press New York 1965.

[6], 278, [2] pp.; 202 × 133 mm.

1760. WAIN, John

Wildtrack. A Poem by John Wain. Macmillan London Melbourne Toronto 1965.

[8], 50, [2] pp.; 221 × 143 mm.

1761. WAIN, John

The Young Visitors. By John Wain. Macmillan London Melbourne Toronto 1965.

[6], 206 pp.; 202 × 133 mm.

1966

1762. ALLAN, R.N.

Soucoupes Volantes!! By R.N. Allan, B.A.(Lond.), Senior Lecturer in French, County of Stafford Training College. Illustrations by Jennetta Vise. Toronto: Macmillan of Canada.

63, [1] pp.; 200 × 130 mm.

Issued in paper.

1763. BOYLE, Joyce

Once Upon a Time. Edited by Joyce Boyle, D.Paed. Macmillan of Canada Toronto.

175, [1] pp.; 233 × 150 mm.
Magic of Reading Series.

1764. CHAUCER, Geoffrey

Geoffrey Chaucer: A Selection of His Works. Edited by Kenneth Kee, Victoria College, University of Toronto. Macmillan of Canada - Toronto, Macmillan & Co Ltd. - London, St. Martin's Press - New York.

xlvi, 232 pp.; 180 × 120 mm.
Issued in paper. Reprinted frequently.
College Classics in English Series.

1765. CLARK, Catherine Anthony

The Hunter And The Medicine Man. By Catherine Anthony Clark. Illustrated by Clare Bice. Toronto: The Macmillan Company of Canada.

[8], 183, [1] pp.; 210 × 139 mm.
Issued in paper.

1766. COGNAC, Marcel

The Many Faces of Quebec. Photographs by Marcel Cognac. Text by Jean-Charles Harvey. Translated by Alta Lind Cook. [Macmillan of Canada/Toronto [and] St. Martin's Press/New York. Originally published in 1964 by le Cercle du Livre de France].

202, [6] pp.; 255 × 220 mm.
Imprint on p. 9.

1767. COOK, Lyn

Lyn Cook, *The Secret of Willow Castle*. Illustrations by Kelly Clark. Macmillan of Canada Toronto.

[12], 234 pp.; 218 × 138 mm.

1768. COOK, Ramsay

Canada and the French-Canadian Question. Ramsay Cook. 1966/Macmillan of Canada/Toronto.

[12], 219, [1] pp.; 213 × 135 mm.
Issued in cloth and paper. Reprinted frequently.

1769. COOPER, William Mansfield

Governments and the University. William Mansfield Cooper, William G. Davis, Alphonse-Marie Parent [and] Thomas R. McConnell. The Macmillan Company of Canada Limited Toronto [and] St. Martin's Press New York in Association with York University 1966.

x, 92 pp.; 220 × 140 mm.
Frank Gerstein Lectures: York University Invitation Series.

1770. CORNELL, Louis L.

Kipling in India. Louis L. Cornell. Macmillan London Melbourne Toronto, St. Martin's Press New York 1966.

xiv, 224 pp.; 222 × 140 mm.

1771. COVELL, Harold M.

[At bottom of page 1:] The Canada Books of Prose and Verse, *Reading Study Book for Our Heritage*. Harold M. Covell [and] John McGechaen. Illustrated by William Wheeler and Robert Kunz. © The Ryerson Press and The Macmillan Company of Canada Limited, 1966 [etc.].

127, [1] pp.; 275 × 210 mm.
Issued in paper.
Canada Books of Prose and Verse Series.

1772. CRAWFORD, Douglas H.

Discovering Mathematics 3. Authors: Douglas H. Crawford, Ph.D., Associate Professor of Mathematics, Queen's University, Kingston [and] Gertrude Bain, B.A., Primary Consultant, Kingston Board of Education. J.M. Dent & Sons (Canada) Limited [and] The Macmillan Company of Canada Limited.

xiv, 305, [1] pp.; 230 × 163 mm.
Discovering Mathematics Series.

1773. DALE, Celia

A Helping Hand. Celia Dale. London Macmillan Melbourne Toronto 1966.
[4], 186, [2] pp.; 218 × 131 mm.

1774. DOW, Marguerite R.

The Magic Mask: A Basic Textbook of Theatre Arts. Marguerite R. Dow, Associate Professor of English, Althouse College of Education, University of Western Ontario. The Macmillan Company of Canada Limited Toronto.
xvi, 367, [1] pp.; 232 × 153 mm.

1775. FINCH, Robert.

Silverthorn Bush and Other Poems. By Robert Finch. 1966 Macmillan of Canada Toronto.

[12], 86 pp.; 220 × 140 mm.

1776. GODDEN, Jon

Jon & Rumer Godden, *Two Under the Indian Sun*. Macmillan London Melbourne Toronto 1966.

199, [1] pp.; 222 × 141 mm.

1777. GODDEN, Rumer

The Dolls' House. By Rumer Godden. Illustrated by Tasha Tudor. Macmillan: London Melbourne Toronto.

135, [1] pp.; 200 × 135 mm.
First published in 1963. Reprinted in 1966. Earlier printing not located.

1778.   GODDEN, Rumer

An Episode of Sparrows. By Rumer Godden. [Quotation]. Toronto: The Macmillan Company of Canada Limited.

[6], 281, [1] pp.; 179 × 122 mm.
Issued in paper. Reissued in 1967 with notes and questions by Dorothy L. Bishop.

1779.   GODWIN, L. Ruth

Full Flight. Edited by L. Ruth Godwin, M.ED., ED.D., Associate Professor, Faculty of Education, University of Saskatchewan, Regina Campus. *Passport To Reading*: A multi-level reading series. General editor: Harold M. Covell, B. ED., M.A., ED.D., Professor of Reading Education, Faculty of Education, University of British Columbia. Associate editors: Grace M. Docter, B.A., English and Guidance, Central High School of Commerce, Toronto, James W. Greig, B.A., ED.D., Principal, St. Andrew's Junior High School, North York, Dorothy Rizer, B.A., M.ED., Faculty of Education, University of British Columbia [and] Tory I. Westermark, B.ED., M.ED., D.ED., Faculty of Education, University of British Columbia. The Macmillan Company of Canada Limited Toronto.

[12], 336 pp.; 234 × 155 mm.
Passport To Reading Series.

1780.   GOODSPEED, D.J.

D.J. Goodspeed, *Ludendorff: Genius Of World War I*. Illustrated With Photographs And Maps. Macmillan of Canada Toronto 1966.

xiv, 335, [1] pp.; 215 × 145 mm.

1781.   GRAY, James H.

The Winter Years: The Depression on the Prairies. By James H. Gray. 1966/Macmillan of Canada/Toronto.

[12], 220, [2] pp.; 232 × 154 mm.
Issued in cloth and paper. Reprinted in 1966, 1967, 1968, 1972 and 1973. Reprinted in the Laurentian Library (No. 38) in 1976.

1781A   GREASON, George K.

Revised Edition, *Canadian Democracy at Work*. George K. Greason, Althouse College of Education, London [and] Roy C. King, Principal, C.B. Parsons Junior High School, North York. Drawings by Dorothy Mould and Vernon Mould. Toronto: The Macmillan Company Of Canada Limited.

[8], 116 pp.; 223 × 145 mm.
First published in 1962 (see 1574). Revised again in 1969 (see 1984), 1971 (see 2099) and 1977 (see 2476A). Issued in paper.

1782.   HOBSBAUM, Philip

In Retreat and Other Poems. Philip Hobsbaum. [Quotation]. Macmillan London Melbourne Toronto [and] St. Martin's Press New York 1966.

x, 51, [1] pp.; 209 × 133 mm.

1783. ISRAEL, Charles E.
The Hostages. By Charles E. Israel. Macmillan of Canada Toronto.
319, [1] pp.; 210 × 142 mm.

1784. JENNINGS, Elizabeth
The Mind Has Mountains. Elizabeth Jennings. [Quotation]. London Macmillan Melbourne Toronto 1966.
[8], 39, [1] pp.; 219 × 133 mm.

1785. JENNINGS, Elizabeth
The Secret Brother and Other Poems for Children. Elizabeth Jennings. Illustrated by Meg Stevens. Macmillan London Melbourne Toronto [and] St. Martin's Press New York 1966.
[8], 40 pp.; 220 × 140 mm.

1786. JEWETT, Eleanore M.
Eleanore M. Jewett, The Hidden Treasure of Glaston. Study material prepared by C.M. Irwin, Head of the English Department, Moira Secondary School, Belleville, Ontario. Illustrated by Frederick T. Chapman. Macmillan of Canada Toronto.
[8], 338 pp.; 195 × 130 mm.

1787. KROETSCH, Robert
The Words of My Roaring. By Robert Kroetsch. Macmillan of Canada Toronto.
[10], 211, [1] pp.; 212 × 143 mm.

1788. LINKLATER, Eric
A Terrible Freedom. Eric Linklater. London Macmillan Melbourne Toronto 1966.
[8], 225, [3] pp.; 209 × 132 mm.

1789. LIVESLEY, Jack
Three Worlds of Drama. Edited by Jack Livesley, B.A., Vice-Principal, Lisgar Collegiate Institute, Ottawa. Toronto: The Macmillan Company of Canada Limited.
[4], 268 pp.; 185 × 120 mm.
Reprinted in paper in 1970.

1790. MacDONALD, J.W.
Edited by J.W. MacDonald, Ontario College of Education [and] J.C.W. Saxton, Ridley College. Illustrated by William Lytle. Four Stages. Toronto: The Macmillan Company of Canada Limited.
[10], 398 pp.; 188 × 122 mm.

1791. MACDONALD, Norman

Canada: Immigration and Colonization 1841-1903. Norman Macdonald, Emeritus Professor, McMaster University. 1966 Macmillan of Canada Toronto.

    xii, 381, [1] pp.; 220 × 140 mm.
    Reprinted in 1968 (cloth) and 1970 (paper).

1792. MACDONALD, Zillah

Prisoner in Louisbourg. Zillah and Colin Macdonald. Macmillan of Canada Toronto.

    [8], 231, [1] pp.; 210 × 140 mm.
    Issued in cloth and paper.

1793. MACMILLAN, Harold

Winds of Change 1914-1939. Harold Macmillan. London Macmillan Melbourne Toronto 1966.

    viii, 664 pp.; 220 × 150 mm.

1794. MARTEL, Suzanne

Surréal 3000. Suzanne Martel. Edited with exercises and vocabulary by H.C. Steels, Etobicoke Collegiate Institute, Islington, Ontario. Illustrated by Lee Clifton. Macmillan of Canada Toronto.

    [6], 201, [1] pp.; 188 × 125 mm.

1795. MILL, John Stuart

John Stuart Mill: A Selection of His Works. Edited by John M. Robson, Victoria College, University of Toronto. Macmillan of Canada - Toronto, Macmillan & Co Ltd - London [and] St. Martin's Press - New York.

    xxxiv, 471 pp.; 183 × 120 mm.
    Issued in paper.
    College Classics in English Series.

1796. MITCHELL, John

A story of the Irish on the Canadian countryside, *The Yellow Briar*. By Patrick Slater [pseud.], with notes and exercises by Dorothy L. Bishop, B.J., M.A., English Department, Lisgar Collegiate Institute, Ottawa, Ontario. Toronto: The Macmillan Company of Canada Limited.

    173, [1] pp.; 188 × 125 mm.
    First published in 1941 (see 919). New edition published in 1970 (see 2071).

1797. MOORE, Evelyn

Teaching the Subjects in the Social Studies: A Handbook for Teachers. Evelyn Moore, Faculty of Education, University of Alberta [and] Edward E. Owen, Faculty of Education, University of Victoria. The Macmillan Company of Canada Limited Toronto.

    [12], 276 pp.; 230 × 145 mm.

1798. MULHOLLAND, Brendan

Almost a Holiday. Brendan Mulholland. Illustrated by Trog. Macmillan London Melbourne Toronto 1966.

viii, 151, [1] pp.; 209 × 133 mm.

1799. NEEDHAM, Richard J.

Needham's Inferno. By Richard J. Needham. Illustrated by Duncan Macpherson. Macmillan of Canada Toronto.

xii, 197, [1] pp.; 218 × 135 mm.
Reprinted in paper in 1967.

1800. NYE, Russell B.

This Almost Chosen People: Essays in the History of American Ideas. By Russell B. Nye. The Macmillan Company of Canada Limited Toronto.

x, 374 pp.; 210 × 140 mm.

1801. OUTRAM, Richard

Exsultate, Jubilate. Richard Outram/1966/The Macmillan Company of Canada Limited Toronto.

89, [1] pp.; 250 × 155 mm.

1802. PATTERSON, Raymond M.

Trail To The Interior. By R.M. Patterson, Macmillan of Canada Toronto, 1966.

xiv, 255, [1] pp.; 215 × 143 mm.
Reprinted in the Laurentian Library (No. 27) in 1974.

1803. POWER, Chubby

A Party Politician: The Memoirs of Chubby Power. Edited by Norman Ward. 1966 Macmillan of Canada Toronto.

[10], 419, [1] pp.; 232 × 145 mm.

1804. PRATT, E.J.

Brébeuf and his Brethren. By E. J. Pratt. Macmillan of Canada.

80 pp.; 175 × 105 mm.
First published in 1940 (see 883). Revised edition with new epilogue published in 1940 (see 884). Issued in paper.

1805. RIZER, Dorothy

Into Orbit. Edited by Dorothy Rizer, B.A., M.ED., Faculty of Education, University of British Columbia and Tory I. Westermark, B.ED., M.ED., D.ED., Faculty of Education, University of Victoria. *Passport To Reading: A multi-level reading series*. General editor: Harold M. Covell, B.ED., M.A., ED.D., Professor of Reading Education and Assistant Director of Elementary Education, Faculty of Education, University of British Columbia. Associate Editors: V. Lawrence Davidson, B.A., Caledonia Junior High School, Dartmouth, Nova Scotia, Grace M. Docter, B.A., Head of Guidance Department, Central High School of Commerce, Toronto, L.

Ruth Godwin, M.ED., ED.D., Associate Professor, Faculty of Education, University of Saskatchewan, Regina Campus, James W. Greig, B.A., ED.D., Associate Professor of Education, Ontario College of Education, Toronto [and] Josephine V. Harris, Director of Special Programmes, Schools Administration Office, Dartmouth, Nova Scotia. The Macmillan Company of Canada Limited Toronto.

[8], 339, [1] pp.; 234 × 155 mm.
Passport To Reading Series.

1806. ROLLAND, Solange Chaput

My Country, Canada or Quebec? Solange Chaput Rolland. [Quotation]. 1966 Macmillan of Canada Toronto.

xiv, 122 pp.; 215 × 130 mm.
Issued in cloth and paper.

1807. ROSS, Murray G.

New Universities in the Modern World. Murray G. Ross, Editor. Macmillan: London Melbourne Toronto. St. Martin's Press: New York.

x, 190 pp.; 220 × 140 mm.

1808. RYGA, George

George Ryga, *Ballad of a Stone-Picker.* Macmillan of Canada, Toronto.

159, [1] pp.; 200 × 135 mm.

1809. SEARY, E.R.

Reading English: A Handbook For Students. By E. R. Seary and G. M. Story. Revised Edition. The Macmillan Company of Canada Limited Toronto.

x, 123, [1] pp.; 195 × 125 mm.
First published in 1958 (see 1450). Revised edition issued in paper.

1810. SHAKESPEARE, William

Julius Caesar. William Shakespeare. Edited by Herman Voaden, M.A., C.D.A., Formerly Director of English, Central High School of Commerce, Toronto. © The Macmillan Company of Canada Limited 1966. Mimeographing or reproducing mechanically in any other way passages from this book without the written permission of the publisher is an infringement of the copyright law. Toronto: The Macmillan Company of Canada Limited.

160 pp.; 180 × 123 mm.
Issued in paper.

1811. SHERK, Paul W.

Senior General Mathematics. Consultant: John I. McKnight, Scarborough Board of Education. Illustrator: D. E. Scovell, David and Mary Thomson Collegiate Institute, Scarborough. [On opposite page: General Editor: Paul W Sherk, Cedarbrae Collegiate Institute, Scarborough. Authors: James W. Fencott [etc.]]. The Macmillan Company of Canada Limited/Toronto.

[8], 312 pp.; 215 × 135 mm.

1812. SIMONSON, H.P.

Your Health and You. H. P. Simonson, B.Sc., B.Ed., Principal, McKernan Junior High School, Edmonton, E.A. Hastie, B.A., Formerly Associate Professor, Faculty of Education, University of Alberta [and] H.A. Doherty, M.Ed., Executive Assistant, Alberta Teachers' Association. Illustrated by G. Fantuz. The Macmillan Company of Canada Limited/Toronto.

[14], 153, [1] pp.; 235 × 165 mm.

1813. THOMPSON, Frances C.

Escape From Grand Pré. By Frances C. Thompson. Illustrated by David Craig. Macmillan of Canada, Toronto.

[8], 118 pp.; 190 × 125 mm.
Issued in cloth and paper.
Buckskin Books Series.

1814. VINCENT, Rodolphe

Quebec: Historic City. Text and Illustrations by Rodolphe Vincent. 1966 Macmillan of Canada Toronto.

28 pp.; 237 × 210 mm.

1815. VOADEN, Herman

Human Values In Drama. Edited by Herman Voaden, M.A., C.D.A., Formerly Director of English, Central High School of Commerce, Toronto. Toronto: The Macmillan Company of Canada Limited.

xvi, 364 pp.; 188 × 125 mm.

1816. VOADEN, Herman

Nobody Waved Goodbye and Other Plays. A Revision of *On Stage*. Edited by Herman Voaden, M.A., C.D.A., Formerly Director of English, Central High School of Commerce, Toronto. The Macmillan Company of Canada Limited Toronto.

xxvi, 453, [1] pp.; 190 × 125 mm.
The title play was published separately in 1971 (see 2120).

1817. WAIN, John

Death of the Hind Legs & other stories. John Wain. Macmillan London Melbourne Toronto 1966.

[6], 185, [1] pp.; 209 × 132 mm.

1818. WAIN, John

A Travelling Woman: A Novel. By John Wain. Macmillan London Melbourne Toronto [and] St. Martin's Press New York 1966.

[8], 207, [1] pp.; 190 × 127 mm.

1819. WARHAFT, Sidney

English Poems, 1250-1800. Sidney Warhaft, John Woodbury [and] Patrick O'Flaherty. Macmillan of Canada Toronto. Macmillan & Co Ltd London. St. Martin's Press - New York.

xviii, 372 pp.; 177 × 115 mm.
Issued in paper.

1820. WEST, Rebecca
The Birds Fall Down. Rebecca West. [Quotation]. London Macmillan Melbourne Toronto 1966.
[8], 428 pp.; 220 × 140 mm.

1821. WEVILL, David
A Christ of The Ice-Floes. David Wevill. Macmillan London Melbourne Toronto [and] St. Martin's Press New York 1966.
viii, 77, [1] pp.; 205 × 130 mm.

1822. WINTER, Ernest H.
Our Century in Prose. Selected and Edited by Ernest H. Winter, M.A., Head of the English Department, Eastdale Collegiate and Vocational Institute, Oshawa, Ontario. The Macmillan Company of Canada Limited Toronto.
xxii, 511, [1] pp.; 207 × 125 mm.

1967

1823. ANDERSEN, Doris
Blood Brothers. Doris Andersen. Illustrated by David Craig. 1967 Macmillan of Canada Toronto.
[6], 136 pp.; 215 × 137 mm.

1824. ARCHIBALD, Harvey N.
Discovering Mathematics 7. Authors: Harvey N. Archibald, B.A., Master of Methods, Toronto Teachers' College, Toronto, Douglas H. Crawford, Ph.D., Associate Professor of Mathematics, Queen's University, Kingston, James F. Tennant, B.A., Principal, Douglas McArthur Public School, Kingston [and] Norman T. Leek, B.A., B. Paed., Inspector of Public Schools, Hamilton Board of Education, Hamilton. J.M. Dent & Sons (Canada) Limited [and] The Macmillan Company of Canada Limited.
xvi, 386 pp.; 230 × 163 mm.
Discovering Mathematics Series.

1825. ARCHIBALD, Harvey N.
Discovering Mathematics 8. Authors: Harvey N. Archibald, B.A., Master of Methods, Toronto Teachers' College, Toronto, Douglas H. Crawford, Ph.D., Associate Professor of Mathematics, Queen's University, Kingston [and] James F. Tennant, B.A., Principal, Duncan McArthur Public School, Kingston. J.M. Dent & Sons (Canada) Limited [and] The Macmillan Company of Canada Limited.
xiv, 377, [1] pp.; 230 × 163 mm.
Discovering Mathematics Series.

1826. BADGLEY, Robin F.

Doctors' Strike: Medical Care and Conflict in Saskatchewan. 1967 /Macmillan of Canada/Toronto. Robin F. Badgley and Samuel Wolfe.

xiv, 201, [1] pp.; 213 × 135 mm.
Issued in cloth and paper.

1827. BESSETTE, Gérard

Incubation. A novel by Gérard Bessette. Translated from the French by Glen Shortliffe. 1967 Macmillan of Canada Toronto.

[6], 143, [1] pp.; 215 × 135 mm.

1828. BROWN, N.E.

Consumer Education. Revised Edition. N. E. Brown, Co-ordinator of Social Studies, Wetaskiwin High School. Toronto: The Macmillan Company of Canada Limited.

[6], 90 pp.; 225 × 143 mm.
First published in 1964 (see 1663). Issued in paper.

1829. BROWNJOHN, Alan

The Lions' Mouths. Poems by Alan Brownjohn. London Macmillan Melbourne Toronto 1967.

x, 54 pp.; 209 × 131 mm.

1830. CARELESS, J.M.S.

Edited by J.M.S. Careless and R. Craig Brown. With a fine-art section of monochrome and colour plates. *The Canadians 1867-1967*. Toronto: Macmillan of Canada 1967.

xx, 856 pp.; 225 × 150 mm.
Reprinted in 1967 (twice). Reprinted in 1968 in two volumes in paper.

1831. CLARKE, Austin C.

The Meeting Point. Austin C. Clarke. Macmillan of Canada Toronto.

[6], 249, [1] pp.; 220 × 140 mm.

1832. CLEMSON, Donovan

Lost Mine. Donovan Clemson. Illustrated by David Craig. 1967 Macmillan of Canada Toronto.

[8], 176 pp.; 217 × 138 mm.
Issued in cloth and paper.

1833. COLLIE, Michael

The House. By Michael Collie. 1967 Macmillan of Canada Toronto.

[8], 37, [1] pp.; 220 × 170 mm.

1834. CONQUEST, Robert

New Lines. An Anthology edited by Robert Conquest. Macmillan London Melbourne Toronto [and] St. Martin's Press New York 1967.

xviii, 91, [3] pp.; 222 × 140 mm.

1835.   CREIGHTON, David
Deeds of Gods and Heroes. David Creighton, Oakville-Trafalgar High School, Oakville, Ontario. The Macmillan Company of Canada Limited Toronto, 1967.

[8], 216 pp.; 217 × 135 mm.

1836.   DUMARESQ, Frances
Into Wonderland. Edited by Frances M. Dumaresq, B.A., B.L.S., Library Consultant, Protestant School Board of Greater Montreal. 1967 Macmillan of Canada Toronto.

224 pp.; 233 × 150 mm.
Magic of Reading Series.

1837.   EASTMAN, H.C.
The Tariff and Competition in Canada. H.C. Eastman and S. Stykolt. Macmillan of Canada/Toronto.

xvi, 400 pp.; 227 × 147 mm.

1838.   ELLIOTT, Charles M.
Discovering Mathematics 4. Authors: Charles M. Elliott, M.A., Ed.D., Superintendent of Public Schools, Oshawa, A.S. Winter, B.A., Principal, Dr. S. J. Phillips Public School, Oshawa [and] Douglas H. Crawford, Ph.D., Associate Professor of Mathematics, Queen's University, Kingston. J.M. Dent & Sons (Canada) Limited [and] The Macmillan Company of Canada Limited.

xiv, 323, [1] pp.; 230 × 163 mm.
Discovering Mathematics Series.

1839.   EPPS, Bernard
Pilgarlic the Death. A novel by Bernard Epps. 1967 Macmillan of Canada Toronto.

[6], 166 pp.; 220 × 133 mm.

1840.   FALKNER, J. Meade
Moonfleet. By J. Meade Falkner. [Quotation]. Toronto: The Macmillan Company of Canada Limited [and] London: Edward Arnold (Publishers) Ltd.

272 pp.; 183 × 120 mm.
New edition published in 1971 (see 2095).

1841.   FINDLEY, Timothy
The Last of the Crazy People. Timothy Findley. Macmillan of Canada Toronto.

[6], 282 pp.; 190 × 130 mm.
The imprint is on a sticker which covers the original publisher's name (Macdonald, London).
Laurentian Library No. 56.

1842. FRACHE, E. June

Fitness For Living. E. June Frache, B.Ed., M.S., Teacher-Program Designer, W.P. Wagner High School, Edmonton [and] E.M. Brown, Formerly Education Supervisor, Alcoholism Foundation of Alberta. Illustrated by Alan Daniel. The Macmillan Company of Canada Limited/Toronto.

[12], 196 pp.; 235 × 165 mm.

1843. GHOSE, Zulfikar

The Murder of Aziz Khan. A novel by Zulfikar Ghose. London Macmillan Melbourne Toronto 1967.

315, [1] pp.; 219 × 138 mm.

1844. GODDEN, Rumer

The River. By Rumer Godden. Macmillan London Melbourne Toronto 1967.

143, [1] pp.; 190 × 123 mm.

1845. GRIGSON, Geoffrey

A Skull in Salop and Other Poems. Geoffrey Grigson. London Macmillan Melbourne Toronto 1967.

[10], 61, [1] pp.; 211 × 132 mm.

1846. GUILLET, Edwin

You'll Never Die John A.!" Edwin C. Guillet. 1967 Macmillan of Canada Toronto.

[10], 148 pp.; 248 × 196 mm.
Issued in paper.

1847. HARE, John

The Literature of France: A Short Introduction. John Hare, Memorial University of Newfoundland. Macmillan of Canada Toronto, St. Martin's Press New York [and] Macmillan & Co Ltd. London 1967.

[10], 177, [1] pp.; 178 × 105 mm.
Issued in paper.

1848. HENDERSON, James

The Time of Your Life: An Anthology of Short Stories. Selected and edited by James Henderson, M.A., Head of the English Department, Oakville-Trafalgar High School, Oakville, Ontario. The Macmillan Company of Canada Limited Toronto.

xx, 224 pp.; 188 × 124 mm.
Revised in 1977 (see 2484).

1849. HILLS, P.J.

Small Scale Organic Preparations. P.J. Hills, B.Sc., A.R.I.C., Senior Science Master, Netherthorpe Grammar School, Staveley, Chesterfield. Toronto: The Macmillan Company of Canada Limited.

vi, 90 pp.; 218 × 140 mm.

1850. HOMEWOOD, M.C.

Les Jeunes Français. Twelve Short Plays To Accompany H.F. Collins's *French Course For Schools Part I*. By M.C. Homewood. Illustrated by B. Biro. The Macmillan Company of Canada Limited Toronto.

vi, 58 pp.; 182 × 120 mm.
Issued in paper.

1851. HOOLE, Arthur H.

The Fundamentals Of Clear Writing With Exercises. Arthur H. Hoole, Honorary Fellow of St. John's College, University of Manitoba. Toronto: The Macmillan Company of Canada Limited.

[8], 282 pp.; 202 × 130 mm.
First published in 1965 (see 1732). Issued in paper.

1852. JACOBSON, Ulah b.

Happy Hours. Edited by Ulah b. Jacobson, B. Ed., Supervisor of Kindergarten and Primary Instruction, Greater Victoria Schools. 1967 Macmillan of Canada Toronto.

208 pp.; 233 × 150 mm.
Magic of Reading Series.

1853. JENNINGS, Elizabeth

Collected Poems 1967. Elizabeth Jennings. Macmillan London Melbourne Toronto 1967.

xvi, 265, [1] pp.; 221 × 140 mm.

1854. JONES, C. Meredith

Les Lettres en France. Edited by C. Meredith Jones And C.A.E. Jensen, University of Manitoba. 1967 Macmillan of Canada/Toronto.

xxxiv, 525, [1] pp.; 238 × 155 mm.

1855. LAPIERRE, Laurier L.

Québec: hier et aujourd'hui. Comité de rédaction: Président: Laurier L. LaPierre, Professeur d'histoire, McGill University et Directeur, Centre d'Études canadiennes-françaises [etc.]. 1967 The Macmillan Company of Canada Limited Toronto.

[14], 306 pp.; 220 × 140 mm.

1856. LEWIS, Elizabeth Foreman

Elizabeth Foreman Lewis, *To Beat a Tiger One Needs A Brother's Help*. Study material prepared by P.W. Diebel, Assistant Superintendent, Hamilton Public Schools [and] R. McBurney, Master, Lakeshore Teachers' College, Toronto. Macmillan of Canada/Toronto.

[10], 258 pp.; 195 × 130 mm.

1857. LOWER, A.R.M.

My First Seventy-Five Years. By Arthur R.M. Lower. 1967 Macmillan of Canada Toronto.

[14], 384 pp.; 226 × 152 mm.

1858.   MacBETH, George

The Colour of Blood. Poems By George MacBeth. Macmillan London Melbourne Toronto 1967.

    [8], 77, [1] pp.; 221 × 141 mm.

1859.   MacLENNAN, Hugh

Return of the Sphinx. Hugh MacLennan. Macmillan of Canada Toronto.

    [10], 303, [1] pp.; 215 × 140 mm.
    Reprinted in the Laurentian Library (No. 10) in 1970.

1860.   MARSHALL, John Stewart

Physics. 2nd edition. J.S. Marshall, McGill University, E.R. Pounder, McGill University [and] R.W. Stewart, University of British Columbia. Macmillan of Canada - Toronto [and] St. Martin's Press - New York.

    x, 1139, [1] pp.; 235 × 158 mm.
    First published in 1957 (see 1404).

1861.   MASSON, Frank N.

Welding Theory And Practice. Frank N. Masson, Head of Welding-Plumbing Dept., H.B. Beal Secondary School, London, Ont. Illustrated by A. Diana. Toronto: The Macmillan Company of Canada Limited.

    [8], 119, [1] pp.; 225 × 157 mm.
    Macmillan Basic Technical Series.

1862.   MAY, Charles Paul

A Book of Canadian Birds. By Charles Paul May. Illustrations by John Crosby. Macmillan of Canada Toronto [and] Macmillan & Co Ltd London.

    [8], 115, [1] pp.; 215 × 135 mm.
    Reprinted in 1975.

1863.   McKAY, W.A.

The Great Canadian Skin Game. By W.A. McKay. Macmillan of Canada/Toronto /1967.

    [6], 88 pp.; 218 × 135 mm.

1864.   MIERTSCHING, Johann

Frozen Ships: The Arctic Diary of Johann Miertsching 1850-1854. Translated and with introduction and notes by L.H. Neatby. 1967 Macmillan of Canada Toronto.

    xviii, 254 pp.; 220 × 135 mm.

1865.   MILLER, Arthur

All My Sons. By Arthur Miller. With study questions by J.W. MacDonald and J.C.W. Saxton. Toronto: The Macmillan Company of Canada Limited.

    95, [1] pp.; 180 × 120 mm.
    Issued in paper.

1866.   MULHOLLAND, Brendan

The Commuter. Brendan Mulholland. Illustrated by Trog. Macmillan London Melbourne Toronto 1967.

[4], 123, [1] pp.; 209 × 133 mm.

1867.   ORR, Andrew A.

Invitation To Drama. Revised Edition. Eight Short Plays For Secondary Schools. Selected And Edited by Andrew A. Orr, M.A. Toronto: Macmillan of Canada.

[10], 284 pp.; 188 × 123 mm.
First published in 1956 (see 1376).

1868.   PACEY, Desmond

The Canada Books of Prose and Verse, *Our Literary Heritage*. Desmond Pacey. The Ryerson Press, Toronto [and] The Macmillan Company of Canada Limited.

[16], 561, [1] pp.; 230 × 160 mm.
Canada Books of Prose and Verse Series.

1869.   PHELAN, Josephine

The Ballad Of D'arcy McGee: Rebel In Exile. Josephine Phelan. Macmillan of Canada Toronto. Illustrated by David Craig.

[8], 132 pp.; 213 × 140 mm.
Issued in cloth and paper.
Great Stories of Canada Series.

1870.   PHILLIPS, R.A.J.

Canada's North. R.A.J. Phillips. 1967/Macmillan of Canada/Toronto.

xiv, 306 pp.; 225 × 150 mm.

1871.   PRUNKL, William R.

Health Around the Clock. William R. Prunkl, B.A., B.Ed., Supervisor, Division II, Edmonton Public School Board [and] Norman E. Lougheed, B.Sc., M.Ed., Principal, Gold Bar Elementary School, Edmonton. Illustrated by A. Diana. The Macmillan Company of Canada Limited/Toronto.

[12], 196 pp.; 235 × 165 mm.

1872.   PRUNKL, William R.

William R. Prunkl, B.A., B.Ed., Supervisor, Division II, Edmonton Public School Board [and] Norman E. Lougheed, B.Sc., M.Ed., Principal, Gold Bar Elementary School, Edmonton. Illustrated by Lee Clifton and Aileen Richardson. *Health Through the Seasons*. The Macmillan Company of Canada Limited/Toronto.

[10], 174 pp.; 235 × 165 mm.

1873. PRUNKL, William R.

A Lifetime of Health. William R. Prunkl, B.A., B.Ed., Supervisor, Division II, Edmonton Public School Board [and] Norman E. Lougheed, B.Sc., M.Ed., Principal, Gold Bar Elementary School, Edmonton. Illustrated by Lee Clifton and Aileen Richardson. The Macmillan Company of Canada Limited/Toronto.

[12], 194 pp.; 235 × 165 mm.

1874. RAYNAULD, André

The Canadian Economic System. André Raynauld, Docteur (en sciences économiques) de l'Université de Paris, Professor and Head, Department of Economics, Université de Montréal. Translated from the French by C.M. Ross, Victoria College, University of Toronto. 1967 The Macmillan Company of Canada Limited Toronto.

[20], 440 pp.; 185 × 125 mm.
Issued in cloth and paper.

1875. RILEY, Louise

Train for Tiger Lily. By Louise Riley. Illustrated By Christine Price. Toronto: The Macmillan Company of Canada.

186 pp.; 210 × 140 mm.
First published in 1954. Reprinted in 1967. Earlier printings not located.

1876. ROSENBLUTH, Gideon

Gideon Rosenbluth, *The Canadian Economy and Disarmament*. 1967 Macmillan of Canada/Toronto.

xii, 189, [1] pp.; 217 × 137 mm.

1877. ROWSE, A.L.

Cornish Stories. A. L. Rowse. Macmillan London Melbourne Toronto 1967.
viii, 152 pp.; 190 × 127 mm.

1878. SANDERS, James B.

A travers les siècles: An Anthology of French Literature. James B. Sanders, University of Western Ontario [and] Douglas G. Creighton, University of Western Ontario. Toronto: The Macmillan Company of Canada Limited.

[12], 356 pp.; 257 × 190 mm.

1879. SCHULL, Joseph

Joseph Schull, *The Nation Makers*. Illustrations by Irma Coucill. Macmillan 1967 Toronto.

[10], 134 pp.; 210 × 135 mm.
Issued in cloth and paper.

1880. *Science and the University*. Lord Bowden, Leo Goldberg, Roger Gaudry [and] Henry Margenau. Macmillan of Canada - Toronto [and] St. Martin's Press - New York in Association with York University 1967.

xii, 104 pp.; 220 × 140 mm.
Frank Gerstein Lectures: York University Invitation Series.

1881.   SCOTT, F.R.

The Blasted Pine. Revised and enlarged edition. An Anthology of Satire, Invective and Disrespectful Verse, Chiefly by Canadian writers. Selected, Arranged and Introduced by F.R. Scott and A.J.M. Smith. Toronto: The Macmillan Company of Canada Limited.

xx, 166 pp.; 194 × 120 mm.
First published in 1957 (see 1410). Revised edition issued in paper. Reprinted in 1971 and 1976.

1882.   SHERK, Paul W.

A teacher's guide to Senior General Mathematics. Paul W. Sherk, Cedarbrae Collegiate Institute, Scarborough, General Editor. The Macmillan Company of Canada Limited/Toronto.

[4], 39, [1] pp.; 207 × 130 mm.
Issued in paper.

1883.   SILLITOE, Alan

A Tree on Fire. Alan Sillitoe. Macmillan 1967 London Melbourne Toronto.

447, [1] pp.; 208 × 128 mm.

1884.   SIMONSON, H.P.

Your Health And Your Community. H.P. Simonson, B.Sc., B.Ed., Principal, Mckernan Junior High School, Edmonton, E.A. Hastie, Formerly Associate Professor, Faculty of Education, University of Alberta, [and] H.A. Doherty, M.Ed., Executive Assistant, Alberta Teachers Association. Illustrated by G. Fantuz. The Macmillan Company of Canada Limited/Toronto.

[10], 205, [1] pp.; 235 × 165 mm.

1885.   STEGNER, Wallace

Wallace Stegner, *Wold Willow: A History, a Story, and a Memory of the Last Plains Frontier*. Toronto: The Macmillan Company of Canada Limited.

[10], 306 pp.; 200 × 125 mm.
Reprinted in the Laurentian Library (No. 59) in 1977.

1886.   SUR, William R.

This is Music: 1. By William R. Sur, Adeline McCall, William R. Fisher [and] Mary R. Tolbert. Adapted for Canadian use by Sherwood Robson, Supervisor of Music, North Vancouver. Illustrator: William Duaan. Canadian Edition. Macmillan of Canada Toronto.

192 pp.; 310 × 228 mm.
This is Music Series.

1887.   SUR, William R.

This is Music: 2. By William R. Sur, Mary R. Tolbert, William R. Fisher [and] Adeline McCall. Adapted for use in Canadian schools by Sherwood Robson, Supervisor of Music, North Vancouver. Illustrator: Nancy Heinlein. Macmillan of Canada Toronto.

168 pp.; 232 × 185 mm.
This is Music Series.

1888. THOMSON, Dale C.

Louis St. Laurent: Canadian. Dale C. Thomson. 1967 Macmillan of Canada Toronto.

[12], 564 pp.; 225 × 150 mm.

1889. THURBER, Walter A.

Exploring Science: Seven. By Walter A. Thurber [and] Robert E. Kilburn. Canadian Edition. 1967 The Macmillan Company of Canada Limited Toronto.

432 pp.; 240 × 160 mm.
Revised in 1971 (see 2130).
Exploring Science Series.

1889A THURBER, Walter A.

Exploring Science: Eight. By Walter A. Thurber [and] Robert E. Kilburn. Canadian Edition. 1967 The Macmillan Company Of Canada Limited Toronto.

429, [1] pp.; 240 × 160 mm.
Revised in 1971 (see 2131).
Exploring Science Series.

1890. THURBER, Walter A.

Exploring Science: Nine. By Walter A. Thurber [and] Robert E. Kilburn. Canadian Edition. 1967 The Macmillan Company of Canada Limited Toronto.

576 pp.; 240 × 160 mm.
Revised in 1971 (see 2132).
Exploring Science Series.

1891. TROOP, Robert

The Hammering. Robert Troop. Macmillan of Canada Toronto.

268 pp.; 200 × 135 mm.

1892. VAN VLIET, M.L.

Physical Education Activities for Secondary Schools: A Program Guide for Teachers and Administrators. M.L. Van Vliet, Ed.D., Dean of the Faculty of Physical Education, University of Alberta, Edmonton [and] M.L. Howell, Ed.D., Faculty of Physical Education, University of Alberta, Edmonton. 1967 Toronto: The Macmillan Company of Canada Limited.

[6], 273, [1] pp.; 270 × 195 mm.
First published in 1956 under the title *Physical Education for Junior and Senior High Schools* (see 1379).

1893. WAIN, John

The Smaller Sky. John Wain. Macmillan London Melbourne Toronto 1967.

184 pp.; 209 × 130 mm.

1894.   WALPOLE, Hugh
The Cathedral: A Novel. By Hugh Walpole. Macmillan London Melbourne
Toronto 1967.
   viii, 531, [1] pp.; 189 × 124 mm.

1895.   WISE, S.F.
Canada Views the United States: Nineteenth-Century Political Attitudes. By
S.F. Wise and Robert Craig Brown. With an Introduction by Richard A.
Preston and a Commentary by David M. Potter. The Macmillan Company of
Canada Limited Toronto.
   xii, 139, [1] pp.; 207 × 140 mm.
   Reprinted in paper in 1972.

1896.   WOOD, Herbert F.
Vimy! Herbert Fairlie Wood. Macmillan of Canada Toronto/1967.
   186 pp.; 220 × 140 mm.

1897.   WOOD, Herbert F.
The Night Riders. John Redmayne [pseud.]. Illustrated by John Lawrence.
Macmillan of Canada Toronto.
   150 pp.; 200 × 130 mm.
   John Redmayne is a pseudonym for Herbert F. Wood and Juliet Wood.

1898.   YEATS, William Butler
The Collected Poems of W.B. Yeats. Macmillan London Melbourne Toronto
1967.
   xviii, 564, [2] pp.; 201 × 130 mm.

1899.   YOUNG, W. Arthur
A Kipling Dictionary. W. Arthur Young and John H. McGivering.
[Quotation]. Macmillan London Melbourne Toronto, St. Martin's Press
New York 1967.
   x, 230 pp.; 223 × 151 mm.

1968

1900.   ANDERSON, Robert N.
Foundation Disciplines and the Study of Education. Robert N. Anderson,
University of Saskatchewan, Regina, Robert F. Lawson, University of Cal-
gary, Randolph L. Schnell, University of Calgary [and] Donald F. Swift,
Oxford University. Macmillan of Canada/Toronto.
   viii, 90 pp.; 235 × 155 mm.

1901.   BATES, Ronald
Changes. Ronald Bates. Toronto: Macmillan of Canada 1968.
   [10], 68 pp.; 205 × 143 mm.
   Issued in cloth and paper.

1902. BERTIN, Leonard

Target 2067: Canada's Second Century. Leonard Bertin. Macmillan of Canada Toronto.

[22], 297, [1] pp.; 232 × 154 mm.

1903. BESSETTE, Gérard

De Québec à Saint-Boniface: Recits Et Nouvelles Du Canada Français. Textes Choisis Et Annotés Par Gérard Bessette. Macmillan of Canada/Toronto.

x, 286 pp.; 220 × 138 mm.
Issued in cloth and paper.

1904. BLISHEN, Bernard R.

Canadian Society: Sociological Perspectives. Third Edition. Edited by Bernard R. Blishen, Frank E. Jones, Kaspar D. Naegele [and] John Porter. 1968 Macmillan of Canada/Toronto.

xvi, 877, [1] pp.; 232 × 155 mm.
First published in 1961 (see 1516). Revised in 1964 (see 1661). The third edition was issued in an abridged form in paper in 1971.

1905. BRADBURY, Ray

Ray Bradbury, *Fahrenheit 451*. Notes and questions prepared by Roy Bentley, M.A., B.Ed., Co-ordinator of English for the Borough of Etobicoke. Macmillan of Canada Toronto.

xvi, 159, [1] pp.; 189 × 125 mm.

1906. BRONTE, Emily

Emily Brontë, *Wuthering Heights*. Edited by Frederick T. Flahiff, St. Michael's College, University of Toronto. Macmillan of Canada - Toronto, Macmillan & Co. Ltd. - London [and] St. Martin's Press - New York.

liv, 368 pp.; 178 × 105 mm.
A school edition, with notes by Linton D. Read, was published in 1960 (see 1480). Issued in paper.
College Classics in English Series.

1907. BRUCE, Charles

News and the Southams. Charles Bruce. 1968 Macmillan of Canada Toronto.

xii, 429, [1] pp.; 228 × 141 mm.

1908. BRUCE, Harry

The Short, Happy Walks of Max MacPherson. Harry Bruce. Illustrated by George Meadows. Macmillan of Canada Toronto 1968.

xiv, 167, [1] pp.; 217 × 135 mm.

1909. BUCKLEY, Helen

Economics for Canadians. Revised Edition. Helen Buckley, Dominion Bureau of Statistics [and] Kenneth Buckley, Professor of Economics, University of Saskatchewan. Toronto: The Macmillan Company of Canada Limited.

x, 224 pp.; 235 × 155 mm.
First published in 1960 (see 1483).

1910.   CAMPBELL, Marjorie Wilkins

The Savage River: Seventy-one Days with Simon Fraser. Marjorie Wilkins
Campbell. Illustrated by Lewis Parker. Macmillan of Canada/Toronto.

[12], 146 pp.; 210 × 133 mm.
Issued in paper.
Great Stories of Canada Series.

1911.   CARD, B.Y.

B.Y Card, Ph.D., Professor of Sociology of Education, Department of
Educational Foundations, University of Alberta, Edmonton. *Trends and
Change in Canadian Society: Their Challenge to Canadian Youth*. Toronto
Macmillan of Canada 1968.

xvi, 206 pp.; 227 × 150 mm.
Issued in paper.

1912.   COLE, Leslie A.

Investigations in Science. Leslie A. Cole and Peter Saxton. General Editor:
J.A. Aikman, Vice-principal, St. Catharines Teachers' College, St.
Catharines, Ontario. Illustrations by Donald Kennedy and Ronald White.
Toronto: The Macmillan Company of Canada Limited.

[10], 363, [1] pp.; 235 × 165 mm.

1913.   CORRIVEAU, Monique

The Wapiti. Monique Corriveau. Translated by J.M. L'Heureux. Illustrated
by Paul Liberovsky. Macmillan of Canada 1968 Toronto.

188 pp.; 220 × 140 mm.
Issued in cloth and paper.

1914.   COVELL, Harold M.

[At bottom of page 1:] *Effective Reading: A Developmental Programme Book
1*. Harold M. Covell [and] John McGechaen. Illustrated by Gus Fantuz and
William Lytle. © The Ryerson Press and the Macmillan Company of Canada
Limited, 1968 [etc.].

88 pp.; 285 × 220 mm.
Issued in cloth and paper.
Effective Reading Books Series.

1915.   COVELL, Harold M.

[At bottom of page:] *Effective Reading: A Developmental Programme Book 4*.
Harold M. Covell [and] John McGechaen. Illustrated by William Wheeler
and Robert Kunz. © The Ryerson Press and the Macmillan Company of
Canada Limited, 1968 [etc.].

143, [1] pp.; 275 × 210 mm.
Issued in paper.
Effective Reading Books Series.

1916. DALE, Peter
The Storms. Peter Dale. Macmillan London Melbourne Toronto 1968.
56 pp.; 209 × 131 mm.

1917. DONNELLY, Murray
Dafoe of the Free Press. Murray Donnelly. 1968 Macmillan of Canada/Toronto.
[16], 207, [1] pp.; 220 × 140 mm.

1918. EAYRS, James
Minutes of the Sixties. James Eayrs. 1968 Macmillan of Canada Toronto.
xiv, 273, [1] pp.; 220 × 140 mm.

1919. FAINLIGHT, Ruth
To See The Matter Clearly And Other Poems. Ruth Fainlight. Macmillan London Melbourne Toronto 1968.
vi, 77, [1] pp.; 208 × 133 mm.

1920. FAIRBAIRNS, Zoë
Live as Family. Zoë Fairbairns. Macmillan London Melbourne Toronto 1968.
[6], 146, [2] pp.; 219 × 132 mm.

1921. FRASER, Frances
The Wind Along the River. By Frances Fraser. Illustrated by Lewis Parker. Macmillan of Canada Toronto 1968.
[10], 83, [1] pp.; 235 × 153 mm.

1922. GODDEN, Rumer
Swan & Turtles. Stories by Rumer Godden. Macmillan London Toronto Melbourne 1968.
218, [2] pp.; 219 × 131 mm.

1923. GODWIN, L. Ruth
Teachers' Manual For Full Flight. By L. Ruth Godwin, M.ED., ED.D., Associate Professor, Faculty of Education, University of Saskatchewan, Regina Campus. Toronto: The Macmillan Company of Canada Limited 1968.
[6], 152 pp.; 214 × 138 mm.
Issued in paper.
Passport to Reading Series.

1924. GRAY, Julia
Longer Poems Selected for Senior Students. With notes and questions by Julia Gray, Richview Collegiate Institute, Islington, Ontario [and] L.H. Newell, University of Toronto Schools, Toronto, Ontario. The Macmillan Company of Canada Limited Toronto.
[6], 169, [1] pp.; 178 × 123 mm.
Issued in paper.

1925. HARDY, Thomas
Thomas Hardy, *Tess of the d'Urbervilles*. Edited by M.W. Steinberg, University of British Columbia. Macmillan of Canada - Toronto.
xxxii, 448 pp.; 178 × 108 mm.
Issued in paper.
College Classics in English Series.

1926. JULIEN, Claude
Claude Julien, *Canada: Europe's Last Chance*. Translated from the French by Penny Williams. With introduction by Blair Fraser. 1968 Macmillan of Canada Toronto.
xiv, 178 pp.; 215 × 135 mm.

1927. KROETSCH, Robert
Alberta. Robert Kroetsch. 1968 Toronto/Macmillan of Canada.
[14], 231, [1] pp.; 220 × 140 mm.
Traveller's Canada Series.

1928. LABARGE, Margaret Wade
Margaret Wade Labarge, *Saint Louis: The Life of Louis IX of France*. Macmillan of Canada Toronto 1968.
303, [1] pp.; 225 × 145 mm.

1929. LANG, H. Murray
Basic Science 2. H.M. Lang, Althouse College of Education, University of Western Ontario, London [and] F.M. Speed, University of Toronto Schools, Toronto. The Macmillan Company of Canada Limited, Toronto.
[12], 396 pp.; 235 × 165 mm.
This is a revision of *Basic General Science 2* published in 1962 (see 1580).

1930. LAURENCE, Margaret
Long Drums and Canons: Nigerian dramatists and novelists 1952-1966. Margaret Laurence. Macmillan London Melbourne Toronto 1968.
209, [1] pp.; 221 × 140 mm.

1931. LEHMANN, John
A Nest of Tigers: Edith, Osbert and Sacheverell Sitwell in their times. John Lehmann. Macmillan: London Melbourne Toronto 1968.
x, 294 pp.; 220 × 138 mm.

1932. LEVINE, Norman
Canadian Winter's Tales. Edited by Norman Levine. Macmillan of Canada/Toronto [and] Macmillan & Co. Ltd./London.
[8], 172 pp.; 210 × 128 mm.
Issued in cloth and paper.

1933. LINKLATER, Eric
The Stories of Eric Linklater. Macmillan London Melbourne Toronto 1968.
377, [1] pp.; 210 × 135 mm.

1934. LOWRY, J.H.

A Course In World Geography. Young & Lowry. *Book III: Regions Of The World, Their Work and Wealth*. By J.H. Lowry, M.A., B.Sc. (Econ.), Senior Geography Master, Cranleigh School. Maps And Diagrams By J.H. Lowry And Peter Jackson. Illustrations By Klaus Meyer. Toronto: The Macmillan Company of Canada Limited.

253, [3] pp.; 230 × 152 mm.

1935. MacBETH, George

The Night of Stones. Poems By George MacBeth. Macmillan London Melbourne Toronto 1968.

[8], 87, [1] pp.; 221 × 140 mm.

1936. MacKENZIE, Jean

Storm Island. Jean MacKenzie. Illustrated by Gordon Rayner. 1968 Macmillan of Canada Toronto.

[8], 115, [1] pp.; 215 × 140 mm.

1937. MAY, Charles Paul

A Book of Reptiles and Amphibians. By Charles Paul May. Illustrations By John Crosby. Macmillan of Canada Toronto.

[10], 117, [1] pp.; 215 × 135 mm.
Issued in cloth and paper.

1938. McCOURT, Edward

Saskatchewan. Edward McCourt. Toronto/Macmillan of Canada/1968.

xiv, 238 pp.; 220 × 140 mm.
Reprinted in 1977 in paper.
Traveller's Canada Series.

1939. McCURDY, Sherburne G.

The Legal Status of the Canadian Teacher. By Sherburne G. McCurdy, Professional Secretary, Newfoundland Teachers' Association, St. John's, Newfoundland. The Macmillan Company of Canada Limited Toronto.

xvi, 187, [1] pp.; 232 × 150 mm.

1940. McGARITY, Daniel P.

Upstage and Down. Edited by Daniel P. McGarity, Head, Department of English - Kenner Collegiate and Vocational Institute, Peterborough, Ontario. Toronto: Macmillan of Canada.

xii, 274 pp.; 187 × 123 mm.

1941. McLEISH, Dougal

The Traitor Game. Dougal McLeish. 1968 Macmillan of Canada Toronto.

[8], 212 pp.; 208 × 140 mm.

1942. MILLER, H.G.

Building Construction: materials and methods. H.G. Miller, Technical Director, General Brock High School, Burlington, Ontario. Illustrated by Tony Langdon and Bernard Loates. Macmillan of Canada Toronto.

[10], 429, [1] pp,; 258 × 178 mm.
Revised metric edition published in 1980 (see 2686).

1943. MILLER, Walter M.

A Canticle for Leibowitz. Walter M. Miller, Jr. Notes and questions prepared by Kenneth J. Weber, B.A., Head of the English Department, W. A. Porter Collegiate Institute, Scarborough, Ontario. Macmillan of Canada Toronto.

xiv, 386 pp.; 190 × 125 mm.
Issued in cloth and paper.
Impact Books Series.

1944. NEEDHAM, Richard J.

The Garden of Needham. Richard J. Needham. Illustrated by Graham Round. Macmillan of Canada Toronto.

[8], 207, [1] pp.; 215 × 140 mm.

1945. O'BRIEN, Mary

The Journals of Mary O'Brien 1828-1838. Edited by Audrey Saunders Miller. 1968 Macmillan of Canada Toronto.

xxii, 314 pp.; 220 × 140 mm.

1946. PATTERSON, Raymond M.

Finlay's River. By R.M. Patterson. Toronto 1968 Macmillan of Canada.

xvi, 315, [1] pp.; 210 × 140 mm.
Reprinted in 1972 in paper. Reprinted in the Laurentian Library (No. 41) in 1976.

1947. PLUNKETT, Thomas J.

Urban Canada and its government: a study of municipal organization. Thomas J. Plunkett. Macmillan of Canada/Toronto/1968.

[12], 178 pp.; 225 × 150 mm.
Issued in cloth and paper.

1948. PRATT, E.J.

Selected Poems of E.J. Pratt. Edited and with an introduction, bibliography and notes by Peter Buitenhuis. Macmillan of Canada/Toronto/1968.

xxxii, 221, [1] pp.; 175 × 105 mm.
Issued in paper.

1949. RICH, John

John Rich, *Interviewing Children and Adolescents*. Macmillan London Melbourne Toronto, St. Martin's Press New York 1968.

viii, 119, [1] pp.; 220 × 150 mm.
Issued in cloth and paper.

1950. ROBERTS, B.A.

The Words We Use: A Study in language, reading, and composition for high school students. B.A. Roberts, M.A. (Oxon.), Co-ordinator for English, Saint John, New Brunswick. Macmillan of Canada Toronto.

viii, 151, [1] pp.; 213 × 133 mm.

1951. SCHULL, Joseph

The Jinker. A novel by Joseph Schull. 1968 Macmillan of Canada Toronto [and] Macmillan & Co. Ltd. London.

[6], 171, [1] pp.; 220 × 145 mm.

1952. SIDE, Ronald K.

Entertainment for All. Edited with adaptations by Ronald K. Side, Master, Hamilton Teachers' College, Hamilton, Ontario. Illustrated by Aileen Richardson. Macmillan of Canada/Toronto.

x, 262 pp.; 195 × 130 mm.

1953. SILLITOE, Alan

Guzman, Go Home and other stories. Alan Sillitoe. Macmillan 1968 London Melbourne Toronto.

169, [1] pp.; 209 × 134 mm.

1954. SILLITOE, Alan

Love in the Environs of Voronezh and Other Poems. Alan Sillitoe. Macmillan 1968 London Melbourne Toronto.

58 pp.; 209 × 132 mm.

1955. SPEED, F.M.

Basic Science. F.M. Speed, University of Toronto Schools, Toronto and H.M. Lang, Althouse College of Education, University of Western Ontario. The Macmillan Company of Canada Limited, Toronto 1968.

[8], 408 pp.; 235 × 165 mm.

This is a revision of *Basic General Science Book 1* published in 1961 (see 1553).

1956. STEVENSON, O.J.

The Talking Wire: The Story of Alexander Graham Bell. By O.J. Stevenson. Illustrated by Lawrence Dresser. Macmillan of Canada Toronto.

viii, 207, [1] pp.; 216 × 143 mm.

First published in 1947. Reprinted frequently. Earlier printings not located.

1957. SUR, William R.

Teacher's Manual for This is Music 2. By William R. Sur, Mary R. Tolbert, William R. Fisher [and] Adeline McCall. Adapted for use in Canadian schools by Sherwood Robson, Supervisor of Music, North Vancouver. Macmillan of Canada Toronto.

viii, 168 pp.; 225 × 180 mm.

This is Music Series.

1958.   SUR, William R.

This is Music 3. By William R. Sur, William R. Fisher, Adeline McCall [and]
Mary R. Tolbert. Adapted for use in Canadian schools by Sherwood Robson,
Supervisor of Music, North Vancouver [and] Mrs. Glenys Purden, Braemar
Elementary School, North Vancouver. Illustrator: Dagmar Wilson. Mac-
millan of Canada Toronto.

176 pp.; 232 × 185 mm.
This is Music Series.

1959.   SUR, William R.

This is Music 4. By William R. Sur, Mary R. Tolbert, William R. Fisher [and]
Gladys Pitcher. Adapted for use in Canadian schools by Paul J. Bourret,
Edmonton Separate School Board [and] Elizabeth Filipkowski, University of
Alberta. Illustrator: Rosalie. Macmillan of Canada Toronto.

192 pp.; 232 × 185 mm.
This is Music Series.

1960.   SUR, William R.

This is Music 5. By William R. Sur, Robert E. Nye, William R. Fisher [and]
Mary R. Tolbert. Adapted for use in Canadian schools by Paul J. Bourret,
Edmonton Separate School Board [and] Elizabeth Filipkowski, University of
Alberta. Illustrator: Winnie Fitch Phelan. Macmillan of Canada Toronto.

215, [1] pp.; 232 × 185 mm.
This is Music Series.

1961.   SUR, William R.

This is Music 6. By William R. Sur, Robert E. Nye, William R. Fisher [and]
Mary R. Tolbert. Adapted for use in Canadian schools by Paul J. Bourret,
Edmonton Separate School Board [and] Elizabeth Filipkowski, University of
Alberta. Illustrator: Gordon Laite. Macmillan of Canada Toronto.

240 pp.; 232 × 185 mm.
This is Music Series.

1962.   TRUDEAU, Pierre Elliott

Pierre Elliott Trudeau, *Federalism and the French Canadians*. With an introduction by John J. Saywell. Macmillan of Canada 1968 Toronto.

xxviii, 212 pp.; 220 × 140 mm.
Reprinted frequently. Reprinted in the Laurentian Library (No. 48) in 1977.

1963.   WADE, Mason

The French Canadians 1760-1967. Mason Wade. Revised edition, in two
volumes. Volume One: 1760-1911. 1968 Macmillan of Canada Toronto,
Macmillan & Co Ltd. London [and] St. Martin's Press New York.

xxiv, 607, [37] pp.; 220 × 140 mm.
First published in 1955 (see 1355). This edition issued in cloth and paper. Reprinted
in the Laurentian Library (No. 33) in 1975.

1964. WADE, Mason

The French Canadians 1760-1967. Mason Wade. Revised edition, in two volumes. Volume Two: 1911-1967. 1968 Macmillan of Canada Toronto, Macmillan & Co Ltd. London [and] St. Martin's Press New York.

xxiii, 608-1128 pp.; 220 × 140 mm.
First published in 1955 (see 1355). This edition issued in cloth and paper. Reprinted in the Laurentian Library (No. 44) in 1976.

1965. WILKINSON, Anne

The Collected Poems Of Anne Wilkinson And A Prose Memoir. Edited, with an introduction, by A.J.M. Smith. The Macmillan Company of Canada Limited 1968 Toronto.

xxii, 212 pp.; 220 × 135 mm.

1966. WILLIAMS, Geoffrey

The Shaping of Modern Europe. Geoffrey Williams. Illustrated by M. Lord, A.R.C.A. Toronto: The Macmillan Company of Canada Limited.

[8], 151, [1] pp.; 220 × 140 mm.
Issued in paper.

1967. YOUNG, Eric W.

A Course In World Geography. Young & Lowry. *Book II: People Round The World*. By Eric W. Young, M.A. Third Edition. Maps And Diagrams By Peter Jackson. Illustrations By Klaus Meyer. Toronto: The Macmillan Company of Canada Limited.

221, [3] pp.; 230 × 152 mm.

1969

1968. AIKMAN, Jack A.

Watching the Weather Change. Jack A. Aikman, Vice-Principal, St. Catharines Teachers' College, St. Catharines, Ontario. Toronto: The Macmillan Company of Canada Limited.

[4], 35, [1] pp.; 230 × 156 mm.
Issued in paper. A metric edition was issued in 1977 (see 2451).
Our Science Program Series.

1969. BREWIS, T.N.

Regional Economic Policies. T.N. Brewis. With an appendix by T.K. Rymes. The Macmillan Company of Canada Limited Toronto.

[16], 303, [1] pp.; 228 × 150 mm.
Reprinted in paper in 1972.

1970. CARR, Albert

Men of Power, *Bismarck*. Albert Carr. Macmillan of Canada Toronto.

31, [1] pp.; 208 × 130 mm.
Issued in paper.
Men of Power Series.

1971. CARR, Albert

Men of Power, *Franco*. Albert Carr. Macmillan of Canada Toronto.

19, [1] pp.; 208 × 130 mm.
Issued in paper.
Men of Power Series.

1972. CARR, Albert

Men of Power, *Hitler*. Albert Carr. Macmillan of Canada Toronto.

20 pp.; 208 × 130 mm.
Issued in paper.
Men of Power Series.

1973. CARR, Albert

Men of Power, *Mao*. Albert Carr. Macmillan of Canada Toronto.

22 pp.; 208 × 130 mm.
Issued in paper.
Men of Power Series.

1974. CARR, Albert

Men of Power, *Mussolini*. Albert Carr. Macmillan of Canada Toronto.

24 pp.; 208 × 130 mm.
Issued in paper.
Men of Power Series.

1975. CARR, Albert

Men of Power, *Stalin*. Albert Carr. Macmillan of Canada Toronto.

20 pp.; 208 × 130 mm.
Issued in paper.
Men of Power Series.

1976. COOK, Ramsay

French-Canadian Nationalism: An Anthology. Edited by Ramsay Cook.
Macmillan of Canada/Toronto/1969.

336 pp.; 225 × 148 mm.
Issued in cloth and paper.

1977. CRAWFORD, Douglas H.

Discovering Mathematics 5. Authors: Douglas H. Crawford, Ph. D., Professor and Head of the Department of Mathematics, McArthur College of
Education, Queen's University, Kingston, James F. Tennant, B.A., Principal, Kingscourt Public School, Kingston, A.S. Winter, B.A., Principal, Dr.
S.J. Phillips Public School, Oshawa [and] Barbara A. Zabel, B.A. J.M. Dent
& Sons (Canada) Limited [and] The Macmillan Company of Canada Limited.

xiv, 354 pp.; 230 × 163 mm.
Discovering Mathematics Series.

1978. DAWE, Alan

Profile of a Nation: Canadian Themes and Styles. Alan Dawe. Macmillan of Canada/Toronto/1969.

xxii, 292 pp.; 224 × 150 mm.
Reprinted in 1970 and 1971. Issued in paper.

1979. DICKENS, Charles

Little Dorrit. By Charles Dickens. Edited by R.D. McMaster, University of Alberta. Macmillan of Canada — Toronto.

xxxiv, 846 pp.; 179 × 120 mm.
Issued in paper.
College Classics in English Series.

1980. DICKSON, Lovat

Lovat Dickson, *H.G. Wells: His Turbulent Life And Times.* Macmillan of Canada Toronto 1969.

xiv, 330, [2] pp.; 243 × 155 mm.

1981. FRASER, Blair

"Blair Fraser Reports": Selections 1944-1968. Edited by John Fraser and Graham Fraser. Macmillan of Canada/Toronto/1969.

xxiv, 312 pp.; 234 × 154 mm.

1982. GALLOWAY, David

The Elizabethan Theatre. Papers given at the International Conference on Elizabethan Theatre held at the University of Waterloo, Ontario, in July 1968. Edited and with an introduction by David Galloway, Department of English, University of Waterloo. Published in collaboration with the University of Waterloo. Macmillan of Canada Toronto.

xiv, 130 pp.; 220 × 138 mm.

1983. GOODSPEED, D.J.

The Road Past Vimy: The Canadian Corps 1914-1918. D.J. Goodspeed. 1969 Macmillan of Canada Toronto.

[10], 185, [1] pp.; 220 × 140 mm.
Issued in cloth and paper.

1984. GREASON, George K.

Third Edition, *Canadian Democracy at Work.* George K. Greason, Program Consultant, Ontario Department of Education [and] Roy C. King, Principal, C.B. Parsons Junior High School, North York. Drawings by Dorothy Mould and Vernon Mould. Toronto: The Macmillan Company of Canada Limited.

[8], 119, [1] pp.; 220 × 145 mm.
First published in 1962 (see 1574). Revised in 1966 (see 1781A). Reprinted with minor revisions in 1971 (see 2099) and 1977 (see 2476A). Issued in paper.

1985.   HALLETT, Fred H.

Machine Shop theory and practice. Revised Edition. Fred H. Hallett, B.Sc., Supervisor of Adult Education, Hamilton Board of Education, Hamilton, Ontario. Illustrated by A. Diana and Keith King. The Macmillan Company of Canada Limited Toronto.

[10], 273, [1] pp.; 235 × 163 mm.
First published in 1961 (see 1536).
Macmillan Basic Technical Series.

1986.   HARRIS, Lawren

Lawren Harris. Edited by Bess Harris and R.G.P. Colgrove and with an introduction by Northrop Frye. [1969 Macmillan of Canada Toronto].

xii, 146, [2] pp.; 254 × 350 mm.
Imprint on verso of half-title. Issued in slipcase. Reprinted in paper in 1976.

1987.   HOBSBAUM, Philip

Coming Out Fighting. Philip Hobsbaum. [Quotation]. Macmillan London Melbourne Toronto 1969.

55, [1] pp.; 209 × 133 mm.

1988.   HORWOOD, Harold

Newfoundland. Harold Horwood. Toronto/Macmillan of Canada/1969.

xii, 244 pp.; 220 × 140 mm.
Reprinted in paper in 1977.
Traveller's Canada Series.

1989.   HORWOOD, R.H.

Bicycles. R. H. Horwood, McArthur College of Education, Queen's University, Kingston, Ontario. The Macmillan Company of Canada Limited 1969.

[28] pp.; 225 × 148 mm.
Issued in paper.
Our Science Program Series.

1990.   HORWOOD, R.H.

Mostly About Pigs. R.H. Horwood, McArthur College of Education, Queen's University, Kingston, Ontario. The Macmillan Company of Canada Limited 1969.

[32] pp.; 225 × 148 mm.
Issued in paper.
Our Science Program Series.

1991.   HORWOOD, R.H.

String. R.H. Horwood, Faculty of Education, Queen's University, Kingston, Ontario. The Macmillan Company of Canada Limited 1969.

[32] pp.; 225 × 148 mm.
Issued in paper.
Our Science Program Series.

1992. HOWELL, Nancy

Sports and Games in Canadian Life 1700 to the Present. Nancy Howell and Maxwell L. Howell. Macmillan of Canada Toronto.

[12], 378 pp.; 225 × 150 mm.
Reprinted in the Laurentian Library (No. 29) in 1975.

1993. IMLACH, George

Hockey Is A Battle. Punch Imlach's own story, with Scott Young. Macmillan of Canada/Toronto/1969.

[10], 203, [1] pp.; 220 × 140 mm.

1994. ISRAEL, Charles E.

Charles E. Israel, *The Labyrinth.* A play for television. Study material prepared by Jack Livesley, Head of Audio-Visual and ETV Services, Collegiate Institute Board of Ottawa. Macmillan of Canada Toronto.

x, 91, [1] pp.; 182 × 120 mm.
Issued in paper.

1995. JENNINGS, Elizabeth

The Animals' Arrival. Elizabeth Jennings. Macmillan London Melbourne Toronto 1969.

[8], 40 pp.; 209 × 131 mm.

1996. KROETSCH, Robert

Robert Kroetsch, *The Studhorse Man.* Macmillan of Canada, Toronto.

168 pp.; 203 × 132 mm.

1997. LOWRY, J.H.

A Course In World Geography. Young & Lowry. *Book IV: The British Isles, Physical and Regional.* By J.H. Lowry, M.A., B.Sc.(Econ.), Senior Geography Master, Cranleigh School. Maps And Diagrams By J.H. Lowry. Illustrations By Klaus Meyer. Toronto: The Macmillan Company of Canada Limited.

288 pp.; 230 × 152 mm.

1998. MACDONALD, John A.

Affectionately Yours: The Letters of Sir John A. Macdonald and His Family. Edited and with an introduction by J.K. Johnson. Toronto/Macmillan of Canada/1969.

[10], 205, [1] pp.; 225 × 145 mm.
Issued in cloth and paper.

1999. MacEWEN, Gwendolyn

The Shadow-Maker. Gwendolyn MacEwen. Toronto: Macmillan of Canada 1969.

[10], 83, [1] pp.; 200 × 135 mm.
Issued in paper.

2000.   MacLENNAN, Hugh
   Hugh MacLennan, *Barometer Rising*. Notes and questions prepared by F.
   Wyatt MacLean, Principal, Bell High School, Ottawa. Macmillan of Canada
   Toronto.
   xiv, 396 pp.; 180 × 120 mm.
   First published in the St. Martin's Classics series in 1948 (see 1191). Issued in paper.

2001.   MACMILLAN, Harold
   Tides Of Fortune 1945-1955. Harold Macmillan. London Macmillan Melbourne Toronto 1969.
   xx, 729, [1] pp.; 220 × 150 mm.

2002.   MALLORY, Enid L.
   Ontario Calls You Camping. Enid L. Mallory. Toronto/Macmillan of
   Canada/1969.
   xii, 180 pp.; 220 × 140 mm.
   Issued in cloth and paper.

2003.   MARSHALL, Tom
   The Silences of Fire. Tom Marshall. Toronto: Macmillan of Canada 1969.
   [12], 72 pp.; 208 × 140 mm.

2004.   MASSEY, Norman Bland
   Patterns For The Teaching Of Science. By Norman Bland Massey, Formerly
   Science Master, London Teachers' College, London, Ontario. Revised Edi-
   tion. The Macmillan Company of Canada Limited Toronto.
   [8], 278 pp.; 220 × 140 mm.
   First published in 1965 (see 1739).

2005.   McCOURT, Edward
   The Yukon and Northwest Territories. Edward McCourt, Macmillan of
   Canada/Toronto/1969.
   [12], 236 pp.; 220 × 140 mm.
   Traveller's Canada Series.

2006.   McKAY, A.G.
   Roman Lyric Poetry: Catullus and Horace. Selected with Commentary by A.
   G. McKay and D.M. Shepherd, McMaster University, Hamilton, Canada.
   Macmillan, St. Martin's Press, 1969.
   274 pp.; 220 × 135 mm.

2007.   McLEISH, Dougal
   The Valentine Victim. Dougal McLeish. Macmillan of Canada Toronto 1969.
   [6], 201, [1], pp.; 208 × 140 mm.

2008. MEASURES, Howard

Howard Measures, *Styles of Address: A Manual Of Usage In Writing And In Speech*. Third Edition. [Quotation]. The Macmillan Company of Canada Limited Toronto.

x, 161, [1] pp.; 220 × 135 mm.
First published in 1962 (see 1590). Reprinted in paper in 1974.

2009. MEYERSON, Martin

The City and the University. Martin Meyerson, Chester Rapkin, John F. Collins [and] Leonard J. Duhl. Macmillan of Canada Toronto in Association with York University.

[10], 81, [1] pp.; 220 × 140 mm.
Frank Gerstein Lectures: York University Invitation Series.

2010. MUNRO, George

[Cover-title:] *Canadian Public Issues through inquiry*. Volume 1, Number 1, October 1969. [Editor: George Munro, Co-ordinator of Social Sciences, Halton County Board of Education. The Macmillan Company of Canada Limited Toronto].

[12] pp.; 275 × 215 mm.
Issued in paper.

2011. MUNRO, George

[Cover-title:] *Canadian Public Issues through inquiry*. Volume 1, Number 2, November 1969. [Editor: George Munro, Co-ordinator of Social Sciences, Halton County Board of Education. The Macmillan Company of Canada Limited Toronto].

[12] pp.; 275 × 215 mm.
Issued in paper.

2012. NEEDHAM, Richard J.

A Friend In Needham or A Writer's Notebook. Richard J. Needham. Illustrated by Randy Jones. Macmillan of Canada Toronto.

[10], 53, [1] pp.; 190 × 125 mm.

2013. PARRY, Hugh

Civilizations at War: The Struggle between Greece and Persia. Hugh Parry, Ph.D., Associate Professor of Classics and Humanities, York University, Toronto. Teacher Consultants: Robert J. Clark, Pauline Johnson Collegiate-Vocational School, Brantford, Ontario [and] Diane P. Rogers, formerly of Oakwood Collegiate Institute, Toronto. Macmillan of Canada/Toronto.

[4], 36 pp.; 225 × 147 mm.
Issued in paper.
The West and the World: Studies in History Series.

2014. PARRY, Hugh

Ideals of Education: Spartan Warrior and Athenian All-round Man. Hugh Parry, Ph.D., Associate Professor of Classics and Humanities, York University, Toronto. Teacher Consultants: Robert J. Clark, Pauline Johnson Collegiate-Vocational School, Brantford, Ontario [and] Diane P. Rogers, formerly of Oakwood Collegiate Institute, Toronto. Macmillan of Canada/Toronto.

[6], 36 pp.; 225 × 147 mm.
Issued in paper.
The West and the World: Studies in History Series.

2015. PARRY, Hugh

The Individual and His Society: Alcibiades—Greek Patriot or Traitor? Hugh Parry, Ph.D., Associate Professor of Classics and Humanities, York University, Toronto. Teacher Consultants: Robert J. Clark, Pauline Johnson Collegiate-Vocational School, Brantford, Ontario [and] Diane P. Rogers, formerly of Oakwood Collegiate Institute, Toronto. Macmillan of Canada/Toronto.

[4], 28 pp.; 225 × 147 mm.
Issued in paper.
The West and the World: Studies in History Series.

2016. PORTER, C.J.

Cross-Currents: Prose from the English-Speaking World. Edited by C.J Porter, Cobourg District Collegiate Institute East. The Macmillan Company of Canada Limited, Toronto.

[8], 308 pp.; 205 × 130 mm.
Revised in 1978 (see 2590). Issued in paper.

2017. REANEY, James

Colours In The Dark. James Reaney. Talonplays with Macmillan of Canada.

90 pp.; 210 × 133 mm.
Issued in paper.

2018. ROBERTS, B.A.

The Canada Books of Prose and Verse, *Teachers' Handbook for Our Literary Heritage*. Prepared by B.A. Roberts, M.A. (Oxon.), Co-ordinator for English, Saint John, New Brunswick. The Ryerson Press [and] The Macmillan Company of Canada Limited.

viii, 160 pp.; 213 × 135 mm.
Issued in paper.
Canada Books of Prose and Verse Series.

2019. ROBERTS, Leslie

Montreal: From Mission Colony to World City. Leslie Roberts. Macmillan of Canada Toronto/1969.

xvi, 356 pp.; 233 × 155 mm.
Issued in cloth and paper.

2020. ROGERS, Diane P.

Inside World Politics. Diane P. Rogers, formerly of Oakwood Collegiate Institute, Toronto and Robert J. Clark, formerly of Pauline Johnson Collegiate-Vocational School, Brantford. Macmillan of Canada/Toronto.

[20], 353, [1] pp.; 230 × 205 mm.

2021. SMITH, Frank A.

Corpse in Handcuffs. Frank A. Smith. Macmillan of Canada Toronto.

176 pp.; 200 × 130 mm.

2022. SOPHOCLES

Sophocles' *King Oedipus*. In the translation by W.B. Yeats. With Selections from *The Poetics of Aristotle* translated by G.M.A. Grube. Edited and with an introduction and notes by Balachandra Rajan, University of Western Ontario. Macmillan of Canada/Toronto.

[8], 99, [1] pp.; 180 × 100 mm.
Issued in paper.

2023. STAVRIANOS, Leften S.

China: A Culture Area in Perspective. Leften S. Stavrianos, Professor of History, Northwestern University [and] Roger F. Hackett, Professor of History, University of Michigan. Macmillan of Canada Toronto.

80 pp.; 257 × 195 mm.
Issued in paper.

2024. STAVRIANOS, Leften S.

Sub-Saharan Africa: A Culture Area in Perspective. Leften S. Stavrianos, Professor of History, Northwestern University [and] Loretta Kreider Andrews, Formerly Teacher, Evanston Township High School. Macmillan of Canada Toronto.

80 pp.; 257 × 195 mm.
Issued in paper.

2025. STEINBECK, John

The Moon Is Down. John Steinbeck. Study material prepared by Lawrence Darby, Head of the English Department, Westview Centennial Secondary School, North York. Macmillan of Canada Toronto.

x, 122 pp.; 188 × 125 mm.

2026. SUR, William R.

Teacher's Manual for This is Music 3. By William R. Sur, William R. Fisher, Adeline McCall [and] Mary R. Tolbert. Adapted for use in Canadian schools by Sherwood Robson, Supervisor of Music, North Vancouver and Mrs. Glenys Purden, Primary Consultant, North Vancouver. Macmillan of Canada Toronto.

xii, 176 pp.; 225 × 180 mm.
This is Music Series.

2027. SUR, William R.

Teacher's Manual for This is Music 4. By William R. Sur, Mary R. Tolbert,
William R. Fisher [and] Gladys Pitcher. Adapted for use in Canadian schools
by Paul J. Bourret, Edmonton Separate School Board [and] Elizabeth Filipkowski, University of Alberta. Macmillan of Canada Toronto.

xviii, 192 pp.; 225 × 180 mm.
This is Music Series.

2028. SUR, William R.

Teacher's Manual for This is Music 5. By William R. Sur, Robert E. Nye,
William R. Fisher [and] Mary R. Tolbert. Adapted for use in Canadian
schools by Paul J. Bourret, Edmonton Separate School Board [and] Elizabeth
Filipkowski, University of Alberta. Macmillan of Canada Toronto.

x, 215, [1] pp.; 225 × 180 mm.
This is Music Series.

2029. SUR, William R.

Teacher's Manual for This is Music 6. By William R. Sur, Robert E. Nye,
William R. Fisher [and] Mary R. Tolbert. Adapted for use in Canadian
schools by Paul J. Bourret, Edmonton Separate School Board [and] Elizabeth
Filipkowski, University of Alberta. Macmillan of Canada Toronto.

x, 240 pp.; 225 × 180 mm.
This is Music Series.

2030. THURBER, Walter A.

Exploring Life Science. By Walter A. Thurber and Robert E. Kilburn.
Canadian Edition. Macmillan of Canada Toronto.

496 pp.; 238 × 165 mm.
Exploring Science Series.

2031. THURBER, Walter A.

Exploring Physical Science. By Walter A. Thurber and Robert E. Kilburn.
Canadian Edition. Macmillan of Canada Toronto.

496 pp.; 238 × 165 mm.
Exploring Science Series.

2032. THURBER, Walter A.

Teacher's Manual: Exploring Earth Science. Canadian Edition. By Walter A.
Thurber [and] Robert E. Kilburn. Toronto: Macmillan of Canada.

[4], 152 pp.; 225 × 150 mm.
Issued in paper.
Exploring Science Series.

2033. TREASE, Geoffrey

Geoffrey Trease, *The Secret Fiord*. Study material prepared by Gordon H.
Budd, Assistant Superintendent of Schools, Windsor, Ontario. Macmillan of
Canada/Toronto 1969.

[8], 232 pp.; 183 × 122 mm.
Issued in paper.
Caravan Books Series.

2034. VARLEY, Peter

Canada. Photographed By Peter Varley. Introduction By Kildare Dobbs. 185 Illustrations, 18 In Colour. Toronto: Macmillan of Canada.

216 pp.; 210 × 145 mm.
First published in 1964 (see 1699). Revised edition published in 1965 (see 1757). This second revision issued in cloth and paper.

2035. YOUNG, Eric W.

A Course In World Geography. Young & Lowry. *Book V: The World Physical and Human*. By Eric W. Young, M.A. Maps and Diagrams By Peter Jackson. Toronto: The Macmillan Company of Canada Limited.

96 pp.; 230 × 152 mm.

1970

2036. ALLINGHAM, Margery

Margery Allingham, *Traitor's Purse*. Study material prepared by Gordon Coggins, M.A., Assistant Professor of English, Brock University, St. Catharines. Macmillan of Canada Toronto.

x, 245, [1] pp.; 180 × 121 mm.
Issued in paper.
Impact Books Series.

2037. BARKER, D.R.

The Story of Ancient Athens. By D.R. Barker. Illustrated by David Chalmers. Macmillan of Canada Toronto.

63, [1] pp.; 238 × 175 mm.
Issued in paper.

2038. BEAMER, B.E.

Experimental Science For The Non-Science Student. B.E. Beamer/W.W. Jackson. Macmillan of Canada.

103, [1] pp.; 278 × 214 mm.
Issued in paper.

2039. BLACKBURN, John H.

John H. Blackburn, *Land of Promise*. Edited and with an introduction by John Archer. Macmillan of Canada/Toronto.

xvi, 238 pp.; 233 × 155 mm.

2040. BROWN, T. Merritt

Specification and Uses of Econometric Models. T. Merritt Brown. The Macmillan Company of Canada Limited Toronto.

487, [1] pp.; 235 × 150 mm.

2041.   BROWNE, Harry
World History 2: The Twentieth Century. Harry Browne. Macmillan of
Canada Toronto.
   viii, 286 pp.; 210 × 145 mm.
   Issued in paper.

2042.   CHEVRIER, Emile D.
Topographic Map and Air Photo Interpretation. Emile D. Chevrier, Head of
the Geography Department, Brookfield High School, Ottawa [and] D.F.W.
Aitkens, Formerly Director of Mapping and Charting, Canadian Forces
Headquarters, Ottawa. The Macmillan Company of Canada Limited, To-
ronto.
   [6], 184 pp.; 302 × 253 mm.
   Published in French in 1980 (see 2677). Issued in paper, spiral-bound.

2043.   COLE, Leslie A.
Investigating Our World. Leslie A. Cole and Peter Saxton. General Editor:
J.A. Aikman, Vice-Principal, St. Catharines Teachers' College, St.
Catharines, Ontario. Illustrations by Frank Zsigo. Toronto: The Macmillan
Company of Canada Limited.
   14, 345, [1] pp.; 235 × 167 mm.

2044.   COOK, Lyn
The Magical Miss Mittens. Lyn Cook. Illustrated by Mary Davies. Macmillan
of Canada Toronto.
   233, [1] pp.; 218 × 135 mm.
   Issued in cloth and paper.

2045.   COWAN, Don
The Sounds of Music. Don Cowan, Faculty of Education, University of
Saskatchewan, Regina. Macmillan of Canada Toronto.
   [6], 144 pp.; 275 × 210 mm.
   Issued in paper, spiral-bound.

2046.   CRAWFORD, Douglas H.
Discovering Mathematics 6. Authors: Douglas H. Crawford, Ph.D., Professor and Chairman, Department of Mathematics, McArthur College of Education, Queen's University, Kingston, James F. Tennant, B.A., Principal,
Kingscourt Public School, Kingston [and] Denis J. Millan, Teacher, Calvin
Park Senior Public School, Kingston. J.M. Dent & Sons (Canada) Limited
[and] The Macmillan Company of Canada Limited.
   xvi, 389, [1] pp.; 230 × 163 mm.
   Discovering Mathematics Series.

2047. CREAL, Michael

The Dynamics of Revolution: France, 1789-1794. Michael Creal, Chairman, Division of Humanities, York University, Toronto. Teacher Consultants: Gary Smith, Associate Professor of History, The College of Education, University of Toronto [and] Robert J. Clark, Assistant Professor of History, Althouse College of Education, University of Western Ontario. Macmillan of Canada/Toronto.

[6], 44, pp.; 225 × 150 mm.
Issued in paper.
The West and the World: Studies in History Series.

2048. CREAL, Michael

The Idea of Progress: The Origins of Modern Optimism. Michael Creal, Chairman, Division of Humanities, York University, Toronto. Consultants: Gary Smith, Associate Professor of History, Faculty of Education, University of Toronto [and] Robert J. Clark, Assistant Professor of History, Althouse College of Education, University of Western Ontario. Macmillan of Canada/Toronto.

[4], 27, [1] pp.; 225 × 150 mm.
Issued in paper.
The West and the World: Studies in History Series.

2049. CREAL, Michael

Voltaire: Passionate Fighter for Liberty. Michael Creal, Chairman, Division of Humanities, York University, Toronto. Teacher Consultants: Gary Smith, Associate Professor of History, Faculty of Education, University of Toronto [and] Robert J. Clark, Assistant Professor of History, Althouse College of Education, University of Western Ontario. Macmillan of Canada/Toronto.

[6], 32 pp.; 225 × 150 mm.
Issued in paper.
The West and the World: Studies in History Series.

2050. CREIGHTON, Donald

Canada's First Century 1867-1967. Donald Creighton. Macmillan of Canada Toronto.

[12], 372 pp.; 230 × 155 mm.
Issued in cloth and paper. Reprinted in 1972 and 1974. Reprinted in the Laurentian Library (No. 43) in 1976.

2051. DAVIDSON, V. Laurence

Anchors Aweigh. Edited by V. Laurence Davidson, B.A., B.ED., Caledonia Junior High School, Dartmouth, Nova Scotia and Josephine V. Harris, B.A., B.ED., Supervisor of Curriculum, Schools Administration Office, Dartmouth, Nova Scotia. *Passport to Reading* is a multi-level reading series [etc.]. The Macmillan Company of Canada Limited, Toronto.

[10], 207, [1] pp.; 234 × 153 mm.
Passport to Reading Series.

2052. DAVIES, Robertson

Fifth Business. A novel by Robertson Davies. Macmillan of Canada/Toronto.

[6], 314 pp.; 220 × 140 mm.

2053. DAVIES, Robertson

[Caption-title on p. 1:] *The Heart of a Merry Christmas*. [On front cover:] Christmas greetings and best wishes for the New Year from The Macmillan Company of Canada Limited, 1970.

[12] pp.; 199 × 136 mm.
Issued in paper. Not for public sale.

2054. FIELDEN, Charlotte

Crying As She Ran. A Novel by Charlotte Fielden. Macmillan of Canada Toronto.

[12], 164 pp.; 223 × 138 mm.
Issued in cloth and paper.

2055. GALLOWAY, David

The Elizabethan Theatre II. Papers given at the Second International Conference on Elizabethan Theatre held at the University of Waterloo, Ontario, in July 1969. Edited and with an introduction by David Galloway, Department of English, University of New Brunswick. Published in collaboration with the University of Waterloo. Macmillan of Canada Toronto.

xvi, 148 pp.; 220 × 138 mm.

2056. GOULSON, Cary F.

Seventeenth-Century Canada: Source Studies. Cary F. Goulson, Associate Professor, Faculty of Education, University of Victoria. Macmillan of Canada/Toronto.

xx, 491, [1] pp.; 227 × 155 mm.
Issued in paper.

2057. GRANATSTEIN, J.L.

The Fuhrer: Adolf Hitler, Master of Germany. J.L. Granatstein, Assistant Professor, Department of History, York University, Toronto. Teacher Consultant: Robert Clark, formerly of Pauline Johnson Collegiate-Vocational School, Brantford, Ontario. Macmillan of Canada/Toronto.

[4], 44 pp.; 225 × 150 mm.
Issued in paper.
The West and the World: Studies in History Series.

2058. GRANATSTEIN, J.L.

Response to Disaster: Germany, France, and the Great Depression. J.L. Granatstein, Assistant Professor, Department of History, York University, Toronto. Teacher Consultant: Robert Clark, formerly of Pauline Johnson Collegiate-Vocational School, Brantford, Ontario. Macmillan of Canada/Toronto.

[4], 44 pp.; 225 × 150 mm.
Issued in paper.
The West and the World: Studies in History Series.

2059. GRANATSTEIN, J.L.

Under Fire: Soldiers and Civilians in World War Two. J.L. Granatstein,
Assistant Professor, Department of History, York University, Toronto.
Teacher Consultant: Robert Clark, formerly of Pauline Johnson
Collegiate-Vocational School, Brantford, Ontario. Macmillan of Canada/To-
ronto.

[4], 60 pp.; 225 × 150 mm.
Issued in paper.
The West and the World: Studies in History Series.

2060. GRAY, James H.

The Boy from Winnipeg. James H. Gray. Illustrated by Myra Lowenthal.
Macmillan of Canada/Toronto.

[10], 204 pp.; 230 × 153 mm.
Reprinted in the Laurentian Library (No. 52) in 1977.

2061. GREENE, E.J.H.

*Reflex French, Integrated Edition: A Comprehensive Course in Modern French
Usage*. By E.J.H. Greene, Manoël Faucher [and] Dennis M. Healy. Illustra-
tions by François Bret, Directeur de l'Ecole des Beaux-Arts de Marseille.
Tapes produced by Edward Marxheimer. Macmillan of Canada Toronto,
Macmillan & Co. Ltd. London [and] St. Martin's Press New York.

xxii, 256 pp.; 220 × 145 mm.
First published in 1960 (see 1492). Reprinted in 1962, 1963 and 1965. Integrated
edition published in 1966. Earlier printing not located.

2062. GREY OWL

The Adventures of Sajo and her Beaver People. By Grey Owl. Toronto: The
Macmillan Company of Canada Limited.

208 pp.; 190 × 125 mm.
Reprinted in 1973 in paper and in the Laurentian Library (No. 55) in 1977 as *Sajo
and the Beaver People*.

2063. KIERAN, Sheila

The Non-Deductible Woman: a handbook for working wives and mothers. Sheila
Kieran. Macmillan of Canada/Toronto.

xiv, 107, [1] pp.; 176 × 105 mm.
Issued in paper.

2064. KILBOURN, William

Canada: A Guide to the Peaceable Kingdom. Edited and with an introduction
by William Kilbourn. Macmillan of Canada Toronto.

xx, 345, [1] pp.; 233 × 154 mm.
Issued in cloth and paper. Reprinted in the Laurentian Library (No. 31) in 1975.

2065. LEVINE, Norman

Norman Levine, *From a Seaside Town*. Macmillan of Canada Toronto.
220 pp.; 200 × 130 mm.

2066.   LEVITT, Kari

Silent Surrender: the multinational corporation in Canada. Kari Levitt. With a preface by Mel Watkins. Macmillan of Canada/Toronto.

> xxii, 185, [1] pp.; 195 × 125 mm.
> There is also a student edition of this title. Issued in cloth and paper. Reprinted in 1972, 1974 and 1975.

2067.   MACKENZIE, Alexander

The Journals and Letters of Sir Alexander Mackenzie. Edited by W. Kaye Lamb. Macmillan of Canada Toronto.

> viii, 551, [1] pp.; 232 × 157 mm.
> The Hakluyt Society, Extra Series No. 41.

2068.   McLAUGHLIN, Lorrie

Shogomoc Sam. Lorrie McLaughlin. Illustrated by Randy Jones. Macmillan of Canada Toronto.

> 61, [1] pp.; 250 × 175 mm.
> Issued in cloth and paper.

2069.   McLEOD, William E.

William E. McLeod, *Personnel Management for Canadians*. Macmillan of Canada/Toronto.

> [14], 186 pp.; 202 × 125 mm.
> Issued in cloth and paper.

2070.   MERSEREAU, M. Grace

Tuned In. Edited by M. Grace Mersereau, Head of the English Department, Ross Sheppard Composite High School, Edmonton, Alberta. Macmillan of Canada.

> [8], 262 pp.; 197 × 125 mm.
> Issued in limp cloth.

2071.   MITCHELL, John

The Yellow Briar: A story of the Irish on the Canadian countryside. By Patrick Slater [pseud.]. With an account of the author by Dorothy Bishop. Illustrated by Alan Daniel. Toronto: Macmillan of Canada.

> [6], 196 pp.; 234 × 155 mm.
> First published in 1941 (see 919). First school edition published in 1966 (see 1796). Issued in cloth and paper.

2072.   MOIR, John S.

Character and Circumstance: Essays in Honour of Donald Grant Creighton. Edited by John S. Moir. Macmillan of Canada/Toronto/1970.

> xiv, 241, [1] pp.; 234 × 154 mm.

2073. MUNRO, George

[Cover-title:] *Canadian Public Issues through inquiry*. Volume 1, Number 4, February 1970. [Editor: George Munro, Co-ordinator of Social Sciences, Halton County Board of Education. The Macmillan Company of Canada Limited Toronto].

[12] pp.; 275 × 215 mm.
Issued in paper.

2074. MUNRO, George

[Cover-title:] *Canadian Public Issues through inquiry*. Volume 1, Number 5, April 1970. [Editor: George Munro, Co-ordinator of Social Sciences, Halton County Board of Education. The Macmillan Company of Canada Limited Toronto].

[12] pp.; 275 × 215 mm.
Issued in paper.

2075. MUNRO, George

[Cover-title:] *Canadian Public Issues through inquiry*. Volume 1, Number 6, May 1970. [Editor: George Munro, Co-ordinator of Social Sciences, Halton County Board of Education. The Macmillan Company of Canada Limited Toronto].

[12] pp.; 275 × 215 mm.
Issued in paper.

2076. *My Toronto*. With a foreword by Peter C. Newman. Toronto: Macmillan of Canada.

[8], 117, [1] pp.; 175 × 105 mm.
Reprinted in 1970 in paper.

2077. NEEDHAM, Richard J.

The Hypodermic Needham. By Richard J. Needham. Illustrated by Franklin. Macmillan of Canada Toronto.

[12], 127, [1] pp.; 218 × 138 mm.

2078. RABY, Ormond

Radio's First Voice: The Story of Reginald Fessenden. Ormond Raby. Macmillan of Canada/Toronto.

[14], 161, [1] pp.; 220 × 140 mm.
Issued in cloth and paper.

2079. SMYTHE, James M.

Elements of Geography: Physical Geography. James M. Smythe, M.A., Head of the Geography Department, Earl Haig Secondary School, North York, Charles G. Brown, B.A., Superintendent of Program and Instruction, Board of Education, North York [and] Eric H. Fors, B.A., Vice-principal, A.Y. Jackson Secondary School, North York. Maps and Diagrams by A. Diana and F. Zsigo. Macmillan of Canada/Toronto.

xii, 292 pp.; 225 × 160 mm.
Physical Geography is a new revison of the first three sections of *Elements of Geography*, first published by Macmillan in 1959 (see 1474). A revised edition was published in 1964 (see 1698). This edition issued in limp cloth. A special revised edition was published in 1976 (see 2435). In 1978 and 1979 English and French metric editions were published (see 2602 and 2655).

2080. STIRLING, Norman

Introduction to Technical Drawing. Revised Edition. Norman Stirling, Technical Director, Courtice Secondary School, Courtice, Ontario. Toronto: The Macmillan Company of Canada Limited.

[10], 293, [1] pp.; 258 × 182 mm.
First published in 1963 (see 1653). Metric edition published in 1977 (see 2517).
Macmillan Basic Technical Series.

2081. SWIFT, W.H.

Educational Administration in Canada: A Memorial to A.W. Reeves. W. H. Swift, Former Deputy Minister of Education, Province of Alberta, In consultation with H.T. Coutts, Dean, Faculty of Education, The University of Alberta. Macmillan of Canada Toronto.

[12], 81, [1] pp.; 233 × 150 mm.

2082. TRUEMAN, R.W.

Our Science Program, *Flights, kites, and Boomerangs*. R.W. Trueman, Vice-Principal, Topcliff Public School, North York. 1970 The Macmillan Company of Canada Limited, Toronto.

31, [1] pp.; 225 × 152 mm.
Issued in paper.
Our Science Program Series.

2083. WILSON, Charles W.

Mapping the Frontier: Charles Wilson's Diary Of The Survey Of The 49th Parallel, 1858-1862, While Secretary Of The British Boundary Commission. Edited and with an introduction by George F.G. Stanley. Toronto: Macmillan of Canada.

[10], 182 pp.; 215 × 140 mm.
Issued in cloth and paper.

2084. WILSON, Clifford

Campbell of the Yukon. Clifford Wilson. Macmillan of Canada.

xxvi, 189, [1] pp.; 217 × 140 mm.

2084A WRIGHT, Richard B.

The Weekend Man. A novel by Richard Wright. Macmillan Toronto [and] London.

[10], 269, [E pp.; 215 × 135 mm.
Reprinted in the Laurentian Library (No. 57) in 1977.

1971

2085. BAIRD, Irene

Irene Baird, *The Climate of Power*. Macmillan of Canada Toronto.

255, [1] pp.; 204 × 130 mm.

2086. BRINKHURST, Ralph O.

This Good, Good Earth: our fight for survival. Ralph O. Brinkhurst [and] Donald A. Chant. Macmillan of Canada/Toronto.

xii, 174 pp.; 218 × 135 mm.
Issued in cloth and paper.

2087. CARELESS, J.M.S.

Edited by J.M.S. Careless, *Colonists & Canadiens 1760-1867*. [Toronto Macmillan of Canada 1971].

x, 278 pp.; 222 × 143 mm.
Imprint on verso of half-title. Issued in cloth and paper.

2088. COOK, Ramsay

The Maple Leaf Forever: Essays on Nationalism and Politics in Canada. Ramsay Cook. Macmillan of Canada Toronto.

[14], 253, [1] pp.; 200 × 125 mm.
Issued in cloth and paper. Reprinted in the Laurentian Library (No. 54) in 1977.

2089. COVELL, Harold M.

[Cover-title:] *Effective Reading 2*. Harold M. Covell/John McGechaen. [©McGraw-Hill Ryerson Limited and the Macmillan Company of Canada Limited, 1971. All rights reserved. No part of this book may be reproduced in any form without permission in writing from the publishers. Printed and bound in Canada].

91, [1] pp.; 279 × 214 mm.
Imprint at foot of p. [1]. Issued in paper.
Effective Reading Books Series.

2090. CREIGHTON, Donald

The Story Of Canada. By Donald Creighton. Macmillan of Canada.

319, [1] pp.; 220 × 138 mm.
First published in 1959 (see 1710A). This revised edition issued in cloth and paper.
Reprinted in the Laurentian Library (No. 34) in 1975.

2091. DAVIS, Glenna

Communication 4. Glenna Davis. Macmillan of Canada/Toronto.

[10], 342 pp.; 233 × 183 mm.
Macmillan Language Program.

2092. DAVIS, Glenna
Idea Book For Teachers: Communication 4. Glenna Davis. Macmillan of Canada/Toronto.
> x, 118 pp.; 225 × 180 mm.
> Issued in paper.
> Macmillan Language Program.

2093. DAWE, Alan
Four Approaches to Prose. Alan Dawe, Vancouver City College. Macmillan of Canada/Toronto.
> xiv, 258 pp.; 214 × 134 mm.
> Issued in paper.

2094. DOERN, G. Bruce
The Structures of Policy-Making in Canada. Edited by G. Bruce Doern and Peter Aucoin. Macmillan of Canada [and] St. Martin's Press.
> [10], 294 pp. + chart; 222 × 145 mm.
> Issued in cloth and paper (the paper issue lacks the St. Martin's Press imprint and is dated on the title-page).

2095. FALKNER, J. Meade
Moonfleet. By J. Meade Falkner. [Quotation]. Edward Arnold (Publishers) Ltd. London [and] The Macmillan Company of Canada Limited Toronto.
> 255, [1] pp.; 175 × 112 mm.
> First published in 1967 (see 1840). Issued in paper.

2096. FETHERLING, Doug
Our Man in Utopia. Doug Fetherling. Illustrated by William Kimber. Macmillan of Canada Toronto.
> [8], 54, [2] pp.; 215 × 140 mm.
> Issued in cloth and paper.

2097. FORSTER, E.M.
Maurice. A novel by E.M. Forster. Macmillan of Canada/Toronto.
> xii, 240 pp.; 223 × 142 mm.

2098. GRAY, James H.
Red Lights on the Prairies. James H. Gray. Macmillan of Canada Toronto.
> xvi, 207, [1] pp.; 235 × 160 mm.

2099. GREASON, George K.
Third Edition. *Canadian Democracy at Work*. George K. Greason, Formerly Head of History Department, Downsview Secondary School, North York [and] Roy C. King, Principal, C.B. Parsons Junior High School, North York. Drawings by Dorothy Mould and Vernon Mould. Toronto: The Macmillan Company of Canada Limited.
> [8], 119, [1] pp.; 215 × 145 mm.
> First published in 1962 (see 1574). Revised in 1966 (see 1781A) and 1969 (see 1984). This edition revised in 1977 (see 2476A). Issued in paper.

2100. GROVE, Jane

Fashion. [Quotation]. Jane Grove. Illustrations by Renate Melinsky. Macmillan of Canada.

    64 pp.; 214 × 145 mm.
    Reprinted in 1973, 1975 and 1979. Issued in paper.

2101. HAMPSON, Cy

Into the Woods Beyond. By Cy Hampson. Macmillan of Canada/Toronto.

    [8], 118 pp.; 233 × 180 mm.

2102. HEFFRON, Dorris

A Nice Fire and some Moonpennies. Dorris Heffron. Macmillan of Canada Toronto.

    160 pp.; 207 × 130 mm.

2103. HENDERSON, Jim

Writers in Conflict. Jim Henderson, M.A., Assistant Co-ordinator, Language Arts, Halton County Board of Education [and] Brian Penman, B.A., Head of the English Department, Oakville-Trafalgar High School. Macmillan of Canada Toronto.

    144 pp.; 268 × 208 mm.
    Issued in paper.

2104. HORTON, John A.

Communication 3. John A. Horton. Macmillan of Canada/Toronto.

    [10], 265, [1] pp.; 233 × 183 mm.
    Macmillan Language Program.

2105. HORTON, John A.

Idea Book: Communication 3. John A. Horton. Macmillan of Canada/Toronto.

    x, 96 pp.; 225 × 180 mm.
    Issued in paper.
    Macmillan Language Program.

2106. IRVING, Robert M.

Crisis: Readings in Environmental Issues and Strategies. Edited by Robert M. Irving and George B. Priddle. Macmillan of Canada - Toronto [and] St. Martin's Press - New York.

    xviii, 354 pp.; 220 × 140 mm.
    Issued in cloth and paper.

2107. JACKSON, Robert J.

Robert J. Jackson [and] Michael B. Stein, *Issues in Comparative Politics: A Text with Readings*. St. Martin's Press New York [and] Macmillan Toronto, London.

    xii, 412 pp.; 233 × 150 mm.
    Issued in paper.

2108. KENYON, W.A.
The Battle for James Bay 1686. W.A. Kenyon [and] J.R. Turnbull. Macmillan of Canada Toronto.
> xviii, 132 pp.; 220 × 140 mm.
> Issued in cloth and paper.

2109. KNOX, Alexander
Alexander Knox, *Night of the White Bear*. Macmillan of Canada Toronto.
> 256 pp.; 205 × 135 mm.

2110. LANGFORD, Cameron
The Winter of the Fisher. Cameron Langford. Macmillan of Canada Toronto.
> 222 pp.; 215 × 145 mm.

2111. LEITCH, Adelaide
The Blue Roan. Adelaide Leitch. Illustrated by Charles Robinson. Macmillan of Canada Toronto.
> [6], 185, [1] pp.; 205 × 135 mm.

2112. LEVINE, Norman
Norman Levine, *I Don't Want to Know Anyone Too Well And Other Stories*. Macmillan.
> 160 pp.; 195 × 130 mm.

2113. MacEWEN, Gwendolyn
King of Egypt, King of Dreams. A novel by Gwendolyn MacEwen. Macmillan of Canada Toronto.
> [10], 287, [1] pp.; 215 × 135 mm.
> Issued in cloth and paper.

2114. MACMILLAN, Harold
Riding The Storm 1956-1959. Harold Macmillan. London Macmillan Melbourne Toronto 1971.
> x, 786 pp.; 220 × 150 mm.

2115. MALLORY, J.R.
The Structure of Canadian Government. J.R. Mallory. Macmillan of Canada Toronto.
> xiv, 418 pp.; 233 × 155 mm.
> Issued in paper.

2116. MANDEL, Eli
English Poems of the Twentieth Century. Selected by Eli Mandel and Desmond Maxwell. Macmillan of Canada/1971.
> [22], 221, [1] pp.; 175 × 102 mm.
> Issued in paper.

2117.   McNAMEE, James

Them damn Canadians hanged Louis Riel! A novel by James McNamee.
Macmillan of Canada/Toronto.

[8], 133, [1] pp.; 220 × 140 mm.
Issued in cloth and paper.

2118.   NORDEGG, Martin

The Possibilities of Canada Are Truly Great: Memoirs 1906-1924. By Martin
Nordegg. Edited and with an Introduction by T.D. Regehr. Macmillan of
Canada.

xvi, 246 pp.; 217 × 140 mm.

2119.   ORMSBY, Margaret A.

Margaret A. Ormsby, *British Columbia: a History.* Macmillan of Canada.

x, 566 pp.; 240 × 160 mm.
First published in 1958 (see 1441). This edition revised. Issued in cloth and paper.

2120.   OWEN, Don

Nobody Waved Good-bye. Don Owen. Edited by Herman Voaden, M.A.,
F.R.S.A., Formerly Director of English, Central High School of Commerce,
Toronto. Macmillan of Canada, Toronto.

[8], 120 pp.; 180 × 123 mm.
First published in 1966 as part of *Nobody Waved Good-bye and Other Plays* (see
1816). Issued in paper.

2121.   PAL, I.-D.

Canadian Economic Issues: Introductory Readings. Edited by I.-D. Pal. Macmillan of Canada 1971.

[12], 630, [2] pp.; 235 × 153 mm.
Issued in cloth and paper.

2122.   RUBINOFF, Lionel

Tradition and Revolution. Ivan Illich, C.S. Holling, George Grant, Robert J.
Liften, Harold Taylor, [and] Jacob Bronowski. Edited by Lionel Rubinoff.
Macmillan of Canada/Toronto, St. Martin's Press/New York in Association
with York University 1971.

[12], 173, [1] pp.; 220 × 140 mm.
Frank Gerstein Lectures: York University Invitation Series.

2123.   SCHULL, Joseph

*The Century of the Sun: The First Hundred Years Of Sun Life Assurance
Company of Canada.* Joseph Schull. 1971 Macmillan of Canada Toronto.

[14], 158 pp.; 220 × 140 mm.
Issued in cloth and paper.

2124.   SCHULL, Joseph

Joseph Schull, *Rebellion: The Rising in French Canada 1837.* Macmillan of
Canada Toronto.

xiv, 226 pp.; 233 × 155 mm.

2125.   SHACK, Sybil F.

Communication 2. Sybil Shack. Macmillan of Canada/Toronto.

[10], 277, [1] pp.; 233 × 183 mm.
Macmillan Language Program.

2126.   SHACK, Sybil F.

Idea Book: Communication 2. Sybil Shack. Macmillan of Canada/Toronto.

x, 158 pp.; 225 × 180 mm.
Issued in paper.
Macmillan Language Program.

2127.   SIMPSON, Leo

A novel by Leo Simpson, *Arkwright*. Macmillan of Canada Toronto.

[14], 442 pp.; 211 × 130 mm.
Issued in cloth and paper.

2128.   SUR, William R.

This is Music for Today: 7. Canadian Edition. William R. Sur [and] Charlotte Dubois. Canadian Edition adapted by Paul J. Bourret, Supervisor of Music, Edmonton Separate School Board and Sherwood Robson, Supervisor of Music, North Vancouver. Macmillan of Canada Toronto.

256 pp.; 265 × 200 mm.
This is Music Series.

2129.   THOMPSON, David

David Thompson, *Travels in Western North America, 1784-1812*. Edited by Victor G. Hopwood. Macmillan of Canada Toronto.

[10], 342 pp.; 224 × 141 mm.
Issued in cloth and paper.

2130.   THURBER, Walter A.

Exploring Science: Stage One. By Walter A. Thurber and Robert E. Kilburn. Macmillan of Canada Toronto.

448 pp.; 235 × 160 mm.
First published as *Exploring Science 7* in 1967 (see 1889). This edition revised.
Exploring Science Series.

2131.   THURBER, Walter A.

Exploring Science: Stage Two. Walter A. Thurber and Robert E. Kilburn. Macmillan of Canada Toronto.

429, [1] pp.; 235 × 160 mm.
First published as *Exploring Science 8* in 1967 (see 1889A). This edition revised.
Exploring Science Series.

2132.   THURBER, Walter A.

Exploring Science: Stage Three. By Walter A. Thurber and Robert E. Kilburn. Macmillan of Canada Toronto.

624 pp.; 235 × 160 mm.
First published as *Exploring Science 9* in 1967 (see 1890). This edition revised.
Exploring Science Series.

2133. THURBER, Walter A.

Teacher's Manual: Exploring Science Stage One. Walter A. Thurber [and] Robert E. Kilburn. Macmillan of Canada Toronto.

[2], 139, [1] pp.; 225 × 150 mm.
Issued in paper.
Exploring Science Series.

2134. THURBER, Walter A.

Teacher's Manual: Exploring Science Stage Two. Walter A. Thurber [and] Robert E. Kilburn. Macmillan of Canada Toronto.

[2], 147, [1] pp.; 225 × 150 mm.
Issued in paper.
Exploring Science Series.

2135. THURBER, Walter A.

Teacher's Manual: Exploring Science Stage Three. Walter A. Thurber [and] Robert E. Kilburn. Macmillan of Canada Toronto.

[4], 254 pp.; 225 × 150 mm.
Issued in paper.
Exploring Science Series.

2136. WATSON, Ulah Jacobson

Resource Book for the Magic of Reading Series. By Ulah Jacobson Watson, B.Ed., Formerly Supervisor of Kindergarten and Primary Instruction, Greater Victoria Schools. Macmillan of Canada/Toronto.

[8], 81, [1] pp.; 210 × 145 mm.
Issued in paper.

2137. YOUNG, Scott

Scott Young [and] George Robertson. *Face-Off: a novel*. Based on an idea created by John F. Bassett. Macmillan of Canada Toronto.

[6], 250 pp.; 220 × 142 mm.

1972

2138. AFFLECK, Muriel A.

Communication 1. Muriel A. Affleck and Katherine G. Therrien. Macmillan of Canada/Toronto.

[10], 246 pp.; 233 × 183 mm.
Macmillan Language Program.

2139. BELL, Robert

Teacher's Guide for Inside World Politics. Prepared by Robert Bell, Ancaster Secondary School, Ancaster, Ontario for *Inside World Politics* by Diane P. Rogers and Robert J. Clark. Macmillan of Canada, 70 Bond Street, Toronto 2, Ontario, 1972.

[4], 129, [1] pp.; 275 × 212 mm.
Issued in paper.

2140. BIRD, Will R.
Will R. Bird, *Angel Cove*. Macmillan of Canada Toronto.
[10], 236 pp.; 217 × 135 mm.

2141. BURROUGHS, Peter
The Canadian Crisis and British Colonial Policy, 1828-1841. By Peter Burroughs, Professor of History, Dalhousie University, Halifax, Nova Scotia.
1972 Macmillan of Canada/Toronto.
viii, 118, [2] pp.; 200 × 130 mm.
Issued in cloth and paper.

2142. COVELL, Harold M.
Dialogue. Edited by Harold M. Covell and James W. Greig. Macmillan of
Canada/Toronto.
[10], 276 pp.; 215 × 155 mm.

2143. COVELL, Harold M.
Viewpoint. Edited by Harold M. Covell and James W. Greig. Macmillan of
Canada/Toronto.
[10], 246 pp.; 215 × 157 mm.

2144. CREIGHTON, Donald
Towards the Discovery of Canada: Selected Essays. Donald Creighton. Macmillan of Canada Toronto.
[8], 315, [1] pp.; 220 × 140 mm.
Issued in cloth and paper.

2145. DAVIES, Robertson
The Manticore. A Novel By Robertson Davies. Macmillan of Canada Toronto.
[8], 280 pp.; 220 × 144 mm.

2146. DIEFENBAKER, John G.
*Those Things We Treasure: A Selection of Speeches on Freedom and in Defence
of Our Parliamentary Heritage*. The Right Honourable John G. Diefenbaker.
Macmillan of Canada Toronto.
x, 170 pp.; 175 × 105 mm.
Issued in paper.

2147. FLIEDNER, Leonard J.
Chemistry: man's servant. Leonard J. Fliedner, Principal, Stuyvesant High
School, New York [and] Louis Teichman, Principal, James M. Kieran
Junior High School, New York. Macmillan of Canada Toronto.
x, 625, [1] pp.; 235 × 160 mm.

2148.   FLIEDNER, Leonard J.

Laboratory Manual for Chemistry: Man's Servant. By Leonard J. Fliedner, Principal, Stuyvesant High School, New York and Louis Teichman, Principal, Margaret Knox Junior High School, New York, Formerly Chairman, Science Department, George Washington High School, New York. Macmillan of Canada Toronto.

    xii, 225, [1] pp.; 273 × 215 mm.
    Issued in paper. Reprinted in 1975.

2149.   FOWKE, Edith

Canadian Vibrations - Canadiennes. Biographical and historical notes Edith Fowke - Notices biographiques et historiques. Consultant on guitar chords Bram Morrison - Conseiller en accords de guitare. Macmillan of Canada.

    [10], 154 pp.; 220 × 140 mm.
    Issued in cloth and paper.

2150.   FOWKE, Edith

A Songbook For Young Voyageurs/Chantons Avec Les Jeunes Voyageurs. Biographical and historical notes, Edith Fowke, Notices biographiques et historiques. Consultant on guitar chords, Bram Morrison, Conseiller en accords de guitare. Macmillan of Canada.

    [10], 154 pp.; 214 × 138 mm.
    Issued in paper.

2151.   FRANCE, Norman

Answer Book for Mathematics for Living. Norman France, M.A., M.Ed., Ph.D., Director of Educational Research, University of Saskatchewan, Regina. Macmillan of Canada/Toronto.

    [66] pp.; 210 × 136 mm.
    Issued in paper.

2152.   FRANCE, Norman

Mathematics For Living. Norman France, M.A., M.Ed., Ph.D., Director of Educational Research, University of Saskatchewan, Regina. Illustrated by Peter Lole. Macmillan of Canada/Toronto.

    [8], 322 pp.; 240 × 165 mm.

2153.   GRAHAME, Gordon Hill

Short Days Ago. Gordon Hill Grahame. Macmillan of Canada Toronto.

    [6], 218 pp.; 225 × 145 mm.

2154.   GRAY, James H.

Booze: The Impact of Whisky on the Prairie West. James H. Gray. Macmillan of Canada/Toronto.

    xvi, 243, [1] pp.; 234 × 153 mm.

2155. HALLETT, Fred H.

Technology for Industrial Manufacturing. Fred H. Hallett, B.Sc., Supervisor of Adult Education, Hamilton Board of Education, Hamilton, Ontario and Albert E. Mills, C. Eng., M.I. Mech. E., P.Eng., Master, School of Technology, Niagara College of Applied Arts and Technology, Welland, Ontario. Macmillan of Canada Toronto.

[10], 676 pp.; 236 × 168 mm.

2156. LUNN, Richard

Space Suits & Gumshoes: An Anthology of Science Fiction and Crime Stories. Selected and edited by Richard Lunn. Macmillan of Canada/Toronto.

[8], 275, [1] pp.; 193 × 123 mm.
Issued in paper.

2157. MacEWEN, Gwendolyn

The Armies of the Moon. Gwendolyn MacEwen. Macmillan of Canada Toronto.

[12], 75, [3] pp.; 220 × 143 mm.
Issued in cloth and paper.

2158. MACMILLAN, Harold

Pointing The Way 1959-1961. Harold Macmillan. London Macmillan Melbourne Toronto 1972.

viii, 504 pp.; 220 × 150 mm.

2159. MAY, Charles Paul

A Book of Insects. By Charles Paul May. Illustrations By John Crosby. St. Martin's Press New York [and] Macmillan of Canada Toronto.

118 pp.; 213 × 140 mm.

2160. MENDEL, Frederick S.

The Book and Life of a Little Man: Reminiscences of Frederick S. Mendel. Macmillan of Canada Toronto.

xvi, 164 pp.; 220 × 140 mm.

2161. MILLER, H.G.

Hand and machine woodwork. Revised Edition. H.G. Miller, Technical Director, General Brock High School, Burlington, Ontario. Illustrated by G. Fantuz, Keith King, and Keith Miller. The Macmillan Company of Canada Limited Toronto.

[12], 242 pp.; 240 × 162 mm.
First published in 1962 (see 1591). Metric edition published in 1978 (see 2581).
Macmillan Basic Technical Series.

2162. MINIFIE, James M.

Homesteader: A Prairie Boyhood Recalled. James M. Minifie. Macmillan of Canada Toronto.

[10], 222 pp.; 233 × 152 mm.
Reprinted in 1973 in paper.

2163. MITCHELL, Ken

Wandering Rafferty. A novel by Ken Mitchell. Macmillan of Canada Toronto.
[10], 210 pp.; 218 × 140 mm.

2164. MUNSTERHJELM, Erik

A Dog Named Wolf. Erik Munsterhjelm. Macmillan of Canada Toronto.
136 pp.; 220 × 140 mm.

2165. NEATBY, H. Blair

The Politics of Chaos: Canada In The Thirties. H. Blair Neatby. Macmillan of
Canada/Toronto.
[8], 196 pp.; 220 × 143 mm.
Issued in cloth and paper.

2166. NEUFELD, E.P.

The Financial System of Canada: Its Growth and Development. E. P. Neufeld.
Macmillan of Canada.
[24], 645, [1] pp.; 240 × 165 mm.

2167. NICHOLS, Ruth

Ruth Nichols, *The Marrow Of The World*. Illustrated by Trina Schart
Hyman. Macmillan of Canada, Toronto.
[8], 168 pp.; 215 × 140 mm.
Reprinted in 1977 in paper.

2168. NORTH, Dick

The Mad Trapper of Rat River. Dick North. Macmillan of Canada/Toronto.
xxii, 144 pp.; 223 × 140 mm.
Reprinted in the Laurentian Library (No. 42) in 1976.

2169. OSTRY, Sylvia

Labour Economics in Canada. Second Edition. Sylvia Ostry [and] Mahmood
A. Zaidi. Volume II of *Labour Policy and Labour Economics in Canada*.
Second Edition by H.D. Woods, Sylvia Ostry [and] Mahmood A. Zaidi.
Macmillan of Canada Toronto.
[14], 354 pp.; 232 × 155 mm.
First published in 1962 (see 1604). Third revised edition published in 1979 (see
2650).

2170. PARRY, Hugh

Julius Caesar: The Legend and the Man. Hugh Parry, Ph.D., Associate
Professor of Humanities, York University, Toronto. Teacher Consultant:
Robert Clark, Department of History, Althouse College of Education, Lon-
don. Macmillan of Canada/Toronto.
[6], 49, [1] pp.; 225 × 147 mm.
Issued in paper.
The West and the World: Studies in History Series.

2171. PARRY, Hugh

Order and Revolution: Cicero and the Conspiracy of Catiline. Hugh Parry, Ph.D., Associate Professor of Humanities, York University, Toronto. Teacher Consultant: Robert Clark, Department of History, Althouse College of Education, London. Macmillan of Canada/Toronto.

[4], 43, [1] pp.; 225 × 147 mm.
Issued in paper.
The West and the World: Studies in History Series.

2172. PARRY, Hugh

People as Possessions: Master and Slave in the Roman World. Hugh Parry, Ph.D., Associate Professor of Humanities, York University, Toronto. Teacher Consultant: Robert Clark, Department of History, Althouse College of Education, London. Macmillan of Canada/Toronto.

[4], 43, [1] pp.; 225 × 147 mm.
Issued in paper.
The West and the World: Studies in History Series.

2173. PATTON, John

Civilization in Perspective. John Patton, History Consultant, Ottawa Board of Education, Ottawa, Ontario. Macmillan of Canada/Toronto.

[12], 312 pp.; 225 × 147 mm.
Issued in paper.
The West and the World: Studies in History Series.

2174. ROCHER, Guy

A General Introduction to Sociology: A Theoretical Perspective. Guy Rocher. Translated from the French by Peta Sheriff. The Macmillan Company of Canada Limited/Toronto.

xxxii, 580 pp.; 213 × 138 mm.

2175. ROGERS, Diane P.

Dimensions of Man. Diane P. Rogers and Norman Sheffe. Teacher Consultant - Joan Morse. Macmillan of Canada/Toronto.

[16], 282 pp.; 233 × 200 mm.

2176. SAWYER, W.W.

An engineering approach to linear algebra. W.W. Sawyer, Professor jointly to the Department of Mathematics and the College of Education, University of Toronto. Macmillan of Canada Toronto.

viii, 304 pp.; 233 × 190 mm.

2177. STACEY, C.P.

Historical Documents of Canada, Volume V: *The Arts of War and Peace 1914-1945*. Edited by C.P. Stacey, Professor of History, University of Toronto, Late Director, Historical Section, Canadian Army. Macmillan of Canada, Toronto.

[29], 656, [1] pp.; 240 × 163 mm.
Historical Documents of Canada Series.

2178.   STEWART, Gordon

A People Highly Favoured of God: The Nova Scotia Yankees and the American Revolution. Gordon Stewart and George Rawlyk. Macmillan of Canada/Toronto.

xxiv, 219, [1] pp.; 230 × 155 mm.

2179.   SWAINSON, Donald

Oliver Mowat's Ontario. Papers presented to the Oliver Mowat Colloquium, Queen's University, November 25-26, 1970. Edited by Donald Swainson. Macmillan of Canada/Toronto.

[8], 235, [1] pp.; 220 × 143 mm.
Issued in cloth and paper.

2180.   WIEBE, Rudy

Stories from Western Canada. A selection by Rudy Wiebe. Macmillan of Canada.

xiv, 274 pp.; 220 × 140 mm.
Issued in cloth and paper.

1973

2181.   AFFLECK, Muriel A.

Idea Book For Teachers: Communication 7. Muriel A. Affleck [and] Katherine G. Therrien. Macmillan of Canada/Toronto.

x, 117, [1] pp.; 225 × 180 mm.
Issued in paper.
Macmillan Language Program.

2182.   ARCHER, Maurice

Introductory Macroeconomics: A Canadian Analysis. Maurice Archer. Macmillan of Canada Toronto.

xiv, 544 pp.; 233 × 153 mm.
Issued in cloth and paper.

2183.   ATKIN, Ronald

Ronald Atkin, *Maintain The Right: The Early History of the North West Mounted Police, 1873-1900.* Macmillan.

400 pp.; 220 × 140 mm.

2184.   BERESFORD-HOWE, Constance

The Book of Eve. A novel by Constance Beresford-Howe. Macmillan of Canada Toronto.

[6], 170 pp.; 219 × 140 mm.

2185.   BERTON, Pierre
   The Golden Trail: The Story of the Klondike Rush. Pierre Berton. Illustrated
   by Alan Daniel. Macmillan of Canada/Toronto.
   [10], 110 pp.; 205 × 130 mm.
   First published in 1954 (see 1304). Revised in 1973. Reprinted in 1974. Issued in
   cloth and paper.
   Great Stories of Canada Series.

2186.   CALLAGHAN, Morley
   An Autumn Penitent. Morley Callaghan. Laurentian Library 16. Macmillan of
   Canada/Toronto.
   [4], 171, [1] pp.; 175 × 105 mm.
   First published in 1929 as part of *A Native Argosy*. Issued in paper.
   Laurentian Library.

2187.   CAMERON, Donald
   Conversations with Canadian Novelists. Donald Cameron. Macmillan of
   Canada/Toronto.
   [8], 160, 160 pp.; 202 × 130 mm.
   Also issued in paper in two volumes.

2188.   CAMPBELL, Marjorie Wilkins
   The North West Company. Marjorie Wilkins Campbell. Toronto: The Macmillan Company of Canada Limited.
   xvi, 295, [1] pp.; 188 × 125 mm.
   First published in 1957 (see 1390). This edition revised. Issued in paper.

2189.   CHEVRIER, Emile D.
   Teacher's Guide To Exercises in Topographic Map and Air Photo Interpretation.
   Emile D. Chevrier [and] D.F.W. Aitkens. Macmillan of Canada.
   [6], 135, [1] pp.; 238 × 150 mm.
   Issued in paper.

2190.   CHILDERHOSE, R.J.
   R.J. Childerhose, *Hockey Fever In Goganne Falls*. Macmillan of Canada.
   [6], 169, [1] pp.; 217 × 138 mm.

2191.   COURTNEY, John C.
   John C. Courtney, *The Selection of National Party Leaders in Canada*. Macmillan of Canada Toronto.
   xvi, 278 pp.; 235 × 155 mm.
   Issued in cloth and paper.

2192.   COVELL, Harold M.
   Challenge. Edited by Harold M. Covell and James W. Greig. Macmillan of
   Canada/Toronto.
   [8], 210, [4] pp.; 214 × 157 mm.
   Issued in paper.
   Action! Series.

2193.   COVELL, Harold M.

[At bottom of page 1:] *Effective Reading: A Developmental Progamme Book 3*. Harold M. Covell [and] John McGechaen. Illustrated by William Wheeler and Robert Kunz. © 1973 The Macmillan Company of Canada Limited, 70 Bond Street, Toronto [etc.].

  127, [1] pp.; 275 × 210 mm.
  Issued in paper.
  Effective Reading Books Series.

2194.   COVELL, Harold M.

Effective Reading 2: A Developmental Reading/Study Skills Programme. By Harold M. Covell, B.Ed., M.A., Ed.D., Professor of Reading Education, Faculty of Education, University of British Columbia and John McGechaen, M.A., Professor of English Education, Faculty of Education, University of British Columbia. The Macmillan Company of Canada Limited.

  [8], 100, [2] pp.; 275 × 210 mm.
  Issued in paper.
  Effective Reading Books Series.

2195.   COVELL, Harold M.

Resource Book for Teachers: Dialogue. By Harold M. Covell and David Martin, Head of the English Department, Gladstone Secondary School, Vancouver, B.C. Consultant James W. Greig. Macmillan of Canada.

  [6], 87, [1] pp.; 215 × 155 mm.

2196.   COVELL, Harold M.

Resource Book For Teachers: Viewpoint. By Harold M. Covell. Consultant James W. Greig. Macmillan of Canada.

  [6], 97, [1] pp.; 215 × 155 mm.

2197.   DAVIDSON, V. Laurence

Teachers' Manual For Anchors Aweigh. By V. Laurence Davidson, B.A., B.ED., Caledonia Junior High School, Dartmouth, Nova Scotia and Josephine V. Harris, B.A., B.ED., Supervisor of Curriculum, Schools Administration Office, Dartmouth, Nova Scotia. Toronto: The Macmillan Company of Canada Limited.

  [6], 113, [1] pp.; 213 × 135 mm.
  Issued in paper.
  Passport to Reading Series.

2198.   DICKSON, Lovat

Lovat Dickson, *Wilderness Man: The strange story of Grey Owl*. Macmillan of Canada/Toronto.

  [12], 283, [1] pp.; 235 × 155 mm.
  Revised and republished in 1976 as Gray Owl: Man of the Wilderness (2380).

2199.   EDUCATIONAL RESEARCH COUNCIL OF AMERICA. SO-
        CIAL SCIENCE STAFF

Concepts and Inquiry: The Educational Research Council Social Science Program. Area Study: Lands of the Middle East. Canadian Edition. Prepared by the Social Science Staff of the Educational Research Council of America. Macmillan of Canada Toronto.

[4], 171, [1] pp.; 200 × 250 mm.
Issued in paper.

2200.   FARRAR, F.S.

Arctic Assignment: The story of the St. Roch. Sgt. F.S. Farrar, RCMP. Illustrated by Merle Smith. Edited by Barrett Bonnezin. Macmillan of Canada/Toronto.

[8], 153, [1] pp.; 204 × 130 mm.
First published in 1955 (see 1338). This edition revised. Reprinted in 1974.
Great Stories of Canada Series.

2201.   GALLOWAY, David

The Elizabethan Theatre III. Papers given at the Third International Conference on Elizabethan Theatre held at the University of Waterloo, Ontario in July 1970. Edited and with an introduction by David Galloway, Department of English, University of New Brunswick. Published in collaboration with the University of Waterloo. Macmillan of Canada Toronto.

xviii, 149, [1] pp.; 220 × 138 mm.

2202.   HOBLEY, L.F.

Introducing Earth Part 1. L.F. Hobley. Macmillan of Canada.

[8], 232 pp.; 200 × 220 mm.
A metric edition of this title was published in 1979 (see 2627).

2203.   HODSON, Bernard A.

Modern Data Processing for Management: A Basic Systems Approach. Bernard A. Hodson. Macmillan of Canada/1973.

[14], 318 pp.; 234 × 155 mm.

2204.   HOLLAND, Vivian

Time Trip. Vivian Holland. Macmillan of Canada.

[4], 27, [1] pp.; 225 × 150 mm.
Issued in paper.

2205.   HORWOOD, R.H.

Inquiry Into Environmental Pollution. R.H. Horwood, Faculty of Education, Queen's University, Kingston, Ontario. Macmillan of Canada Toronto.

[12], 116 pp.; 210 × 135 mm.
Issued in paper.

2206. HORWOOD, R.H.

Trees. R. H. Horwood, Faculty of Education, Queen's University, Kingston, Ontario. The Macmillan Company of Canada Limited.

32 pp.; 225 × 148 mm.
Issued in paper.
Our Science Program Series.

2207. JAMIESON, Stuart

Industrial Relations in Canada. Second edition. Stuart Jamieson. Macmillan of Canada/Toronto 1973.

[8], 156 pp.; 220 × 140 mm.
First published in 1957 (see 1420). Issued in cloth and paper.

2208. KENDAL, Wallis

Just Gin. Wallis Kendal. Illustrated by Ib Ohlsson. Macmillan of Canada Toronto.

159, [1] pp.; 217 × 144 mm.

2209. LAURENDEAU, André

André Laurendeau, *Witness for Quebec*. Essays Selected and Translated by Philip Stratford. Introduction by Claude Ryan. Macmillan of Canada Toronto.

[22], 290, [6] pp.; 220 × 140 mm.
Issued in cloth and paper.

2210. LOUBSER, Leon

Our Changing Environment, *Making Electricity*. Program Co-ordinator/Author Leon Loubser. Designer Don Kletke. Maclean-Hunter Learning Materials Company. Affiliated with Macmillan of Canada Educational Division.

47, [1] pp.; 220 × 250 mm.
Issued in paper.
The Changing Environment Series.

2210A MACDONALD, Molly Anne

[Cover-title:] *The Royal Canadian Mounted Police* [Author: Molly Anne Macdonald. Illustrations: Douglas Anderson and Communication Art Associates. Design: Keith Sturgess. Editor: William F. Waller. Published by the Macmillan Commercial Productions Unit, for the Macmillan Company of Canada. © 1973 The Macmillan Press Ltd.].

[36] pp.; 300 × 210 mm.
Author statement and imprint on inside back cover. Issued in paper.

2211. MITCHELL, W.O.

The Vanishing Point. A novel by W.O. Mitchell. Macmillan of Canada, Toronto.

[6], 393, [1] pp.; 223 × 140 mm.
Reprinted in the Laurentian Library (No. 25) in 1975.

2212.   MORSE, Joan

Teacher's Guide for Dimensions of Man. By Diane P. Rogers and Norman
Sheffe. Prepared by Joan Morse, Wentworth County Board of Education.
Macmillan of Canada.

> [4], 131, [1] pp.; 215 × 190 mm.
> Issued in paper.

2213.   MUSGRAVE, Susan

Grave-dirt and selected strawberries. Susan Musgrave. Macmillan of Canada
Toronto.

> [10], 115, [1] pp.; 210 × 135 mm.
> Issued in paper.

2214.   PRATSON, Frederick

A Guide To Atlantic Canada. Frederick Pratson. The Chatham Press, Inc.,
Riverside, Connecticut [and] Macmillan of Canada, Toronto.

> 160 pp.; 225 × 150 mm.

2215.   PRESTHUS, Robert

Elite Accommodation in Canadian Politics. Robert Presthus. Macmillan of
Canada Toronto.

> xii, 372 pp.; 233 × 155 mm.

2216.   ROBINSON, Sinclair

Practical Handbook of Canadian French. Sinclair Robinson [and] Donald
Smith. *Manuel Pratique du Français Canadien*. Macmillan of Canada Toronto.

> [14], 172 pp.; 195 × 135 mm.
> Issued in cloth and paper.

2217.   SHACKLETON, Philip

Philip Shackleton, *The Furniture of Old Ontario*. Macmillan of Canada Toronto.

> [12], 299, [1] pp.; 310 × 230 mm.
> Reprinted in 1973 and 1974. Reprinted in 1978 in a reduced format with black and
> white illustrations.

2218.   SIMPSON, Leo

The Peacock Papers. A novel by Leo Simpson. Macmillan of Canada Toronto.

> [6], 226 pp.; 220 × 143 mm.

2219.   SMALLWOOD, Joey

I Chose Canada: The Memoirs of the Honourable Joseph R. "Joey" Smallwood.
Macmillan of Canada/Toronto.

> [12], 600 pp.; 233 × 155 mm.

2220.   THOMPSON, Kent

Stories from Atlantic Canada. A selection by Kent Thompson. Macmillan of
Canada.

> xvi, 231, [1] pp.; 220 × 140 mm.
> Issued in cloth and paper.

2221. THOMPSON, Kent

The Tenants were Corrie and Tennie. A novel by Kent Thompson. Macmillan of Canada/Toronto [and] St. Martin's Press/New York.

[8], 200 pp.; 220 × 140 mm.

2222. THURBER, Walter A.

Exploring Science Stage One Record Book. Walter A. Thurber, Robert E. Kilburn [and] Douglas B. Seager. Macmillan of Canada.

vi, 234 pp.; 275 × 210 mm.
Issued in paper.
Exploring Science Series.

2223. THURBER, Walter A.

Exploring Science Stage Two Record Book. Walter A. Thurber, Robert E. Kilburn [and] Douglas B. Seager. Macmillan of Canada.

vi, 212 pp.; 275 × 210 mm.
Issued in paper.
Exploring Science Series.

2224. THURBER, Walter A.

Exploring Science Stage Three Record Book. Walter A. Thurber, Robert E. Kilburn [and] Douglas B. Seager. Macmillan of Canada.

vi, 325, [1] pp.; 275 × 210 mm.
Issued in paper.
Exploring Science Series.

2225. TRUEMAN, R.W.

Our Science Program, *Snow*. R.W. Trueman, Vice-Principal, Shoreham Public School, North York. 1973 The Macmillan Company of Canada Limited, Toronto.

32 pp.; 225 × 152 mm.
Metric edition published in 1977 (see 2519). Issued in paper.
Our Science Program Series.

2226. TRUEMAN, R.W.

Teacher's Guide for Introducing Earth Part 1 by L.F. Hobley. Prepared by R.W. Trueman, Principal, Greenland Road Public School, North York. Macmillan of Canada.

[4], 168 pp.; 234 × 151 mm.

2227. WALLACE, Keith E.

Driving. Keith E. Wallace [and] Jack Greening. Maclean-Hunter Learning Materials Company, 481 University Avenue, Toronto M5W 1A7.

[8], 104 pp.; 215 × 275 mm.
Issued in paper.

2228. WESTERMARK, Tory I.

Poetry is for People. Tory I. Westermark, University of British Columbia [and] Bryan N.S. Gooch, University of Victoria. Macmillan of Canada.

[8], 216 pp.; 214 × 138 mm.
Issued in paper.

2229. WIGLE, Robert

Mathematical Pursuits One. Robert Wigle, Mathematics Consultant, North York Board of Education, Paul Dowling, Mathematics Department, Ancaster High and Vocational School, Ancaster, Ontario [and] Paul Jennings, Assistant Head of the Mathematics Department, T.L. Kennedy Secondary School, Mississauga, Ontario. Macmillan of Canada.

[8], 356 pp.; 233 × 155 mm.
Also issued in an SI edition in 1975.
Mathematical Pursuits Series.

2230. WILSON, J. Tuzo

Unglazed China. J. Tuzo Wilson. Macmillan of Canada Toronto.

xvi, 336 pp.; 213 × 137 mm.

2231. WOLFE, Samuel

The Family Doctor. Samuel Wolfe & Robin F. Badgley. With the collaboration of Richard V. Kasills, John D. Bury, John Z. Carson, Reynold J.M. Gold, Robert A. Spasoff [and] Genevieve Teed. Macmillan of Canada/Toronto.

[12], 201, [1] pp.; 220 × 143 mm.
Issued in cloth and paper.

2231A WOODCOCK, George

Canada and the Canadians. By George Woodcock. With Photographs by Ingeborg Woodcock. Macmillan of Canada, Toronto.

346 pp., 215 × 136 mm.
Issued in paper.

2232. WOODS, H.D.

Labour Policy in Canada. Second edition. H.D. Woods. Volume I of *Labour Policy and Labour Economics in Canada*. Second edition by H.D. Woods, Sylvia Ostry [and] Mahmood A. Zaidi. Macmillan of Canada Toronto.

[10], 377, [1] pp.; 234 × 156 mm.
First published in 1962 (see 1604).

2233. WOOLLATT, Richard

Sights And Sounds. Richard Woollatt, Nelson High School, Burlington, Ontario & Raymond Souster. Macmillan of Canada.

[8], 216 pp.; 213 × 137 mm.
Issued in paper.

2234. WRIGHT, Richard B.
In the Middle of a Life. A novel by Richard B. Wright. Macmillan Toronto
and London.
   [10], 305, [1] pp.; 215 × 143 mm.

2235. YOUNG, Scott
Silent Frank Cochrane: The North's First Great Politician. Scott Young &
Astrid Young. Macmillan of Canada Toronto.
   [6], 218 pp.; 220 × 140 mm.

1974

2236. ALLAN, Andrew
Andrew Allan: A Self-Portrait. Introduction by Harry J. Boyle. Macmillan of
Canada Toronto.
   [8], 199, [1] pp.; 221 × 142 mm.

2237. ANDERSEN, Doris
Slave of the Haida. Doris Andersen. Macmillan of Canada/Toronto.
   [8], 166 pp.; 220 × 140 mm.
   Reprinted in 1978 in paper.
   Great Stories of Canada Series.

2238. ARCHER, Maurice
Introductory Microeconomics: A Canadian Analysis. Maurice Archer. Macmillan of Canada Toronto.
   [12], 418 pp.; 233 × 153 mm.
   Issued in cloth and paper.

2239. *L'Atlas National Du Canada*. Quatrième Edition (Revisée). Publié par The
Macmillan Company of Canada Limited, Toronto, Ontario, avec le concours
du ministère de l'Energie, des Mines et des Ressources et d'Information
Canada. Ottawa, Canada 1974.
   [16], 254, [12] pp.; 375 × 270 mm.
   Also published in English as *The National Atlas of Canada* (see 2282).

2240. BAIRD, David M.
A Guide to Geology for Visitors to Canada's National Parks. David M. Baird,
PH.D., D.SC., F.R.S.C. Macmillan of Canada/Toronto. In Co-operation
With Indian and Northern Affairs/Affaires indiennes et du Nord [and] Parks
Canada/Parcs Canada.
   160 pp.; 175 × 125 mm.
   This revised edition issued in paper.

2241. BLACKLOCK, Les

The High West. Photographs by Les Blacklock. Text by Andy Russell.
Macmillan of Canada Toronto.

141, [1] pp.; 275 × 220 mm.
Reprinted in 1976. Issued in paper.

2242. BUSKIRK, Richard H.

Modern Management and Machiavelli. Richard H. Buskirk. Macmillan of
Canada.

xii, 291, [1] pp.; 212 × 138 mm.

2243. CAMERON, David

Nationalism, Self-Determination and the Quebec Question. David Cameron.
Canadian Controversies Series. Macmillan of Canada/1974.

xiv, 177, [1] pp.; 220 × 143 mm.
Issued in cloth and paper.
Canadian Controversies Series.

2244. CAMPBELL, Marjorie Freeman

Torso. Marjorie Freeman Campbell. Macmillan of Canada/Toronto.

x, 198 pp.; 220 × 140 mm.

2245. CAMPBELL, Marjorie Wilkins

The Nor'Westers: The Fight for the Fur Trade. Marjorie Wilkins Campbell.
Illustrated by Gordon Maclean. Macmillan of Canada/Toronto.

[8], 128 pp.; 204 × 130 mm.
First published in 1954 (see 1309). This revised edition issued in cloth and paper.
Great Stories of Canada Series.

2246. CLARK, Robert J.

Canadian Issues and Alternatives. Robert J. Clark, Editor-in-Chief, Assistant
Professor, Faculty of Education, University of Western Ontario, London,
Ontario, Robert Remnant, Master Teacher of History Social-Sciences, Sud-
bury, Ontario, John Patton, Ottawa Board of Education, Ottawa, Ontario,
Cary Goulson, Associate Professor, Faculty of Education, University of
Victoria, Victoria, B.C. [and] Eric Fors, Vice-Principal, A.Y. Jackson Sec-
ondary School, Willowdale, Ontario. Macmillan of Canada/Toronto.

[12], 241, [1] pp.; 235 × 175 mm.
Reprinted with corrections in 1979 (see 2612).

2247. COLLIE, Michael

New Brunswick. Michael Collie. Toronto/Macmillan of Canada.

xxii, 148 pp.; 223 × 142 mm.
Traveller's Canada Series.

2248.   COVELL, Harold M.

[Cover-title:] *Individual Study Material: Challenge*. By Harold M. Covell and David Martin, Head of the English Department, Gladstone Secondary School, Vancouver, B.C. Consultant: James W. Greig. Macmillan of Canada.

[2], 33, [1] pp.; 213 × 156 mm.
Issued in paper.

2249.   COVELL, Harold M.

Individual Study Material: Dialogue. By Harold M. Covell and David Martin, Head of the English Department, Gladstone Secondary School, Vancouver, B.C. Consultant: James W. Greig. Macmillan of Canada.

[2], 25, [1] pp.; 213 × 156 mm.
Issued in paper.

2250.   COVELL, Harold M.

Resource Book For Teachers: Challenge. By Harold M. Covell and David Martin, Head of the English Department, Gladstone Secondary School, Vancouver, B.C. Consultant: James W. Greig. Macmillan of Canada.

[6], 93, [1] pp.; 213 × 156 mm.
Issued in paper.

2251.   CREIGHTON, Donald

Canada: The Heroic Beginnings. Donald Creighton. Macmillan of Canada/Toronto. In co-operation with Indian and Northern Affairs [-] Affaires indiennes et du Nord [and] Parks Canada [-] Parcs Canada.

255, [1] pp.; 272 × 215 mm.

2252.   DEACON, William Arthur

The Four Jameses. William Arthur Deacon. Introduction by Doug Fetherling. Macmillan/Toronto.

204 pp.; 188 × 130 mm.
Issued in paper.

2253.   DICHTER, Ernest

The Naked Manager. Ernest Dichter. Macmillan of Canada.

xii, 156 pp.; 213 × 140 mm.

2254.   DOERN, G. Bruce

Issues in Canadian Public Policy. Edited by G. Bruce Doern and V. Seymour Wilson. Macmillan of Canada/1974.

[8], 355, [1] pp.; 220 × 140 mm.
Issued in cloth and paper.

2255.   DUNN, Philippa

Pine Mountain Adventures, *Changing Fortunes*. Author: Philippa Dunn.
Reading Consultant: Diane Johnson. Illustrator: Larry Hall. Maclean-
Hunter Learning Materials Company.

[6], 105, [1] pp.; 225 × 150 mm.
Issued in paper.
Pine Mountain Adventures Series.

2256.   DUNN, Philippa

Pine Mountain Adventures, *End of a Legend*. Author: Philippa Dunn.
Reading Consultant: Dianne Johnson. Illustrator: Larry Hall. Maclean-
Hunter Learning Materials Company.

[6], 109, [1] pp.; 225 × 150 mm.
Issued in paper.
Pine Mountain Adventures Series.

2257.   DUNN, Philippa

Pine Mountain Adventures, *Turning Point*. Author: Philippa Dunn. Reading Consultant: Dianne Johnson. Illustrator: Larry Hall. Maclean-Hunter
Learning Materials Company.

[6], 109, [1] pp.; 225 × 150 mm.
Issued in paper.
Pine Mountain Adventures Series.

2258.   EPP, Frank H.

Mennonites in Canada, 1786-1920: The History of a Separate People. Frank H.
Epp. Illustrations by Douglas Ratchford. Macmillan of Canada Toronto.

480 pp.; 240 × 158 mm.

2259.   FERGUSON, Robert D.

Man from St. Malo: The Story of Jacques Cartier. Robert D. Ferguson.
Illustrated by Merle Smith. Macmillan of Canada/Toronto.

[10], 123, [1] pp.; 205 × 130 mm.
First published in 1959 (see 1465). This edition revised. Issued in cloth and paper.
Great Stories of Canada Series.

2260.   FICE, R.H.C.

*Macmillan Discovery Project: The Sea: Sailing Ships For Discovery And
Trade*. R.H.C. Fice and Iris Simkiss. [Table of Contents]. Macmillan of
Canada.

31, [1] pp.; 246 × 188 mm.
Issued in paper.

2261.   FICE, R.H.C.

Macmillan Discovery Project: The Sea: Weather And Navigation. R.H.C. Fice
and Iris Simkiss. [Table of Contents]. Macmillan of Canada.

31, [1] pp.; 246 × 188 mm.
Issued in paper.

2262. FREY, Cecelia
Breakaway. Cecelia Frey. Macmillan of Canada/Toronto.
[8], 183, [1] pp.; 220 × 143 mm.

2263. HAIG-BROWN, Roderick
Captain of the Discovery: The Story of Captain George Vancouver. Roderick
Haig-Brown. Illustrated by Gordon Maclean. Macmillan of Canada/To-
ronto.
[6], 174 pp.; 205 × 130 mm.
First published in 1956 (see 1371). This edition revised.
Great Stories of Canada Series.

2264. HAMILTON, William B.
Local History In Atlantic Canada. William B. Hamilton. Macmillan of
Canada.
xvi, 241, [1] pp.; 233 × 153 mm.

2265. HIBBARD, G.R.
The Elizabethan Theatre IV. Papers given at the Fourth International Conference on Elizabethan Theatre held at the University of Waterloo, Ontario, in
July 1972. Edited and with an introduction by G.R. Hibbard, Department of
English, University of Waterloo. Published in collaboration with the University of Waterloo. Macmillan of Canada Toronto.
xvi, 175, [1] pp.; 220 × 140 mm.

2266. HOBLEY, L.F.
Introducing Earth Part 2. L.F. Hobley. Macmillan of Canada.
[8], 240 pp.; 200 × 220 mm.
A metric edition of this title was published in 1979 (see 2628).

2267. JACKSON, Robert J.
The Canadian Legislative System: Politicians and Policy-Making. Robert J.
Jackson and Michael M. Atkinson. Canadian Controversies Series. Macmil-
lan of Canada/1974.
xii, 196 pp.; 220 × 140 mm.
Revised in 1980 (see 2682). Issued in cloth and paper.
Canadian Controversies Series.

2268. KEIRSTEAD, B.S.
Economics Canada: Selected Readings. Edited by B.S. Keirstead, J.R.G.
Brander, J.F. Earl and C.M. Waddell. Macmillan of Canada.
[12], 495, [1] pp.; 235 × 155 mm.
Issued in cloth and paper.

2269.   LANG, H. Murray

Inquiries Into Biology, *The Cell*. H. Murray Lang, Associate Professor, The Faculty of Education, University of Toronto, Edwin G. Palfery, Science Chairman, Mimico High School, Borough of Etobicoke [and] Ed L.R. Van Nieuwenhove, Head of Science, Woburn Collegiate Institute, Borough of Scarborough. Macmillan of Canada.

[4], 44 pp.; 277 × 213 mm.
Issued in paper.
Inquiries into Biology Series.

2270.   LANG, H. Murray

Inquiries Into Biology, *The Cell: Teacher's Guide*. H. Murray Lang, Associate Professor, The Faculty of Education, University of Toronto, Edwin G. Palfery, Science Chairman, Mimico High School, Borough of Etobicoke [and] Ed. L.R. Van Nieuwenhove, Head of Science, Woburn Collegiate Institute, Borough of Scarborough. Macmillan of Canada.

[2], 35, [1] pp.; 277 × 213 mm.
Issued in paper.
Inquiries into Biology Series.

2271.   LANG, H. Murray

Inquiries Into Biology, *What is Life?* H. Murray Lang, Associate Professor, The Faculty of Education, University of Toronto, Edwin G. Palfery, Science Chairman, Mimico High School, Borough of Etobicoke [and] Ed L.R. Van Nieuwenhove, Head of Science, Woburn Collegiate Institute, Borough of Scarborough. Macmillan of Canada.

[4], 44 pp.; 277 × 213 mm.
Issued in paper.
Inquiries into Biology Series.

2272.   LANG, H. Murray

Inquiries Into Biology, *What Is Life? Teacher's Guide*. H. Murray Lang, Associate Professor, The Faculty of Education, University of Toronto, Edwin G. Palfery, Science Chairman, Mimico High School, Borough of Etobicoke [and] Ed L.R. Van Nieuwenhove, Head of Science, Woburn Collegiate Institute, Borough of Scarborough. Macmillan of Canada.

[2], 32 pp.; 277 × 213 mm.
Issued in paper.
Inquiries into Biology Series.

2273.   LEE, Dennis

Alligator Pie. The poems were written by Dennis Lee. The pictures were drawn by Frank Newfeld. Macmillan of Canada.

64 pp.; 260 × 193 mm.
Issued in cloth and paper. Reprinted frequently.

2274.   LEE, Dennis
Nicolas Knock And Other People. Poems By Dennis Lee. Pictures By Frank
Newfeld. Macmillan of Canada.
> 64 pp.; 260 × 193 mm.
> Issued in cloth and paper. Reprinted frequently.

2275.   LOCHHEAD, Douglas
100 Poems of Nineteenth Century Canada. Selected by Douglas Lochhead and
Raymond Souster. Macmillan of Canada.
> xviii, 218 pp.; 213 × 135 mm.
> Issued in cloth and paper.

2276.   LONGSTRETH, T. Morris
The Scarlet Force: The Making of the Mounted Police. T. Morris Longstreth.
Illustrated by Alan Daniel. Macmillan of Canada/Toronto.
> [10], 154 pp.; 205 × 130 mm.
> First published in 1953 (see 1297). Revised in 1964 (see 1683). This edition further
> revised.
> Great Stories of Canada Series.

2277.   MacEWEN, Gwendolyn
Gwendolyn MacEwen, *Magic Animals: Selected Poems Old And New*. Macmillan of Canada Toronto.
> 154 pp.; 220 × 140 mm.
> Issued in cloth and paper.

2278.   MacLENNAN, Hugh
Rivers Of Canada. Hugh MacLennan. With The Camera Of John de Visser.
Macmillan of Canada/Toronto.
> 270 pp.; 310 × 230 mm.
> *Rivers of Canada* is a revised and enlarged edition of *Seven Rivers of Canada* (see
> 1542).

2279.   MANTHORPE, Jonathan
The Power & The Tories: Ontario Politics — 1943 To The Present. Jonathan
Manthorpe. Macmillan of Canada.
> [10], 305, [1] pp.; 233 × 155 mm.

2280.   MERSEREAU, M. Grace
Singing Under Ice. Edited by M. Grace Mersereau, Head of the English
Department, Harry Ainlay Composite High School, Edmonton, Alberta.
Macmillan of Canada.
> [8], 264 pp.; 197 × 125 mm.
> Issued in paper.

2281.   MIGUÉ, Jean-Luc
The Price of Health. Jean-Luc Migué and Gérard Bélanger. Translated from
the French by Nicole Fredette and James Robinson. Macmillan of Canada.
> x, 229, [1] pp.; 222 × 140 mm.
> Issued in cloth and paper.

2282.   *The National Atlas Of Canada*. Fourth Edition (Revised). Published by
The Macmillan Company of Canada Limited, Toronto, Ontario, in associa-
tion with the Department of Energy, Mines and Resources and Information
Canada, Ottawa, Canada 1974.

> [16], 254, [12] pp.; 375 × 270 mm.
> Also published in French as *L'Atlas National du Canada* (see 2239).

2283.   NELLES, H.V.

*The Politics of Development: Forests, Mines & Hydro-Electric Power in On-
tario, 1849-1941*. H.V. Nelles. Macmillan of Canada.

> xiv, 514 pp.; 240 × 167 mm.
> Reprinted in 1975 in paper.

2284.   NICOL, Eric

Letters To My Son. Eric Nicol. Illustrations by Roy Peterson. Macmillan of
Canada/Toronto.

> [8], 182 pp.; 220 × 140 mm.

2285.   POWE, Bruce

The Last Days of the American Empire. Bruce Powe. Macmillan of Canada
Toronto, 1974.

> xiv, 326 pp.; 217 × 143 mm.

2286.   RITCHIE, Carson I.A.

The Eskimo And His Art. Carson I.A. Ritchie. Macmillan of Canada Toronto.

> 80 pp.; 293 × 215 mm.

2287.   RITCHIE, Charles

Charles Ritchie, *The Siren Years: A Canadian Diplomat Abroad 1937-1945*.
Macmillan of Canada Toronto.

> 216 pp.; 220 × 140 mm.
> Reprinted in the Laurentian Library (No. 50) in 1977.

2288.   ROWLAND, Wade

Fuelling Canada's Future. Wade Rowland. Macmillan of Canada 1974.

> [10], 161, [1] pp.; 220 × 140 mm.
> Issued in cloth and paper.

2289.   SCAMMELL, W.M.

International Trade and Payments. W.M. Scammell. The Macmillan Company of Canada Limited Toronto.

> xiv, 607, [1] pp.; 240 × 155 mm.

2290.   SCHROEDER, Andreas

Stories From Pacific & Arctic Canada. A selection by Andreas Schroeder &
Rudy Wiebe. Macmillan of Canada.

> xvi, 284 pp.; 220 × 140 mm.
> Issued in cloth and paper.

2291.   SELLEKAERTS, Willy
Econometrics and Economic Theory: Essays in Honour of Jan Tinbergen. Edited by Willy Sellekaerts. Macmillan of Canada.
 viii, 298 pp.; 220 × 135 mm.

2292.   SELLEKAERTS, Willy
Economic Development and Planning: Essays in Honour of Jan Tinbergen. Edited by Willy Sellekaerts. Macmillan of Canada.
 xxiv, 266 pp.; 220 × 135 mm.

2293.   SELLEKAERTS, Willy
International Trade and Finance: Essays in Honour of Jan Tinbergen. Edited by Willy Sellekaerts. Macmillan of Canada.
 viii, 292 pp.; 220 × 135 mm.

2294.   STANLEY, George F.G.
Canada's Soldiers: The Military History of an Unmilitary People. Third Edition. By George F.G. Stanley. Maps by C.C.J. Bond. Macmillan of Canada/Toronto.
 [14], 487, [1] pp.; 235 × 155 mm.
 First published in 1954 (see 1328). Revised in 1960 (see 1506).

2295.   STENSON, Fred
Lonesome Hero. Fred Stenson. Macmillan of Canada/Toronto.
 [8], 182 pp.; 220 × 143 mm.

2296.   STEWART, Walter
Hard to Swallow: Why food prices keep rising — and what can be done about it. Walter Stewart. Macmillan of Canada Toronto.
 [6], 218 pp.; 230 × 150 mm.
 Issued in cloth and paper.

2297.   STUDNICKI-GIZBERT, K.W.
Papers and discussions from the Conference on Canadian National Transport Policy held at York University, Toronto, in May 1972. *Issues in Canadian Transport Policy*. Edited and with an introduction by K.W. Studnicki-Gizbert. Published in collaboration with the University of Toronto/York University Joint Program in Transportation. Macmillan of Canada/Toronto 1974.
 xvi, 476 pp.; 233 × 152 mm.

2298.   TARDIF, Louis M.R.
A Canadian Topliner, *Singled Out*. Louis M.R. Tardif. Macmillan of Canada.
 [2], 188, [2] pp.; 175 × 105 mm.
 Issued in paper.
 Topliner Series.

2298A TRUEMAN, R.W.

Teacher's Guide for Introducing Earth Part 2 by L.F. Hobley. Prepared by R.W. Trueman, Principal, Greenland Road Public School, North York. Macmillan of Canada.

[4], 241, [1] pp.; 234 × 151 mm.

2299. TRUSS, Jan

Bird at the Window. Jan Truss. Macmillan of Canada/Toronto 1974.

[8], 178 pp.; 220 × 140 mm.
This title was also issued in the Alberta Heritage Collection.

2300. WARKENTIN, Germaine

Stories from Ontario. A Selection by Germaine Warkentin. Macmillan of Canada.

xvi, 272 pp.; 220 × 140 mm.
Issued in cloth and paper.

2301. WAYMAN, Tom

For and Against the Moon: Blues, Yells, and Chuckles. Tom Wayman. Macmillan of Canada/Toronto.

157, [1] pp.; 130 × 210 mm.
Issued in paper.

2302. WIGHT, Oliver W.

Production and Inventory Management in the Computer Age. Oliver W. Wight, President, Oliver Wight, Inc. Macmillan of Canada.

xii, 284 pp.; 230 × 150 mm.

2303. WIGLE, Robert

Mathematical Pursuits Two. Robert Wigle, Head of Mathematics Department, Delhi District Secondary School, Delhi, Ontario, Paul Dowling, Mathematics Department, Ancaster High and Vocational School, Ancaster, Ontario [and] Paul Jennings, Assistant Head of the Mathematics Department, T.L. Kennedy Secondary School, Mississauga, Ontario. Macmillan of Canada.

x, 353, [1] pp.; 233 × 155 mm.
Mathematical Pursuits Series.

1975

2304. ABRAHAMSON, Una

The Canadian Guide to Home Entertaining. Una Abrahamson. Macmillan of Canada/Toronto 1975.

176 pp.; 271 × 217 mm.

2305. AIKMAN, J.A.

Sound. J.A. Aikman. Macmillan of Canada.

[6], 27, [1] pp.; 225 × 150 mm.
Issued in paper.

2306. ANGUS, Terry

Themes in Canadian Literature, *The Prairie Experience*. Edited by Terry Angus. General Editor, David Arnason. Macmillan of Canada.

[6], 122 pp.; 225 × 145 mm.
Issued in paper.
Themes in Canadian Literature Series.

2307. ARCHER, Maurice

Canada's Economic Problems and Policies. Maurice Archer. Macmillan of Canada/Toronto.

xii, 211, [1] pp.; 220 × 142 mm.
Issued in cloth and paper.

2308. ARNASON, David

Themes in Canadian Literature, *Isolation in Canadian Literature*. Edited by David Arnason. Questions and Bibliography by Alice K. Hale. General Editor, David Arnason. Macmillan of Canada.

[6], 122 pp.; 225 × 145 mm.
Issued in paper.
Themes in Canadian Literature Series.

2309. BAILEY, Leuba

Themes in Canadian Literature, *The Immigrant Experience*. Edited by Leuba Bailey. General Editor, David Arnason. Macmillan of Canada.

[6], 122 pp.; 225 × 145 mm.
Issued in paper.
Themes in Canadian Literature Series.

2310. BATTEN, Jack

The Leafs in Autumn. Jack Batten. Macmillan of Canada/Toronto.

[12], 143, [1] pp.; 220 × 142 mm.

2311. BOYLE, Harry J.

Harry J. Boyle, *The Luck of the Irish: A Canadian Fable*. Macmillan of Canada/Toronto.

[8], 160 pp.; 220 × 145 mm.

2312. BROWN, Robert Craig

Robert Laird Borden: A Biography, Volume I: 1854-1914. By Robert Craig Brown. Macmillan of Canada/Toronto.

xii, 306 pp.; 235 × 155 mm.

2313. CALLAGHAN, Morley

A Fine and Private Place. A Novel by Morley Callaghan. Macmillan of Canada Toronto.

[4], 213, [1] pp.; 214 × 140 mm.

2314. COLES, Don
Sometimes All Over. Poems by Don Coles. Macmillan of Canada.
89, [1] pp.; 214 × 138 mm.
Issued in paper.

2315. COSBIE, W.G.
The Toronto General Hospital 1819-1965: A Chronicle. W.G. Cosbie, M.D.
Macmillan of Canada Toronto.
x, 373, [1] pp.; 235 × 153 mm.

2316. CRAIG, John
Close Doesn't Count. John Craig. Macmillan of Canada, Toronto.
[4], 176 pp.; 220 × 138 mm.

2317. DAVIES, Robertson
Question Time. A play by Robertson Davies. Macmillan of Canada Toronto.
xviii, 70 pp.; 214 × 139 mm.
Issued in paper.

2318. DAVIES, Robertson
World of Wonders. Robertson Davies. Macmillan of Canada Toronto.
[8], 358 pp.; 222 × 145 mm.

2319. DEWDNEY, Selwyn
They Shared to Survive: The Native Peoples of Canada. Selwyn Dewdney.
Illustrated by Franklin Arbuckle. Macmillan of Canada/Toronto.
[4], 210, [10] pp.; 233 × 160 mm.
Issued in cloth and paper.

2320. DIEFENBAKER, John G.
One Canada: Memoirs of the Right Honourable John G. Diefenbaker: The Crusading Years 1895-1956. Macmillan of Canada Toronto.
xvi, 298 pp.; 233 × 150 mm.
Second volume published in 1976 (see 2381) and third volume in 1977 (see 2464).
Reprinted frequently.

2321. FULTON, David
Design For Small Communities: A Report of Interdesign '74/Ontario. Edited by
David Fulton. Sanctioned by the International Council of Societies of Industrial Design, Brussels, Belgium. A Project of The Association Of Canadian
Industrial Designers In Co-operation With The Government of Ontario.
Macmillan of Canada.
[10], 141, [1] pp.; 275 × 213 mm.
Issued in paper.

2322.   GIDNEY, R.D.

Man and Machine: What Price? R.D. Gidney, Faculty of Education, University of Western Ontario. Consultant: R.J. Clark, Faculty of Education, University of Western Ontario. Macmillan of Canada/Toronto.

[6], 60 pp.; 225 × 150 mm.
Issued in paper.
The West and the World: Studies in History Series.

2323.   GIDNEY, R.D.

Robert Owen: Realist or Visionary? R.D. Gidney, Faculty of Education, University of Western Ontario. Consultant: R.J. Clark, Faculty of Education, University of Western Ontario. Macmillan of Canada/Toronto.

[4], 57, [1] pp.; 225 × 150 mm.
Issued in paper.
The West and the World: Studies in History Series.

2324.   GIDNEY, R.D.

Votes for the People: The Chartist Movement, 1839. R.D. Gidney, Faculty of Education, University of Western Ontario. Consultant: R.J. Clark, Faculty of Education, University of Western Ontario. Macmillan of Canada/Toronto.

[4], 52 pp.; 225 × 150 mm.
Issued in paper.
The West and the World: Studies in History Series.

2325.   GOLD, Joseph

In the Name of Language! Edited by Joseph Gold. Macmillan of Canada [and] Maclean-Hunter Press.

xiv, 209, [1] pp.; 220 × 140 mm.
Issued in cloth and paper.

2326.   GRAY, James H.

James H. Gray, *The Roar of the Twenties*. Macmillan of Canada Toronto.

[10], 358 pp.; 235 × 155 mm.

2327.   GREENING, Jack

Driving: Teacher's Guide. Jack Greening [and] Keith Wallace. Maclean-Hunter Learning Materials Company.

[6], 81, [1] pp.; 270 × 210 mm.
Issued in paper.

2328.   GREGORY, Lady

Lady Gregory, *Selected Plays*. Chosen and Introduced by Elizabeth Coxhead. Foreword by Sean O'Casey. Macmillan of Canada [and] Maclean-Hunter Press.

269, [1] pp.; 213 × 134 mm.
Issued in paper.

2329. GROSMAN, Brian A.

Police Command: Decisions & Discretion. Brian A. Grosman. Macmillan of Canada.

[12], 154 pp.; 220 × 140 mm.
Issued in cloth and paper.

2329A HARPER, George Mills

Yeats Studies Series. General Editors: Robert O'Driscoll and Lorna Reynolds. *Yeats and The Occult*. Edited By George Mills Harper. Macmillan of Canada [and] Maclean-Hunter Press.

xxii, 322 pp.; 220 × 140 mm.
Yeats Studies Series.

2330. HARPER, Peter

Social Studies Primary Resource Book, *Project Five to Nine*. Peter Harper, Project Director. John Burdikin, Muriel A. Carriere, Mary C.L. James, Shirley Koleszar, Sharon Olsen, Florence Padgett, Elizabeth M. Peters, Claudia C. Silverton, [and] Rose Marie Williams. Macmillan of Canada.

[4], 76 pp.; 275 × 210 mm.
Issued in paper.
Macmillan Elementary Social Studies Program.

2331. HIBBARD, G.R.

The Elizabethan Theatre V. Papers given at the Fifth International Conference on Elizabethan Theatre held at the University of Waterloo, Ontario in July 1973. Edited and with an introduction by G. R. Hibbard, Department of English, University of Waterloo. Published in collaboration with the University of Waterloo. Macmillan of Canada.

xviii, 158 pp.; 220 × 140 mm.

2332. HODGINS, Jack

Themes in Canadian Literature, *The Frontier Experience*. Edited by Jack Hodgins. General Editor, David Arnason. Macmillan of Canada.

[6], 122 pp.; 225 × 145 mm.
Issued in paper.
Themes in Canadian Literature Series.

2333. KOSTASH, Myrna

Her Own Woman: Profiles of Ten Canadian Women. By Myrna Kostash, Melinda McCracken, Valerie Miner, Erna Paris, [and] Heather Robertson. Macmillan of Canada Toronto.

x, 212, [2] pp.; 220 × 135 mm.
Issued in cloth and paper.

2334. KUDRNA, Dennis A.

Purchasing Manager's Decision Handbook. By Dennis A. Kudrna. Macmillan of Canada.

xii, 221, [1] pp.; 235 × 154 mm.

2335. LANG, H. Murray

Inquiries into Biology, *Diversity of Life*. H. Murray Lang, Associate Professor, The Faculty of Education, University of Toronto, Edwin G. Palfery, Science Chairman, Mimico High School, Borough of Etobicoke [and] Ed L. R. Van Nieuwenhove, Head of Science, Woburn Collegiate Institute, Borough of Scarborough. Macmillan of Canada.

[4], 70 pp.; 277 × 213 mm.
Issued in paper.
Inquiries into Biology Series.

2336. LANG, H. Murray

Inquiries into Biology, *Interdependence of Life*. H. Murray Lang, Associate Professor, The Faculty of Education, University of Toronto, Edwin G. Palfery, Science Chairman, Mimico High School, Borough of Etobicoke, [and] Ed L.R. Van Nieuwenhove, Head of Science, Woburn Collegiate Institute, Borough of Scarborough. Macmillan of Canada.

[6], 68 pp.; 277 × 213 mm.
Issued in paper.
Inquiries into Biology Series.

2337. LANG, H. Murray

Inquiries into Biology, *Microbiology*. H. Murray Lang, Associate Professor, The Faculty of Education, University of Toronto, Edwin G. Palfery, Science Chairman, Mimico High School, Borough of Etobicoke [and] Ed L.R. Van Nieuwenhove, Head of Science, Woburn Collegiate Institute, Borough of Scarborough. Macmillan of Canada.

[6], 67, [1] pp.; 277 × 213 mm.
Issued in paper.
Inquiries into Biology Series.

2338. MacDONALD, Donald C.

Government and Politics of Ontario. Edited by Donald C. MacDonald. Macmillan of Canada [and] Maclean-Hunter Press.

xii, 370 pp.; 220 × 140 mm.
Issued in cloth and paper.

2339. *Man in Society: Poverty*. Maclean-Hunter Learning Materials Company [and] the Macmillan Company of Canada.

40 pp.; 202 × 200 mm.
Issued in paper.

2340. McCULLOUGH, Elizabeth

Themes in Canadian Literature, *The Role of Woman in Canadian Literature*. Edited by Elizabeth McCullough. General Editor, David Arnason. Macmillan of Canada.

[6], 120 pp.; 225 × 145 mm.
Issued in paper.
Themes in Canadian Literature Series.

2341. MILLER, Orlo
Death to the Donnellys. A novel by Orlo Miller. Macmillan of Canada/Toronto.
[4], 228 pp.; 220 × 140 mm.

2342. MINGAY, G.E.
Arthur Young and His Times. Edited by G.E. Mingay, Professor of Agrarian History, University of Kent at Canterbury. Macmillan of Canada/Maclean-Hunter Press.
[8], 264 pp.; 220 × 140 mm.

2343. MONET, Jean
Estate Planning for Canadians. By Jean Monet, Q.C. of the Quebec Bar, with the assistance of Stephen D. Hart of the Quebec Bar. Macmillan of Canada Toronto.
xiv, 378 pp.; 210 × 135 mm.

2344. MOWAT, William
Themes in Canadian Literature, *Native Peoples in Canadian Literature*. Edited by William and Christine Mowat. General Editor, David Arnason. Macmillan of Canada.
[6], 122 pp.; 225 × 145 mm.
Issued in paper.
Themes in Canadian Literature Series.

2345. NADER, George A.
Cities of Canada: Volume One: Theoretical, Historical and Planning Perspectives. George A. Nader, Trent University. Macmillan of Canada.
xii, 404 pp.; 233 × 155 mm.

2346. NOWLAN, Michael O.
Themes in Canadian Literature, *The Maritime Experience*. Edited by Michael O. Nowlan. General Editor, David Arnason. Macmillan of Canada.
[6], 122 pp.; 225 × 145 mm.
Issued in paper.
Themes in Canadian Literature Series.

2347. O'DRISCOLL, Robert
Yeats Studies Series, *Yeats and the Theatre*. Edited by Robert O'Driscoll and Lorna Reynolds. Maclean-Hunter Press [and] Macmillan of Canada.
xiv, 288 pp.; 220 × 140 mm.
Yeats Studies Series.

2348. PAUPST, James C.
The Sleep Book. By Dr. James C. Paupst. With Toni Robinson. Macmillan of Canada Toronto.
xvi, 173, [1] pp.; 210 × 140 mm.

2349. RICHARDSON, Boyce

Strangers Devour the Land: The Cree hunters of the James Bay area versus Premier Bourassa and the James Bay Development Corporation. Boyce Richardson. Macmillan of Canada.

  xxii, 342, xiv, [4] pp.; 242 × 163 mm.
  Reprinted in the Laurentian Library (No. 47) in 1977.

2350. ROBINSON, Helier J.

Renascent Rationalism. Helier J. Robinson. Macmillan of Canada [and] Maclean-Hunter Press.

  xiv, 290 pp.; 220 × 140 mm.

2351. ROSS, Alexander

The Risk Takers. By Alexander Ross. A Financial Post/Macmillan Book. Maclean-Hunter Limited.

  [10], 177, [1] pp.; 233 × 155 mm.
  Issued in cloth and paper.

2352. ROWAT, Donald C.

Donald C. Rowat, *Your Local Government: A Sketch of the Municipal System of Canada*. Macmillan of Canada Toronto.

  xii, 131, [1] pp.; 215 × 135 mm.
  First published in 1955 (see 1353). This edition revised.

2353. SAWYER, John A.

John A. Sawyer, *Macroeconomics: Theory and Policy in the Canadian Economy*. Macmillan of Canada/Toronto.

  [10], 406 pp.; 233 × 155 mm.

2354. SCHLESINGER, Benjamin

The Chatelaine Guide to Marriage. Edited by Benjamin Schlesinger, Ph. D. Macmillan of Canada/Toronto.

  [6], 218 pp.; 212 × 135 mm.
  Issued in paper.

2355. SCHULL, Joseph

Edward Blake: The Man of the Other Way (1833-1881). Joseph Schull. Macmillan of Canada.

  xiv, 257, [1] pp.; 235 × 155 mm.

2356. SPEED, F.M.

Investigations in Behaviour and Elementary Neurobiology. F.M. Speed and J.J.B. Smith. Macmillan of Canada.

  189, [1] pp.; 240 × 184 mm.
  Issued in limp cloth.

2357.   STECKNER, Tillmann

Automotive Mechanics, Operation Sheets, Level I. Tillmann Steckner, Technical Department, A.B. Lucas Secondary School, London, Ontario. ISBN 0-7705-1352-2. Macmillan of Canada.

> 76 pp.; 275 × 215 mm.
> Issued in paper.

2358.   STECKNER, Tillmann

Automotive Mechanics, Operation Sheets, Level 2. Tillmann Steckner, Technical Department, A.B. Lucas Secondary School, London, Ontario. ISBN 0-7705-1353-0. Macmillan of Canada.

> 162 pp.; 275 × 215 mm.
> Issued in paper.

2359.   STECKNER, Tillmann

Tillmann Steckner, B.A., Technical Department, A.B. Lucas Secondary School, London, Ontario. A Completely Revised Edition of *Automotive Mechanics: Principles and Operation*, by Mervin J. McGuffin, Area Superintendent, Board of Education, London, Ontario. *Automotive Mechanics and Technology*. Macmillan of Canada.

> viii, 312 pp.; 257 × 182 mm.

2360.   STEVENS, John

Themes in Canadian Literature, *The Urban Experience*. Edited by John Stevens. General Editor, David Arnason. Macmillan of Canada.

> [6], 121, [1] pp.; 225 × 145 mm.
> Issued in paper.
> Themes in Canadian Literature Series.

2361.   TOLTON, C.D.E.

André Gide and the Art of Autobiography: A Study of Si le grain ne meurt. C.D.E. Tolton. Macmillan of Canada [and] Maclean-Hunter Press.

> [6], 122 pp.; 218 × 140 mm.

2362.   TRUEMAN, R.W.

Our Science Program, *Simple Solutions*. R.W. Trueman, Principal, Greenland Road Public School, North York, Ontario. [...] © 1975 The Macmillan Company of Canada Limited, [etc.].

> 31, [1] pp.; 225 × 152 mm.
> Issued in paper.
> Our Science Program Series.

2363.   VOADEN, Herman

Look Both Ways: Theatre Experiences. Editor: Herman Voaden, C.M., M.A., C.D.A., F.R.S.A., Former Head of English Department, Central High School of Commerce, Toronto. Associate Editors: J.C. Adams, M.A., Head of English Department, Central High School of Commerce, Toronto [etc.]. Macmillan of Canada.

> xvi, 237, [1] pp.; 225 × 150 mm.
> Issued in paper.

2364. WAYMAN, Tom

Money and Rain: Tom Wayman Live! Macmillan of Canada/Toronto.

x, 150 pp.; 133 × 210 mm.
Issued in paper.

2365. WOOLLATT, Richard

Teaching Notes: Sights and Sounds. Richard Woollatt & Raymond Souster. Macmillan of Canada.

[4], 49, [1] pp.; 210 × 135 mm.
Issued in paper.

2366. YEATES, Maurice H.

La grand'rue de Quebec à Windsor. Maurice Yeates. Publié par The Macmillan Company of Canada Limited, Toronto (Ontario), en coopération avec le Ministère d'Etat aux Affaires urbaines et Information Canada, Ottawa, Canada, 1975.

xxx, 470 pp.; 220 × 145 mm.
Also issued in English (see 2367).

2367. YEATES, Maurice H.

Main Street: Windsor to Quebec City. Maurice Yeates. Published by The Macmillan Company of Canada Limited, Toronto, Ontario in association with the Ministry of State for Urban Affairs and Information Canada, Ottawa, Canada, 1975.

xiv, 431, [1] pp.; 220 × 145 mm.
Also issued in French (see 2366).

2368. ZASLOW, Morris

Reading The Rocks. Morris Zaslow. The Story of The Geological Survey of Canada 1842-1972. Published by The Macmillan Company of Canada Limited, Toronto, Ontario, in association with the Department of Energy, Mines and Resources and Information Canada, Ottawa, Canada, 1975.

[8], 599, [1] pp.; 280 × 220 mm.

1976

2369. ALLINGHAM, Michael

Resource Allocation and Economic Policy. Edited by Michael Allingham and M.L. Burstein. Macmillan of Canada/Maclean-Hunter Press.

xiv, 251, [1] pp.; 221 × 140 mm.

2370. ARNASON, David

Nineteenth Century Canadian Stories. Selected by David Arnason. Macmillan of Canada.

xii, 212 pp.; 214 × 136 mm.
Issued in cloth and paper.

2371.   BAKER, H.S.

Organization for Economic Cooperation and Development, Review of Educational Policies in Canada (Western Region). *Education Purposes and Structures*. H.S. Baker. Macmillan of Canada.

[4], 37, [1] pp.; 270 × 210 mm.
Issued in paper.

2372.   *Cambridge Latin Course: Unit I*. Drawings by Joy Mellor and Leslie Jones. Macmillan of Canada 1976.

13 pamphlets individually paginated in a box; 207 × 145 mm.
The Cambridge Latin Course: Unit I is the first in a series of 5 Latin courses designed for students. Thirteen pamphlets are included in this box, the contents of which are: 1) Caecilius, 2) in villa, 3) Pantaganthus, 4) in foro, 5) in theatro, 6) Felix, 7) Cena, 8) gladiatores, 9) thermae, 10) rhetor, 11) candidatus, 12) Mons Vesuvius, and i) words and phrases.
Cambridge Latin Series.

2373.   *Cambridge Latin Course: Unit II*. Drawings by Joy Mellor and Leslie Jones. Macmillan of Canada 1976.

10 pamphlets individually paginated in a box; 207 × 145 mm.
The Cambridge Latin Course: Unit II is the second in a series of 5 Latin courses designed for students. Ten pamphlets are included in this box, the contents of which are 13) in Britannia, 14) apud Salvium, 15) Rex Cagidubnus, 16) in palatio, 17) Alexandria, 18) Eutychus et Clemens, 19) Aegyptii, 20) medias, i) words and phrases, and ii) information about the language.
Cambridge Latin Series.

2374.   *Cambridge Latin Course: Unit III*. Drawings by Joy Mellor and Leslie Jones. Macmillan of Canada 1976.

13 pamphlets individually paginated in a box; 207 × 145 mm.
The Cambridge Latin Course: Unit III is the third in a series of 5 Latin courses designed for students. Thirteen pamphlets are included in this box, the contents of which are: 21) Aquae Sulis, 22) defixio, 23) fuga, 24) Deva, 25) pax, 26) Roma, 27) Euphrasyne, 28) Paris, 29 Confarreatio, 30) consilium, 31) annales, i) Words and Phrases, and ii) information about the language.
Cambridge Latin Series.

2375.   *Cambridge Latin Course: Unit IV*. Drawings by Joy Mellor and Leslie Jones. Macmillan of Canada 1976.

8 pamphlets individually paginated in a box; 207 × 145 mm.
The Cambridge Latin Course: Unit IV is the fourth in a series of 5 Latin courses designed for students. Eight pamphlets are included in this box, the contents of which are i) Bithynia, ii) odi et amo, iii) miser Catulle, iv) domi, v) vivite mortales meneo, vi) mors omnibus instat, vii) mira arte and viii) words and phrases.
Cambridge Latin Series.

2376.   *Cambridge Latin Course: Unit V*. Drawings by Joy Mellor and Leslie Jones. Macmillan of Canada 1976.

3 pamphlets individually paginated in a box; 207 × 145 mm.
The Cambridge Latin Course: Unit V is the last in a series of 5 Latin courses designed for students. Three pamphlets are included in this box, the contents of which are i) Nero et Agrippina ii) Dido et Aeneas and iii) words and phrases.
Cambridge Latin Series.

2377. COFFEY, Peter

The External Economic Relations of the EEC. Peter Coffey, Senior Research Fellow and Head of the Economics Section, Europa Instituut, University of Amsterdam. Macmillan of Canada [and] Maclean-Hunter Press.

xiv, 118 pp.; 220 × 138 mm.

2378. CRYSDALE, Stewart

Religion in Canadian Society. Edited by Stewart Crysdale and Les Wheatcroft. Macmillan of Canada [and] Maclean-Hunter Press.

xiv, 498 pp.; 233 × 153 mm.
Issued in cloth and paper.

2379. DALY, Ronald C.

The Macmillan School Atlas. New Metric Edition. Ronald C. Daly, B.A., M.Ed., Principal, Fairmount Park Senior School, Toronto, Formerly Social Studies Consultant, Toronto Board of Education. Maps and illustrations by John R. Waller. The Macmillan Company of Canada Limited Toronto.

124, [4] pp.; 276 × 218 mm.
First published in 1965 (see 1712).

2380. DICKSON, Lovat

Grey Owl: Man of the Wilderness. Lovat Dickson. Macmillan of Canada.

[12], 173, [1] pp.; 189 × 132 mm.
An earlier version was published in 1973 as *Wilderness Man: The Strange Story of Grey Owl* (see 2198). Issued in paper.

2381. DIEFENBAKER, John G.

One Canada: Memoirs of the Right Honourable John G. Diefenbaker: The Years of Achievement 1957-1962. Macmillan of Canada Toronto.

xviii, 330 pp.; 233 × 150 mm.
First volume published in 1975 (see 2320) and third volume in 1977 (see 2464).

2382. DUNKELMAN, Ben

Dual Allegiance. An Autobiography by Ben Dunkelman. Macmillan of Canada Toronto.

xiv, 336 pp.; 234 × 150 mm.

2383. EVANS, Douglas

The Politics of Energy: The Emergence of the Superstate. Douglas Evans. Macmillan of Canada [and] Maclean-Hunter Press.

xii, 155, [1] pp.; 222 × 140 mm.

2384. FLANNERY, James W.

W.B. Yeats and the Idea of a Theatre: The Early Abbey Theatre in Theory and Practice. James W. Flannery. Macmillan of Canada.

xxii, 404 pp.; 222 × 142 mm.

2385.   FLETCHER, G.A.

The Discount Houses in London: Principles, Operation and Change. G.A.
Fletcher, B.A., M. Sc. (Econ.), Lecturer in Economics, University of Liverpool. Macmillan of Canada/Maclean-Hunter Press.

  xiv, 298 pp.; 222 × 144 mm.

2386.   FLOWERS, Betty

Browning and the Modern Tradition. Betty S. Flowers. Macmillan of Canada
[and] Maclean-Hunter Press.

  [8], 208 pp.; 220 × 140 mm.

2387.   FODERARO, Salvatore

Independent Africa. Salvatore Foderaro, Professor of Law, University of
Rome. Translated from the Italian. Macmillan of Canada [and] Maclean-
Hunter Press.

  183, [1] pp.; 220 × 152 mm.

2388.   FOLEY, James

Themes in Canadian Literature, *The Search for Canadian Identity*. Edited by
James Foley. General Editor, David Arnason. Macmillan of Canada.

  [6], 122 pp.; 225 × 145 mm.
  Issued in paper.
  Themes in Canadian Literature Series.

2389.   FORD, Theresa

Themes in Canadian Literature, *Canadian Humour and Satire*. Edited by
Theresa Ford. General Editor, David Arnason. Macmillan of Canada.

  [6], 122 pp.; 225 × 145 mm.
  Issued in paper.
  Themes in Canadian Literature Series.

2390.   GAGNE, Wallace

Nationalism, Technology and the Future of Canada. Edited by Wallace Gagne.
Macmillan of Canada [and] Maclean-Hunter Press.

  [8], 167, [1] pp.; 220 × 142 mm.
  Issued in cloth and paper.

2391.   GALBRAITH, John S.

The Little Emperor: Governor Simpson of the Hudson's Bay Company. John S.
Galbraith. Macmillan of Canada Toronto.

  x, 232 pp.; 235 × 155 mm.

2392.   GIFFORD, Tony

The Play's The Thing: Four Original Television Dramas. Edited by Tony
Gifford, Utilization Officer, Educational Media Division, Ontario Educational Communications Authority. Macmillan of Canada.

  183, [1] pp.; 210 × 135 mm.
  Issued in paper.

2393. GREEN, Alan G.

Immigration and the Postwar Canadian Economy. Alan G. Green. Macmillan of Canada [and] Maclean-Hunter Press.

    xviii, 312 pp.; 234 × 157 mm.

2394. HALE, Alice K.

Themes in Canadian Literature, *The Depression in Canadian Literature.* Edited by Alice K. Hale and Sheila A. Brooks. General Editor, David Arnason. Macmillan of Canada.

    [6], 114 pp.; 225 × 145 mm.
Issued in paper.
Themes in Canadian Literature Series.

2395. HANSON, Eric J.

Organization for Economic Cooperation and Development, Review of Educational Policies in Canada (Western Region). *Financing in Educational Services in Western Canada.* Eric J. Hanson, Professor Emeritus/University of Alberta. Macmillan of Canada.

    [4], 134, [12] pp.; 272 × 207 mm.
Issued in paper.

2396. HENDERSON, Jim

The Language Box: An Elementary School Communications Kit. Jim Henderson [and] John A. Myers. Macmillan of Canada.

    213 × 130 mm.
Box consisting of Teacher's Handbook, Student Record Folder and 300 cards. Also in this series is a Language Box Specimen Kit consisting of Teacher's Handbook, specimen cards, Student Record Folder, and Descriptive Leaflet.
Language Box Series.

2397. HODGINS, Jack

Spit Delaney's Island. Selected Stories by Jack Hodgins. Macmillan of Canada Toronto.

    [8], 199, [1] pp.; 234 × 155 mm.
Reprinted in the Laurentian Library (No. 58) in 1977. Issued in cloth and paper.

2398. HODGINS, Jack

Themes in Canadian Literature, *The West Coast Experience.* Edited by Jack Hodgins. General Editor, David Arnason. Macmillan of Canada.

    [6], 120 pp.; 225 × 145 mm.
Issued in paper.
Themes in Canadian Literature Series.

2399. HULME, George

The Life and Death of Adolf Hitler. By George Hulme. Macmillan of Canada [and] Maclean-Hunter Press.

    [6], 246 pp.; 240 × 158 mm.

2400. HUTCHISON, Bruce
The Far Side of the Street. Bruce Hutchison. Macmillan of Canada Toronto.
[12], 420 pp.; 233 × 150 mm.

2401. JAKOBER, Marie
The Mind Gods: A Novel of the Future. Marie Jakober. Macmillan of Canada.
Toronto.
[10], 165, [1] pp.; 220 × 144 mm.

2402. JANES, J. Robert
Geology and the New Global Tectonics: An Introduction to Physical and Historical Geology. J. Robert Janes, B.A.Sc., M.Eng. Macmillan of Canada.
[12], 468 pp.; 235 × 175 mm.

2403. KELLY, William
Policy in Canada. William and Nora Kelly. Macmillan of Canada [and]
Maclean-Hunter Press.
xii, 704 pp.; 234 × 155 mm.

2404. KENNEDY, Betty
Gerhard: A Love Story. Betty Kennedy. Macmillan of Canada/Toronto.
[8], 71, [1] pp.; 206 × 138 mm.
Issued in cloth and paper.

2405. KILBOURN, William
The Toronto Book: An Anthology of Writings Past and Present. Edited by
William Kilbourn. Macmillan of Canada/Toronto.
290 pp.; 233 × 155 mm.

2406. KIRKPATRICK, A.M.
Crime and You. A.M. Kirkpatrick and W.T. McGrath. Macmillan of Canada
[and] Maclean-Hunter Press.
xiv, 170 pp.; 220 × 140 mm.
Issued in cloth and paper.

2407. LANG, H. Murray
Inquiries into Biology, *Diversity of Life: Teacher's Guide*. H. Murray Lang,
Associate Professor, The Faculty of Education, University of Toronto,
Edwin G. Palfery, Science Chairman, Mimico High School, Borough of
Etobicoke and Ed L.R. Van Nieuwenhove, Head of Science, Woburn Collegiate Institute, Borough of Scarborough. Macmillan of Canada.
[2], 43, [1] pp.; 277 × 213 mm.
Issued in paper.
Inquiries into Biology Series.

2408. LANG, H. Murray

Inquiries into Biology, *Interdependence of Life: Teacher's Guide*. H. Murray Lang, Associate Professor, The Faculty of Education, University of Toronto, Edwin G. Palfery, Vice-Principal, Alderwood Collegiate Institute, Borough of Etobicoke [and] Ed L.R. Van Nieuwenhove, Head of Science, Woburn Collegiate Institute, Borough of Scarborough. Macmillan of Canada.

[2], 39, [1] pp.; 277 × 213 mm.
Issued in paper.
Inquiries into Biology Series.

2409. LANG, H. Murray

Inquiries into Biology, *Microbiology: Teacher's Guide*. H. Murray Lang, Associate Professor, The Faculty of Education, University of Toronto, Edwin G. Palfery, Science Chairman, Mimico High School, Borough of Etobicoke, [and] Ed L.R. Van Nieuwenhove, Head of Science, Woburn Collegiate Institute, Borough of Scarborough. Macmillan of Canada.

[2], 38 pp.; 277 × 213 mm.
Issued in paper.
Inquiries into Biology Series.

2410. LYON, Peyton V.

Canada and the Third World. Edited by Peyton V. Lyon and Tareq V. Ismael. Macmillan of Canada [and] Maclean-Hunter Press.

l, 342 pp.; 220 × 140 mm.
Issued in cloth and paper.
Canadian Controversies Series.

2411. MacLAREN, Roy

Roy MacLaren, *Canadians in Russia, 1918-1919*. Macmillan of Canada [and] Maclean-Hunter Press.

x, 301, [1] pp.; 234 × 155 mm.

2412. MARCHAND, Philip

Philip Marchand, *Just Looking, Thank You: An Amused Observer's View of Canadian Lifestyles*. Macmillan of Canada Toronto.

xvi, 208 pp.; 220 × 140 mm.

2413. MARTIN, Wilfred B.W.

The Negotiated Order of the School. Wilfred B.W. Martin. Macmillan of Canada [and] Maclean-Hunter Press.

xvi, 191, [1] pp.; 220 × 140 mm.

2414. McDONALD, Neil

Egerton Ryerson and His Times. Edited by Neil McDonald and Alf Chaiton. Macmillan of Canada.

[12], 319, [1] pp.; 220 × 140 mm.
Issued in cloth and paper. Reprinted in 1978.

2415.   McGARRY, James P.

Place Names in the Writings of William Butler Yeats. By James P. McGarry. Edited and with additional material by Edward Malins and a Preface by Kathleen Raine. Macmillan of Canada [and] Maclean-Hunter Press.

> 99, [1] pp.; 220 × 140 mm.

2416.   McGRATH, W.T.

Crime and Its Treatment in Canada. Second Edition. Edited by W.T. McGrath. Macmillan of Canada [and] Maclean-Hunter Press.

> [12], 610 pp.; 232 × 155 mm.
> First published in 1965 (see 1742). Issued in cloth and paper.

2417.   McLACHLAN, Ian

The Seventh Hexagram. A novel by Ian McLachlan. Macmillan of Canada, Toronto.

> [10], 278 pp.; 235 × 158 mm.

2418.   MINIFIE, James M.

James M. Minifie, *Expatriate*. Introduction by Leland Stowe. L'Envoie by Hugh Keenleyside. Macmillan of Canada Toronto.

> x, 214 pp.; 235 × 153 mm.

2418A   MITCHELL, W.O.

W.O. Mitchell. *Who Has Seen The Wind*. Illustrated by William Kurelek. Macmillan of Canada Toronto.

> [14], 301, [5] pp.; 255 × 215 mm.
> First published in 1947 (see 1145). A school edition was published in 1960 (see 1501). Reprinted in paper in 1971 in the St. Martin's Classics Series. Published in the Laurentian Library (No.14) in 1972. This edition reprinted in 1978.

2419.   MOORE, George

Hail and Farewell: Ave, Salve, Vale. George Moore. Edited by Richard Cave. Macmillan of Canada [and] Maclean-Hunter Press.

> 774 pp.; 238 × 158 mm.

2420.   NADER, George A.

Cities of Canada: Volume Two: Profiles of Fifteen Metropolitan Centres. George A. Nader, Trent University. Macmillan of Canada [and] Maclean-Hunter Press.

> xiv, 460 pp.; 233 × 155 mm.

2421.   NEW, William H.

Modern Canadian Essays. Edited by William H. New. Macmillan of Canada.

> xii, 187, [1] pp.; 215 × 138 mm.
> Issued in paper.

2422.   NICHOLS, Ruth

Song Of The Pearl. Ruth Nichols. Macmillan of Canada, Toronto.

> [8], 158 pp.; 210 × 140 mm.

2423. O'DRISCOLL, Robert

Robert O'Driscoll, *An Ascendancy of the Heart: Ferguson and the Beginnings of Modern Irish Literature in English*. With an Introduction by Maire Cruise O'Brien. Macmillan of Canada/Maclean-Hunter Press.

84 pp.; 220 × 140 mm.

2424. OGELSBY, J.C.M.

Gringos From the Far North: Essays in the History of Canadian-Latin American Relations 1866-1968. J.C.M. Ogelsby. Macmillan of Canada [and] Maclean-Hunter Press.

xvi, 346 pp.; 233 × 155 mm.

2425. PAMMETT, Jon H.

Foundations of Political Culture: Political Socialization in Canada. Edited by Jon H. Pammett and Michael S. Whittington. Macmillan of Canada [and] Maclean-Hunter Press.

xii, 318 pp.; 233 × 155 mm.

2426. PENTON, M. James

Jehovah's Witnesses in Canada: Champions of Freedom of Speech and Worship. M. James Penton. Macmillan of Canada [and] Maclean-Hunter Press.

xii, 388 pp.; 234 × 155 mm.

2427. PRESLEY, John R.

Currency Areas: Theory and Practice. John R. Presley and Geoffrey E.J. Dennis. Macmillan of Canada/Maclean-Hunter Press.

[10], 114 pp.; 220 × 140 mm.

2428. RAMSDEN, Madeleine

Dreams and Challenges: Writing Poetry. Madeleine Ramsden, Head of English Department, Louis Riel Collegiate, St. Boniface, Manitoba. Consultant: Robert Ireland, Co-ordinator of Language Arts, Metropolitan Separate School Board, Toronto. Macmillan of Canada.

[14], 108 pp.; 225 × 148 mm.

2429. RAMSDEN, Madeleine

Teacher's Handbook: Dreams and Challenges: Writing Poetry. Madeleine Ramsden, Head of English Department, Louis Riel Collegiate, St. Boniface, Manitoba. Macmillan of Canada.

[14], 40 pp.; 227 × 150 mm.
Issued in paper.

2430. RAMU, G.N.

Introduction to Canadian Society: Sociological Analysis. Edited by G.N. Ramu [and] Stuart D. Johnson. Macmillan of Canada [and] Maclean-Hunter Press.

x, 530 pp.; 232 × 155 mm.

2431. REGEHR, T.D.

The Canadian Northern Railway: Pioneer Road of the Northern Prairies 1895-1918. T.D. Regehr. Macmillan of Canada [and] Maclean-Hunter Press.

xvi, 543, [1] pp.; 230 × 153 mm.

2432. ROYLE, Edward

The Infidel Tradition from Paine to Bradlaugh. Edited by Edward Royle, University of York. [Quotation]. Macmillan of Canada/Maclean-Hunter Press.

xviii, 228 pp.; 222 × 136 mm.
History in Depth Series.

2433. SCHULL, Joseph

Edward Blake: Leader and Exile (1881-1912). Joseph Schull. Macmillan of Canada Toronto.

xiv, 266 pp.; 235 × 155 mm.

2434. SMITH, Peter Seaborn

Oil and Politics In Modern Brazil. Macmillan of Canada/Maclean-Hunter Press.

[12], 289, [1] pp.; 230 × 153 mm.

2435. SMYTHE, James M.

Special Revised Edition, *Elements of Geography*. James M. Smythe, M.A., Head of the Geography Department, Earl Haig Secondary School, North York, Charles G. Brown, B.A., Assistant Director of Education, Board of Education, North York, Eric H. Fors, B.A., Vice-Principal, Westview Centennial Secondary School, North York. Maps and Diagrams by A. Diana and F. Zsigo. Macmillan of Canada/Toronto.

xii, 526 pp.; 235 × 165 mm.
Elements of Geography: Special Revised Edition, contains the new revision of the first three sections published separately as *Physical Geography* in 1970 (see 2079) and the last three sections, updated, of *Elements of Geography: Revised Edition*, 1964 (see 1698). First published in 1959 (see 1474). In 1978 a metric edition of the 1970 *Physical Geography* edition was published (see 2602). In 1979 a French metric edition was published (see 2655).

2436. STACEY, C.P.

Mackenzie King And The Atlantic Triangle. The 1976 Joanne Goodman Lectures, Delivered at the University of Western Ontario. By C.P. Stacey, Late University Professor, University of Toronto. Macmillan of Canada/Maclean-Hunter Press.

xviii, 74 pp.; 220 × 140 mm.

2437. STACEY, C.P.

A Very Double Life: The Private World of Mackenzie King. C.P. Stacey. Macmillan of Canada Toronto.

256 pp.; 233 × 155 mm.
Reprinted in the Laurentian Library (No. 46) in 1977.

2438.   STANTON, Charles R.
Canadian Forestry: The View Beyond The Trees. By Chas. R. Stanton. [Contents Listed]. Macmillan of Canada [and] Maclean-Hunter Press. Cette publication est disponible en français sous le titre *La foresterie au Canada — Au delà des arbres*.
> 70 pp.; 275 × 213 mm.
> Issued in paper.

2439.   STERN, Robert M.
Price Elasticities in International Trade: An Annotated Bibliography. By Robert M. Stern, Jonathan Francis and Bruce Schumacher. Macmillan of Canada/Maclean-Hunter Press.
> xvi, 363, [1] pp.; 222 × 141 mm.

2440.   STEVENS, John
Themes in Canadian Literature, *The Ontario Experience*. Edited by John Stevens. General Editor, David Arnason. Macmillan of Canada.
> [6], 122 pp.; 225 × 145 mm.
> Issued in paper.
> Themes in Canadian Literature Series.

2441.   STEWART, Walter
But Not in Canada! Walter Stewart. Macmillan of Canada.
> [8], 258 pp.; 220 × 140 mm.

2442.   SUKNASKI, Andrew
Wood Mountain Poems. Andrew Suknaski. Macmillan of Canada/Toronto.
> 127, [1] pp.; 210 × 133 mm.
> Issued in paper.

2443.   THOMAS, Nicholas
A Guide To Prehistoric England. Nicholas Thomas. Macmillan of Canada [and] Maclean-Hunter Press.
> 270 pp.; 220 × 142 mm.

2444.   TOMLINSON, B.R.
The Indian National Congress and the Raj, 1929-1942: The Penultimate Phase. Macmillan of Canada/Maclean-Hunter Press.
> [8], 208 pp.; 222 × 144 mm.

2445.   WIEBE, Rudy
Double Vision: An Anthology of Twentieth-Century Stories in English. Selected by Rudy Wiebe, University of Alberta. Macmillan of Canada.
> xiv, 331, [1] pp.; 188 × 130 mm.
> Issued in paper.

2446. WIGLE, Robert

Teacher's Guide: Mathematical Pursuits One. Robert Wigle, Head of the Mathematics Department, Delhi District Secondary School, Delhi, Ontario, Paul Dowling, Mathematics Department, Delhi District Secondary School, Delhi, Ontario [and] Paul Jennings, Associate Chairman of Pure Science, Lester B. Pearson Secondary School, Burlington, Ontario. Macmillan of Canada.

[2], 64 pp.; 272 × 208 mm.
Issued in paper.

2447. WIGLE, Robert

Teacher's Guide: Mathematical Pursuits Two. Robert Wigle, Head of the Mathematics Department, Delhi District Secondary School, Delhi, Ontario, Paul Dowling, Mathematics Department, Delhi District Secondary School, Delhi, Ontario [and] Paul Jennings, Associate Chairman of Pure Science, Lester B. Pearson Secondary School, Burlington, Ontario. Macmillan of Canada.

[2], 51, [1] pp.; 272 × 208 mm.
Issued in paper.

2448. WILSON, Betty

André Tom Macgregor. Betty Wilson. Macmillan of Canada Toronto.

[6], 162 pp.; 220 × 140 mm.

2449. WILSON, Lionel

Themes in Canadian Literature, *The Artist in Canadian Literature*. Edited by Lionel Wilson. General Editor, David Arnason. Macmillan of Canada.

[6], 122 pp.; 225 × 145 mm.
Issued in paper.
Themes in Canadian Literature Series.

2450. WRIGHT, Richard B.

Farthing's Fortunes. Richard B. Wright. Macmillan of Canada/Toronto.

xiv, 333, [1] pp.; 235 × 160 mm.

1977

2451. AIKMAN, J.A

Watching the Weather Change. Metric edition. Jack A. Aikman, Formerly Vice-Principal, St. Catharines Teachers' College, St. Catharines, Ontario. Toronto: The Macmillan Company of Canada Limited.

[4], 35, [1] pp.; 226 × 149 mm.
First published in 1969 (see 1968).
Our Science Program Series.

2452.   ALLEN, Robert Thomas
Robert Thomas Allen, *My Childhood and Yours: Happy Memories of Growing Up*. Macmillan of Canada, Toronto.
   [8], 167, [1] pp.; 220 × 137 mm.

2453.   ANDERSON, Allan
Remembering the Farm: Memories of Farming, Ranching and Rural Life in Canada, Past and Present. Allan Anderson. Macmillan of Canada Toronto.
   xviii, 287, [1] pp.; 233 × 155 mm.
   Reprinted in 1978 (cloth) and 1979 (paper).

2454.   BERCUSON, David Jay
Canada and the Burden of Unity. Edited by David Jay Bercuson. Macmillan of Canada.
   [12], 191, [1] pp.; 220 × 142 mm.
   Issued in paper.

2455.   BERESFORD-HOWE, Constance
A Population of One. A Novel By Constance Beresford-Howe. Macmillan of Canada/Toronto.
   [12], 201, [1] pp.; 220 × 140 mm.

2456.   BRITTON, Edward
The Community of the Vill: A Study in the History of the Family and Village Life in Fourteenth-Century England. Edward Britton. Macmillan of Canada.
   xx, 291, [1] pp.; 233 × 155 mm.

2457.   BRUCE, Harry
Lifeline: The Story of the Atlantic Ferries and Coastal Boats. Harry Bruce. Macmillan of Canada/Toronto.
   xviii, 249, [1] pp.; 220 × 140 mm.

2458.   CALLAGHAN, Morley
Close to the Sun Again. A New Novel By Morley Callaghan. Macmillan of Canada/Toronto.
   [6], 169, [1] pp.; 220 × 138 mm.

2458A   *The Celtic Way Of Life*. Macmillan of Canada/Maclean-HunterPress.
   136 pp.; 215 × 148 mm.

2459.   CHARNIN, Martin
Annie. A Theatre Memoir by Martin Charnin, Lyricist and Director of the Broadway Musical. Macmillan of Canada Toronto.
   134 pp.; 275 × 205 mm.
   Issued in paper.

2460.   CHERNICK, Beryl A.

In Touch: Putting Sex Back Into Love and Marriage. By Beryl A. Chernick, MD, PH.D., and Avinoam B. Chernick, MD, FRCS(C), FACOG. Adapted by Jeniva Berger. Macmillan of Canada Toronto.

[10], 182 pp.; 220 × 140 mm.

2461.   CURZON, Gerard

The Multinational Enterprise in a Hostile World. Proceedings of a conference held in Geneva under the auspices of the Graduate Institute of International Studies, l'Institut Universitaire d'Etudes Européennes and the Center for Education in International Management. Edited by Gerard Curzon and Victoria Curzon with the collaboration of Lawrence G. Franko and Henri Schwamm. Macmillan of Canada/Maclean-Hunter Press.

x, 147, [1] pp.; 220 × 140 mm.

2462.   DARLING, Christopher

Kain & Augustyn. A Photographic Study by Christopher Darling. Text by John Fraser. Foreword by Rudolf Nureyev. A Jonathan-James Book. Macmillan of Canada.

160 pp.; 285 × 218 mm.
Issued in cloth and paper.

2463.   DAVIES, Robertson

One Half of Robertson Davies: Provocative Pronouncements on a Wide Range of Topics. By Robertson Davies. Macmillan of Canada/Toronto.

[8], 286 pp.; 223 × 143 mm.

2464.   DIEFENBAKER, John G.

One Canada: Memoirs of the Right Honourable John G. Diefenbaker: The Tumultuous Years 1962-1967. Macmillan of Canada Toronto.

xxvi, 309, [1] pp.; 233 × 150 mm.
First volume published in 1975 (see 2320) and second volume in 1976 (see 2381).

2465.   ENGLISH, John

Mackenzie King: Widening the Debate. Edited by John English/J.O. Stubbs. Macmillan of Canada.

x, 253, [1] pp.; 220 × 140 mm.

2466.   FAZAKAS, Ray

The Donnelly Album. The Complete and Authentic Account Illustrated with Photographs of Canada's Famous Feuding Family. Ray Fazakas. Macmillan of Canada Toronto.

[8], 311, [1] pp.; 270 × 215 mm.
Issued in cloth and paper.

2467.   FEACHEM, Richard
Guide to Prehistoric Scotland. Richard Feachem. Macmillan of Canada/Maclean-Hunter Press.
223, [1] pp.; 222 × 144 mm.

2468.   FERGUSON, Trevor
High Water Chants. A novel by Trevor Ferguson. Macmillan of Canada.
[12], 268 pp.; 220 × 140 mm.

2469.   FINNERAN, Richard J.
The Correspondence of Robert Bridges and W.B. Yeats. Edited by Richard J. Finneran. Macmillan of Canada.
xviii, 68 pp.; 220 × 140 mm.

2470.   GALBRAITH, John Kenneth
From the works of John Kenneth Galbraith, *The Galbraith Reader*. Selected and arranged with narrative comment by the editors of Gambit. Gambit, Ipswich & Macmillan of Canada, 1977.
xiv, 496 pp.; 239 × 157 mm.

2471.   GEDGE, Pauline
Child of the Morning. By Pauline Gedge. The Macmillan Company of Canada Limited 1977.
[8], 403, [1] pp.; 237 × 157 mm.

2472.   GEHLE, Quentin L.
The Writing Process. Quentin L. Gehle [and] Duncan J. Rollo. Macmillan of Canada.
xvi, 268, [2] pp.; 230 × 160 mm.
Issued in paper.

2473.   GIBSON, Norman J.
Economic Activity in Ireland: A Study of Two Open Economies. Editors Norman J. Gibson and John E. Spencer. Contributors: W. Black, J.A. Bristow, P.T. Geary, N.J. Gibson, M.J. Harrison. D. McAleese, J.W. O'Hagan, J.E. Spencer, [and] B.M. Walsh. Gill and Macmillan, Macmillan of Canada [and] Maclean-Hunter Press.
xxii, 272 pp.; 220 × 140 mm.

2474.   GODFREY, C.
Four-Figure Tables. By C. Godfrey and A.W. Siddons. Macmillan of Canada 1977.
46 pp.; 213 × 135 mm.
Issued in paper.

2475.   GOODSPEED, D.J.

The German Wars 1914-1945. D.J. Goodspeed. Illustrated with maps. Macmillan of Canada/Toronto 1977.

xvi, 561, [1] pp.; 238 × 160 mm.

2476.   GORDON, Esmé

The Royal Scottish Academy of Painting Sculpture & Architecture 1826-1976. Esmé Gordon. Macmillan of Canada/Maclean-Hunter Press. With A Foreword By His Royal Highness, The Prince Philip, Duke of Edinburgh, O.M., K.G., K.T., Honorary Member of the Royal Scottish Academy.

xxiv, 272 pp.; 252 × 190 mm.

2476A   GREASON, George K.

Third Edition, *Canadian Democracy at Work.* George K. Greason, Formerly Head of History Department, Downsview Secondary School, North York [and] Roy C. King, C.W. Jefferys Secondary School, North York. Drawings by Dorothy Mould and Vernon Mould. Toronto: The Macmillan Company Of Canada Limited.

[8], 119, [1] pp.; 223 × 145 mm.
First published in 1962 (see 1574). Revised in 1966 (see 1781A) and 1969 (see 1984). Third edition revised in 1971 (see 2099). This edition also revised.

2477.   GREIG, James W.

Over the Horizon. Edited by James W. Greig, B.A., ED.D., Co-ordinator of Continuing Education and Graduate Studies, The Faculty of Education, University of Toronto. Macmillan of Canada.

[10], 310 pp.; 233 × 155 mm.
First published in 1964 (see 1678A). This edition revised.
Passport to Reading Series.

2478.   GRUMEZA, Ion

Nadia: The Success Secrets of the Amazing Romanian Gymnast. By Ion Grumeza. Edited by Fred Kerner. Drawings by Lisa Craig Wesson. Photographs by Bruce Curtis, Bob Greene, Joe DiMaggio and others. The K.S. Giniger Company, Inc. Publishers, New York. Distributed by Hawthorn Books, Inc., New York. In Canada: The Macmillan Company of Canada, Ltd., Toronto.

127, [1] pp.; 230 × 145 mm.
Reprinted in 1977 (twice). Issued in paper.

2479.   HABERMAN, Arthur

The Making of the Modern Age: Europe and the West Since 1789. Arthur Haberman, Associate Professor of History and Humanities Associate Dean, Faculty of Education, York University, Toronto. Study material and bibliography by Robert Remnant, History Department, Lasalle Secondary School, Sudbury, Ontario. Macmillan of Canada.

[10], 336 pp.; 245 × 175 mm.

2480. HAND, J.G.

Investigative Science, *The Investigative Cycle — Chemistry*. By J.G. Hand, Science Department, Hill Park Secondary School, Hamilton, Ontario, G.W. Kocsis, Assistant Head of Biology, Hill Park Secondary School, Hamilton, Ontario, S.G. Percival, Chairman of Pure Science, Lester B. Pearson High School, Burlington, Ontario [and] C.F. Reid, Head of Science, Hill Park Secondary School, Hamilton, Ontario. Macmillan of Canada.

[2], 30 pp.; 230 × 172 mm.
Issued in paper.
Investigative Science Series.

2481. HAND, J.G.

Investigative Science, *Skills and Techniques*. J.G. Hand, Science Department, Hill Park Secondary School, Hamilton, Ontario, G.W. Kocsis, Assistant Head of Biology, Hill Park Secondary School, Hamilton, Ontario, S.G. Percival, Chairman of Pure Science, Lester B. Pearson High School, Burlington, Ontario [and] C.F. Reid, Head of Science, Hill Park Secondary School, Hamilton, Ontario. Macmillan of Canada.

[2], 70 pp.; 230 × 172 mm.
Issued in paper.
Investigative Science Series.

2482. HAND, J.G.

Investigative Science, *Water Management*. J.G. Hand, Science Department, Hill Park Secondary School, Hamilton, Ontario, G.W. Kocsis, Assistant Head of Biology, Hill Park Secondary School, Hamilton, Ontario, S.G. Percival, Chairman of Pure Science, Lester B. Pearson High School, Burlington, Ontario [and] C.F. Reid, Head of Science, Hill Park Secondary School, Hamilton, Ontario. Macmillan of Canada.

[2], 31, [1] pp.; 230 × 172 mm.
Issued in paper.
Investigative Science Series.

2483. HEGGIE, Grace F.

Canadian Political Parties 1867-1968: A Historical Bibliography. Compiled And Edited By Grace F. Heggie. Macmillan of Canada.

[16], 603, [1] pp.; 257 × 168 mm.

2484. HENDERSON, Jim

The Time of Your Life: An Anthology of Short Stories. Revised Edition. Selected and edited by Jim Henderson, M.A., Co-ordinator, Language Study Centre, Toronto Board of Education. Macmillan of Canada.

xviii, 239, [1] pp.; 180 × 123 mm.
First published in 1967 (see 1848). Issued in paper.

2485. HIGGINS, Donald J.H.

Urban Canada: Its Government and Politics. Donald J.H. Higgins. Macmillan of Canada.

[10], 322 pp.; 226 × 147 mm.

2486.   HODGINS, Jack
The Invention of the World. A Novel By Jack Hodgins. Macmillan of Canada/Toronto.
    xii, 354 pp.; 220 × 140 mm.

2487.   HUME, John R.
The Industrial Archaeology of Scotland. II. The Highlands and Islands. John R. Hume. Macmillan of Canada.
    335, [1] pp.; 220 × 143 mm.

2488.   IRELAND, Robert J.
The Macmillan Spelling Series: 4. Revised Edition. Robert J. Ireland. General Editor: George E. Flower, Dean, Faculty of Education, McGill University, Montreal. Designed by Glyphics, Division of Kerrigan O'Grady Limited. Illustrated by Heather Collins. © 1977, Macmillan of Canada.
    112 pp.; 233 × 155 mm.
    First published in 1961 (see 1529).
    Macmillan Spelling Series.

2489.   JACK, Donald
The Story of CFRB: *Sinc, Betty, And The Morning Man.* By Donald Jack. Macmillan of Canada Toronto.
    [8], 166 pp.; 213 × 138 mm.
    Issued in paper.

2490.   JONAS, George
George Jonas and Barbara Amiel, *By Persons Unknown: The Strange Death of Christine Demeter.* Macmillan of Canada Toronto.
    x, 349, [1] pp.; 233 × 155 mm.

2491.   LAMB, James B.
The Corvette Navy: True Stories From Canada's Atlantic War. James B. Lamb. Macmillan of Canada/Toronto.
    [8], 179, [1] pp.; 220 × 140 mm.

2492.   LEE, Dennis
Garbage Delight. The poems were written by Dennis Lee. The pictures were drawn by Frank Newfeld. Macmillan of Canada Toronto.
    64 pp.; 260 × 193 mm.

2493.   McAULIFFE, C.A.
The Chemistry of Mercury. Edited by C.A. McAuliffe, University of Manchester Institute of Science and Technology. Macmillan of Canada/Maclean-Hunter Press.
    viii, 288 p.; 240 × 158 mm.

2494.   McCONNELL, W.H.

W.H. McConnell, *Commentary on the British North America Act*. Macmillan of Canada.

  x, 469, [1] pp.; 233 × 155 mm.

2495.   McFEE, Oonah

A Novel. *Sandbars*. Oonah McFee. Macmillan of Canada.

  [10], 357, [1] pp.; 220 × 140 mm.

2496.   McKAY, Heather

Heather McKay's Complete Book of Squash. By Heather McKay with Jack Batten. A Jonathan-James Book. Macmillan of Canada, Toronto.

  143, [1] pp.; 213 × 187 mm.
  Issued in paper.

2497.   METTAM, Roger

Government And Society In Louis XIV's France. Edited by Roger Mettam. Macmillan of Canada/Maclean-Hunter Press.

  xviii, 270 pp.; 222 × 141 mm.
  History in Depth Series.

2498.   MITCHELL, Ken

Everybody Gets Something Here. Stories by Ken Mitchell. Macmillan of Canada Toronto.

  [6], 122 pp.; 220 × 140 mm.
  Issued in cloth and paper.

2499.   MITCHELL, Peter M.

China: Tradition and Revolution. Peter M. Mitchell, Department of History, York University. Study material prepared by Douglas M. Parker, Head of History, Thistletown Collegiate Institute, Rexdale, Ontario. Macmillan of Canada/Toronto.

  [6], 234 pp.; 225 × 150 mm.
  Issued in paper.
  The West and the World: Studies in History Series.

2500.   NOWLAN, Michael O.

Themes in Canadian Literature, *Canadian Myths and Legends*. Edited by Michael O. Nowlan. General Editor, David Arnason. Macmillan of Canada.

  [6], 118 pp.; 225 × 145 mm.
  Issued in paper.
  Themes in Canadian Literature Series.

2501. NOWLAN, Michael O.

[Cover-title:] *Question Time*. A Play By Robertson Davies. *Comments and Exercises* by Michael O. Nowlan, Head of the English Department, Oromocto Senior High School, Oromocto, New Brunswick. Macmillan of Canada.

8 pp.; 210 × 130 mm.
Issued in paper.

2502. O'BOYLE, Sean

Sean O'Boyle, *The Irish Song Tradition*. Macmillan of Canada/Maclean-Hunter Press.

93, [1] pp.; 220 × 142 mm.

2503. O'DAY, Alan

Alan O'Day, *The English Face of Irish Nationalism: Parnellite Involvement in British Politics 1880-86*. Gill and Macmillan, Macmillan of Canada [and] Maclean-Hunter Press.

x, 210 pp.; 221 × 140 mm.

2504. O'LEARY, Grattan

Grattan O'Leary, *Recollections of People, Press, and Politics*. Foreword by Robert L. Stanfield. Introduction and Personal Postcript by I. Norman Smith. Macmillan of Canada/Toronto.

xvi, 208 pp.; 233 × 150 mm.

2505. PEARCE, G.F.

Engineering Graphics and Descriptive Geometry in 3-D. G.F. Pearce. The Macmillan Company of Canada.

[6], 375, [1] pp.; 278 × 220 mm.
Issued in paper.

2506. PENNER, Philip G.

Language on Paper: Writing Systems, English Punctuation, English Spelling. Philip G. Penner [and] Ruth E. McConnell, University of British Columbia. Macmillan of Canada.

[10], 182 pp.; 231 × 174 mm.
Issued in paper.

2507. PENNER, Philip G.

Learning Language. A Revision of *Learning English*. Philip G. Penner, [and] Ruth E. McConnell, University of British Columbia. Macmillan of Canada.

[16], 334 pp.; 235 × 175 mm.
First published in 1963 as *Learning English* (see 1645).

2508. PENNER, Philip G.

Teacher's Handbook: Learning Language. P.G. Penner, [and] R.E. McConnell, University of British Columbia. Macmillan of Canada.

[6], 99, [1] pp.; 225 × 145 mm.
Issued in paper.

2509. PUNNETT, R.M.

The Prime Minister in Canadian Government and Politics. R.M. Punnett.
Canadian Controversies Series. Macmillan of Canada [and] Maclean-Hunter
Press.

    viii, 168 pp.; 220 × 140 mm.
    Issued in cloth and paper.
    Canadian Controversies Series.

2510. RITCHIE, Charles

An Appetite for Life: The Education of a Young Diarist 1924-1927. Charles
Ritchie. Macmillan of Canada Toronto.

    xiv, 173, [1] pp.; 220 × 140 mm.

2511. ROCHE, Richard

Saltees: Islands of birds and legends. Richard Roche, with a section on the bird
life by Oscar Merne. Photographs by George Gmelch, Brendan Hearne [and]
Richard Mills. Macmillan of Canada.

    151, [1] pp.; 251 × 188 mm.

2512. SHACK, Sybil F.

The Macmillan Spelling Series: 3. Revised Edition. Sybil Shack. General
Editor: George E. Flower, Dean, Faculty of Education, McGill University,
Montreal. Designed by Glyphics, Division of Kerrigan O'Grady Limited.
Illustrated by Heather Collins. © 1977, Macmillan of Canada.

    160 pp.; 233 × 155 mm.
    First published in 1960 (see 1488).
    Macmillan Spelling Series.

2513. SLOAN, Glenna Davis

A Canadian Topliner, *Spotlight on Liz*. Glenna Davis Sloan. Macmillan of
Canada.

    [2], 124, [2] pp.; 175 × 105 mm.
    Issued in paper.
    Topliner Series.

2514. SMITH, Ronald W.

Sociology: An Introduction. Ronald W. Smith [and] Frederick W. Preston,
Both of The University of Nevada, Las Vegas. Macmillan of Canada.

    xiv, 575, [1] pp.; 240 × 190 mm.

2515. STACEY, C.P.

C.P. Stacey, *Canada and the Age of Conflict: A History of Canadian External
Policies. Volume 1: 1867-1921*. Macmillan of Canada.

    [12], 410 pp.; 234 × 156 mm.
    Reprinted in paper in 1979.

2516.   STEINHAUER, Paul D.

Psychological Problems of the Child and His Family: A Textbook of Basic Child and Adolescent Psychiatry for Students and Practitioners of Medicine and the Mental Health Professions. Edited by Paul D. Steinhauer and Quentin Rae-Grant. Macmillan of Canada.

xiv, 459, [1] pp.; 233 × 155 mm.

2517.   STIRLING, Norman

Introduction to Technical Drawing. Metric Edition. Norman Stirling, Director of Technical Education, Courtice Secondary School, Courtice, Ontario. Macmillan of Canada.

[10], 369, [1] pp.; 258 × 180 mm.
First published in 1963 (see 1653). Revised edition published in 1970 (see 2080).
Macmillan Basic Technical Series.

2518.   SUTHERLAND, Ronald

Ronald Sutherland, *The New Hero: Essays in Comparative Quebec/Canadian Literature.* Macmillan of Canada/Toronto.

xvi, 118 pp.; 210 × 135 mm.
Issued in paper.

2519.   TRUEMAN, R.W.

Our Science Program, *Snow.* Metric Edition. R.W. Trueman, Principal, Greenland Road Public School, North York. 1977 The Macmillan Company of Canada Limited.

32 pp.; 225 × 152 mm.
First published in 1973 (see 2225). Issued in paper.
Our Science Program Series.

2520.   VASS, Ben

Countdown Canada: A Conceptual Geography Study. Ben Vass, Co-ordinator of Geography, Board of Education for the Borough of North York, Roy Alderdice, Head of the Geography Department, C.W. Jefferys Secondary School, North York [and] George Sled, Head of the Geography Department, Victoria Park Secondary School, North York. Macmillan of Canada.

[8], 227, [1] pp.; 283 × 217 mm.

2521.   WAYMAN, Tom

Free Time. Industrial Poems By Tom Wayman. Macmillan of Canada Toronto.

128 pp.; 130 × 205 mm.
Issued in paper.

2522.   WEIR, Joan Sherman

A Canadian Topliner, *Exile at the Rocking Seven.* Joan Sherman Weir. Macmillan of Canada.

[2], 145, [3] pp.; 175 × 105 mm.
Issued in paper.
Topliner Series.

2523. WIGLE, Robert

Mathematical Pursuits Three. Robert Wigle, Head of Mathematics Department, Delhi District Secondary School, Delhi, Ontario, Paul Dowling,
Mathematics Department, Delhi District Secondary School, Delhi, Ontario
[and] Paul Jennings, Associate Chairman of Pure Science, Lester B. Pearson
High School, Burlington, Ontario. Macmillan of Canada.

x, 422 pp.; 233 × 155 mm.
Mathematical Pursuits Series.

1978

2524. AMIRAULT, Ernest J.

*Canada's Hospitality Law: A Survey of the Law Governing the Operation of
Hotels, Motels, Restaurants, Lodges, Travel Agencies, and Tourist Establish-
ments in Canada*. Ernest J. Amirault, B.A., LL.B., Professor of Business
Law, Ryerson Polytechnical Institute [and] Maurice Archer, B.Sc.
(ECON.), M.A., Professor of Business Management, Ryerson Polytechnical
Institute. Macmillan of Canada.

[18], 333, [1] pp.; 225 × 148 mm.
Issued in paper.

2525. ANDERSON, Allan

Allan Anderson [and] Betty Tomlinson, *Greetings From Canada: An Album
of Unique Canadian Postcards from the Edwardian Era 1900-1916*. Macmillan
of Canada Toronto.

xx, 188 pp.; 228 × 293 mm.
Issued in hard covers and paper.

2526. ANDERSON, Doris

Doris Anderson, *Two Women*. Macmillan of Canada Toronto.

[8], 243, [1] pp.; 220 × 143 mm.

2527. ARCHER, Maurice

Introduction to Economics: A Canadian Analysis. Maurice Archer. Macmillan
of Canada.

x, 614 pp.; 225 × 150 mm.
Issued in paper.

2528. ARCHER, Maurice

Starting and Managing Your Own Small Business. Maurice Archer and Jerry
White. A Financial Post/Macmillan Book.

[8], 291, [1] pp.; 225 × 145 mm.
Issued in paper.
Canadian Small Business Series.

2529. BACKHOUSE, Constance

The Secret Oppression: Sexual Harassment of Working Women. Constance
Backhouse and Leah Cohen. Macmillan of Canada Toronto.

   [12], 208 pp.; 233 × 154 mm.

2530. BAIN, George

Clem Watkins, Jr. [pseud.], *Letters From Lilac 1965-1973*. Edited and
selected by George Bain. Macmillan of Canada Toronto.

   [8], 187, [5] pp.; 222 × 136 mm.

2531. BAXTER, Angus

Angus Baxter, *In Search of Your Roots: A Guide For Canadians Seeking Their
Ancestors*. Macmillan of Canada Toronto.

   [14], 293, [1] pp.; 233 × 155 mm.
   Revised and updated in 1980 (see 2673).

2532. BERESFORD-HOWE, Constance

The Unreasoning Heart. By Constance Beresford-Howe. [Quotation]. Macmillan of Canada Toronto.

   [4], 236 pp.; 188 × 132 mm.
   Issued in paper.
   Laurentian Library.

2533. BERKOWITZ, S.D.

Canada's Third Option. Edited by S.D. Berkowitz & Robert K. Logan.
Macmillan of Canada.

   [14], 282 pp.; 213 × 133 mm.
   Issued in paper.

2534. BLISS, Michael

*A Canadian Millionaire: The Life and Business Times of Sir Joseph Flavelle,
Bart. 1858-1939*. Michael Bliss. Macmillan of Canada.

   xiv, 562 pp.; 236 × 157 mm.

2535. BOULOGNE, Jean

The Making of a Gymnast. By Jean Boulogne. With photographs by Carl de
Baldo and others, and illustrations by Lynn T. Wilton. A Giniger Book
published in association with Hawthorn Books, Inc., New York, A Howard
& Windham Company. In Canada: The Macmillan Company of Canada,
Ltd., Toronto.

   96 pp.; 283 × 217 mm.
   Issued in cloth and paper.

2536. CALLAGHAN, Morley

No Man's Meat & The Enchanted Pimp. By Morley Callaghan. Macmillan of
Canada.

   [6], 170 pp.; 222 × 139 mm.

2537.   CAMPBELL, Colin

The Canadian Senate: A Lobby From Within. Colin Campbell. Canadian Controversies Series. Macmillan of Canada.

   [8], 184 pp.; 220 × 143 mm.
   Issued in cloth and paper.
   Canadian Controversies Series.

2538.   CLERY, Val

Edited by Val Clery, *Canada from the Newsstands: A Selection From The Best Canadian Journalism Of The Past Thirty Years*. Macmillan of Canada Toronto.

   [8], 291, [1] pp.; 235 × 151 mm.
   Issued in cloth and paper.

2539.   CLERY, Val

Doors. Text by Val Clery. Photographs by Gordon Beck, John Bigg, Bill Brooks, John de Visser, Peter Dominick, Ted Grant, Rudi Haas, Jennifer Harper, G.J. Harris, Uta Hoffmann, Charles Kadin, Fiona Mee, Bill McLaughlin, Barry Moscrop, Wim Noordhoek, Murray Sumner and Robert van der Hilst. A Jonathan-James Book. Macmillan of Canada, Toronto.

   [144] pp.; 217 × 217 mm.

2540.   CLERY, Val

Windows. Text by Val Clery. Photographs by Gordon Beck, Bill Brooks, John de Visser, Jennifer Harper, Henry Less, Bill McLaughlin, Wim Noordhoek, Peter Paterson, Murray Sumner and Richard Vroom. A Jonathan-James Book. Macmillan of Canada, Toronto.

   [168] pp.; 217 × 217 mm.

2541.   DAWE, Alan

Copyright Canada: A Prose Rhetoric and Sampler. Alan Dawe, Chairman, English and Modern Languages Division, Vancouver Community College, Langara, B.C. [Quotation]. Macmillan of Canada.

   [10], 243, [1] pp.; 277 × 216 mm.
   Issued in paper.

2542.   de SANTANA, Hubert

Danby: Images of Sport. By Hubert de Santana. Published by Amberley House Limited, Toronto. Distributed by Macmillan of Canada, Toronto.

   64 pp.; 235 × 272 mm.

2543.   DOERN, G. Bruce

The Regulatory Process in Canada. Edited by G. Bruce Doern. Macmillan of Canada.

   [14], 365, [1] pp.; 226 × 150 mm.
   Issued in paper.

2544.   FERGUSSON, Donald A.

From the Farthest Hebrides. BHO NA H-INNSE GALL AS IOMAL-LAICHE. General Editor, Donald A. Fergusson. Gaelic Editor, Aonaghus Iain MacDhamhnuill. Music Editor, Jean F. Gillespie London. Macmillan of Canada.

xiv, 321, [1] pp.; 260 × 202 mm.

2545.   FLOWER, George E.

Individualized Spelling Exercises: The Macmillan Spelling Series 3.Revised Edition. General Editor: Dr. George E. Flower, Dean of the Faculty of Education, McGill University, Montreal. 1978, The Macmillan Company of Canada Limited.

[Duplicating Masters for 39 Units]; 275 × 210 mm.
Issued in paper.
Macmillan Spelling Series.

2546.   FLOWER, George E.

Individualized Spelling Exercises: The Macmillan Spelling Series 4.Revised Edition. General Editor: Dr. George E. Flower, Dean of the Faculty of Education, McGill University, Montreal. 1978, The Macmillan Company of Canada Limited.

[Duplicating Masters for 39 Units]; 275 × 210 mm.
Issued in paper.
Macmillan Spelling Series.

2547.   FLOWER, George E.

Individualized Spelling Exercises: The Macmillan Spelling Series 6. Revised Edition. General Editor: Dr. George E. Flower, Dean of the Faculty of Education, McGill University, Montreal. 1978, The Macmillan Company of Canada Limited.

[Duplicating Masters for 39 Units]; 275 × 210 mm.
Issued in paper.
Macmillan Spelling Series.

2548.   FLOWER, George E.

Individualized Spelling Exercises: The Macmillan Spelling Series 7. Revised Edition. General Editor: Dr. George E. Flower, Dean of the Faculty of Education, McGill University, Montreal. 1978, The Macmillan Company of Canada Limited.

[Duplicating Masters for 39 Units]; 275 × 210 mm.
Issued in paper.
Macmillan Spelling Series.

2549.   FLOWER, George E.

Individualized Spelling Exercises: The Macmillan Spelling Series 8. Revised Edition. General Editor: Dr. George E. Flower, Dean of the Faculty of Education, McGill University, Montreal. 1978, The Macmillan Company of Canada Limited.

[Duplicating Masters for 39 Units]; 275 × 210 mm.
Issued in paper.
Macmillan Spelling Series.

2550.   FLOWER, George E.

The Macmillan Spelling Series: 2. Revised Edition. Irene Knapik, Gerry Levert, Cathie Neagle, Robin Schollen. General Editor: George E. Flower, Dean, Faculty of Education, McGill University, Montreal. Authors: Robert F. Bornhold, K.H.D. Hall, Robert J. Ireland, Irene Knapik, Gerry Levert, Gordon F. Mann, Cathie Neagle, Robin Schollen [and] Sybil Shack. Designed by Blair Kerrigan/Glyphics. Illustrated by Heather Collins/Glyphics. Macmillan of Canada 1978.

> 128 pp.; 233 × 190 mm.
> First published in 1960 (see 1486).
> Macmillan Spelling Series.

2551.   GEDGE, Pauline

The Eagle and The Raven. A novel by Pauline Gedge. Macmillan of Canada Toronto 1978.

> [6], 694 pp.; 235 × 155 mm.

2552.   GLENDAY, Daniel

Modernization and the Canadian State. Edited by Daniel Glenday, Hubert Guindon [and] Allan Turowetz. Macmillan of Canada.

> [8], 456 pp.; 225 × 145 mm.
> Issued in paper.

2553.   GRAY, James H.

Troublemaker!: A Personal History. James H. Gray. Macmillan of Canada/Toronto.

> xii, 307, [1] pp.; 235 × 150 mm.

2554.   GRAY, John M.

Fun Tomorrow: Learning to be a Publisher and Much Else. John Morgan Gray. Macmillan of Canada, Toronto.

> [10], 347, [1] pp.; 233 × 150 mm.

2555.   HAMILTON, William B.

William B. Hamilton, *The Macmillan Book of Canadian Place Names.* Macmillan of Canada Toronto.

> xii, 340 pp.; 235 × 160 mm.

2556.   HAND, J.G.

Investigative Science, *Chemistry Concepts.* J.G. Hand, Science Department, Hill Park Secondary School, Hamilton, Ontario, G.W. Kocsis, Assistant Head of Biology, Hill Park Secondary School, Hamilton, Ontario, S.G. Percival, Chairman of Pure Science, Lester B. Pearson High School, Burlington, Ontario [and] C.F. Reid, Head of Science, Hill Park Secondary School, Hamilton, Ontario. Macmillan of Canada.

> [4], 37, [1] pp.; 230 × 172 mm.
> Issued in paper.
> Investigative Science Series.

2557. HAND, J.G.

Investigative Science, *Forensic Science and Criminology*. J.G. Hand, Science Department, Hill Park Secondary School, Hamilton, Ontario, G.W. Kocsis, Assistant Head of Biology, Hill Park Secondary School, Hamilton, Ontario, S.G. Percival, Chairman of Pure Science, Lester B. Pearson High School, Burlington, Ontario [and] C.F. Reid, Head of Science, Hill Park Secondary School, Hamilton, Ontario. Macmillan of Canada.

[4], 39, [1] pp.; 230 × 172 mm.
Issued in paper.
Investigative Science Series.

2558. HAND, J.G.

Investigative Science, *Product Analysis—Juices*. J.G. Hand, Science Department, Hill Park Secondary School, Hamilton, Ontario, G.W. Kocsis, Assistant Head of Biology, Hill Park Secondary School, Hamilton, Ontario, S.G. Percival, Chairman of Pure Science, Lester B. Pearson High School, Burlington, Ontario, [and] C.F. Reid, Head of Science, Hill Park Secondary School, Hamilton, Ontario. Macmillan of Canada.

[4], 43, [1] pp.; 230 × 172 mm.
Issued in paper.
Investigative Science Series.

2559. HARDY, W.G.

The Scarlet Mantle: A Novel of Julius Caesar. By W.G. Hardy. Macmillan of Canada Toronto.

xvi, 462 pp.; 230 × 155 mm.

2560. HIBBARD, G.R.

The Elizabethan Theatre VI. Papers given at the Sixth International Conference on Elizabethan Theatre held at the University of Waterloo, Ontario, in July 1975. Edited and with an introduction by G.R. Hibbard, Department of English, University of Waterloo. Published in collaboration with the University of Waterloo. Macmillan of Canada.

xiv, 161, [1] pp.; 220 × 140 mm.

2561. HOWARD, John

Rusting Out, Burning Out, Blowing Out: Stress and Survival on the Job. Dr. John Howard, Dr. David Cunningham, [and] Dr. Peter Rechnitzer. A Financial Post/Macmillan Book.

136 pp.; 225 × 145 mm.
Issued in paper.

2562. HUNT, John R.

A Canadian Topliner, *The Search*. John R. Hunt. Macmillan of Canada.
[2], 123, [1] pp. + ad.; 177 × 106 mm.
Topliner Series.

2563. IRELAND, Robert J.

A Canadian Topliner, *Ernie*. Robert J. Ireland. Macmillan of Canada.

[2], 125, [1] pp.; 177 × 112 mm.
Topliner Series.

2564. IRELAND, Robert J.

The Macmillan Spelling Series: 6. Revised Edition. Robert J. Ireland. General Editor: George E. Flower, Dean, Faculty of Education, McGill University, Montreal. Designed by Glyphics, Division of Kerrigan O'Grady Limited. Illustrated by Heather Collins. 1978, Macmillan of Canada.

128 pp.; 233 × 155 mm.
First published in 1961 (see 1531).
Macmillan Spelling Series.

2565. IRELAND, Robert J.

The Macmillan Spelling Series: 8. Revised Edition. Robert J. Ireland. General Editor: George E. Flower, Dean, Faculty of Education, McGill University, Montreal. Designed by Glyphics, Division of Kerrigan O'Grady Limited. Illustrated by Heather Collins. 1978, Macmillan of Canada.

127, [1] pp.; 233 × 155 mm.
First published in 1961 (see 1629).
Macmillan Spelling Series.

2566. IRELAND, Robert J.

The Macmillan Spelling Series: Teacher's Handbook 4. Revised Edition. Robert J. Ireland, Co-ordinator of Language Arts, Metropolitan Separate School Board, Toronto. Macmillan of Canada.

[4], 171, [1] pp.; 223 × 145 mm.
Macmillan Spelling Series.

2567. IRELAND, Robert J.

The Macmillan Spelling Series: Teacher's Handbook 6. Revised Edition. Robert J. Ireland, Assistant Superintendent of Curriculum (Language Arts), Metropolitan Separate School Board, Toronto. Macmillan of Canada.

[4], 193, [1] pp.; 223 × 145 mm.
Macmillan Spelling Series.

2568. IRELAND, Robert J.

The Macmillan Spelling Series: Teacher's Handbook 8. Revised Edition. Robert J. Ireland, Assistant Superintendent of Curriculum (Language Arts), Metropolitan Separate School Board, Toronto. Macmillan of Canada.

[4], 213, [1] pp.; 223 × 145 mm.
Macmillan Spelling Series.

2569. JAMES, Janet Craig

A Canadian Topliner, *Peppy Baker*. Janet Craig James. Macmillan of Canada.

[2], 135, [5] pp.; 176 × 116 mm.
Issued in paper.
Topliner Series.

2570. JOHNSON, John

Taxi! True Stories From Behind The Wheel. John Johnson. Macmillan of Canada/Toronto.

xiv, 224 pp.; 220 × 140 mm.

2571. No entry

2572. KNEIDER, A.P.

How to Make Money in a Retail Store of Your Own. A.P. Kneider. A Financial Post/Macmillan Book.

xii, 250 pp.; 233 × 150 mm.
Issued in cloth and paper.
Canadian Small Business Series.

2573. LANG, H. Murray

Inquiries into Biology, *The Functioning Animal*. H. Murray Lang, Professor and Chairman of Science Education, The Faculty of Education, University of Toronto, Edwin G. Palfery, Vice-Principal, Alderwood Collegiate Institute, Borough of Etobicoke [and] Ed L.R. Van Nieuwenhove, Vice-Principal, Cedarbrae Collegiate Institute, Borough of Scarborough. Macmillan of Canada.

[6], 79, [1] pp.; 277 × 213 mm.
Issued in paper.
Inquiries into Biology Series.

2574. LANG, H. Murray

Inquiries into Biology, *The Functioning Animal: Teacher's Guide*. H. Murray Lang, Professor and Chairman of Science Education, The Faculty of Education, University of Toronto, Edwin G. Palfery, Vice-Principal, Alderwood Collegiate Institute, Borough of Etobicoke [and] Ed L.R. Van Nieuwenhove, Vice-Principal, Cedarbrae Collegiate Institute, Borough of Scarborough. Macmillan of Canada.

[2], 35, [1] pp.; 277 × 213 mm.
Issued in paper.
Inquiries into Biology Series.

2575. LANG, H. Murray

Inquiries into Biology: *Selection for Survival*. H. Murray Lang, Professor and Chairman of Science Education, The Faculty of Education, University of Toronto. Edwin G. Palfery, Vice-Principal, Alderwood Collegiate Institute, Borough of Etobicoke. Ed L.R. Van Nieuwenhove, Vice-Principal, Cedarbrae Collegiate Institute, Borough of Scarborough. Macmillan of Canada.

[4], 74, pp.; 277 × 213 mm.
Issued in paper.
Inquiries into Biology Series.

2576.   LANG, H. Murray

Inquiries into Biology, *Selection for Survival: Teacher's Guide*. H. Murray
Lang, Professor and Chairman of Science Education, The Faculty of Educa-
tion, University of Toronto, Edwin G. Palfery, Vice-Principal, Alderwood
Collegiate Institute, Borough of Etobicoke [and] Ed L.R. Van Nieuwenhove,
Vice-Principal, Cedarbrae Collegiate Institute, Borough of Scarborough.
Macmillan of Canada.

> [2], 36 pp.; 277 × 213 mm.
> Issued in paper.
> Inquiries into Biology Series.

2577.   LEGATE, David M.

Stephen Leacock: A Biography. By David M. Legate. Macmillan of Canada
Toronto.

> [14], 296 pp.; 188 × 130 mm.
> Issued in paper.
> Laurentian Library.

2578.   MacLENNAN, Hugh

The Other Side of Hugh MacLennan: Selected Essays Old and New. Edited by
Elspeth Cameron. Macmillan of Canada/Toronto.

> xiv, 301, [1] pp.; 220 × 140 mm.

2579.   MACPHERSON, Duncan

[Cover-title:] *Macpherson Editorial Cartoons 1978: 136 Selected Cartoons by
Duncan Macpherson*. Introduction by Christina McCall Newman.

> [138] pp.; 229 × 236 mm.
> Issued in paper.

2579A   McCARTHY, Michael J.

A Canadian Topliner, *The Journey Home*. Michael J. McCarthy. Macmillan
of Canada.

> [2], 146, [4] pp.; 178 × 107 mm.
> Issued in paper.
> Topliner Series.

2580.   McNEIL, Bill

Bill McNeil, *Voice of the Pioneer*. Pioneers of all sorts — prospectors, scien-
tists, homesteaders, teachers, bush pilots and many others — tell their
fascinating stories here, as they have told them on Canada's best-loved radio
program. Macmillan of Canada Toronto.

> xiv, 257, [1] pp.; 235 × 152 mm.
> Reprinted in 1979 (cloth) and 1980 (paper).

2581.   MILLER, H.G.

Hand and Machine Woodwork. Metric Edition. H.G. Miller, Formerly Technical Director, General Brock High School, Burlington, Ontario. Illustrated
by G. Fantuz, Keith King, and Keith Miller. Macmillan of Canada.

> [10], 242 pp.; 235 × 155 mm.
> First published in 1962 (see 1591). Revised in 1972 (see 2161).

2582.   MILLER, Orlo

Orlo Miller, *Twenty Mortal Murders: Bizarre Murder Cases From Canada's Past*. Macmillan of Canada Toronto.

xiv, 226 pp.; 220 × 140 mm.

2583.   MUNRO, Alice

Who Do You Think You Are?. Stories by Alice Munro. Macmillan of Canada/Toronto.

[12], 206 pp.; 223 × 143 mm.

2584.   NICHOLS, Ruth

The Left-Handed Spirit. Ruth Nichols. Macmillan of Canada/Toronto.

[4], 220 pp.; 215 × 140 mm.

2585.   PENNER, Philip G.

Language on Paper: Teacher's Handbook. P.G. Penner [and] R.E. McConnell, University of British Columbia. Macmillan of Canada.

[4], 19, [1] pp.; 225 × 150 mm.
Issued in paper.

2586.   PENNER, Philip G.

Language: Speech and Writing. Philip G. Penner [and] Ruth E. McConnell, University of British Columbia. Macmillan of Canada.

[10], 293, [1] pp.; 235 × 175 mm.

2587.   PHIDD, Richard W.

The Politics and Management of Canadian Economic Policy. Richard W. Phidd [and] G. Bruce Doern. Macmillan of Canada.

[10], 598 pp.; 225 × 148 mm.

2588.   PHILLIPS, P.T.

The View From the Pulpit: Victorian Ministers and Society. Edited And With An Introduction By P.T. Phillips. Macmillan of Canada.

[10], 326 pp.; 234 × 145 mm.

2589.   PILLES, Herb

Affection: Showing We Care. Herb Pilles/Lucinda Doucette/Dale McLean. Macmillan of Canada.

Portfolio; 260 × 300 mm.
This is a portfolio consisting of 8 open-ended stories, 6 col. posters, 3 sets of 10 col. role-playing cards, and teacher's guide.

2590.   PORTER, C.J.

Cross-Currents: Prose from the English-Speaking World. Revised Edition. Edited by C.J. Porter. Macmillan of Canada.

[12], 305, [1] pp.; 197 × 123 mm.
First published in 1969 (see 2016). Issued in paper.

2591. PYKE, Linda

Linda Pyke, *Prisoner*. Macmillan of Canada/Toronto.

[8], 87, [1] pp.; 225 × 150 mm.
Issued in paper.

2592. RADWANSKI, George

Trudeau. George Radwanski. Macmillan of Canada Toronto.

xii, 372 pp.; 233 × 155 mm.

2593. SENIOR, Hereward

Hereward Senior, *The Fenians and Canada*. Macmillan of Canada.

x, 176 pp.; 210 × 133 mm.
Issued in paper.

2594. SETON, Ernest Thompson

Animal Tracks and Hunter Signs. Ernest Thompson Seton. Macmillan of Canada, Toronto.

160 pp.; 187 × 130 mm.
Issued in paper.
Laurentian Library.

2595. SHACK, Sybil F.

The Macmillan Spelling Series: 5. Revised Edition. Sybil Shack. General Editor: George E. Flower, Dean, Faculty of Education, McGill University, Montreal. Designed by Glyphics, Division of Kerrigan O'Grady Limited. Illustrated by Heather Collins. 1978, Macmillan of Canada.

128 pp.; 233 × 155 mm.
First published in 1961 (see 1529A).
Macmillan Spelling Series.

2596. SHACK, Sybil F.

The Macmillan Spelling Series: 7. Revised Edition. Sybil Shack. General Editor: George E. Flower, Dean, Faculty of Education, McGill University, Montreal. Designed by Glyphics, Division of Kerrigan O'Grady Limited. Illustrated by Heather Collins. 1978, Macmillan of Canada.

127, [1] pp.; 233 × 155 mm.
First published in 1962 (see 1571).
Macmillan Spelling Series.

2597. SHACK, Sybil F.

The Macmillan Spelling Series: Teacher's Handbook 3. Revised Edition. Sybil Shack, Formerly Principal, Winnipeg School Division No. 1. Macmillan of Canada.

[4], 195, [1] pp.; 223 × 145 mm.
Issued in paper.
Macmillan Spelling Series.

2598.   SHACK, Sybil F.
The Macmillan Spelling Series: Teacher's Handbook 5. Revised Edition. Sybil Shack, Formerly Principal, Winnipeg School Division No. 1. Macmillan of Canada.

> [4], 202 pp.; 223 × 145 mm.
> Issued in paper.
> Macmillan Spelling Series.

2599.   SHACK, Sybil F.
The Macmillan Spelling Series: Teacher's Handbook 7. Revised Edition. Sybil Shack, Formerly Principal, Winnipeg School Division No. 1. Macmillan of Canada.

> [4], 193, [1] pp.; 223 × 145 mm.
> Issued in paper.
> Macmillan Spelling Series.

2600.   SMITH, Philip
The Treasure-Seekers: The Men Who Built Home Oil. Philip Smith. Macmillan of Canada/Toronto.

> x, 310 pp.; 230 × 150 mm.

2601.   SMITH, Ross E.
Successful People Management: How to get and keep good employees. Ross E. Smith. A Financial Post/Macmillan Book.

> [10], 221, [1] pp.; 225 × 145 mm.
> Issued in paper.
> Canadian Small Business Series.

2602.   SMYTHE, James M.
Physical Geography. Metric Edition. James M. Smythe, M.A., Head of the Geography Department, Earl Haig Secondary School, North York, Charles G. Brown, B.A., Director and Secretary-Treasurer, Metropolitan Toronto School Board, Eric H. Fors, B.A., Supervisor of Planning, Board of Education, North York [and] Robert C. Lord, B.A., Head of the Geography Department, Clarkson Secondary School, Mississauga. Maps and Diagrams by A. Diana, F. Zsigo and J. Loates. Macmillan of Canada/Toronto.

> x, 342 pp.; 230 × 160 mm.
> This is the metric edition of the 1970 *Physical Geography*, a revised edition consisting of the first three parts of *Elements of Geography* published by Macmillan in 1959 (see 1474, 1698, 2079 and 2435). A French metric edition was published in 1979 (see 2655).

2603.   STEVENS, John
Canadian Stories of Action and Adventure. Edited by John Stevens and Roger J. Smith, Faculty of Education, University of Toronto. Macmillan of Canada.

> xiv, 218 pp.; 182 × 125 mm.
> Issued in paper.

2604. SUKNASKI, Andrew

Andrew Suknaski, *The ghosts call you poor*. Macmillan of Canada Toronto.

[10], 117, [1] pp.; 213 × 137 mm.
Issued in paper.

2605. TECKERT, Harry E.

You and the Law: What every small business owner needs to know. Harry E.
Teckert and Michael J. McDonald. A Financial Post/Macmillan Book.

[10], 324 pp.; 225 × 145 mm.
Issued in paper.
Canadian Small Business Series.

2606. WALLACE, W. Stewart

The Macmillan Dictionary of Canadian Biography. Edited by W. Stewart
Wallace. Fourth Edition. Revised, Enlarged and Updated by W.A. McKay.
Macmillan of Canada Toronto.

[10], 914 pp.; 240 × 165 mm.
First published in 1926 under the title *The Dictionary of Canadian Biography* (see
298). Revised and enlarged in 1945 in two volumes (see 1094 and 1095). Third
edition published in 1963 (see 1657).

2607. WIGLE, Robert

Mathematical Pursuits Four. Robert Wigle, Mathematics Department, Delhi
District Secondary School, Delhi, Ontario, Paul Dowling, Formerly of the
Mathematics Department, Delhi District Secondary School, Delhi, Ontario
[and] Paul Jennings, Associate Chairman of Pure Sciences, Lester B. Pearson
High School, Burlington, Ontario. Macmillan of Canada.

x, 390 pp.; 233 × 155 mm.
Mathematical Pursuits Series.

1979

2608. ANDERSON, Allan

*Salt Water, Fresh Water: Over a hundred Canadians who work on the water —
fishermen, guides, pilots, divers, rum-runners, whalers, tugboat skippers, and
many more — pass along their vivid stories of life afloat past and present*. Allan
Anderson. Macmillan of Canada Toronto.

xviii, 391, [1] pp.; 233 × 155 mm.

2609. ARTIBISE, Alan F.J.

The Usable Urban Past: Planning and Politics in the Modern Canadian City.
Edited With Introductions By Alan F.J. Artibise And Gilbert A. Stelter. The
Carleton Library No. 119. Published by Macmillan of Canada in association
with the Institute of Canadian Studies, Carleton University.

[10], 383, [3] pp.; 188 × 125 mm.
Issued in paper.
Carleton Library.

2610.   BORNHOLD, Robert F.

[Cover-title:] *Individualized Spelling Exercises*. The Macmillan Spelling Series. Revised Edition: 2. Duplicator Masters.

[66 forms, interleaved]; 278 × 214 mm.
Macmillan Spelling Series.

2611.   CAMPBELL, Colin

The Superbureaucrats: Structure and Behaviour in Central Agencies. Colin Campbell and George Szablowski. Macmillan of Canada.

xii, 286 pp.; 213 × 135 mm.
Issued in paper.

2612.   CLARK, Robert J.

Canadian Issues and Alternatives. Robert J. Clark, Editor-in-Chief, Assistant Professor, Faculty of Education, University of Western Ontario, London, Ontario, Robert Remnant, History Department, Lasalle Secondary School, Sudbury, Ontario, John Patton, Ottawa Board of Education, Ottawa, Ontario [and] Cary Goulson, Associate Professor, Faculty of Education, University of Victoria, Victoria, British Columbia. Macmillan of Canada/Toronto.

[12], 257, [1] pp.; 235 × 175 mm.
First published in 1974 (see 2246). This edition revised.

2613.   COLES, Don

Anniversaries. Poems by Don Coles. Macmillan of Canada Toronto.

75, [5] pp.; 215 × 137 mm.
Issued in paper.

2614.   DERMER, Jerry

Financial Accounting: A Canadian Perspective. Jerry Dermer, Faculty of Management Studies, University of Toronto [and] Joel Amernic, Department of Political Economy, University of Toronto. Macmillan of Canada.

xxiv, 792 pp.; 234 × 155 mm.

2615.   DOERN, G. Bruce

Public Policy In Canada: Organization, Process, and Management. Edited by G. Bruce Doern and Peter Aucoin. Macmillan of Canada.

xx, 339, [1] pp.; 188 × 124 mm.
Issued in paper.

2616.   DRACHE, Arthur

The Financial Post Book of Tax Tactics: Tips from a professional tax planner. By Arthur Drache. Financial Post/Macmillan.

144 pp.; 225 × 145 mm.
Issued in paper.

2617.   DROBOT, Eve

Words For Sale: More than two dozen professionals show how you can make money in the fast-growing Canadian magazine market. Edited by Eve Drobot & Hal Tennant for the Periodical Writers Association of Canada. Macmillan of Canada.

xviii, 189, [1] pp.; 212 × 137 mm.
Issued in cloth and paper.

2618. EMSON, H.E.

The Doctor and the Law: A Practical Handbook for the Canadian Physician.
H.E. Emson, M.A., M.D., FRCP(C). Macmillan of Canada.

[12], 235, [1] pp.; 226 × 148 mm.
Issued in paper.

2619. FETHERLING, Doug

Canada and the Great Stock Market Crash: *Gold Diggers of 1929.* Doug
Fetherling. Macmillan of Canada Toronto.

xii, 180 pp.; 220 × 140 mm.

2620. GALLANT, Mavis

From the Fifteenth District. A Novella and Eight Short Stories. Mavis Gallant.
Macmillan of Canada/Toronto.

[8], 243, [1] pp.; 212 × 140 mm.

2621. GARGRAVE, Anthony

*How to Win an Election: The Complete Practical Guide to Organizing and
Winning any Election Campaign.* Anthony Gargrave & Raymond Hull. Macmillan of Canada/Toronto.

xii, 228 pp.; 235 × 150 mm.

2622. GOVIER, Katherine

Random Descent. A Novel by Katherine Govier. Macmillan of Canada Toronto.

[8], 228 pp.; 220 × 140 mm.

2623. HAMMOND, Ruth

Public Relations For Small Business: What it is and why you need it. Ruth
Hammond and W. Forbes LeClair. A Financial Post/Macmillan Book.

xii, 112 pp.; 228 × 150 mm.
Issued in paper.

2624. HAND, J.G.

Teacher's Guide: Investigative Science — Chemistry. J.G. Hand, Science
Department, Hill Park Secondary School, Hamilton, Ontario, G.W. Kocsis,
Assistant Head of Biology, Hill Park Secondary School, Hamilton, Ontario,
S.G. Percival, Chairman of Pure Sciences, Lester B. Pearson High School,
Burlington, Ontario [and] C.F. Reid, Head of Science, Hill Park Secondary
School, Hamilton, Ontario. Macmillan of Canada.

[4], 54 pp.; 230 × 172 mm.
Issued in paper.
Investigative Science Series.

2625.   HARDY, W.G.

The Bloodied Toga: A Novel Of Julius Caesar. By W.G. Hardy. Macmillan of Canada Toronto.

[12], 510 pp.; 233 × 150 mm.

2626.   HESSE, M.G.

Themes in Canadian Literature, General Editor: David Arnason. *Childhood and Youth in Canadian Literature*. Edited by M.G. Hesse. Macmillan of Canada.

[6], 122 pp,; 225 × 145 mm.
Issued in paper.
Themes in Canadian Literature Series.

2627.   HOBLEY, L.F.

Introducing Earth, SI Metric Edition Part 1. L.F. Hobley. Introductory section by John C. Washington, White Oaks Secondary School, Oakville, Ontario. Macmillan of Canada.

xxxviii, 232 pp.; 200 × 220 mm.
First published in 1973 (see 2202).

2628.   HOBLEY, L.F.

Introducing Earth, SI Metric Edition Part 2. L.F. Hobley. Introductory section by John C. Washington, White Oaks Secondary School, Oakville, Ontario. Macmillan of Canada.

xxx, 240 pp.; 200 × 220 mm.
First published in 1974 (see 2266).

2629.   HODGINS, Jack

Jack Hodgins, *The Resurrection of Joseph Bourne, Or A Word Or Two On Those Port Annie Miracles*. Macmillan of Canada Toronto.

[12], 271, [1] pp.; 220 × 140 mm.

2630.   HOWARD, Richard B.

Richard B. Howard, *Upper Canada College 1829-1979: Colborne's Legacy*. Macmillan of Canada, Toronto.

xviii, 462 pp.; 261 × 196 mm.

2631.   HUNDEY, Ian

Canada: Immigrants & Settlers. Ian Hundey, Newmarket High School, Newmarket, Ontario, with Larry Milberry. Macmillan of Canada.

[14], 327, [1] pp.; 195 × 217 mm.
Macmillan Elementary Social Studies Program.

2632.   IRELAND, Robert J.

The Macmillan Spelling Series: Worktext 4. Revised Edition. Robert J. Ireland. Macmillan of Canada.

128 pp.; 277 × 215 mm.
Issued in paper.
Macmillan Spelling Series.

2633.   IRELAND, Robert J.

Spelling Across the Curriculum: A Student Handbook. By Robert J. Ireland. Macmillan of Canada/Toronto.

  xviii, 172 pp.; 213 × 135 mm.
  Issued in paper.

2634.   IRELAND, Robert J.

Spelling Across the Curriculum. Robert J. Ireland, Assistant Superintendent of Curriculum (Language Arts), Metropolitan Separate School Board, Toronto. *Teacher's Guide*. Macmillan of Canada, 70 Bond Street Toronto M5B 1X3.

  [4], 24 pp.; 270 × 210 mm.
  Issued in paper.

2635.   KENNEDY, Betty

Hurricane Hazel. Betty Kennedy. Macmillan of Canada Toronto.

  xii, 176 pp.; 233 × 155 mm.

2636.   KNAPIK, Irene

The Macmillan Spelling Series: Teacher's Handbook 2. Revised Edition. Irene Knapik, Gerry Levert, Cathie Neagle, Robin Schollen, St. Barnabas Separate School, Metropolitan School Board, Toronto. Macmillan of Canada.

  [4], 172 pp.; 210 × 135 mm.
  Issued in paper.
  Macmillan Spelling Series.

2637.   LADELL, John

Inheritance: Ontario's Century Farms Past and Present. John and Monica Ladell. Illustrations by Bert Hoferichter, MPA. Macmillan of Canada Toronto.

  xx, 274 pp.; 232 × 155 mm.

2638.   LAIDLAW, Robert

The McGregors: A Novel of an Ontario Pioneer Family. Robert Laidlaw. Macmillan of Canada/Toronto.

  x, 166 pp.; 220 × 138 mm.

2639.   LAMB, James B.

Press Gang: Post-War Life in the World of Canadian Newspapers. (By the author of *The Corvette Navy*.) James B. Lamb. Macmillan of Canada/Toronto.

  [10], 204 pp.; 220 × 140 mm.

2640.   LANG, H. Murray

Inquiries into Biology, *Continuity of Life*. H. Murray Lang, Professor and Chairman of Science Education, The Faculty of Education, University of Toronto, Edwin G. Palfery, Vice-Principal, Alderwood Collegiate Institute, Borough of Etobicoke [and] Ed L.R. Van Nieuwenhove, Vice-Principal, Cedarbrae Collegiate Institute, Borough of Scarborough. Macmillan of Canada.

[6], 62 pp.; 277 × 213 mm.
Issued in paper.
Inquiries into Biology Series.

2641.   LANG, H. Murray

Inquiries into Biology, *Continuity of Life: Teacher's Guide*. H. Murray Lang,
Professor and Chairman of Science Education, The Faculty of Education,
University of Toronto, Edwin G. Palfery, Vice-Principal, Alderwood Col-
legiate Institute, Borough of Etobicoke [and] Ed L.R. Van Nieuwenhove,
Vice-Principal, Cedarbrae Collegiate Institute, Borough of Scarborough.
Macmillan of Canada.

[2], 36 pp.; 277 × 213 mm.
Issued in paper.
Inquiries into Biology Series.

2642.   LAWRENCE, Hal

Hal Lawrence, *A Bloody War: One Man's Memories of the Canadian Navy
1939-1945*. Macmillan of Canada/Toronto.

x, 193, [1] pp.; 234 × 150 mm.

2643.   LEE, Dennis

Alligator Pie Calendar 1979. Text Dennis Lee 1978. Design and illustrations
Frank Newfeld 1978. [The Macmillan Company of Canada 70 Bond Street,
Toronto.]

28 pp.; 330 × 245 mm.
In envelope. Issued in paper.

2644.   LeSUEUR, William Dawson

William Lyon MacKenzie: A Reinterpretation. By William Dawson LeSueur.
Edited and with an Introduction by A.B. McKillop. The Carleton Library
No. 111. Published by Macmillan of Canada, Limited, in association with the
Institute of Canadian Studies, Carleton University.

liv, 430, [4] pp.; 190 × 125 mm.
Issued in paper.
Carleton Library.

2645.   LYON, Peyton V.

Canada as an International Actor. Peyton V. Lyon and Brian W. Tomlin.
Canadian Controversies Series. Macmillan of Canada.

xiv, 209, [1] pp.; 210 × 135 mm.
Canadian Controversies Series.

2645A MACPHERSON, Duncan

[Cover-title:] *Macpherson Editorial Cartoons 1979: 132 Selected Cartoons by
Duncan Macpherson*. Introduction by George Bain.

[136] pp.; 229 × 236 mm.
Issued in paper.

2646.   MacPHERSON, Ian

Each for All: A History of the Co-operative Movement in English Canada, 1900-1945. Ian MacPherson. The Carleton Library No. 116. Published by Macmillan of Canada in association with the Institute of Canadian Studies, Carleton University.

  xiv, 258 pp.; 190 × 125 mm.
  Issued in paper.
  Carleton Library.

2647.   MISHLER, William

Political Participation in Canada: Prospects for Democratic Citizenship. William Mishler. Canadian Controversies Series. Macmillan of Canada.

  viii, 167, [1] pp.; 210 × 135 mm.
  Issued in paper.
  Canadian Controversies Series.

2648.   NICHOLSON, Norman L.

The Boundaries of the Canadian Confederation. Norman L. Nicholson. The Carleton Library No. 115. Published by Macmillan of Canada in association with The Institute of Canadian Studies, Carleton University.

  xii, 252 pp.; 190 × 125 mm.
  Issued in paper.
  Carleton Library.

2649.   *Organization of the Government of Canada 1978/1979*. Published by the Macmillan Company of Canada Ltd., in cooperation with Treasury Board Canada and the Canadian Government Publishing Centre, Supply and Services Canada.

  viii, 613, [1] pp.; 225 × 160 mm.

2650.   OSTRY, Sylvia

Labour Economics in Canada. Third Edition. Sylvia Ostry [and] Mahmood A. Zaidi. With the assistance of Gail Cook Johnson. Macmillan of Canada Toronto.

  xiv, 418 pp.; 225 × 145 mm.
  First published in 1962 (see 1604). Second edition published in 1972 (see 2169).
  Issued in paper.

2651.   PORTER, Marion R.

Does Money Matter? Prospects for Higher Education in Ontario. Marion R. Porter, John Porter, and Bernard R. Blishen. The Carleton Library No. 110. Published by Macmillan of Canada in association with the Institute of Canadian Studies, Carleton University.

  xx, 211, [1] pp.; 189 × 126 mm.
  Issued in paper.
  Carleton Library.

2652. RAMU, G.N.
Courtship, Marriage, and the Family in Canada. Edited by G.N. Ramu.
Macmillan of Canada.
[10], 219, [1] pp.; 225 × 145 mm.

2653. RANGER, Robin
Arms and Politics 1958-1978: Arms Control in a Changing Political Context.
Robin Ranger. Macmillan of Canada.
viii, 280 pp.; 225 × 150 mm.

2654. SAINT-PIERRE, Gaston
Themes in Canadian Literature, General Editor: David Arnason. *The
French Canadian Experience.* Edited by Gaston Saint-Pierre. Macmillan of
Canada.
[6], 122 pp.; 226 × 148 mm.
Issued in paper.
Themes in Canadian Literature Series.

2655. SMYTHE, James M.
Géographie Physique. Édition métrique. James M. Smythe, M.A., Directeur
du Département de géographie, Earl Haig Secondary School, North York,
Charles G. Brown, B.A., Directeur et Secrétaire-trésorier, Commission
scolaire de Toronto métropolitain, Eric H. Fors, B.A., Directeur-adjoint,
Westview Centennial Secondary School, North York [and] Robert C. Lord,
B.A., Directeur du Département de géographie, Clarkson Secondary School,
Mississauga. Ouvrage traduit par Fernand Grenier, Télé-université, Univer-
sité du Québec. Cartes et graphiques réalisés par A. Diana, F. Zsigo et J.
Loates. Macmillan of Canada/Toronto.
x, 340 pp.; 230 × 160 mm.
See 2602 for notes on the English edition of this title.

2656. SNYDER, J. Christopher
"The comprehensive guide to registered tax-shelter plans." 1980 edition.
How to be sure you have the right R.R.S.P. (or RHOSP or DPSP or IAA). By
J. Christopher Snyder. A Financial Post/Macmillan Book.
[4], 154 pp.; 225 × 145 mm.
Issued in paper.

2657. STEVENSON, Garth
Unfulfilled Union: Canadian Federalism and National Unity. Garth Steven-
son. Canadian Controversies Series. Macmillan of Canada.
xii, 257, [1] pp.; 210 × 134 mm.
Issued in paper.
Canadian Controversies Series.

2658. SUCH, Peter
Dolphin's Wake. A novel by Peter Such. Macmillan of Canada.
[8], 229, [1] pp.; 220 × 140 mm.

2659.   Transport Canada Air: *Flight Training Manual*. Third Edition. Macmillan of Canada Toronto.

> viii, 197, [1] pp.; 275 × 214 mm.
> Issued in paper.

2660.   TRUEMAN, R.W.

Teacher's Guide for Introducing Earth Part 1/SI Metric Edition By L.F. Hobley. Prepared by R.W. Trueman, Principal, Greenland Road Public School, North York. Macmillan of Canada.

> [4], 172 pp.; 225 × 150 mm.
> Issued in paper.

2661.   TRUEMAN, R.W.

Teacher's Guide for Introducing Earth Part 2/SI Metric Edition By L.F. Hobley. Prepared by R. W. Trueman, Principal, Greenland Road Public School, North York. Macmillan of Canada.

> [4], 247, [1] pp.; 225 × 150 mm.
> Issued in paper.

2662.   VASS, Ben

Countdown Canada: A Conceptual Geography Study. Teacher's Guide. Ben Vass, Co-ordinator of Geography, Board of Education for the Borough of North York, Roy Alderdice, Head of the Geography Department, C.W. Jefferys Secondary School, North York [and] George Sled, Head of the Geography Department, Victoria Park Secondary School, North York. Macmillan of Canada.

> 192 pp.; 270 × 200 mm.

2663.   WEIR, Carolyn

The Right Honourable John George Diefenbaker: A Pictorial Tribute. By Carolyn Weir. Macmillan of Canada Toronto.

> [128] pp.; 215 × 215 mm.
> Issued in paper.

2664.   WHITE, Walter L.

Canadian Confederation: A Decision-Making Analysis. W.L. White, R.H. Wagenberg, R.C. Nelson [and] W.C. Soderlund. The Carleton Library No. 117. Published by Macmillan of Canada in association with the Institute of Canadian Studies, Carleton University.

> xii, 164 pp.; 190 × 127 mm.
> Issued in paper.
> Carleton Library.

2665.   WIGLE, Robert

Teacher's Guide: Mathematical Pursuits Three. Robert Wigle, Mathematics Department, Delhi District Secondary School, Delhi, Ontario, Paul Dowling, Formerly of the Mathematics Department, Delhi District Secondary School, Delhi, Ontario [and] Paul Jennings, Associate Chairman of Pure Science, Lester B. Pearson High School, Burlington, Ontario. Macmillan of Canada.

[2], 84 pp.; 272 × 208 mm.
Issued in paper.

2666. WIGLE, Robert

Teacher's Guide: Mathematical Pursuits Four. Robert Wigle, Mathematics Department, Delhi District Secondary School, Delhi, Ontario, Paul Dowling, Formerly of the Mathematics Department, Delhi District Secondary School, Delhi, Ontario [and] Paul Jennings, Associate Chairman of Pure Science, Lester B. Pearson High School, Burlington, Ontario. Macmillan of Canada.

[4], 95, [1] pp.; 272 × 208 mm.
Issued in paper.

2667. WINKLER, Alan

Concepts and Challenges in Science 1. Canadian SI Edition. Alan Winkler, Leonard Bernstein, Martin Schachter [and] Stanley Wolfe. Stanley Wolfe, Project Co-ordinator. Macmillan of Canada.

[6], 281, [1] pp.; 283 × 215 mm.

2668. WINKLER, Alan

Concepts and Challenges in Science 2. Canadian SI Edition. Alan Winkler, Leonard Bernstein, Martin Schachter [and] Stanley Wolfe. Stanley Wolfe, Project Co-ordinator. Macmillan of Canada.

[8], 262 pp.; 283 × 215 mm.

2669. WINKLER, Alan

Concepts and Challenges in Science 3. Canadian SI Edition. Alan Winkler, Leonard Bernstein, Martin Schachter [and] Stanley Wolfe. Stanley Wolfe, Project Co-ordinator. Macmillan of Canada.

[6], 266 pp.; 283 × 215 mm.

2670. WINKS, Robin

The Relevance of Canadian History: U.S. and Imperial Perspectives. The 1977 Joanne Goodman Lectures Delivered at the University of Western Ontario. By Robin W. Winks, Professor of History, Master of Berkeley College, Yale University. Macmillan of Canada.

xvi, 99, [1] pp.; 220 × 140 mm.

2671. WRIGHT, Laurali

Neighbours. Laurali Wright. Macmillan of Canada/Toronto.

[10], 258 pp.; 220 × 140 mm.

1980

2672. AMIEL, Barbara

Confessions. By Barbara Amiel. Macmillan of Canada Toronto.

[10], 241, [1] pp.; 233 × 152 mm.

2673. BAXTER, Angus

Angus Baxter, *In Search of Your Roots: A Guide For Canadians Seeking Their Ancestors*. Macmillan of Canada Toronto.

[14], 293, [1] pp.; 225 × 149 mm.
First published in 1978 (see 2531). This edition revised and updated. Issued in paper.

2674. BROWN, Robert Craig

Robert Laird Borden: A Biography: Volume II: 1914-1937. By Robert Craig Brown. Macmillan of Canada/Toronto.

xiv, 256 pp.; 235 × 155 mm.

2675. BYERS, Gerald L.

Marketing for Small Business: What it is and why you need it. Gerald L. Byers and Harry E. Teckert. A Financial Post/Macmillan Book.

xii, 228 pp.; 227 × 148 mm.
Canadian Small Business Series.

2676. CANADA. ENERGY, MINES AND RESOURCES CANADA

Canada Gazetteer Atlas. Published by Macmillan of Canada — a Division of Maclean-Hunter Limited, in co-operation with Energy, Mines and Resources Canada and the Canadian Government Publishing Centre, Supply and Services Canada, 1980.

[11], 164, [1] pp.; 455 × 330 mm.

2677. CHEVRIER, Emile D.

Topologie: Initiation aux cartes topographiques et aux photos aériennes. Émile D. Chevrier, Chef de section de géographie, École secondaire Sir John A. Macdonald, Ottawa [et] D.F.W. Aitkens, Ex-directeur des levés et de la cartographie, forces armées canadiennes Ottawa. Adaptation: Hervé Boudreault, Professeur-géographe, École Secondaire De La Salle, Ottawa, Robert Branalt, Ex-conseiller pedagogique, Ministère de l'Education de l'Ontario, Ottawa [et] Jean-Jacques Foisy, Chef de section de géographie, École secondaire De La Salle, Ottawa. The Macmillan Company of Canada Limited Toronto.

[8], 184 pp.; 310 × 255 mm.
First published in English in 1970 (see 2042). Issued in a binder.

2678. CLEAVER, Elizabeth

Petrouchka. Adapted from Igor Stravinsky and Alexandre Benois by Elizabeth Cleaver. Macmillan of Canada, Toronto.

[32] pp.; 220 × 277 mm.

2679. GRIFFITHS, Barry

Canada: Our Home. Barry Griffiths, Principal, Gulfstream Public School, North York, Ontario [and] J.M. Daly, Principal, St. Paul Separate School, Kingston, Ontario. Macmillan of Canada. A Canadian Company.

[6], 183, [1] pp.; 233 × 178 mm.
Macmillan Elementary Social Studies Program.

2680. HOUSE, J.D.

The Last of the Free Enterprisers: The Oilmen of Calgary. J.D. House.
[Quotation]. The Carleton Library No. 122. Published by Macmillan of
Canada, A Canadian Company, in association with the Institute of Canadian
Studies, Carleton University.

x, 230 pp.; 189 × 126 mm.
Issued in paper.
Carleton Library.

2681. HUNDEY, Ian

Canada: Builders of the Nation. Ian Hundey, Newmarket High School,
Newmarket, Ontario. Macmillan of Canada.

[12], 338 pp.; 195 × 217 mm.

2682. JACKSON, Robert J.

The Canadian Legislative System: Politicians and Policymaking. Second, Revised Edition. Robert J. Jackson and Michael M. Atkinson. Canadian Controversies Series. Macmillan of Canada.

xvi, 222 pp.; 210 × 130 mm.
First published in 1974 (see 2267).
Canadian Controversies Series.

2683. KUSHNER, Donn

Donn Kushner, *The Violin-Maker's Gift.* Illustrated by Doug Panton. Macmillan of Canada Toronto.

[6], 74 pp.; 222 × 138 mm.

2684. LEE, Dennis

[Cover-title:] The Dennis Lee & Frank Newfeld 1980 *Alligator Pie Calendar.*
Text: Dennis Lee 1979/Design And Illustrations: Frank Newfeld 1979.
[Back-cover:] Printed In Canada For The Macmillan Company of Canada, 70
Bond Street, Toronto, M5B 1X3.

28 pp.; 330 × 245 mm.
Issued in paper.

2685. MARR, William L.

Canada: An Economic History. William L. Marr and Donald G. Paterson.
Macmillan of Canada. A Canadian Company.

xx, 539, [1] pp.; 225 × 145 mm.
Issued in paper.

2686. MILLER, H.G.

Building Construction: Materials and methods. Revised Metric Edition. H.G.
Miller, Formerly Technical Director, General Brock High School, Bur-
lington, Ontario. Illustrated by Tony Langdon, Bernard Loates, and Bio-
Medical Productions. Macmillan of Canada — A Canadian Company.

[10], 455, [1] pp.; 258 × 178 mm.
First published in 1968 (see 1942).

2687. MORTON, W.L.

Contexts of Canada's Past. Selected Essays of W.L. Morton. Edited and with an Introduction by A.B. McKillop. The Carleton Library No. 123. Published by Macmillan of Canada in association with the Institute of Canadian Studies, Carleton University.

[10], 289, [1] pp.; 190 × 126 mm.
Issued in paper.
Carleton Library.

2688. PERRY, Robert L.

The Financial Post's New Money Management Book: Lots of ways to protect your cash from shrinkage and the tax man. Edited by Robert L. Perry. Financial Post/Macmillan.

[6], 154 pp.; 225 × 145 mm.
First published in 1976 under the title *Money Management Book*.
Issued in paper.

2689. WHITE, Larry

How to Make Advertising Work for Your Small Business. Larry White. A Financial Post/Macmillan Book.

xiv, 236 pp.; 225 × 148 mm.
Issued in paper.
Canadian Small Business Series.

2690. WIEBE, Rudy

More Stories from Western Canada. Edited by Rudy Wiebe and Aritha Van Herk. Macmillan of Canada.

viii, 296 pp.; 189 × 125 mm.
Issued in paper.

2691. WORZEL, Richard

Making Your Money Grow: How to Plan Your Own Successful Investment Strategy In Today's Market. By Richard Worzel. Financial Post/Macmillan.

[10], 166 pp.; 223 × 145 mm.
Issued in paper.